This text is dedicated to a longtime friend
Wayne Koch
whose encouragement so many years ago requires a huge thank you.

Series in Finance

Thomson Business and Professional Publishing Series in Finance

Introductory Courses

Personal Finance
New! Boone/Kurtz/Hearth: Planning Your Financial Future, 4e, 2006
Gitman/Joehnk: Personal Financial Planning, 10e, 2005

Survey of Finance
New! Besley/Brigham: Principles of Finance, 3e, 2006
Mayo: Financial Institutions: Investments, and Management: An Introduction, 8e, 2004

Entrepreneurial Finance
New! Leach/Melicher: Entrepreneurial Finance, 2e, 2006
Stancill: Entrepreneurial Finance For New and Emerging Businesses, 1e, 2004

Corporate Finance

Corporate Finance/Financial Management – Undergraduate
Besley/Brigham: Essentials of Managerial Finance, 13e, 2005
Brigham/Houston: Fundamentals of Financial Management, Concise 4e, 2004
Brigham/Houston: Fundamentals of Financial Management, 10e, 2004
Lasher: Practical Financial Management, 4e, 2005
New! Megginson/Smart: Introduction to Corporate Finance,1e, 2006
New! Moyer/McGuigan/Kretlow: Contemporary Financial Management, 10e, 2006
Moyer/McGuigan/Rao: Contemporary Financial Management Fundamentals, 1e, 2005

Corporate Finance/Financial Management – Undergraduate / Supplemental Products
Mayes/Shank: Financial Analysis with Microsoft® Excel 2002, 3e, 2004

International Finance
Butler: Multinational Finance, 3e, 2004
New! Crum/Brigham/Houston: Fundamentals of International Finance, 1e, 2005
New! Madura: International Financial Management, 8e, 2006

Intermediate/Advanced Undergraduate Corporate Finance
Brigham/Daves: Intermediate Financial Management, 8e, 2004

Intermediate/Advanced Undergraduate Corporate Finance / Supplemental Products
New! Brigham/Buzzard: Cases for Topics in Financial Management, 2006
    Visit **http://www.textchoice.com** for more information.
Klein/Brigham: Finance Online Case Library 2005, 2e, 2005
Mayes/Shank: Financial Analysis with Microsoft® Excel 2002, 3e, 2004

Capital Budgeting/Long Term Capital Budgeting
Seitz/Ellison: Capital Budgeting and Long-Term Financing Decisions, 4e, 2005

Working Capital Management/Short Term Financial Management
Maness/Zietlow: Short-Term Financial Management, 3e, 2005

Valuation
Daves/Ehrhardt/Shrieves: Corporate Valuation: A Guide for Managers and
    Investors, 1e, 2004

Financial Analysis & Planning
Harrington: Corporate Financial Analysis in a Global Environment, 7e, 2004

MBA/Graduate Corporate Finance
Brigham/Ehrhardt: Financial Management: Theory and Practice, 11e, 2005
New! Ehrhardt/Brigham: Corporate Finance: A Focused Approach, 2e. 2006
Hawawini/Viallet: Finance for Executives: Managing for Value Creation, 2e,
    2002
Smart/Megginson/Gitman: Corporate Finance, 1e, 2004

MBA/Graduate Corporate Finance /Supplemental Products
New! Brigham/Buzzard: Cases for Topics in Financial Management, 2006
    Visit **http://www.textchoice.com** for more information.
Klein/Brigham: Finance Online Case Library
    Visit **http://www.textchoice.com** for more information.
Mayes/Shank: Financial Analysis with Microsoft® Excel 2002, 3e, 2004

Investments Courses
Investments – Undergraduate
Hearth/Zaima: Contemporary Investments: Security and Portfolio Analysis, 4e,
    2004
New! Mayo: Basic Investments, 1e, 2006
New! Mayo: Investments: An Introduction, 8e, 2005
New! Reilly/Norton: Investments, 7e, 2006
StockNavigator: Online Stock Simulation
    Visit **http://stocknavigator.swlearning.com** for more information.
Strong: Practical Investment Management, 3e, 2004

Derivatives/Futures and Options
Chance: An Introduction to Derivatives and Risk Management, 6e, 2004
Strong: Derivatives: An Introduction, 2e, 2005
Stulz: Risk Management and Derivatives, 1e, 2003

Fixed Income
New! Grieves/Griffiths; A Fixed Income Internship: Volume 1: Introduction to
Fixed Income Analytics, 1e, 2006
Sundaresan: Fixed Income Markets and Their Derivatives, 2e, 2002

Real Options
New! Shockley: An Applied Course in Real Options Valuation, 1e, 2006

MBA/Graduate Investments
New! Reilly/Brown: Investment Analysis and Portfolio Management, 8e, 2006
New! Strong: Portfolio Construction, Management, and Protection, 4e, 2006

Financial Institutions Courses
Financial Institutions and Markets
New! Madura: Financial Markets and Institutions, 7e, 2006

Financial Institutions Management
Gardner/Mills/Cooperman: Managing Financial Institutions, 5e, 2005

Money & Capital Markets
Liaw: Capital Markets, 1e, 2004

Commercial Banking/Bank Management
New! Koch/MacDonald: Bank Management, 6e, 2006

Insurance
Risk Management and Insurance/Introduction to Insurance
Trieschmann/Hoyt/Sommer: Risk Management and Insurance, 12e, 2005

Certification
NASD – National Association of Securities Dealers
Thomson South-Western: NASD Exam for Series 6: Preparation Guide, 1e, 2004
Thomson South-Western: NASD Stockbroker Series 7 Exam: Preparation Guide,
1e, 2004

Brief Contents

Contents

Preface

"Nothing venture, nothing win . . . In for a penny, in for a pound." I admit that I'm misusing Gilbert and Sullivan's quote, which applies to love. However, I think it also applies to investments, except that you need to add "nothing venture, nothing lost." Of course, investing is not a game in which you win or lose (neither is love). The goal of investing is to earn a return (win), but to earn that return you must accept risk (lose). Studies of investment returns suggest that over time you should earn a positive return, though during many periods (e.g., 2000–2002) you would have sustained losses.

Virtually everyone makes investments. Even if you do not select specific assets such as IBM stock, you may participate in a pension plan that requires you to select among alternatives available to you. All investment alternatives have common characteristics, such as the sources of return and the risk you must bear. You must determine how much risk you are willing to bear, since a higher return is necessarily associated with accepting more risk. The basic goal is to earn a positive return over a period of time so that you achieve your investment objectives and stay within your risk tolerance.

You must also determine how actively you want to manage your portfolio. You need not actively trade your assets to actively manage your portfolio. You may acquire specific assets—such as a certificate of deposit, a mutual fund, or a stock—and infrequently alter your portfolio. But even passive portfolio management requires some supervision as your financial situation changes (e.g., you get married), you grow older, and your resources change (e.g., you obtain a better-paying job with different benefits).

Some individuals find investing and portfolio management daunting because it appears to require specialized knowledge or they expect to have to work with sophisticated professionals. However, you may find investing fascinating and exciting because you can actively participate in the investing process and see the results of your decisions. One purpose of this text is to help you make more informed investment decisions. Ultimately you will have to put this knowledge to use and construct your personal portfolio. Not all of your investment decisions will be profitable, but over time (unless you overreach and take foolish chances) the value of your portfolio should grow.

INVESTMENT COURSES

Who were Babe Ruth, Roger Maris, and Mickey Mantle? Did you ever see Rudolf Nureyev or Mikhail Baryshnikov perform? Who said "Do, or do not. There is no try"?

You probably never took a course in baseball, but any baseball fan knows that Maris and Mantle were in a battle to break Babe Ruth's record of 60 homeruns in a season. It is unlikely that you took a course in ballet, but you may have seen on the stage, movies, or TV those two famous Russian ballet dancers who defected to the West during the Cold War. If you are a Star Wars fan, you should remember Yoda's advice to Luke Skywalker concerning the correct way to approach a task. Even if you completed a course on film, I doubt you covered that quote from *The Empire Strikes Back*.

I never completed a course on baseball, ballet, or film, but somehow I obtained and assimilated knowledge of baseball, ballet, movies, and a variety of other topics. That also applies to investments. I learned a considerable amount of information from doing: having to make my own investment decisions. You, too, will learn from making investment decisions. Prior knowledge learned from courses and readings cannot decrease your ability to make those decisions.

If you are reading this text, you probably are taking a formal college-level course on investments. As with any course, you bring prior knowledge and experience. Many textbooks on investments are written for students with considerable background in accounting, economics, and finance. Not every student taking a course in investments has such a background. In writing this text, I assumed that you know time value of money concepts and that you can analyze financial statements. If you lack this background in compounding and discounting or the application of ratios to a financial statement, some of this text may be difficult. After the first chapter, I have included a self-test to help you determine your level of knowledge and ability to use these key concepts. I then suggest how any deficiencies may be corrected and have included a review of time value at the end of the text.

Basic Investments is essentially what its name implies: the fundamental investment alternatives, their sources of risk and return, techniques used to value stocks and bonds, and methods to manage (but not erase) risks. The text covers descriptive material (e.g., the mechanics of buying stocks) and theoretical concepts (e.g., portfolio construction and efficient markets). The theory, however, has practical implications and always contributes to your ability to manage your portfolio and help you achieve your investment objectives.

Some of the concepts and the investment alternatives (for example, derivatives) may be difficult to understand. Thomas Alva Edison said "There is no substitution for hard work." While I cannot give you a shortcut to learning this material, I do assume that you have a desire to tackle a fascinating subject and that you are willing to devote real energy to the learning process. If you take Edison's advice, this text should significantly increase your knowledge of investments and help you construct a portfolio to meet your financial goals.

·•●LEARNING AIDS

The architect Mies van der Rohe used the phrase "Less is more" and applied it to his work, which includes the New York State Theater in Lincoln Center for the Performing Arts. The building's simple promenade vividly illustrates "less is more." This book has learning aids, but their number is fewer rather than more and limited to those that I believe you may use. For example, my students indicated that few of them read learning objectives placed at the beginning of a chapter or the questions at the end of the chapter. So I have placed only learning objectives at the end of each chapter. If you did not learn these concepts while reading the text material, you may use these objectives as an indication of important topics and concepts to reread and study.

Important terms are in **bold** print in the text and in the index. Definitions are provided in the margin. Calculator solutions for time value illustrations also appear in the margin. This use of the margin avoids breaking the flow of the text material and succinctly presents the illustration.

The Internet is probably one of your primary sources of information (or at least the initial source). For this reason, Web addresses are provided throughout this text. Over time, Web addresses or a site's coverage may change. You need both flexibility when using these sources and a dosage of skepticism, since material found through the Internet may be biased or purposely misleading. I also encourage you to perform your own searches, since you may find different sites with more or better information that best meets your specific needs.

An Instructor's Manual and Test Bank is available to instructors who adopt this text. The manual includes teaching guides and solutions for the problems at the end of each chapter as well as true-false and multiple-choice test questions and answers. Additional problems are also provided for homework assignments or extra test items.

Acknowledgments

A textbook requires input from many individuals in addition to the author. Over the years, I have received many reviews from people who offered suggestions for improvements. This book is no exception. The following individuals provided advice and help that improved the final manuscript for *Basic Investments*:

Eddie Ary, Ouachita Baptist University
Bruce Brown, College of Financial Planning
Pamela L. Hall, Western Washington University
Dr. Zahid Iqbal, Texas Southern University
John Kensinger, University of North Texas
Malek Lashgari, University of Hartford
Jim Lock, North Virginia Community College
Paul Maloney, Providence College
Cheryl McGaughey, Angelo State University
Ron Meier, College of Financial Planning
Jim Milanese, University of North Carolina, Greensboro
Zane Dennick Ream, Robert Morris University
Frederick P. Schadler, East Carolina University
Anne Macy Terry, West Texas A&M University.

I appreciate the time and effort that each of these instructors took to communicate their suggestions.

The PowerPoint slides were created by Anne Piotrowski. Her willingness to work through various styles and possible presentations greatly enhanced the final product. She deserves a special "thank you" for her efforts.

At this point in the preface, it is traditional for the authors to thank members of the editorial and production staff for their help in bringing the book to fruition. I wish to thank Mike Reynolds, my executive editor; Dave Shaut, Vice-President and Editor-in-Chief; Dan Plofchan, Production Editor; and John Barans, Technology Project Editor. I also want to extend a special thanks to my Senior Developmental Editor, Trish Taylor, for her continued support and understanding and to

Margaret Trejo of Trejo Production for her efficient and supportive handling of the process of converting manuscript into finished product. And I need to thank members of my immediate family, especially Sharon, Chloe, Stella, Tess, Nell, Dash, and Tinker, for their patience during the long process of creation and production.

I encourage readers to contact me with suggestions and comments. Please feel free to write me at the School of Business, The College of New Jersey, Box 7718, Ewing NJ 08628-0718 or, if you prefer, please use my e-mail address, mayoher@tcnj.edu.

Basic Investments

An Introduction to *Basic Investments*

In 1986, Microsoft first sold its stock to the general public. Within ten years, the stock's value had increased over 5,000 percent. A $10,000 investment was worth over $500,000. In the same year, Worlds of Wonder also sold its stock to the public. Ten years later, the company was defunct. A $10,000 investment was worth nothing. These are two examples of emerging firms that could do well or could fail. Would investing in large, well-established companies generate more consistent returns? The answer depends, of course, on which stocks you purchased and when. In 1972, Xerox stock reached a high of $171.87 a share. The price subsequently declined and did not exceed the old high until 26 years later in 1998. Obviously, limiting your investments to large firms does not ensure a positive return.

Today the investment environment is even more dynamic. World events occur rapidly—events that alter the values of specific assets. You have so many assets from which to choose. The amount of information available to you is staggering, and it is continually growing. The accessibility of personal computers and the dissemination of information on the Internet increase your ability to track investments and to perform investment analysis. Furthermore, the recessions of the early 1990s and 2000s, the large decline in stock prices during 2000–2002, the historic decline in interest rates during 2001–2003, and the frequent changes in the tax laws have increased investor awareness of the importance of financial planning, asset selection, and portfolio construction.

As you work your way through this text, you will be bombarded with many alternatives and strategies. I cannot help you make investment decisions, but I can help you learn about your choices. This is, of course, the purpose of any textbook in investments, but unlike many textbooks, this one will often address you individually. I cannot teach you to make wise investments, nor can I assure that learning this material will result in your making profitable investments. (You should be skeptical of anyone who makes such a claim!) But I can explain techniques for analyzing and valuing financial assets, their sources of risk, and how these risks may be managed, if not eliminated. It is your job to learn the material, determine which parts are most relevant for you, and then apply them.

PORTFOLIO CONSTRUCTION AND PLANNING

Investment decisions are about making choices. Once you have earned income, you have two basic choices: to spend it or to save it. If you choose to save, you face a second decision: What to do with the savings? Each saver must decide where to invest this command over resources (goods and services) that is currently not being used. This is an important decision because these assets are the means by which you transfer today's purchasing power to the future. In effect, you must decide on a **portfolio** of assets to own. (Notice that I will boldface terms and place them in the margin. I have also constructed an index that helps you find a particular topic.) A portfolio is simply a combination of assets designed to serve as a store of value. Poor management of these assets may destroy the portfolio's value, and you will then not achieve your financial goals.

portfolio
A combination of assets (owned by an investor) to serve as a store of value.

There are many assets (e.g., stocks, bonds, derivatives) that you may include in your portfolio. This textbook will discuss many of them, but the stress will be on long-term financial assets. While you may hold a portion of the portfolio in short-term assets, such as savings accounts, these assets do not present the problem of valuation and choice that accompanies the decision to purchase a stock or a bond. Understanding the nature of long-term assets (i.e., how they are bought and sold, how they are valued, and how they may be used in portfolio construction) is the primary focus of this text.

Several factors affect the construction of a portfolio. These include your financial goals, the risks involved, the taxes that will be imposed on any gain, and your knowledge of the available opportunities and alternative investments. This text will cover a wide range of alternative investments, their use in a portfolio, the risks associated with owning them, and their valuation.

There are many reasons for saving and accumulating assets. You may postpone current consumption to accumulate funds to make the down payment on a house, finance a child's education, start a business, meet financial emergencies, finance retirement, leave a sizable estate, or even accumulate for the sake of accumulating. For any or all of these reasons, people acquire portfolios of assets rather than spend all their current income.

The motives for saving should dictate, or at least affect, the composition of the portfolio. Not all assets are appropriate to meet specific financial goals. For example, savings that are held to meet emergencies, such as an extended illness or unemployment, should not be invested in assets whose return and safety of principal are uncertain. Instead, emphasis should be placed on safety of principal and assets that may be readily converted into cash (that is, liquid assets such as savings accounts or shares in money market mutual funds). The emphasis should not be on long-term growth and high returns. However, the funds should not sit idle; they should be invested in relatively safe assets that offer modest returns.

Other goals, such as financing retirement or a child's education, have a longer and more certain time horizon. The investor knows approximately when the funds will be needed and so can construct a portfolio with a long-term horizon. Bonds that mature when the funds will be needed or common stocks that offer the potential for growth would be more appropriate than savings accounts or certificates of deposit. The longer time period means you can acquire long-term assets that may offer a higher yield.

Most investors have several financial goals that must be met simultaneously. Thus, it is not surprising to learn that their portfolios contain a variety of assets. Of course, priorities and needs differ. The individual who is employed in a cyclical industry and may be laid off during a recession may place more stress on funds to cover unemployment than would the tenured professor. An individual with a poor medical history may own more safe, short-term investments than the person with good health. Medical coverage or disability insurance will also affect your need for funds to cover a short-term emergency. If you have this coverage, more of the portfolio may be directed toward other financial goals.

In addition to financial goals, willingness to bear risk plays an important role in constructing a portfolio. Some individuals are more able to assume risk. These persons will tend to select assets on which the return involves greater risk to obtain the specified investment goals. For example, if you want to build a retirement fund, you can choose from a variety of possible investments. However, not all investments are equal with regard to risk and potential return. Those investors who are more willing to accept risk may construct portfolios with assets involving greater risk that may earn higher returns.

Taxes may also affect the composition of your portfolio. Income such as interest and realized capital gains are taxed. When a person dies, the federal government taxes the value of the estate, and many states levy a tax on an individual's inheritance. Such taxes and the desire to reduce them affect the composition of each investor's portfolio.

Portfolio decisions are obviously important. They set a general framework for the asset allocation of the portfolio among various types of investments. Individuals, however, rarely construct a portfolio all at once but acquire assets one at a time. The decision revolves around which specific asset to purchase: Which mutual fund? Which bond? or Which stock? Security analysis considers the merits of the individual asset. Portfolio management determines the impact that the specific asset has on the portfolio.

A large portion of this text is devoted to descriptions and analysis of individual securities, because it is impossible to know an asset's effect on the portfolio without first knowing its characteristics. Stocks and bonds differ with regard to risk, potential return, and valuation. Even within a type of asset such as bonds there can be considerable variation. For example, a corporate bond is different from a municipal bond, and a convertible bond differs from a straight bond that lacks the conversion feature. You need to know these differences as well as the relative merits and risks associated with each of the assets. Then you can construct a portfolio that will help you realize your financial goals.

Preliminary Definitions

I went to the doctor and he said, "You have a contusion." I asked, "What is a contusion?" and he said, "A bruise." My mind thought: "A bruise by another name is still a bruise" and immediately wanted to ask (but did not), "Why not call it a bruise?"

Every discipline or profession has its own terminology. The field of investments is no different. Some of the jargon is colorful (e.g., *bull* and *bear*); some is descriptive (e.g., *primary* and *secondary* markets); and some, like *contusion*, seem to confuse or muddy the waters (e.g., *purchasing power risk*, which is the risk associated with loss from inflation). In order to proceed, we need a common ground. What follows is a series of basic definitions, and the best time to learn them is now, since I will use these terms throughout this text.

Let's start with the word *investments*. Unfortunately, this term is ambiguous; it has more than one meaning. In an economics class, the term "investment" refers to the purchase of a physical asset such as plant, equipment, or inventory. In a corporate finance course, the term could apply to any asset such as the purchase of plant, equipment, accounts receivable, or marketable securities. For most individuals, the word denotes buying stock or bonds (or maybe a house), but it probably does not mean purchasing plant, equipment, or inventory.

In either case, the firm or the individual wants a productive asset. The difference in the definitions (that is, the usage of the word) rests on the aggregate change in productive assets. When firms invest in plant and equipment, there is a net increase in productive assets. This increase generally does not occur when individuals purchase stocks and bonds. Instead, for every investment by the buyer there is an equal *dis*investment by the seller. These buyers and sellers are trading one asset for another: The seller trades the security for cash, and the buyer trades cash for the security. These transactions occur in secondhand markets, and for that reason securities markets are often referred to as **secondary markets**. Only when the securities are initially issued and sold in the **primary market** is there an investment in an *economic* sense. Then and only then does the firm receive the money that it, in turn, may use to purchase plant, equipment, or inventory.

In this text, the word investment is used in the layperson's sense. Purchase of an asset for the purpose of storing value (and, it is hoped, increasing that value over time) will be called an *investment*, even if in the aggregate there is only a transfer of ownership from a seller to a buyer. The purchases of stocks, bonds, options, commodity contracts, and even antiques and real estate are all considered to be investments if the individual's intent is to transfer purchasing power to the future. If these assets are acting as stores of value, they are investments for that individual.

Assets have **value** because of the future benefits they offer. The process of determining what an asset is worth today is called **valuation**. An investor appraises the asset and assigns a current value to it based on the belief that the asset will generate cash flows (e.g., interest) or will appreciate in price. After computing this value, the individual compares it with the current market price to determine if the asset is currently overpriced or underpriced.

In some cases this valuation is relatively easy. For example, the bonds of the federal government pay a fixed amount of interest each year and mature at a specified date. Thus, the future cash flows are known. However, the future cash flows of other assets are not so readily identified. For example, although an investor may anticipate future dividends, neither their payment nor their amount can be known with certainty. Forecasting future benefits may be difficult, but it is still crucial to the *process of valuation*. Without forecasts and a valuation of the asset, the investor cannot know if the asset should be purchased or sold.

Because the valuation of assets is complicated and the future is uncertain, people may have different estimates of future cash flows. It is therefore easy to understand why two individuals may have completely divergent views on the worth of a particular security. One person may believe that an asset is overvalued and hence seek to sell it, while another may seek to buy it in the belief that it is undervalued. Valuation may be subjective, which leads to one person's buying while the other is selling. That does not mean that one person is necessarily irrational or incompetent. People's goals and perceptions (or estimates) of an asset's potential may change, affecting their valuation of the specific asset.

An investment is made because the investor anticipates a **return**. The total return on an investment is what the investor earns. This may be in the form of

---

secondary market
A market for buying and selling previously issued securities.

primary market
The initial sale of securities.

value
What something is worth; the present value of future benefits.

valuation
The process of determining the current worth of an asset.

return
The sum of income plus capital gains earned on an investment in an asset.

income
The flow of money or its equivalent produced by an asset; dividends and interest.

capital gain
An increase in the value of a capital asset, such as a stock.

rate of return
The annual percentage return realized on an investment.

risk
The possibility of loss; the uncertainty of future returns.

speculation
An investment that offers a potentially large return but is also very risky; a reasonable probability that the investment will produce a loss.

income, such as dividends and interest, or in the form of **capital gains**, or appreciation if the asset's price rises. Not all assets offer both income and capital appreciation. Some stocks pay no current dividends but may appreciate in value. Other assets, including savings accounts, do not appreciate in value. The return is solely the interest income.

Return is frequently expressed in percentages, such as the **rate of return**, which is the annualized return that is earned by the investment relative to its cost. Before purchasing an asset, the investor anticipates that the return will be greater than that of other assets of similar risk. Without this anticipation, the purchase would not be made. The *realized* return may, of course, be quite different from the *anticipated* rate of return. That is the element of risk.

Risk is the uncertainty that the anticipated return will be achieved. The investor must be willing to bear this risk to achieve the expected return. Even relatively safe investments involve some risk; there is no completely safe investment. For example, savings accounts that are insured still involve some element of risk of loss. If the rate of inflation exceeds the rate of interest that is earned on these insured accounts, you suffer a loss of purchasing power.

A term that is frequently used in conjunction with risk is **speculation**. Many years ago virtually all investments were called "speculations." Today the word implies a high degree of risk. However, risk is not synonymous with speculation. Speculation has the connotation of gambling, in which the odds are against the player. Many securities are risky, but over a period of years you should earn a positive return. The odds are not really against the investor, and such investments are not speculations.

The term *speculation* is rarely used in this text, and when it is employed, the implication is that you run a good chance of losing the funds invested in the speculative asset. Although a particular speculation may pay off handsomely, you should not expect that many such gambles will reap large returns. After adjusting for the larger amount of risk that must be borne, the anticipated return may not justify the risk involved.

EFFICIENT AND COMPETITIVE MARKETS

Have you ever been fishing? (If not, substitute playing golf or some similar activity.) Did you catch any fish? Which fish did you talk about? The answer to that question is probably the "big one" or the "big one that got away." What is more important, of course, is the size of the average fish (or average golf score). If you go fishing several times, you will not catch a "big one" every time or even frequently. The average size of the fish you catch becomes the norm. And other individuals who fish in the same waters will have comparable results. Unless they have special skills or knowledge, most individuals' catch should be similar to and approach the average size of fish that is caught.

In many ways, the fishing analogy applies to investing. Individuals tend to talk about the big return ("I bought X and it doubled within a week") or the lost opportunity ("I bought Plain and Fancy Doughnuts of America. It rose 80 percent within an hour and I did not sell"). But what matters is the return you earn after making many investments over an extended period of time. Unless you have special skills or knowledge, that return should tend to be comparable to the return earned by other investors in comparable investments.

Why is this so? The answer lies in the reality that investors participate in *efficient* and *competitive* financial markets. Economics teaches that markets with many participants (i.e., buyers and sellers) who may enter and exit freely will be competitive. That certainly describes financial markets. Investors may participate freely in the purchase and sale of stocks and bonds. Virtually anyone, from a child to a grandmother, may own a financial asset, even if it is just a savings account. Many firms, including banks, insurance companies, and mutual funds, compete for investors' funds. The financial markets are among the most (and perhaps *the* most) competitive of all markets.

Financial markets tend to be very efficient. As is explained throughout this text, security prices depend on future cash flows, such as interest or dividend payments. If new information suggests that these flows will be altered, the market rapidly adjusts the asset's price. Thus, an efficient financial market implies that a security's current price embodies all the known information concerning the potential return and risk associated with the particular asset. If an asset, such as a stock, were undervalued and offered an excessive return, investors would seek to buy it, which would drive the price up and reduce the return that subsequent investors would earn. Conversely, if the asset were overvalued and offered an inferior return, investors would seek to sell it, which would drive down its price and increase the return to subsequent investors. The fact that there are sufficient informed investors means that a security's price will reflect the investment community's consensus regarding the asset's true value and also that the expected return will be consistent with the amount of risk the investor must bear to earn the return.

The concept of an efficient financial market has an important and sobering corollary. Efficient markets imply that investors (or at least the vast majority of investors) cannot expect on average to beat the market *consistently*. Of course, that does not mean an individual will never select an asset that does exceedingly well. Individuals can earn large returns on particular assets, as the stockholders of many firms know. Certainly the investor who bought Heller Financial stock on July 29, 2001, for $35.90 and sold it one day later on July 30, 2001, for $52.99 made a large return on that investment. (The reason for the large increase was that GE announced on July 30, 2001, that it would acquire Heller Financial for a premium over the previous day's closing price.) The concept of efficient markets implies that this investor will not consistently select those individual securities that earn abnormally large returns.

If investors cannot expect to outperform the market consistently, they also should not consistently underperform the market. (That is, you would not always be the investor who *sold* Heller Financial just prior to the large increase in its price.) Of course, some securities may decline in price and inflict large losses on their owners, but efficient markets imply that individuals who construct well-diversified portfolios will not always select the stocks and bonds of firms that fail. If such individuals do exist, they will soon lose their resources and will no longer be able to participate in financial markets.

Thus, efficient financial markets imply that you should, over an extended period of time, earn neither excessively positive nor excessively negative returns. Instead, returns should mirror the returns earned by the financial markets as a whole and the risk assumed by the investor. As is covered in Chapter 4, the Ibbotson studies (which are considered the benchmark for aggregate returns) indicate that the historical return on investments in stock in the country's largest firms has been approximately 11 percent annually. Smaller, but riskier, companies have generated higher returns. These historical returns are consistent with the risk/ return trade-off, that higher returns require more risk. In an efficient market framework, it would be reasonable to assume that over an extended period of time the typical investor earns returns that are consistent with these historical returns.

Although security prices and returns are ultimately determined by the interaction of supply and demand (sellers and buyers), there is little the individual investor can do to affect a security's price. Instead you should select among the alternatives to build a portfolio that is consistent with your financial goals and willingness to bear risk. That is, you allocate your resources to construct a well-diversified portfolio that, over time, meets your reasons for saving and postponing current spending.

THE AUTHOR'S PERSPECTIVE AND INVESTMENT PHILOSOPHY

Financial textbooks present material that is factual (e.g., the features of bonds), theoretical (e.g., the theory of portfolio construction and diversification), and the result of empirical studies. This text is no exception. It tries to avoid the author's bias or perspective. In reality, however, an author's viewpoint cannot be completely disregarded. It affects the space devoted to a topic and how the topic is covered.

The first tenet that affects my perspective is a belief that investment decisions are made in exceedingly competitive financial markets (the efficient markets referred to earlier). Information is disseminated so rapidly that few individual investors are able to take advantage of new information. This theme of efficient markets reappears throughout the book. You could conclude that the reality of efficient markets ends your chances of making good investments, but that is the wrong conclusion. The presence of efficient markets ensures that you can make investments on a level playing field. In other words, the return you earn does not have to be inferior to the returns generated by more seasoned or professional investors.

A second tenet that affects my perspective is my investment philosophy. I began the first version of an investment book during the 1970s, so it is possible to infer how long I have been investing. Over the years I have developed my personal investment strategy that stresses patience and long-term wealth accumulation. Additional considerations are taxation and transaction costs. The philosophy and strategies of other individuals and portfolio managers may be the exact opposite. They may have a shorter time horizon and may be less concerned with current taxes or the costs of buying and selling securities.

Understanding yourself and specifying financial goals are important when developing an investment philosophy and making investment decisions. If your investments cause you to worry (frequently expressed as causing you to lose sleep), you need to look inside yourself to determine why. If I had to buy and sell securities frequently, I would have a conflict with my personality and long-term financial goals. As a graduate student, I would often buy and sell for small gains. I found such trading to be fun and stimulating, but I observed that stocks I sold always seemed to rise and those I did not sell always seemed to decline. In effect, I violated one of investing's cardinal rules: "Let your winners run but cut your losses." It was many years before I realized that a buy-and-sell strategy (a trading strategy) did not work for me. Part of the reason was my inability to sell the losers. (Behavioral finance might suggest that I had a problem with "letting go" or that I wanted to avoid the "pain of regret" in which I refused to face the reality that I had made a bad investment decision.) I also had failed to specify why I was investing. I was treating investment as a game and not a means to reach a financial goal.

Your background also affects your investment strategies. I grew up in a family of homebuilders. As would be expected, family members had a bias, which I continue to have, for companies related to real estate (e.g., the real estate investment trusts discussed in Chapter 13). Natural resources for building (e.g., trees for lumber), building materials (e.g., plumbing supplies), and appliances for homes were often the topic of discussion at dinner. Such companies as Georgia-Pacific (lumber) or Maytag (appliances) I remember from childhood. The same applies to such companies as the local gas and electric (Dominion Resources) or phone utility (AT&T before divestiture), because I grew up with their names.

In addition to efficient markets, financial goals, and your background, the time you have to devote to investing affects your decisions. I teach courses in finance, have contact with former students who work in the area, and know investment professionals. Daily news coverage, programs like *The Nightly Business Report* on public TV, 1-800 phone numbers, and materials I have retained, such as annual reports, mean I can obtain information even when I am away from my personal computer and the Internet! I think about some topic in finance and investments every day, holidays and vacations included.

Most individuals do not have such continuous contact with investments. Their jobs and family obligations preclude it. These individuals may not develop financial goals and investment strategies, but their need for financial planning does not disappear. When individuals lack time or believe they do not have expertise, they may use professional financial planners or other professionals, such as brokers, to facilitate the construction of a diversified portfolio. The growth in the popularity of mutual funds is partially explained by individuals who do not want to select specific securities and who turn over that process to portfolio managers. These investors, however, continue to need specific investment goals and strategies, and they still must select the portfolio managers!

Your background, time available to devote to investments, and financial goals may produce an investment philosophy and strategy that differ from mine. The material in this text presents alternative investments and strategies, some of which I have not used (and would not use). I will, however, try to present all the material in an unbiased manner so that you may draw your own conclusions and develop your own financial goals, investment philosophy, and strategy.

THE PLAN FOR *BASIC INVESTMENTS*

You will be buying and selling securities in efficient financial markets and competing with many investors, professional security analysts, and portfolio managers. You need a certain amount of basic information concerning investments. This text will help you learn that essential basic knowledge about securities: their features, their sources of return, and the risk associated with each asset. Perhaps because investing is concerned with your money and the potential for large gains or losses, it seems more mysterious and exciting than it is. I don't want to suck the life out of your enthusiasm for investing, but I do want you to make investment decisions with your "eyes wide open." You need fundamental knowledge and realistic expectations.

The number of alternatives available to you is mind-boggling. Shares in thousands of corporations are actively traded. Corporations, the federal government, and state and local governments issue a variety of debt instruments that range in maturity from a few days to 30 or more years. If you do not want to select individual securities, you can choose among over 8,000 mutual funds. More than 10,000 commercial banks and thrift institutions offer a variety of savings and time deposits (certificates of deposit). Real estate, options, futures, and even collectibles further increase the number of possible alternatives. And, as if there were insufficient domestic choices, you may purchase foreign securities. The problem is not one of availability but one of choice.

This text is divided into three parts. The first covers the basic background. The first chapter considers how securities come into existence (the primary market for initial public offerings) and their subsequent trading in the secondary markets (the securities markets such as the New York Stock Exchange and the Nasdaq stock market). Chapter 2 covers the framework for investment decisions: financial planning and taxation as it applies to investments. Since none of us likes paying taxes, a considerable amount of the chapter is devoted to sheltering returns from taxation, especially the importance of long-term capital gains and pension plans. Chapter 3 explains sources of risk, how risk is measured, and the importance of constructing diversified portfolios that reduce risk exposure. Chapter 4, the last chapter in Part 1, discusses various measures of the market, such as the Dow Jones industrial average, and historical returns that securities have achieved over extended periods of time.

Part 2 is devoted to the securities that investors include in their portfolios. Chapter 5 describes the features of common stock, which represents ownership (equity) in a corporation. Chapters 6 through 8 consider methods for analyzing and valuing common stocks for possible inclusion in your portfolio. Chapters 9 through 11 expand your horizon to bonds and preferred stock. Chapters 9 and 10 describe the features and the variety of corporate and government bonds. Chapter 11 is devoted to the pricing of bonds.

After completing the material in Chapters 5 through 11, you may decide to let someone else manage your resources. Chapter 12 covers the basics of selecting investment companies, especially mutual funds. Chapter 13 considers a variety of specialized investment companies and ends with a discussion of how you may compare the performance (i.e., benchmark) of mutual fund portfolio managers.

Part 3 widens your choices by adding derivative securities: options and futures contracts. Chapter 14 covers put and call options to sell and buy stock. This chapter describes the basic features of options, the advantages and risks associated with buying and selling options, and how they may be used in combination with stocks to manage risk. Chapter 15 is devoted to futures, which are contracts to buy or sell a commodity or financial asset. Since these are among the riskiest of all assets, it is highly unlikely that you will even participate in the market for futures. You, however, may become employed by a corporation that does use these contracts to hedge its operations and financial decisions.

The text ends with a postscript. The primary purpose of this postscript is to remind you of the importance of establishing financial goals, allocating your assets among the alternatives to meet those goals, and the efficient market hypothesis. If you learn nothing but the importance of diversification, you will have learned a major lesson in investments. The efficient market hypothesis is almost as important. While not everyone agrees that markets are efficient, there is general agreement among professionals and academics that it is exceedingly hard to beat the market (that is, to outperform the market consistently over a period of time).

The efficient market implies that many techniques used to analyze and select securities will not generate superior results. This is a sobering hypothesis. You need always to be aware of the efficient market hypothesis and its implications.

Before proceeding to Chapter 1, I have one final point. All textbooks make assumptions concerning your background. I have assumed that you know two important topics: the time value of money and the analysis of financial statements using ratios. For these topics, I have provided a self-test section before Chapter 2. (You will be faced with situations that involve time value in Chapter 2, so the self-test can't wait until later in the text.) Essentially, the self-tests are practice problems. If you can solve and interpret the problems, then you don't need additional work; if you have difficulty completing the problems, suggestions are provided to help you correct any deficiency.

INTERNET APPLICATIONS

The Internet facilitates inclusion of current investment applications and problems. However, as one anonymous reviewer put it: "I had a very bad experience using web based applications. . . . It was amazing how many of the links no longer worked. In many cases when the links still worked, the content had been revised to such an extent that the questions were either not answered or required exhaustive searches."

I sympathize. I hate being frustrated, so to reduce the probability of creating frustration for you, the applications in this book are generic, include alternatives, and, in many cases, provide several addresses. Addresses will be monitored and changed as necessary. A list of updates can be found on the book's Web page at **http://mayo.swlearning.com**. (You can always do an Internet search to find a new address or additional addresses. Remember, the purpose of these applications is not that you complete a specific task but rather to familiarize you with locating and applying information concerning investments.)

APPLICATION FOR AN INTRODUCTION TO *BASIC INVESTMENTS*

The study of finance may lead to a variety of possible careers. If you are contemplating a career in finance, you need to be aware of professional certifications, including the Chartered Financial Analyst (CFA) sponsored by the CFA Institute (formerly the Association for Investment Management and Research) and the Certified Financial Planner (CFP) authorized through the Certified Financial Planner Board of Standards.

The CFA primarily interests individuals who want to become financial analysts and portfolio managers. The CPF primarily interests individuals who want to work with people and small businesses to develop and execute financial plans that encompass investments and tax management, estate planning, and risk management. Both certifications have educational and work experience requirements. Your first Internet assignment is to find the CFA and CFP requirements for certification. These may be found at **http://www.cfainstitute.org** and **http://www.cfp-board.org**, respectively.

CURRENCY WITH THOMSON ONE: INTRODUCTION

Keeping current is important for making investment decisions. One method to maintain currency is to use a database such as Thomson ONE: Business School Edition, which is available to students using this text. If you acquired a new copy, the database is available at no additional cost for a period of four months. Follow the instructions on the registration card that comes with the text to access the database.

Throughout out this text, there are illustrations, examples, and problems that employ data from a variety of sources (e.g., the Federal Reserve). Some of this information is also available in Thomson ONE: Business School Edition, and selected chapters have problems and exercises requesting that you use the Thomson ONE: Business School Edition database. By completing these problems and exercises, you will be using current information and becoming familiar with a resource that is employed by professional financial analysts.

These exercises are built upon the financial statements of four firms in three industries:

Pharmaceuticals

Bristol-Myers Squibb (BMY)

Johnson & Johnson (JNJ)

Schering Plough (SGP)

Wyeth (WYE)

Retail

Limited Brands (LTD)

Lowe's (LOW)

Nordstrom, Inc. (JWN)

Pier 1 (PIR)

Telecommunications

Bell South (BLS)

SBC Communications (SBC)

Sprint (FON)

Verizon (VZ)

While each company is in one of the three industries, they do differ. For example, Verizon and SBC provide local phone service to different geographical regions but compete head-to-head in providing long-distance service. Each stock is actively traded and the ticker symbols are provided in the parentheses. You may access specific company information in the Thomson ONE: Business School Edition database by using either its name or the symbol.

PART

1 • • •

The Basics of Investing

When I was much younger, I wanted to buy stocks. In retrospect, I had little knowledge of investments on which to base my decisions, but that didn't stop me from buying stocks. I remember the first one I bought. Its price went nowhere, so I sold that stock and bought another. Its price rose dramatically, and I eventually sold it to make the down payment on my first house. Today the stock is worth less than what I sold it for. The first stock, however, rose dramatically after I sold it. Think about my experience: I sold a stock that subsequently did well and sold a stock that subsequently did poorly. One good decision and one poor decision, but the good decision had nothing to do with my knowledge of investing. It was the result of my needing cash.

No matter how much you learn about investing, you will make some good decisions and some bad decisions. As the title of this text implies, *Basic Investments* covers the basics for making investment decisions: how securities are bought and sold, the features of various financial assets, the importance of diversification, and several tools to help you manage risk. Notice that this list does not include how to outperform the market. (You should be skeptical of anyone or any book that makes that claim.) This text may not increase your ability to make consistently good decisions, but it may help you make fewer bad ones. Certainly you will be better informed than I was when I bought my first stock.

This text has three parts. Part 1 starts with the initial public offerings (IPOs) of securities and their subsequent trading in the secondary markets (Chapter 1). You will learn the difference between long and short positions, cash and margin accounts, and the mechanics of buying and selling securities. Chapter 2 considers your need for establishing investment goals and financial planning. This chapter also covers taxation and how it may affect your investment decisions. Chapters 3 and 4 cover risk and return. Chapter 3 is devoted to sources of risk, and how risk may be measured and managed through the construction of a diversified portfolio. If you learn only one concept concerning investments, the importance of diversification would be my candidate for that concept. Part 1 ends with the sources of investment returns, the computation of aggregate measures of the securities markets, and the historical returns that broad classes of financial assets have earned over extended periods of time.

CHAPTER

1 • • •

Securities Markets

On April 12, 2004, over 3.1 million shares of IBM traded on the New York Stock Exchange. In all, over 3.1 billion shares traded that day on the exchange. Not one penny of the proceeds of those sales went to the firms whose shares were bought and sold. Instead, all those transactions were among investors. Obviously, many individuals were altering their portfolios through buying or selling those existing securities.

This buying and selling of securities has a certain mystique or fascination for both the novice and the seasoned investor. Investors may be drawn to securities by the excitement generated by trading securities. Perhaps the fascination is the result of the fact that large sums can be earned (or lost) through investments in stocks and bonds. For whatever reason, investors (including you) need to understand how securities markets work and the mechanics for buying and selling securities.

This chapter explains the creation of securities and the mechanics of buying and selling stocks and bonds. The chapter begins with the transfer of funds from savers to firms, which occurs when firms issue new securities. These new issues may be sold directly to buyers or through investment bankers, who often guarantee the sale so that the issuing firm raises a specified amount of funds. Once the securities are issued and initially sold, secondary markets develop in which these securities continue to be bought and sold. The bulk of the chapter describes how you buy and sell securities, the role of brokers, types of security orders and accounts, and the cost of buying and selling securities. The chapter ends with a brief discussion of the regulation of the securities industry and the role of the Securities Investor Protection Corporation (SIPC), which insures investors against losses incurred from the failure of a brokerage firm.

•⦿THE CREATION OF SECURITIES

There are basically only two methods for transferring funds to business. One is the direct investment, which occurs when new securities are issued and purchased by investors or when individuals invest in partnerships or proprietorships. The second method is the indirect transfer through a financial intermediary such as a commercial bank. Essentially the bank issues a variety of accounts or securities to raise funds which are subsequently lent to the firms, governments, or individuals in need of funds. The financial intermediary stands between the ultimate supplier and the ultimate user of the funds and facilitates the flow of money and credit between suppliers and users.

While you may personally invest in a savings account or other instrument issued by a financial intermediary, courses in investments are primary concerned with the creation of stocks and bonds and their subsequent trading in the securities markets. These stocks and bonds may be sold directly to investors or through investment bankers, who facilitate the initial sale of the securities.

The direct sale of an entire issue of bonds or stock to an investor (or group of investors) or to a financial institution, such as a pension fund or a life insurance company, is called a **private placement**. The primary advantages of a private placement to the firm are the elimination of the cost of selling securities to the general public and the ready availability of large amounts of cash. In addition, the firm does not have to meet the disclosure requirements that are necessary to sell securities to the general public. This disclosure of information is for the protection of the investing public; it is presumed that the financial institution can protect itself by requiring information as a precondition for granting a loan. The disclosure requirements are both a cost to the firm when securities are issued to the public and a possible source of information to its competitors that the firm may wish to avoid divulging. An additional advantage of a private placement to both the firm and the financial institution is that the terms of securities may be tailored to meet both parties' needs.

A private placement has similar advantages for the firm that is investing the funds. A substantial amount of money may be invested at one time, and the maturity date can be set to meet the lender's needs. In addition, brokerage fees associated with purchasing securities are avoided. The financial intermediary can gain more control over the firm that receives the funds by building restrictive covenants into the agreement. These covenants may restrict the firm from issuing additional securities without the prior permission of the lender and may limit the firm's dividends, its merger activity, and the types of investments that it may make. All these restrictive covenants are designed to protect the lender from risk of loss and are part of any private sale of securities from a firm to a financial institution. Because each sale is separately negotiated, the individual terms vary with the bargaining powers of the parties and the economic conditions at the time of the agreement.

Private placements are especially important for small, emerging firms. The size of these firms or the risk associated with them often precludes their raising funds from traditional sources such as commercial banks. Firms that do make private placements of securities issued by emerging firms are called **venture capitalists**. Venture capital is a major source of finance for small firms or firms developing new technologies. The venture capitalists thus fill a void by acquiring securities issued by small firms with exceptional growth potential.

private placement
The nonpublic sale of securities.

venture capitalist
Firm specializing in investing in the securities, especially stock, of small, emerging companies.

Of course, many small firms do not realize this potential, and venture capitalists often sustain large losses on their investments. Success, however, can generate a very large return. In a sense, it is a numbers game. If a venture capitalist invests in five projects and four fail, the one large gain can more than offset the investments in the four losers.

THE ISSUING AND SELLING OF NEW SECURITIES

investment banker
An underwriter, a firm that sells new issues of securities to the general public.

initial public offering (IPO)
The first sale of common stock to the general public.

Firms, in addition to acquiring funds through private placements, may issue new securities and sell them to the general public, usually through **investment bankers**. If this sale is the first sale of common stock to the general public, it is referred to as an **initial public offering (IPO)**. Firms sell securities when internally generated funds are insufficient to finance the desired level of investment spending and when the firm believes it to be advantageous to obtain outside funding from the general public instead of from a financial intermediary. Such outside funding may increase public interest in the firm and its securities and may also bypass some of the restrictive covenants that are required by financial institutions.

The following section addresses the sale of new securities to the general public through an investment banker. It covers the role played by the investment banker, the mechanics of selling new securities, and the potential volatility of the new-issue market. Exhibit 1.1 (p. 18), which is the title page for the prospectus of new issue of Yahoo! Inc. common stock, illustrates the process of an initial public offering. Although the discussion is limited to the sale of stock, the process also applies to new issues of corporate bonds sold to the general public.

The Role of Investment Bankers

A corporation can market its securities directly to the public. For example, Dominion Resources had a dividend reinvestment plan, in which cash dividends are used to purchase additional stock, and, at one time, had a stock purchase plan for customers in which they made cash contributions to buy stock with their electric bill payments. If a firm does directly sell shares to the general public, the formal offer to sell these securities must be made by a prospectus, and the securities must be registered with the Securities and Exchange Commission (SEC). This process of registering the securities and their subsequent sale to the general public is discussed below.

Direct plans to sell securities to the general public involve expenses, so many firms employ investment bankers to market new securities. In effect, an investment banker serves as a middleman to channel money from investors to firms that need the capital. Although investment bankers are conduits through which the money flows, they are not financial intermediaries, since they do not create claims on themselves. With a financial intermediary, the investor has a claim on the intermediary. With an investment banker, however, the investor's claim is on the firm that issues the securities and not on the investment banker who facilitated the initial sale.

Investment banking is an important but often confusing financial practice, partly because of the misnomer. An *investment banker* is often not a banker and generally does not invest. Instead, the investment banker is usually a brokerage firm, such as Goldman, Sachs & Co., Donaldson, Lufkin & Jenrette Securities Corporation, and Montgomery Securities. Although these brokerage firms may own securities, they do not necessarily buy and hold the newly issued securities on

EXHIBIT 1.1   Title Page for the Prospectus of an Issue of Common Stock of Yahoo! Inc.

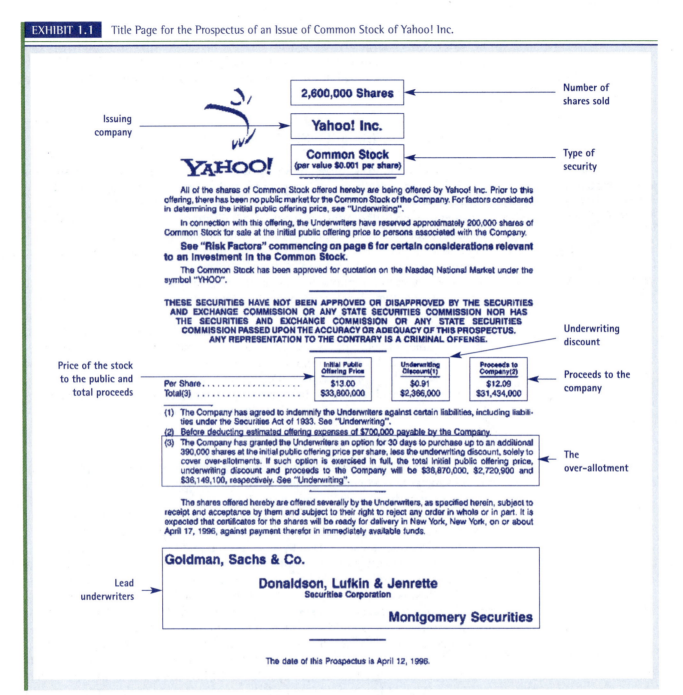

their own account for investment purposes. (When an investment bank does commit its own funds and buys the securities as an investment, it is referred to as a *merchant bank* and its activity as *merchant banking*.)

The Mechanics of Underwriting

underwriting
The process by which securities are sold to the general public and in which the investment banker buys the securities from the issuing firm.

If a firm needs funds from an external source, it can approach an investment banker to discuss an underwriting. The term **underwriting** refers to the process of selling new securities. In an underwriting the firm that is selling the securities, and not the firm that is issuing the shares, bears the risk associated with the sale. The investment banker *buys the securities with the intention of reselling them*. If it fails to sell the securities, the investment banker must still pay the agreed-upon sum to the firm at the time of the offering (i.e., the sale) of the securities. Failure to sell the securities imposes losses on the underwriter, who must remit funds for securities that have not been sold.

The firm in need of financing and the investment banker discuss the amount of funds needed, the type of security to be issued, the price and any special features of the security, and the cost to the firm of issuing the securities. All these factors are negotiated by the firm seeking capital and the investment banker. If mutually acceptable terms are reached, the investment banker will be the intermediary through which the securities are sold by the firm to the general public.

originating house
An investment banker that makes an agreement with a firm to sell a new issue of securities and forms the syndicate to market them.

syndicate
A selling group assembled to market an issue of securities.

Because an underwriting starts with a particular brokerage firm that manages the underwriting, that firm is called the **originating house**. The originating house need not be a single firm if the negotiation involves several investment bankers. In this case, several firms can jointly underwrite and sell the securities to the general public.

The originating house does not usually sell all the securities by itself but instead forms a **syndicate** to market them. The syndicate is a group of brokerage houses that join together to underwrite a specific sale of securities. The members of the syndicate may bring in additional brokerage firms to help distribute the securities. The firm that manages the sale is frequently referred to as the *lead underwriter*. It is the lead underwriter that allocates the specific number of securities each member of the syndicate is responsible for selling. In the Yahoo! illustration, 17 additional firms joined the three lead underwriters to sell the securities.

The use of a syndicate has several advantages. First, the syndicate may have access to more potential buyers for the securities. Second, by using a syndicate the number of securities that each brokerage firm must sell is reduced. The increase in the number of potential customers and the decrease in the amount that each broker must sell increases the probability that the entire issue of securities will be sold. Thus, syndication makes possible both the sale of a large offering of securities and a reduction in the risk borne by each member.

Types of Agreements

best-efforts agreement
Agreement with an investment banker who does not guarantee the sale of a security but who agrees to make the best effort to sell it.

firm commitment
Agreement with an investment banker who guarantees a sale of securities by agreeing to purchase the entire issue at a specified price.

The agreement between the investment bankers and the firm may be one of two types. The investment bankers may make a **best-efforts agreement** in which they agree to make their best effort to sell the securities but do not guarantee that a specified amount of money will be raised. The risk of selling the securities rests with the firm issuing the securities. If the investment bankers are unable to find buyers, the firm does not receive the desired amount of money.

The alternative is a **firm commitment**, an underwriting in which the investment bankers purchase (i.e., underwrite) the entire issue of securities at a specified price and subsequently sell them to the general public. Most sales of new securities are made through firm commitments, and best-effort sales are generally limited to small security issues by less well known firms. In an underwriting, the investment bankers pay the expenses with the anticipation of recouping these costs through the sale. Because the underwriters have agreed to purchase the entire issue, they must pay the firm for all the securities even if the syndicate is unable to sell them. Thus, the risk of the sale rests with the underwriters.

It is for this reason that the pricing of the underwritten securities is crucial. If the initial offer price is too high, the syndicate will be unable to sell the securities. When this occurs, the investment bankers have two choices: (1) to maintain the offer price and hold the securities in inventory until they are sold or (2) to let the market find a lower price level that will induce investors to purchase the securities. Neither choice benefits the investment bankers. If the underwriters purchase the securities and hold them in inventory, they either must tie up their own funds, which could be earning a return elsewhere, or must borrow funds to pay for the securities. The investment bankers pay interest on these borrowed funds. Thus, the decision to support the offer price of the securities requires the investment bankers to invest their own capital or, more likely, to borrow substantial amounts of capital. In either case, the profit margins on the underwriting are substantially decreased, and the investment bankers may even experience a loss on the underwriting.

Instead of supporting the price, the underwriters may choose to let the price of the securities fall. The inventory of unsold securities can then be sold, and the underwriters will not tie up capital or have to borrow money from their sources of credit. If the underwriters make this choice, they take losses when the securities are sold at less than cost. But they also cause the customers who bought the securities at the initial offer price to sustain a loss. The underwriters certainly do not want to inflict losses on these customers, because if they experience losses continually, the underwriters' market for future security issues will vanish. Therefore, the investment banks try not to overprice a new issue of securities, for overpricing will ultimately result in their suffering losses.

There is also an incentive to avoid underpricing new securities. If the issue is underpriced, all the securities will be readily sold and their price will rise because demand will have exceeded supply. The buyers of the securities will be satisfied, for the price of the securities will have increased as a result of the underpricing. The initial purchasers of the securities reap windfall profits, but these gains are really at the expense of the company whose securities were underpriced. If the underwriters had assigned a higher price to the securities, the company would have raised more capital. Underwriting is a very competitive business, and each security issue is negotiated individually; hence, if one investment banker consistently underprices securities, firms will choose competitors to underwrite their securities.

Although there are reasons for the underwriters to avoid either underpricing or overpricing, there is a greater incentive to underprice the securities. Underpricing facilitates the sale and generates immediate profits for the initial buyers. One academic study did find that *initial* purchases earned higher returns as the buyers were given a price incentive to buy the new offering.[1] Subsequent buyers, how-

---

1. See Roger G. Ibbotson, "Price Performance of Common Stock New Issues," *Journal of Financial Economics* (September 1975): 235–272. For additional literature on IPOs, consult Seth Anderson, *Initial Public Offerings* (Boston: Kluwer Academic Publishers, 1995) and Jay R. Ritter, "Initial Public Offerings," *Contemporary Financial Digest* (Spring 1998): 5–30.

    A wealth of information on IPOs may be found at Hoover's IPO Central (**http://www.hoovers .com/global/ipoc/**).

ever, did not fare as well, and any initial underpricing appears to disappear soon after the original offering. In addition, many initial public offerings subsequently underperform the market during the first years after the original sale.

Marketing New Securities

Once the terms of the sale have been agreed upon, the managing house may issue a **preliminary prospectus**. The preliminary prospectus is often referred to as a *red herring*, a term that connotes the document should be read with caution as it is not final and complete. (The phrase "red herring" is derived from British fugitives' rubbing herring across their trails to confuse pursuing bloodhounds.) The preliminary prospectus informs potential buyers that the securities are being registered with the **Securities and Exchange Commission (SEC)** and may subsequently be offered for sale. **Registration** refers to the disclosure of information concerning the firm, the securities being offered for sale, and the use of the proceeds from the sale.[2]

The cost of printing the red herring is borne by the issuing firm. This preliminary prospectus describes the company and the securities to be issued; it includes the firm's income statement and balance sheets, its current activities (such as a pending merger or labor negotiation), the regulatory bodies to which it is subject, and the nature of its competition. The preliminary prospectus is thus a detailed document concerning the company and is, unfortunately, usually tedious reading.

The preliminary prospectus does not include the price of the securities. That will be determined on the day that the securities are issued. If security prices decline or rise, the price of the new securities may be adjusted for the change in market conditions. In fact, if prices decline sufficiently, the firm has the option of postponing or even canceling the underwriting.

After the SEC accepts the registration statement, a final prospectus is published. (Exhibit 1.1 is the title page to the Yahoo! final prospectus.) The SEC does not approve the issue as to its investment worth but rather sees that all required information has been provided and that the prospectus is complete in format and content. Except for changes that are required by the SEC, the final prospectus is virtually identical to the preliminary prospectus. Information regarding the price of the security, the proceeds to the company, the underwriting discount, along with any more recent financial data is added. As may be seen in Exhibit 1.1, Yahoo! Inc. issued 2,600,000 shares of common stock at a price of $13.00 to raise a total of $33,800,000. The cost of the underwriting (also called *flotation costs* or *underwriting discount*) is the difference between the price of securities to the public and the proceeds received by the firm. In this example, the cost is $0.91 a share for a total cost of $2,366,000, which is 7.5 percent of the proceeds received by Yahoo!

The issuing company frequently grants the underwriter an over-allotment to cover the sale of additional shares if there is sufficient demand. In this illustration, Yahoo! granted the underwriters the option to purchase an additional 390,000 shares, which would raise the total proceeds received by Yahoo! to $36,149,100.

The late 1990s saw a large increase in the number of IPOs, many of which were very speculative at best. Many companies, especially those related to technology in general and the Internet in particular, raised large amounts of capital. Their stock prices rose dramatically and just as dramatically fell. Ask Jeeves went public

preliminary prospectus (red herring)
Initial document detailing the financial condition of a firm that must be filed with the SEC to register a new issue of securities.

Securities and Exchange Commission (SEC)
Government agency that enforces the federal securities laws.

registration
Process of filing information with the SEC concerning a proposed sale of securities to the general public.

2. While there are exceptions, generally unregistered corporate securities may not be sold to the general public. The debt of governments (e.g., state and municipal bonds), however, is not registered with the SEC and may be sold to the general public. Information concerning the SEC may be obtained from **http://www.sec.gov**, the Securities and Exchange Commission's home page.

in July 1999 at a price of $14. It closed after the first day of trading at $64.94 and reached almost $200 in September. In July 2001, the stock was trading for about $2. Another highflyer, Ariba, saw its stock decline from $242 to $4 in less than a year.

While the late 1990s may be considered an aberration, they were not unique. In a sense, it was a repeat of the late 1960s when stocks of franchising and nursing home companies went public, rose dramatically, and subsequently declined. For example, Four Seasons Nursing Homes went public on May 10, 1968, at $11 a share. The stock rose to $102, but within two years the company was bankrupt and the stock sold for $0.16. In retrospect, a price of $102 seems absurd. The company had 3.4 million shares outstanding, so at a price of $102, the value of the company was $346.8 million ($102 × 3.4). The firm had revenues of only $19.3 million and earnings of less than $2 million, so it made no sense in terms of earnings capacity to value the firm in excess of $300 million.

The new-issue market in the late 1990s, however, was different in one very important respect. Ask Jeeves and Ariba didn't have earnings, and even at the collapsed price of $4 a share, the total market value of Ariba exceeded $1 billion. When the price of that stock reached $242, the total value of the company exceeded $60 billion! So if it made little sense to value Four Seasons Nursing Homes, which actually had earnings, at $300 million, it would make even less sense to value Ariba at $60 billion when it was operating at a loss. (This question of valuation is an essential question, perhaps the most important question, in finance. The process of valuation and techniques used to analyze a stock are covered in Chapter 7.)

The lure of large gains is, of course, what attracts speculative investors. All firms were small at one time, and each one had to go public to have a market for its shares. Someone bought the shares of IBM, Microsoft, and Johnson & Johnson when these firms went public. The ability to spot the companies that promise the greatest growth for the future is rare. However, the new-issue market has offered and continues to offer the opportunity to invest in emerging firms, some of which may produce substantial returns for those investors or speculators who are willing to accept the risk. It is the possibility of such large rewards that makes the new-issue market so exciting. However, if the past is an indicator of the future, many small, emerging firms that go public will fail and will inflict significant losses on those investors who have accepted this risk by purchasing their securities.

Shelf-Registrations

The preceding discussion was cast in terms of firms initially selling their stock to the general public (i.e., the "initial public offering" or "going public"). Firms that have previously issued securities and are currently public also raise funds by selling new securities. If the sales are to the general public, the same basic procedure applies. The new securities must be registered with and approved by the SEC before they may be sold to the public, and the firm often uses the services of an investment banker to facilitate the sale.

There are, however, differences between an initial public offering and the sale of additional securities by a publicly held firm. The first major difference concerns the price of the securities. Because a market already exists for the firm's stock, the problem of an appropriate price for the additional shares is virtually eliminated. This price will approximate the market price on the date of issue. Second, because the firm must periodically publish information (for instance, the annual report) and file documents with the SEC, there is less need for a detailed prospectus.

Many publicly held firms construct a prospectus describing a proposed issue of new securities and file it with the SEC. This document is called a *shelf-registration*. After the shelf-registration has been accepted by the SEC, the firm may sell the securities whenever the need for funds arises. Such shelf-registrations offer the issuing firm considerable flexibility because the securities do not have to be issued but can be quickly sold if the firm deems that the conditions are optimal for the sale.

SECONDARY MARKETS AND THE ROLE OF MARKET MAKERS

While securities are issued in the primary market, all subsequent transactions are in the secondary markets. If you have bought a stock, it is highly unlikely that you purchased the security as part of the IPO. Instead you bought it in one of the secondary markets.

This section covers security dealers (market makers) and their role in secondary markets. Securities are bought and sold every day by investors who never meet each other. The market transfers stocks and bonds from individuals who are selling to those who are buying. This transfer may occur on an organized exchange located in one geographical area, such as the New York Stock Exchange (**http://www. nyse.com**), which is sometimes referred to as the "Big Board," or the American Stock Exchange, the AMEX (**http://www.amex.com**) or "the curb".[3] Trading on either exchange is not automatic. A company must apply to have its securities accepted for trading. If the company meets the conditions set by the exchange, the securities are "listed" and may be bought and sold through the exchange.[4]

over-the-counter (OTC) market
The informal secondary market for unlisted securities.

Securities of public companies with shares that are not listed on an exchange are traded **over-the-counter (OTC)**. The most important OTC market is the Nasdaq stock market (**http://www.nasdaq.com**). Nasdaq is an acronym for National Association of Securities Dealers Automated Quotation system, which is the system of communication for over-the-counter price quotations.[5] (Some companies such as Microsoft and Intel choose *not* to have their shares traded on one of the exchanges.) All major unlisted stocks are included in the Nasdaq stock market. You may readily obtain bid and ask prices for many OTC stocks and bonds by simply entering the security's symbol into the system.

dealers
Market makers who buy and sell securities for their own accounts.

In either case—a listed or an unlisted security—professional security dealers make markets in stocks and bonds and facilitate their transfer from sellers to buyers. The Securities and Exchange Act of 1934 defines a **dealer** as anyone engages in the "business of buying and selling for his *own account*." Dealers in the OTC markets are referred to as "market makers," and dealers in listed securities on the

---

3. For histories of the New York and American stock exchanges, consult Robert Sobel, *The Big Board: A History of the New York Stock Market* (New York: The Free Press, 1965) and Robert Sobel, *The Curbstone Brokers: The Origins of the American Stock Exchange* (New York: Macmillan, 1970). For a history of the evolution of the stock market, see B. Mark Smith, *Toward Rational Exuberance* (New York: Farrar, Straus and Giroux, 2001).

4. Delistings do occur. For example, the NYSE delisted the stock of Aurora Foods and Mirant stock in July 2003 after each firm filed for bankruptcy. Over time, however, the number of listed securities has increased. While 1,536 stocks were traded on the NYSE in 1973, the 2003 NYSE Annual Report showed that the number had grown to over 2,959 issues of 2,783 companies.

5. For reference books on the Nasdaq stock market that also provide information on trading procedures, see Leo M. Loll Jr. and Julian G. Buckley, *The Over-the-Counter Securities Markets* (Englewood Cliffs, NJ: Prentice Hall, 1986) and the National Association of Securities Dealers, *The NASDAQ Handbook*, rev. ed. (Chicago: Probus Publishing, 1992).

specialist
A market maker on the New York Stock Exchange who maintains an orderly market in the security.

round lot
The general unit of trading in a security, such as 100 shares.

odd lot
A unit of trading, such as 22 shares, that is smaller than the general unit of sale.

bid and ask
Prices at which a security dealer offers to buy and sell stock.

spread
The difference between the bid and the ask prices.

NYSE or AMEX are referred to as **specialists**.[6] No matter what the name, all of these dealers offer to buy securities from any seller and to sell securities to any purchaser. In effect, they make markets in securities.

Transactions are made in either round lots or odd lots. A **round lot** is the normal unit of trading, and for stocks that is usually 100 shares. Smaller transactions such as 37 shares are called **odd lots**. As you might expect, the vast majority of trades are round lots or multiples of round lots.

Security dealers quote prices on a **bid and ask** basis; they buy at one price (the bid) and sell at the other price (the ask). For example, a market maker may be willing to purchase a specific stock for $20 and sell for $21. The security is then quoted "20–21," which are the bid and ask prices. For example, as I write this, the quote for New Plan Excel is 23.56–23.61, which means I can currently buy the stock for $23.61 and sell it for $23.56. (New Plan Excel is a real estate investment trust. This type of security is discussed in Chapter 13.)

The difference between the bid and the ask is the **spread** (i.e., the $0.05 difference between $23.61 and $23.56 for New Plan). The spread, like brokerage commissions, is part of the cost of investing. These two costs should not be confused. The spread is one source of compensation for maintaining a market in the security. The broker's commission is compensation for executing your purchase or sell orders.

While the spread is a primary source of compensation for market makers, it is not their only source. Market makers also earn income when they receive dividends and interest from the securities they own. Another source of profit is an increase in security prices, for the value of the dealers' portfolios rises. These profits are a necessary element of securities markets because they induce the market makers to serve the crucial functions of buying and selling securities and of bearing the risk of loss from unforeseen price declines. These market makers guarantee to buy and sell at the prices they announce. Thus, an investor knows what the securities are worth at any given time and is assured that there is a place to sell current security holdings or to purchase additional securities. For this service, the market makers must be compensated, and this compensation is generated through the spread between the bid and ask prices, dividends and interest earned, and profits on the inventory of securities should their prices rise. (Of course, the market makers must bear any losses on securities that they hold when prices fall.)

Determination of Prices

equilibrium price
A price that equates supply and demand.

Although the bid and ask prices are quoted by market makers, the security prices are set by the demand from all buyers and the supply from all sellers of securities. Market makers try to quote an **equilibrium price** that equates the supply with the demand. If market makers bid too low a price, too few shares will be offered to satisfy the demand. If they ask too high a price, too few shares will be purchased, which will result in a glut, or excess shares, in their portfolios.

Could market makers set a security's equilibrium price? For large companies the answer is probably no. If the market makers tried to establish a price above the equilibrium price that is set by supply and demand, they would have to absorb all of the excess supply of securities that would be offered at the artificially higher price. Conversely, if the market makers attempted to establish a price below the equilibrium price, they would have to sell a sufficient number of securities to meet the excess demand that would exist at the artificially lower price. The buying of

---

6. As of January 2004, 443 individuals operated as specialists. See the New York Stock Exchange annual report or *Fact Book* available at the NYSE Web site: **http://www.nyse.com**.

securities requires the delivery of the securities sold. Market makers do not have an infinite well of money with which to purchase the securities nor an unlimited supply of securities to deliver. They may increase or decrease their inventory, but they cannot support the price indefinitely by buying securities, nor can they prevent a price increase by selling them.

Although market makers cannot set the market price, they perform an extremely important role: They maintain an orderly market in securities so that buyers and sellers will have an established market in which to trade. To establish this orderly market, the market makers offer to buy and sell at the quoted bid and ask prices but guarantee only one round-lot transaction at these prices. If a market maker sets too low a price for a certain stock, a large quantity will be demanded by investors. The market maker is required to sell only one round lot at this price and then may increase the bid and ask prices. The increase in the price of the stock will (1) induce some holders of the stock to sell their shares and (2) induce some investors who wanted to purchase the stock to drop out of the market.

If the market maker sets too high a price for the stock, a large quantity of shares will be offered for sale, but these shares will remain unsold. If the market maker is unable to or does not want to absorb all these shares, the security dealer may purchase a round lot and then lower the bid and ask prices. The decline in the price of the stock will (1) induce some potential sellers to hold their stock and (2) induce some investors to enter the market by purchasing the shares, thereby reducing any of the market maker's surplus inventory.

Reporting of Transactions

Daily transactions on the listed exchanges are reported by the financial press (e.g., *The Wall Street Journal*). Weekly summaries are also reported in several publications (e.g., *The New York Times* and *Barron's*). Although there is variation in this reporting, a detailed format may appear as follows:

	52 WEEKS									
YTD %CHG	HI	LO	STOCK	(SYM)	DIV	YLD%	PE	VOL 100S	LAST	NET CHG
+4.1	99.38	45.83	BigGrn	BGN	2.16	4.2	30	20046	51.63	−1.75

The YTD %CHG represents the percentage change in the price of the stock during the current calendar year, so in this illustration the current price of the stock is 4.1 percent higher than the close at the end of the previous year. The HI and LO represent the high and low prices of the stock ($99.38 and $45.83, respectively) during the past 52 weeks. Notice that the percentage change in the price of the stock covers only the calendar year while the high and low prices cover the preceding 12 months.

Next is the name of the company (usually in abbreviated form) and the ticker symbol in bold print (BigGrn **BGN**). The DIV represents the firm's annual dividend paid during the preceding 12 months or the annual dividend rate based on four quarterly payments. The YLD % is the dividend divided by the price of the stock ($2.16/$51.63 = 4.2%). This dividend yield is a measure of the flow of income produced by an investment in BigGrn. (Dividends are discussed in detail in Chapter 5.)

PE is the ratio of the price of the stock to the company's per-share earnings. This price/earnings (P/E) ratio is a measure of value and tells what the market is currently paying for $1 of the firm's earnings. P/E ratios permit comparisons of firms relative to their earnings and, as is explained in Chapter 7, is one analytical tool that is often used in the selection of stock.

The last entries concern trading during the day. Vol 100s is the volume of shares traded expressed in hundreds, so 20046 represents 2,004,600 shares. LAST represents the closing price of the stock ($51.63) and NET CHG is the change from the closing price on the previous day of trading. In this illustration the price of the stock declined $1.75 from the previous day of trading.

The reporting of Nasdaq national-market issues is essentially the same as the reporting of NYSE-listed securities. In addition to the Nasdaq national-market issues, some financial papers report smaller, less actively traded Nasdaq stocks, called Nasdaq small cap issues or bulletin board issues. There are even securities whose prices are not reported in the financial press but are available in the "pink sheets." For example, after being delisted from the NYSE, the stocks of Mirant and Aurora Foods continued to trade in the pink sheets. Many, perhaps most, of the securities quoted in the pink sheets sell for less than $1.00. As of January 2004, Mirant was $0.38 and Aurora Foods was $0.01, if you could find a quote.

Composite Transactions

With the development of the Nasdaq stock market, the distinction between the various exchanges and the over-the-counter market is being erased. Since New York Stock Exchange securities trade on other exchanges, the actual reporting of New York Stock Exchange listings includes all the trades and is reported as the NYSE-Composite transactions. The bulk of the transactions in listed securities, however, still occurs on the NYSE.

third market
Over-the-counter market for securities listed on an exchange.

In addition to the primary market (the initial sale of the security) and the secondary market (subsequent trading in the security), there is also the **third market**, which is over-the-counter trading in listed securities. While any trades in listed securities off the exchange may be referred to as the third market, the bulk of these trades are large transactions. Such large trades (i.e., 10,000 shares or more) are called *blocks*, and the market makers who organize and execute the trades are referred to as *block positioners*.

The participants in the third market are usually institutional investors, such as pension plans, mutual funds, or insurance companies, who want to buy or sell large amounts of stocks in listed securities, such as the stock of IBM, which trades on the NYSE. The institutional investor works through a large brokerage firm that completes the transaction. If the investor desires to buy a large position, the brokerage firm (or security dealer) seeks potential sellers. After the required seller (or sellers, for a sufficiently large block) is found, the securities are traded off the floor of the exchange.

In the *fourth market*, the financial institutions do not use brokerage firms or security dealers but may trade securities through a computerized system, such as *Instinet* (**http://www.instinet.com**), which provides bid and ask price quotations and executes orders. This system is limited to those financial institutions that subscribe to the service. Transactions through Instinet are reported in the financial press through the composite transactions just like trades on the various exchanges.

Block trades, the third market, and the fourth market offer financial institutions two advantages: lower commissions and quicker executions. Competition among brokerage firms for this business has reduced the commission fees. In addition, the effort and time required to put together a block to purchase or to find buyers for a sale is reduced through the development of block trading and over-the-counter trading of listed securities. The effect of this trading and the change in the regulatory environment for financial institutions has led to a national market for the execution of security orders, since these orders need not go through an exchange in a particular geographical area.

THE MECHANICS OF INVESTING IN SECURITIES

broker
An agent who handles buy and sell orders for an investor.

Individual investors usually purchase stocks and bonds through **brokers**, who buy and sell securities for their customers' accounts. (Some brokerage firms use different titles, such as "account executive" or "assistant vice president." These individuals perform the traditional functions of "brokers.") While a few companies (e.g., ExxonMobil) offer investors the option to purchase shares directly from the corporation, the majority of purchases are made through brokerage firms, such as Merrill Lynch or A.G. Edwards. Many brokerage firms also act as market makers and may be referred to as "broker-dealers" since different divisions within the firm perform both functions. The firm has individuals who buy and sell for the firm's account (i.e., are security dealers) and other individuals who buy and sell for customers' accounts (i.e., are brokers).

The broker services an individual's account and is the *investor's agent* who executes buy and sell orders. To be permitted to buy and sell securities, brokers must pass a proficiency examination administered by the National Association of Securities Dealers. Once the individual has passed the test, he or she is referred to as a **registered representative** and can buy and sell securities for customers' accounts.

registered representative
A person who buys and sells securities for customers; a broker.

Although registered representatives must pass this proficiency examination, you should not assume that the broker is an expert. There are many aspects of investing, and even an individual who spends a considerable portion of the working day servicing accounts cannot be an expert on all the aspects of investing. Thus, many recommendations are based on research that is done by analysts employed by the brokerage firm rather than by individual salespersons.

You should also realize that brokers make their living through buying and selling for their customers' accounts. Thus, a broker's advice may be colored by the desire to secure commissions. You may request advice, but often it is given unsolicited. You are, however, ultimately responsible for the investment decisions and must weigh the impact of a specific investment decision in terms of fulfilling your financial goals.

Selecting a brokerage firm can be a difficult task. Full-service firms offer more services, which may include estate planning, life insurance, and the management of your portfolio. Service comes with a price, however. Full-service brokerage firms may assess a fee that is a percentage of the assets managed (e.g., 1 percent on the first $1,000,000 with a $10,000 minimum fee) or charge commissions for individual trades. Small accounts are discouraged through higher fees and higher commissions (as a percentage of the size of the account or of the size of the trade).

The Long and Short Positions

Essentially, an investor has only two courses of action, which involve opposite positions. They are frequently referred to as the *bull* and *bear* positions and are symbolized by a statue, which is located outside the NYSE, of a bull and a bear locked in mortal combat.[7]

If an investor expects a security's price to rise, the security is purchased. The investor takes a **long position** in the security in anticipation of the price increase. The investor is **bullish** because he or she believes that the price will rise. The long position earns profits for the investor if the price rises after the security has been purchased. For example, if an investor buys 100 shares of AB&C for $55 (i.e., $5,500 plus brokerage fees) and the price rises to $60, the profit on the long position is $5 per share (i.e., $500 on 100 shares before commissions).

Opposite the long position is the **short position (bearish)**, in which the investor anticipates that the security's price will fall. The investor sells the security and holds cash or places the funds in interest-bearing short-term securities, such as Treasury bills or a savings account. Some investors who are particularly bearish or who are willing to speculate on the decline in prices may even "sell short," which is a sale for future delivery. (The process of selling short is discussed later in this section.)

Types of Orders

After an investor decides to purchase a security, a buy order is placed with the broker. The investor may ask the broker to buy the security at the best price currently available, which is the asking price set by the market maker. Such a request is a **market order**. The investor is not assured of receiving the security at the currently quoted price, since that price may change by the time the order is executed. However, the order is generally executed at or very near the asking price.

The investor may enter a **limit order** and specify a price below the current asking price and wait until the price declines to the specified level. Such an order may be placed for one day (i.e., a **day order**), or the order may remain in effect indefinitely (i.e., a **good-till-canceled order**). Such an order remains on the books of the broker until it is either executed or canceled. If the price of the security does not decline to the specified level, the purchase is never made. While a good-till-30canceled order may remain in effect indefinitely, brokerage firms generally have a time limit (e.g., one month or three months) that specifies when the order will be canceled if it has not been executed.

After purchasing the security an investor may place a **stop order** to sell, which may be at a higher or lower price. Once the stock reaches that price, the stop order becomes a market order. An investor who desires to limit potential losses may place a stop-loss order, which specifies the price below the cost of the security at which the broker is authorized to sell. For example, if an investor buys a stock for $50 a share, a stop-loss order at $45 limits the loss to $5 a share, plus the commission fees for the purchase and the sale. If the price of the stock should fall to $45, the stop-loss order becomes a market order, and the stock is sold. (Since the order is now a market order, there is no assurance that the investor will get $45. If there is an influx of sell orders, the sale may occur at less than $45.) Such a sale protects the investor from riding the price of the stock down to $40 or lower. Of course, if the stock rebounds from $45 to $50, the investor has sold out at the bottom price.

long position
Owning assets for their income and possible price appreciation.

bullish
Expecting that prices will rise.

short position
Selling borrowed assets for possible price deterioration; being short in a security or a commodity.

bearish
Expecting that prices will decline.

market order
An order to buy or sell at the current market price or quote.

limit order
An order placed with a broker to buy or sell at a specified price.

day order
An order placed with a broker that is canceled at the end of the day if it is not executed.

good-till-canceled order
An order placed with a broker that remains in effect until it is executed by the broker or canceled by the investor.

stop order
A purchase or sell order designed to limit an investor's loss or to assure a profit on a position in a security.

---

7. The derivations of "bull" and "bear" are lost in time. "Bearish" may originate from trading in pelts when bearskins were sold before the bears were caught. Bullbaiting and bearbaiting were also sports in the eighteenth century. See Steele Commager, "Watch Your Language," *Forbes* (October 27, 1980): 113–116.

The investor may also place a stop-sell order above the purchase price. For example, the investor who purchases a stock at $50 may place a sell order at $60. Should the price of the stock reach $60, the order becomes a market order, and the stock is sold. Such an order limits the potential profit, for if the stock's price continues to rise, the investor who has already sold the stock does not continue to gain. However, the investor has protected the profit that resulted as the price increased from $50 to $60. In many cases the investor watches the stock's price rise, decides not to sell, and then watches the price subsequently decline. Stop-sell orders are designed to reduce this possibility.

Because both limit orders and stop orders specify a price, they are easy to confuse. The limit order specifies a price at which a stock is to be bought or sold. (The purchase could be made at a lower price, and the sale could occur at a higher price.) Limits orders are filled in order of receipt. A limit order to buy stock at $10 may not be executed if other investors have previously entered purchase orders at that price.[8]

A stop order also specifies a price. Once the price is reached, the order becomes a market order and is executed. Since the stop becomes a market order, the actual price at which it is executed may not necessarily be the specified price. For example, an investor buys a stock for $25 and enters a "stop-loss order" to sell at $20 to limit the possible loss on the stock. If the price declines to $20, the stop loss becomes a market order and stock is sold. As mentioned before, the investor may anticipate receiving $20, but there is no guarantee that the stock will be sold at that price. If, for example, the stock reported lower earnings and the price immediately dropped from $25 to $19, the stop-loss order would be executed at $19 instead of the specified $20.

If the investor were unwilling to accept a price less than $20, the individual could enter the sale order as a "stop-limit" order that combines a stop-loss with a limit order. However, the stock would not be sold if the price declined through the specified price before the limit order was executed. If, after the earnings announcement the price immediately dropped from $22 to $19, a stop-limit order at $20 would not be executed unless the stock subsequently rose to $20. With any limit order there is no assurance that the order will be executed. In other words, investors cannot have their cake and eat it too. Once the specified price is reached, a stop order guarantees an execution but not the price, whereas a limit order guarantees the price but not an execution.

Once the purchase has been made, the broker sends the investor a **confirmation statement**, an example of which is shown in Exhibit 1.2 (p. 30). This confirmation statement gives the number of shares and name of the security purchased (100 shares of Clevepak Corporation), the unit price ($12.13), and the total amount that is due ($1,264.76).[9] The amount that is due includes both the price of the securities and the transaction fees. The major transaction fee is the brokerage firm's commission, but there may also be state transfer fees and other miscellaneous fees. The investor has three business days after the trade date (the day the security is purchased—April 12, 200X) to pay the amount that is due. The settlement date (the day the payment is due—April 15, 200X) is three business days after the trade date, and this time difference is frequently referred to as $T + 3$.

confirmation statement
A statement received from a brokerage firm detailing the sale or purchase of a security and specifying a settlement date.

---

8. Since individuals tend to think in terms of simple numbers such as $10 or $15, it may be a wise strategy to enter the buy order at $10.05, so that the order would be executed before all orders placed at $10. The same applies to sell orders. A limit to sell at $13 is executed once the stock price rises to $13 and prior sell orders are executed. A sell order at $12.90 stands before all sell orders at $13.

9. The CUSIP in the confirmation statement (1667661) refers to the Committee for Uniform Securities Identification Procedures, which assigns a unique number for each security issue.

EXHIBIT 1.2	Confirmation Statement for the Purchase of 100 Shares of Clevepak Corporation

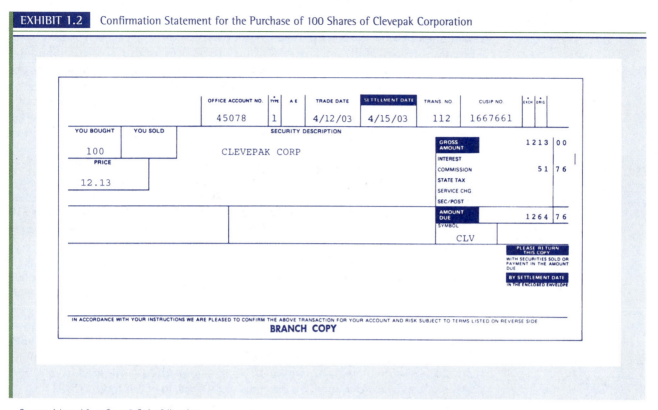

Source: Adapted from Scott & Stringfellow, Inc.

• **margin**
The amount that an investor must put down to buy securities on credit.

• **margin requirement**
The minimum percentage, established by the Federal Reserve, that the investor must put up in cash to buy securities.

Cash and Margin Accounts

The investor must pay for the securities as they are purchased. This can be done either with cash or with a combination of cash and borrowed funds. The latter is called buying on **margin**. The investor then has either a cash account or a margin account. A cash account is what the name implies: The investor pays the entire cost of the securities (i.e., $1,264.76 in Exhibit 1.2) in cash.

When an investor uses margin—that is, purchases the security partially with cash and partially with credit supplied by the broker—he or she makes an initial payment that is similar to a down payment on a house and borrows the remaining funds necessary to make the purchase. To open a margin account, the investor signs an agreement with the broker that gives the use of the securities and some control over the account to the broker. The securities serve as collateral for the loan. Should the amount of collateral on the account fall below a specified level, the broker can require that the investor put more assets in the account. This is called a *margin call*, and it may be satisfied by cash or additional securities. If the investor fails to meet a margin call, the broker will sell some securities in the account to raise the cash needed to protect the loan.

The **margin requirement** is the minimum percentage of the total price that the investor must pay and is set by the Federal Reserve Board. Individual brokers, however, may require more margin. The minimum payment required of the investor is the value of the securities times the margin requirement. Thus, if the margin requirement is 60 percent and the price of 100 shares is $1,000, the investor must supply $600 in cash and borrow $400 from the broker, who in turn borrows the funds from a commercial bank. The investor pays interest to the broker on $400. The interest rate will depend on the rate that the broker must pay to the lending institution. The investor, of course, may avoid the interest charges by paying the entire $1,000 and not using borrowed funds.

Investors use margin to increase the potential return on the investment. When they expect the price of the security to rise, some investors pay for part of their purchases with borrowed funds. If the price rises from 10 to 14, the profit is $400. If the investor pays the entire $1,000, the percentage return is 40 percent ($400/ $1,000). However, if the investor uses margin and pays for the stock with $600 in equity and $400 in borrowed funds, the investor's percentage return is increased to 67 percent ($400/$600). In this case, the use of margin is favorable because it increases the investor's return on the invested funds.

Of course, if *the price of the stock falls*, the reverse occurs — that is, *the percentage loss is greater*. If the price falls to $7, the investor loses $300 before commissions on the sale. The percentage loss is 30 percent. However, if the investor uses margin, the percentage loss is increased to 50 percent. Because the investor has borrowed money and thus reduced the amount of funds that he or she has committed to the investment, the percentage loss is greater. The use of margin magnifies not only the potential gain but also the potential loss. Because the potential loss is increased, buying securities on credit increases the element of risk that must be borne by the investor.

The previous example illustrated the potential magnification of the percentage return on a margin purchase versus a cash purchase. The example was an oversimplification because it excluded commissions, interest on any borrowed funds, and dividends received (if any). The following is a more complete illustration.

Assume the investor buys 100 shares of stock for $10 a share and sells it for $14. Also assume the margin requirement is 60 percent, the commission rate is 5 percent of the purchase or sale price, the interest rate is 10 percent, and the stock pays a dividend of $1.00 a share. The following illustrates the two positions:

	Cash	Margin
Sale price	$1,400	$1,400
Commission	70	70
Proceeds of sale	1,330	1,330
Loan repayment	0	420
Cash received	1,330	910
Dividends received	$ 100	$ 100
Interest paid	0	42

Percentage earned on the cash purchase:

$$\frac{\$1,330 + \$100 - \$1,050}{\$1,050} = 36.2\%$$

Percentage earned on the margin purchase:

$$\frac{\$1,330 - \$1,050 + \$100 - \$42}{\$630} = 53.7\%$$

Notice that the profit on the purchase and sale ($1,330 – $1,050) and the dividend payment are the same in both cases. The difference in the percentage earned is the result of having to pay interest ($42) and the fact that the investor put up only 60 percent of the funds ($630) and borrowed $420. It is the commitment of less than the full purchase price plus commissions and borrowing the balance that is the source of the magnification of the percentage return.

The percentage returns are also different from those in the simple illustration. When commissions, interest, and dividends are included, the return on the all-cash investment is 36.2 percent versus 30 percent in the simplified illustration. The return on the margin investment is 53.7 percent instead of 67 percent because the commissions and interest consume part of the return.

Maintenance Margin

The margin requirement establishes the minimum amount the investor must deposit (and the maximum amount the investor may borrow) when purchasing a security. If the price of the stock subsequently rises, the investor's position improves because the amount borrowed as a proportion of the total value of the stock declines. If, however, the value of the stock falls, the investor's position deteriorates and the amount owed becomes a larger proportion of the value of the stock.

maintenance margin
The minimum equity required for a margin position.

In order to protect the broker from the investor's defaulting (not repaying the loan), a second margin requirement is established. This **maintenance margin** sets the minimum equity the investor must have in the position. If the stock's price declines sufficiently so that the investor violates the maintenance margin requirement, the investor receives a *margin call* and must advance additional funds or the broker will sell the stock and close the position. (Actually, maintenance margin applies to the account as a whole. The investor receives a margin call when the value of the portfolio does not meet the maintenance margin requirement.)

Delivery of Securities

Once the shares have been purchased and paid for, the investor must decide whether to leave the securities with the broker or to take delivery. (In the case of a margin account, the investor *must* leave the securities with the broker.) If the shares are left with the broker, they will be registered in the brokerage firm's name (i.e., in the **street name**). The brokerage firm then becomes custodian of the securities, is responsible for them, and sends a statement of the securities that are being held in the street name to the investor. The statement (usually monthly) also includes any transactions that have taken place and any dividends and interest that have been received.[10] The investor may either leave the dividends and interest payments to accumulate or receive payment from the broker.

street name
The registration of securities in a brokerage firm's name instead of in the buyer's name.

The main advantage of leaving the securities with the brokerage is convenience, and the vast majority of investors do have their securities registered in street

---

10. Statements sent by brokerage firms may include considerably more information, including (1) the asset allocation of the various investments by type (e.g., stocks, fixed income, money market mutual funds), (2) year-to-date portfolio performance and major stock indexes, (3) cost basis of the securities and unrealized gains, and (4) dividends to be received in the next period.

name. My broker told me that only 5 percent of his customers take delivery. Some brokerage firms charge a service fee to have securities delivered, which obviously discourages delivery.

If you choose to take delivery of the securities, you will receive the stock certificates or bonds. Because the certificates may become negotiable, you may suffer a loss if they are stolen. Therefore, care should be taken to store them in a safe place such as a lock box or safe-deposit box in a bank.[11] If the certificates are lost or destroyed, they can be replaced, but only at considerable expense in terms of money and effort. For example, the financial statements of Dominion Resources direct stockholders who lose certificates to write the transfer agent for instructions on how to obtain replacements. Bond is required to protect the stockholder and the transfer agent should the lost certificates return to circulation. The cost of the bond is 2 percent of the stock's current market value *(not your cost)* plus a processing fee.

The Cost of Investing

commissions
Fees charged by brokers for executing orders.

Investing, like everything else, is not free. You must pay certain costs, the most obvious of which are **commission fees**. There may also be transfer fees, but these tend to be trivial. Commission costs are not trivial, and for small investors they may constitute a substantial portion of the total amount spent on the investment. Commission rates are supposed to be set by supply and demand, but in reality only large investors (e.g., financial institutions such as insurance companies or mutual funds) are able to negotiate commissions with brokerage firms. These institutions do such a large dollar volume that they are able to negotiate lower rates. For these institutions, the commission rates (as a percentage of the dollar amount of the transaction) may be small.

You, however, do not have this influence and generally have to accept the rate that is offered by the brokerage firm. Although the fee schedule may not be made public by the brokerage firm, the registered representative will generally tell (if asked) what the fee will be before executing the transaction.

In general, commission rates are quoted in terms of round lots of 100 shares. Most firms also set a minimum commission fee (e.g., $50) that may cover all transactions involving $1,000 or less. Then, as the value of the 100 shares increases to greater than $1,000, the fee also increases. However, this commission fee as a percentage of the dollar value of the transaction will usually fall.

discount broker
A broker who charges lower commissions on security purchases and sales.

Some brokerage firms, known as **discount brokers**, offer lower commissions. (Full-service brokers may offer discounts, but the investor must ask for them. Receiving the requested discount will depend on such factors as the volume of trades generated by the investor.) Discount brokerage firms may not offer the range of services available through the full-service brokerage houses, but if the individual does not need these services, discount brokers may help to reduce the cost of investing by decreasing commissions.

Investors may further reduce commission costs by trading on-line. Firms that offer this service initially charged substantially lower commissions than were assessed by discount brokers. Even discount brokerage firms like Charles Schwab offered its customers discounts from its regular commissions if investors used its electronic trading system. Obviously, if you feel comfortable using on-line trading and do not need regular brokerage services, you may be able to obtain substantial reductions in the cost of buying and selling securities.

---

11. My late sister had stock certificates all over the house. When I would visit, it was not unusual to see a certificate mixed in with junk mail. How she knew what she owned was a mystery to me.

Even among the on-line brokers there are differences in commissions and services. Fees and commissions tend to vary with the size of the account and the account's trading activity. These differences make it difficult to generalize about which type of account or which firm is best or cheapest. One possible source of assistance to help you select among the various on-line brokers is the review published annually by the American Association of Individual Investors (**http://aaii.com**).

Impact of the Spread on the Cost of Investing

While commissions and other fees are explicit costs, there is also an important implicit cost: the spread between the bid and the ask price of a security. As was explained earlier in this chapter, you pay the ask price but receive only the bid price when you sell securities. This spread should be viewed as a cost of investing. If you want to buy a stock that is quoted 20–21, you will have to pay $2,100 plus the commission. If the commission is a minimum of $50 a trade, the cost of a round trip (a purchase and a sale) is substantial. You pay $2,150 to buy the stock that you could immediately sell for $1,950. When you add the $100 spread and the two $50 commissions, that's a total cost of $200. The bid price must rise 2 points to $22 to cover both the commissions and the spread. You may think this example is an exaggeration. If you limit trades to stocks with a spread of only a penny (22.00–22.01) and trade on-line for $10 a trade, the stock's bid price must rise to $22.21 to cover the total cost of a 100-share purchase and sale.

THE SHORT SALE

How do you make money in the securities markets? The obvious answer is to buy at low prices and to sell at high prices. For most people this implies that you first buy the security and then sell it at some later date. Can you sell the security first and buy it back later at a lower price? The answer is yes, for a **short sale** reverses the order. You sell the security first with the intention of purchasing it in the future at a lower price.

Because the sale precedes the purchase, the investor does not own the securities that are being sold short. Selling something that you do not own may sound illegal, but there are many examples of such short selling in normal business relationships. A magazine publisher who sells a subscription, a professional such as a lawyer, engineer, or teacher who signs a contract for future services, and a manufacturer who signs a contract for future delivery are all making short sales. When your school collected the semester's tuition, it established a short position; it contracted for the future delivery of educational services. If the cost of fulfilling the contract increases, the short seller loses. If the cost declines, the short seller profits. Selling securities short is essentially no different: It is a current sale with a contract for future delivery. If the securities are subsequently purchased at a lower price, the short seller will profit. However, if the cost of the securities rises in the future, the short seller will suffer a loss.

For many individuals, the short sale and how it is executed are difficult to understand. The mechanics may be illustrated with an example. Suppose a stock is selling for $50 and you think it will appreciate. You purchase 100 shares of the stock (establish a long position) for a total cost of $5,000. If the price rises to $75, you will earn $2,500 ($7,500 – $5,000) if you sell the shares.

The short sale reverses the process: you sell the stock first and buy it back at some time in the future. Suppose you think the stock is *overpriced* and that the price will *fall*. You certainly would not buy the stock. Instead you sell 100 shares that you do not own. Because you sold the stock, you must make delivery. (Remember, the buyer does not know that you are selling the stock short and does not care.) To make delivery, you borrow 100 shares from your broker. The broker borrows the stock from clients who have left securities registered in street name. (If you have a margin account, one part of the margin agreement permits the brokerage firm to lend the shares. If you registered the shares in a cash account, the brokerage firm cannot lend the shares to a short seller.)

Although you have sold the stock, the proceeds of the sale are not remitted to you but are held by the broker. These proceeds will subsequently be used to repurchase the stock. (In the jargon of the securities market, such repurchases are referred to a *covering* the *short sale*.) Because you borrowed the stock, you must deposit with the broker an amount equal to the margin requirement for the purchase of the stock. Thus, if the margin requirement is 60 percent, you must deposit $3,000 ($5,000 × 0.6) with the broker. These funds protect the broker (i.e., they are the short seller's collateral) and they are returned to you, the short seller, plus any profits or minus any losses when you buy the shares and close your position (i.e., return the shares to the broker).

This flow of certificates and money is illustrated in Figure 1.1. The broker receives the $5,000 proceeds from the buyer and the $3,000 margin from you. You receive nothing, but the borrowed securities flow through your account en route to the buyer. Your account statement will indicate that you are short the 100 shares, which is the exact opposite of what would happen if you had purchased the 100 shares. If you had bought 100 shares, your account would indicate that you own (have a long position on) the stock.

It the price of the stock declines to $40, you can buy the stock for $4,000. This purchase is no different from any purchase. The stock is then returned to the broker; in effect the loan of the stock is repaid. You have made a profit of $1,000 because the stock was purchased for $4,000 and sold for $5,000. The broker returns your $3,000 margin. Since only $4,000 of the $5,000 original sales proceeds were used to repurchase the stock, the broker also remits the $1,000 difference (your

---

FIGURE 1.1   *The Flow of Money and Certificates in a Short Sale*

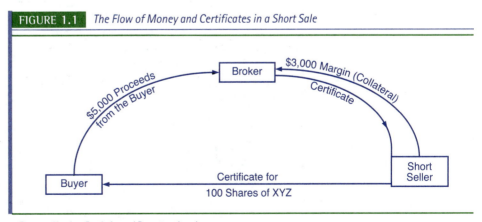

Source: *Hershey Foods Annual Report,* various issues.

$1,000 profit). This process is illustrated in Figure 1.2. The 100 shares are purchased for $4,000. The stock is returned to the broker, and the broker returns the $3,000 margin plus the $1,000 profit.

If the price of the stock had risen to $60 and you purchased the shares and returned them to the broker, your short position would have resulted in a $1,000 loss. The proceeds from the short sale would have been insufficient to purchase the shares. One thousand dollars of the collateral would have had to be used in addition to the proceeds to buy the stock and cover the short position. The broker would owe you only what was left of the collateral ($2,000) after the transactions had been completed.

Although the previous transactions may sound complicated, they really are not. All that has occurred is that you bought and sold a security. Instead of first purchasing the security and then selling it, you initially sold the security and subsequently purchased the shares to cover the short position. Because the sale occurred first, there is additional bookkeeping to account for the borrowed securities, but the transaction itself is not complicated.

Unfortunately, some individuals believe that short selling is gambling. They believe that if investors sell short and the price of the stock rises substantially, the losses could result in financial ruin. However, short sellers can protect themselves by placing stop-loss purchase orders to cover the short position if the stock's price rises to a particular level. Furthermore, if these investors fail to place stop-loss orders, the brokers will cover the position for them once their collateral has shrunk and can no longer support the short position. In effect, the short seller receives a margin call. Thus, the amount that an investor can lose is limited by the collateral. Short selling really involves no greater risk than purchasing securities, for investors who buy securities can lose all their invested funds.

Actually, selling short is consistent with a rational approach to the selection of securities. If you analyze a company and find that its securities are overpriced, you will certainly not buy the securities, and any that you currently own should be sold. In addition, if you have confidence in the analysis and believe that the price will decline, you may sell short. The short sale, then, is the logical strategy given

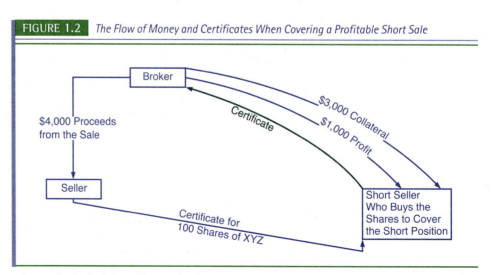

FIGURE 1.2   *The Flow of Money and Certificates When Covering a Profitable Short Sale*

Source: *Hershey Foods Annual Report,* various issues.

the basic analysis. Securities that are overpriced should be considered for short sales, just as securities that are undervalued are the logical choice for purchase.

Short selling is not limited to individual investors; market makers may also sell short. If there is an influx of orders to buy, the market makers may partially satisfy this demand by selling short. They will then repurchase the shares in the future to cover the short position after the influx of orders has subsided. Frequently, this transaction can be profitable. After the speculative increase in price that results from the increased demand, the price of the security may decline. When this occurs, the market makers profit because they sell short when the price rises but cover their positions after the price subsequently falls.

The Uptick Rule

There is one important constraint on your ability to sell short: the *uptick* rule. You may buy stock and sell existing holdings at will, but the uptick rule is a major constraint on selling short, which is designed to stop price manipulation by short sellers.

Uptick refers to the direction of price change. If the price of a stock moves up from the previous trade, that is an uptick. If the price of the stock declines from the previous trade, that is a downtick. Short sales can be executed only when the previous change in the price of the stock was an uptick. Thus, if the price of the stock moves from $10 to $9.90, a short sale cannot be executed. If, however, the price moves back to $10 from $9.90, that is an uptick and a short sale may be made. (An uptick refers to the last change in price. If a stock trades for $10 and then trades for $9.90, $9.90, $9.90, and $9.90, the last change was down. Until the stock rises [e.g., to $9.92], the last change was a downtick.)

The purpose of the uptick rule is to reduce the ability of investors and speculators to manipulate the market. Without this regulation, short sellers could borrow large quantities of stock that, when sold, would drive down the stock's price. By such manipulation, the short sellers could guarantee themselves profits. By instituting the uptick rule, the SEC has reduced the ability of short sellers to manipulate the market for their own benefit.

REGULATION

full disclosure laws
The federal and state laws requiring publicly held firms to disclose financial and other information that may affect the value of their securities.

Like many industries, the securities industry is subject to a substantial degree of regulation both from the federal and from state governments. Since the majority of securities are traded across state lines, most regulation is at the federal level.

The purpose of these laws is to protect the investor by ensuring honest and fair practices. The laws require that the investor be provided with information upon which to base decisions. Hence, these acts are frequently referred to as the **full disclosure laws**, because publicly owned companies must inform the public of certain facts relating to their firms. The regulations also attempt to prevent fraud and the manipulation of stock prices. However, they do not try to protect investors from their own folly and greed. The purpose of legislation governing the securities industry is not to ensure that investors will profit from their investments; instead, the laws try to provide fair market practices while allowing investors to make their own mistakes.

Although current federal regulation developed during the 1930s as a direct result of the debacle in the securities markets during the early part of that decade, state regulations started in 1911 with the pioneering legislation in the state of Kansas. These state laws are frequently called *blue sky laws* because fraudulent securities were referred to as pieces of blue sky. Although there are differences among the state laws, they generally require that (1) security firms and brokers be licensed, (2) financial information concerning issues of new securities be filed with state regulatory bodies, (3) new securities meet specific standards before they are sold, and (4) regulatory bodies be established to enforce the laws.

The Federal Securities Laws

The first modern federal legislation governing the securities industry was the Securities Act of 1933, which primarily concerns the issuing of new securities. It requires that new securities be "registered" with the Securities and Exchange Commission (SEC). As was previously discussed, registration consists of supplying the SEC with information concerning the firm, the nature of its business and competition, and its financial position. This information is then summarized in the prospectus (refer to Exhibit 1.1), which makes the formal offer to sell the securities to the public.

Although the Securities Act of 1933 applies only to new issues, the Securities Exchange Act of 1934 (and subsequent amendments) extends the regulation to existing securities. This act forbids market manipulation, deception and misrepresentation of facts, and fraudulent practices. The SEC was also created by this act to enforce the laws pertaining to the securities industry. A summary of the SEC's objectives is provided in Exhibit 1.3.

Under the Securities Exchange Act of 1934, publicly held companies are required to keep current the information on file with the SEC. This is achieved by having the firm file an annual report (called the *10-K report*) with the SEC. The 10-K report contains a substantial amount of factual information concerning the firm, and this information is usually sent in summary form to the stockholders in the company's annual report. (Companies must upon request and without charge send a copy of

---

EXHIBIT 1.3   Summary of the Objectives of the SEC

1 To ensure that individuals have sufficient information to make informed investment decisions.
2 To provide the public with information by the registration of corporate securities prior to their sale to the general public, and to require timely and regular disclosure of corporate information and financial statements.
3 To prevent manipulation of security prices by regulating trading in the securities markets; by requiring insiders to register the buying and selling of securities; and by regulating the activities of corporate officers and directors.
4 To regulate investment companies (e.g., mutual funds) and investment advisors.
5 To work in conjunction with the Federal Reserve to limit the use of credit to acquire securities.
6 To supervise the regulation of member firms, brokers, and security dealers by working with the National Association of Securities Dealers, which is the self-regulatory association of brokers and dealers.

Information concerning the SEC may be found in Samuel L. Hayes III, ed., *Wall Street and Regulation* (Boston: Harvard Business School Press, 1987) and K. Fred Skousen, *An Introduction to the SEC*, 5th ed. (Cincinnati: South-Western/Thomson Learning, 1990).
The most recent information concerning the SEC may be found at its Web site: http://www.sec.gov.

the 10-K report to stockholders. The 10-K report may also be obtained from EDGAR, which is described in Chapter 5 in the section on sources of information.)

Firms are also required to release any information during the year that may materially affect the value of their securities. Information concerning new discoveries, lawsuits, or a merger must be disseminated to the general public. The SEC has the power to suspend trading in a company's securities for up to ten days if, in its opinion, the public interest and the protection of investors necessitate such a ban on trading. If a firm fails to keep investors informed, the SEC can suspend trading pending the release of the required information. Such a suspension is a drastic act and is seldom used, for most companies frequently issue news releases that inform the investing public of significant changes affecting the firm. Sometimes the company itself asks to have trading in its securities halted until a news release can be prepared and disseminated.

The disclosure laws do not require that the company tell everything about its operations. All firms have trade secrets that they do not want known by their competitors. The purpose of the full disclosure laws is not to restrict the corporation but (1) to inform the investors so that they can make intelligent decisions and (2) to prevent a firm's employees from using privileged information for personal gain.

It should be obvious that employees, ranging from president of the company to mailroom clerk, may have access to information before it reaches the general public. Such information (called *inside information*) may significantly enhance the employees' ability to make profits by buying or selling the company's securities before the announcement is made. Such profiteering from inside information is illegal. Officers and directors of the company must report their holdings and any changes in their holdings of the firm's securities to the SEC. (The use of reports of insider transactions to forecast stock prices is discussed in Chapter 2 in the section on the efficient market hypothesis.) Thus, it is possible for the SEC to determine if transactions have been made prior to any public announcement that affected the value of the securities. If insiders do profit illegally from the use of such information, they may be prosecuted under criminal law and their gains may have to be surrendered to the firm.

Sarbanes–Oxley Act of 2002

The large increase in stock prices experienced during 1998 and into 2000, and the subsequent decline in prices, may partially be attributed to fraudulent (or at least questionable) accounting practices and securities analysts' touting of stocks. These scandals led to the creation of the Sarbanes-Oxley Act, which was intended to restore public confidence in the securities markets. While it is too early to determine the ramifications of Sarbanes-Oxley, its range and coverage are extensive. The main provisions encompass:

- The independence of auditors and the creation of the Public Company Accounting Oversight Board
- Corporate responsibility and financial disclosure
- Conflicts of interest and corporate fraud and accountability

Sarbanes-Oxley created the Public Company Accounting Oversight Board, whose purpose is to oversee the auditing of the financial statements of publicly held companies. The board has the power to establish audit reporting rules and standards and to enforce compliance by public accounting firms. Firms and individuals who conduct audits are prohibited from performing nonaudit services for clients that they audit.

Corporate responsibility and financial disclosure require a publicly held firm's chief executive officer (CEO) and chief financial officer (CFO) to certify that the financial statements do not contain untrue statements or material omissions. These officers are also responsible for internal controls to ensure that they receive accurate information upon which to base their certifications of the financial statements. Corporate personnel cannot exert improper influence on auditors to accept misleading financial statements. Directors and executive officers are also banned from trading in the firm's securities during blackout periods when the firm's pensions are not permitted to trade the securities. Personal loans to executives and directors are prohibited, and senior management must disclose purchases and sales of the firm's securities within two business days. (The previous requirement for disclosure was ten days after the close of the calendar month.)

Conflicts of interest revolve around the roles played by securities analysts and by investment bankers. Investment bankers facilitate a firm's raising of funds. Analysts determine if securities are under- or overvalued. Both are employed by financial firms such as Merrill Lynch. If a securities analyst determines that a stock is overvalued, this will damage the relationship between the investment bankers and the firm wishing to sell the securities. Hence, there is an obvious conflict of interest between the securities analysts and the investment bankers working for the same financial firm.

These two divisions need to be independent of each other. While the financial firms asserted that a "firewall" did exist between the investment bankers and the securities analysts, the actions of the securities analysts often implied the opposite. Sarbanes-Oxley seeks to strengthen the firewall. Investment bankers' ability to preapprove a securities analyst's research reports is restricted. Individuals concerned with investment banking activities cannot supervise securities analysts. Retaliation against securities analysts for negative reports is prohibited. An analyst must disclose whether he or she owns securities or received compensation from the companies covered by the analyst. Penalties for violating Sarbanes-Oxley and existing corporate fraud laws that prohibit the destruction of documents and impeding or obstructing investigations were increased, with penalties including fines and imprisonment of up to 20 years.

Other Regulations

Although the Securities Act of 1933, the Securities Exchange Act of 1934, and the Sarbanes-Oxley Act of 2002 are the backbone of securities regulation, other laws pertaining to specific areas of investments have been enacted. These include the Investment Advisers Act of 1940, which applies to investment advisory services and individuals who are compensated for advising about securities.[12] These individuals must register with the SEC and must disclose their backgrounds, business affiliations, and the compensation charged for their services. Failure to register with the SEC can lead to an injunction against supplying the service or to prosecution for violating securities laws.

SECURITIES INVESTOR PROTECTION CORPORATION

Most investors are aware that accounts in virtually all commercial banks are insured by the Federal Deposit Insurance Corporation (FDIC—**http://www.fdic.gov**). As of

---

12. Securities and Exchange Commission, *The Work of the Securities and Exchange Commission* (Washington, DC: Government Printing Office, 1978), p. 17.

2004, should an insured commercial bank fail, the FDIC reimburses the depositor for any losses up to $100,000. If a depositor has more than $100,000 on account at the time of the commercial bank's failure, the depositor becomes a general creditor for the additional funds.

This insurance has greatly increased the stability of the commercial banking system. Small depositors know that their funds are safe and therefore do not panic if a commercial bank fails (as one occasionally does). This stability simply did not exist before the formation of the FDIC. When panicky depositors tried to make withdrawals, some commercial banks could not meet the sudden requests for cash. Many had to close, which only increased the panic that had caused the initial withdrawals. Since the advent of the FDIC, however, such panic and withdrawals should not occur because the FDIC reimburses depositors (up to the limit) for any losses they sustain.

Securities Investor Protection Corporation (SIPC)
The agency that insures investors against failures by brokerage firms.

Like commercial banks, brokerage firms are also insured by an agency that was created by the federal government—the **Securities Investor Protection Corporation (SIPC)**. The SIPC (**http://www.sipc.org**) is managed by a seven-member board of directors. Five members are appointed by the president of the United States, and their appointments must be confirmed by the Senate. Two of the five represent the general public, and three represent the securities industry. The remaining two members are selected by the secretary of the treasury and the Federal Reserve board of governors.

The SIPC performs a role similar to that of the FDIC. Its objective is to preserve public confidence in the securities markets and industry. Although the SIPC does not protect investors from losses resulting from fluctuations in security prices, it does insure investors against losses arising from the failure of a brokerage firm. The insurance provided by the SIPC protects a customer's cash and securities up to $500,000.[13] If a brokerage firm fails, the SIPC reimburses the firm's customers up to this specified limit. If a customer's claims exceed the $500,000 limit, that customer becomes a general creditor for the remainder of the funds.

The cost of this insurance is paid for by the brokerage firms that are members of the SIPC. All brokers and dealers that are registered with the Securities and Exchange Commission (SEC) and all members of national security exchanges must be members of the SIPC. Most security dealers are thus covered by the SIPC insurance. Some firms have even chosen to supplement this coverage by purchasing additional insurance from private insurance firms.

FOREIGN SECURITIES

Foreign companies, like U.S. companies, issue a variety of securities to raise funds. These securities subsequently trade on foreign exchanges or foreign over-the-counter markets. For example, there are stock exchanges in London, Paris, Tokyo, and other foreign financial centers. Unless Americans and other foreigners are forbidden to acquire these securities, you can buy and sell stocks through these exchanges in much the same way you may buy domestic stocks and bonds.

By far, the easiest way to acquire foreign stocks is to purchase the shares of firms that are traded in the United States on an exchange or through the Nasdaq stock market. Exhibit 1.4 (p. 42) provides a sample of these stocks and includes the company, the country of origin, its primary industry, and where the shares are traded.

---

13. Only $100,000 of the $500,000 insurance applies to cash balances on an account.

EXHIBIT 1.4   Selected Foreign Securities Traded on the New York Stock Exchange and through Nasdaq

Firm	Country of Origin	Primary Industry	Where Traded in the United States
Alcan Aluminum	Canada	Aluminum	NYSE
Campbell Resources	Canada	Gold mining	NYSE
Hitachi	Japan	Electronics	NYSE
Japan Airlines	Japan	Airline	Nasdaq
KLM Royal Dutch Airlines	Netherlands	Airline	NYSE
Kloof Gold Mines	South Africa	Gold mining	Nasdaq
Sony	Japan	Electronics	NYSE
TDK	Japan	Electronics	NYSE
Volkswagenwerk	Germany	Automobiles	Nasdaq

● **American Depository Receipts (ADRs) and American Depository Shares**
Receipts issued for foreign securities held by a trustee.

As you may see in the exhibit, many foreign stocks, such as SONY and Royal Dutch Airlines, are traded on the New York Stock Exchange. Others are traded on the AMEX and through the Nasdaq stock market. The majority of the firms whose securities are actively traded in the United States are either Japanese or Canadian.

These domestic markets do not actually trade the foreign shares but trade receipts for the stock, called **American Depository Receipts (ADRs)** or **American Depository Shares**. These receipts are created by large financial institutions such as commercial banks. The ADRs are sold to the public and continue to trade in the United States.[14]

There are two types of ADRs. *Sponsored* ADRs are created when the firm wants the securities to trade in the United States. The firm employs a bank to perform the paperwork to create the ADRs and to act as transfer agent. In this case the costs are absorbed by the firm. All ADRs listed on the NYSE and AMEX are sponsored ADRs. *Unsponsored* ADRs are created when a brokerage firm believes there will be sufficient interest in a stock or bond to make a market in the security. The brokerage firm buys a block of securities and hires a commercial bank to create the ADRs and to act as transfer agent. However, fees for this service and for converting dividend payments from the foreign currency into U.S. dollars will be paid by the stockholders, not the issuing firm.

The creation of ADRs greatly facilitates trading in foreign securities. Stocks are quoted in dollars instead of the currency of the company. Dividend payments are in dollars, and the securities have to comply with U.S. regulations. If, however, there are no ADRs for the specific stock you want to purchase, you may still instruct your broker to buy the shares in the appropriate foreign market. Trading practices need to coincide with U.S. practice, but such differences are often more a matter of detail than substance (e.g., settlement date may not be three days as in the United States) and they are diminishing with increased global investing.

---

14. Information concerning foreign securities (e.g., financials, earnings estimates, prices, and linkages to the company) may be found at **http://www.adr.com**, a Web site that is a joint project of JPMorgan and Thomson Financial.

SUMMARY

All firms must have a source of funds with which to acquire assets and retire outstanding liabilities as they come due. Besides retaining earnings, a firm may obtain these funds from savers who are not currently using all their income to buy goods and services. The transfer of these savings may occur directly when firms issue new securities, or indirectly through a financial intermediary.

When a firm issues new stocks or bonds, it usually employs the services of an investment banker to facilitate the sale of the securities by acting as a middleman between the firm and the savers. In many cases, investment bankers underwrite the issue of new securities, which means that they guarantee a specified amount of money to the issuing firm and then sell the securities to the public. Because the underwriters are obligated to remit the specified amount for the securities, they bear the risk of the sale.

Once the securities are issued, they are traded on organized exchanges, such as the NYSE, or in the informal over-the-counter markets, including the Nasdaq stock market. Securities are bought through brokers, who buy and sell for their customers' accounts. The brokers obtain the securities from dealers, who make markets in them. These dealers offer to buy and sell at specified prices (quotes), which are called the bid and the ask. Brokers and investors obtain these prices through a sophisticated electronic system that transmits the quotes from the various dealers.

After securities are purchased, the investor must pay for them with either cash or a combination of cash and borrowed funds. When the investor uses borrowed funds, that individual is buying on margin. Buying on margin increases both the potential percentage return and the potential risk of loss for the investor.

Investors may take delivery of their securities or leave them with the brokerage firm. Leaving securities registered in the street name offers the advantage of convenience because the brokerage firm becomes the custodian of the certificates. Since the advent of the SIPC and its insurance protection, there is little risk of loss to the investor from leaving securities with the brokerage firm.

Investors establish long or short positions. With a long position, the investor purchases stock in anticipation of its price rising. If the price of the stock rises, you may sell it for a profit. With a short position, the investor sells borrowed stock in anticipation of its price declining. If the price of the stock falls, you may repurchase it at the lower price and return it to the lender. The position generates a profit because the selling price exceeds the purchase price.

Both the long and short positions are the logical outcomes of security analysis. If you think a stock is underpriced, a long position (i.e., purchase of the stock) should be established. If you think a stock is overvalued, a short position would be sensible. If you are correct in either case, the position will generate a profit. Either position may, however, generate a loss if prices move against your anticipated price change.

The federal laws governing the securities industry are enforced by the Securities and Exchange Commission (SEC). The purpose of these laws is to ensure that individual investors have access to information upon which to base investment decisions. Publicly owned firms must supply investors with financial statements and make timely disclosure of information that may affect the value of the firms' securities.

Investors' accounts with brokerage firms are insured by the Securities Investor Protection Corporation (SIPC). This insurance covers up to $500,000 worth of securities held by the broker for the investor. The intent of SIPC is to increase public confidence in the securities industry by reducing the risk of loss to investors from failure by brokerage firms.

Investors living in the United States may assume a global view and acquire stocks and bonds issued in foreign countries. These securities may be bought and sold through U.S. brokers in much the same way that investors acquire domestic securities. American depository receipts (ADRs) representing foreign securities have been created to facilitate trading in foreign stocks. These ADRs are denominated in dollars, their prices are quoted in dollars, and their units of trading are consistent with those in the United States.

Learning Objectives

Now that you have completed this chapter, you should be able to:

1. Explain the role of the investment banker and the financial intermediary such as a commercial bank.
2. Identify the components necessary for the sale of securities to the general public.
3. Differentiate the risk associated with a best-efforts sale of securities with an underwriting.
4. Explain the role of market makers.
5. Demonstrate the process of buying or selling a stock.
6. Differentiate among the types of securities orders and identify the cost of investing in stocks and bonds.
7. Compare cash and margin accounts and their impact on return and risk.
8. Contrast long and short positions and explain the sources of risk and return in each position.
9. State the purpose of the Securities and Exchange Commission (SEC) and the Securities Investor Protection Corporation (SIPC) and the role of regulation in the securities markets.

PROBLEMS

1) A stock sells for $10 per share. You purchase 100 shares for $10 a share (i.e., for $1,000), and after a year the price rises to $17.50. What will be the percentage return on your investment if you bought the stock on margin and the margin requirement was (a) 25 percent, (b) 50 percent, and (c) 75 percent? (Ignore commissions, dividends, and interest expense.)

2) Repeat Problem 1 to determine the percentage return on your investment but in this case suppose the price of the stock falls to $7.50 per share. What generalization can be inferred from your answers to Problems 1 and 2?

3) Investor A makes a cash purchase of 100 shares of AB&C common stock for $55 a share. Investor B also buys 100 shares of AB&C but uses margin. Each holds the stock for one year, during which dividends of $5 a share are distributed. Commissions are 2 percent of the value of a purchase or sale; the

margin requirement is 60 percent, and the interest rate is 10 percent annually on borrowed funds. What is the percentage earned by each investor if he or she sells the stock after one year for (a) $40, (b) $55, (c) $60, and (d) $70? If the margin requirement had been 40 percent, what would have been the annual percentage returns? What conclusion do these percentage returns imply?

4) An investor sells a stock short for $36 a share. A year later, the investor covers the position at $30 a share. If the margin requirement is 60 percent, what is the percentage return earned on the investment? Redo the calculations, assuming the price of the stock is $42 when the investor closes the position.

Internet Application for Chapter 1   The Basics of Investing

One successful portfolio manager, Peter Lynch, has suggested that you should buy stocks in companies that you know or whose products you use. Since that strategy may be as good a starting point as any, I have identified several stocks to consider:

Anheuser-Busch Co (BUD)

Guitar Center (GTRC)

Harley Davidson (HDI)

Pfizer (PFE)

Former students of mine selected these companies for inclusion in the student investment fund. If these firms do not appeal to you, substitute FedEx Corp (FDX), Heinz Co. (HNZ), Merck & Co. (MRK) or Pier 1 Imports (PIR).

To buy these stocks, you will need to open an account with a brokerage firm. The minimum amount necessary to open an account, commissions, and other fees (e.g., an inactivity fee) vary among full-service, discount, and on-line brokerage firms. Compare the commissions and fees for several of the following brokerage firms. (You may select additional or different firms if you prefer.) Which kind of firm appears to best meet your needs?

AmeriTrade   http://www.ameritrade.com

E*Trade   https://us.etrade.com

Fidelity Investments   http://www.fidelity.com

Merrill Lynch Direct   http://www.mldirect.com

Schwab   http://www.schwab.com

Scottrade   http://www.scottrade.com

TD Waterhouse   http://www.tdwaterhouse.com

TEST YOURSELF: *Time Value of Money and Analysis of Financial Statements*

Whenever you do something, you bring knowledge to that activity. For example, if you attend an Eagles-Cowboys game, you bring knowledge of football and, perhaps, the rivalry between the two teams. If you attend a performance of the Nutcracker, you bring your knowledge of music, ballet, and, perhaps, the rivalry between the Nutcracker and the Mouse King.

When you take a course, you use knowledge acquired in prior courses. The ability to solve time value of money problems and to analyze a firm's financial statements using ratios is often assumed knowledge for a course in investments. Problems concerning the future or the present value of a dollar and the present or future value of an annuity permeate investments and appear frequently throughout this text. You will not be able to grasp a significant portion of this text if you cannot solve time value problems.

Ratios are often used to analyze a firm's financial statements. A particular firm's ratios may be compared over time (a time-series analysis) to determine changes in performance or financial condition. Or the firm's ratios may be compared to other firms in the same industry (a cross-sectional analysis). Many of these ratios appear throughout this text. For example, the debt ratio (debt/total assets) measures a firm's usage of debt financing and is an indicator of risk. Even if you are not being asked to compute the ratio, you need to know how the ratio is used and how to interpret it (i.e., you need to know what the ratio indicates).

TIME VALUE OF MONEY

What follows is a series of 20 problems. Please do them to test your ability to solve time value problems. Answers are provided at the end of this test and solved using interest tables and a financial calculator. (Interest tables are provided as an appendix to the text if you prefer to use them.) Once again there is an assumption: you know how to use a financial calculator. If you cannot, perhaps you know how to solve the problems using Excel. There are often several ways to reach a destination, and that applies to solving time value problems. It is the ability to obtain the answers and interpret them that is important and not the specific technique used to solve the numerical problem.

*If you are unable to solve these problems, you need help! One possible solution is to locate time value of money explanations, problems, and applications by doing an Internet search using "time value of money calculators." One possible site is **http://www .TeachMeFinance.com**. Another possible tool for solving the problems is the Investment Analysis Calculator, which may be located at **http://www.swcollege.com/finance/ mayo**. Click on the link to the calculator and use it to solve a variety of problems concerning investments.*

Another possible solution is to use the Time Value Review at the end of this text. This review walks you through the basics of time value and illustrates the future and present values of single payments and annuities. Several additional problems (with answers) are provided so that you may once again test your ability to solve time value problems.

Problems

1) A saver places $1,000 in a certificate of deposit that matures after ten years and pays 5 percent interest, which is compounded annually until the certificate matures.
   a) How much interest will the saver earn if the interest is left to accumulate?

Interactive e-lectures
See a visual explanation and example of time value at
http://mayoxtra.swlearning.com

Interactive e-lectures
See a visual explanation and example of annuities at
http://mayoxtra.swlearning.com

   b) How much interest will the save earn if the interest is withdrawn each year?
   c) Why are the answers to a and b different?

2) A self-employed person deposits $3,000 annually in a retirement account that earns 8 percent.
   a) How much will be in the account when the individual retires at the age of 65 if the savings program starts when the person is age 40?
   b) How much additional money will be in the account if the saver defers retirement until age 70?
   c) How much money will be in the account if the saver discontinues the contributions at age 65 but does not retire and start taking distributions until age 70?

3) A 45-year-old woman decides to put funds into a retirement plan. She can save $2,000 a year and and 9 percent on this savings. How much will she have accumulated if she retires at age 65? At retirement how much can she withdraw each year for 20 years from the accumulated savings if the savings continue to earn 9 percent?

4) If a father wants to have $100,000 to send a newborn child to college, how much must he invest annually for 18 years if he earns 9 percent on his funds?

5) A widow currently has a $93,000 investment yielding 9 percent annually. Can she withdraw $16,000 a year for the next ten years?

6) An investment generates $10,000 per year for 25 years. If an investor can earn 10 percent on other investments, what is the current value of this investment? If its current price is $120,000, should the investor buy it?

7) a) If a person currently earns $10,000 and inflation continues at 4 percent for 10 years, how much must the person make to maintain purchasing power?
   b) If a person bought a $50,000 home in 1970 and sold it in 2000, what would be the value of the house if the annual rate of price appreciation were 5 percent during the 30 years?

8) You purchase a stock for $20 and expect its price to grow annually at a rate of 8 percent.
   a) What price are you expecting after five years?
   b) If the rate of increase in the price doubled from 8 percent to 16 percent, would that double the *increase* in the price? Why?

9) An investment offers to pay you $10,000 a year for five years. If it costs $33,250, what will be your rate of return on the investment?

10) You are offered $900 after five years or $150 a year for five years. If you can earn 6 percent on your funds, which offer will you accept? If you can earn 14 percent on your funds, which offer will you accept? Why are your answers different?

11) You purchase a townhouse for $85,000. After a down payment of $18,000, you obtain a mortgage loan at 9 percent that requires annual payments for 15 years.
   a) What are the annual payments?
   b) How much of the first payment goes to pay the interest?
   c) What is the remaining mortgage balance after the first payment is made?

12) You want your salary to double in six years. At what annual rate of growth must your salary increase to achieve your goal?

13) Each year you invest $2,000 in an account that earns 10 percent annually. How long will it take for your to accumulate $50,000?

14) Auntie Erin sells her house for $100,000. She invests the money to earn 7 percent annually. If her life expectancy is 10 years, what is the maximum amount she can annually spend on a nursing home, doctors, and taxes?

15) A firm must choose between two investment alternatives, each costing $100,000. The first alternative generates $35,000 a year for four years. The second pays one large lump sum of

$157,400 at the end of the fourth year. If the firm can raise the required funds to make the investment at an annual cost of 10 percent, which alternative should be preferred? Would the answer be different if the cost of funds were 7 percent?

16) Uncle Fred recently died and left $325,000 to his 50-year-old favorite niece. She immediately spent $100,000 on a town home but decided to invest the balance so she could retire at age 65. What rate of return must she earn on her investment over the next 15 years to permit her to withdraw $75,000 at the end of each year through age 80 if her funds earn 10 percent during retirement?

17) You purchase a stock for $10,000 and collect $400 at the end of each year in dividends. You sell the stock for $11,300 after four years. What was the annual return on your $10,000 investment?

18) A $1,000,000 state lottery prize is spread evenly over 10 years ($100,000 a year), or you may take a lump distribution of $654,000. If you can earn 7 percent, which alternative is better?

19) You purchase a building for $900,000, collect annual rent (after expenses) of $120,000, and sell the building for $1,000,000 after three years. What is the annual return on this investment?

20) You buy a stock for $1,000 and expect to sell it for $900 after four years but also expect to collect dividends of $120 a year. Prove that the return on this investment is less than 10 percent.

Answers

1) **a)** $1,000(1 + .05)^{10} = x$

   $x = \$1,000(1.629) = \$1,629$

   1.629 is the interest factor for the future value of $1 for 10 years at 5%.

   Financial Calculator Solution:
   PV = –1000
   N = 10
   I = 5
   PMT = 0
   FV = ?
   FV = 1629

   b) If the interest is withdrawn each year, the investor receives $50 annually and $500 over the lifetime of the investment.

   c) The difference in the amount of interest ($629 - $500 = $129) is the result of compounding.

2) **a)** $x = \$3,000(73.106) = \$219,318$

   73.106 is the interest factor for the future sum of an annuity of $1 at 8% for 25 years.

   Financial Calculator Solution:
   PV = 0
   N = 25
   I = 8
   PMT = –3000
   FV = ?
   FV = 219318

   b) $x = \$3,000(113.283) = \$339,849$

   113.283 is the interest factor for the future sum of an annuity of $1 at 8% for 30 years.

Financial Calculator Solution:

 PV = 0
 N = 30
 I = 8
 PMT = −3000
 FV = ?
 FV = 339850

The additional funds:

$339,849 − $219,318 = $120,531

($120,532 if a financial calculator is used.)

c) In this question the individual stops making the contribution but does not draw on the fund. The amount grows to:

$219,318(1 + .08)^5 = $219,318(1.469) = $322,178

1.469 is the interest factor for the future value of $1at 8% for five years.

Financial Calculator Solution:

 PV = −219318
 N = 5
 I = 8
 PMT = 0
 FV = ?
 FV = 322250

(The big difference between the answers is the result of rounding $[1.08]^5$ to three places.)

3) $2,000(51.160) = $102,320

84.701 is the interest factor for the future value of an annuity of $1 at 9% for 20 years.

Financial Calculator Solution:

 PV = 0
 N = 20
 I = 9
 PMT = −2000
 FV = ?
 FV = 102320

The individual has accumulated $102,320. This will permit withdrawals of $11,210 a year for 20 years:

$$\$102,320 = \frac{x}{(1 + .07)} + \ldots + \frac{x}{(1 + .07)^{20}}$$

$102,320 = x(9.128)

x = $11,210

Financial Calculator Solution:

 PV = 102320
 N = 20
 I = 9
 FV = 0
 PMT = ?
 PMT = 11209.

4) x(41.301) = $100,000

$x = \$100,000/41.301 = \$2,421$

41.301 is the interest factor for the future sum of an annuity of $1 at 9% for 18 years.

Financial Calculator Solution:
  PV = 0
  N = 18
  I = 9
  FV = 100000
  PMT = ?
  PMT = −2421

5) To answer this question, determine the amount that can be withdrawn:

$\$93,000 = x(\text{PVAIF})$

$\$93,000 = x(6.418)$

$x = \$14,490.50$

Financial Calculator Solution:
  PV = 93000
  N = 10
  I = 9
  FV = 0
  PMT = ?
  PMT = −14491

She can withdraw only $14,491 and not $16,000.

6) This problem is an introduction to valuation. It asks what is the present value of a series of future payments (i.e., illustrates discounted cash flow):

$$x = \frac{\$10,000}{(1 + .10)} + \ldots + \frac{10,000}{(1 + .10)^{25}}$$

$x = \$10,000(9.077) = \$90,770$

9.077 is the interest factor for the present value of an annuity of $1 at 10% for 25 years.

Financial Calculator Solution:
  N = 25
  I = 10
  PMT = 10000
  FV = 0
  PV = ?
  PV = −90770

If this investment costs $120,000, it is overpriced and should not be purchased, since it is worth only $90,770.

7) a) $\$10,000(1 + .04)^{10} = x$

$\$10,000(1.480) = \$14,800$

1.480 is the interest factor for the future value of $1 at 4% for ten years.

Financial Calculator Solution:
  PV = −10000
  N = 10
  I = 4
  PMT = 0
  FV = ?
  FV = 14802.

If the annual rate of inflation is 4%, then it will take $14,800 to purchase $10,000 worth of goods bought ten years previously.

b) $\$50,000(1 + .05)^{30} = x$

$\$50,000(4.322) = \$216,100$

4.322 is the interest factor for the future value of $1 at 5% for 30 years.

Financial Calculator Solution:

PV = −50000
N = 30
I = 5
PMT = 0
FV = ?
FV = 216097

8) a) $\$20(1 + .08)^5 = P_5$

$\$20(1.469) = \$29.38$

1.469 is the interest factor for the future value of $1 at 6% for five years.

Financial Calculator Solution:

PV = −20
N = 5
I = 8
PMT = 0
FV = ?
FV = 29.39

b) $\$20(1 + .16)^5 = P_5$

$\$20(2.100) = \$42.00$

2.100 is the interest factor for the future value of $1 at 16% for five years.

Financial Calculator Solution:

PV = −20
N = 5
I = 16
PMT = 0
FV = ?
FV = 42.01

Doubling the growth rate (8% to 16%) more than doubles the price appreciation: $9.38 at 8% versus $22.00 at 16%.

9) $\$10,000(PVAIF) = \$33,520$

$PVAIF = \$33,520/\$10,000 = 3.352$

Look up 3.352 in the interest table for the present value of an annuity of $1 to determine that the rate of return is 15%.

Financial Calculator Solution:

PV = −33520
N = 5
PMT = 10000
FV = 0
I = ?
I = 15

10) At 6%:

$150(5.637) = $845.55 < $900

5.637 is the interest factor for the future value of an annuity of $1 at 6% for five years.

Financial Calculator Solution:
    PV = 0
    N = 5
    I = 6
    PMT = −150
    FV = ?
    FV = 846

At 14%:

$150(6.610) = $991.50 > $900

6.610 is the interest factor for the future value of an annuity of $1 at 14% for five years.

Financial Calculator Solution:
    PV = 0
    N = 5
    I = 14
    PMT = −150
    FV = ?
    FV = 992

The higher interest rate favors early payments, which are assumed to be reinvested at the higher rate. Thus, in this example the $150 payments received in the early years produce the higher terminal value when they compound at 14%. (Notice the negative sign for the payments. The interpretation is that cash outflows (investments) of $150 each payment will produce the terminal value. This problem may also be solved by determining the present values of both sets of payments.)

11) Amount of the mortgage: $85,000 − $18,000 = $67,000

   a) The periodic payment required by the mortgage:

      $67,000(*PVAIF*) = x

      x = 67,000/8.060 = $8,312.65

   Financial Calculator Solution:
       PV = 67000
       N = 15
       I = 9
       FV = 0
       PMT = ?
       PMT = −8311.95.

   b) Interest: $67,000 × .09 = $6,030

   c) Principal repayment: $8,312.65 − $6,030 = $2,282.65

      Balance owed: $67,000 − $2,282.65 = $64,717.35

12) $1(1 + x)^6 = $2

   (1 + x)^6 = interest factor = 2/1 = 2

   x = 12%

   Look up 2 in the interest table for the future value of $1 under six years and determine the growth rate to be approximately 12%.

   Financial Calculator Solution:
       PV = −1

    N = 6
    PMT = 0
    FV = 2
    I = ?
    I = 12.25

13) ($2,000)(FVAIF at 10% for x years) = $50,000

interest factor = $50,000/$2,000 = 25

Look up 25 in the interest table for the future value of an annuity of $1 at 10% and determine the number to be approximately 13 years.

Financial Calculator Solution:
    PV = 0
    I = 10
    PMT = -2000
    FV = 50000
    N = ?
    N = 13.14.

14) x (7.024) = $100,000

x = $100,000/7.024 = $14,237

7.024 is the interest factor for the present value of an annuity of $1 at 7% for 10 years.

Financial Calculator Solution:
    PV = 100000
    N = 10
    I = 7
    FV = 0
    PMT = ?
    PMT = -14238.

15) Determine the present value of each investment alternative:

A: $35,000(3.170) = $110,950

B: $157,400 (0.683) = $107,504.

The first alternative has the larger present value and is preferred.

Financial Calculator Solution:

N = 4	N = 4
I = 10	I = 10
PMT = 35000	PMT = 0
FV = 0	FV = 157400
PV = ?	PV = ?
PV = -110,945.	PV = -107500

By varying the cost of funds, the second alternative may be preferred. At 7 percent the present values are

A: $35,000(3.387) = $118,545

B: $157,400(0.763) = $120,096.20

and the second alternative is preferred.

Financial Calculator Solution:

N = 4	N = 4
I = 7	I = 7
PMT = 35000	PMT = 0

FV = 0	FV = 157400
PV = ?	PV = ?
PV = –118552	PV = –120080

16) First, determine the amount necessary to permit the $75,000 annual withdrawal. Then determine the amount necessary to invest annually to obtain that required amount.

The required amount is

$75,000(*PVAIF*, 15*N*, 10%) = ?

$75,000(7.606) = $570,450.

Financial Calculator Solution:
    PMT = 75000
    N = 15
    I = 10
    FV = 0
    PV = ?
    PV = 570455.96

To obtain this amount, the $225,000 must earn 6.4%.

$225,000(1 + r)^{15} = $570,450

FVIF, 15*N*, ?*I* = $570,450/$225,000 = 2.533

Since the interest factor for the future value of $1 is 2.533, the required annual return is between 6 and 7 percent.

Financial Calculator Solution:
    PV = 225000
    PMT = 0
    N = 15
    FV = 570455.96
    I = ?
    I = 6.4

17) $10,000 = $400(*PVAIF*, 4*N*, ?*I*) + $11,300(*PVIF*, 4*N*, ?*I*)

At 7 percent:

PV = $400(3.387) + $11,300(0.763) = $9,977

The return is approximately 7 percent.

Financial Calculator Solution:
    PV = –10000
    N = 4
    PMT = 400
    FV = 11300
    I = ?
    I = 6.93.

18) Determine the present value of the annuity and compare the amount to the lump sum payment.

PV = $100,000(*PVAIF*, 7*I*, 10*N*)

    = $100,000(7.024) = $702,400

The annuity payments are preferred.

Financial Calculator Solution:
    FV = 0
    PMT = 100000
    N = 10

$$I = 7$$
$$PV = ?$$
$$PV = -702358$$

19) $900,000 = $120,000(*PVAIF*, 3*N*, ?*I*)
               + $1,000,000(*PVIF*, 3*N*, ?*I*)

At 16 percent:

PV = $120,000(2.246) + $1,000,000(0.641)

   = $269,520 + $641,000 = $910,520

The return is exceeds 16 percent.

Financial Calculator Solution:
   PV = −900000
   N = 3
   PMT = 12000
   FV = 1000000
   I = ?
   I = 16.49

20) $1,000 = $120(*PVAIF*, 4*N*, ?*I*) + $900(*PVIF*, 4*N*, ?*I*)

At 10 percent:

PV = $120(3.170) + $900(0.683) = $380 + $615 = $995

The return is approximately 10 percent.

Financial Calculator Solution:
   PV = −1000
   N = 4
   PMT = 120
   FV = 900
   I = ?
   I = 9.84

RATIO ANALYSIS OF FINANCIAL STATEMENTS

The computation of ratios is perceptibly simpler than solving time value problems. You will probably rarely do the calculations yourself, but if you obtain ratios through an Internet source such as Yahoo! Finance, you should know the ratios' definitions and what each ratio is measuring.

In order to review the analysis of financial statements, please compute the following ratios using the financial statements for Hershey Foods Corporation for 2003.

- Current ratio
- Quick ratio
- Inventory turnover
- Receivables turnover
- Average collection period (days sales outstanding)
- Operating profit margin

- Net profit margin
- Return on assets
- Return on equity
- Debt/net worth
- Debt ratio
- Times-interest-earned

In order to calculate the ratios, use the following balance sheet (Exhibit T.1) and income statement (Exhibit T.2).

EXHIBIT T.1	Hershey Foods Corporation Consolidated Balance Sheet	
December 31, (in millions)	**2003**	**2002**
ASSETS		
Current assets		
Cash and cash equivalents	$114.8	$297.7
Accounts receivable	420.9	371.0
Inventories	492.9	503.3
Other	103.0	91.6
Total current assets	1,131.6	1,263.6
Property, plant, and equipment	1,661.9	1,486.1
Other assets	789.0	730.9
Total assets	$3,582.5	$3,480.6
LIABILITIES AND STOCKHOLDERS' EQUITY		
Current liabilities		
Accounts payable	$573.3	$518.7
Other	12.5	28.1
Total current liabilities	585.8	546.8
Long-term debt	968.5	851.8
Other long-term liabilities	370.8	362.2
Deferred income taxes	377.6	348.0
Total liabilities	2,302.7	2,108.8
Stockholders' equity		
Common stock	180.0	180.0
Additional paid-in capital	4.0	0.6
Retained earnings	3,264.0	2,991.1
Treasury stock repurchased at cost	(2,147.4)	(1,808.2)
Other adjustments	(20.7)	8.2
Total stockholders' equity	1,279.9	1,371.7
Total liabilities and stockholders' equity	$3,582.5	$3,480.6

Source: Adapted from *Hershey Foods Corporation Proxy Statement* and *2003 Annual Report to Stockholders.*

SUMMARY OF RATIO DEFINITIONS

Liquidity ratios:

Current ratio:

$$\frac{\text{Current assets}}{\text{Current liabilities}}$$

Quick ratio:

$$\frac{\text{Current assets} - \text{inventory}}{\text{Current liabilities}}$$

Activity ratios

Inventory turnover:

$$\frac{\text{Sales}}{\text{Average inventory}}$$

or

EXHIBIT T.2	Hershey Foods Corporation Statement of Income	

For the years ended December 31, (in millions except per-share data)	2003	2002
Net Sales	$4,172.6	$4,120.3
Costs and expenses		
Cost of goods sold	2,544.7	2,561.1
Selling, marketing, and administrative	831.4	861.0
Other	(1.7)	(3.8)
Earnings before interest and taxes	798.1	702.0
Interest expense	65.3	64.4
Provision for income taxes	267.9	234.0
Net income	$464.9	$403.6
Net income per share	$3.48	$2.96
Net income per share—diluted	$3.46	$2.93
Cash dividends per share	$1.445	$1.26

Source: Adapted from *Hershey Foods Corporation Proxy Statement* and *2003 Annual Report to Stockholders.*

$$\frac{\text{Cost of goods sold}}{\text{Average inventory}}$$

(The denominator may be defined as year-end inventory instead of average inventory.)

Average collection period:

$$\frac{\text{Receivables}}{\text{Sales per day}}$$

Receivables turnover:

$$\frac{\text{Annual credit sales}}{\text{Accounts receivable}}$$

or

$$\frac{\text{Annual sales}}{\text{Accounts receivable}}$$

(If credit sales are not given, the first definition of receivables turnover cannot be computed.)

Operating profit margin:

$$\frac{\text{Earnings before interest and taxes}}{\text{Sales}}$$

Net profit margin:

$$\frac{\text{Earnings after taxes}}{\text{Sales}}$$

Return on assets:

$$\frac{\text{Earnings after taxes}}{\text{Total assets}}$$

Return on equity:

$$\frac{\text{Earnings after taxes}}{\text{Equity}}$$

Leverage and coverage ratios

Debt/net worth:

$$\frac{\text{Debt}}{\text{Equity}}$$

Debt ratio:

$$\frac{\text{Debt}}{\text{Total assets}}$$

Times-interest-earned:

$$\frac{\text{Earnings before interest and taxes}}{\text{Interest expense}}$$

The calculations:

Current ratio:

$$\frac{\text{current assets}}{\text{current liabilities}} = \frac{\$1{,}131.6}{\$585.8} = 1.93$$

Quick ratio:

$$\frac{\text{current assets minus inventory}}{\text{current liabilities}} = \frac{\$638.7}{\$585.8} = 1.09$$

Inventory turnover:

$$\frac{\text{sales}}{\text{inventory}} = \frac{\$4{,}172.6}{\$492.9} = 8.47$$

or

$$\frac{\text{cost of goods sold}}{\text{inventory}} = \frac{\$2{,}544.7}{\$492.9} = 5.16$$

This calculation uses year-end inventory and not average inventory. Inventory turnover may also be defined as sales/average inventory.

Receivables turnover:

$$\frac{\text{annual credit sales}}{\text{accounts receivable}}$$

or

$$\frac{\text{annual sales}}{\text{accounts receivable}} = \frac{\$4{,}172.6}{\$420.9} = 9.9$$

Since credit sales are not given; the first definition of receivables turnover cannot be computed.

Average collection period:

$$\frac{\text{receivables}}{\text{sales per day}} = \frac{\$420/9}{\$4,172.6/360} = 36.3 \text{ days}$$

Operating profit margin:

$$\frac{\text{earnings before interest and taxes}}{\text{sales}} = \frac{\$798.1}{\$4,172.6} = 19.1\%$$

Net profit margin:

$$\frac{\text{earnings after taxes}}{\text{sales}} = \frac{\$464.9}{\$4,172.6} = 11.1\%$$

Return on assets:

$$\frac{\text{earnings after taxes}}{\text{total assets}} = \frac{\$464.9}{\$3,582.5} = 13\%$$

Return on equity:

$$\frac{\text{earnings after taxes}}{\text{equity}} = \frac{\$464.9}{\$1,279.9} = 36.3\%$$

Debt/net worth:

$$\frac{\text{debt}}{\text{equity}} = \frac{\$2,302.6}{\$1,279.9} = 1.8$$

Debt ratio:

$$\frac{\text{debt}}{\text{total assets}} = \frac{\$2,302.6}{\$3,582.5} = 64.3\%$$

Times-interest-earned:

$$\frac{\text{earnings before interest and taxes}}{\text{interest expense}} = \frac{\$798.1}{\$65.3} = 12.22$$

Now repeat the analysis using more recent financial statements; that is, perform a time-series analysis to determine if Hershey's financial condition has changed. Obtain Hershey's financial statements for the next several years (e.g., 2004 through 2006). The financial statements may be found in the company's annual report or at its Web site. You may also find the statements at the SEC's EDGAR (http://www.sec.gov) or Mergent Online (http://www.mergentonline.com).

You could also perform a cross-sectional analysis that compares Hershey to its competitors. However, Hershey Foods is an unusual firm. It has only two major competitors (Nestle and Mars) for its primary products. Nestle is a foreign firm, so the financial statement may not be comparable to Hershey's. Mars is privately held, so financial information is not available. This means you will not be able to perform a cross-section analysis that compares the three competitors' financial statements.

CHAPTER

2 ● ● ●

Portfolio Planning in an Efficient Market Context

Many of life's activities, such as a wedding, a trip, or a job search, involve planning. Shouldn't investing also involving planning? The answer is obviously "Yes!" Planning is always preceded by a specified general goal or specific objective. The same principle applies to investing. Why are you deferring current consumption and investing? Are you saving to accumulate money for a down payment on a house? Are you worried that your job will be terminated? Are you accumulating assets to cover expenses if you are no longer employed or become disabled? Unless you are investing solely for the fun of it, your portfolio is designed to meet one or more specified objectives. This chapter is primarily concerned with financial planning and the allocation of your assets to meet your objectives.

How you construct that portfolio and allocate your resources among various alternative investments is to some extent affected by taxation. Taxes reduce the return you get to keep. Various tax shelters exist, and some were created to encourage you to pursue specific financial objectives such as saving for retirement. While the tax laws and their application to investments are exceedingly complex, this chapter emphasizes only two: the taxation of capital gains and losses and the deferral of income taxes through investments in pension plans.

The last two topics covered in this chapter are the allocation of assets and the efficiency of financial markets. The allocation of your assets among the various classes of assets has an important impact on the return your portfolio achieves. In addition, you make investments in efficient financial markets. The efficacy of financial markets suggests that you cannot expect to do exceptionally well on a consistent basis. Instead, the return you earn will depend on the risk you accept and the return on the market as a whole. The chapter ends with coverage of this sobering topic, the efficient market hypothesis. The implication of this hypothesis is important to investment decision making, and the efficient market hypothesis permeates this text. You do not have to accept this hypothesis, but if you are not aware of it, you may make investment decisions with false hope.

THE PROCESS OF FINANCIAL PLANNING

Before constructing a portfolio, you should start by defining its purpose. There have to be some objective(s) to guide the selection of assets, since not all securities will meet specific objectives. Your next step is to analyze your resources and environment. These change over your lifetime and you need to be aware of your resources and the source of income with which you have to work. You then construct a financial plan designed to fulfill the investment objectives within the environmental and financial constraints.

The Specification of Investment Goals and Objectives

The purpose of investing is to transfer purchasing power from the present to the future. A portfolio is a store of value designed to meet your reasons for postponing the consumption of goods and services from the present to the future. Several reasons for saving and investing may include:

1. The capacity to meet financial emergencies;
2. The financing of specific future purchases, such as the down payment for a home;
3. The provision for income at retirement;
4. The ability to leave a sizable estate to heirs or to charity;
5. The ability to speculate or receive enjoyment from accumulating and managing wealth.

In addition to these specific investment goals, many individuals have general financial objectives that are related to their age, income, and wealth. Individuals go through phases, often referred to as a **financial life cycle**. The cycle has three stages: (1) a period of accumulation, (2) a period of preservation, and (3) a period of the use or depletion of the investor's assets.

During the period of accumulation, the individual generates income but expenditures on housing, transportation, and education often exceed cash inflows, which increases debt. Even during this period when you have substantial debt (e.g., a mortgage, car payments, or student loans) you can start the process of accumulating assets, especially by participating in tax-deferred pension plans. Such participation, especially if the employee's contributions are matched by the employer, may be one of the best investment strategies any individual can follow.

Another desirable strategy during the period of asset accumulation is to restructure or retire debt. While stocks and bonds have uncertain returns, retiring debt has an assured return, the interest savings. This return can be substantial if the debt being retired is the balance owed on credit cards. Certainly the returns on many financial assets are less than the high interest rates charged on many credit card balances and argue that credit card debt reduction is a desirable, even superior, alternative to investing in stocks and bonds.

During the period of preservation, income often exceeds expenditures. Individuals reduce debt (e.g., pay off the mortgages on their homes) and continue to accumulate assets. The emphasis, however, may change to preservation of existing assets in addition to the continued accumulation of wealth. Since investors will need a substantial amount of wealth upon reaching retirement, they must continue to take moderate or prudent risk to earn a sufficient return. Without that return they may not have the funds that are needed to finance their retirement.

financial life cycle
The stages of life during which individuals accumulate and subsequently use financial assets.

During the period when assets are consumed, most individuals will no longer have salary or wage income. Even though a pension and Social Security replace lost income, many individuals must draw down their assets to meet expenditures. While the assets that are retained continue to earn a return, both the amount of risk and return are reduced as safety of principal becomes increasingly important.

A large variety of assets (e.g., stocks, bonds, and mutual funds) are available to meet your financial goals as you go through your financial life cycles. Within each type of asset there is an almost unlimited number of choices. However, each of the various assets has common characteristics: liquidity/marketability, potential return, risk, and tax implications.

You do not spend your stocks or bonds. The ability to convert the asset into cash is obviously important. The ease of converting an asset to cash is an asset's liquidity. For many assets this liquidity depends on the asset's marketability, the existence of a secondary market in which the asset may be sold. The potential return from an investment is either the income it generates (e.g., interest), price appreciation, or a combination of both. All investments involve risk that is either specific to the asset or to the type of asset. (The management of risk is crucial to portfolio management, and the methods and strategies for risk management are discussed throughout this text.) Last, federal, state, and local taxation permeates investment decisions since income, capital gains, and wealth are all subject to tax, the tax rates on income, capital gains, and wealth differ.

An Analysis of the Individual's Financial Resources

Financial planning requires an analysis of your financial resources. This may be done by constructing two financial statements. The first one enumerates what is owned and owed, and the other enumerates cash receipts and disbursements. The former is, of course, a balance sheet, whereas the latter is a cash budget.

The entries for an individual's balance sheet are given in Exhibit 2.1 (p. 64). It lists all the individual's assets and liabilities. The difference between these assets and liabilities is the individual's net worth (which would be your "estate" if you were to die at the time the balance sheet is constructed). For clarity, you should list short-term assets and then long-term assets, and the same should be done with liabilities. In effect, your balance sheet is no different from a firm's balance sheet.

The entries for the balance sheet given in Exhibit 2.1 consider the financial position as of the present and as of some specified time in the future (such as retirement. (Many of the various entries are the content of the subsequent chapters in this text.) For the purpose of financial planning, it is advisable to construct your current financial position as well as to project what that position will be at some time in the future. Such a projection is often referred to as a **pro forma financial statement**. The construction of a pro forma balance sheet will require that you make assumptions concerning (1) your ability to accumulate assets and retire liabilities and (2) the rate of return that will be achieved by the assets. While the resulting projections will depend on the assumptions, the projections often bring into sharp focus future financial needs and can help in establishing current investment strategies.

The balance sheets in Exhibit 2.1 are more detailed than is necessary for most individuals. Few individual investors will have entries for each asset or liability enumerated in the exhibit. For example, you may not be eligible for Keogh accounts. Also, some of the entries may not apply now but may apply in the future. For example, if you have not started an IRA but intend to, this should be included in the projected balance sheet even though it is not currently applicable.

pro forma financial statement
A projected or forecasted financial statement.

EXHIBIT 2.1	An Individual's Balance Sheet and the Determination of Net Worth		
		Present	**Future**
ASSETS			
1. Bank deposits			
a. Cash, checking accounts		___	___
b. Savings accounts		___	___
c. Certificates of deposit		___	___
d. Money market accounts		___	___
e. Other		___	___
	Subtotal	___	___
2. Liquid financial assets			
a. Money market mutual funds		___	___
b. Treasury bills		___	___
c. Series EE and I bonds		___	___
	Subtotal	___	___
3. Retirement and savings plans			
a. IRA accounts:			
Tax-deferred IRA		___	
Roth IRA		___	
b. Keogh accounts		___	
c. Employee savings and investment plan:			
d. Employee stock		___	___
e. Other		___	___
	Subtotal	___	___
4. Financial assets			
a. Treasury bonds		___	___
b. GNMAs and other federal agency debt		___	___
c. Corporate bonds		___	___
d. Municipal bonds		___	___
e. Corporate stock		___	___
f. Mutual funds			
Bond funds		___	___
Stock funds		___	___
	Subtotal	___	___
5. Tangible assets			
a. Real estate:		___	___
Home and vacation properties		___	___
Investment properties		___	___
b. Personal tangible property (e.g., cars, silver, furniture, jewelry, boats)		___	___
	Subtotal	___	___
Total Assets		___	___

(continued on next page)

EXHIBIT 2.1	An Individual's Balance Sheet and the Determination of Net Worth		
		Present	**Future**
LIABILITIES			
1. Short-term			
a. Current portion of mortgage owed		_____	_____
b. Current portion of car payments		_____	_____
c. Credit card balances		_____	_____
d. Miscellaneous		_____	_____
	Subtotal	_____	_____
2. Long-term			
a. Mortgage balance owed		_____	_____
b. Balance owed on car or other tangible assets		_____	_____
c. Bank loans		_____	_____
d. Other		_____	_____
	Subtotal	_____	_____
Total Liabilities		_____	_____
SUMMARY			
Total assets		_____	_____
Total liabilities		_____	_____
NET WORTH (value of estate: assets minus liabilities)		_____	_____

cash budget
A financial statement enumerating cash receipts and cash disbursements.

The mechanics of constructing a balance sheet are relatively easy. The difficult part is enumerating the assets and placing values on them. Such valuation is easy for publicly traded securities, such as stocks and bonds. The problem concerns placing values on tangible personal assets, such as collectibles or real estate. Since the purpose of constructing a balance sheet is to determine your financial condition, it is advisable to be conservative in estimating the value of these assets. If, for example, an individual had to sell antiques to finance living expenses, it would be better to underestimate than to overestimate the prices for which these assets may be sold.

After you enumerate what is owned and what is owed and thereby determine your net worth, the next step is to analyze the flow of receipts and disbursements. This is done by constructing a **cash budget**. Exhibit 2.2 (p. 66) shows the entries needed for the construction of a cash budget. It lists all the sources of receipts (e.g., salary, interest, and rental income) and all the disbursements (e.g., mortgage payments, living expenses, and taxes). As with the balance sheet, the cash budget may be constructed for the present or projected for a specific time in the future (e.g., at retirement). Exhibit 2.2 thus provides for both a current annual cash budget and a pro forma cash budget. Although the cash budget illustrated in this exhibit is for one year, cash budgets may be constructed to cover other time periods, such as monthly receipts and disbursements.

As with the balance sheet in Exhibit 2.1, the entries in Exhibit 2.2 are probably too detailed for many individuals. If your receipts exceed disbursements, the excess receipts become a source of funds that should be invested to meet future financial needs. It is possible that after constructing such a cash budget, you will perceive ways to increase receipts and decrease disbursements and thus generate additional funds for investment.

EXHIBIT 2.2   An Individual's Cash Budget for One Year

	Present	Future
CASH RECEIPTS		
Salary (after withholding)	_____	_____
Social Security	_____	_____
Pension	_____	_____
Interest from savings	_____	_____
Dividends on stock	_____	_____
Commissions & bonuses	_____	_____
Royalties, fees	_____	_____
Distributions from businesses	_____	_____
Net rental income	_____	_____
Veterans' benefits	_____	_____
Annuity payments	_____	_____
Distributions from trusts	_____	_____
Distributions from IRA, Keogh, and 401(k) accounts	_____	_____
Other receipts	_____	_____
Total Receipts	_____	_____

	Present	Future
CASH DISBURSEMENTS		
1. Housing	_____	_____
a. Mortgage payments	_____	_____
b. Rent	_____	_____
c. Maintenance	_____	_____
d. Utilities and fuel	_____	_____
e. Property taxes	_____	_____
2. Food and personal expenditures		
a. Dining at home	_____	_____
b. Dining out	_____	_____
c. Personal care	_____	_____
d. Clothing	_____	_____
e. Recreation and travel	_____	_____
f. Furniture, appliances	_____	_____
g. Hobbies	_____	_____
3. Transportation		
a. Automobile payments	_____	_____
b. Operating expenses	_____	_____
c. Public transportation	_____	_____
4. Medical		
a. Insurance	_____	_____
b. Deductibles paid	_____	_____
c. Miscellaneous expense	_____	_____

(continued on next page)

EXHIBIT 2.2	An Individual's Cash Budget for One Year		
		Present	**Future**
CASH DISBURSEMENTS			
5. Insurance			
a. Life insurance			
b. Homeowner's insurance		_____	_____
c. Automobile insurance		_____	_____
d. Other		_____	_____
6. Estimated taxes		_____	_____
7. Other disbursements			
a. Gifts		_____	_____
b. Contributions		_____	_____
c. Miscellaneous		_____	_____
Total Disbursements		_____	_____
SUMMARY			
Total receipts		_____	_____
Total disbursements		_____	_____
Difference between receipts and disbursements		_____	_____

Establishing Financial Plans

After specifying goals and analyzing your financial position, you can establish a financial plan or course of action. This plan is the strategy by which you will fulfill your financial goals. Although plans will vary among individuals, the importance of such a plan applies to all. It is the means to the end—the means to financial success and security.

Plans require the establishment of priorities. Those financial goals that are most important should be fulfilled first. After investments have been made to satisfy these needs, the next most important goals should be attacked. In this way the investor systematically saves and invests to meet the specified goals. For example, you may determine the following goals and their priority:

- Funds to meet financial emergencies
- Funds to finance a child's education
- Funds to finance retirement

The initial goal, then, is sufficient liquid assets to cover emergencies (e.g., unemployment or extended illness). After this goal has been met, you proceed to accumulate assets designed to finance the child's college education. The process is continued until all the goals have been met.

The Capacity to Meet Financial Emergencies While this financial goal can be well defined, planning to have funds to meet financial emergencies involves uncertainty. You do not know when (or even if) the money will be needed. While long-term securities may be used to meet a financial goal that has an identifiable time period, they would probably be inappropriate to meet the goal of having sufficient funds to deal with emergencies. Assets that are very liquid (i.e., that are easily converted into cash) should be chosen to fulfill this investment goal, such as certificates of deposit with a commercial bank and money market mutual funds.

The Financing of Identifiable Future Purchases, Such as a Child's Education While it is impossible to know when the funds will be needed for an emergency, this uncertainty need not apply to other future purchases of goods and services. The desire to purchase a specified good or service often has a known time dimension. Financing an education and planning for retirement are both examples of expenditures that will occur at a particular time in the future. Although there may be some deviation in the time of the actual occurrence, you know approximately when these events will happen and can plan to have the funds to finance the purchase.

Consider the financing of a child's college education. If the child is currently eight years old, the funds for a college education will be needed in approximately ten years. Even though the future cost of the education is not known, parents know when the funds will be needed and can systematically accumulate assets to meet this anticipated expense. The assets should be long-term since the funds will not be needed for many years, and they should be relatively safe since the parents would not want to lose the funds.

Altering Financial Plans

Financial planning is the backbone of portfolio construction, but you must realize that goals and financial conditions do change. Such changes may alter the general financial plan. The birth of a child, the death of a spouse, a promotion, or a new job are just some of the many possible events that shape our lives and can alter our financial goals. You must be willing to adjust financial plans accordingly.

Firms also change, so their securities may no longer be appropriate for an individual's portfolio. For example, AT&T is different today than it was prior to the spin-off of Lucent, NCR, and AT&T Wireless. In effect, AT&T converted itself into a more focused firm and no longer serves the needs of investors who previously acquired AT&T as a low-risk, moderate-growth stock.

One of the most important facets of investing—taxation—is also subject to change. Taxes alter the environment in which investment decisions are made. Some changes encourage investing or favor specific securities that you may acquire. Changes in the tax laws can have a profound impact on your portfolio and thus require you to reassess the composition of the portfolio and make appropriate adjustments. It is only possible to conjecture as to what future changes in the tax code may be enacted. Since you need to be aware of current tax laws, they are discussed later in this chapter.

Finally, you must be willing to realize that not all investments will achieve their anticipated return or serve the purpose for which they were acquired. That is the nature of risk; the future is uncertain. If a particular asset is no longer appropriate or the anticipated return has not been realized, you should be willing to liquidate that asset and acquire an alternative. This does not mean that you should continuously turn over the portfolio. Such a course of action may be counterproductive and perhaps may even reduce the return as you pay the fees associated with the sale of one asset and the purchase of another. However, you should not become so enamored with particular assets that they are an end unto themselves instead of a means to meet specified financial goals.

••THE TAX ENVIRONMENT

Financial planning and the execution of those plans cannot be performed in a vacuum. Constructing a financial plan and choosing to save more and spend less may be a responsible act, but it may affect other members of your family. I realize that if you are an undergraduate, you may not have many responsibilities other than to yourself. But you will have more responsibilities in the future, and financial planning concerns your future and your capacity to meet those responsibilities.

Your ability to plan financially will be improved by knowing the investment alternatives covered in this text. Planning will also be improved if you have basic knowledge of taxation. There are so many levels of taxation. Sales taxes are levied on purchases, excise taxes are levied on specific items such as gasoline, you pay tolls to ride on some roads, and property taxes are levied against the value of your home. While these taxes are important, especially as a source of revenue for a particular government, they rarely affect investment decisions. Estate taxes and income taxes, however, are crucial considerations to financial planning and the management of your portfolio.

Estate taxes are levied as of the date of your death on the value of your assets (after deducting any liabilities). Estate taxes are obviously important when planning for the disbursement of your wealth. The number of estates affected by these taxes is relatively small, so this basic text will not cover estate taxes. (If you do accumulate a sizable portfolio, you will become aware of the need for estate planning. At that time you should consult an estate lawyer and/or financial planner for help.)

Income taxes are an entirely different matter. Of course, you would not have to pay any income taxes if you did not have taxable income. However, the returns on your investments (i.e., dividends, interest, and capital gains) are all subject to federal income tax. These taxes affect your investment decisions. If the taxes on all sources of income and investment return were the same, the impact would be less, but taxes are not evenly applied to earned income and investment returns. These differences revolve around the tax rates and the timing of when the taxes are levied.

Income taxes are levied by the federal government and by many state governments and even some localities. A tax is **progressive** if the tax rate increases as the tax base (income) rises. If the tax rate declines as the base increases, the tax is **regressive**. If the tax rate remains constant, the tax is **proportionate**. The federal personal income tax is progressive because as your income rises, the tax rate increases. For example, as of January 2004, the income tax rates for a married couple filing a joint return for 2003 were

- **progressive tax**
  A tax whose rate increases as the tax base increases.

- **regressive tax**
  A tax whose rate declines as the tax base increases.

- **proportionate tax**
  A tax whose rate remains constant as the tax base changes.

Taxable Income	Marginal Tax Rate
$0 – 14,000	10%
14,001 – 56,800	15
56,801 – 114,650	25
114, 651 – 174,700	28
174,701 – 311,950	33
311,951	35

Given this tax schedule, a couple with taxable income of $14,000 owes federal income taxes of $1,400 (0.10 × $14,000). If taxable income is $60,000, the taxes owed are $8,620 ($14,000 × 0.10 + 42,800 × 0.15 + 3,200 × 0.25 = $8,620). This tax is 14.37 percent ($8,620/$60,000) of the couple's taxable income.

marginal tax rate
The tax rate paid on an additional last dollar of taxable income; an individual's tax bracket.

tax shelter
An asset or investment that defers, reduces, or avoids taxation.

capital gain
The increase in the value of an asset such as a stock or a bond.

capital loss
A decrease in the value of an asset such as a stock or a bond.

The right-hand column (i.e., the tax rate on additional income) is often referred to as the **marginal tax rate**. As may be seen from the schedule, the tax rate increases as income increases, which indicates that the federal income tax structure is progressive. The tax brackets (e.g., $56,801 – 114,650) change every year, because the brackets are adjusted for inflation. That means there is a *cost of-living (COLA) adjustment*. As prices increase, the tax brackets are raised so you are not taxed at a higher rate solely as the result of inflation.

Since additional investment returns are subject to tax at higher marginal tax rates, the question becomes, can you do anything to reduce taxes owed? The answer is Yes; there are several tax shelters available to all federal taxpayers. As the name implies, a **tax shelter** is something that protects against taxes; the tax shelter either *avoids, reduces, or defers* taxes. An example of a tax shelter that avoids taxation is the municipal bond discussed in Chapter 10. The interest on these bonds is exempt from federal income taxation. An example of a tax shelter that reduces income is the deductibility of interest on mortgages and property taxes. A home is, in part, an investment, and the deductibility of these expenses associated with home ownership reduces your federal taxes. This tax saving makes ownership less expensive and more attractive. Tax-deferred retirement plans, as the name implies, permit you to defer taxes. You do not avoid paying the tax; it is postponed until some time in the future. In effect, you have the free use of funds until the tax must be paid, which may be many years into the future.

You do not have to be wealthy to use these shelters. Long-term capital gains and retirement accounts, covered in the next sections, are tax shelters that every investor should use. They should be part of your financial plan and investment strategy. You should also realize that it is possible to make costly mistakes in an attempt to avoid paying taxes. You should never let taxes drive your investment decisions. Instead you should make prudent investment decisions that take advantage of shelters that avoid, reduce, or defer your tax obligations.

CAPITAL GAINS AND LOSSES

Many investments are purchased and subsequently sold. If the sale results in a profit, that profit is considered a **capital gain**; if the sale results in a loss, that is a **capital loss**. If the gain or loss is realized within a year, it is a *short-term* capital gain or loss. If the sale occurs after a year from the date of purchase, it is a *long-term* gain or loss.

Short-term capital gains are taxed at the individual's marginal tax rate. Thus, if you buy a stock for $10,000 and sell it for $13,000 after nine months, the $3,000 short-term capital gain is taxed as any other source of taxable income. If the stock had been held for 15 months, the $3,000 long-term capital gain would be taxed at either 5 or 15 percent, depending on your marginal tax rate. Taxpayers in the 10 and 15 percent brackets pay 5 percent and all others pay 15 percent. Thus, for individuals in the 33 percent marginal tax bracket, long-term capital gains are taxed at 15 percent. An individual in the 33 percent tax bracket would pay $990 on a $3,000 short-term capital gain, while a $3,000 long-term capital gain generates $450 in taxes, a reduction of $540.

The investor may use capital losses to offset capital gains. If the investor bought a second stock for $15,000 and sold it for $12,000, the $3,000 loss would offset the $3,000 capital gain. This offsetting of capital gains by capital losses applies to both short- and long-term gains. However, there is a specified order in which losses offset gains.

Initially short-term losses are used to offset short-term gains, and long-term losses are used to offset long-term gains. If there is a net short-term loss (i.e., short-term losses exceed short-term gains), it is used to offset long-term gains. For example, if an investor has realized net short-term losses of $3,000, that short-term loss may be used to offset up to $3,000 in long-term capital gains. If net short-term losses are less than long-term gains, the resulting net capital gain is taxed as long-term.

If there is a net long-term loss (i.e., long-term losses exceed long-term gains), the loss is used to offset short-term gains. For example, $3,000 in net long-term capital losses is used to offset up to $3,000 in short-term capital gains.[1] If net long-term losses are less than short-term gains, the resulting net capital gain is taxed as short-term.

If the investor has a net short- or long-term capital loss after subtracting short- or long-term capital gains, that net capital loss is used to offset income from other sources, such as dividends or interest. However, only $3,000 in capital losses may be used in a given year to offset income from other sources. If you have a larger loss (e.g., $5,000), only $3,000 may be used in the current year. The remainder ($2,000) is carried forward to offset capital gains or income received in future years. Under this system of carry-forward, a current capital loss of $10,000 offsets only $3,000 in current income and the remaining $7,000 is carried forward to offset capital gains and income in subsequent years. If you have no capital gains in the second year, only $3,000 of the remaining loss offsets income in the second year and the balance ($4,000) is carried forward to the third year. In the case of a large capital loss, this $3,000 limitation may be an incentive for you to take gains in the current year rather than carry forward the loss.

Even if capital gains were taxed at the same rate as ordinary income, they are still illustrative of a tax shelter. The taxes on capital gains may be deferred indefinitely, because investment profits are taxed only after they have been realized. Many profits on security positions are only **paper profits**, because some investors do not sell the securities and realize the gains. The tax laws encourage such retention of securities by taxing the gains only when they are realized.

paper profits
Price appreciation that has not been realized.

Capital gains taxes can be avoided entirely if the individual holds the securities until he or she dies. The value of securities is taxed as part of the deceased's estate. The securities are then transferred through the deceased's will to other individuals, such as children or grandchildren, and the cost basis becomes the security's value as of the date of death. For example, suppose your grandfather owns shares of IBM that were purchased in the 1960s. The current value of the shares is probably many times their cost. If he were to sell these shares, he would incur a large capital gain. However, if he holds the shares until he dies, their new cost basis becomes the current value of the shares, and the capital gains tax on the appreciation is avoided.[2]

PENSION PLANS

One tax shelter that may also ease the burden of retirement is the pension plan. Many firms contribute to these plans for their employees. The funds are invested

---

1. The $3,000 limitation applies to joint returns. If you are filing a single return, the limitation is $1,500.
2. Under current tax law, the estate tax is being phased out and scheduled to be repealed in 2010. Because Congress can change the tax laws, whether the complete abolition of the estate tax will occur is conjecture. If the estate tax is abolished, the ability to step up a security's cost basis and avoid capital gains taxes will also disappear.

in income-earning assets, such as stocks and bonds. In some cases, the employee is required to make payments in addition to the employer's contributions. The amount of the employer's contribution is usually related to the employee's earnings. These contributions are not included in taxable income, so the worker does not have to pay taxes on the employer's payments to the pension plan. Instead, the funds are taxed when the worker retires and starts to use the money that has accumulated through the plan.

Deductible IRAs

One criticism of employer-sponsored pension plans was that they were not available to all workers. However, Congress passed legislation that enables all employees as well as the self-employed to establish their own pension plans; thus, the tax shelter that was previously provided only through employer-sponsored pension plans is now available to all workers. An employee who is not covered by a pension plan may set up an **individual retirement account (IRA)**. In 1981 Congress passed additional legislation that extended IRAs to all employees, even if they were already participating in an employer-sponsored pension plan.

IRA
A retirement plan (individual retirement account) that is available to workers.

As of January 2004, you may open an account with a financial institution, such as a commercial bank, brokerage firm, or mutual fund company, and may deposit up to $3,000 per year. The funds must be earned, which means that any employee who earns $3,000 or more may place as much as $3,000 in an IRA account. However, if your source of income is dividends or interest, these funds cannot be placed in an IRA.

The amount invested in the IRA is deducted from your taxable income. Income earned by the funds in the account is also not taxed. All taxes are deferred until the funds are withdrawn from the IRA, and then they are taxed as ordinary income. If you prematurely withdraw the funds (before age 59½), the money is taxed as ordinary income and a penalty tax is added.

IRA accounts soon became one of the most popular tax shelters, but Congress placed important restrictions on the deductibility of the IRA contribution. For workers *covered by a pension plan*, full deductibility is applicable only for couples filing a joint return with adjusted gross income (in 2003) of *less than* $60,000. (For single workers covered by a pension plan the limit is $40,000.) Note that adjusted gross income is used and not earned income. If an individual earns a modest salary but has significant amounts of interest or dividend income, this additional income counts when determining the deductibility of IRA contributions. Once the cutoff level of income is reached, the deductibility of the contribution is reduced, so that it is completely phased out once the couple reaches adjusted gross income of $70,000 ($50,000 for individuals).

It is important to emphasize that the complete loss of deductibility of the IRA contribution applies only to workers filing a joint return who earn more than $70,000 ($50,000 filing a single return). For the majority of workers, the deductibility of the IRA contribution still applies. And the deductibility still applies to any individual, no matter what the level of income, who is not covered by an employer-sponsored pension plan.

Keogh account (HR-10 plan)
A retirement plan that is available to self-employed individuals.

Keogh Accounts

Self-employed persons may establish a pension plan called a **Keogh account** or **HR-10 plan**. The account is named after the congressman who sponsored the enabling legislation. A Keogh is similar to an IRA or a company-sponsored pension plan. The individual places funds in the account and deducts the amount from taxable income. The maximum annual contribution is the lesser of 25 percent of income or $35,000. (Future limits will be adjusted for inflation.) The funds placed in the account earn a return that (like the initial contributions) will not be taxed until the funds are withdrawn. As in the case of the IRA, there is a penalty for premature withdrawals before age 59½ and withdrawals must start after reaching the age of 70½.

The determination of the amount an individual may contribute to a Keogh account is somewhat confusing. The individual may contribute up to 25 percent of net earned income, but the calculation of net earned income subtracts the pension contribution as a business expense. The effect is that the individual can contribute 20 percent of income before the contribution. Consider a self-employed individual who earns $100,000 before the pension contribution. If that individual contributes $20,000 (i.e., 20 percent of $100,000), he or she has contributed 25 percent of income after deducting the pension contribution:

Net income after contribution: $100,000 – $20,000 = $80,000.

Contribution as percent of net earned income: $20,000/$80,000 = 25%.

It is probably easier to determine the maximum possible contribution by taking 20 percent of income before the contribution than by determining 25 percent of net earned income.[3]

A self-employed person may open an IRA in addition to a Keogh account. The contribution to the IRA, however, may not be deductible from taxable income if the individual's income exceeds the limits discussed above. If the self-employed person has funds to finance only one account, it is probably more advantageous to have the Keogh account since the amount that may be contributed (and sheltered from current income taxes) is larger.

If a self-employed person does open a Keogh plan, it must also apply to other people employed by this individual. There are some exceptions, such as new and young employees; however, if a self-employed individual establishes a Keogh account for himself or herself, other regular employees cannot be excluded. By establishing the account, the self-employed individual takes on fiduciary responsibilities for the management of Keogh accounts for his or her employees. This individual can avoid these responsibilities by establishing a Simplified Employee Pension (SEP) plan. SEPs were designed by Congress to encourage small employers to establish pension plans for their employees while avoiding the complexities of the pension laws.

401(k) Plans

Many employers now offer supplementary retirement accounts (SRAs), which are often referred to as *401(k) plans*. These programs permit individuals to contribute a portion of their earned income, up to a specified limit, to a savings plan. The contribution is deducted from the individual's earnings before determining taxable

---

3. The formula for determining the maximum contribution is

$$\frac{\text{Income} \times 0.25}{1 + 0.25}.$$

If the individual's income is $100,000, the maximum contribution is

$$\frac{\$100,000 \times 0.25}{1 + 0.25} = \frac{\$25,000}{1.25} = \$20,000.$$

income; thus, a 401(k) plan has the same effect on the employee's federal income taxes as IRAs and Keogh accounts. The funds may be invested in one of several plans offered by the company. These often include a stock fund, a bond fund, and a money market fund. The individual has the choice as to the distribution of the contributions among the plans and may be allowed to shift the funds at periodic intervals.

403(b) Plans

Nonprofit organizations, such as hospitals, religious organizations, foundations, and public and private schools, may offer similar salary reduction plans, referred to as *403(b) plans*. They work essentially in the same way as 401(k) plans for employees of for-profit organizations. In both cases, the employee's income is reduced by the contribution so that federal income tax is deferred until the funds are withdrawn from the account. The contributions are invested, and the tax on the earnings is also deferred until the funds are withdrawn.

Nondeductible IRAs—The Roth IRA

In 1997, enabling legislation created the Roth IRA, named after its sponsor, Senator Roth from Delaware. Like the deductible IRA, the Roth IRA is designed to encourage saving for retirement and is an illustration of a tax shelter. However, unlike the traditional IRA in which the contributions are deducted up front, the Roth IRA's advantage occurs when the funds are withdrawn. While the contributions are not tax deductible, the withdrawals are not subject to income tax. As was explained earlier, withdrawals from a deductible IRA are subject to income taxation.

Like the deductible IRA, the Roth IRA is subject to limitations concerning the amount of the contribution. For 2003–2004 the limitation is $3,000 annually for an individual's account. Contributions may be made as long as adjusted gross income is less than $150,000 ($95,000 if single). For adjusted gross income in excess of these levels, the contributions are phased out. Complete phaseout occurs at adjusted gross incomes of $160,000 and $110,000, respectively. (These phaseout income limitations are more generous than the limitations for deductible IRAs and may encourage the individual to select the Roth IRA in preference to the deductible IRA.)

The individual can have both types of IRAs but cannot contribute $3,000 to both. Thus, the investor could invest $1,500 in each account (for a total of $3,000), but that strategy avoids the important question: Which is better, the deductible or the nondeductible IRA?

Although it may appear that the nondeductible IRA is preferred because all the return on the investments is exempt from taxation, that is not necessarily the correct choice. Instead, the choice depends on the investor's current income tax bracket and anticipated tax bracket in the future when the funds are withdrawn. In general, if the tax bracket is higher when the contributions are made, the deductible IRA should be preferred. The converse would be true if the investor expects to be in a higher tax bracket when the funds are withdrawn. Then the nondeductible IRA should be preferred. If the tax brackets are the same, it may not matter which IRA the individual chooses. (There are other differences between the deductible and the nondeductible plans, such as mandatory withdrawal from a deductible IRA starting at age 70½. The nondeductible IRA does not have mandatory withdrawals. Such differences may favor one plan over the other independently of the individual's tax bracket.)

ASSET ALLOCATION

Now that you are aware of the need to identify financial goals, construct financial plans, and avail yourself of various tax shelters, you need to be aware of portfolio construction. Financial assets are acquired one at a time and combined in your portfolio. This portfolio, which manages your risk exposure while achieving your financial goals, may have a variety of assets ranging from savings accounts to corporate bonds and common stocks to mutual funds. Even within a type of asset such as the corporate bond, there is a spectrum of different features. This variety of assets is, of course, the content of much of the remainder of this text. As you proceed, you will realize that many assets may not be appropriate to meet some financial goals and that financial assets that are appropriate under one set of circumstances may not be appropriate when the circumstances change.

As you read more about investing, you may encounter the phrase "asset allocation." This is an ambiguous term frequently used concerning investing and portfolio construction. In some contexts "asset allocation" means determining the proportion of your assets in different classes of assets (e.g., 60 percent stock, 30 percent fixed income, and 10 percent cash). In other cases "asset allocation" may imply altering your portfolio in response to changing economic or market conditions (e.g., shifting from stocks to cash in anticipation of declining stock prices). Last, "asset allocation" simply refers to the process of constructing a diversified portfolio (e.g., selecting different stocks and bonds to reduce risk without reducing return).

The broadest definition is the first, which suggests that asset allocation is part of the planning process that determines the optimal allocation prior to the selection of specific assets. That is, asset allocation establishes portfolio policy. The other two definitions imply that asset allocation is an operational concept that guides changes in the portfolio.

Asset Allocation as Policy

Asset allocation as part of the financial plan may be illustrated by an individual with only two financial goals: funds for emergencies (such as unemployment) and funds for retirement. The pie charts in Figure 2.1 (p. 76) represent asset allocations designed to meet these two goals at three different points in an individual's life. In the first, the individual is 30 years old and has only a modest amount of assets ($50,000). The allocation policy determines that 60 percent of funds should be used to meet financial emergencies with 40 percent designated for growth. After making this determination, 60 percent of the assets are invested in liquid assets and the remaining funds are allocated to more volatile stocks or growth mutual funds whose potential higher returns are more suited for a long-term financial goal. If the value of these assets were to increase, then some would be sold and the funds transferred into liquid assets to maintain the 60–40 proportion of the portfolio.

In the second pie chart, the individual is now 50 years old and has assets of $300,000. The appropriate allocation is determined to be 15 percent to meet emergencies and 85 percent for growth. Even though the absolute amount of funds necessary to meet the first goal has been increased from $30,000 to $45,000, these funds constitute a smaller percentage of the portfolio. Since retirement is closer, the type of growth security may be less volatile and offer a smaller return than the assets selected when the individual was 30 years old. Once again, if the value of assets designed to meet the growth objective were to change, the individual would alter the portfolio to maintain the 15–85 asset allocation.

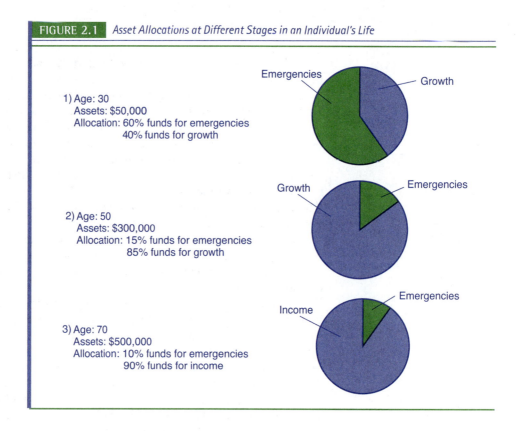

FIGURE 2.1 *Asset Allocations at Different Stages in an Individual's Life*

1) Age: 30
   Assets: $50,000
   Allocation: 60% funds for emergencies
              40% funds for growth

2) Age: 50
   Assets: $300,000
   Allocation: 15% funds for emergencies
              85% funds for growth

3) Age: 70
   Assets: $500,000
   Allocation: 10% funds for emergencies
              90% funds for income

In the third chart, the individual is now 70 with $500,000 in assets. The need for funds to meet emergencies such as unemployment ceases, but other possible emergencies such as illness may become important. The optimal allocation is determined to be 10 percent for emergencies and 90 percent for income during retirement. The specific assets (e.g., individual stocks and bonds or mutual funds) produce dividend and interest income and expose the individual to less risk than the growth stocks that were appropriate when the individual was younger. Once again, if the value of these income-producing assets were to change, the individual would alter the portfolio to maintain the 10–90 asset allocation.

Changing the portfolio to maintain a percentage allocation implies that the portfolio requires active supervision. Since security prices change daily, this supervision can be taken to an extreme in which the portfolio is rebalanced every day. This extreme may be avoided by defining the percentages as ranges instead of single points. For example, an asset allocation may be 30 to 40 percent liquid assets and 70 to 60 percent growth securities. As long as the components of the portfolio remain within the specified range, no adjustments are required.

The Importance of Asset Allocation

Asset allocation took on an entirely new dimension with the publication in 1986 of an article by Brinson, Hood, and Beebower and later confirmation in a subsequent publication. Essentially, the authors wanted to decompose the return earned by a portfolio manager into three components: (1) investment policy, (2) market timing, and (3) security selection.[4] The decomposition would then determine the portfolio manager's contribution, since the components could be compared to a passive benchmark portfolio, such as the S&P 500 stock index.

While total returns may be compared to a benchmark, part of the return depends on the investment policy, which may be *independent of the portfolio manager's decision-making power*. For example, suppose a corporation employs a money management firm to oversee its pension plan. The corporation sets the general policy that 30 to 40 percent of the portfolio should be in fixed-income securities and 70 to 60 percent should be in equities. This policy decision is independent of the portfolio manager's decision as to how to execute the policy. The portfolio manager's choices are limited to which fixed-income securities and which stocks will be in the portfolio and when to move from one type of security to the other to maintain the specified allocation.

Brinson, Hood, and Beebower determined a method to isolate each factor's contribution. In effect, their method determined the relative importance of the investment policy, market timing, and security selection. Their results, however, startled the investment management community, since 93.6 percent of the observed variation in returns was attributed to the investment policy. The impact of market timing and security selection was minor and (to make matters worse) actually reduced the average return and increased the variability of the return. A passive strategy of buying the stock index generated a higher return than attempting market timing and selecting individual assets.

This seminal work in asset allocation has been expanded. One study identified 11 variables that suggested an active allocation strategy produced higher returns.[5] A more recent study concluded that the portfolio manager's discretion to change the policy also affects the results.[6] Permitting the portfolio manager to alter the proportions changes the relative importance of policy, timing, and security selection. Timing and security selection then have a larger impact on total return, but the total amount of variation in returns that was explained by the active management of the portfolio was still small. The policy that determined the asset allocation, however, remained a major determinant of the total return.

THE EFFICIENT MARKET HYPOTHESIS

The previous section indicated that your allocation among various classes of assets is exceedingly important. The specific stocks and bonds that you acquire have little impact on the return you earn. Instead that return is highly dependent on the distribution of the portfolio among the various classes of securities. Why may this be true? Shouldn't you, or at least professional money managers, do better?

Perhaps it is conceit that makes some individuals (perhaps even you) believe that they can do better than the average investor and can "beat the market." Certainly there has to be a technique, a magic bullet, that produces superior results?

4. Gary P. Brinson, L. Randolph Hood, and Gilbert L. Beebower, "Determinants of Portfolio Performance," *Financial Analysts Journal* (July–August 1986): 39–44; and Gary P. Brinson, B. D. Singer, and Gilbert L. Beebower, "Determinants of Portfolio Performance II: An Update," *Financial Analysts Journal* (May–June 1991): 40–48.
5. R. C. Klemkosky and R. Bharati, "Time-Varying Expected Returns and Asset Allocation," *Journal of Portfolio Management* (summer 1995): 80–88.
6. Warren E. Bitters, *The New Science of Asset Allocation* (Chicago, IL: Glenlake Publishing, 1997).

efficient market hypothesis (EMH)
A theory that security prices correctly measure the firm's future earnings and dividends and that investors should not consistently outperform the market on a risk-adjusted basis.

This section discusses the efficient market hypothesis.[7] Once you understand that hypothesis and its implications, the conclusion concerning asset allocation and its impact on your return should not be so surprising.

The **efficient market hypothesis (EMH)** suggests that investors cannot expect to outperform the market consistently on a risk-adjusted basis. Notice that the hypothesis does not say that you will not outperform the market, since obviously some investors may do exceptionally well for a period of time. Being an occasional winner is not what is important, however, since most investors have a longer time horizon. The efficient market hypothesis suggests that you will not outperform the market on a risk-adjusted basis over an extended period of time.

The efficient market hypothesis is based on several assumptions, including (1) the fact that there are a large number of competing participants in the securities markets, (2) information is readily available and virtually costless to obtain, and (3) transaction costs are small. The first two conditions seem obvious. That there are a large number of participants cannot be denied. Brokerage firms, insurance companies, investment and asset management firms, and many individuals spend countless hours analyzing financial statements, seeking to determine the value of a company. The amount of information available on investments is nothing short of staggering, and the cost of obtaining much of the information used in security analysis is often trivial.

The third condition may not hold for individual investors, who must pay commissions to brokerage firms for executing orders. The condition may apply to financial institutions, such as trust departments and mutual funds. These institutions pay only a few cents per share, and this insignificant cost does not affect their investment decisions. Today, as a result of electronic trading, even the individual investor may now be able to buy and sell stock at a cost that is comparable to financial institutions. However, investors who continue to use traditional full-service brokers pay substantial commissions to trade stocks, and these commissions do affect an investment's return.

Because securities markets are highly competitive, information is readily available, and transactions may be executed with minimal transaction costs, the efficient market hypothesis argues that security prices adjust rapidly to new information and must reflect all known information concerning the firm. Since security prices fully incorporate known information and prices change rapidly, day-to-day price changes will follow in a *random walk* over time. A random walk essentially means that price changes are unpredictable and patterns formed are accidental. If prices do follow a random walk, trading rules are useless, and various techniques, such as charting, moving averages, or odd-lot purchases relative to sales, cannot lead to superior security selection. (These techniques are discussed in Chapter 8.)

The conventional choice of the term *random walk* to describe the pattern of changes in security prices is perhaps unfortunate for two reasons. First, it is reasonable to expect that over a period of time, stock prices will rise as firms and the economy grow.

Second, the phrase *random walk* is often misinterpreted as meaning that security prices are randomly determined, an interpretation that is completely backwards. It is *changes* in security prices that are random. Security prices themselves are rationally and efficiently determined by such fundamental considerations as

7. For a lucid book on efficient markets and their implication for following a passive investment strategy, see Burton G. Malkiel, *A Random Walk Down Wall Street* (New York: W.W. Norton, 2003). This classic is currently in its 8th edition and should be in every investor's library, including yours.

earnings, interest rates, dividend policy, and the economic environment. Changes in these variables are quickly reflected in a security's price. All known information is embodied in the current price, and only new information alters that price. New information has to be unpredictable; if it were predictable, the information would be known and stock prices would have already adjusted for that information. Hence, new information *must be random*, and security prices should change randomly in response to that information. If changes in security prices were not random and could be predicted, then some investors could consistently outperform the market (i.e., earn a return in excess of the expected return given the amount of risk) and securities markets would not be efficient.

Because security prices incorporate all known information concerning a firm, the current price of a stock must properly value the firm's future growth and dividends. Today's price, then, is a true measure of the security's worth. Security analysis that is designed to determine if the stock is over- or underpriced is futile, because the stock is neither. If prices were not true measures of the firm's worth, an opportunity to earn excess returns would exist. Investors who recognized these opportunities (e.g., that a particular stock is undervalued) and took advantage of the mispricing (e.g., bought the undervalued stock) would consistently outperform the market on a risk-adjusted basis.

The Speed of Price Adjustments

For security markets to be efficient, security prices must adjust rapidly. The efficient market hypothesis asserts that the market prices adjust extremely rapidly as new information is disseminated. In the modern world of advanced communication, information is rapidly dispersed in the investment community. The market then adjusts security prices in accordance with the impact of the news on the firm's future earnings and dividends. By the time that the individual investor has learned the information, security prices probably will have already changed. Thus, the investor will not be able to profit from acting on the information.

This adjustment process is illustrated in Figure 2.2 (p. 80), which plots the price of AMR (American Airlines) stock. In early October, AMR received a buyout offer at $120, and the stock rose quickly and dramatically. However, the offer was terminated on October 16, and the price of the stock fell 22.13 points from $98.63 to $76.50. Such price behavior is exactly what the efficient market hypothesis suggests: The market adjusts very rapidly to new information. By the time the announcement was reported in the financial press on October 17, it was too late for the individual investor to react, as the price change had already occurred. Today, with announcements being rapidly disseminated via the Internet, it is unlikely that many, if any, individuals could receive and act on the information before the price changes. Once the announcement has been made, the stock's market makers will immediately alter the bid and ask prices to adjust for the new information.

If the market were not so efficient and prices did not adjust rapidly, some investors would be able to adjust their holdings and take advantage of differences in investors' knowledge. Consider the broken line in Figure 2.2. If some investors knew that the agreement had been terminated but others did not, the former could sell their holdings to those who were not informed. The price then might fall over a period of time as the knowledgeable sellers accepted progressively lower prices in order to unload their stock. Of course, if a sufficient number of investors had learned quickly of the termination, the price decline would be rapid as these investors adjusted their valuations of the stock in accordance with the new information. That

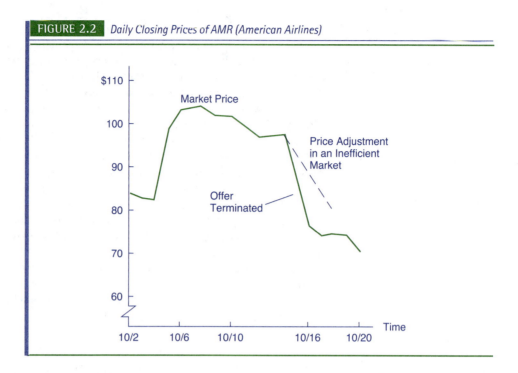

FIGURE 2.2   *Daily Closing Prices of AMR (American Airlines)*

is exactly what happened, because a sufficient number of investors were rapidly informed and the efficient market quickly adjusted the stock's price.

If an investor were able to anticipate the termination of the merger before it was announced, that individual could avoid the price decline. Obviously, some investors did sell their shares just before the announcement, but it is also evident that some individuals bought those shares. Certainly one reason for learning the material and performing the various types of analysis throughout this text is to increase your ability to anticipate events before they occur. However, you should realize that considerable evidence supports the efficient market hypothesis and strongly suggests few investors will, over a period of time, outperform the market consistently.

Forms of the Efficient Market Hypothesis

The previous discussion of the efficient market hypothesis suggested that financial markets are efficient. The competition among investors, the rapid dissemination of information, and the swiftness with which security prices adjust to this information produce efficient financial markets in which you cannot expect to consistently outperform the market. Instead, you can expect to earn a return that is consistent with the amount of risk you bear.

While you may know that financial markets are efficient, you may not know *how* efficient. The degree of efficiency is important, because it determines the value the individual investor places on various types of analysis to select securities. If financial markets are inefficient, then many techniques may aid you in selecting securities, and these techniques should lead to superior results. However, as markets become more efficient and various tools of analysis become well known, their usefulness for security selection is reduced. They will no longer produce superior results (i.e., beat the market on a risk-adjusted basis).

You may believe that the financial markets are weakly efficient, semistrongly efficient, or strongly efficient. The *weak form* of the efficient market hypothesis suggests that the fundamental analysis discussed in Chapters 6 and 7 may produce superior investment results but that the technical analysis discussed in Chapter 8 will not. Thus, studying past price behavior and other technical indicators of the market will not produce superior investment results.

The *semistrong* form of the efficient market hypothesis asserts that the current price of a stock reflects all the public's information concerning the company. This knowledge includes both the firm's history and the information learned through studying the firm's financial statements, its industry, and the general economic environment. Analysis of this material cannot be expected to produce superior investment results. Notice that the hypothesis does not state that the analysis cannot produce superior results. It just asserts that superior results should not be expected. However, there is the implication that even if the analysis of information produces superior results in some cases, it will not produce superior results over many investment decisions. Hence, you should not expect to beat the market on a consistent basis.

This conclusion should not be surprising to anyone who thinks about the investment process. Many investors and analysts study the same information. Their thought processes and training are similar, and they are in competition with one another. Certainly, if one perceives a fundamental change in a particular firm, this information will be readily transferred to other investors, and the price of the security will change. The competition among the potential buyers and the potential sellers will result in the security's price reflecting the firm's intrinsic worth.

As may be expected, the investment community is not particularly elated with this conclusion. It implies that the fundamental analysis considered in Chapters 6 and 7 will not produce superior investment results. Thus, neither technical nor fundamental analysis will generate consistently superior investment performance. Of course, if the individual analyst is able to perceive fundamental changes before other analysts do, that individual can outperform the market as a whole. However, few, if any, individuals should be able to consistently perceive such changes. Thus, there is little reason to expect investors to achieve *consistently* superior investment results.

There is, however, one major exception to this general conclusion of the semistrong form of the efficient market hypothesis. If the investor has access to *inside information*, that individual may consistently achieve superior results. In effect, this individual has information that is not known by the general investing public. Such privileged information as dividend cuts or increments, new discoveries, or potential takeovers may have a significant impact on the value of the firm and its securities. If the investor has advance knowledge of such events and has the time to act, he or she should be able to achieve superior investment returns.

Of course, most investors do not have access to inside information or at least do not have access to information concerning a number of firms. An individual may have access to privileged information concerning a firm for which he or she works. But the use of such information for personal gain is *illegal*.[8] To achieve continuous superior results, the individual would have to have a continuous supply of correct inside information and to use it illegally. Probably few, if any, investors have this

---

8. Martha Stewart's legal problems started when prosecutors alleged that she had sold Imclone stock based on a tip from an insider. Even though she was not an insider, a sale based on information received from an insider is also illegal.

continuous supply, which may explain why both fundamentalists and technical analysts watch sales and purchases by insiders as a means to glean a clue as to the true future potential of the firm as seen by its management.

The *strong form* of the efficient market hypothesis asserts that the current price of a stock reflects all known (i.e., public) information and all privileged or inside information concerning the firm. Thus, even access to inside information cannot be expected to result in superior investment performance. Once again, this does not mean that an individual who acts on inside information cannot achieve superior results. It means that these results cannot be expected and that success in one case will tend to be offset by failure in other cases, so over time the investor will not achieve superior results.

This conclusion rests on a very important assumption: Inside information cannot be kept inside! Too many people know about the activities of a firm. This information is discerned by a sufficient number of investors, and the prices of the firm's securities adjust for the informational content of this inside knowledge. Notice that the conclusion that the price of the stock still reflects its intrinsic value does not require that all investors know this additional information. All that is necessary is for a sufficient number to know. Furthermore, the knowledge need not be acquired illegally. It is virtually impossible to keep some information secret, and there is a continual flow of rumors concerning a firm's activities. Denial by the firm is not sufficient to stop this spread of rumors, and when some are later confirmed, it only increases the credibility of future rumors as a possible means to gain inside information.

Although considerable empirical work has been designed to verify the forms of the efficient market hypothesis, these tests generally support only the weak and semistrong forms. The use of privileged information may result in superior investment performance, but the use of publicly known information cannot be expected to produce superior investments. Thus, neither technical nor fundamental analysis may help you, because the current price of a stock fully incorporates this information.

IMPLICATIONS OF THE EFFICIENT MARKET HYPOTHESIS

The efficient market hypothesis reappears throughout this text. And each time it appears, it will remind you that outperforming the market over a period of time is difficult, if not impossible, to achieve. Ultimately, you must decide how efficient you believe financial markets are and whether there are exceptions to the basic theory such as insider purchases and sales that you can exploit.

You also have to decide how actively you want to participate in the management of your portfolio. If, for example, you believe that markets are efficient and that you have neither the time nor the inclination to manage the portfolio, then employing someone else to manage the funds is a logical and reasonable approach to portfolio management. (In that case you might consider turning to Chapter 12 and skipping all the material, except Chapter 3 on risk measurement, in between.) If you do not want to employ someone, you can still passively manage your portfolio. At one extreme you could allocate your entire portfolio among a variety of investments such as savings accounts and index funds. (In that case, you may skip to the end of Chapter 13 to the material on index and exchange-traded funds.)

If you don't believe that markets are efficient or you don't want to delegate investment decisions, then you will need to manage your own portfolio. The extreme case of active management is the "day trader," who buys and sells virtually every day. Of course, this strategy requires a large investment of time. Day traders devote all their working hours to making trades. All of their energies and thought processes have to be devoted to perceiving price movements and making trades. Day trading is not free. These individuals pay commissions, and even if the cost per trade is small, the total cost of all the trades can be substantial. Day traders also must pay income taxes on their gains. There is no tax shelter for day traders such as lower taxes through long-term capital gains.

Between the two extremes of doing little and passively holding financial assets or actively trading every day, there is a wide spectrum of possibilities. You need to look inside yourself and determine what works for you. That is, you need to develop a financial plan, determine how to execute the plan, and determine how actively you want to manage your portfolio. It is easy to infer from the efficient market hypothesis that all you have to do is randomly select a diversified portfolio and hold it indefinitely. There is no need to change the portfolio. You just buy and hold.

This naïve policy fails to consider why you saved and acquired your portfolio. A simple buy-and-hold strategy ignores your portfolio's objectives. Over time your financial goals will change and the allocation of your portfolio among various financial assets should change. The naïve buy-and-hold strategy also does not consider your tax environment and any tax shelters that may be available to you. Like your financial goals, the tax laws *will be revised during your lifetime*. These revisions may require that you alter your portfolio, especially to take advantage of any changes that are favorable to you.

The importance of the efficient market hypothesis is not that investment decision making is useless. Instead the hypothesis brings to your attention the environment in which you make financial decisions. While the hypothesis suggests that you will not consistently make investments that produce superior returns, it also implies that over time you should earn a return that is consistent with the market return and the amount of risk that you accept. The theory implies that you should acquire a portfolio that meets your financial goals and that you should not chase whatever investment fad is currently being reported on TV or in the financial press.

The remainder of this text will explain the features of various investments and how you might analyze these assets for possible inclusion in your portfolio. Since all investments involve risk, the sources of risk associated with these investments and how you may use different assets to help manage risk are also covered. Knowledge of this material should help you achieve your financial goals. (I cannot determine your financial goals and your risk tolerance. Those you will have to determine for yourself.) The more you know about investments, the greater is the probability that you will make fewer bad investment decisions.

Unless you are a very conservative, passive investor, you will make mistakes. Even if the first company you invest in goes bankrupt, the experience will make you a better investor. The combination of knowledge concerning investments and efficient markets suggests that over time your investments will produce positive results. The movie *Parenthood* compares life and parenting to a roller coaster and shows how exciting life and parenting can be. That simile also applies to financial planning, portfolio construction, and investing. There is no denying that buying a stock and watching it appreciate can be fun and exciting. And even stocks that produce losses can make wonderful conversation. I have made good and bad investment decisions (and will continue to do so), but after many years of investing, I continue to enjoy the ride.

SUMMARY

Financial planning starts with specifying your financial goals. While each individual has different goals, common objectives include accumulating funds to cover emergencies, financing specific purchases such as a home, providing for children's education, and supplementing retirement income. After specifying your goals, you need to assess your financial resources and spending. This assessment may be achieved by constructing your current balance sheet and cash budget. These financial statements will facilitate determining what you currently own, what you owe, and what you currently spend.

Financial planning is not done in a vacuum. Federal and state taxes play an important role in investment planning and decision making. The federal income tax is progressive, which means that your marginal tax rate rises as your income increases. You may be able to shelter current income from taxation. For example, gains on profitable sales of securities are considered capital gains, and long-term capital gains are taxed at lower rates than income from other sources such as interest and earnings. Pension plans such as the IRA, the Keogh account, and the 401(k) are also illustrations of a tax shelter. Contributions to the plans are not subject to current income tax but are taxed when the funds are withdrawn from the pension plans. An alternative pension plan, the Roth IRA, does not shelter income from current taxation, but withdrawals from the plan are not taxed, so that your returns on investments in the Roth IRA avoid federal income taxation.

Part of the financial planning process is the allocation of your assets over different investment classes. This allocation tends to vary over your lifetime as you go through periods of accumulation, preservation, and withdrawal. Asset allocation is also important because the return you earn is affected by your choices of classes of assets. A portfolio consisting of relatively safe investments will generate a smaller return than a portfolio allocated to riskier securities.

Investments are made in efficient financial markets. This efficiency implies that it is difficult to outperform the market on a consistent basis. While there is general agreement that financial markets are efficient, there is disagreement as to the degree of efficiency. The weak form of the efficient market hypothesis suggests that the technical analysis discussed in Chapter 8 will not lead to superior investment results. You will not beat the market! The semistrong form adds the fundamental analysis discussed in Chapters 6 and 7 and suggests that these methods for identifying securities for purchase or sale also will not produce consistent superior results. The strong form suggests that even access to inside information will not produce superior investment results.

How strongly you believe the efficient market hypothesis affects your approach to investments. Even if, however, you firmly believe that the securities markets are efficient and that you cannot beat the market over a period of time, that does not absolve you of developing financial plans. Even passive portfolio management requires that you construct a portfolio designed to meet your financial objectives. The difference between active and passive strategies is built around how frequently you alter and rebalance the portfolio and trade specific investments. The difference is not between identifying goals and constructing a portfolio to meet those goals.

Learning Objectives

Now that you have completed this chapter, you should be able to:

1. Enumerate possible financial objectives.
2. Construct your balance sheet and cash budget.
3. Identify the taxes that affect investment decisions.
4. Illustrate how capital losses are used to offset capital gains and ordinary income.
5. Demonstrate how pension plans, IRAs, Keogh accounts, and 401(k) accounts are tax shelters.
6. Explain the importance of asset allocation and its possible impact on a portfolio's return.
7. Differentiate the three forms of the efficient market hypothesis.
8. Isolate how your belief in the degree of market efficiency affects your selection of securities.

PROBLEMS

This chapter has several problems for you to work that apply to the material in this chapter. The problems, however, were not illustrated in the chapter. The first four apply to taxes you owe, and you should be able to do them if you read the material on taxes closely. Five through seven apply time value of money to IRA accounts. (They would also apply to Keogh accounts and 401[k] plans). These problems illustrate how much you will have in the plan under different assumptions and how to determine how long the amount accumulated in the IRA will last if you withdraw a specified amount or how much you may withdraw each year based on your expected life span.

1) **a)** An individual in the 28 percent federal income tax bracket and 15 percent long-term capital gains tax bracket bought and sold the following securities during the year:

	Cost Basis of Stock	Proceeds of Sale
ABC	$24,500	$28,600
DEF	35,400	31,000
GHI	31,000	36,000

What are the taxes owed on the short-term capital gains?

b) An individual in the 35 percent federal income tax bracket and 15 percent long-term capital gains tax bracket bought and sold the following securities during the year:

	Cost Basis of Stock	Proceeds of Sale
ABC	$34,600	$28,600
DEF	29,400	31,000
GHI	21,500	19,000

What are the taxes owed or saved as a result of these sales?

2) An investor is in the 33 percent tax bracket and pays long-term capital gains taxes of 15 percent. What are the taxes owed (or saved in the cases of losses) in the current tax year for each of the following situations?

    a) Net short-term capital gains of $3,000; net long-term capital gains of $4,000

    b) Net short-term capital gains of $3,000; net long-term capital losses of $4,000

    c) Net short-term capital losses of $3,000; net long-term capital gains of $4,000

    d) Net short-term capital gains of $3,000; net long-term capital losses of $2,000

    e) Net short-term capital losses of $4,000; net long-term capital gains of $3,000

    f) Net short-term capital losses of $1,000; net long-term capital losses of $1,500

    g) Net short-term capital losses of $3,000; net long-term capital losses of $2,000

3) You are in the 28 percent income tax bracket and pay long-term capital gains taxes of 15 percent. What are the taxes owed or saved in the current year for each of the following sets of transactions?

    a) You buy 100 shares of ZYX for $10 and after seven months sell it on December 31, 200X, for $23. You buy 100 shares of WER for $10 and after fifteen months sell it on December 31, 200X, for $7. You buy 100 shares of DFG for $10 and after nine months, on December 31, 200X, it is selling for $15.

    b) You buy 100 shares of ZYX for $60 and after seven months sell it on December 31, 200Y, for $37. You buy 100 shares of WER for $60 and after fifteen months sell it on December 31, 200Y, for $67. You buy 100 shares of DFG for $60 and after nine months sell it on December 31, 200Y, for $76.

    c) On January 2, 200X, you buy 100 shares of ZYX for $40 and sell it for $31 after twenty-two months. On January 2, 200X, you buy 100 shares of WER for $40 and sell it for $27 after fifteen months. On January 2, 200X, you buy 100 shares of DFG for $40 and sell it for $16 after eighteen months.

    d) On January 2, 200X, you buy 100 shares of ZYX for $60. On October 2, 200X, you sell 100 shares of ZYX for $40. On November 10, 200X, you purchase 100 shares of ZYX for $25.

4) You are in the 25 percent income tax bracket. What are the taxes owed or saved if you

    a) Contribute $2,000 to a 401(k) plan

    b) Contribute $2,000 to a Roth IRA

    c) Withdraw $2,000 from a traditional IRA

    d) Withdraw $2,000 from a Keogh account

5) You are 60 years old. Currently, you have $10,000 invested in an IRA and have just received a lump-sum distribution of $50,000 from a pension plan, which you roll over into an IRA. You continue to make $2,000 annual payments to the regular IRA and expect to earn 9 percent on these funds until you start withdrawing the money at age 70 (i.e., after ten years). The IRA rollover will earn 9 percent for the same duration.

        a) How much will you have when you start to make withdrawals at age 70?

        b) If your funds continue to earn 9 percent annually and you withdraw $17,000 annually, how long will it take to exhaust your funds?

        c) If your funds continue to earn 9 percent annually and your life expectancy is 18 years, what is the maximum you may withdraw each year?

6) Bob places $1,000 a year in his IRA for ten years and then invests $2,000 a year for the next ten years. Mary places $2,000 a year in her IRA for ten years and then invests $1,000 a year for the next ten years. They both have invested $30,000. If they earn 8 percent annually, how much more will Mary have earned than Bob at the end of 20 years?

7) Bob and Barbara are 55 and 50 years old. Bob annually contributes $1,500 to Barbara's IRA. They plan to make contributions until Bob retires at age 65 and then to leave the funds in as long as possible (i.e., age 70 to ease calculations).

    Mike and Mary are 55 and 50 years old. Mike annually contributes $2,000 to Mike's IRA. They plan to make contributions until Mike retires at age 65 and then leave the funds in as long as possible (i.e., age 70 to ease calculations). Both Barbara's and Mike's IRAs yield 10 percent annually.

    The combined life expectancy of both couples is to age 85 of the wife. What will be each couple's annual withdrawal from the IRA based on life expectancy?

    This is a tricky problem. You have to think through how long the funds will be in the accounts before withdrawals occur and for how many years the withdrawals will occur. (Hint: analyze each person's age.)

Internet Application for Chapter 2 Portfolio Planning in an Efficient Market Context

Taxes affect financial planning. Use the Internet to answer the following questions.

1) What is the marginal tax bracket for a single individual and compare it with the marginal tax bracket for a couple filing a joint return if their taxable incomes are $50,000, $75,000, or $150,000?

2) What is the maximum amount that taxpayers in the above tax brackets can contribute to a Roth IRA?

3) What are the current maximum tax rates on long-term capital gains and on short-term capital gains?

4) Are contributions to your college's alumni fund tax deductible?

One way to answer these questions is to go to the IRS Web site at **http://www.irs.ustreas.gov**. Other sites you may use for tax information include TurboTax (**http://www.turbotax.com**) and 1040.com (**http://www.1040.com**).

CHAPTER

3 ...

The Measurement of Risk and Return

I n February 2004, the Mega Millions jackpot reached $230 million. People drove for miles and stood in long lines to buy a ticket. The odds of winning were 135,145,920 to 1. These odds were obviously not on any individual's side. Perhaps the buyers should have listened to George Patton, who in *War as I Knew It* wrote, "Take calculated risks; that is quite different from being rash." All investments involve risk because the future is uncertain, but the possible returns on investments are perceptibly more certain than the returns on a state-sponsored lottery.

This chapter is an introduction to the sources and measurements of risk and how these measurements are used in portfolio theory. Risk may be measured by a standard deviation, which measures the dispersion (or variability) around a central tendency, such as an average return. Risk also may be measured by a beta coefficient, which is an index of the volatility of a security's return relative to the return on the market. Much of this chapter is devoted to an exposition of these measures of risk and the reduction of risk through the construction of diversified portfolios. This chapter also lays a foundation for security valuation and performance evaluation. These crucial topics are developed in Chapter 8 on stock valuation and Chapter 12 on mutual fund performance.

Part of this chapter is devoted to illustrating how statistical tools such as the standard deviation or a least-squares regression equation are calculated. These illustrations mean that you will not have to take any given results on faith, since the actual calculation is provided. I will, however, be honest with you. I do not perform these calculations when making an investment decision. (If I had to do them, I would use a computer program such as Excel, which has easy-to-use programs for executing elementary descriptive statistics and regression analysis.) However, statistical concepts appear in the academic and professional literature on investments, and they even appear in the popular press designed for the serious investor. Thus, you need a basic understanding of these statistical concepts and their application to help you make informed investment decisions.

SOURCES OF RETURN

Investments are made to earn a return. To earn the return, you must accept the possibility of loss. Portfolio theory is concerned with risk and return. Its purpose is to determine the combination of risk and return that allows you to achieve the highest return for a given level of risk. Initially, this chapter considers various usages for the term *return*, followed by a discussion of the measurement of risk. Risk and return are then combined in the discussion of portfolio construction.

The word *return* is often modified by an adjective, including the *expected return*, the *required return*, and the *realized return*. The **expected return** is the anticipated flow of income and/or price appreciation. An investment may offer a return from either of two sources. The first source is the flow of income that may be generated by the investment. A savings account pays interest income. The second source of return is capital appreciation. If you buy stock and its price subsequently increases, you earn a capital gain. All investments offer the investor potential income and/or capital appreciation. Some investments, like the savings account, offer only income, whereas other investments, such as an investment in land, may offer only capital appreciation. In fact, some investments may require that expenditures (e.g., property tax on the land) be made by the investor.

This expected return is summarized in Equation 3.1:

expected return
The sum of the anticipated dividend yield and capital gains.

$$(3.1) \qquad E(r) = \frac{E(D)}{P} + E(g).$$

The symbols are

$E(r)$ the expected return (as a percentage)
$E(D)$ the expected dividend (or interest in the case of a debt instrument)
P the price of the asset
$E(g)$ the expected growth in the value of the asset (i.e., the capital gain).

If you buy a stock for $10 and expect to earn a dividend of $0.60 and sell the stock for $12, the expected return is

$$E(r) = \frac{\$0.60}{\$10} + \frac{\$12 - \$10}{\$10} = 0.06 + 0.20 = 26\%.$$

You expect to earn a return of 26 percent.[1]

It is important to realize that this return is anticipated. The yield that is achieved on the investment is not known until after the investment is sold and converted to cash. It is important to differentiate between the *expected return*, the *required return*, and the *realized return*. The expected return is the incentive for accepting risk, and it must be compared to your **required return**, which is the return necessary to induce the investor to bear the risk associated with a particular investment. The required return includes (1) what you may earn on alternative investments, such as the risk-free return available on Treasury bills, and (2) a premium for bearing risk that includes compensation for fluctuations in security prices. Since the required return includes a measure of risk, the discussion of the required return must be postponed until the measurement of risk is covered.

required return
The return necessary to induce the investor to purchase an asset.

1. Since the time period has not been specified, this return should not be confused with an annual rate of return. In Chapter 4, returns that do not specify the time period are referred to as *holding period returns*. The calculation of *annual rates of return* is also addressed in Chapter 4.

realized return
The sum of income and capital gains earned on an investment.

The **realized return** is the return actually earned on an investment and is essentially the sum of the flow of income generated by the asset and the capital gain. The realized return may, and often does, differ from the expected and required returns.

The realized return is summarized by Equation 3.2:

(3.2)
$$r = \frac{D}{P} + g.$$

This is essentially the same as the equation for expected return with the expected value sign, E, removed. If an investor buys a stock for $10 and collects $0.60 in dividends, and the stock appreciates by 20 percent, the realized return is

$$r = \frac{\$0.60}{\$10} + \frac{\$12 - \$10}{\$10} = 0.06 + 0.20 = 26\%.$$

Expected Return Expressed as a Probability

Probability theory measures or indicates the likelihood of something occurring. If you are certain that something will happen, the probability is 100 percent. (Remember the old joke about death and taxes.) The sum of all the probabilities of the possible outcomes is 100 percent. The expected value (the anticipated outcome) is the sum of each outcome multiplied by the probability of occurrence. For example, you are considering purchasing a stock. The possible returns and your estimate of their occurring are as follows:

Return	Probability
3%	10%
10	45
12	40
20	5

The sum of all the probabilities is 100 percent, and the returns encompass all the possible outcomes. The expected value or, in this illustration, the expected return $[E(r)]$ is the probability of the outcome times each individual price. That expected value is

$$E(r) = (0.10).03 + (0.45).10 + (0.40).12 + (0.05).20$$
$$= 0.003 + 0.045 + 0.048 + 0.01 = 0.106 = 10.6\%.$$

Each of the expected returns is weighted by the probability of occurrence. The results are then added to determine the expected return, 10.6%.

While it is possible that the return on the stock could be as low as 3 percent or as high as 20 percent, their weights are relatively small. They contribute only modestly to the expected return. The return of 10 percent carries more weight (45 percent) in the determination of the expected return. Notice, however, that the expected return is not 10 percent, nor is it any of the four possible outcomes. The expected return is a weighted average in which each outcome is weighted by the probability of the outcome occurring.

You may also use this information to construct cumulative probabilities. Cumulative probability distributions answer questions such as, What is the probability that the return will be least 10 percent, or What is the probability that I will not earn 12 percent? The answer to the former question is 90 percent

(45% + 40% + 5%) percent, because that percentage includes all the probabilities that the return will be 10 percent or greater. The answer to the second question is 55 percent, because it includes all the probabilities that the stock's return will be less than 12 percent.

Probability lends itself to studying different situations. By changing the individual probabilities, the outcome (the expected value) is altered. For example, the probabilities in the preceding example could be changed, which would affect the weighted average (i.e., the expected return). If the individual returns remain the same but their probability of occurring are changed as follows:

Return	Probability
3%	20%
10	35
12	40
20	5

the expected return $[E(r)]$ becomes

$$E(r) = (0.20).03 + (0.35).10 + (0.40).12 + (0.05).20$$
$$= 0.006 + 0.035 + 0.048 + 0.01 = 0.099 = 9.9\%$$

A greater weight is now assigned to the lowest return, which has the effect of reducing the expected return from 10.6 percent to 9.9 percent.

Sources of Risk

Risk is concerned with the uncertainty that your realized return will not equal your expected return. There are several sources of risk, and these are frequently classified as diversifiable (or unsystematic) risk or nondiversifiable (or systematic) risk. Diversifiable risk refers to the risk associated with the specific asset and is reduced through the construction of a diversified portfolio. Nondiversifiable risk refers to the risk associated with (1) fluctuating security prices in general, (2) fluctuating interest rates, (3) reinvestment rates, (4) the loss of purchasing power through inflation, and (5) loss from changes in the value of exchange rates. These sources of risk are not affected by the construction of a diversified portfolio.

Nondiversifiable Risk

Asset returns tend to move together. If security prices rise in general, the price of a specific security tends to rise with the market. Conversely, if the market were to decline, the value of an individual security would also tend to fall. Thus there is a systematic relationship between the price of a specific asset, such as a common stock, and the market as a whole. As long as investors buy securities, they cannot avoid bearing this source of systematic risk.

Asset values are also affected by changes in interest rates. As is explained in Chapter 11, rising interest rates depress the prices of fixed-income securities, such as long-term bonds and preferred stock. Conversely, if interest rates fall, the value of these assets rises. A systematic negative (i.e., inverse) relationship exists between the prices of fixed-income securities and changes in interest rates. As long as investors acquire fixed-income securities, they must bear the risk associated with fluctuations in interest rates.

Common stock prices are also affected by changes in interest rates. Just as there is a negative relationship between interest rates and the prices of fixed-income securities, the same relationship exists between common stock and interest rates. First, future cash flows from common stocks are being discounted at higher rates, so their present values are lower. In addition, higher rates make fixed-income securities more attractive, so investors buy bonds and other fixed-income investments in preference to common stock. The movement from stock to higher-paying debt instruments tends to depress stock prices. The converse is true when interest rates fall. The rotation from lower-yielding fixed-income securities to equities should lead to higher stock prices.

Investors receive payments, such as dividends or interest, that may be reinvested. When yields change (e.g., when interest rates rise or decline), the amount received on these reinvested funds also changes. This, then, is the source of reinvestment risk. In the early 1980s, when interest rates were relatively high, investors benefited when their funds were reinvested. However, in the 2000s, when yields were the lowest in 40 years, many investors' incomes declined as they earned less on reinvested funds. This was particularly true for savers such as retirees with low-risk investments such as certificates of deposit (CDs). When higher-yielding CDs came due, investors had to accept lower interest yields when they renewed the certificates.

Investors must also endure the loss of purchasing power through inflation. It is obvious that rising prices of goods and services erode the purchasing power of both investors' income and assets. Like fluctuating security prices or changes in interest rates, there is nothing the individual can do to stop inflation; therefore, the goal should be to earn a return that exceeds the rate of inflation. If the investor cannot earn such a return, he or she may benefit more from spending the funds and consuming goods now.

The last source of systematic risk is the risk associated with changes in the value of currencies. If investors acquire foreign investments, the proceeds of the sale of the foreign asset must be converted from the foreign currency into the domestic currency before they may be spent. (The funds, of course, may be spent in the foreign country without the conversion.) Since the values of currencies change, the value of the foreign investments will rise or decline with changes in the value of the currencies. If the value of the foreign currency rises, the value of the foreign investment increases and the domestic investor gains. The converse occurs when the price of the foreign currency declines. (You may also have to endure political risks if investments are made in unstable countries with unstable governments.)

You can avoid exchange-rate risk by not acquiring foreign assets and, of course, miss the opportunities such investments may offer. However, you may still bear some of this risk because many firms are affected by changes in the value of foreign currencies. Many U.S. firms invest abroad. For example, over two-thirds of the Coca-Cola Company's revenues are generated abroad. Even if a company does not invest abroad, it may compete with foreign firms in domestic markets. Hence investors who do not own foreign assets are affected, albeit indirectly, by changes in the value of foreign currencies relative to their own.

Diversifiable Risk

Besides the sources of nondiversifiable systematic risk, you also face the unsystematic, diversifiable risk associated with each asset. Since you buy specific assets, for example, the common stock of IBM or bonds issued by the township of Princeton, you must bear the risk associated with each specific investment.

For firms, the sources of unsystematic risk are the business and financial risks associated with the operation. Business risk refers to the nature of the firm's operations, and financial risk refers to how the firm finances its assets (i.e., whether the firm uses a substantial or modest amount of debt financing). For example, the business risk associated with United or Delta Airlines is affected by such factors as the cost of fuel, the legal and regulatory environment, the capacity of planes, and seasonal changes in demand. Financial risk for airlines depends on how the airline finances its planes and other assets — that is, whether the assets were acquired by issuing bonds, preferred stock, or common stock; by leasing; or by borrowing from other sources.

Unsystematic risk applies to all classes of investments. For example, government securities such as municipal securities are subject to asset-specific risk. A municipal government's operations and how it chooses to finance them are the sources of this unsystematic risk. Some local governments have their own police force while others rely on state or county police. One local government may rely on property taxes as its primary source of revenues while another may tax earned income. A decline in property values or an increase in unemployment may decrease tax revenues and increase the unsystematic risk associated with their debt obligations.

You cannot anticipate all the events that will affect a particular firm or government. A strike, a natural disaster, or an increase in insurance costs may affect the value of a firm's or government's securities in positive or negative ways. In either case, the possibility of these events occurring increases the unsystematic risk associated with investing in a specific asset.

Total (Portfolio) Risk

portfolio risk
The total risk associated with owning a portfolio; the sum of systematic and unsystematic risk.

diversification
The process of accumulating different securities to reduce the risk of loss.

The combination of systematic and unsystematic risk is defined as the total risk (or **portfolio risk**) that you bear. Unsystematic risk may be significantly reduced through **diversification**, which occurs when you purchase the securities of firms in different industries. Buying the stock of five telecommunication companies is not considered diversification, because the events that affect one company tend to affect the others. A diversified portfolio may consist of stocks and bonds issued by a communications company, an electric utility, an insurance firm, a commercial bank, an oil refinery, a retail business, and a manufacturing firm. This is a diversified mixture of industries and types of assets. The impact of particular events on the earnings and growth of one firm need not apply to all the firms; therefore, the risk of loss in owning the portfolio is reduced.

How diversification reduces risk is illustrated in Figure 3.1, which shows the price performance of three stocks and their composite. Stock A's price initially falls, then rises, and starts to fall again. Stock B's price ultimately rises but tends to fluctuate. Stock C's price fluctuates the least of the three but ends up with only a modest gain. Purchasing stock B and holding it would have produced a substantial profit, while A would have generated a moderate loss.

The last quadrant illustrates what happens if the investor buys an equal dollar amount of each stock (i.e., buys a diversified portfolio). (The statistical condition that must be met to achieve diversification is discussed later in this chapter.) The value of the portfolio as a whole may rise even though the value of an individual security may not, and the fluctuation in the value of the portfolio is less than the fluctuations in individual security prices. By diversifying the portfolio, you are able to reduce the risk of loss. Of course, you also give up the possibility of a large gain.

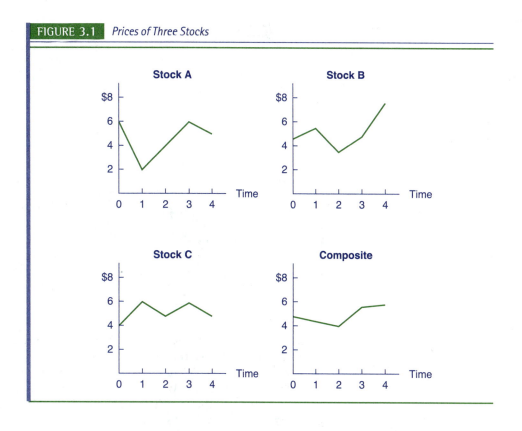

FIGURE 3.1   *Prices of Three Stocks*

In effect, a diversified portfolio reduces the element of unsystematic risk. The risk associated with each individual investment is reduced by accumulating a diversified portfolio of assets. Even if one company fails (or does extremely well), the impact on the portfolio as a whole is reduced through diversification. Distributing investments among different industries, however, does not eliminate market risk and the other types of systematic risk. The value of a group of securities will tend to follow the market values in general. The price movements of securities will be mirrored by the diversified portfolio; hence, the investor cannot eliminate this source of systematic risk.

How many securities are necessary to achieve a diversified portfolio that reduces and almost eliminates unsystematic risk? The answer may be "surprisingly few." Several studies have found that risk has been significantly reduced in portfolios consisting of from 10 to 15 securities.[2]

This reduction in unsystematic risk is illustrated in Figure 3.2 (p. 96). The vertical axis measures units of risk, and the horizontal axis gives the number of securities. Since systematic risk is independent of the number of securities in the portfolio, this element of risk is illustrated by a line, *AB*, that runs parallel to the

2. For further discussion, see the following: John Evans and Stephen Archer, "Diversification and the Reduction of Dispersion: An Empirical Analysis," *Journal of Finance* (December 1968): 761–767; Bruce D. Fielitz, "Indirect versus Direct Diversification," *Financial Management* (winter 1974): 54–62; William Sharpe, "Risk, Market Sensitivity and Diversification," *Financial Analysts Journal* (January–February 1972): 74–79, and Meir Statman, "How Many Stocks Make a Diversified Portfolio?" *Journal of Financial and Quantitative Analysis* (September 1987): 353–364. However, George Frankfurter suggests that even well-diversified portfolios have a substantial amount of nonsystematic risk. See his "Efficient Portfolios and Nonsystematic Risk," *The Financial Review* (fall 1981): 1–11.

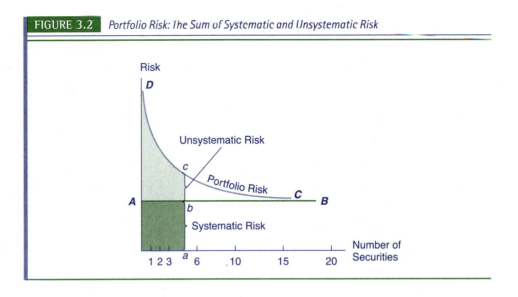

FIGURE 3.2   *Portfolio Risk: The Sum of Systematic and Unsystematic Risk*

horizontal axis. Regardless of the number of securities that you own, the amount of nondiversifiable risk remains the same.[3]

Portfolio risk (i.e., the sum of systematic and unsystematic risk) is indicated by line *CD*. The difference between line *AB* and line *CD* is the unsystematic risk associated with the specific securities in the portfolio. The amount of unsystematic risk depends on the number of securities held. As this number increases, unsystematic risk diminishes; this reduction in risk is illustrated in Figure 3.2 where line *CD* approaches line *AB*. For portfolios consisting of ten or more securities, the risk involved is primarily systematic.

Such diversified portfolios, as mentioned previously, do not consist of ten public utilities but of a cross section of stocks. Investing $20,000 in ten stocks (i.e., $2,000 for each) may achieve a reasonably well diversified portfolio. Although such a portfolio costs more in commissions than two $10,000 purchases, you achieve a diversified mixture of securities, which should reduce the risk of loss associated with investment in a specific security. Unfortunately, you must still bear the systematic risk associated with movements in the markets, the risk of loss in purchasing power that results from inflation, and the other sources of nondiversifiable risk.

THE MEASUREMENT OF RISK

Portfolio theory determines the combination of risk and return that allows you to achieve the highest return for a given level of risk. The previous section addressed the expected and realized return; the measurement of risk is the focus of the next sections of this text.

---

3. The sources of systematic risk may be managed through techniques that are covered throughout this text. For example, you bear less market risk by constructing a portfolio that is less responsive to changes in security prices. (See the discussion of beta coefficients later in this chapter.) Interest rate and reinvestment rate risk may be managed using "duration" (covered in Chapter 11). Exchange-rate risk may be reduced through the use of derivatives (Chapters 14 and 15).

Risk is concerned with the uncertainty regarding whether the realized return will equal the expected return. The measurement of risk places emphasis either on the extent to which the return varies from the average return or on the volatility of the return relative to the return on the market. The variability of returns is measured by a statistical concept called the *standard deviation*, while volatility is measured by what has been termed a *beta coefficient*. (In terms of Figure 3.2, the standard deviation measures the total risk — that is, the distance *ac*. The beta measures systematic risk — distance *ab*. As may be seen in the figure, total risk approaches systematic risk as the portfolio becomes more diversified, so that in a well-diversified portfolio, the two measures of risk are essentially equal.) This section considers the standard deviation as a measure of risk. Beta coefficients are covered later in the chapter.

Dispersion Around an Investment's Return

One measure of risk measures the variability or dispersion around a central value such as an average. If there is not much difference between the average and the individual observations, the dispersion is small. If the individual observations differ considerably from the average, the dispersion is large. The larger the dispersion, the greater is the risk when this concept is applied to investments.

This concept may be demonstrated by a simple example. Consider two investments, both a which have an average return of 15 percent:

Stock A	Stock B
13.5%	11.0%
14.0	11.5
14.25	12.0
14.5	12.5
15.0	15.0
15.5	17.5
15.75	18.0
16.0	18.5
16.5	19.0

Although the average return is the same for both stocks, there is an obvious difference in the individual returns. Stock A's returns are close to the 15 percent average, but stock B's returns are closer to the high and low values. The returns of stock A cluster around the average return. Because there is less variability in returns, it is the less risky of the two securities.

These differences in risk are illustrated in Figure 3.3 (p. 98), which plots returns on the horizontal axis and the frequency of their occurrence on the vertical axis. (This is basically the same information that was previously given for stocks A and B, except that more observations would be necessary to construct such a graph. While only nine observations are used in the illustration, the figure is drawn as if there were a large number of observations.) Most of stock A's returns are close to the average return, so the frequency distribution is higher and narrower. The frequency distribution for stock B's return is lower and wider, which indicates a greater dispersion in that stock's returns.

The large dispersion around the average return implies that the stock involves greater risk because the investor can be less certain of the stock's return. The larger

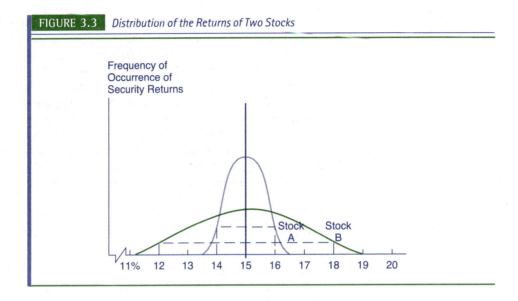

FIGURE 3.3   *Distribution of the Returns of Two Stocks*

the dispersion, the greater is the chance of a large loss from the investment, and, correspondingly, the greater is the chance of a large gain. However, this potential for increased gain is concomitant with bearing more risk. Stock A involves less risk; it has the smaller dispersion. But it also has less potential for a large gain. A reduction in risk also means a reduction in possible return on the investment.

Standard Deviation as a Measure of Risk: One Asset

This dispersion around the mean value (i.e., the average return) is measured by the standard deviation. Since the standard deviation measures the tendency for the individual returns to cluster around the average return and is a measure of the variability of the return, it may be used as a measure of risk. The larger the dispersion, the greater the standard deviation and the larger the risk associated with the particular security.

The equation for the computation of the standard deviation (σ) is

(3.3)
$$\sigma = \sqrt{\frac{\Sigma(r_n - \bar{r})^2}{n-1}}$$

This equation states that the standard deviation is the square root of the sum of the squared differences between the individual observation (r_n) and the average ($\bar{r}$), divided by the number of observations (n) minus 1.[4]

----

4. The subscript n represents the total observations from 1 through n. The line over the r indicates that the number is the average of all the observations. The $n-1$ represents the degrees of freedom, because there can be only $n-1$ independent observations. Consider the following analogy. If you know (1) the average of a series of 10 numbers and (2) 9 of the 10 numbers, the remaining number can be determined. It cannot be independent, so there are only $10-1$ (i.e., $n-1$) independent numbers.

When computing the standard deviation from sample data, $n-1$ is generally used in the denominator. However, the difference between n and $n-1$ is very small for large numbers of observations. For large samples, n and $n-1$ are virtually the same, and n may be used instead of $n-1$. When all observations are known (i.e., when computing the standard deviation of a population), n is also used. See, for instance, a text of statistics, such as David R. Anderson, Dennis J. Sweeney, and Thomas A. Williams, *Statistics for Business and Economics*, 8th ed. (Cincinnati: South-Western/ Thomson Learning, 2002).

The calculation of the standard deviation for stock A's return is provided in Exhibit 3.1 (p. 100). The exhibit has two parts. In the first, the standard deviation is computed for the returns of stock A, which are historical returns. The standard deviation may also be computed for expected values. In the second part, the standard deviation is computed for expected values using the expected returns and their weights from the illustration in the section: Expected Return Expressed as a Probability. As may be seen in Exhibit 3.1, the standard deviation for stock A is 1.01. You must now interpret this result. Plus and minus 1 standard deviation has been shown to encompass 68 percent of all observations. In this case that would be 68 percent of all the returns. Since the standard deviation for stock A's return is 1.01, that means approximately two-thirds of the returns fall between 13.99 and 16.01 percent. These answers are simply the average return (15 percent) plus 1.01 and minus 1.01 percent (i.e., plus and minus the standard deviation).

For stock B the standard deviation is 3.30, so approximately 68 percent of the returns fall between 11.7 and 18.3 percent. Stock B's returns have a wider dispersion from the average return, and this fact is indicated by the greater standard deviation.

These differences in the standard deviations are illustrated in Figure 3.4 (p. 102), which reproduces Figure 3.3 but adds the standard deviations. The average return for both stocks is 15 percent, but the standard deviation is greater for stock B than for stock A (i.e., 3.30 for B versus 1.01 for A). By computing the standard deviation, the analyst quantifies risk. This will help in the selection of individual securities, since the investor will prefer those assets with the least risk for a given expected return.

If this were an illustration of selecting between two securities, the individual would select investment A because it has the lower standard deviation for a given return. If this were an illustration comparing the historical or actual returns between two investments, the individual would conclude that investment A had outperformed investment B since the returns were the same but B's return had been more variable.

Such comparisons are easy when the returns are the same, because the analysis is limited to comparing the standard deviations. The comparisons are also easy when the standard deviations are the same, because then the analysis is limited to comparing the returns. Such simple comparisons are rare, since investment returns and standard deviations often differ. Investment A may offer a return of 10 percent with a standard deviation of 4 percent, while investment B offers a return of 14 percent with a standard deviation of 6 percent. Since neither the returns nor the standard deviations are the same, they may not be compared. Investment A offers the lower return and less risk; therefore, it cannot be concluded that it is the superior investment.

This inability to compare may be overcome by computing the *coefficient of variation* (CV), which divides the standard deviation by the return. The coefficient of variation is a relative measure of risk and is used to adjust for differences in scale. It is defined as the standard deviation divided by the mean:

Average rates of return (and their standard deviations) are illustrations of samples, because not every possible period is included. Even computations of annual rates of return are samples because the annual returns may be computed for January 1, 20X0 through January 1, 20X1 but exclude rates computed using January 2, 20X0 through January 2, 20X1; January 3, 20X0 through January 3, 20X3; etc. The presumption is that if enough periods are included in the computation, the results are representative of all possible outcomes (representative of the population). The large samples would also mean that the difference between n and $n-1$ is small and should not affect the estimate of the variability around the mean.

EXHIBIT 3.1   Computation of Standard Deviations

A) Computation for Stock A

1 For the range of possible returns, subtract the average return from the individual observations.
2 Square this difference.
3 Add these squared differences.
4 Divide this sum by the number of observations less 1.
5 Take the square root.

For stock A, the standard deviation is determined as follows:

Individual Return	Average Return	Difference	Difference Squared
13.50%	15%	−1.5	2.2500
14	15	−1	1.0000
14.25	15	−0.75	0.5625
14.50	15	−0.5	0.25
15	15	0	0
15.50	15	0.5	0.25
15.75	15	0.75	0.5625
16	15	1	1.000
16.50	15	1.5	2.2500

The sum of the squared differences: 8.1250.

The sum of the squared differences divided by the number of observations less 1:

$$\frac{8.1250}{8} = 1.0156.$$

The standard deviation (the square root):

$$\sqrt{1.0156} = \pm1.01$$

(A square root is a positive [+] or negative [−] number. For example, the square root of 9 is +3 *and* −3 since (3)(3) = 9 *and* (−3)(−3) = 9. However, in the calculation of the standard deviation, only positive numbers are used—that is, the sum of the squared differences—so the square root must be a positive number.)

(3.4)
$$CV = \frac{\text{The standard deviation}}{\text{The average}}$$

If, for example, firm A had average earnings of $100 with a standard deviation of $10, while firm B's average earnings were $100,000 with a standard deviation of $100, the coefficients of variation would be

$$CV_A = \frac{\$10}{\$100} = 0.1 \text{ and } CV_B = \frac{\$100}{\$100,000} = 0.001.$$

From this perspective, B's earnings are less variable than A's even though B's standard deviation is larger. When the coefficient of variation is applied to returns and their standard deviations (i.e., the standard deviation of the return divided by the average return), higher coefficients of variation imply more risk, because a higher numerical value means more variability per unit of return.

EXHIBIT 3.1   Computation of Standard Deviations *(continued)*

B) Computation of the Standard Deviation for an Average Expected Value
The returns and their probabilities:

Return	Probability
3%	10%
10	45
12	40
20	5

The expected value (return) was
$$E(r) = (0.10).03 + (0.45).10 + (0.40).12 + (0.05).20$$
$$= 0.003 + 0.045 + 0.048 + 0.01 = 0.106 = 10.6\%$$

The calculation of the standard deviation:

Individual Return	Expected Return	Difference	Difference Squared and Weighted by the Probability
3%	10.6%	-7.6	57.76)(0.10) = 5.776
10	10.6	-.6	(0.36)(0.45) = 0.162
12	10.6	1.4	(1.96)(0.40) = 0.784
20	10.6	9.4	(88.36)(0.05) = 4.418
			11.14

standard deviation: $\sqrt{11.14} = 3.338$

(The sum of the weighted squared difference is referred to as the "variance." The standard deviation is the square root of the variance ($\sqrt{11.14} = 3.338$) and is a weighted average of the differences from the expected value.)

THE RETURN AND STANDARD DEVIATION OF A PORTFOLIO

Although the preceding discussion was limited to the return on an individual security and the dispersion around that return, the concepts can be applied to an entire portfolio. A portfolio also has an average return and a dispersion around that return. The investor is concerned not only with the return and the risk associated with each investment but also with the return and risk associated with the portfolio as a whole. This aggregate is, of course, the result of the individual investments and of each one's weight in the portfolio (i.e., the value of each asset, expressed in percentages, in proportion to the total value of the portfolio).

Consider a portfolio consisting of the following three stocks:

Stock	Return
1	8.3%
2	10.6
3	12.3

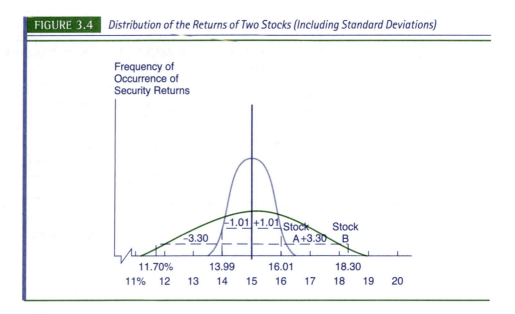

FIGURE 3.4   *Distribution of the Returns of Two Stocks (Including Standard Deviations)*

If 25 percent of the total value of the portfolio is invested in stocks 1 and 2 and 50 percent is invested in stock 3, the return is more heavily weighted in favor of stock 3. The return is a weighted average of each return times its proportion in the portfolio.

Return	x	Weight (Percentage Value of Stock in Proportion to Total Value of Portfolio)	=	Weighted Average
8.3%	x	0.25	=	2.075%
10.6	x	0.25	=	2.650
12.3	x	0.50	=	6.150

The return is the sum of these weighted averages.

$$2.075\%$$
$$2.650$$
$$\underline{6.150}$$
$$10.875\%$$

The previous example is generalized in Equation 3.5, which states that the return on a portfolio r_p is a weighted average of the returns of the individual assets $[(r_1) \dots (r_n)]$, each weighted by its proportion in the portfolio $(w_1 \dots w_n)$:

(3.5) $$r_p = w_1(r_1) + w_2(r_2) + \dots + w_n(r_n).$$

Thus, if a portfolio has 20 securities, each plays a role in the determination of the portfolio's return. The extent of that role depends on the weight that each asset has in the portfolio. Obviously those securities that compose the largest part of the individual's portfolio have the largest impact on the portfolio's return.[5]

Unfortunately, an aggregate measure of the portfolio's risk (i.e., the portfolio's standard deviation) is more difficult to construct than the weighted average of the returns. This is because security prices are *not independent of each other*. However, while security prices do move together, there can be considerable difference in these price movements. For example, prices of stocks of firms in home building may be more sensitive to recession than stock prices of utilities, whose prices may decline only moderately. These relationships among the assets in the portfolio must be considered in the construction of a measure of risk associated with the entire portfolio. These inner relationships among stocks are called *covariation*. Covariation considers both the variability of the individual asset and its relationship with the other assets in the portfolio.

Since the determination of a portfolio's standard deviation becomes very complicated for a portfolio of many assets, the following illustrations will be limited to portfolios of only two assets. Three cases are illustrated in Figure 3.5 (p. 104). In the first case, the two assets' returns move exactly together; in the second, the two assets' returns move exactly opposite; and in the third, the returns are independent of each other. While these examples are simple, they do illustrate how a portfolio's standard deviation is determined and the effect of the relationships among the assets in the portfolio on the risk associated with the portfolio as a whole.

The standard deviation of the returns on a portfolio (S_d) with two assets is given in Equation 3.6:

(3.6)
$$S_d = \sqrt{w_a^2 S_a^2 + w_b^2 S_b^2 + 2 w_a w_b \, \text{cov}_{ab}}$$

Although this looks formidable, it says that the standard deviation of the portfolio's return is the square root of the sum of (1) the squared standard deviation of the return of the first asset (S_a) times its squared weight in the portfolio (w_a) plus (2) the squared standard deviation on the second asset (S_b) times its squared weight (w_b) in the portfolio plus (3) 2.0 times the weight of the first asset times the weight of the second asset times the covariance (cov) of the two assets.[6]

---

5. The same general equation may be applied to expected returns, in which case the expected return on a portfolio, $E(r_p)$, is a weighted average of the expected returns of the individual assets [$(E(r_1) \ldots E(r_n)$], each weighted by its proportion in the portfolio ($w_1 \ldots w_n$):

   $E(r_p) = w_1 E(r_1) + w_2 E(r_2) + \ldots + w_n E(r_n)$.

6. While Equation 3.6 expresses the standard deviation of a portfolio consisting of two assets, most portfolios consist of more than two assets. The standard deviations of portfolios consisting of more assets are computed in the same manner, but the calculation is considerably more complex. For a three-security portfolio, the calculation requires portfolio weights for securities a, b, and c, and the covariance of *ab*, *ac*, and *bc*. For a six-security portfolio, the calculation requires each security's weight and the covariance of *ab, ac, ad, ae, af, bc, bd, be, bf, cd, ce, cf, de, df,* and *ef* for a total of 15 covariances. The number of required covariances is

   $$\frac{(n^2 - n)}{2},$$

   in which *n* is the number of securities in the portfolios. For a six-security portfolio that is

   $$\frac{(6^2 - 6)}{2} = 15.$$

   For a portfolio with 100 securities, the required number of covariances is

   $$\frac{(100^2 - 100)}{2} = 4,950.$$

   While such calculations can be performed by computers, a two-security portfolio is sufficient to illustrate the computation of the portfolio standard deviation and its implication for diversification.

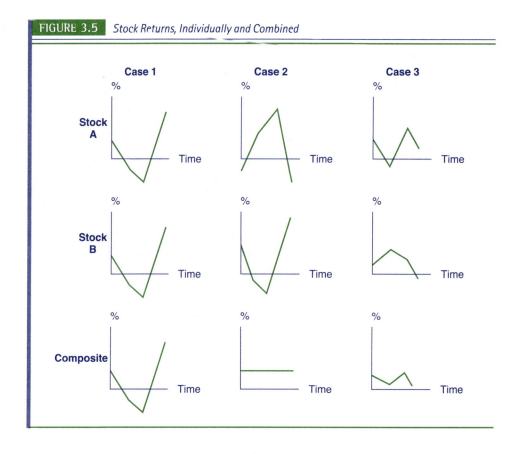

FIGURE 3.5   *Stock Returns, Individually and Combined*

The calculations of the covariance and the correlation coefficients are illustrated later in this chapter. As is also explained, the correlation coefficient combines the standard deviations of the two variables and their covariance. Thus, the covariance is computed before the correlation coefficient. However, it is often convenient to express the covariance of the returns on assets a and b (cov_{ab}) in terms of the correlation coefficient:

(3.7) $cov_{ab} = S_a \times S_b \times$ **(correlation coefficient of *a* and *b*).**

For this discussion, it is necessary to know only that the numerical values of the correlation coefficient range from +1.0 for perfect positive correlation to –1.0 for perfect negative correlation.

To illustrate the determination of the portfolio's standard deviation, consider the returns earned by the stocks A and B, the standard deviations of their returns, and the standard deviations of a portfolio equally invested in each security. The numerical calculations for three cases are illustrated in Exhibit 3.2, and Figure 3.5 plots the individual and the portfolio return.

In case 1 the securities move exactly together. Their standard deviations are equal, and the correlation coefficient of their returns is 1.0. In this case, there is no impact on the portfolio's standard deviation. Case 2 is the exact opposite. The returns for the two stocks move exactly opposite of each other. While their standard deviations are equal, the correlation coefficient of the returns is –1.0. In this case, the portfolio standard deviation is 0.0. There is no variability in the portfolio return.

In the last case, the returns do not move together or against each other. In the first and third years, they both generated positive returns, but in the other two years one generated a loss while the other produced a positive return. In this illustration the correlation coefficient between the returns is –0.524, and the standard deviation of the portfolio is 4.11, which does not equal the standard deviation of the returns of either of the two stocks.

What does the above imply about risk and its management? In the first case, the standard deviation of the portfolio is the same as the standard deviation of the

EXHIBIT 3.2   Calculation of Portfolio Standard Deviations

Case 1 Perfect Positive Correlation (Correlation Coefficient = 1.0)

Year	Return on Security A	Return on Security B	Return on Portfolio
1	10%	10%	10%
2	–12	–12	–12
3	–25	–25	–25
4	37	37	37
Average return	2.5%	2.5%	2.5%
Standard deviation of security returns	27.16	27.16	?

$$S_d = \sqrt{w_a^2 S_a^2 + w_b^2 S_b^2 + 2w_a w_b cov_{ab}}$$

$$= \sqrt{w_a^2 S_a^2 + w_b^2 S_b^2 + 2w_a w_b S_a S_b \text{Correlation Coefficient}_{ab}}$$

$$= \sqrt{0.5^2(27.16)^2 + 0.5^2(27.16)^2 + 2(0.5)(0.5)(27.16)(27.16)(1)}$$

$$= 27.16.$$

Case 2 Perfect Negative Correlation (Correlation Coefficient = –1.0)

Year	Return on Security A	Return on Security B	Return on Portfolio
1	–15%	25%	5%
2	12	–2	5
3	25	–15	5
4	–37	47	5
Average return	–3.75%	13.75%	5%
Standard deviation of security returns	27.73	27.73	?

$$S_d = \sqrt{w_a^2 S_a^2 + w_b^2 S_b^2 + 2 w_a w_b cov_{ab}}$$

$$= \sqrt{0.5^2(27.73)^2 + 0.5^2(27.73)^2 + 2(0.5)(0.5)(27.73)(27.73)(-1)}$$

$$= 0.$$

EXHIBIT 3.2	Calculation of Portfolio Standard Deviations *(continued)*

Case 3 Partial Negative Correlation (Correlation Coefficient = −0.524)

Year	Return on Security A	Return on Security B	Return on Portfolio
1	10%	2%	6%
2	−8	12	2
3	14	65	10
4	4	−2	1
Average return	5%	4.5%	4.75%
Standard deviation of security returns	9.59	5.97	?

$$S_d = \sqrt{w_a^2 S_a^2 + w_b^2 S_b^2 + 2\,w_a w_b \text{cov}_{ab}}$$

$$= \sqrt{0.5^2(9.59)^2 + 0.5^2(5.97)^2 + 2(0.5)(0.5)(9.59)(5.97)(-0.524)}$$

$$= 4.11.$$

two assets. Combining these assets in the portfolio has no impact on the risk associated with the portfolio. In Case 2, the portfolio's risk is reduced to zero (i.e., the portfolio's standard deviation is zero). This indicates that combining these assets whose returns fluctuate exactly in opposite directions has the effect on the portfolio of completely erasing risk. The fluctuations associated with one asset are exactly offset by the fluctuations in the other asset, so there is no variability in the portfolio's return.

Notice that in the second case the elimination of risk does not eliminate the positive return. Of course, if one asset yielded a return of +10 percent while the other asset yielded –10 percent, the net return is 0 percent. That is, however, a special case. If in one period the return on one asset is +15 percent while the other is –5 percent, the net is 5 percent. (Remember: The return is a weighted average of the individual returns, so in this illustration the return is (0.5) (0.15) + (0.5) (–0.05) = 0.05 = 5%.) If, in the next period, the first asset yielded –1 percent while the other yielded 11 percent, the net is still 5 percent. The swing in the first asset's return is –16 percent (+15 to –1), while the swing in the second asset's return is +16 percent (–5 to +11). The movements are exactly opposite, so the correlation coefficient would be –1.0, but the return on a portfolio *equally* invested in the two securities would be +5 percent for both periods.

In the third case, which is the most realistic of the three illustrations, the standard deviation of the portfolio is less than the standard deviations of the individual assets. The risk associated with the portfolio as a whole is less than the risk associated with either of the individual assets. Even though the assets' returns do fluctuate, the fluctuations partially offset each other, so that by combining these assets in the portfolio, the investor reduces exposure to risk with almost no reduction in the return.

Diversification and the reduction in unsystematic risk require that assets' returns *not be highly positively correlated.* When there is a high positive correlation (as in Case

1), there is no risk reduction. When the returns are perfectly negatively correlated (as in Case 2), risk is erased (i.e., there is no variability in the combined returns). If one asset's return falls, the decline is exactly offset by the increase in the return earned by the other asset. The effect is to achieve a risk-free return. In the third case, there is neither a perfect positive nor a perfect negative correlation. However, there is risk reduction, because the returns are poorly correlated. The lower the positive correlation or the greater the negative correlation among the returns, the greater will be the risk reduction achieved by combining the various assets in the portfolio.

While the above illustration is extended, it points out a major consideration in the selection of assets to be included in a portfolio. The individual asset's expected return and risk are important, but the asset's impact on the portfolio as a whole is also important. The asset's return and the variability of that return should be considered in a portfolio context. It is quite possible that the inclusion of a volatile asset will reduce the risk exposure of the portfolio as a whole if the return is negatively correlated with the returns offered by the other assets in the portfolio. Failure to consider the relationships among the assets in the portfolio could prove to be counterproductive if including the asset reduces the portfolio's potential return without reducing the variability of the portfolio's return (i.e., without reducing the element of risk).

RISK REDUCTION THROUGH DIVERSIFICATION: AN ILLUSTRATION

The previous discussion has been abstract, but the concept of diversification through securities whose returns are not positively correlated may be illustrated by considering the returns earned on two specific stocks, Public Service Enterprise Group and Mobil Corporation. Public Service Enterprise Group is primarily an electric and gas utility whose stock price fell with higher interest rates and inflation. Prior to its merger with Exxon, Mobil was a resource company whose stock price rose during inflation in response to higher oil prices but fell during the 1980s as oil prices weakened and inflation receded.

The annual returns (dividends plus price change) on investments in these two stocks are given in Figure 3.6 (p. 108) for the period 1971 through 1991. As may be seen in the graph, there were several periods when the returns on the two stocks moved in opposite directions. For example, during 1971 and 1978, an investment in Public Service Enterprise Group generated a loss while an investment in Mobil produced profits. However, the converse occurred during 1981 as the trend in Public Service Enterprise Group's stock price started to improve. From 1980 to 1985 the price of Public Service Enterprise Group doubled, but the price of Mobil's stock declined so that most of the return earned on Mobil's stock during the mid-1980s was its dividend.

Figure 3.7 presents a scatter diagram of the returns on these two stocks for 1971–1991. The horizontal axis presents the average annual return on Public Service Enterprise Group, while the vertical axis presents the average annual return on Mobil Corporation. As may be seen in the graph, the individual points lie throughout the plane representing the returns. For example, point A represents a positive return on Mobil but a negative return on Public Service Enterprise Group, and point B represents a positive return on Public Service Enterprise Group but a negative return on Mobil.

FIGURE 3.6 *Annual Returns for Mobil and PSEG: Individually and Combined*

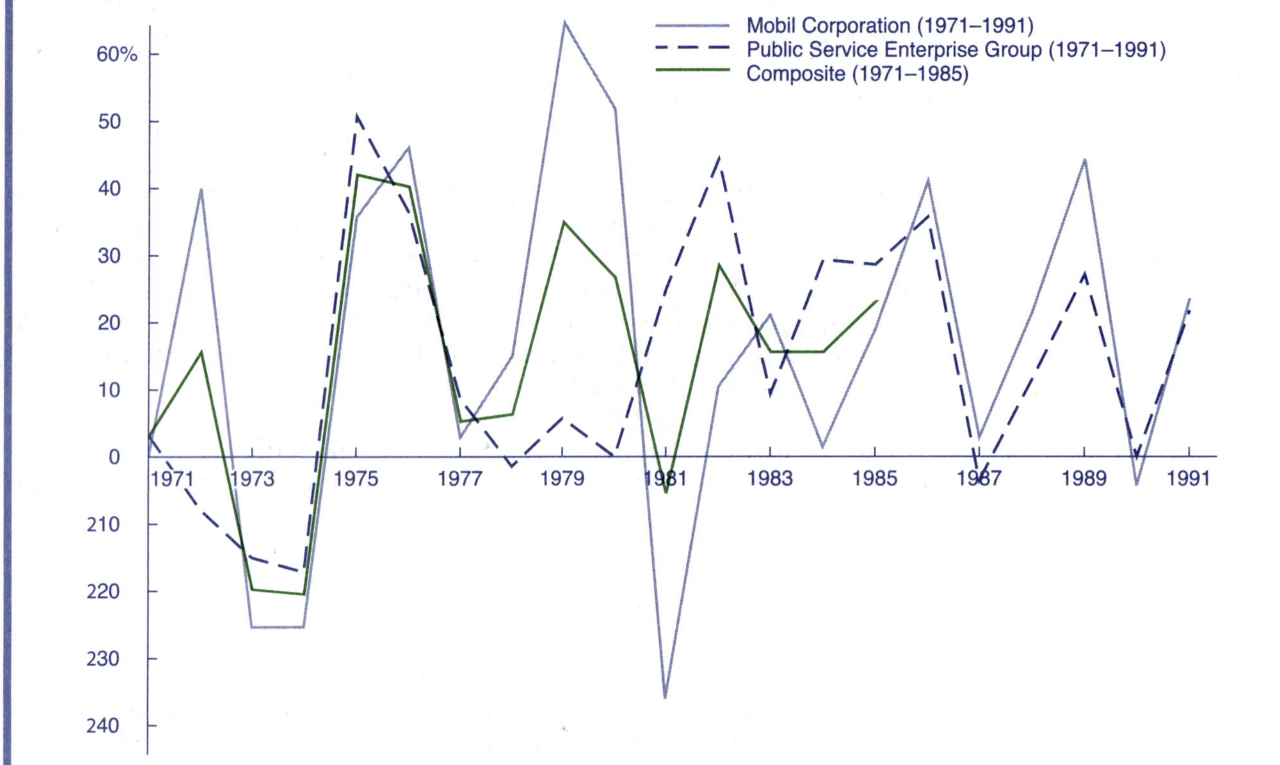

Combining these securities in a portfolio reduces the individual's risk exposure, as is also shown in Figures 3.6 and 3.7. The line representing the composite return in Figure 3.6 runs between the lines representing the returns on the individual securities. Over the entire time period, the average annual returns on Mobil and Public Service Enterprise Group were 16.6 and 13.0 percent, respectively. The average annual return on the composite was 14.8 percent. The risk reduction (i.e., the reduction in the dispersion of the returns) can be seen by comparing the standard deviations of the returns. For the individual stocks, the standard deviations were 26.5 percent and 19.4 percent, respectively, for Mobil and Public Service Enterprise Group. However, the standard deviation for the composite return was 18.9, so the dispersion of the returns associated with the portfolio is less than the dispersion of the returns on either stock by itself.[7]

In this illustration the correlation coefficient between the two returns is 0.34. This lack of correlation is visible in Figure 3.7. If there were a high positive correlation between the two returns, the points would lie close to the line XY. Instead, the points are scattered throughout the figure. Thus, there is little correlation

7. The calculation is
$$= \sqrt{(0.05)^2(26.5)^2 + (0.5)^2(19.4)^2 + 2(0.5)(0.5)(26.5)(19.4)(0.34)}$$
$$= 18.9$$

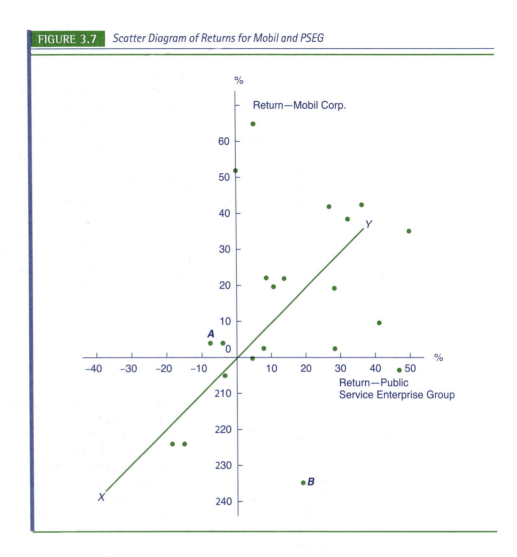

FIGURE 3.7   *Scatter Diagram of Returns for Mobil and PSEG*

between the two returns, which is why combining the two securities reduces the individual's risk exposure.

It should be noted that combining these two stocks achieved diversification in the past because their returns were not highly correlated. Such diversification, however, may not be achieved in the future if the returns become highly positively correlated. This higher correlation appears to have occurred since 1985. The annual returns plotted in Figure 3.6 appear to have moved together from 1985 through 1991. This movement suggests that investing in these two stocks had little impact on diversification after 1985. This inference is confirmed because the correlation coefficient for years 1971 through 1985 is 0.231, but 0.884 for years 1986 through 1991.

Although diversification is a prime goal because it reduces your risk exposure without necessarily reducing the portfolio's return, you are faced with the problem of identifying those assets whose returns will not be positively correlated in the future. Unfortunately, the returns on many financial assets are positively correlated. In addition, as illustrated in Figure 7.6, returns that are negatively correlated under one set of economic conditions may not be negatively correlated in a different economic environment.

THE COMPUTATION OF COVARIANCE AND THE CORRELATION COEFFICIENT

As the preceding material indicates, correlation coefficients are exceedingly important to the construction of well-diversified portfolios. This section illustrates how covariance and correlation coefficients are calculated. If you already know how to perform the calculations or are comfortable with using a computer program such as Excel to compute these statistics, proceed to the next section on the second measure of risk, the beta coefficient.

To illustrate the calculation of covariance and the correlation coefficient, consider the following annual returns for two stocks.

	Return	
Year	Fund A	Fund B
1	10%	17%
2	14	3
3	8	16
4	8	21
5	10	3
Average return	10%	12%

The average return is 10 percent for A and 12 percent for B. (The standard deviations of the returns are 2.449 and 8.426, respectively.)

Both stocks have positive returns, and the higher return for B is associated with more variability—that is, a higher standard deviation. There is also variability between the returns in a given year. For example, A did well in year 5 when B earned a small return, but B did very well in year 4 when A earned a modest return. Covariance and correlation measure the variability of the returns on A and B relative to each other and indicate if the returns move together or inversely.

The covariance is found by considering simultaneously how the individual returns of A differ from its average and how the individual returns of B differ from its average. The differences are multiplied together, summed, and the sum is divided by the number of observations minus 1 ($n - 1$). For the previous returns, the calculation of the covariance is as follows:

Average Return on A	Individual Return on A	Difference	Average Return on B	Individual Return on B	Difference	Product of the Difference
10%	10	0	12%	17	−5	0
10	14	−4	12	3	9	−36
10	8	2	12	16	−4	−8
10	8	2	12	21	−9	−18
10	10	0	12	3	9	0
				The sum of the product of the differences:		−62

To determine the covariance (cov_{AB}), the sum of the product of the differences is divided by the number of observations minus 1:

$$cov_{AB} = \frac{-62}{5-1} = -15.5.$$

Notice that unlike the computation for the standard deviation, the differences are not squared, so the final answer can have a negative number. The negative number indicates that the variables move in opposite directions, and a positive number indicates they move in the same direction. Large numerical values indicate a strong relationship between the variables, while small numbers indicate a weak relationship between the variables.

Since the covariance is an absolute number, it is often converted into the *correlation coefficient*, which measures the strength of the relationship and is easier to interpret than the covariance. The correlation coefficient (R_{AB}) is defined as

(3.8)
$$R_{AB} = \frac{\text{Covariance of AB}}{\text{(Standard deviation of A)(Standard deviation of B)}}$$

In this example, the correlation coefficient of AB is

$$R_{AB} = \frac{-15.5}{(2.499)(8.426)} = -0.7511.$$

A correlation coefficient of –0.7511 indicates a strong negative relationship between the two variables.

The correlation coefficient is often converted into the *coefficient of determination*, which is the correlation coefficient squared and is often referred to as R^2. The coefficient of determination gives the proportion of the variation in one variable explained by the other variable. In the preceding illustration, the coefficient of determination is 0.5641 ((–0.7511)(–0.7511)), which indicates that 56.41 percent of the variation in fund A's return is explained by the variation in fund B's return. (Correspondingly, 56.41 percent of the variation in B's return is explained by A's return. No causality is claimed by the coefficient of determination. It is the job of the analyst to determine if one of the variables is dependent on the other.) Obviously, some other variable(s) must explain the remaining 43.59 percent of the variation.

Since the R^2 gives the proportion of the variation in one variable explained by the other, it is an important statistic in investments. For example, Morningstar reports the volatility of a mutual fund's return relative to the return on the market. This volatility is measured by a *beta coefficient*, which is covered next in this chapter. The beta has little meaning if the relationship between the fund's return and the market return is weak. The strength of the relationship is indicated by the R^2. If the $R^2 = 0.13$, the beta has little meaning, since the variation in the return is caused by something other than the movement in the market (i.e., the stock has little market risk). If the $R^2 = 0.94$, it is reasonable to conclude that the variability of the return is primarily the result of the variability of the market (i.e., the stock's primary source of risk is movements in the market).

BETA COEFFICIENTS

When you construct a well-diversified portfolio, the unsystematic sources of risk are swept away. That leaves the systematic risk as the relevant source of risk. A

beta coefficient
An index of risk; a measure of the systematic risk associated with a particular stock.

beta coefficient is a measure of the systematic risk associated with the stock. It is an index of the volatility of the stock relative to the volatility of the market.

Please do not confuse a beta coefficient with the correlation coefficient that could be computed relating the return on a stock to return on the market. The numerical value of the correlation coefficient would be bounded by +1.0 to –1.0. The numerical value of a beta coefficient can exceed these limits.

If a stock has a beta of 1.0, the stock's return moves exactly with the market. A 10 percent return on the market could be expected to generate a 10 percent return on the stock. (Correspondingly, a 10 percent decline in the market will generate a 10 percent decline in the stock.) A beta coefficient of 0.7 indicates the stock will rise by only 7 percent as the result of a 10 percent increase in the market. Correspondingly, the stock would fall only by 7 percent if the market were to decline by 10 percent. A beta coefficient of 1.2 means that the stock could be expected to rise by 12 percent if the market return were 10 percent, but the stock would fall if 12 percent if the market were to decline by 10 percent.

The greater the beta coefficient, the more systematic market risk is associated with the individual stock. While high beta coefficients may imply larger gains during rising markets, they also imply larger losses during declining markets. For this reason, stocks with higher betas are sometimes referred to as *aggressive*. The converse is true for stocks with low beta coefficients, which should earn lower returns than the market during periods of rising stock prices but earn higher (or less negative) returns than the market during periods of declining prices. Such stocks are referred to *as defensive*.

This relationship between the return on a specific security and the market index as a whole is illustrated in Figures 3.8 and 3.9. In each graph the horizontal

FIGURE 3.8   *Stock with a Beta Coefficient of Greater Than 1.0*

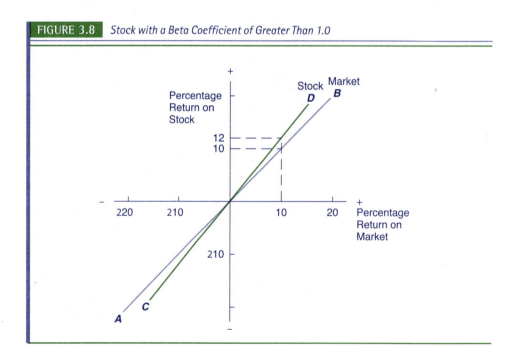

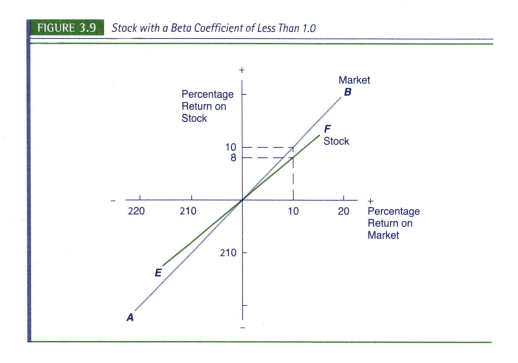

FIGURE 3.9   *Stock with a Beta Coefficient of Less Than 1.0*

axis represents the percentage return on the market and the vertical axis represents the percentage return on the individual stock. The line *AB*, which represents the market, is the same in both graphs. It is a positive-sloped line that runs through the point of origin and is equidistant from both axes (i.e., it makes a 45-degree angle with each axis).

Figure 3.8 illustrates a stock with a beta coefficient of greater than 1. Line *CD* represents a stock whose return rose and declined more than the market. In this case the beta coefficient is 1.2, so when the return on the market index is 10 percent, this stock's return is 12 percent.

Figure 3.9 illustrates a stock with a beta coefficient of less than 1. Line *EF* represents a stock whose return rose (and declined) more slowly than that of the market. In this case the beta coefficient is 0.8, so when the market's return is 10 percent, this stock's return is 8 percent.

The Calculation of Beta: Regression Analysis

Beta coefficients are calculated by a statistical technique called "regression analysis" or "least squares." Simple linear regression estimates an equation between an independent variable and a dependent variable; it regresses one variable on the other. ("Multiple regression" has more than one independent variable.) In the case of estimating beta coefficients, the two variables are the return on the stock and the return on the market.

While correlation coefficients do not imply causality, regression analysis does imply a causal relationship, because variables are specified as *independent* and *dependent*. Consider the following data relating the independent variable, the return on the market (r_m), and the dependent variable, the return on a stock (r_s).

Return on the Market (r_m)	Return on a Stock (r_s)
14%	13%
12	13
10	12
10	9
5	4
2	-1
-1	2
-5	-7
-7	-8
-12	-10

Each pair of observations represents the return on the market and the return on the stock for a period of time, such as a week or a year. The data are plotted in Figure 3.10, with each point representing one set of observations. For example, point *A* represents a 4 percent return on the stock in response to a 5 percent increase in the market. Point *B* represents a –7.0 percent return on the stock and a –5.0 percent return on the market.

FIGURE 3.10 *Observations Relating the Return on a Stock to the Return on the Market*

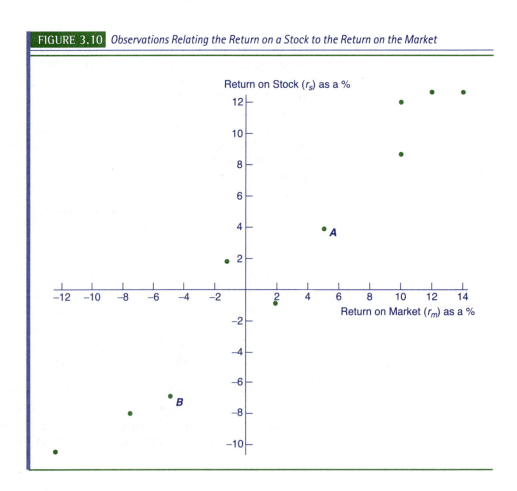

The individual points like *A* and *B* tell little about the relationship between the return on the market and the return on the stock, but all the observations, taken as a whole, may. In this illustration, the points suggest a strong positive relationship between the return on the market and the return on the stock, but inferences from visual inspection may be inaccurate.

Regression analysis confirms the relationship by estimating a linear equation relating the return on the market—the independent variable—and the return on the stock—the dependent variable. The general form of the equation is

(3.9)
$$r_s = a + br_m + e$$

in which r_s and r_m are the return on the stock and the return on the market, respectively, a is the Y-intercept, b is the slope of the line, and e is an error term. (The analysis assumes that the error term is equal to 0, since errors should be both positive and negative and tend to cancel out. If the errors do not cancel out, the equation is misspecified.)

Although the actual computations of the intercept and slope are performed by a computer, a manual demonstration of the process is presented in Exhibit 3.3, from which the following equation is derived:

$$r_s = -0.000597 + 0.9856\ r_m.$$

The Y-intercept is –0.000597 and the slope of the line is +0.9856. *This slope is the stock's beta coefficient.* This equation is given as line XY in Figure 3.11 (p. 116),

EXHIBIT 3.3   Manual Calculation of a Simple Linear Regression Equation

$X(r_m)$	$Y(r_s)$	X^2	Y^2	XY
0.14	0.13	0.0196	0.0169	0.0182
0.12	0.13	0.0144	0.0169	0.0156
0.10	0.12	0.0100	0.0144	0.0120
0.10	0.09	0.0100	0.0081	0.0090
0.05	0.04	0.0025	0.0016	0.0020
0.02	-0.01	0.0004	0.0001	-0.0002
-0.01	0.02	0.0001	0.0004	-0.0002
-0.05	-0.07	0.0025	0.0049	0.0035
-0.07	-0.08	0.0049	0.0064	0.0056
-0.12	-0.10	0.0144	0.0100	0.0120
$\Sigma X = 0.28$	$\Sigma Y = 0.27$	$\Sigma X^2 = 0.0788$	$\Sigma Y^2 = 0.0797$	$\Sigma XY = 0.775$

n = the number of observations (10)

$$b = \frac{n\Sigma XY - (\Sigma X)(\Sigma Y)}{n\ \Sigma X^2 - (\Sigma X)^2}$$

$$= \frac{(10)(0.0775) - (0.28)(0.27)}{(10)(0.0788) - (0.28)(0.28)}$$

$$= \frac{0.7750 - 0.0756}{0.7880 - 0.0784} = 0.9856$$

The a is computed as follows:

$$a = \frac{\Sigma Y}{n} - b\frac{\Sigma X}{n}$$

$$= \frac{0.27}{10} - (0.9856)\frac{0.28}{10} = -0.000597$$

The estimated equation is $r_s = -0.000597 + 0.9856\ r_m$.

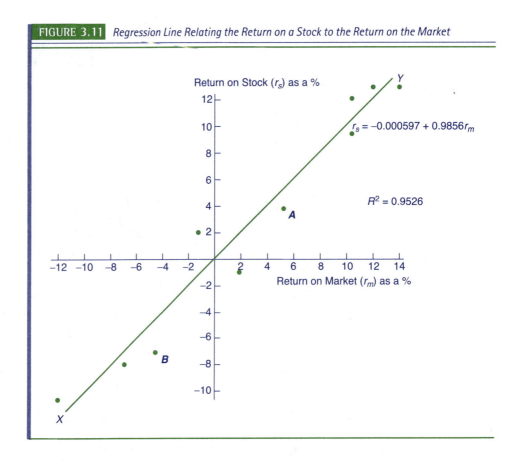

FIGURE 3.11   *Regression Line Relating the Return on a Stock to the Return on the Market*

which reproduces Figure 3.10 but adds the regression line. As may be seen from the graph, line *XY* runs through the individual points. Some of the observations are above the line, while others fall below it. Some of the individual points are close to the line, while others appear farther away. The closer the points are to the line, the stronger is the relationship between the two variables.

Since the individual observations lie close to the estimated regression line, that suggests a high correlation between the two variables. In this illustration, the actual correlation coefficient is 0.976, which indicates a very strong relationship between the return on the stock and the return on the market. The coefficient of determination, the R^2, is 0.9526, which indicates that over 95 percent of the return on the stock is explained by the return on the market.

A small R^2 (e.g., $R^2 = 0.25$) would suggest that other factors affected the stock's return. The stock would have more unsystematic, diversifiable risk, and the beta coefficient may be a poor predictor of the stock's future performance. That, however, need not imply that the beta is useless. A portfolio beta, which is an aggregate of the individual betas, may be a good predictor of the return you can expect from movements in the market. Factors that adversely affect the return on one security may be offset by factors that enhance the return earned on other securities in the portfolio. In effect, the errors cancel.

Computing beta coefficients for a significant number of securities is obviously a time-consuming, tedious job even if you use a computer program such as Excel to perform the calculations. Fortunately, you may obtain beta coefficients from several sources. For example, the *Value Line Investment Survey* (**http:// www.valueline.com**) supplies beta coefficients for the stocks covered by the service. Beta coefficients may also be found through a variety of Internet sites such as

Money Central   **http://www.moneycentral.msn.com/investor**

Reuters   **http://www.investor.reuters.com**

Yahoo!   **http://finance.yahoo.com**.

You should be warned that betas for the same stock from different sources may vary. Beta coefficients are calculated with historical data. Although such data may be accumulated and tabulated for many years, this does not mean that each source uses the same data for the same time periods. Hence, the resulting betas often differ, and there is no correct answer as to which source provides the appropriate beta for you to use in a current analysis of a stock or portfolio.

Beta coefficients are used as part of the Capital Asset Pricing Model (CAPM). Specifically, they are employed in the security market line, which specifies a relationship between risk and return. The security market line may be used to specify a required return on an investment or to judge performance. Both of these applications are developed and illustrated in subsequent chapters in this text.

BETA AND THE SECURITY MARKET LINE

Beta's primary use in finance has been its incorporation into the Capital Asset Pricing Model (CAPM) as the key variable that explains individual security returns. The relationship between risk, as measured by beta, and an asset's return is specified in the security market line (SML). The security market line stipulates the return on a stock (r_s) as

(3.10)
$$r_s = r_f + (r_m - r_f)\beta.$$

The return on a stock depends on the risk-free rate of interest (r_f) and a risk premium composed of the extent to which the return on the market (r_m) exceeds the risk-free rate and the individual stock's beta coefficient. This relationship (i.e., the security market line) is shown in Figure 3.12 (p. 118).

In addition to being a theory of the determination of security returns, the Capital Asset Pricing Model plays an important role in the valuation of securities and the analysis of portfolio performance. For example, in Chapter 7, the security market line component of the CAPM is used to determine the required return for an investment in common stock. This return is then used in the dividend-growth model to determine the value of a common stock. The model is also used in portfolio evaluation in Chapter 13, in which a realized return is compared to the required return specified by using the Capital Asset Pricing Model. Thus, the CAPM not only is an integral part of the theory of portfolio construction and the determination of security returns but also establishes a criterion for assessing portfolio performance.

Portfolio Betas

The security market line relates a particular stock's beta to the security's return. However, beta coefficients may also be computed for an entire portfolio and

FIGURE 3.12 *Security Market Line*

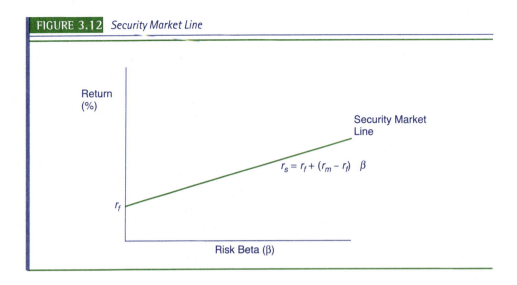

related to the portfolio's return. If a portfolio is well diversified, its beta is an appropriate index of the portfolio's risk, since diversification virtually eliminates the portfolio's unsystematic risk. The portfolio beta is a weighted average of each security in the portfolio and its beta. Thus, if a portfolio has the following stocks and their betas,

Stock	Amount Invested	Percent of Portfolio	Beta
A	$100	10%	0.9
B	200	20	1.2
C	300	30	1.6
D	400	40	1.7

the portfolio's beta is

$$(0.1)(0.9) + (0.2)(1.2) + (0.3)(1.6) + (0.4)(1.7) = 1.49.$$

This portfolio's beta is greater than 1.0, which indicates that the portfolio is more volatile than the market. Of course, the portfolio beta would have been different if the weights were different. If the portfolio had been more heavily weighted in stock A instead of stock D, for example, the numerical value of the beta would have been lower.

In addition to betas for individual stocks, betas may be computed for portfolios or mutual funds. For example, Morningstar provides beta coefficients for the mutual funds in its database, and the American Association of Individual Investors supplies betas for the funds covered by its *Guide to the Top Mutual Funds*. The interpretation of these betas is essentially the same as that for common stock. A numerical value of beta that is greater than 1.0 suggests an aggressive mutual fund whose return is more volatile than the market. A numerical value less than 1.0 suggests the opposite: that the fund has less market risk. (Morningstar also provides the coefficient of determination, [R^2]. A small R^2 would suggest that nonmarket factors are the primary contributors to the variability of the fund's return.)

SUMMARY

Because the future is uncertain, all investments involve risk. The return the investor anticipates through income and/or capital appreciation may differ considerably from the realized return. This deviation of the realized return from the expected return is the risk associated with investing.

Risk emanates from several sources, which include fluctuations in market prices, fluctuations in interest rates, changes in reinvestment rates, fluctuations in exchange rates, and loss of purchasing power through inflation. These sources of risk are often referred to as *systematic risk* because the returns on assets tend to move together (i.e., there is a systematic relationship between security returns and market returns). Systematic risk is also referred to as *nondiversifiable risk* because it is not reduced by the construction of a diversified portfolio.

Diversification does, however, reduce *unsystematic risk*, which applies to the specific firm and encompasses the nature of the firm's operation and its financing. Because unsystematic risk applies only to the individual asset, there is no systematic relationship between the source of risk and the market as a whole. A portfolio composed of 10 to 15 unrelated assets—for example, stocks in companies in different industries or different types of assets, such as common stock, bonds, mutual funds, and real estate—virtually eradicates the impact of unsystematic risk on the portfolio as a whole.

Risk may be measured by the standard deviation, which measures the dispersion around a central tendency, such as an asset's or a portfolio's average return. If the individual returns differ considerably from the average returns, the dispersion is larger (i.e., the standard deviation is larger) and the risk associated with the asset is increased.

An alternative measure of risk, the beta coefficient, measures the responsiveness or volatility of an asset's return relative to the return on the market as a whole. If the beta coefficient exceeds 1, the stock's return is more volatile than the return on the market; but if the beta is less than 1, the return on the stock is less volatile. Since the beta coefficient relates the return on the stock to the market's return, it is an index of the systematic risk associated with the stock.

Learning Objectives

Now that you have completed this chapter, you should be able to:

1. Calculate expected returns and differentiate between expected and realized returns.
2. Identify the sources of risk.
3. Differentiate nondiversifiable systematic risk from diversifiable unsystematic risk.
4. Explain how the standard deviation, the coefficient of variation, and beta coefficients are used as measures of risk.
5. Identify the relationship between securities that is necessary to achieve diversification.

6. Interpret the differences among beta coefficients of 1.5, 1.0, and 0.5.
7. Explain how beta coefficients are used in the Capital Asset Pricing Model and differentiate the components of the security market line.

PROBLEMS

1) You are considering three stocks with the following expected dividend yields and capital gains:

	Dividend Yield	Capital Gain
A	10%	0%
B	5	5
C	0	10

a) What is the expected return on each stock?
b) How may transactions costs and capital gains taxes affect your choices among the three securities?

2) A portfolio consists of assets with the following expected returns:

	Expected Return	Weight in Portfolio
Real estate	16%	20%
Low-quality bonds	15	10
AT&T stock	12	30
Savings account	5	40

a) What is the expected return on the portfolio?
b) What will be the expected return if you reduce your holdings of the AT&T stock to 15 percent and put the funds into real estate investments?

3) You are given the following information concerning two stocks:

	A	B
Expected return	10%	14%
Standard deviation of the expected return	3.0	5.0
Correlation coefficient of the returns		−.1

a) What is the expected return on a portfolio consisting of 40 percent in stock A and 60 percent in stock B?
b) What is the standard deviation of this portfolio?
c) Discuss the risk and return associated with investing (a) all your funds in stock A, (b) all your funds in stock B, and (c) 40 percent in A and 60 percent in B. (This answer *must* use the numerical information in your answers derived above.)

4) You are given the following information:

Expected return on stock A	12%
Expected return on stock B	20%
Standard deviation of returns:	
stock A	1.0
stock B	6.0
Correlation coefficient of the returns on stocks A and B	+2

a) What are the expected returns and standard deviations of a portfolio consisting of:
  1) 100 percent in stock A?
  2) 100 percent in stock B?
  3) 50 percent in each stock?
  4) 25 percent in stock A and 75 percent in stock B?
  5) 75 percent in stock A and 25 percent in stock B?

b) Compare the above returns and the risk associated with each portfolio.

c) Redo the calculations assuming that the correlation coefficient of the returns on the two stocks is –0.6. What is the impact of this difference in the correlation coefficient?

5) What is the beta of a portfolio consisting of one share of each of the following stocks given their respective prices and beta coefficients?

Stock	Price	Beta
A	$10	1.4
B	24	0.8
C	41	1.3
D	19	1.8

How would the portfolio beta differ if an equal dollar amount were invested in each stock?

6) What should be the return on a stock according to the security market line if the risk-free rate is 6 percent, the return on the market is 10 percent, and the stock's beta is 0.5? If the beta had been 2.0, what should be the return?

Internet Application for Chapter 3
The Measurement of Risk and Return

Beta coefficients provide you with an indication of the market risk associated with a particular stock. Several sources offer beta coefficients. For example, the *Value Line Investment Survey* (http://www.valueline.com) provides betas to its subscribers. Beta coefficients are also available in several other Internet sites, such as those listed below.

Find the beta coefficients from at least three sources for the four stocks you are following (BUD, GTRC, HDI, and PFE or the alternatives) and rank them for market risk. Do the betas offered at the various sites differ?

Possible Internet sites for financial information are

Business Week Online http://www.businessweek.com

CBS MarketWatch http://cbs.marketwatch.com

Kiplinger.com http://kiplinger.com

Morningstar.com http://www.morningstar.com

Money Central http://moneycentral.msn.com/investor

Nasdaq http://www.nasdaq.com

Reuters http://investor.reuters.com

Yahoo! http://finance.yahoo.com.

Zacks.com http://www.zacks.com

You will be asked to use these sites in subsequent chapters to locate additional information. Remember: Not all information may be available at all sites, and the data may differ among various sites. Since you will be making investment decisions, it is your obligation to determine which sources best fit your needs.

THOMSON ONE
Business School Edition

Currency with Thomson ONE: Business School Edition

All investments involve risk. Beta coefficients are an index of the market risk associated with a stock. Using the Thomson ONE: Business School Edition database, rank the betas for four stocks in each of the three industry groups. Which are the most and least risky stocks based on their beta coefficients? Based on an average beta, which industry has the most systematic, market risk?

Now that you know the market risk associated with each stock, consider the following additional questions. Do your rankings help you construct a diversified portfolio? Would combining one of the stocks from one industry (e.g., pharmaceuticals) with another from a different industry (e.g., retail) help diversify a portfolio? What additional information would you need to answer that question?

CHAPTER

4 • • •

Investment Returns

From 1996 through 1999, the Standard & Poor's 500 stock index rose 26.435 percent annually. Is it reasonable to expect that stock prices will continue to increase at 26.435 percent? At that rate, $1,000 will grow to $108,980 in 20 years. If you could invest $1,000 each year for 20 years, you would accumulate $408,473.

As was proved during 2000-2002, such returns do not continue indefinitely. What return is it reasonable to assume will occur? What return has the stock market achieved over an extended period of time, such as 20 years? As this chapter will show, the large companies that compose the S&P 500 stock index have averaged about 11 percent annually. Even at that rate, $1,000 grows to $8,062 in 20 years, and $1,000 invested every year for 20 years grows to $64,203. Of course, you won't get to keep the entire amount because you will have to pay taxes on the gains. However, even if combined state and federal taxes consume 20 percent of the total, you still walk away with $6,450 and $51,362, respectively.

Historical market returns are important because they give you perspective and are useful when forecasting future returns, at least over an extended period of time. The dividend-growth valuation model presented in Chapter 7 has three components, one of which is the return on the market. The market's historical return is often used as a proxy for or forecast of future returns and may be used in that model.

Aggregate measures of the market and the historical returns earned by investments in stocks are the primary focus of this chapter. The first section discusses the construction of aggregate measures of the securities markets. These include the Dow Jones averages, the Standard & Poor's 500 stock index, the New York Stock Exchange index, the Wilshire 5000 Total Market stock index, and selected specialized indexes that have recently been developed.

The second section is devoted to historical returns earned on investments in securities. The coverage includes various methods employed to compute and show returns and academic studies of returns actually realized. The chapter concludes with a discussion of buying stock systematically to smooth out fluctuations in prices and returns experienced from year to year.

••MEASURES OF STOCK PERFORMANCE: AVERAGES AND INDEXES

You would think that constructing an aggregate measure of the stock market is easy, but there are several crucial questions, and how they are answered affects the resulting measure. For example, which companies should be included in an index? Do you include all the companies listed on the New York Stock Exchange? Is the index limited to only large companies, and, if so, what is the definition of "large"? Should the index exclude certain types of companies such as utilities, or should the index be specialized and include only certain types of companies such as utilities?

A second set of questions concerns the weight to be given to each security. For example, consider two stocks. Company A has 1 million shares outstanding and the stock sells for $10. Company B has 10 million shares outstanding, and its stock sells for $20. The total market value (or capitalization) of A is $10 million while the total market value of B is $200 million. How should these two securities be weighted? There are several choices: (1) treat each stock's price equally, (2) adjust for B's larger number of shares, or (3) use an equal dollar amount invested in each stock.

A Price-Weighted Arithmetic Average

The first choice is the arithmetic average of both stocks. The two prices are treated equally and the average price is

$$\frac{(\$10 + \$20)}{2} = \$15.$$

If the prices of the stocks rise to $18 and $22, respectively, the new average price is

$$\frac{(\$18 + \$22)}{2} = \$20.$$

In both calculations, the simple average gives equal weight to each stock price and does not recognize the difference in the number of shares outstanding.

A Value-Weighted Average

An alternative means used to measure stock performance is to construct an average that allows for differences in the number of shares each company has outstanding. If the preceding numbers are used, the total value of A and B is

Price × Number of shares = Total value
$$\$10 \times 1,000,000 = \$10,000,000$$
$$+$$
$$\underline{\$20 \times 10,000,000 = 200,000,000}$$
$$\$210,000,000.$$

The average price of a share of stock is

Average price = Total value of all shares ÷ Total number of shares
$$\text{Average price} = \frac{\$210,000,000}{(10,000,000 + 1,000,000)}$$
$$= \$19.09.$$

If the prices of the stocks rise to $18 and $22, respectively, the new total value of all shares is

$$\$18 \times 1,000,000 = \$\ 18,000,000$$
$$+$$
$$\$22 \times 10,000,000 = \ 220,000,000$$
$$\overline{\$238,000,000.}$$

The average value of a share of stock becomes

$$\text{Average price} = \frac{\$238,000,000}{(10,000,000 + 1,000,000)}$$
$$= \$21.64.$$

The value-weighted average gives more weight to companies with more shares outstanding, and that affects the average.

An Equal–Weighted Average

An alternative to the price-weighted and the value-weighted averages is the equal-weighted average price, which assumes an equal dollar invested in each stock. If, in the preceding illustration, $100 is invested in each stock, the investor would acquire 10 shares of stock A and 5 shares of stock B. The total cost of the 15 shares is $200, so the average price of a share is

$$\frac{\$200}{15} = \$13.33.$$

If the prices of the stocks rise to $18 and $22, respectively, the value of the shares is

$$\$180 + \$110 = \$290.$$

The new average value of a share is

$$\frac{\$290}{15} = \$19.33.$$

A Geometric Average

A fourth alternative means to calculate an aggregate measure of security prices is to construct a geometric average. Instead of adding the prices of the various stocks and dividing by the number of entries, a geometric average multiplies the various prices and then takes the nth root with n equal to the number of stocks. For example, if the prices of two stocks are $10 and $20, the geometric average is

$$\text{Average price} = \sqrt[2]{(\$10)(\$20)} = \$14.14.$$

If the prices of the stocks rise to $18 and $22, the new geometric average price is

$$\text{Average price} = \sqrt[2]{(\$18)(\$22)} = \$19.90.$$

As this discussion indicates, there are several ways to view an aggregate market price. Each of these methods produces a different average price, and when the stock prices are changed, the changes in the averages differ. In the illustration, the simple average rose from $15 to $20 for a 33.3 percent increase, but the value-weighted average price rose from $19.09 to $21.64, which is only a 13.34 percent increase. The equal-weighted average rose from $13.33 to $19.33, a 45 percent increase, while the geometric average price rose from $14.14 to $19.90, a 40.74 percent increase.

As is discussed later in this chapter, annual returns are often computed using geometric averages. Compounding, which the arithmetic average does not consider, is exceedingly important in investments. If the purpose is to compare the *order of returns*, the investment with the higher arithmetic average will also be the higher compound return. The order of the returns is not changed. If the purpose is to determine the *true annualized return*, then *compounding* must be considered—which requires computing the geometric average and not the arithmetic average.

Different Movements in Price Averages

The previous discussion illustrated how different types of stock price averages may be computed, resulting in different percentage changes in the averages. Even though the percentage changes vary, it would seem reasonable to assume that the average prices change in the same direction. However, that need not be the case; consider three stocks with the following prices and number of shares outstanding:

Stock	A	B	C
Number of shares outstanding	1,000	10,000	3,000
Price as of 1/1/0X	$10	$15	$25
Price as of 1/1/0Y	18	13	25

The price-weighted averages for the two years are

$$\frac{(\$10 + \$15 + \$25)}{3} = \$16.67$$

$$\frac{(\$18 + \$13 + \$25)}{3} = \$18.66.$$

The value-weighted averages are

$$\frac{(\$10 \times 1,000) + (\$15 \times 10,000) + (\$25 \times 3,000)}{14,000} = 16.78$$

$$\frac{(\$18 \times 1,000) + (\$13 \times 10,000) + (\$25 \times 3,000)}{14,000} = \$15.93.$$

These examples show that the average value of a share of stock differs in each case, and the price change can move in opposite directions.[1] The value of a share of stock

---

1. The geometric averages are

$$\sqrt[3]{(\$10 \times \$15 \times \$25)} = \$15.54$$

and

$$\sqrt[3]{(\$18 \times \$13 \times \$25)} = \$18.02.$$

Geometric averages may be computed using any electronic calculator with a y^x key. Take the reciprocal of the exponent and express it as a decimal (i.e., convert the 3 into ⅓, expressed as .3333). The average price for the first stock is $(\$10)(\$15)(\$25)^{.3333}$; use the y^x key to perform the calculation. Thus, the geometric average price of a share of this stock is

$$\sqrt[3]{(\$10 \times \$15 \times \$25)} = (\$10)(\$15)(\$25)^{.3333} = \$15.54.$$

rose from $16.67 to $18.66 according to the simple average, but when the value-weighted average was used, the price of a share decreased from $16.78 to $15.93.

The previous discussion covered the calculation of average price. Average price is generally converted into an index whose advantage is ease of comparison over time. In the example of price-weighted average, the initial price was $16.67. This amount could be used as the base year to which all subsequent years are compared. In the second year, the average price rose to $18.66. The new average price is expressed relative to the average in the initial year, which is called the base year:

$$\frac{\$18.66}{\$16.67} = 1.1193.$$

The result, 1.1193, means that the current price is 0.1193 (1.1193 – 1), or 11.9 percent greater than the prior year's price. If the price rises to $19.56 in the next year, then the increase relative to the base year is

$$\frac{\$19.56}{\$16.67} = 1.1734.$$

Thus, the price in the second year is 17.34 percent higher than in the initial year.

THE DOW JONES AVERAGES

Dow Jones Industrial Average
An average of the stock prices of 30 large firms.

One of the first measures of stock prices was the average developed by Charles Dow.[2] Initially, the average consisted of the stock from only 11 companies, but it was later expanded to include more firms. Today, this average is called the **Dow Jones Industrial Average**, and it is probably the best known and most widely quoted average of stock prices.

The Dow Jones Industrial Average is a simple price-weighted average. Initially, it was computed by summing the price of the stocks of 30 companies and then dividing by 30. Over time, the divisor has been changed so that substitutions of one firm for another or a stock split has no impact on the average. If the computation were simply the sum of the current prices of 30 divided by 30, the substitution of one stock for another or a stock split would affect the average.

To see the possible impact of substituting one stock for another, consider an average that is computed using three stocks (A, B, and C) whose prices are $12, $35, and $67, respectively. The average price is $38. For some reason, the composition of the average is changed. Stock B is dropped and replaced by stock D, whose price is $80. The average price is now $53 [($12 + 35 + 80)/30]. The substitution of D for B has caused the average to increase even though there has been no change in stock prices. To avoid this problem, the divisor is changed from 3 to the number that does not change the average. To find the divisor, set up the following equation:

$$(\$12 + 67 + 80)/X = \$38.$$

Solving for X gives a divisor of 4.1842. When the prices of stocks A, C, and D are summed and divided by 4.1842, the average price is

$$(\$12 + 67 + 80)/4.1842 = \$38,$$

---

2. In 1882 Edward Jones joined Charles Dow to form a partnership that grew into Dow, Jones and Company. Information on the Dow Jones averages may be found at http://www.djindexes.com.

so the average price has not been altered by the substitution of stock D for B.

A similar situation occurs when one of the stocks is split. (Stock splits and their impact on the price of a share is covered in Chapter 5.) Suppose stock D is split 2 for 1 so its price becomes $40 instead of $80 (two new shares at $40 = one old share at $80). The investor's wealth has not changed; the individual continues to hold stock worth a total of $159 ($12 + 67 + 40 + 40). The price average, however, becomes ($12 + 67 + 40)/4.1842 = $28.44 instead of $38. According to the average, the stock is worth less. The average has been affected by something other than a price movement—in this case, the stock split. Once again, this problem is solved by changing the divisor so that the average price remains $38. To find the divisor, set up the following equation:

$$(\$12 + 67 + 40)/X = \$38.$$

Solving for X gives a divisor of 3.1316. When the individual prices of stocks A, C, and D are summed and divided by 3.1316, the average price is

$$(\$12 + 67 + 40)/3.1316 = \$38,$$

so the average price has not been altered by the stock split.

While the Dow Jones Industrial Average (and the Utility Average, the Transportation Average, and the Composite Average) are adjusted for stock splits, stock dividends in excess of 10 percent, and the substitution of one firm for another, no adjustment is made for the distribution of cash dividends. Hence, the average declines when stocks like ExxonMobil go ex-div (pay a dividend) and their prices decline. (The reason for a stock's price to decline when the firm pays a dividend is also explained in Chapter 5.)

The failure to include dividend payments means that the annual percentage change in the Dow Jones Industrial Average understates the true return. This failure to include the dividend can have an amazing impact when compounding is considered. Suppose the average rises 8 percent annually when dividends are excluded but the return is 10 percent when dividends are included and reinvested. (The dividend yield on the Dow Jones Industrial Average was 2.04% as of May 2004.) Over 20 years, $1,000 grows to $4,661 at 8 percent but to $6,728 at 10 percent. If the time period is extended to 50 years, these values become $46,902 and $117,391, respectively.[3]

This understatement of the true annual return is, of course, true for all stock indexes that do not add back the dividend payment. The bias is greater for those indexes that cover the largest companies, since they tend to pay dividends. Although some small cap stocks do distribute dividends, they tend to pay out a smaller proportion of their earnings, and the dividend constitutes a small, perhaps even trivial, part of the total return.

The Dow Jones Industrial Average for the period from 1950 through 2003 is presented in Figure 4.1, which plots the high and low values of the average for each year. During the 1960s and 1970s, the Dow Jones Industrial Average (like the stock market) was erratic and certainly did not experience the steady growth achieved during the 1950s. In 1970 and in 1974 the Dow Jones Industrial Average even fell below the high achieved in 1959. The period from 1985 through 1999, however, showed a different pattern, as stock prices soared and the Dow Jones

---

3. One study found that from its inception through December 31, 1998, the Dow Jones Industrial Average grew from 40.94 to 9,181.43, for a 5.42 percent annual growth rate. However, if dividends had been reinvested, the Dow Jones would have been 652,230.87, for an annual growth rate of 9.89 percent. See Roger G. Clarke and Meir Statman, "The DJIA Crossed 652,230," *The Journal of Portfolio Management* (winter 2000): 89–93.

FIGURE 4.1   *Annual Price Range of the Dow Jones Industrial Average, 1950–2003*

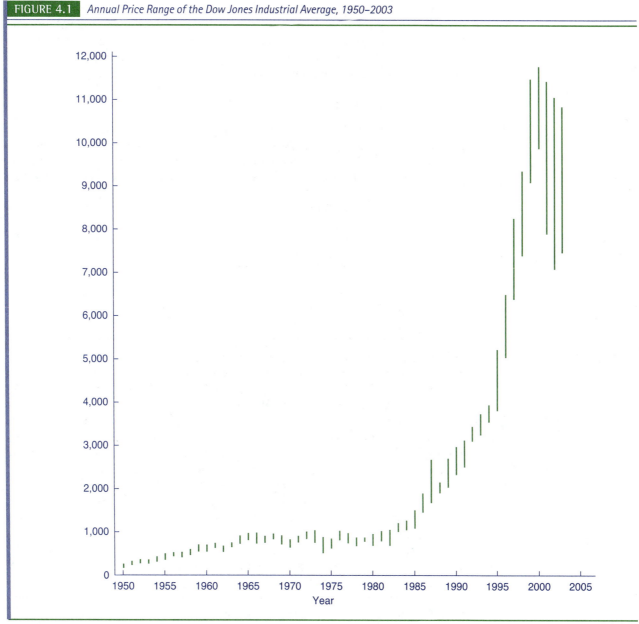

Source: First issue of *The Wall Street Journal* for each year.

Industrial Average rose to 11,497 at the end of 1999. This continual growth came to a crashing end in 2000, when the average declined 6.2 percent and continued to decline through 2002. Even in 2004, the Dow Jones Industrial Average traded below 10,000, some 15 percent below the 1999 closing average.

In addition to the industrial average, Dow Jones computes an average for transportation stocks, utility stocks, and a composite of the 65 stocks included in the separate averages. (Dow Jones also has developed specialty indexes covering specific industries [e.g., Internet Services], countries [e.g., the Japan 100 index], or world markets [e.g., the Global Equity Portfolio]). The firms in these averages are among the largest in terms of sales and assets and among the best known in the country.

This small number of firms is one source of criticism of the Dow Jones averages. It is argued that the small sample is not indicative of the market as a whole. For this reason, broader-based indexes such as the NYSE index or the Standard & Poor's 500 stock index may be better indicators of general market performance (These indexes are discussed later in this chapter.)

Graphical Illustrations

While a picture may be worth 1,000 words, pictures can be misleading. So, before proceeding to the discussion of other indexes of stock prices, you need to consider the composition of graphs (i.e., the pictures) used to illustrate indexes of stock prices. The choice of the scale affects the picture and can influence your perception of the performance of the stock market.

This impact may be illustrated by the following monthly range of stock prices and percentage increases:

Month	Price of Stock	Percentage Change in Monthly Highs
January	$ 5–10	—
February	10–15	50
March	15–20	33
April	20–25	25

Even though the monthly price increases are equal ($5), the percentage increments decline. The investor who bought the stock at $10 and sold it for $15 made $5 and earned a return of 50 percent. The investor who bought it at $20 and sold for $25 also made $5, but the return was only 25 percent.

These monthly prices may be plotted on graph paper that uses absolute dollar units for the vertical axis. This is done on the left-hand side of Figure 4.2. Such a graph gives the appearance that equal price movements yield equal percentage changes. However, this is not so, as the preceding illustration demonstrates.

To avoid this problem, a different scale can be used, as illustrated in the right-hand side of Figure 4.2. Here, equal units on the vertical axis represent percentage change. Thus, a price movement from $10 to $15 appears to be greater than one from $20 to $25, because in percentage terms it *is* greater.

The impact of using the percentage scale may be seen by comparing Figures 4.1 and 4.3. Both present the annual price range of the Dow Jones Industrial Average, but Figure 4.1 uses an absolute scale while Figure 4.3 (p. 132) expresses prices in relative terms. The general shape is the same in both cases, but the large absolute increase in the Dow Jones Industrial Average during the late 1990s is considerably less impressive in Figure 4.3. Because absolute price changes are reduced to relative price changes, graphs like Figure 4.3 are better indicators of security price movements and the returns investors earn. Several of the figures in this text that indicate movements in stock prices are constructed to show relative price changes rather than absolute prices.

OTHER MAJOR INDEXES OF STOCK PRICES

Standard & Poor's 500 stock index
A value-weighted index of 500 stocks.

Unlike the Dow Jones Industrial Average, the **Standard & Poor's 500 stock index** (commonly referred to as the S&P 500) is a value-weighted index. The index was 10 in the base year, 1943. Thus, if the index is currently 100, the value of these

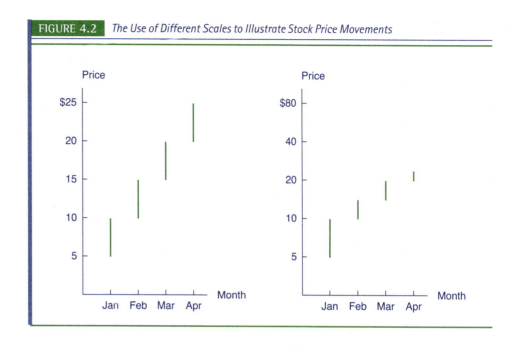

FIGURE 4.2   *The Use of Different Scales to Illustrate Stock Price Movements*

stocks is ten times their value in 1943. Standard & Poor's also computes an index of 400 industrial stocks and indexes of 20 transportation, 40 utility, and 40 financial companies.

Since the S&P 500 is a value-weighted index, large capitalization stocks such as Microsoft and ExxonMobil, whose market values were $283.1 billion and $282.9 billion as of May 2004, have more impact on the index than Alcoa, whose market value was $27.2 billion. Although the number of stocks in the S&P 500 remains constant, the composition of the index changes over time. Mergers and acquisitions are one cause of changes in the index as a firm is acquired and is replaced in the index by another stock. A financially weak firm whose stock has experienced a major decline in value may be dropped in favor of a company in better financial condition. Also, if the market value of a company declines, it may be dropped from the index and replaced by a stock with a larger capitalization. In August 2003, McDermott International was dropped and MedcoHealth Solutions was added. The reason given for the switch was the decline in McDermott's market capitalization.

The impact on the price of the stock that is added is usually positive. Any increase, however, is not the result of the company's receiving favorable recognition but of buying by the index funds, which must now include the stock in their portfolios. Conversely, if a firm is dropped from the index, the index funds will sell their positions, which may cause the price of the stock to decline.

The **New York Stock Exchange** composite index includes all common stock listed on the NYSE. Like the Standard & Poor's indexes, the NYSE index is a value-weighted index. In 2002, the NYSE reconstituted the composite index to include all common stocks, the American Depository Receipts (ADRs) of foreign stocks traded on the exchange, and real estate investment trusts (REITs) and to exclude preferred stocks, closed-end funds, exchange-traded funds, and derivatives. (Each of these types of securities is covered in various places in this text. See the index for specific locations.) The composite index's base was changed from 50 to 5,000 as of

NYSE composite index
New York Stock Exchange index; an index of prices of all the stocks listed on the New York Stock Exchange.

FIGURE 4.3   *Annual Price Range of the Dow Jones Industrial Average, 1950–2003*

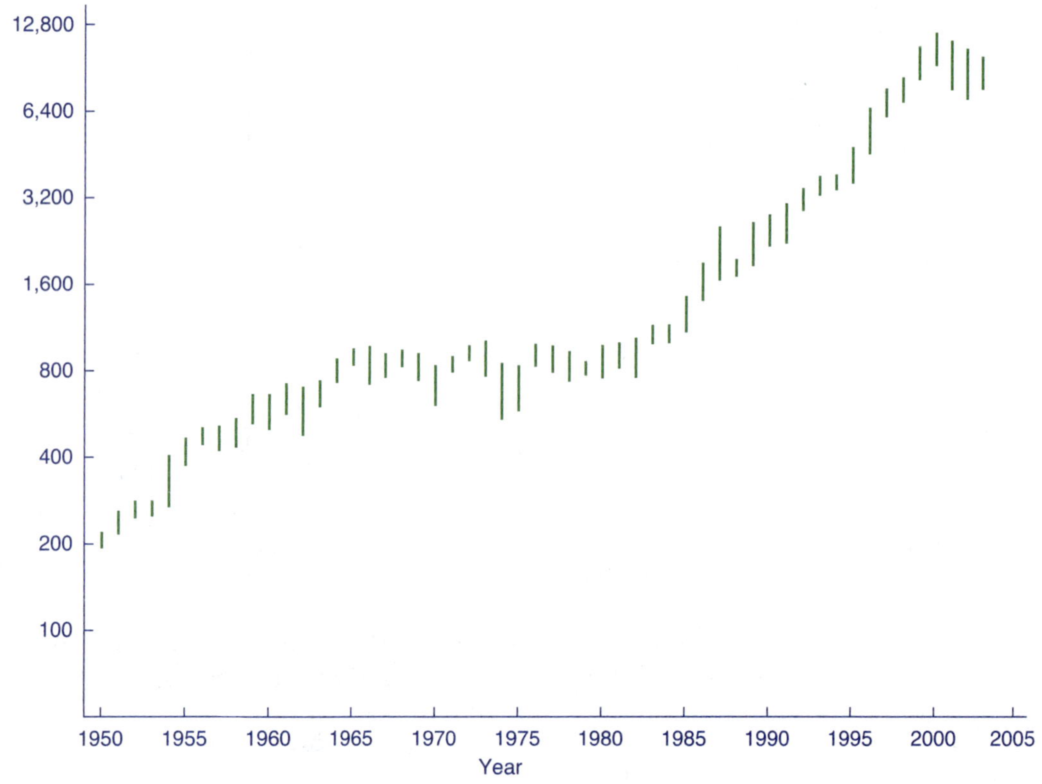

Source: First issue of *The Wall Street Journal* for each year.

December 31, 2002. Returns on the index are now reported for both price changes and for price changes plus dividends. (For information on the revised NYSE composite index, consult the NYSE Web page: **http://www.nyse.com**.

Value Line computes an index of more than 1,700 stocks that includes stocks traded on the New York Stock Exchange and on Nasdaq. Unlike the Dow Jones Industrial Average, which is a simple arithmetic average, and the S&P 500, which is a value-weighted average, the Value Line index is a geometric average that gives equal weight to each stock included in the average.

The Wilshire 5000 stock index is the broadest-based aggregate measure of stock prices. It is constructed using all stocks traded on the New York and American stock exchanges plus the actively traded over-the-counter stocks (i.e., virtually every publicly traded U.S. company). Other stock indexes include the American Stock Exchange index, which is a value-weighted index that encompasses all the common stocks on that exchange. The National Association of Security Dealers Automatic Quotation System (Nasdaq) index of over-the-counter stocks covers more than 3,000 issues. The National Association of Securities Dealers also publishes nonindustrial OTC indexes for banking and insurance. A summary of major aggregate measures of the U.S. stock market (including their coverage and means of computation) is given in Exhibit 4.1.

EXHIBIT 4.1   The Coverage and Computation of Selected Aggregate Measures of U.S. Stock Markets

Market Measure	Coverage	Computation
Dow Jones Industrial Average	30 large firms	Price-weighted arithmetic average
Standard & Poor's 500 stock index	500 actively traded stocks (400 industrial, 20 transportation, 40 utility, and 40 financial firms)	Value-weighted
Standard & Poor's 400 stock index	400 industrial companies	Value-weighted
Standard & Poor's 100 stock index	100 large cap stocks	Value-weighted
Standard & Poor's MidCap index	400 medium-sized firms with median market values (stock price times number of shares outstanding) of approximately $2 billion	Value-weighted
NYSE composite index	All stocks listed on the NYSE	Value-weighted
AMEX composite index	All stocks listed on the AMEX	Value-weighted
Value Line average	Approximately 1,700 stocks covered by the Value Line Investment Survey	Equally-weighted geometric average
National Association of Securities Dealers (Nasdaq) composite index	3,000 over-the-counter stocks	Value-weighted
Wilshire 5000 index	Approximately 7,000 NYSE, AMEX, and Nasdaq stocks	Value-weighted

Initially, market indexes covered some concept of the market as a whole. Now, however, a variety of indexes have been developed, many of which are devoted to a subsection of the market, such as all stocks that meet a certain condition or belong to a particular subgroup. Examples of these indexes include the Nasdaq Industrials, Nasdaq Banks, Nasdaq Computer, and Nasdaq Telecommunications indexes. Additional indexes and their components include:

Russell 1000	the largest 1,000 firms
Russell 2000	next-largest 2,000 firms
Russell 3000	combines the firms in the Russell 1000 and Russell 2000
Standard & Poor's 400 MidCap	index of moderate-sized firms
Standard & Poor's 600 SmallCap	index of relatively small firms
Standard & Poor's 1500 Index	combines all the stocks in the S&P 500, S&P 400 MidCap, and the S&P 600 SmallCap indexes

Many of these indexes are reported daily in *The Wall Street Journal* or are available through other sources, especially on the Internet, such as Yahoo! (**http://finance.yahoo.com**). There are also stock indexes of foreign stock markets such as the Japanese Nikkei 225 stock average, the London Financial Times Stock Exchange 100, and the Toronto Stock Exchange 300 composite index.

As may be seen in Exhibit 4.1 and the preceding list, a large variety of indexes exists. While it may seem unnecessary to have so many indexes (and obviously you cannot follow all of them), each index can serve an important purpose. Chapter 13 on mutual funds shows that assessing a portfolio manager's performance requires a benchmark for comparison. While a large cap growth fund may be compared to the S&P 500 stock index, such a comparison would not be valid for the manager of a fund that specialized in energy stocks or small cap stocks. This question of comparability, of course, applies to any specialized investment portfolio and has led to the creation of specialized indexes. If assessment is going to be based on market comparisons, then appropriate measures of the relevant market's performance are necessary.

In addition to indexes of stock prices, there are also aggregate measures of the bond market, such as the Dow Jones composite corporate bond average of ten public utility and ten industrial bonds. Actually, there are several hundred different bond indexes that include the Lehman Brothers aggregate index, the Merrill Lynch Domestic Master Index, and the Salomon Brothers corporate bond index. These indexes are similar, and individual issues are weighted by their market value. Specialized bonds such as high-yield, variable-rate, and convertible bonds are excluded. (The various types of bonds, their features, and valuation are covered in Chapters 8–10.)

PRICE FLUCTUATIONS

The increase in stock prices over time is illustrated in Figure 4.4, which plots the Dow Jones Industrial Average, the Standard & Poor's 500 stock index, and the NYSE composite index for 1980 through 2000. (The Dow Jones values have been divided by 10 to put them on a common basis with the other two indexes. Since the NYSE composite index was subsequently reconstituted and the base year changed, the figure extends only through 2000.) All three aggregate measures show the large increase in stock prices that occurred during the period from 1980 through 1999. The Dow Jones Industrial Average increased at an annual rae of 12.6 percent, while the other two indexes increased at 12.1 and 11.5 percent, respectively. The figure also shows the decline in stock prices that started in 2000 and did not end until 2003.

As would be expected, all three aggregate measures of the stock market move together, but the amount of movement does vary. For example, from January 1986 to January 1989, the Dow Jones Industrial Average rose by 39 percent, but the NYSE composite index rose only 31 percent. Generally, the correlation among the various aggregate measures is very high.[4] Some differences, however, do exist in the variability of these aggregate measures. The standard deviations of the

---

4. Merrill Lynch Quantitative Analysis Group has estimated the correlation coefficients relating the S&P 500 and the Dow Jones Industrial Average to be 0.95, and the correlation coefficient between the S&P 500 and the NYSe composite index approximated 1.0. The correlation coefficient of the monthly price changes for the data used in Figure 4.4 for the S&P 500 and the NYSE composite is 0.99. The NYSE reported that the correlation between its index and the S&P 500 is 0.968. For correlation coefficients between the NYSE composite index and other indexes, see the NYSE Web page, **http://www.nyse.com**.

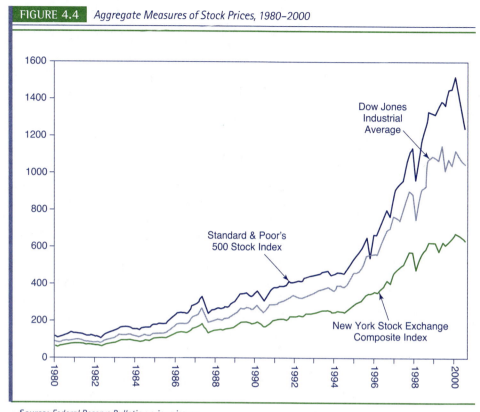

FIGURE 4.4 *Aggregate Measures of Stock Prices, 1980–2000*

Source: *Federal Reserve Bulletin,* various issues.

monthly return based on the data used to construct Figure 4.4 were 6.1 percent for the Dow Jones Industrial Average and 6.5 percent for the S&P 500. The standard deviation for the NYSE composite index was slightly lower (5.9 percent).

Figure 4.4 also shows the security prices can and do fall. One particularly severe decline occurred in October 1987 when the Dow experienced its largest one-day decline, in excess of 20 percent. However, in a matter of months, stock prices had rebounded and exceeded the highs reached prior to the October debacle. A similar large decline, but over a more extended period of time, occurred during 2000–2002. However, the markets had not completely recovered, and stock prices had not reached new highs, as of June 2004.

RETURNS ON INVESTMENTS IN COMMON STOCK

holding period return (HPR)

Total return (income plus price appreciation during a specified time period) divided by the cost of the investment.

What returns have been earned on investments in securities? To answer this question, you should consider the purchase price of the security, the sale price, the flow of income (such as dividends or interest), and how long you owned the asset. The easiest (and perhaps the most misleading) return is the **holding period return (HPR)**. It is derived by dividing the gain (or loss) plus any income by the price paid for the asset. That is,

(4.1)
$$HPR = \frac{P_1 + D - P_0}{P_0},$$

in which P_1 is the sale price, D is the income, and P_0 is the purchase price. If you buy a stock for $40, collect dividends of $2, and sell the stock for $50, the holding period return is

$$\text{HPR} = \frac{\$50 + \$2 - \$40}{\$40} = 30\%.$$

The holding period return has a major weakness because it fails to consider how long it took to earn the return. This problem is immediately apparent if the information in the previous example had been a stock that cost $40, paid annual dividends of $1, and was sold at the end of the *second* year for $50. Given this information, what is the return? While the holding period return remains the same, 30 percent is obviously higher than the true annual return. If the time period is greater than a year, the holding period return *overstates* the true annual return. (Conversely, for a period that is less than a year, the holding period return understates the true annual return.)

Because the holding period return is easy to compute, it is frequently used, producing misleading results. Consider the following example. You buy a stock for $10 per share and sells it after ten years for $20. What is the holding period return on the investment? This simple question can produce several misleading answers. You may respond by answering, "I doubled my money!" or "I made 100 percent!" That certainly sounds impressive, but it completely disregards the *length of time* needed to double your money. You may compute the arithmetic average and assert that you made 10 percent annually (100% ÷ 10 years). This figure is less impressive than the claim that the return is 100 percent, but it is also misleading because it fails to consider compounding. Some of the return earned during the first year in turn earned a return in subsequent years, which was not taken into consideration when you averaged the return over the ten years.

The correct way to determine the **rate of return** that was earned is to phrase the question as follows: "At what rate does $10 grow to $20 after ten years?" You should recognize this as another example of the time value of money. The equation used to answer this question is

$$P_0(1 + r)^n = P_n,$$

in which P_0 is the cost of the security, r is the rate of return per period, n is the number of periods (e.g., years), and P_n is the price at which the security is sold. When the proper values are substituted, the equation becomes

$$\$10(1 + r)^{10} = \$20,$$

which asks at what rate $10 will grow for ten years to become $20. The answer is:

$$\$10(1 + r)^{10} = \$20.00,$$
$$(1 + r)^{10} = 2,$$
$$r = \sqrt[10]{2} - 1 = 1.0718 - 1 = 7.18\%,$$

so the annual rate of return is 7.18 percent. The correct rate of return on the investment (excluding any dividend income) is considerably less impressive than "I doubled my money!" or "I made 10 percent each year."

In the previous illustration, you know the beginning and the ending values. Suppose you computed each year's percentage return and averaged them. Is this

rate of return
The discount rate that equates the cost of an investment with the cash flows generated by the investment.

Calculator Solution	
Function Key	Data Input
PV =	−10
FV =	20
PMT =	0
N =	10
I =	?
Function Key	Answer
I =	7.18

approach acceptable? For example, suppose you bought a stock for $20 and its price rose to $25. The return is 25 percent ($5/$20). The next year the price declined back to $20, for a 20 percent loss (–$5/$25). You obviously earned nothing over the time period and the rate of return should indicate this fact.

If, however, you average the annual returns, the investment will have generated a positive return:

$$\frac{25\% - 20\%}{2} = 2.5\%.$$

Owing to the magic of numbers, you have earned a 2.5 percent positive return, even though the investment produced neither a gain nor a loss. Unless you want to overstate your return, *do not average positive and negative percentage changes.*

The correct method to determine the annualized return is to compute a geometric average. In the first year, the stock rose from $20 to $25 (or $25 ÷ $20 = 1.25). In the second year, the stock declined from $25 to $20 (or $20 ÷ $25 = 0.8). The geometric average is

$$\sqrt[2]{(1.25)(0.80)} = 1.00,$$

so the return is 1.00 – 1.00 = 0.0%. (Notice that you subtract 1.0 to get the net change. Look back at the earlier illustration of the return earned on the $10 stock that you sold after ten years for $20. You subtracted 1.0 from the 1.0718 to determine the return of 7.18 percent. In effect, the 1.0 that you subtract represents the amount initially invested.)

Geometric averages are often used to obtain rates of return over a period of years. Suppose the annual rates of return are as follows:

Year	Rate of Return
1	25%
2	3
3	–18
4	–10
5	15

The geometric average return is

$$\sqrt[5]{(1.25(1.03)(0.82)(0.90)(1.15)} - 1 = 0.0179 = 1.79\%$$

This annual return is lower than the arithmetic return of 3 percent that would be obtained by adding each of the returns and dividing by 5. As in the previous example, the averaging of positive and negative annual returns (i.e., the computation of an arithmetic average) overstates the true return.

The inclusion of income makes the calculation of the return more difficult. Consider the example that started this section in which you bought a stock for $40, collected $2 in dividends for two years, and then sold the stock for $50. What is the rate of return? The holding period return is overstated because it fails to consider the time value of money. If you compute the rate of growth and consider only the original cost and the terminal value, the rate of return is understated because the dividend payments are excluded.

internal rate of return
Percentage return that equates the present value of an investment's cash inflows with its cost.

These problems are avoided by computing an investment's **internal rate of return**, an approach that determines the rate that equates the present value of all an investment's future cash inflows with the present cost of the investment. An example of an internal rate of return is the yield to maturity on a bond (discussed in Chapter 11). Since the yield to maturity equates the present value of the cash inflows (the interest and principal repayment) with the present cost of the investment, it is the true, annualized rate of return.

The general equation for the internal rate of return (r) for a stock is

(4.2)
$$P_0 = \frac{D_1}{(1 + r)} + \ldots + \frac{D_n}{(1 + r)^n} + \frac{P_n}{(1 + r)^n}.$$

Interactive e-lectures

See a visual explanation and example of measuring returns at

http://mayoxtra.swlearning.com

in which D is the annual dividend received in n years, and P_n is the price received for the stock in the nth year.

If the internal rate of return were computed for the previous illustration of a stock that cost $40, paid an annual dividend of $1, and was sold at the end of the second year for $50, the equation to be solved is

$$\$40 = \frac{\$1}{(1 + r)} + \frac{\$1}{(1 + r)^2} + \frac{\$50}{(1 + r)^2}$$

Notice that there are three cash inflows: the dividend received each year and the sale price. The internal rate of return equates *all* cash inflows to the investor with the cost of the investment. These cash inflows include periodic payments as well as the sale price. (The calculation for the holding period return combined the dividend plus the capital gain on the investment and treated them as occurring at the end as a single cash inflow.)

There is no easy, manual solution to this equation. Even if you try to solve by trial and error using an interest table, the answer will be only an approximation. However, a financial calculator or program such as Excel can readily and accurately solve the problem. When the data are entered into a financial calculator, the internal rate of return on the investment, 14.17 percent, is readily determined. This 14.17 percent is the true, annualized rate of return on the investment. (The use of a financial calculator facilitates the computation of the internal rate of return, but calculators do have weaknesses. In this illustration, the yearly payments are equal and are entered into the calculator as an annuity. If the yearly payments were unequal, each payment would have to be individually entered. Because calculators limit the number of individual entries, they may not be used to determine the internal rate of return for problems with large numbers of cash inflows.)

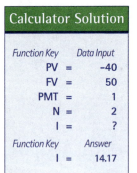

Calculator Solution

Function Key	Data Input
PV =	–40
FV =	50
PMT =	1
N =	2
I =	?
Function Key	Answer
I =	14.17

The internal rate of return has two potential problems. The first concerns the reinvestment of cash inflows you received. The internal rate of return assumes that cash inflows are *reinvested at the investment's internal rate.* In the preceding illustration that means the $1 received in the first year is reinvested at 14.17 percent. If the dividend annualized payment is reinvested at a lower rate or not reinvested (e.g., it is spent), the true annualized return on the investment will be less than the rate determined by the equation. Conversely, if you earn more than 14.17 percent when the $1 is reinvested, the true return on the investment will exceed the internal rate of return determined by the equation.

The second problem occurs when you make more than one purchase of the security. While the problem is not insurmountable, it makes the calculation more difficult. Suppose you buy one share for $40 at the beginning of the first year, buy a second share for $42 at the end of the first year, and sell both shares at the end of the second year for $50 each. The firm pays an annual dividend of $1, so $1 is collected at the end of year 1 and $2 at the end of year 2. What is the return on the investment?

To answer this question using the internal rate of return, you must equate the present value of the cash inflows and the cash outflows. The cash flows are as follows:

Time	Year 0	End of Year 1	End of Year 2
Cash outflow	$40	$42	–
Cash inflow	–	$1	$2 + $100

There are two cash outflows (the purchases of $40 and $42) that occur in the present (year 0) and at the end of year 1. There are two cash inflows, the $1 dividend received at the end of year 1 and the $2 dividend at the end of year 2 plus the cash from the sale of the shares ($100) at the end of year 2. The equation for the internal rate of return is

$$\$40 + \frac{42}{(1+r)} = \frac{\$1}{(1+r)} + \frac{2+100}{(1+r)^2}$$

and the internal rate of return is 16.46 percent.

In this example, you own one share during the first year and two shares during the second year. The return in the second year has more impact on the overall return than the rate earned during the first year when you owned only one share. Since the number of shares and hence the amount invested differ each year, this approach to determining rates of return is sometimes referred to as a **dollar-weighted rate of return**.

An alternative to the dollar-weighted or internal rate of return is the **time-weighted return**, which ignores the amount of funds invested during each time period. This technique computes the return for each period and averages the results. In effect, it computes the holding period return for each period and averages them. In the illustration, the initial price was $40; you collected $1 in dividends and had stock worth $42 at the end of the year. The return for the first year was

$$(\$42 + 1 - 40) \div 40 = 7.5.$$

During the second year, a share rose from $42 to $50 and paid a $1 dividend. The return was

$$(\$50 + 1 - 42) \div 42 = 21.43\%.$$

The simple average return is

$$(7.5\% + 21.43) \div 2 = 14.47\%,$$

and the geometric average return is

$$\sqrt{(1.075)(1.2143)} - 1 = \sqrt{1.3054} - 1 = 1.1425 - 1 = 14.25\%.$$

As discussed earlier, the geometric average is the true compound rate, while the simple average tends to overstate the true annual rate of return and should not be used.

dollar–weighted rate of return
The rate that equates the present value of cash inflows and cash outflows; the internal rate of return.

time–weighted rate of return
Average of individual holding period returns.

In this illustration, the dollar-weighted return (i.e., the internal rate of return) is higher than the time-weighted return. This is because the stock performed better in the second year when you owned more shares. The results would have been reversed if the stock had performed better the first year than during the second year (i.e., 21.4 percent in year 1 and 7.5 percent in year 2). In that case, the larger amount invested would have earned the smaller return, so the dollar-weighted return would have been less than the time-weighted return.

Which of the two methods, the dollar-weighted return or the time-weighted return, is preferred? There is no absolute right answer. Because you are concerned with the return earned on *all* the dollars invested, the dollar-weighted return would appear to be superior. However, there is an argument for the use of a time-weighted return to evaluate the performance of a portfolio manager. For example, a firm may make periodic contributions to its employee pension plan. Because the timing and amount of the cash inflows are beyond the pension plan manager's control, the use of a dollar-weighted return is inappropriate. Thus, money managers often use a time-weighted return instead of a dollar-weighted return to evaluate portfolio performance.[5]

STUDIES OF INVESTMENT RETURNS

Several studies have been conducted by academicians on the returns earned by investments in common stocks. (Brokerage firms, investment advisory services, and other financial institutions have also computed returns, but you should be skeptical of the results. See, for instance, the discussion of returns earned by mutual funds in Chapter 12 in the section on the consistency of returns.) One of the first studies found that the annual rates of return from investments in all common stocks listed on the NYSE from 1926 to 1965 was 9.5 percent.[6] The returns were even higher during the 1950s and early 1960s when the country and the stock market experienced prosperity and rapid growth. During this period, the annual rates of return approximated 15 percent.

Ibbotson and Sinquefield initially extended the results of previous studies to 1981.[7] Their study was more comprehensive than the previous studies in that it considered not only stocks but also corporate bonds, federal government bonds and bills, and the rate of inflation. Since 1981 the results have been updated annually, and this work is generally considered to be the most definitive study of rates of return on alternative investments.[8] A summary of the results is presented in Exhibit 4.2. As may be seen in the exhibit, the annual rate of return for common stocks as measured by the Standard & Poor's 500 common stock index was 10.2 percent. If only smaller stocks are considered, the annual rate of return rises to 12.1 percent. Ibbotson Associates defines small stocks as the lowest one-fifth of New York Stock Exchange firms in total value (i.e., price times number of shares outstanding).

5. The CFA Institute (**http://www.cfainstitute.org**) *requires* its members to calculate time-weighted returns at least quarterly using a geometric average. The purpose of the calculation is to inform clients of the portfolio manager's performance. The portfolio managers must also present measures of risk, such as the standard deviations of the returns.
6. Lawrence Fisher and James H. Lorie, "Rates of Return on Investments in Common Stock: The Year-by-Year Record, 1926–1965," *Journal of Business* 40 (July 1968): 1–26.
7. Robert Ibbotson and Rex Sinquefield, *Stocks, Bonds, Bills, and Inflation: The Past and the Future* (Charlottesville, VA: Financial Analysts Research Foundation, 1982).
8. The annual updates are published by Ibbotson Associates in *The Stocks, Bonds, Bills, and Inflation (SBBI) Yearbook*. Information concerning SBBI is available at **http://www.ibbotson.com**.

EXHIBIT 4.2	Annual Rates of Return, 1926–2002, Estimated by Ibbotson Associates	
Security	**Annual Rate of Return**	**Standard Deviation of Return**
Large company common stocks	10.2%	20.5%
Small company stocks	12.1	33.2
Long-term corporate bonds	5.9	8.7
Long-term government bonds	5.5	9.4
Treasury bills	3.8	3.2
Rate of Inflation	3.0	4.4

Source: *Stocks, Bonds, and Inflation, 2003 Yearbook* (Chicago: Ibbotson Associates, 2003) (Data in the *SBBI Yearbook* updated annually.)

Exhibit 4.2 includes the annual rates of return earned by long-term corporate debt, federal government bonds, and Treasury bills. In addition, the exhibit includes the standard deviation of each rate of return, which indicates the associated risk. As would be expected, the risk is largest for the small stocks. While their annual return was 12.1 percent, the standard deviation was 33.2 percent, which means that in 68 percent of the years the annual return ranged from 45.3 percent to –21.1 percent. This is a very large range in returns when compared to that of Treasury bills, which had a standard deviation of 3.2 percent. Obviously, if you limit the portfolio to riskier securities and are forced to sell the stocks, you could sustain a large loss if the sale occurred during a declining market. Conversely, over a period of years, the riskier stocks produced a higher return.

Exhibit 4.2 gives the annual rate of inflation, and it is interesting to note that the rate earned on Treasury bills slightly exceeded the rate of inflation. This suggests that the investor who is concerned with maintaining purchasing power can meet this goal (at least before federal income taxes are considered) by acquiring Treasury bills. The exhibit also suggests that over time, the yield on stocks tends to be approximately 7 percent above the rate on Treasury bills. This information may be important when trying to establish a return necessary to justify purchasing equities. For example, a current yield on Treasury bills of 2.5 percent suggests that a return of 9.5 percent may be necessary to justify purchasing a corporation's common stock (before adjusting for the risk associated with the specific company).

Because the results in Exhibit 4.2 may have been affected by the returns earned during the depression of the 1930s, Exhibit 4.3 (p. 142) presents the returns for more recent time periods: 1945–1995, 1980–1995, and 1988–2002. For all three periods, the returns on stocks exceeded the returns presented in Exhibit 4.2. Exhibit 4.3 also indicates considerable range in the returns. During 1954, the return on large stocks exceeded 50 percent, while the losses in 1974 exceeded 25 percent. The returns on small stocks experienced an even greater range, from a high of 83.6 percent in 1967 to a loss of 30.9 percent in 1973. Even during the most recent time period, 1988–2002, the returns on large stocks ranged from 37.4 percent to –22.1 percent, and the range in the returns on small stocks was even larger (44.6 percent to –21.6 percent). Perhaps the most unexpected result revealed in Exhibit 4.3 is the performance of small stocks compared to large stocks. During 1980–1995, the smaller stocks earned a lower return, indicating that the additional risk associated with investments in smaller companies did not generate corresponding higher returns.

EXHIBIT 4.3	Average, Highest, and Lowest Returns: 1945–1995, 1980–1995, and 1988–2002					
		1945–1995		**1980–1995**		**1988–2002**
Large company stocks	average return	12.4%		15.8%		11.5%
	highest return	52.6 (1954)		37.4 (1995)		37.4 (1995)
	lowest return	−26.5 (1974)		−4.9 (1981)		−22.1 (2002)
Small company stocks	average return	14.7		15.6		12.3
	highest return	83.6 (1967)		44.6 (1991)		44.6 (1991)
	lowest return	−30.9 (1973)		−21.6 (1990)		−21.6 (1990)
Rate of Inflation	average	4.3		4.4		3.0
	highest	18.2 (1945)		12.4 (1980)		6.1 (1990)
	lowest	0.4 (1955)		1.1 (1986)		1.5 (2001)

Source: *Stocks, Bonds, Bills, and Inflation, 2003 Yearbook* (Chicago: Ibbotson Associates, 2003).

Exhibits 4.2 and 4.3 indicate that investments in common stock have generated positive returns, but the standard deviations in Exhibit 4.2 and the lowest returns in Exhibit 10.3 confirm that investment in stocks can produce losses over short periods of time. While the –26.5 percent return in 1974 was the worst case for the large companies and –30.9 percent in 1973 the worst for the small companies, these two years were not unique. Common stocks generated negative returns during 14 of the 58 years from 1945 through 2002.

This pattern of returns changes when longer time periods are considered. Exhibit 4.4 presents the high–low returns for time periods varying from one year to twenty years. As the number of years increases, the range of the return diminishes *and* the worst-case scenario improves. Over all ten-year time periods, investments in stock *did not produce a loss*. The worst case for common stocks and small stocks occurred from 1965 through 1974 when they earned annualized returns of 1.4 percent and 3.2 percent, respectively.

For twenty-year time periods, the range of returns continued to decline and the minimum returns increased. The worst period for stocks (1959 through 1978) generated annual returns of 6.53 percent, and for the small stocks the lowest return was 8.21 percent earned during 1955 through 1974. In addition, for every ten-year period since 1974, common stock annual returns have exceeded 10 percent. These results suggest that if you take a long perspective, you should earn positive returns on investments in common stocks. If you do sustain losses during a particular period, perseverance and patience should be rewarded and the losses erased.

You may ask whether securities traded in a particular market, such as the Nasdaq stock market, generate higher returns than the stocks traded on another market such as the New York Stock Exchange. The data in Exhibits 4.2 through 4.4 do suggest that small stocks often generate higher returns than large stocks. However, the time period for the comparison is important. Figure 4.5 (p. 144) plots the Nasdaq market index and the S&P 500 stock index. While Nasdaq stocks such as Microsoft are in the S&P 500, the composition of the two indexes differs. Figure 4.5 has two parts. (Each index has been adjusted to establish a common starting value: 100 for 1980–1994 and 500 for 1995–2003.) Part a (1980–1994) indicates that the Nasdaq rose more than the S&P 500, about 11 percent annually versus 10 percent for the S&P 500. Part b indicates a similar result from the beginning value in 1995 to the ending value in 2003. But those returns do not hold if a different time period

EXHIBIT 4.4	Highest and Lowest Returns for Different Time Horizons (since 1946)	
	Common Stocks	**Small Company Stocks**
One-year		
Lowest return	−26.5% (1974)	−30.9% (1973)
Highest return	52.6% (1954)	83.6% (1967)
Five-year time horizon:		
Lowest return	−2.4% (1970–1974)	−12.6% (1970–1974)
Highest return	28.6% (1995–1999)	39.8% (1975–1979)
Ten-year time horizon:		
Lowest return	1.4% (1965–1974)	3.2% (1965–1974)
Highest return	20.1% (1949–1958)	30.4% (1975–1984)
Twenty-year time horizon:		
Lowest return	6.5% (1959–1978)	8.2% (1955–1974)
Highest return	17.9% (1980–1999)	20.3% (1975–1994)

Source: Chicago: Ibbotson Associates, 2003, various pages.

is selected as the starting point for comparing the returns. Figure 4.5 clearly illustrates the large increase experienced by Nasdaq stocks starting in 1998 and continuing into 2000 and the subsequent large decline that started in 2000 and continued through 2002. If you purchased Nasdaq stocks during 1999 and held them until the end of 2003, you sustained a loss. As of June 2004, the Nasdaq index remained below its closing value of December 2000, and more than 60 percent below its peak of 5,133 in May 2000. (The S&P 500 was 26 percent below its September 2000 high of 1,531, so the general results were the same, just less severe.)

The Reinvestment Assumption

Before jumping to conclusions as to what an investor in the stock market will earn, you should realize that studies of investment return are aggregates. Your portfolio may not mirror the market return. In addition, historical returns may not be indicators of future returns. Studies of historical returns make a crucial assumption that investors may not be able to fulfill. The studies compute internal rates of return that assume that cash inflows are reinvested at the internal rate. For most individuals, that assumption does not apply. While it obviously does not apply if you spend the payments, the assumption still would not apply even if the income were reinvested. Because you would have to pay income taxes on the dividend and interest income, the funds available would be reduced. If all the funds were reinvested, you would have to pay the tax from other sources. In either case, the comparability of the historical returns with the return you earn is diminished. (This is, of course, the same problem covered in Chapter 8. In that discussion, the fund's return is stated before tax while the individual has to pay the income tax on the distributions, so the realized returns are after tax.)

At best, historical returns may be taken as starting points in the valuation of stock. They may be used in the capital asset pricing model to help determine the required return, which in turn is used as the discount factor in the dividend-growth model. Thus, historical returns are important to the determination of whether a stock is overvalued or undervalued.

FIGURE 4.5 *S&P 500 Stock Index and Nasdaq Stock Index, 1980–2003*

Source: Data from Commodity Systems, Inc. (CSI) available through Yahoo! at http://finance.yahoo.com under the section "Historical Prices."

REDUCING THE IMPACT OF PRICE FLUCTUATIONS: AVERAGING

One strategy for accumulating shares and reducing the impact of security price fluctuations is to "average" the position. By buying shares at different times, you accumulate the shares at different prices. Such a policy may be achieved through the dividend reinvestment plans offered by mutual funds and many companies.

An alternative is for the investor to systematically purchase shares of stock through a broker. There are two basic methods for achieving this averaging: the periodic purchase of shares and the purchase of additional shares if the stock's price falls.

Periodic Purchases

Under the periodic purchase plan, you buy additional shares of a stock at regular intervals. For example, you may elect to buy $2,000 worth of a stock every quarter or every month. This purchase is made at the appropriate interval, no matter what the price of the stock is. Since the dollar amount is the same, this technique is referred to as **dollar cost averaging**.

The effect of such a program is illustrated in Exhibit 4.5, which shows the number of shares of EMEC stock purchased at various prices when $2,000 is invested each quarter. The first column gives the dates of purchase, and the second column presents the various prices of the stock; the third and fourth columns list the number of shares purchased and the total number of shares held in the position. The last column presents the average price of the stock held in the position. You should notice that when the price of the stock declines, $2,000 buys more shares. For example, at $33 per share, $2,000 buys only 60 shares, but at $18 per share you receive 111 shares. Because more shares are acquired when the price of the stock falls, this has the effect of pulling down the average cost of a share. In this example, after two years the average cost of the stock had fallen to $23.85 and you had accumulated 671 shares. If the price of the stock subsequently rises, you will earn more profits on the lower-priced shares and thus will increase the return on the entire position.

Averaging Down

Some investors find it difficult to purchase stock periodically, especially if the price of the stock has increased. Instead, they prefer to purchase additional shares of the stock only if the price declines. Such investors are following a policy of averaging down. Averaging down is a means by which the investor reduces the average cost basis of an investment in a particular security. By buying more shares as the price declines, the average cost of a share is reduced. This may be particularly rewarding

> **dollar cost averaging**
> *The purchase of securities at different intervals to reduce the impact of price fluctuations.*

EXHIBIT 4.5   Average Position When $2,000 in EMEC Stock is Purchased Each Quarter

Date	Price of Stock	Number of Shares Purchased	Cumulative Number of Shares Owned	Average Cost of Share
1/1/X0	$25	80	80	$25.00
4/1/X0	28	71	151	26.50
7/1/X0	33	60	211	28.44
10/1/X0	27	74	285	28.07
1/1/X1	21	95	380	26.32
4/1/X1	18	111	491	24.44
7/1/X1	20	100	591	23.69
10/1/X1	25	80	671	23.85

if the price subsequently rises, because the investor has accumulated shares at decreased prices and earns a gain when the price increases. The investor may dollar cost average, which means that the same dollar amount is spent on shares each time a purchase is made. Or the investor may average down by purchasing the same number of shares (i.e., **share averaging**) every time a purchase is made.

Exhibit 4.6 illustrates these averaging down strategies. The price of the stock is given in column 1. Column 2 uses the dollar cost averaging method; the investor purchases $1,000 worth of stock every time the price declines by $5. As is readily seen in column 2, the number of shares in each successive purchase is larger. The last entries in the column give the total amount that the investor has spent ($5,000), the total number of shares that have been purchased (289), and the average cost of the shares ($17.30). The average cost of the total position has declined perceptibly below the $30 price of the initial commitment. However, if the price of the stock were to increase to $30, the entire position would be worth $8,670. The investor would have made a profit of $3,670 and earned a gain of 73 percent on the entire position.

Column 3 in Exhibit 4.6 illustrates the share averaging method, which means that the same number of shares are bought every time the investor makes a purchase. When the price declines by $5, the investor buys 100 shares. If the price of the stock were to fall to $10, the investor would have accumulated 500 shares under share averaging, for a total cost of $10,000. If the price of the stock were to return to $30, the entire position would be worth $15,000, and the investor's profit would be $5,000, for a gain of 50 percent.

There is a greater reduction in the average cost of the entire position with dollar cost averaging than with share averaging. When you dollar cost average, the amount spent is held constant and the number of shares purchased varies. When you share average, the number of shares purchased is held constant and the dollar amount varies. Because you purchase a fixed number of shares with share averaging regardless of how low the price falls, the average cost of a share in the position is not reduced to the extent that it is with dollar cost averaging.

The preceding discussion and examples explain the essentials of averaging. You may choose any number of variations on this basic concept. For example, you may choose to average down on declines of any dollar amount in the price of the

EXHIBIT 4.6   Averaging Down Strategies

Price of the Stock	Number of Shares Purchased ($1,000 Each Purchase)	Cost of 100 Shares
$30	33	$ 3,000
25	40	2,500
20	50	2,000
15	66	1,500
10	100	1,000
	289 shares	$10,000
	(for a cost of $5,000 and an average cost of $17.30 per share)	(500 shares, for a cost of $10,000 and an average cost of $20 per share)

stock or may select any dollar amount to invest for periodic purchases or for averaging down. The effect is the same—that is, to reduce the average cost basis of the position in that particular security.

Averaging down obviously requires that you have the funds to acquire the additional shares once the price has declined. In addition, dollar cost averaging will involve purchasing odd lots (33 shares, for example) or combinations of odd and even lots (such as 133 shares, composed of one round lot of 100 shares and one odd lot of 33 shares). Such purchases may not be cost-efficient when considering commissions. Dividend reinvestment plans that permit additional contributions may alleviate the problem of commission costs, but the purchases then cannot be made at a particular desired price. Instead, you must accept the price on the day the funds are invested.

If you follow a policy of dollar cost averaging, you should not assume the strategy will lead to a positive return. The stock's price may continue to decline, or many years may pass before the price of the security rises to its previous level. You should view the funds spent on the initial investment as a fixed or sunk cost that *should not influence the decision to buy additional shares*. This type of reasoning is difficult to put into practice. Many individuals will not readily admit that they have made a poor investment. Unfortunately, they then follow a program of averaging down in the belief that it will vindicate their initial investment decision.

You should not automatically follow a policy of averaging down. Before additional purchases are made, the stock should be reanalyzed. If the potential of the company has deteriorated (which may be why the price of the stock has fallen), you would be wiser to discontinue the policy of averaging down, sell the stock, and take a tax loss. If the stock lacks potential, it makes no sense to throw good money (the money used to buy the additional shares) after bad (the money previously invested in the stock). Some questions that you should ask are "Does the firm still have potential?" or "Is there a substantive reason for maintaining the current position in the stock?" If the answer is yes, then averaging down and periodic purchases are two means of accumulating shares while reducing their average cost basis. Such strategies reduce the impact of security price fluctuations, but it cannot be assumed the strategies produce superior returns, since excess returns are inconsistent with the efficient market hypothesis. Averaging strategies do, however, offer a means to systematically accumulate securities.

SUMMARY

Security prices fluctuate daily. Many averages and indices have been developed that track these price movements. Aggregate measures of the market include the Dow Jones averages, Standard & Poor's stock indexes, the NYSE index, the Russell stock indexes, and the Value Line stock index. There are even measures of segments of the market (e.g., large cap stocks) or sectors (e.g., tech stocks).

The composition and method of calculation of each measure differ. The composition ranges from the Dow Jones Industrial Average of 30 companies to the

Russell 5000, which encompasses over 7,000 companies. The method of calculation is based on averages, which include price-weighted averages (e.g., the Dow Jones industrials), value-weighted averages (e.g., the S&P 500), and geometric averages (e.g., the Value Line index).

An index may be used to compute stock returns. Just as there are several ways to calculate an average, there are several ways to compute a return. The holding period return is the percent change in the price of the investment over the entire time period. The holding period return may also include any income generated by the investment. Since the holding period return does not consider time, it does not include the impact of compounding and often overstates the true, compounded return. Dollar-weighted returns and time-weighted returns do include the impact of time. The dollar-weighted return (or internal rate of return) equates the present value of an investment's cash inflows with the investment's cash outflows. The time-weighted return is a geometric average of each period's return.

While studies of common stock returns have found that investors have earned an annual return in excess of 10 percent, there has been considerable variation from year to year. The late 1990s produced exceptional returns in excess of 25 percent annually, but 2000-2002 produced one of the strongest reversals ever experienced by investors, and by the end of 2003, market indexes were considerably below their historic highs.

Averaging is one strategy designed to reduce the impact of security price fluctuations. You may make periodic purchases (dollar cost averaging) or buy additional shares after the price has declined (averaging down). Such strategies may reduce the average cost of the stock in the position and generate larger returns. But to earn the higher returns, the price of the stock must rise, and such price increases are not assured.

Learning Objectives

Now that you have completed this chapter, you should be able to:

1. Differentiate among a simple price-weighted average, a value-weighted average, an equal-weighted average, and a geometric average.
2. Contrast the Dow Jones average with other aggregate measures such as the S&P 500 stock index.
3. Explain the difference between the holding period and the annualized rate of return.
4. Compute the return on an investment.
5. Compare the risk and returns associated with alternative investments based on the Ibbotson Associated studies of returns.
6. Execute dollar cost averaging and averaging down strategies.

PROBLEMS

1) Given the following information concerning four stocks,

	Price	Number of Shares
Stock A	$10	100,000
Stock B	17	50,000
Stock C	13	150,000
Stock D	20	200,000

a) Construct a simple price-weighted average, a value-weighted average, and a geometric average.

b) What is the percentage increase in each average if the stocks' prices become:

1) A: $10, B: $17, C: $13, D: $40

2) A: $10, B: $34, C: $13, D: $20?

c) Why were the percentage changes different in (1) and (2)?

2) You are given the following information concerning four stocks:

Stock		A	B	C	D
Shares outstanding		1,000	300	2,000	400
Price	20X0	$50	30	20	60
	20X1	50	30	40	60
	20X2	50	60	20	60

a) Using 20X0 as the base year, construct three aggregate measures of the market that simulate the Dow Jones Industrial Average, the S&P 500 stock index, and the Value Line stock index (i.e., a simple average, a value-weighted average, and a geometric average).

b) What is the percentage change in each aggregate market measure from 20X0 to 20X1, and 20X0 to 20X2? Why are the results different even though only one stock's price changed and in each case the price that changed doubled?

c) If you were managing funds and wanted a source to compare your results, which market measure would you prefer to use in 20X2?

3) An investor buys a stock for $35 and sells it for $56.38 after five years.

a) What is the holding period return?

b) What is the true annual rate of return?

4) A stock costs $80 and pays a $4 dividend each year for three years.

a) If an investor buys the stock for $80 and sells it for $100 after three years, what is the annual rate of return?

b) What would be the annualized return if the purchase price were $60?

c) What would be the annualized return if the dividend were $1 annually and the purchase price were $80 and the sale price were $100?

5) You purchase a stock for $100 that pays an annual dividend of $5.50. At the beginning of the second year, you purchase an additional share for $130. At the end of the second year, you sell both shares for $140. Determine the dollar-weighted return and the time-weighted compounded (i.e., geometric) return on this investment. Repeat the process but assume that the second share was purchased for $110 instead of $130. Why do the rates of return differ?

6) You purchase shares in an investment company such as a mutual fund for $35 a share. The fund makes the following cash payments called "distributions":

Year	Distribution
1	$1.00
2	3.15
3	2.09
4	1.71

At the end of the fourth year, you sell the shares for $41. What was the dollar-weighted rate of return on your investment?

7) You invest $100 in a mutual fund that grows 10 percent annually for four years. Then the fund experiences an exceptionally bad year and declines by 60 percent. After the bad year, the fund resumes its 10 percent annual return for the next four years.

   a) What is the average percentage change for the nine years?

   b) If you liquidate the fund after nine years, how much do you receive?

   c) What is the annualized return on this investment using a dollar-weighted calculation and using a time-weighted calculation?

8) You read that stock A is trading for $50 and is down 50 percent for the year. Stock B is also trading for $50 but has risen 100 percent for the year. If the investor had purchased one share of each stock at the beginning of the year, what can you conclude has happened to the value of the portfolio?

9) You believe that QED stock may be a good investment and decide to buy 100 shares at $40. You subsequently buy an additional $4,000 worth of the stock every time the stock's price declines by an additional $5. If the stock's price declines to $28 and rebounds to $44, at which time you sell your holdings, what is your profit? (Assume that no fractional shares may be purchased.)

10) On January 31, 2001, you bought 100 shares of Avaya (AV) for $17.50 a share. Subsequent prices of AV were

January 1, 2002	$ 8.60
January 1, 2003	2.50
January 1, 2004	17.50

You owned the stock for three years (2001 through 2004). What were your (1) holding period return, (2) average percentage return, and (3) true return on this investment?

11) Determine the Dow Jones Industrial Average as of your date of birth and as of your most recent birthday. What was the annualized rate of return on the average between the two dates? Since this return does not include dividend income, it understates the return. Assume that you collected dividends of 2 percent and compare your return with the data for stock returns in Exhibit 4.2. (Information on the Dow Jones averages and indexes may be found at **http://www.djindexes.com**.)

Internet Application for Chapter 4 Investment Returns

Assume that three years ago you purchased each of the four stocks you are following.

What was your holding period return and three-year compounded return for each stock?

If you had bought an equal-dollar amount in each stock, did you earn a higher return over the last three years compared to a major measure of the market such as the S&P 500 (ticker symbol: ^GSPC) stock index? If you bought one share of each stock, what adjustment would you have to make when computing your aggregate return?

Did you include any dividend payments in the computation of the returns? If not, do you think the exclusion significantly understated your individual stock returns and the returns that you compared to the aggregate measure of the stock market? Explain your answers to these questions.

THOMSON ONE
Business School Edition

Currency with Thomson ONE: Business School Edition

Stock indexes give you a measure of where the market has been and where it may be going. Markets often move in trends, so that if an index is rising, that suggests that stocks will continue to increase. (The topic is developed in Chapter 8 on technical analysis.) Go to the Thomson ONE: Business School Edition database and obtain the pattern for the last six months for at least two stock indexes and determine the current trend in the index and whether the current level of the index is greater or less than the index average. Interpret the results and determine if each index is indicating the same direction for stock prices or if they are contradicting each other.

2 • • •

The Basic Investment Alternatives

Now that you know the basic background for making investment decisions, let's move forward to specific financial assets that you might include in your portfolio. These are the securities that the word *investments* generally implies: stocks, bonds, and mutual funds. (Nontraditional financial assets such as options and futures are considered in Part 3 on derivatives.)

Chapters 5 through 8 and 9 through 11 are devoted to stocks and bonds, respectively. I realize that you might not have considered bonds as an integral part of your portfolio, but that omission is a mistake. Bonds can generate a flow of interest income; you may speculate on their price changes, and, most importantly, they may be used to help diversify your portfolio. These securities deserve serious consideration by any investor.

The chapters devoted to stocks and bonds cover the features that differentiate each security, techniques for analyzing these assets, and the process of valuing them. Valuation is, of course, the crucial concept covered in Part 2, because it helps answer the question: Is the security under- or overvalued? The answer to this question determines whether you are a buyer or a seller.

After covering Chapter 5 through 11, you may decide that you do not have the inclination or the time to select individual securities. Part 2 then ends with two chapters devoted to investment companies: their features, the advantages they offer, their sources of return, and the risks associated with these investments. Chapter 12 is a basic introduction to investment companies, while Chapter 13 is devoted to specialized funds that offer alternatives to the traditional mutual fund. There are important advantages to delegating the decision to select individual stocks and bonds, but you should not conclude that these portfolio managers will generate superior returns for you. Investors have to pay fees and expenses to have their funds professionally managed, and these fees and expenses reduce your net return. As is stressed in several places in this text, financial markets are competitive and efficient. That implies that few investors, including professional portfolio managers and security analysts, will over time consistently outperform the market on a risk-adjusted basis.

CHAPTER

5 • • •

Corporate Stock

During 2003, Cornerstone Realty Income (TCR) paid a dividend of $0.80. At the year-end price of $9, that was a dividend yield of 8.9 percent. Berkshire Hathaway (BRKa) paid no dividend, but one share of its stock commanded a price of $84,250. Dominion Resources (D) paid $2.58, an amount that had not changed for over eight years, but Coca-Cola (KO) raised its dividend for the 41st consecutive year. Obviously dividends differ among various firms!

This chapter concerns stock, common stock and preferred stock. Corporations issue shares of stock, which represent ownership (equity) in the firm, and these shares subsequently trade in the secondary markets. Initially this chapter covers the features of common stock followed by the features of preferred stock. Two important differences between these two types of securities are the dividend and the priority of claims. Preferred stock pays a fixed dividend while common stock pays a variable dividend (if it pays a dividend at all). Preferred stock also has a prior claim on the firm's assets and earnings.

Dividends are important because they are a source (along with capital gains) of your return on an investment in stock. This chapter covers dividend policy, the process by which dividends are distributed, and dividend reinvestment plans. The chapter also includes stock dividends and stock splits; neither alters the firm's assets, liabilities, and equity, but both alter the number of shares outstanding.

Before acquiring stock, you should analyze the firm to determine if its securities are under- or overvalued. The coverage of several methods used for valuation is deferred to Chapter 7. This chapter, however, lays an important foundation and ends with a discussion of sources of corporate information, corporate filings with the SEC, and how these sources may be easily obtained. Of course, you will have to apply the information and do the analysis necessary to make an informed investment decision.

•••THE CORPORATE FORM OF BUSINESS AND THE RIGHTS OF COMMON STOCKHOLDERS

stock
A security representing ownership in a corporation.

certificate of incorporation
A document creating a corporation.

charter
A document specifying the relationship between a firm and the state in which it is incorporated.

bylaws
A document specifying the relationship between a corporation and its stockholders.

voting rights
The rights of stockholders to vote their shares.

director
A person who is elected by stockholders to determine the goals and policies of the firm.

A corporation is an artificial legal economic unit established (i.e., chartered) by a state. **Stock**, both common and preferred, represents ownership, or equity, in a corporation. Under state laws, the firm is issued a **certificate of incorporation** that indicates the name of the corporation, the location of its principal office, its purpose, and the number of shares of stock that are authorized (i.e., the number of shares that the firm may issue). In addition to a certificate of incorporation, the firm receives a **charter** that specifies the relationship between the corporation and the state. At the initial meeting of stockholders, **bylaws** are established that set the rules by which the firm is governed, including such issues as the **voting rights** of the stockholders.

In the eyes of the law, a corporation is a legal entity that is separate from its owners. It may enter into contracts and is legally responsible for its obligations. Creditors may sue the corporation for payment if it defaults on its obligations, but the creditors cannot sue the stockholders. Therefore, you know that if you purchase stock in a publicly held corporation such as General Motors, the maximum that can be lost is the amount of the investment.[1] Occasionally, a large corporation (e.g., Enron) does go bankrupt, but owing to limited liability, its stockholders cannot be sued by its creditors.

Because stock represents ownership in a corporation, investors who purchase shares obtain all the rights of ownership. These rights include the option to vote the shares. The stockholders elect a board of **directors** that selects the firm's management. Management is then responsible to the board of directors, which in turn is responsible to the firm's stockholders. If the stockholders do not think that the board is doing a competent job, they may elect another board to represent them.

For publicly held corporations, such democracy rarely works. Stockholders are usually widely dispersed, while the firm's management and board of directors generally form a cohesive unit. Rarely does the individual investor's vote mean much.[2] However, there is always the possibility that if the firm does poorly, another firm may offer to buy the outstanding stock held by the public. Once such purchases are made, the stock's new owners may remove the board of directors and establish new management. To some extent this encourages a corporation's board of directors and management to pursue the goal of increasing the value of the firm's stock.

A stockholder generally has one vote for each share owned, but there are two ways to distribute this vote. With the traditional method of voting, each share gives the stockholder the right to vote for one individual for *each* seat on the board of directors. Under this system, if a majority group voted as a block, a minority group could never elect a representative. The alternative system, **cumulative voting**, gives minority stockholders a means to obtain representation on the firm's

cumulative voting
A voting scheme that encourages minority representation by permitting each stockholder to cast all of his or her votes for one candidate for the firm's board of directors.

---

1. Stockholders in privately held corporations who pledge their personal assets to secure loans do not have limited liability. If the corporation defaults, the creditors may seize the assets that the stockholders have pledged. In this event, the liability of the shareholders is not limited to their investment in the firm.
2. Exceptions do occur. In 1994, Kmart stockholders defeated a proposal to create separate classes of stock representing minority positions in four specialty units. One of the biggest occurred when Penn Central stockholders voted down a merger with Colt Industries. Management supported the merger but lost the vote: 10,245,440 shares against versus 10,104,220 shares in favor. For evidence of the impact of proxy fights on stockholder returns, see Lisa F. Borstadt and Thomas J. Swirlein, "The Efficient Monitoring Role of Proxy Contests: An Empirical Analysis of Post-Contest Control Changes and Firm Performance," *Financial Management* (autumn 1992): 22–34.

board. While cumulative voting is voluntary in most states, it is mandatory in several, including California, Illinois, and Michigan.

How cumulative voting works is best explained by a brief example. Suppose a firm has a board of directors composed of five members. With traditional voting, a stockholder with 100 shares may vote 100 votes for a candidate for each seat. The total 500 votes are split among the seats. Under cumulative voting, the individual may cast the entire 500 votes for a candidate for one seat. Of course, then the stockholder cannot vote for anyone running for the remaining four seats.

A minority group of stockholders can use the cumulative method of voting to elect a representative to the firm's board of directors. By banding together and casting all their votes for a specific candidate, the minority may be able to win a seat. Although this technique cannot be used to win a majority, it does offer the opportunity for representation that is not possible through the traditional method of distributing votes (i.e., one vote for each elected position). As would be expected, management rarely supports the cumulative voting system.

Since stockholders are owners, they are entitled to the firm's earnings. These earnings may be distributed in the form of cash dividends, or they may be retained by the corporation. If they are retained, your investment in the firm is increased (i.e., the stockholder's equity increases). However, for every class of stock, the individual investor's relative position is not altered. Some owners of common stock cannot receive cash dividends, whereas others have their earnings reinvested. The distribution or retention of earnings applies equally to all stockholders.[3]

Although limited liability is one of the advantages of investing in publicly held corporations, stock ownership does involve risk. As long as the firm prospers, it may be able to pay dividends and grow. However, if earnings fluctuate, dividends and growth may also fluctuate. It is the owners—the stockholders—who bear the business risk associated with these fluctuations. If the firm should default on its debt, it can be taken to court by its creditors to enforce its obligations. If the firm should fail or become bankrupt, the stockholders have the last claim on its assets. Only after all the creditors have been paid will the stockholders receive any funds. In many cases of bankruptcy, this amounts to nothing. Even if the corporation survives bankruptcy proceedings, the amount received by the stockholders is uncertain.

Preemptive Rights

preemptive rights
The right of current stockholders to maintain their proportionate ownership in the firm.

rights offering
Sale of new securities to stockholders.

Some stockholders have **preemptive rights**, which is their prerogative to maintain their proportionate ownership in the firm. If the firm wants to sell additional shares to the general public, these new shares must be offered initially to the existing stockholders in a sale called a **rights offering**. If the stockholders wish to maintain their proportionate ownership in the firm, they can exercise their rights by purchasing the new shares. However, if they do not want to take advantage of this offering, they may sell their privilege to whoever wants to purchase the new shares.

Preemptive rights may be illustrated by a simple example. If a firm has 1,000 shares outstanding and you own 100 shares, you own 10 percent of the firm's stock. If the firm wants to sell 400 new shares and the stockholders have preemptive rights, these new shares must be offered to the existing stockholders before they are sold to the general public. You would have the right to purchase 40, or 10 percent, of the

3. Some corporations have different classes of stock. For example, Food Lion, Inc., has two classes of common stock, both of which are publicly traded. The class A stock does not have voting power while the class B does. However, if management chooses to pay dividends to the class B stock, it must pay a larger dividend to the class A stock.

new shares. If you make the purchase, then your relative position is maintained, for you own 10 percent of the firm both before and after the sale of the new stock.

Although preemptive rights are required in some states for incorporation, their importance has diminished and the number of rights offerings has declined. Some firms have changed their bylaws in order to eliminate preemptive rights. For example, AT&T asked its stockholders to relinquish these rights. The rationale for this request was that issuing new shares through rights offerings was more expensive than selling the shares to the general public through an underwriting. Investors who desired to maintain their relative position could purchase the new shares, and all stockholders would benefit through the cost savings and the flexibility given to the firm's management. Most stockholders accepted management's request and voted to relinquish their preemptive rights. Now AT&T does not have to offer any new shares to its current stockholders before it offers them publicly.

PREFERRED STOCK

Firms may issue both preferred and common stock. (Some firms even have issued a preference stock, which is subordinated to preferred stock but has preference over common stock. Such stock is another level of preferred stock, and in this text no distinction is made between the two.) As the name implies, **preferred stock** holds a position superior to common stock. For example, preferred stockholders receive dividend payments before common stockholders and, in case of liquidation, are compensated before common stockholders. However, preferred stock lacks some of the features associated with common stock, such as the right to vote the shares. In addition, preferred stock dividends are usually fixed and cannot grow if the firm prospers and its earnings grow. This difference between the dividends of preferred stock and common stock is exceedingly important, as it affects how the two securities are analyzed and valued. For this reason the valuation of preferred stock is covered with the valuation of fixed income securities (i.e., bonds) in Chapter 11.

While most firms have only one issue of common stock, they may have several issues of preferred stock. As may be seen in Exhibit 5.1, Virginia Electric and Power (a division of Dominion Resources) has eight issues of preferred stock. In 7 cases the dividend is fixed. Thus, for the series $5.00 preferred, the annual dividend is $5.00, which is distributed at the rate of $1.25 per quarter.

The dividend is expressed either as a dollar amount or as a percentage based on the preferred stock's par value. The par value is the stated value of the shares and is also the price at which the shares were initially sold. In the case of the Virginia Electric $5.00 preferred, the par value is $100, so the dividend rate is 5.0 percent based on the par value.

Preferred stock dividends are paid from the firm's earnings. If the firm does not have the earnings, it may not declare and pay the preferred stock dividends. If the firm should omit the preferred stock's dividend, the dividend is said to be *in arrears*. The firm does not have to remove this **arrearage**. In most cases, however, any omitted dividends have to be paid in the future before dividends may be paid to the holders of the common stock. Such cases in which the preferred stock's dividends accumulate are called **cumulative preferred**. Most preferred stock is cumulative, but there are examples of **noncumulative preferred stocks** whose dividends do not have to be made up if missed. For investors holding preferred stock in firms experiencing financial difficulty, forcing the firm to pay dividends to erase the arrearage may further weaken it. Once the firm has regained its profitability, eras-

preferred stock
A class of stock (i.e., equity) that has a prior claim to common stock on the firm's earnings and assets in case of liquidation.

arrearage
Cumulative preferred dividends that have not been paid.

cumulative preferred stock
A preferred stock whose dividends accumulate if they are not paid.

noncumulative preferred stock
Preferred stock whose dividends do not accumulate if the firm misses a dividend payment.

| EXHIBIT 5.1 | The Preferred Stocks of Virginia Electric and Power |

Preferred Stock Not Subject to Mandatory Retirement	
Annual Dividend per Share	**Outstanding Shares**
$4.04	12,926
4.20	14,797
4.12	32,534
4.80	73,206
5.00	106,677
7.05	500,000
6.98	600,000
Money market preferred (with a variable rate after 12/20/07)	1,250,000

Source: 2003 Dominion Resources *Annual Report.*

ing the arrearage may become important not only to holders of the stock but also to the company, as a demonstration of its improved financial condition.

Once the preferred stock is issued, management may never have to concern itself with retiring the stock. It is perpetual. This is both an advantage and a disadvantage. If the firm does not have to use funds to retire the stock, the funds may be employed elsewhere, such as the purchase of plant and equipment. However, if management were to want to change the firm's capital structure, it might have difficulty retiring the preferred stock. If the preferred stock has to be repurchased, the price may have to be bid up to induce holders to sell the shares. The firm may avoid this problem by making the preferred stock callable. For example, the Virginia Electric and Power variable rate preferred stock in Exhibit 5.1 is callable and may be retired by the company under certain conditions. (Call features are common with bonds and are discussed in more detail in Chapters 9 and 11.)

COMMON STOCK CASH DIVIDENDS

dividend
A payment to stockholders that is usually in cash but may be in stock or property.

regular dividends
Steady dividend payments that are distributed at regular intervals.

extra dividend
A sum paid in addition to the firm's regular dividend.

Corporations may pay their stockholders dividends, which can be in the form of cash or additional shares. A **dividend** is a distribution from earnings. Companies that pay cash dividends often have a dividend policy that is known to the investment community. Even if the policy is not explicitly stated by management, the continuation of such practices as paying quarterly dividends implies a specific policy.

While most American companies that distribute cash dividends pay a **regular dividend** on a quarterly basis, there are other types of dividend policies. For example, some companies pay a quarterly dividend plus an additional or **extra dividend**. In September 2003, SBC Communications declared its regular quarterly dividend plus an extra dividend because the company had strong cash flows. Such a policy is appropriate for a firm with fluctuating cash flows. Management may not want to increase the dividend and then have difficulty maintaining the higher dividend. By having a set cash payment that is supplemented with extras in good years, management is able to maintain a fixed payment that is relatively assured and supplement the cash dividend when the extra is warranted by earnings and cash flow.

Other firms pay cash dividends that are **irregular**: There is no set dividend payment. For example, real estate investment trusts (frequently referred to as

irregular dividends
Dividend payments that either do not occur in regular intervals or vary in amount.

payout ratio
The ratio of dividends to earnings.

retention ratio
The ratio of earnings not distributed to earnings.

REITs and discussed in Chapter 13) are required by law to distribute their earnings to maintain their favorable tax status. These trusts are, in effect, closed-end investment companies and pay no corporate income tax; instead, their earnings are distributed and the stockholders pay the tax. To ensure this favorable tax treatment, REITs must distribute at least 90 percent of their earnings. Since the earnings of such trusts fluctuate, the cash dividends also fluctuate. The special tax laws pertaining to REITs cause them to have irregular dividend payments.

Since management seeks to maximize the wealth of the stockholders, the dividend decision should depend on who has the better use for the funds, the stockholders or the firm. If management can earn a higher return on the funds, then retaining and reinvesting the earnings is the logical choice. Management, however, probably does not know the stockholders' alternative uses for the funds and thus pursues a policy that it believes is in the stockholders' best interest. Stockholders who do not like the dividend policy may sell their shares. If sellers exceed buyers, the price will fall, and management will be made aware of the investors' attitude toward the dividend policy.

Management may view dividend policy as the distribution of a certain proportion of the firm's earnings. This policy may be expressed in terms of a **payout ratio**, which is the proportion of the earnings that the firm distributes. Conversely, the **retention ratio** is the proportion of the earnings that are not paid out and are retained. For example, Hershey Foods earned $2.93 in 2002 and paid cash dividends of $1.26. The payout ratio is 43.0 percent ($1.26/$2.93), and the retention ratio is $1.67/$2.93 = 57.0 percent. (The retention ratio is also equal to 1 – payout ratio, which is 1 – 0.43 = 57.0 percent for Hershey Foods.)

For some firms, the payout ratio has remained relatively stable over time. Such consistency suggests that management views the dividend policy in terms of distributing a certain proportion of the firm's earnings to stockholders. The obvious implication is that higher earnings will lead to higher dividends as management seeks to maintain the payout ratio.[4]

Management, however, rarely increases the cash dividend immediately when earnings increase because it wants to be certain that the higher level of earnings will be maintained. The managements of many publicly held corporations are reluctant to reduce the dividend because the decrease may be interpreted as a sign of financial weakness. In addition, a decrease in earnings may not imply that the firm's capacity to pay the dividend has diminished. For example, an increase in noncash expenses, such as depreciation, reduces earnings but not cash, and the same applies to a write-down of the book value of an asset. In both cases, the firm's capacity to pay the dividend is not affected, because the expense does not affect cash. Management then maintains the dividend payment to signal that the firm's financial condition has not deteriorated.[5]

This pattern is illustrated in Figure 5.1, which presents the quarterly per-share earnings (after extraordinary gains and losses) and the cash dividend for Hershey Foods for 1998–2003. As may be seen in the figure, earnings fluctuate more than the cash dividend. The declines in earnings experienced during the first two quarters of each year do not lead to dividend cuts. The increases in earnings during the

---

4. SCANA's management stated in the company's *2001 First Quarter Interim Report* that the "goal is to increase the common stock dividend at a rate that reflects the growth in our principal businesses, while maintaining a payout ratio of 50–55 percent of earnings."

5. A survey of corporate managers suggests that management (1) is concerned with dividend continuity, (2) believes dividends help maintain or increase stock prices, and (3) believes dividend payments indicate the future prospects of the firm. These results are reported in H. Kent Baker, Gail E. Farrelly, and Richard B. Edelman, "A Survey of Management Views on Dividends Policy," *Financial Management* (autumn 1985): 78–84.

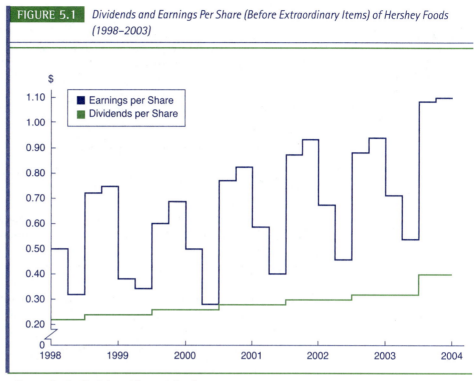

FIGURE 5.1   *Dividends and Earnings Per Share (Before Extraordinary Items) of Hershey Foods (1998–2003)*

Source: *Hershey Foods Annual Report*, various issues.

last two quarters do not lead to dividend increments. Instead, the pattern of rising earnings during the six years is associated with the steady annual increments in the cash dividend.

While U.S. firms tend to follow a policy of quarterly dividend distributions, firms in other countries may not. Many foreign firms often make only two payments. The first payment may be called a "preliminary" dividend and the second (made at the end of the firm's fiscal year) may be called a "final" dividend. For example, SONY paid $0.054 in March 2002 and then distributed almost twice as much ($0.105) in September 2002.

Even if the cash payments from foreign firms occur at regular intervals, the dollar amount tends to vary. This variation is the result of fluctuation in the dollar value of each currency. If the value of the dollar falls relative to the euro, for example, any dividends that are distributed in euros translate into more dollars when the euros are converted. The converse is also true. If the dollar value of the euro should fall, the dividend buys fewer dollars when the currency is converted. Americans who want predictable flows of dividends are usually advised to purchase American stocks and avoid foreign securities.

The Distribution of Dividends

The process by which dividends are distributed occurs over time. First, the firm's directors meet. When they declare a dividend, two important dates are established. The first date determines who is to receive the dividend. On the **date of record**, the ownership books of the corporation are closed, and everyone who owns stock in the company at the end of that day receives the dividend.

date of record
The day on which an investor must own shares in order to receive the dividend payment.

If the stock is purchased after the date of record, you do not receive the dividend. The stock is traded **ex-dividend**, for the price of the stock does not include the dividend payment. This **ex-dividend date** is two trading days prior to the date of record, because the settlement date for a stock purchase is three working days after the transaction.

This process is illustrated by the following time line:

Declaration date	Ex div date	Date of record	Distribution date
(January 2)	(January 30)	(February 1)	(March 1)

On January 2, the board of directors declares a dividend to be paid March 1 to all stockholders of record February 1. To receive the dividend, you must own the stock at the close of trading on February 1. To own the stock on February 1, the stock must have been purchased on or before January 29. If the stock is bought January 29, settlement will occur after three days on February 1 (assuming three workdays), so the investor owns the stock on February 1. If you buy the stock on January 30, you do not own the stock on February 1 (the seller owns the stock) and you cannot be the owner of record on February 1. On January 30, the stock trades exclusive of the dividend (ex-dividend or "ex-div"), and the buyer does not receive the dividend.

In the financial press, transactions in the stock on the ex-dividend date are indicated by an x for "ex-div." The following entry indicates the stock of Reynolds and Reynolds traded exclusive of the dividend.

	DIV	%	PE	100s	LAST	NET CHG
Reyn&Reyn REY x	.44	2.0	17	1453	22.50	+0.31

The $0.11 (i.e., $0.44 ÷ 4) quarterly dividend will be paid to whoever bought the stock on the previous day and will not be paid to investors who purchased the stock on the ex-dividend date.

You should realize that buying or selling stock on the ex-dividend date may not result in a windfall gain or a substantial loss. If a stock that pays a $1.00 dividend is worth $100 on the day before it goes ex-dividend, it cannot be worth $100 on the ex-dividend date. If it were worth $100 on both days, investors would purchase the stock for $100 the day before the ex-dividend date, sell it for $100 on the ex-dividend date, and collect the $1 dividend. If investors could do this, the price would exceed $100 on the day preceding the ex-dividend date and would be less than $100 on the ex-dividend date. In effect, this price pattern does occur because this stock would sell for $100 and then be worth $100 minus $1 on the ex-dividend date.

This price change is illustrated in the previous example. There was an increase in the price of Reynolds and Reynolds stock for the ex-dividend date. This indicates that the closing price on the previous day was $22.30 and not $22.19 (22.50 – 0.31), as might be expected. Since the current buyers will not receive the dividend, the net change in the price of the stock is reduced for the dividend. The net change is figured from the adjusted price (i.e., $22.30 minus the $0.11 dividend). If the stock had closed at 23.00, the net change would have been +0.81, and if it had closed at 22.00, the net change would have been –0.19.

The second important date established when a dividend is declared is the day on which the dividend is paid, or the **distribution date**. The distribution date may be several weeks after the date of record, as the company must determine who the owners were as of the date of record and process the dividend checks. The company may not perform this task itself; instead, it may use the services of its commercial bank, for which the bank charges a fee. The day that the dividend is received by the stockholder is thus likely to be many weeks after the board of directors announces the dividend payment. For example, the distribution date for a Black & Decker dividend that was declared on July 17 was September 25, which was almost two weeks after the date of record, September 14.

Many firms try to maintain consistency in their dividend payment dates. Textron makes payments on the first business days of January, April, July, and October. Public Service Enterprise Group pays its dividends on the last days of March, June, September, and December. Such consistency in payments is beneficial to investors and the firm, as both can plan for this receipt and disbursement.

••STOCK DIVIDENDS

stock dividend
A dividend paid in stock.

recapitalization
An alteration in a firm's sources of finance, such as the substitution of long-term debt for equity.

Some firms make a practice of paying stock dividends in addition to or in lieu of cash dividends. **Stock dividends** are a form of **recapitalization** and do *not* affect the assets or liabilities of the firm. Since the assets and their management produce income for the firm, a stock dividend does not by itself increase the potential earning power of the company. Some investors, however, may believe that stock dividends will enhance the earning capacity of the firm and consequently the value of the stock. They mistakenly believe that the stock dividend increases the firm's assets.

The following balance sheet demonstrates the transactions that occur when a firm issues a stock dividend:

Assets		Liabilities and Equity	
Total assets	$10,000,000	Total liabilities	$2,500,000
		Equity: $2 par common stock	2,000,000
		(2,000,000 shares authorized;	
		1,000,000 outstanding)	
		Additional paid-in capital	500,000
		Retained earnings	5,000,000

Since a stock dividend is only a recapitalization, the assets and the liabilities are not affected by the declaration and payment of the stock dividend. However, the entries in the equity section of the balance sheet are affected. The stock dividend transfers amounts from retained earnings to common stock and additional paid-in capital. The amount transferred depends on (1) the number of new shares issued through the stock dividend and (2) the market price of the stock.

If the company in the preceding example issued a 10 percent stock dividend when the price of the common stock was $20 per share, 100,000 shares would be issued with a market value of $2,000,000. This amount is subtracted from retained earnings and transferred to common stock and additional paid-in capital. The amount transferred to common stock will be 100,000 times the par value of the stock ($2 × 100,000 = $200,000). The remaining amount ($1,800,000) is transferred to additional paid-in capital. The balance sheet then becomes:

Assets		Liabilities and Equity	
Total assets	$10,000,000	Total liabilities	$2,500,000
		Equity: $2 par common stock	2,200,000
		(2,000,000 shares authorized;	
		1,100,000 outstanding)	
		Additional paid-in capital	2,300,000
		Retained earnings	3,000,000

You should note that no funds (i.e., money) have been transferred. While there has been an increase in the number of shares outstanding, there has been no increase in cash and no increase in assets that may be used to earn profits. All that has happened is a recapitalization: The equity entries have been altered.

The major misconception concerning the stock dividend is that it increases the ability of the firm to grow. If the stock dividend is a substitute for a cash dividend, then this belief may be partially true, because the firm retains the cash that would have been paid to stockholders if a cash dividend had been declared. However, the firm will still have the cash even if it does not pay the stock dividend. Hence, the decision to pay the stock dividend does not increase the amount of cash; it is the decision *not to pay* the cash dividend that conserves the money. When a stock dividend is paid in lieu of cash, it may even be interpreted as a screen: The stock dividend is hiding management's reluctance to pay cash dividends.

Although the stock dividend does not increase the wealth of the stockholder, it does increase the number of shares owned. In the previous example, a stockholder who owned 100 shares before the stock dividend had $2,000 worth of stock. After the stock dividend is distributed, this stockholder owns 110 shares that are also worth $2,000, for the price of the stock falls from $20 to $18.18. The price of the stock declines because there are 10 percent more shares outstanding, but there has been no increase in the firm's assets and earning power. The old shares have been diluted, and hence the price of the stock must decline to indicate this **dilution**.

If the price of the stock did not fall to adjust for the stock dividend, all companies could make their stockholders wealthier by declaring stock dividends. However, because the stock dividend does not increase the assets or earning power of the firm, investors are not willing to pay the former price for a larger number of shares; hence, the market price must fall to adjust for the dilution of the old shares.

> **dilution**
> *A reduction in earnings per share due to the issuing of new securities.*

THE STOCK SPLIT

After the price of a stock has risen substantially, management may decide to split the stock. The rationale for the **stock split** is that it lowers the price of the stock and makes it more accessible to investors. For example, when Finova split its stock 2 for 1, management stated in the *Annual Report* that "the split would help broaden our investor base." The management of MindSpring went even further in a 1999 press release announcing a 2-for-1 split: "This action will help widen the distribution and enhance the marketability of MindSpring's common stock, and bring the price per share . . . into a range which should generate increased interest from current and new shareholders." Implicit in this reasoning are the beliefs that investors prefer lower-priced shares and that reducing the price of the stock benefits the current stockholders by widening the market for their stock.

Like the stock dividend, the stock split is a recapitalization. It does not affect the assets or liabilities of the firm, nor does it increase its earning power. The wealth of the stockholder is increased only if investors prefer lower-priced stocks, which will increase the demand for this stock.

The balance sheet used previously for illustrating the stock dividend may also be used to illustrate a 2-for-1 stock split. In a 2-for-1 stock split, one old share becomes two new shares, and the par value of the old stock is halved. There are no

> **stock split**
> *Recapitalization that affects the number of shares outstanding, their par value, the earnings per share, and the price of the stock.*

changes in the additional paid-in capital or retained earnings. The new balance sheet becomes:

Assets		Liabilities and Equity	
Total assets	$10,000,000	Total liabilities	$2,500,000
		Equity: $1 par common stock	2,000,000
		(2,000,000 shares authorized;	
		2,000,000 outstanding)	
		Additional paid-in capital	500,000
		Retained earnings	5,000,000

There are now twice as many shares outstanding, and each new share is worth half as much as one old share. If the stock had sold for $80 before the split, each share becomes worth $40. The stockholder with 100 old shares worth $8,000 now owns 200 shares worth $8,000 (i.e., $40 × 200).

An easy way to find the price of the stock after the split is to multiply the stock's price before the split by the reciprocal of the terms of the split. For example, if a stock is selling for $54 per share and is split 3 for 2, then the price of the stock after the split will be $54 × ⅔ = $36. Such price adjustments must occur because the old shares are diluted and the earning capacity of the firm is not increased.

Stock splits may use any combination of terms. Exhibit 5.2 illustrates the terms of several stock splits in 2003. Although 2-for-1 splits are the most common, there can be unusual terms, such as the 5-for-4 split of Baldwin & Lyons. There is no obvious explanation for such terms except that management wanted to reduce the stock's price to a particular level and selected the terms that would achieve the desired price.

There are also reverse splits, such as the Ascential Software 1-for-4 split. A reverse split reduces the number of shares and raises the price of the stock. The purpose of such a split is to add respectability to the stock (i.e., to raise the price above the level of the "cats and dogs"). Since some investors will not buy low-priced stock and since commissions on such purchases are often higher (at least for full-service brokers), it may be in the best interest of all stockholders to raise the stock's price through a reverse split. (As you might expect, reverse splits were

EXHIBIT 5.2   Selected Stock Splits Distributed in 2003

Rent-A-Center	5 for 2
Arrow International	2 for 1
Metrologic Instruments	2 for 1
Oshkosh Truck	2 for 1
Southwest Bancorp(OK)	2 for 1
Barr Laboratories	3 for 2
Hibbett Sporting Goods	3 for 2
Lannett	3 for 2
Baldwin & Lyons	5 for 4
Ascential Software	1 for 4

common during 2003 after the severe price declines experienced in the 2000–2002 bear market.)

Stock splits, like stock dividends, do not increase the assets or earning capacity of the firm. The split does decrease the price of the stock and thereby may increase its marketability. Thus, the split stock may be more widely distributed, which increases investor interest in the company. This wider distribution may increase the wealth of the current stockholders over time.

Academic studies, however, are inconclusive as to whether stock splits or stock dividends increase the value of stock.[6] These studies generally show that other factors, such as increased earnings, increased cash dividends, or a rise in the general market, result in higher prices for individual stocks. In fact, stock splits generally occur after the price of the stock has risen. Instead of being a harbinger of good news, they mirror an increase in the firm's earnings and growth.

THE TAXATION OF STOCK DIVIDENDS AND STOCK SPLITS

The federal government taxes cash dividends. Does it also tax shares received in stock dividends and stock splits? The answer is No. There is no taxation of stock dividends and stock splits unless the investor sells the shares.

If you bought 100 shares for $5,000 ($50 a share) and the firm pays a 10 percent stock dividend, your 100 shares become 110 shares. The total cost remains $5,000 and the cost basis per share is $45.45 ($5,000/110). As long as you do not sell the shares, there is no taxable transaction. If you sell the entire 110 shares, the cost basis is $5,000. If, however, you sell only part of the 110 shares, your cost basis is figured using the adjusted $45.45 cost per share. If you sell 50 shares, the cost basis is $2,272.50.

If the firm splits the stock, your cost basis is also adjusted for the split. If you own 100 shares that cost $5,000 ($50 a share) and the stock is split 2 for 1, you now have 200 shares that cost $5,000. The cost basis is adjusted to $25 a share. If you sell 100 shares for $40 a share, your capital gain is $1,500 ($4,000 – $2,500) and is taxed at the appropriate capital gains tax rate. If you sell 50 shares for $10 share, your capital loss is $750 ($500 – $1,250). That loss may then be used to offset capital gains from other transactions.

DIVIDEND REINVESTMENT PLANS

dividend reinvestment plan (DRIP)
A plan that permits stockholders to have cash dividends reinvested in stock instead of received in cash.

Many corporations that pay cash dividends also have **dividend reinvestment plans (DRIPs)** in which the cash dividends are used to purchase additional shares of stock. Dividend reinvestment programs started in the 1960s, but the expansion

---

6. See, for instance, Michael T. Maloney and J. Harold Mulherin, "The Effect of Splitting on the Ex: A Microstructure Reconciliation," *Financial Management* (winter 1992): 44–59. This article has over 50 references on the impact of stock splits. Evidence that stock splits may increase investors' wealth is provided in David L. Ikenberry, Graeme Rankine, and Earl K. Stice, "What Do Stock Splits Really Signal," *Journal of Financial and Quantitative Analysis* (September 1996): 357–375. For an extensive review of the literature on stock splits and stock dividends, refer to H. Kent Baker, Aaron L. Philips, and Gary E. Powell, "The Stock Distribution Puzzle: A Synthesis of the Literature on Stock Splits and Stock Dividends," *Financial Practice and Education* (spring/summer 1995): 24–37.

of the programs occurred in the early 1970s, so that currently more than 2,000 companies offer some version of the dividend reinvestment plan.[7]

Types of Dividend Reinvestment Plans

There are two general types of dividend reinvestment programs. In most plans a bank acts on behalf of the corporation and its stockholders. The bank collects the cash dividends for the stockholders and in some plans offers the stockholders the option of making additional cash contributions. The bank pools all the funds and purchases the stock on the open market (i.e., in the secondary market). Since the bank is able to purchase a larger block of shares, it receives a reduction in the per-share commission cost of the purchase. This reduced brokerage fee applies to all the shares purchased by the bank. Thus, all investors, ranging from the smallest to the largest, receive this advantage. The bank does charge a fee for its service, but this fee is usually modest, does not offset the savings in brokerage fees, and in some cases is paid for by the firm.

In the second type of reinvestment plan, the company issues new shares of stock for the cash dividend, and the money is directly rechanneled to the company. The investor may also have the option of making additional cash contributions. This type of plan offers the investor an additional advantage in that the brokerage fees are completely circumvented. The entire amount of the cash dividend is used to purchase shares, with the cost of issuing the new shares being paid by the company.

Some brokerage firms also offer dividend reinvestment plans. For example, Charles Schwab will reinvest dividends for stock registered in street name. Referred to as the *StockBuilder Plan*, Schwab purchases the shares for the investor and charges a small fee for the service. Schwab benefits by any profits on the spread between the bid and ask prices on securities bought and sold and by inducing individuals to invest through Schwab instead of competing brokerage firms.

Advantages of Dividend Reinvestment Plans

Dividend reinvestment plans offer advantages to both firms and investors. For stockholders, the advantages include the purchase of shares at a reduction in commissions. Even reinvestment plans in which the fees are paid by the stockholder offer this savings. Both types of plans are particularly attractive to the small investor, for few brokerage firms are willing to buy $100 worth of stock, and substantial commissions are charged on such small transactions.

Perhaps the most important advantage to investors is the fact that the plans are automatic. The investor does not receive the dividends, for the proceeds are automatically reinvested. For any investor who lacks the discipline to save, such forced saving may be a means to systematically accumulate shares. For the firm,

7. Mergent's annual *Dividend Record* lists the firms traded on the NYSE and AMEX that offer dividend reinvestment plans. The American Association of Individual Investors annually publishes similar information and includes phone numbers, minimum-maximum optional cash purchases, fees, and discounts (if available). There is even an investment advisory service, the DRIP Investor (http://www.dripinvestor.com), which provides timely information on the plans. Information concerning dividend reinvestment plans is readily available on the Internet from DRIP Central (http://www.dripcentral.com) and Netstock Direct (http://www.netstockdirect.com). Netstock Direct not only provides detailed plan summaries but its software also allows companies to publish their plans. Links to the firms provide investors with immediate access to each firm's dividend reinvestment or direct purchase stock plan.

the primary advantages are the goodwill that is achieved by providing another service for its stockholders. The plans that involve the issue of new shares also raise new equity capital. This automatic flow of new equity reduces the need for the sale of shares through underwriters.

The Internal Revenue Service considers dividends that are reinvested to be no different from cash dividends that are received. Such dividends are subject to federal income taxation. The exclusion from federal income taxation of dividend income that is reinvested has been considered as one possible change in the tax code, but as of 2004 the change had not been enacted.

REPURCHASES OF STOCK

stock repurchase
The buying of stock by the issuing corporation.

A firm with excess cash may choose to repurchase some of its outstanding shares of stock or to liquidate the corporation. This section briefly covers **stock repurchases**. A repurchase is in effect a partial liquidation, as it decreases the number of shares outstanding. This reduction should increase the earnings per share because the earnings are spread over fewer shares.

While the repurchase of shares is a partial liquidation, it may also be viewed as an alternative to the payment of cash dividends. Instead of distributing the money as cash dividends, the firm offers to purchase shares from stockholders. If the stockholders believe that the firm's potential is sufficient to warrant the retention of the shares, they do not have to sell them. If the shares are sold back to the company, any resulting profits will be taxed as capital gains.

There are several reasons why management may choose to repurchase stock. Management may need to use the shares for another purpose, such as exercising stock options that have been granted to employees.[8] Management may want to alter the capital structure of the firm and use less equity financing relative to debt financing. The total equity of the firm is reduced by the repurchase, so that the return on the firm's equity may be increased. Since repurchases reduce the number of outstanding shares, the firm's earnings per share should be increased. These increases in the return on equity and the earnings per share could lead to a higher stock price.

Management may also repurchase shares to reduce the chance of an unwanted takeover attempt. If management believes the firm has generated excess cash and may become a takeover candidate, then repurchasing the shares can serve two purposes: (1) It increases earnings per share and possibly increases the stock's price, and (2) it decreases the probability of an unsolicited attempted takeover. (The repurchase will also increase management's proportionate ownership and strengthen its control over the firm, assuming that management does not participate in the repurchase.)

The potential impact of repurchasing shares may be seen when Teledyne bought 8.7 million shares at $200 for a total outlay of $1.74 billion. Teledyne initially offered to repurchase 5 million shares. At that time the stock was selling for $156, so the offer represented a 28 percent premium over the current price. The large premium induced more than 5 million shares to be tendered. While Teledyne

---

8. Repurchased shares are usually held in the firm's "treasury" for future use. While the cost of the repurchased shares reduces the firm's equity, the shares are not retired but held by the company. If the shares were retired and management subsequently wanted to issue the stock to employees or the general public, the shares would have to be reregistered with the SEC in order for them to be publicly traded.

could have prorated its purchases, it chose to accept all the shares. The repurchase reduced the number of shares outstanding from 20 million to 11.3 million and raised per-share earnings by more than $7. After the repurchase the price of the stock did not decline back to $156 but continued to grow and *sold for more than $240 a share within a few weeks*. Such behavior by investors suggests that the repurchase served the best interests of the remaining stockholders.

SOURCES OF CORPORATE INFORMATION

Publicly held firms are required by both federal and state laws, including the full-disclosure laws, to publish annual and quarterly reports. Furthermore, the SEC requires publicly held firms to publish news bulletins detailing any pertinent changes that may affect the value of their securities. These news releases will cover such items as announcements of major new products, merger activity, dividend payments, new financing or refinancing of existing debt, stock repurchases, and management changes.

Although publicly held corporations do send stockholders information, the Internet has become an important, perhaps even favored, means for these companies to communicate with stockholders and the general public. Publicly held American firms have Web pages that are readily accessed. Because the information that firms are required to disseminate is available through the Internet, many firms have stopped sending to stockholders material other than the annual report.

The easiest way to obtain information from the corporation may be to use the firm's Web address. For example, suppose you want information from Hershey Foods. Go to **http://www.hersheys.com**. (If you do not know the Web address, do a search on Google using the company's name.) Because Hershey Foods is a consumer products company, a substantial proportion of the available material concerns its products, but there is also a section on investor relations, which includes:

1. Investors' overview
2. Analyst coverage
3. Annual reports
4. Corporate governance
5. Dividend history
6. Earnings estimates
7. Financial releases
8. Fundamentals
9. SEC filings
10. Stock purchase plans

The Annual Report

One of the most important publication is the firm's annual report. This report covers a wide variety of topics and generally includes a corporate overview and descriptions of the firm's business, audited financial statements, management's discussions of the firm's operations and financial condition, and a letter from the corporation's president or chief executive officer or both.

Although the annual report includes a substantial amount of factual and financial information, it should be viewed as a public relations document. It is frequently printed on expensive paper and filled with colorful pictures of products and of smiling employees. There are exceptions. For example, Verizon's 2002 annual report contains no pictures, and is printed on recycled paper to demonstrate the company's "commitment to protecting the environment." Prior to 1991, the company published the colorful, public relations type of annual report favored by most firms.

The typical annual report begins with a letter from the president of the company to the stockholders. The chair of the board of directors also frequently signs this letter. The letter reviews the highlights of the year and points out certain noteworthy events, such as a dividend increase or a merger. It may also forecast events in the immediate future, such as next year's sales growth and earnings.

After the letter to the stockholders, the annual report may describe the various components of the business. For example, it may illustrate with words and pictures the various products that the firm makes, the type of research and development in which the company is engaged, the particular application of the firm's goods and services in different industries, and the outlook for the firm's products in the various industries in which it operates.

After the descriptive material, there follows a set of financial statements. These statements include the balance sheet as of the end of the firm's fiscal year, its income statement for the fiscal year, and the statement of cash flows. A summary of financial information for the past several years may also be given. This summary permits the investor to view the firm's growth in sales, earnings, and dividends as well as the book value of the stock. Since the financial data have been audited, the investors may assume that the information is accurate and that the appropriate accounting principles have been applied consistently. Without this audit, year-by-year comparisons may be meaningless.

SEC Filings

Firms must file several documents with the Securities and Exchange Commission (SEC), which are available to investors. The *10-K report* is the firm's annual report to the SEC. Because it gives a much more detailed statement of the firm's fundamental financial position than is provided in the stockholders' annual report, the 10-K is the basic source of data for the professional financial analyst. The contents of the 10-K include audited financial statements, breakdowns of sales and expenses by product lines, more detailed information about legal proceedings, management compensation including deferred compensation and incentive options, and environmental issues. Some of these items may involve considerable future costs and may take years to resolve, which could be detrimental to future earnings and the financial health of the company. Although the 10-K is not automatically sent to stockholders, a company must supply stockholders this document upon written request, and it is generally available through the company's Web site. (Some firms send stockholders the 10-K as the firm's annual report.)

The *10-Q report* is the firm's quarterly report to the SEC. Like the 10-K, it is a detailed report of the firm's financial condition. (The quarterly report that firms send to some stockholders is basically a summary of the 10-Q.) The *8-K report* must be filed with the SEC within 15 days after an event that may materially affect the value of the firm's securities. This document often details materials previously announced through a press release.

Individuals as well as firms may have to file forms with the SEC. Any stockholder who acquires 5 percent of a publicly held corporation's stock must submit a *13-D report*. This document requires crucial information, such as the intentions of the stockholder acquiring the large stake. Many takeover attempts start with the acquiring stockholder accumulating a substantial stake in the corporation. The required filing of the 13-D means that once the position reaches 5 percent of the outstanding shares, the buyer's intentions can no longer be hidden.

The SEC may be reached through its Web address: **http://www.sec.gov**. The SEC home page includes investor assistance and complaints, basic information concerning the SEC and its rule-making and enforcement powers, and specialized information for small business. The home page also provides entry to the EDGAR database.

Of all the information available from the SEC, perhaps the EDGAR database is the most important. EDGAR is an acronym for Electronic Data Gathering Analysis and Retrieval, which is the government's database of SEC filings by public companies and mutual funds. Data collection began in 1994 with a phase-in period. As of May 1996, all publicly held companies were required to file financial information electronically. From this site, you may obtain (download) a firm's 10-K or 10-Q.

If you want only the data a firm files with the government, EDGAR should be sufficient. Although EDGAR is a major source of free data, the data may not be in a useful form. Several firms have processed this data into more useful forms and sell their services by subscription. See, for instance, EDGAR Online (**http://www.edgar-online.com**).

In addition to the company's Web page and filings with the SEC, you may find information on a specific firm from a variety of Internet sources. Several possibilities are provided in the next two chapters on fundamental analysis, stock valuation, and security selection. Much of this material is redundant. Since the data may be tabulated and reported at different times, competing sources may provide different data. Occasionally the data from different sources are contradictory. Since you must ultimately be responsible for your investment decisions, I would suggest that you initially sample several sources to determine the specific Internet sites that best meet your needs.

Inside Information

In addition to the sources that have been previously discussed, there is the possibility of an investor's obtaining *inside information*. Inside information is not available to the general public, and it may be of value in guiding investments in a particular firm. For example, news of a dividend cut or increment may affect a stock's price. Such knowledge before it is made public should increase the individual's ability to make profitable investment decisions. However, the use of such information for personal gain by employees of the firm, brokers or investment managers, or anyone else is illegal.

The reasons for insiders buying or selling their shares are varied. For example, an individual may be using the proceeds of a sale to retire personal debt or an executive may be exercising an option to buy the stock. Such transactions are legal and are done for reasonable, legitimate financial purposes. However, some financial analysts and investors believe that inside transactions offer a clue to management's perception of the future price performance of the stock. If many insiders sell their shares, this may be interpreted as a bearish sign, indicating that the market price of the stock will decline in the future. Conversely, a large number of purchases by insiders implies that management expects the price of the stock to rise. Such purchases by insiders are interpreted as being bullish. The reason for these interpretations is obvious: If managers believe that the firm's earnings are growing, they will buy the stock. Insiders' purchases and sales may mirror management's view of the company's potential.

Because officers, directors, and other insiders must file purchases and sales with the SEC, this information is public. (The value of this information may be asymmetric. While insiders will buy in anticipation of a price increase, a sale need not imply that the price of the stock will decline. Insiders may have other reasons for selling, such as a desire to lock in gains from stock options or to obtain funds for other purposes.) Once again, the investor is faced with the problem of putting the information collected by the SEC into useful form. Several Internet sources offer information concerning insider purchases and sales but may charge for the service. Possible sources include Dow Jones (**http://www.dowjones.com/corp/index/html**) and MarketEdge (**http://www.marketedge.com**).

SUMMARY

A corporation is an economic unit created (i.e., chartered) by a state. Ownership in the corporation is represented by shares of stock, which may be transferred from one individual to another. Investors in publicly held corporations have limited liability, and common stockholders may vote their shares for the firm's board of directors, who are responsible for selecting the corporation's management.

In addition to common stock, some corporations issue preferred stock, which pays a fixed dividend and is similar to other fixed-income securities such as bonds. Preferred stock has a position superior to common stock. Dividends are distributed to preferred stock before common stock, but preferred stockholders have few of the rights granted common stockholders. Preferred stockholders do not have voting rights and their dividends cannot increase as the firm prospers and its earnings and common stock dividends grow.

After a firm has earned profits, it may either retain them or distribute them in the form of cash dividends. Many publicly held corporations follow a stated dividend policy and distribute quarterly cash dividends. A few firms supplement this dividend with extra dividends if earnings warrant the additional distribution. Some firms pay irregular dividends that vary in amount from quarter to quarter.

Dividends are related to the firm's capacity to pay them. As earnings rise, dividends also tend to increase, but there is usually a lag between higher earnings and increased dividends. Most managements are reluctant to cut dividends and thus do not raise the dividend until they believe that the higher level of earnings can be sustained.

In addition to cash dividends, some firms distribute stock dividends. These dividends and stock splits do not increase the earning capacity of the firm. Instead, they are recapitalizations that alter the number of shares the firm has outstanding. Since stock dividends and stock splits do not alter the firm's earning capacity, they do not increase the wealth of the stockholders. The price of the stock adjusts for the change in the number of shares that results from stock dividends and stock splits, and the stock distributions are not subject to federal income or capital gains taxation.

Many firms offer their stockholders the option of having their dividends reinvested in the firm's stock. This is achieved either through the firm's issuing new shares or purchasing existing shares. Dividend reinvestment plans offer the stockholders the advantages of forced savings and a reduction in brokerage fees.

Instead of paying cash dividends, a firm may offer to repurchase some of its existing shares. Such repurchases reduce the number of shares outstanding and may enhance the growth in the firm's per-share earnings because there will be fewer shares outstanding. Any profits earned on such repurchases are taxed as capital gains.

Corporations publish a substantial amount of information. A summary of the firm's products, services, accomplishments, and financial performance is provided to stockholders in the annual report. In addition to the annual report, a publicly held firm must file with the SEC a variety of forms that include the 10-Q report and the 10-K report, which provide detailed financial information for each quarter and fiscal year. Insiders and anyone owning 5 percent of the stock must also file with the SEC, detailing their purchases and sales of the corporation's stock. All of this information is readily available through the Internet and through access to the SEC's database, EDGAR.

Learning Objectives

Now that you have completed this chapter, you should be able to:

1. Summarize the rights of common stockholders.
2. Compare and contrast the features of common stock and preferred stock.
3. List the important dates for the distribution of dividends.
4. Explain why changes in cash dividends generally follow changes in earnings.
5. Determine the impact of stock dividends and stock splits on a firm's assets, liabilities, equity, earning capacity, and the price of the firm's stock.
6. Identify the advantages and costs associated with dividend reinvestment plans.
7. Analyze the tax implication of stock dividends, stock splits, dividend reinvestment plans, and corporate stock repurchases.
8. Name several sources of corporate information and how they may be obtained.

PROBLEMS

1) A firm has the following items on its balance sheet:

Cash	$ 20,000,000
Inventory	134,000,000
Notes payable to bank	31,500,000
Common stock ($10 par; 1,000,000 shares outstanding)	10,000,000
Retained earnings	98,500,000

Describe how each of these accounts would appear after:
   a) A cash dividend of $1 per share
   b) A 10 percent stock dividend (fair market value of stock is $13 per share)
   c) A 3-for-1 stock split
   d) A 1-for-2 reverse stock split
2) A company whose stock is selling for $60 has the following balance sheet:

Assets	$10,000,000	Liabilities	$14,000,000
		Preferred stock	1,000,000
		Common stock ($12 par;	
		100,000 shares outstanding)	1,200,000
		Paid–in capital	1,800,000
		Retained earnings	12,000,000

   a) Construct a new balance sheet showing the effects of a 3-for-1 stock split. What is the new price of the stock?
   b) Construct a new balance sheet showing the effects of a 10 percent stock dividend. What will be the approximate new price of the stock?
3) You purchase 100 shares of stock for $40 a share. The company currently pays a cash dividend of $2, so the dividend yield is 5 percent ($2/$40). You sign up for the dividend reinvestment plan. If the price of stock and the dividend do not change, how many shares will you have in the plan at the end of ten years? What would be the impact on this number of shares if (1) the dividend were increased or (2) the price of the stock rose?

Internet Application for Chapter 5   Corporate Stock

To analyze and value your firms, you will need basic information concerning each firm such as earnings and dividends. What are the earnings per share (EPS) and dividends per share for each firm? Are the data you located for the last fiscal year, the last three months, or the last twelve months? Which data do you think are more relevant to use?

Currency with Thomson ONE: Business School Edition

Returns from investments in stock come from growth (capital gains) and income (dividends). Using the Thomson ONE: Business School Edition database, determine the following for each of the firms:

Dividends and dividend yield

Earnings per share

Payout ratio

Return on equity

Earnings estimates.

Based solely on this information, which two companies in each industry appear to be the strongest?

6 • • •

The Basics of Fundamental Analysis

Many events affect investment decisions. Some events cause securities markets to react; others do not. On April 18, 2001, the Federal Reserve unexpectedly lowered interest rates and the Dow Jones Industrial Average rose 372 points. Subsequently, on May 15 and July 26, the Federal Reserve again lowered interest rates, and the stock market yawned. Within a few months of the inauguration of President George W. Bush, the federal income tax code was, again, altered. During the first quarter of 2001, the rate of economic growth continued to decline, but the economy did continue to expand, although at a slower rate. In the second quarter, the country entered a recession and ended its record expansion of no recession for ten years.

Do these events matter from the investor's perspective? The answer is ambiguous. The positive response to the April 18th decline in interest rates certainly affected investors owning securities. But the May 15th decline had no immediate impact. The changes in the tax code will result in investors paying lower income tax rates, but the impact for many individuals may be marginal at best. The lower rate of economic growth certainly did affect some industries, especially technology companies, and firms within those industries were adversely affected. Many employees were let go; some firms folded, and those that survived saw their stock prices decline.

This chapter considers the aggregate economic environment in which investment decisions are made. This macroeconomic framework is a precursor to the methods of stock valuation and selection that follow in the next chapter. Emphasis is placed on the Federal Reserve's monetary policy and the federal government's fiscal policy, especially the impact on interest rates. Since the risk-free rate is part of the required return in the Capital Asset Pricing Model, anything that affects the rate of interest should affect security prices. The chapter also considers the impact on specific industries, since firms operate within an industry. The chapter ends with a discussion of specific ratios used to analyze a firm's financial position.

The material in this chapter and the subsequent chapter form the backbone of fundamental analysis. You should realize that two chapters cannot cover these important topics in depth; entire books have been written on each topic alone. This text can include only the basic methods and tools used in fundamental analysis and the valuation of common stock. You should also remember the concept of efficient financial markets and that analysis of the economic environment and the valuation of a firm's securities will not by themselves lead to superior investment decisions.

THE LOGICAL PROGRESSION OF FUNDAMENTAL ANALYSIS

Fundamental analysis has a logical progression from the general to the specific. First, the analyst considers the economic environment, which may give some indication of the future direction of security prices. For example, rising inflation and interest rates argue that security prices should tend to fall. Second, the analyst considers the industry, since industries react differently to changes in the economic environment. The demand for durable items, such as cars, major appliances, and housing, tends to respond to changes in the level of economic activity, while the demand for other products, such as necessities (e.g., food) and some consumer goods, tends to be less responsive to changes in economic activity.

After considering the economy and the industry, the analyst considers the individual firm, since what applies to the economy or the industry may not apply to a specific firm. Some firms do poorly even when the general economy prospers. From 1999 through 2003, US Airways Group operated at a loss even when some airlines generated record profits. The converse is also true, since some firms do well and grow during periods of economic stagnation. These stocks may be good purchases even if it appears that the market as a whole will decline.

It may be difficult to justify purchasing stock when it appears that the economy or an industry is doing poorly. Some analysts, however, believe that this is the best time to purchase stock. If many investors are selling, security prices will be driven down, so that the buyer may be purchasing the stock at an undervalued price. These analysts are referred to as **contrarians**. Being a contrarian and going against the general sentiment is not easy. (A similar type of approach is also one of the tools of technical analysis explained in Chapter 8. In technical analysis a contrarian emphasizes doing the opposite of what investment advisory services are recommending.)

Many financial analysts and investors who use fundamental analysis are not contrarians. Instead, they follow the general logic of fundamental analysis of considering the economy, the industry, and the firm's performance and position within its industry. They use the analysis to help identify what they believe to be the general direction of the market and undervalued securities.

contrarians
Investors who go against the consensus concerning investment strategy.

THE ECONOMIC ENVIRONMENT

All investment decisions are made within the economic environment. This environment varies as the economy goes through stages of prosperity. These stages are often referred to as the **business cycle**. The name is perhaps a poor choice, since the word *cycle* suggests a regularly repeated sequence of events, such as the seasons of the year. The economy does not follow a regularly repeated sequence of events. Instead, the term *business cycle* refers to a pattern of changing economic output and growth: an initial period of rapid growth followed by a period of slow growth or even stagnation after which the economy contracts.

While each business cycle differs, there are common characteristics that are illustrated in Figure 6.1. Starting from a point of neutrality (t_1), the economy expands, reaching a peak at t_2. The economy then declines, reaching a trough at t_3 and subsequently starts to rebound to repeat the pattern. The peak may be accompanied by an increased rate of inflation as the economy gets "overheated." Since in the aggregate, prices of goods and services generally do not fall, there is no "deflation" (i.e., a period of *falling* prices, which is the opposite of inflation). Instead, the

business cycle
An economic pattern of expansion and contraction.

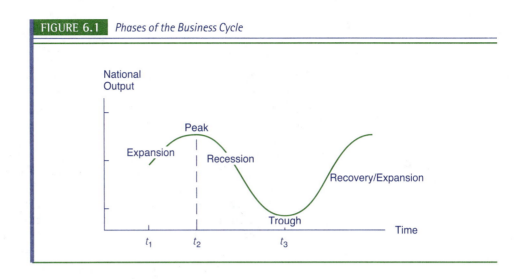

FIGURE 6.1 *Phases of the Business Cycle*

levels of employment and output tend to decline. Such a period of economic contraction is called a **recession**.

recession
A period of rising unemployment and declining national output.

One of the major advances within the social sciences is the increased understanding of events that affect the phases of the business cycle and of the causes of economic growth. This understanding has led to the development of tools, such as monetary and fiscal policy, that can alleviate the swings in economic activity. Unfortunately for policymakers, outside events also affect the level of economic activity. The capacity of policymakers to control the economy is constrained by these ever-changing social and political events.

⦿MEASURES OF ECONOMIC ACTIVITY

gross domestic product (GDP)
Total value of all final goods and services newly produced within a country by domestic factors of production.

Economic activity is measured by aggregate indicators such as the level of production and national output. Perhaps the most commonly quoted measure is **gross domestic product (GDP)**, which is the total dollar value of all *final* goods and services newly produced within the country's boundaries with *domestic* factors of production. Cars made in the United States by Toyota are included in GDP, while IBM computers produced in Europe are not. Gross domestic product has replaced gross national product (GNP) as the primary measure of a nation's aggregate national output. (GNP is the total value of all final goods and services newly produced by an economy and includes income generated abroad—that is, income earned abroad by U.S. firms is added and income earned in the United States by foreign firms is subtracted.) The change from GNP to GDP emphasizes the country's output of goods and services within its geographical boundaries. Alternative measures of economic activity stress prices and employment. Emphasis is often placed on unemployment, especially the rate of unemployment, which measures output lost.

GDP may be computed by adding the expenditures of the sectors of an economy or by adding all sources of income. From the individual investor's perspective, the former is more useful since corporate earnings are related to expenditures by the various sectors of the economy. These expenditures are personal consumption (C), gross private domestic investment (I), government spending (G), and net exports (E). The sum, GDP, is often indicated by the following equation:

(6.1)   **GDP = C + I + G + E**

Equation 6.1 points out the importance to economic activity of personal spending and investment in plant, equipment, and inventory by firms, government spending, and the exporting of goods. Government taxation, of course, reduces the ability of individuals and firms to spend, but the tax revenues are spent — they contribute to the nation's GDP. Correspondingly, the importing of goods increases the GDP of other nations, while foreign spending here increases gross domestic product. (In a sense the Mercantilists of the fifteenth through the seventeenth centuries had it right: Export goods and receive gold. Perhaps they placed the emphasis incorrectly on the accumulation of wealth and national power. They should have said, "Export goods and increase the domestic economy by increasing output and employment.")

Since the GDP is the sum of spending by each sector, if one sector of the economy were to decline, then GDP would also decline if another sector did not increase. For example, political pressure to reduce federal government spending puts pressure on business to expand jobs and invest in plant and equipment. Without such expansion in the business sector to offset the decline in government spending, consumer income and spending may not rise and the economy may stagnate.

Equation 6.1 also points out the importance of fiscal and monetary policies on the nation's economy. Excluding the direct impact of government spending, the thrust of a specific policy is its effect on the firms' and consumers' ability to, or incentive to, spend. For example, lower interest rates encourage additional spending by firms on plant, equipment, and inventory and by individuals on durable goods such as cars and homes. Higher interest rates have the opposite effect. These changes in business and consumer spending have an immediate impact on the aggregate level of output; that is, they affect the level of GDP.

Over time, the nation's output grows, but the rate of growth varies. The level of employment also rises as the economy grows, but the rate of employment (and unemployment) varies from year to year. From 1964 to 1990, the economy experienced four periods of recession as determined by the National Bureau of Economic Research (NBER): December 1969–November 1970, November 1973–March 1975, January 1980–July 1980, and July 1981–November 1982. The length of the recessions varied from a few months in 1980 to almost a year and a half from 1981 to 1982. The periods of economic growth also varied from the short period of growth in late 1980 to mid-1981, to the long period of growth that started at the end of 1982 and lasted to July 1990. That recession ended in March 1991, and the subsequent period of economic expansion continued until the spring of 2001.

This variability in the length of the periods of recession and expansion and the variation in the rate of growth verifies that there is no readily identifiable, repeating business cycle. If the economy did go through identifiable patterns, they would be readily recognized by policymakers, who would adjust their strategies in an effort to stop (or at least reduce) the impact of economic stagnation or inflation. Even though the economy does not follow precise patterns, growth in the macro economy is closely watched by investors and financial analysts, since changes in the level of economic activity often bring responses from the federal government or the Federal Reserve in the form of economic policy.

Investors and financial analysts follow various indicators of economic activity to forecast the direction of the economy, to anticipate changes in national economic policy, and to help formulate possible investment strategies. Hence the emphasis is placed on *leading* indicators of economic activity. The National Bureau of Economic Research tabulates a series of economic indicators. Eleven are leading indicators, four are coincident indicators, and seven are lagging indicators. The data are reported individually for each series, and the NBER groups these indicators into three composite indexes.

The Conference Board also publishes composite economic indicators. As with the NBER indicators, some are leading while others are coincident and lagging indicators. The ten leading indicators are:

1. Average weekly hours of manufacturing production workers
2. Average weekly initial claims for unemployment insurance
3. Manufacturers' new orders (consumer goods and materials)
4. Time for deliveries
5. Manufacturers' new orders of nondefense capital goods
6. Building permits, new private housing units
7. Stock prices (S&P 500 stock index)
8. Money supply (M-2)
9. Interest rate spread (difference between ten-year Treasury bond yields and short-term rates)
10. Index of consumer expectations

Measures of Consumer Confidence

One leading economic indicator that receives special attention is a measure of consumer sentiment or confidence. Consumer confidence affects spending, which has an impact on corporate profits and levels of employment. Two such measures include the Consumer Confidence Index (CCI) and the Consumer Sentiment Index (CSI). The CCI is published monthly by the Consumer Research Center of the Conference Board (**http://www.conference-board.org**) in the *Consumer Confidence Survey* and in the *Statistical Bulletin*; the CSI is published monthly by the Survey Research Center of the University of Michigan and is available by subscription. The CSI is used by the Department of Commerce as one of its leading indicators. Both the CCI and the CSI provide indicators of consumer attitudes by focusing on (1) consumer perceptions of business conditions, (2) consumer perceptions of their financial condition, and (3) consumer willingness to purchase durables, such as automobiles, homes, and other large dollar-cost items. An increase in confidence forecasts that consumers will increase spending, which leads to economic growth.

The absolute level of either index does not measure consumer optimism or pessimism. However, the level may be compared to previous economic periods, and changes in the indexes suggest changes in consumer optimism or pessimism. A decline in consumer confidence forecasts a reduction in the level of economic activity. Individuals who are worried about losing their jobs or who anticipate a decline in income will demand fewer goods and services and will not borrow to finance durable purchases. An increase in the indexes has, of course, the opposite implication. To some extent, a reduction in consumer confidence and a resulting decline in the demand for goods and services may be a self-fulfilling prophecy. If consumers do cut back and purchase fewer goods and services, firms will have to contract, laying off workers and cutting payrolls.

From your perspective, the change in the economy resulting from a change in consumer confidence could lead to a shift in your portfolio. A reduction in confidence that leads to economic contraction argues for movement out of growth companies into defensive stocks such as utilities or large firms (IBM or Merck) and debt instruments (i.e., to alter your asset allocation from equities to debt and cash). The reduction in the level of economic activity should hurt firms' earnings and reduce their capacity to pay dividends or reinvest funds. However, the lower level of economic activity may induce the Federal Reserve to pursue a stimulatory monetary policy. At least initially, an easy-money policy will reduce interest rates, as the Federal Reserve puts money into the economy. Investors with long-term debt instruments in their portfolios should experience capital gains as bond prices rise in response to lower interest rates.

While investors may follow leading indicators to help formulate investment strategies, the usefulness of the index of leading indicators for trading in stocks is limited, because *stock prices are one of the leading indicators.* By the time the index of indicators has given a signal, stock prices have (probably) already changed. It is still possible, however, that one of the specific leading indicators leads the stock market. For example, if changes in the stock market precede changes in economic activity by four months and changes in the money supply precede the change in economic activity by seven months, then changes in the money supply might predict changes in the stock market three months before the event. Unfortunately, there is variation in the individual components of the leading indicators. While a specific indicator may lead one recession by three months, it may lead another recession by nine months. One indicator by itself is not an accurate forecaster. (If it were, there would be no need for an *index* of leading indicators.)

In addition, it is virtually impossible to tell when an indicator has changed. Peaks and valleys (i.e., changes in the indicators) are generally determined after the fact. It is impossible to tell when a recession has started (or ended) until the change has occurred, and the same principle would apply to a specific indicator's forecasting changes in stock prices.

This inability to forecast changes in stock prices is consistent with the efficient market hypothesis. If one variable or an index of several variables could be used to forecast the direction of stock prices, individuals using the technique would consistently outperform the market. Such performance is unlikely using publicly known information, so the inability to use economic data to forecast stock prices is further support for the semistrong form of the efficient market hypothesis.

The Consumer Price Index

In addition to aggregate measures of economic activity and leading indicators, measures of inflation can have an important impact on investor behavior. Inflation is a general rise in prices and was previously discussed as an important source of risk. While prices are expressed in units of a currency (e.g., dollars), inflation is generally measured by an index. Two commonly used indexes are the Consumer Price Index (CPI) and the Producer Price Index (PPI). The CPI is calculated by the Bureau of Labor Statistics and measures the cost of a basket of goods and services over time. The PPI is calculated by the U.S. Department of Labor and measures the wholesale cost of goods over a period of time. Since goods are manufactured prior to their sale to consumers, changes in the Producer Price Index often forecast changes in the Consumer Price Index. (Information concerning federal government statistics such as the Consumer Price Index may be found through the Bureau of Labor Statistics home site: **http://www.stats.bls.gov**).

While aggregate prices are measured by an index, the rate of inflation is measured by changes in the index. If the CPI rises from 100 to 105.6 during the year, the annual rate of inflation is 5.6 percent. Over time, there has been considerable variation in the rate of inflation. During 1930, the inflation rate was –6.0 percent (i.e., prices in the aggregate fell). During 1980, the rate was 12.4 percent. Exhibit 4.2 reported that the annual rate of inflation for 1926 through 2002 was 3.0 percent, with a standard deviation of 4.4. This result indicates that for 68 percent of the years, the rate of inflation ranged from a low of –1.4 percent to a high of 7.4 percent. For the 1962–2003 period, there were no years in which consumer prices fell.

The impact of inflation on individuals varies with their consumption of goods and services. Since inflation is a general rise in prices and the Consumer Price Index measures the price of a basket of goods and services, the impact on you depends on the extent to which you consume the particular goods whose prices are inflating. For example, higher housing costs do not affect individuals equally. Homeowners seeking to sell may benefit from the higher prices at the expense of those seeking to acquire housing. Prices also do not rise evenly over geographic areas. Heating costs may rise more in the north than in the south, and correspondingly the cost of air-conditioning may rise more in the south than the north.

While the effects of inflation vary among individuals, its impact on interest rates is the same for all individuals, firms, or governments who borrow or who lend funds. An increase in the rate of inflation will increase interest rates as investors seek a higher return to maintain the purchasing power of their funds. In addition, the Federal Reserve will pursue a tight-money policy designed to curb inflation. Such a policy drives up interest rates on short-term federal government securities. This increase in short-term rates permeates all interest rates, so that the policy is felt by all borrowers.

Inflation can have a negative impact on the stock market. Although higher prices of goods and services sold could lead to increased earnings, firms have to purchase inputs, so inflation increases the cost of production. Replacing aging plant and equipment becomes more costly, and inventory, labor, and financing costs rise in response to inflation. Discounted cash flow models of valuation, such as the dividend-growth model presented in Chapter 7, also suggest that inflation should tend to depress stock prices. Cash flows may not grow as rapidly as consumer prices during periods of rapid inflation, and the required return rises as investors seek to earn higher returns to compensate for the loss of purchasing power. When both of these factors are applied to future cash flows, they indicate that inflation will lower stock prices.

THE FEDERAL RESERVE

Federal Reserve
The central bank of the United States.

In addition to forecasts of aggregate economic activity, investors are concerned with the monetary policy of the **Federal Reserve** (the "Fed"). The Federal Reserve is the country's central bank.[1] Although in many countries the treasury and the central bank are one and the same, in the United States they are independent of each other. Such independence is an example of the checks and balances of the U.S. political system. However, both the U.S. Treasury and the Federal Reserve share the same general goals of full employment, stable prices, and economic growth.

---

1. For a concise introduction to the structure and role of the Federal Reserve, obtain Board of Governors, *The Federal Reserve System: Purposes and Functions*, 8th ed. (Washington, DC: Government Printing Office, 1994). Publications of the Federal Reserve include the *Federal Reserve Bulletin*. This monthly publication reports financial data, including interest rates, employment, gross domestic product, and the money supply. Materials published by the Federal Reserve may be found at its Web address: http://www.federalreserve.gov.

The Federal Reserve pursues these economic goals through its impact on the supply of money and the cost of credit. Monetary policy refers to changes in the supply of money and credit. When the Federal Reserve wants to increase the supply of money and credit to help expand the level of income and employment, it follows an *easy* monetary policy. When it desires to contract the supply of money and credit to help fight inflation, it pursues a *tight* monetary policy.

The Impact of the Federal Reserve on Interest Rates

The Federal Reserve seeks to affect the level of economic activity by changing interest rates or the supply of money. Through its impact on the cost of credit, the Federal Reserve seeks to control inflation or to stimulate employment and economic growth. The Federal Reserve affects interest rates through its power to change the money supply by using the tools of monetary policy: the reserve requirements of banks, the discount rate, and open market operations.

The Federal Reserve influences the money supply and interest rates through the lending capacity of the fractional reserve banking system. Depository institutions (commercial banks and savings institutions, such as savings and loan associations) must hold reserves against their deposit liabilities. The amount of these reserves is determined by the Federal Reserve. Any transaction that affects banks' reserves affects their capacity to lend.

When a cash deposit is made in a bank, the cash becomes part of the bank's reserves. These reserves are divided into *required reserves* and *excess reserves*. This division depends on the **reserve requirement**, which is the percentage set by the Federal Reserve that depository institutions must hold against deposit liabilities. (Deposit liabilities are primarily checking and savings accounts, but the Federal reserve may set reserve requirements against other accounts, such as time deposits.) If the reserve requirement is 10 percent and $100 cash is deposited, $10 must be held against the deposit (the required reserve) and $90 is available for lending (the excess reserves).

Any transaction that affects the banking system's reserves or any change in the reserve requirement alters the system's ability to expand the supply of money. By lowering the reserve requirement, the Federal Reserve instantly creates new excess reserves (and new lending capacity). According to the previous illustration, if the reserve requirement were lowered from 10 percent to 5 percent, $95 instead of $90 of the $100 deposit would be considered excess reserves, so each bank could lend more and create more credit.[2] These additional loans will be magnified as the new money works its way through the fractional reserve banking system. Thus, by lowering the reserve requirement, the Federal Reserve increases the capacity of

reserve requirement
The percentage of cash that banks must hold against their deposit liabilities.

---

2. The actual amount of the expansion depends on what happens to the new funds generated by the loans. If the money does not return to the banking system (i.e., people retain cash), the money supply does not expand. However, since the vast majority of transactions use checks instead of cash, it is reasonable to assume that the funds created by the new loans will be returned to the banking system, permitting the system to expand further.

Another drain on the banking system occurs when the money is used to purchase foreign goods and services. The money leaves the country and lodges in foreign banks, which increases the foreign banks' capacity to lend but reduces the American lending capacity. Fortunately for the U.S. economy, the dollar is an international currency. U.S. payments for foreign goods result in increased deposits in foreign banks, but unless the dollars are converted into the local currency, these banks maintain deposits in U.S. banks. Foreign banks then can make loans denominated in dollars; since U.S. bank deposits are maintained, the American banking system does not contract.

The process of loan creation through the fractional reserve banking system is explained in money and banking texts. See, for instance, Frederic S. Miskin, *The Economics of Money, Banking, and Financial Markets*, 7th ed. (Reading, MA: Pearson Addison-Wesley, 2003).

discount rate
The rate of interest that the Federal Reserve charges banks for borrowing reserves.

banks to lend, and when they do lend, they effect an increase in the supply of credit and money within the economic system.

The **discount rate** is the interest rate the Federal Reserve charges depository institutions for borrowing reserves. When banks borrow from the Federal Reserve, they receive excess reserves. When these reserves are loaned, they expand the supply of money and credit. Depository institutions may also borrow from the Federal Reserve when they determine that they have insufficient reserves to meet their reserve requirements. In that case, borrowing the required reserves would not expand the supply of money and credit, because the expansion had already occurred at the time the loans were made. By borrowing the necessary reserves, banks will not have to liquidate assets in order to obtain the funds to meet their reserve requirements. Such liquidations would cause the system to contract, so in this case, borrowing the reserves from the Federal Reserve maintains the supply of money and credit.

While changes in the reserve requirement and the discount rate can affect the supply of money and credit, they are infrequently used. Since 1963, the reserve requirement for checking accounts has been changed only eight times. During 1994, the Fed increased the discount rate from 3 percent to 5.25 percent over a period of 13 months to slow down the economy and help maintain the economic expansion. After a decrease to 5 percent in January 1996, the rate was not changed again until October 1998, when it was lowered to 4.75 percent.

During 2000 and 2001, the Federal Reserve used the discount rate more aggressively. Starting with a rate increase in November 1999, the Federal Reserve continued to increase the discount rate from 4.75 percent to 6 percent in June 1999. The increases were designed to dampen the economy, which was growing at a rate that was believed to be unsustainable and would lead to inflationary pressure. Then in January 2001, the Federal Reserve reversed the process and decreased the rate from 6 percent on January 1 to 1.25 percent on December 11. These unprecedented decreases were designed to rejuvenate an economy whose rate of growth had declined from 5.3 percent during the first half of 2000. By the second quarter of 2001, economic growth turned negative, and the economy entered its first recession in ten years.

While the Federal Reserve does change the discount rate, such changes may be more symbolic than substantive. There are other, more effective (and subtler) means to alter the supply of money and credit. Instead of relying on the discount rate and the reserve requirement, the Federal Reserve uses the **federal funds rate** (or *Fed funds rate*) and open market operations. While the term *federal funds rate* includes the words *federal* and *rate*, this rate should not be confused with the discount rate or the rate on federal government debt. The federal funds rate is the interest charged by banks when they lend reserves to each other. Banks with excess reserves can put those funds to work by lending them to other banks in the federal funds market. Thus, the bank converts a sterile asset into an income-earning asset, and the bank in need of reserves acquires them without having to borrow from the Federal Reserve.

federal funds rate
The rate of interest a bank charges another for borrowing reserves.

Unlike the discount rate, the federal funds rate is not set by the Federal Reserve. Instead, it is established by the interaction of the demand and supply of funds available in the federal funds market. The Federal Reserve, however, can affect the supply of funds and thereby affect the federal funds rate. During the 1990s and early 2000s, the Federal Reserve preferred to set a target federal funds rate and changed that target as a tool of monetary policy instead of changing the discount rate.

open market operations

The buying or selling of Treasury securities by the Federal Reserve.

The target federal funds rate is achieved through the most important tool of monetary policy, open market operations. **Open market operations** is the buying and selling of securities (primarily U.S. Treasury bills) by the Federal Reserve. The Federal Reserve may buy or sell these securities in any quantity at any time. When the Federal Reserve follows an expansionary policy, it purchases Treasury bills. When the Federal Reserve pays for the securities, the funds are deposited into commercial banks, which puts reserves into the banking system. Because only a percentage of the reserves will be required against the deposit liabilities, the remainder become excess reserves. When these newly created excess reserves are loaned by the banking system, the supply of money and credit is increased.

A tight (contractionary) monetary policy is designed to drain reserves from the banking system. The Federal Reserve sells securities, which are then purchased by the general public or banks. When the securities are paid for, funds flow from deposits to the Federal Reserve. The effect is to reduce the reserves of depository institutions. Because only a small percentage of the lost reserves are required, the majority become lost excess reserves. The reduction in excess reserves then decreases the banks' capacity to lend and thus contracts the supply of money and credit.

Open market operations have a direct and immediate impact on interest rates. When the Federal Reserve purchases Treasury bills, demand is increased. This drives up prices (and, as is explained in Chapter 11, simultaneously drives down yields) in order to induce investors to sell the securities. The opposite occurs when the Federal Reserve sells Treasury bills. In that case, the Fed increases the supply, which reduces their price (and simultaneously increases their yields) and induces investors to purchase the securities. Thus, by altering the demand for and supply of U.S. Treasury bills, the Federal Reserve affects their prices and their yields.

The change in yields on Treasury bills is transferred to all other yields. If the rate on Treasury bills rises, the rate on other short-term securities must also rise. In addition, short-term rates tend to be less than long-term rates, so the increase in short-term rates will be transferred to long-term rates. Of course, the amount of change in each rate varies, since other factors also affect interest rates. Still, the general conclusion remains that all rates should rise in response to the Treasury bill rate increase.

The opposite impact occurs when the Federal Reserve puts reserves into the banking system. The initial impact will be to drive down the Treasury bill rate, which in turn will cause interest rates in general to decline. The extent to which rates fall and which specific rates decline then depends on the other factors. For example, if investors/lenders anticipate that easy money may lead to inflation, the expectation of increased inflation may cause long-term rates to remain stable or even rise even though current short-term rates have fallen.

The actual impact of any change in the supply of money and loanable funds is difficult to isolate, because the Federal Reserve uses monetary policy to pursue more than one economic goal. Over time, the Federal Reserve must increase the money supply to facilitate economic growth. If the money supply grows too slowly, it will put pressure on interest rates and there will be insufficient funds to sustain the growth. Conversely, the Federal Reserve does not want to increase the money supply too rapidly, because excess monetary expansion will lead to inflationary pressure.

The Impact of Monetary Policy on Stock Prices

It is relatively easy to perceive a relationship between monetary policy and interest rates. All interest rates are interrelated, so that if the Fed affects short-term rates, the impact is transferred to other rates. The impact on stock prices is harder to trace because the linkage could occur in several ways. Also other factors are simultaneously affecting stock prices, which muddies the waters.

First, there is the possible impact of changes in monetary policy on earnings. Higher interest rates imply higher costs of funds, which reduce earnings. As was discussed in the previous chapter, corporate earnings may be distributed as cash dividends or retained to finance growth. Since returns depend on dividends and capital gains, anything that reduces earnings has the potential to reduce returns. Hence, taken by itself (as you remember from economics: change one variable and hold all the others constant), higher interest rates should lead to lower stock prices. Conversely, lower interest rates should lead to higher stock prices by increasing earnings.

The second linkage between changes in interest rates and stock prices is the impact on the required return specified by the security market line component of the Capital Asset Pricing Model (Chapter 3) and applied in the next chapter on stock valuation. That required return is used to discount future cash flows to determine the current value of a stock. When the Fed raises interest rates, the required return is increased, which drives down stock prices. The converse occurs when a lower interest rate decreases the required return and raises present values (i.e., increases stock prices).

Since changes in interest rates can have an impact on stock prices, it is not surprising that investors watch the Fed with the hope of determining the next change in monetary policy. (Notice the importance of determining the next change before it happens. Once the change has occurred, efficient markets suggest the impact will rapidly be reflected in prices.) This "Fed watching" primarily revolves around the meetings of the Federal Open Market Committee (FOMC) and statements of the chair of the Board of Governors of the Federal Reserve. The FOMC is individually the most powerful component of the Fed because it has control over open market operations. The committee consists of 12 members, 7 of whom are the members of the Board of Governors. (The remaining members are presidents of one of the 12 Federal Reserve district banks. Membership rotates among 11 of the district bank presidents. The president of the New York district bank is a permanent member.)

The most important individual member of the Fed is the chair of the Board of Governors. During the 1990s and into the 2000s, Alan Greenspan, an economist who served as head of the Council of Economic Advisors to President Ford, has been chair. His frequent testimony to Congress is eagerly anticipated for clues to future Fed actions. The market often (but not always) reacts to statements from Chairman Greenspan, but the reaction may be short-lived. For example, his "irrational exuberance" comment, which implied that he thought security prices were too high, resulted in the Dow Jones Industrial Average declining 145 points the next day. However, the average rose more than 1,000 points within six months after the "irrational exuberance" comment. (Hindsight is, of course, 20/20; the large decline in the market during 2000-2002 suggests that Chairman Greenspan was correct, but premature.)

FISCAL POLICY

fiscal policy
Taxation, expenditures, and debt management of the federal government.

In addition to the monetary policy of the Federal Reserve, the fiscal policy of the federal government can have an important impact on the security markets. **Fiscal policy** is taxation, expenditures, and debt management by the federal government.[3] Like monetary policy, fiscal policy may be used to pursue the economic goals of price stability, full employment, and economic growth.

Obviously, taxation can have an impact on security prices. Corporate income taxes reduce corporate earnings and hence reduce firms' capacity to pay dividends and to retain earnings for growth. Personal income taxes reduce disposable income. This reduces demand for goods and services as well as savings that would be invested in some asset. Federal taxes also affect the demand for specific securities, such as the tax-exempt bond discussed in Chapter 10. Thus the tax policies may affect not only the level of security prices but also relative prices, as certain types of assets receive favorable tax treatment.

The potential impact of the federal government's fiscal policy is not limited to taxation. Expenditures can also affect security prices. This should be obvious with regard to the specific products bought by the government. Such purchases may increase a particular firm's earnings and help enhance its stock's price. However, expenditures in general, especially **deficit spending**, in which expenditures exceed revenues, can affect the financial markets and security prices.

> **deficit spending**
> *Government expenditures exceeding government revenues.*

When the federal government's expenditures exceed revenues, the federal government may obtain funds to finance this deficit from three sources: (1) the general public, (2) banks, and (3) the Federal Reserve. When the federal government sells securities to the general public to finance the deficit, these securities compete directly with all other securities for the funds of savers. This increased supply of federal government securities will tend to decrease security prices and increase their yields.

A similar conclusion applies to sales of Treasury securities to banks. If the banks lend money to the federal government, they cannot lend these funds to individuals and businesses. The effect will be to raise the cost of loans as the banks ration their supply of loanable funds. Higher borrowing costs should tend to reduce security prices for several reasons. First, higher costs should reduce corporate earnings, which will have an impact on dividends and growth rates. Second, higher borrowing costs should reduce the attractiveness of buying securities on credit (i.e., margin) and thus reduce the demand for securities. Third, the higher costs of borrowing will encourage banks to raise the rates they pay depositors. Since all short-term rates are highly correlated, increases in one rate will be transferred to other rates. Once again, the higher interest rates in general produce lower security prices.

If the Federal Reserve were to finance the federal government's deficit, the impact would be the same as if the Fed had purchased securities through open market operations. In either case, the money supply would be expanded. In effect, when the Fed buys the securities issued to finance the federal government's deficit, the Fed is monetizing the debt because new money is created.

> **surplus**
> *Receipts exceeding disbursements.*

The opposite of deficit spending is a **surplus**, in which government revenues exceed government expenditures. Prior to the late 1990s, the federal government had not had a budgetary surplus since the Nixon administration. Once receipts did exceed disbursements, the issue arose as to what should be done with the surplus.

As expected, politicians had different ideas as to how to use the surplus. These included reducing taxes and increasing spending on specific programs. The former would decrease government revenues while the latter would increase disbursements, either of which would consume the surplus. Other suggestions

---

3. See the Council of Economic Advisors, *Economic Report of the President.* This annual publication reports the fiscal policy (i.e., taxation and expenditures) of the federal government and is available at **http://www.gpoaccess.gov/eop/index.html**.

included reducing part of the outstanding federal debt. Reducing the debt would, of course, restore the funds to the general public or commercial banks when these investors sold their securities back to the federal government.

··•INDUSTRY ANALYSIS

Industries go through a cycle that is analogous to the life cycle experienced by individuals. Initially, technology generates a product that spawns an industry. For example, the development of small chips led to the personal computer industry. In other cases, change in one area causes the rebirth of another. Film studios had many movies that were occasionally shown in rereleases or on late-night TV, but the development of home video cameras, videocassettes, and videotape players generated a new market for an old product: the rental and sale of movies on cassettes and subsequently DVDs for home use.

Initially, many firms enter a rapidly expanding industry, but as the number of participants increases, the markets become saturated. The rate of growth declines, producing a phase of consolidation. Some firms fail and cease operations while others merge with stronger firms. The benefits to the surviving firms include a larger market share and increased capacity to survive. A mature industry will tend to have a few remaining participants that share a stable market. Such markets may continue to grow, but the rate of growth is modest.

This life-cycle pattern of growth is illustrated in Figure 6.2 (p. 188), which shows the initial rapid growth in sales (t_0 to t_1), followed by the reduction in the rate of growth (t_1 to t_2), and the inevitable period of maturity (t_2 to t_3). In some cases, the industry may even start to decline as total sales diminish (t_3 and on). In a declining industry the competition can be especially fierce as the participants fight for the declining market.

The time necessary for this life cycle can be long or very short, depending on the rate of technological change, the amount of funds necessary to start operations, and the legal barriers to entry and competition, such as patents. Ease of entry will rapidly saturate the market. Today it may be difficult to realize that McDonald's and Burger King were once two of many rapidly growing fast-food enterprises serving primarily hamburgers. For each of these firms to have survived, Americans would have had to eat hamburgers for breakfast, lunch, and dinner. Only a handful of the initial entrants survived, and today the market is dominated by a few large firms.

In some cases, saturated domestic markets have encouraged firms to expand abroad. Deteriorating domestic cigarette sales have driven R. J. Reynolds and Phillip Morris to expand foreign markets in an effort to maintain sales and profitability. According to the 2003 annual report, over 70 percent of Coca-Cola's revenues were generated by foreign sales.

If management has insight and perceives the decline in its industry, it may alter the firm's core businesses by diversifying into other areas still offering potential growth. For example, increased use of cars and planes led to a decline in the demand for long-distance bus travel. Greyhound, the former leader in city-to-city bus travel, sold its bus operations.[4] While the company continued to manufacture buses for sale to urban and inter-city transit systems, it no longer operated a bus system. In addition, Greyhound's management diversified into consumer products

---

4. The buyers of the bus operations took the new firm public in 1991, so Greyhound was reborn as a publicly held long-distance bus company.

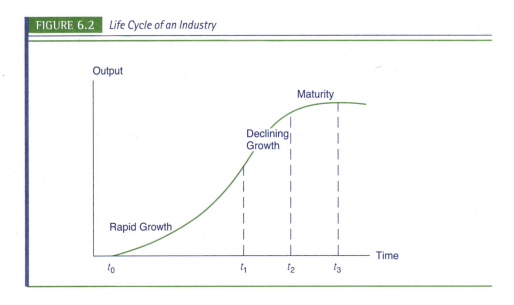

FIGURE 6.2   *Life Cycle of an Industry*

(e.g., Dial soaps and Purex laundry products) and services (e.g., Dobbs, which provides catering to airlines) and then changed the firm's name to Dial Corp. to acknowledge the firm's new configuration.[5]

In addition to going through a cycle of growth and decay, industries respond to the level of economic activity. Some industries tend to be cyclical and move with the economy. Examples of **cyclical industries** include automobiles and construction. Since consumers can defer such high-priced items from one year to the next, sales in these industries tend to be exaggerated by economic fluctuations. Car sales and housing starts vary from year to year, and, as would be expected, earnings of firms in these industries also tend to fluctuate.

These fluctuations in the revenues and earnings of a cyclical firm are illustrated by Lennar, which builds moderately priced homes primarily in Florida, Texas, and Arizona, and, as noted, whose sales and earnings tend to be cyclical. This was evident during the late 1980s when both revenues and earnings rose rapidly, mirroring economic growth. Sales went from $154 million in 1984 to almost $400 million in 1989, and earnings per share rose from $0.22 to $0.93 during the same period. The weaker economy in the early 1990s had a major impact on Lennar's revenues, and earnings per share fell to $0.45.

The second half of the 1990s was a period of rapid economic expansion. As a result of acquisitions and economic expansion, Lennar's revenues and earnings grew rapidly. From 1995 through 2000, revenues more than quadrupled, and earnings per share rose from $1.95 in 1995 to $3.64 in 2000. The economy slipped into recession during 2001; however, Lennar did not experience a decline in earnings. Instead it reported per-share earnings of $6.01 and $7.72 in 2001 and 2002, respectively. Just because a firm operates in a cyclical industry does not mean that it must experience declining earnings during periods of economic contraction. Recessions are not evenly spread throughout the economy or through each geo-

cyclical industry
An industry whose sales and profits are sensitive to changes in the level of economic activity.

5. Dial subsequently sold the operations that manufactured buses and, in 1997, split into two companies—Dial, the manufacturer of consumer products, and Viad, a provider of services, such as contracting for trade shows, food services, and money order processing.

graphical region. The influx of people into the regions served by Lennar produced higher earnings even though the aggregate economy stagnated.

While some industries are cyclical, others are not. Many firms operate in industries that are stable and experience growth even when the economy is in recession. For example, food processors, selected retailers, and producers of staples operate in industries that are not prone to recession. People have to eat and these purchases cannot be deferred. Even a company such as Hershey Foods may experience growth during recession because consumers may defer spending on big-ticket items (e.g., new cars) but continue to treat themselves to candy.

The fact that some firms are in cyclical industries while others are in more stable industries does not imply that you should purchase securities in the latter group to the exclusion of those in the former. Security markets tend to smooth out the fluctuations in earnings so the firm's value is related to its performance over time. As the valuation models presented in Chapter 7 indicate, cash flows, such as dividend income, and the growth in the firm's earnings over many years (all properly discounted back to the present) ultimately determine the value of the shares. The fact that a firm is in a cyclical industry does not by itself imply that the firm's securities are inferior investments. It indicates that returns from such investments may be more variable (i.e., riskier).

Perhaps the ideal investment is in a firm in a growing industry. Demand for the firm's output can be anticipated to increase, and even if more companies enter the market, the expansion of the market itself will permit the firm to maintain its profits in the face of increased competition. Identifying such industries is not easy. Airlines were considered a growth industry but fell on hard times, and mergers consolidated the industry. Technology-oriented industries, such as those that produce copiers and computers, have provided excellent examples of growth, but they stagnated during 2001–2003.

In addition to studying the type of industry, the financial analyst considers such factors as government regulations, labor conditions, and the financing requirements of the industry. While all industries are subject to regulation, some are more heavily regulated than others. For example, utilities such as electric and gas are subject to a large amount of regulation concerning the price firms may charge and the returns they may earn for their stockholders.[6] This regulatory climate varies from state to state. If a utility operates in a state whose utility commission tends to be more stringent, that utility will often experience lower returns on assets and equity. This tends to result in lower dividends and a lower stock price.

Labor conditions also affect the analysis of an industry. The presence of labor unions or the industry's need for skilled labor can affect earnings. Unions such as those organized in airlines (e.g., the pilots' union) or mining (e.g., the United Mine Workers) can affect earnings through strikes and expensive contracts. The need for specialized labor such as engineers can also have an impact on earnings as firms pay generous salaries in an effort to bid away skilled workers from other firms. An analysis of previous labor negotiations or the supply of available skilled labor can give the financial analyst insight into the risk associated with the industry as a whole.

---

6. Electric and gas utilities are currently undergoing deregulation, but the process of deregulating differs among the states. Some states are requiring that utilities separate transmission and distribution from the generation of electricity. Other states permit utilities to own both generation and distribution, but the firms must open their transmission lines to other suppliers. And some states have not started the deregulation process. The California experience illustrates one possible impact on consumers and electric companies. Deregulation has led to brownouts and the bankruptcy of Pacific Gas and Electric, when the utility had to pay more under deregulation for power but was precluded by regulation from passing on the higher costs to consumers.

Financing requirements also can have an impact on firms' earnings. Industries that are growing or use a large amount of plant and equipment need more funds than more stable and less capital-intensive industries. For example, firms with oil operations need a substantial amount of plant and equipment, since drilling for oil requires investments in rigs, completed wells require transportation systems, and oil refining requires investment in plant and equipment. Differences in the amount of assets used to generate sales are illustrated in Exhibit 6.1, which presents the ratio of revenues to total assets for several firms with sales in excess of $1 billion. The table ranks the firms from the lowest to highest sales to total assets and lists each firm's industry. As may be expected, an electric and gas utility, such as Public Service Enterprise, must have substantial investment in plant and equipment to generate revenues. For every $1 in revenues, the firm had over $3 in assets. An appliance manufacturer (Maytag) or medical distributor (Owens & Minor) may not need large investments in plant and equipment to generate sales. Owens & Minor generates $4 for every $1 invested in assets.

The more assets needed to generate sales, the larger is the potential impact on earnings. All assets necessitate a source of funds. Debt financing requires future cash outflows (principal repayments and interest expense). Additional equity financing spreads earnings over more shares, which may decrease earnings per share. Thus, this need for funds to finance investments in plant and equipment can affect the valuation of a firm's stock because the financing may reduce total earnings or earnings per share.

ANALYSIS OF THE FIRM

After completing an analysis of the economy and the industry, the financial analyst turns to the individual firm. Much of the analysis is built around the firm's financial statements, using a variety of ratios. (See the self-test on time value of money and the analysis of financial statements.) You may compute a large number of ratios, but the ratios may be classified into liquidity, activity, profitability, leverage, and coverage. Liquidity ratios (e.g., the current ratio and the quick ratio), activity ratios (e.g., inventory turnover, days sales outstanding, or receivables

EXHIBIT 6.1   Ratio of Revenues to Total Assets for Selected Firms with Revenues and Assets in Excess of $1 Billion

Firm	Industry	Revenues	Assets	Sales to Total Assets
Corning	Fiber optics	$3.2	$11.5	0.28
Public Service Enterprise Group	Gas and electric utility	8.4	25.7	0.33
Heinz	Food products	8.2	9.2	0.89
Maytag	Appliances	4.7	3.1	1.50
Owens & Minor	Medical supplies distributor	4.0	1.0	4.00

Source: 2002 Annual Reports.

turnover), and coverage ratios (times-interest-earned) are primarily used by creditors such as bondholders. Since creditors are paid in cash, the ability of the firm to generate funds is obviously important. The speed with which it sells its inventory and how rapidly it collects its receivables are crucial to creditors. Inventory sitting on the shelves and outstanding receivables cannot be used to pay interest and retire payables.

Stockholders are primarily concerned with leverage and profitability. Leverage ratios (e.g., debt to equity or the debt ratio) measure the extent to which the firm uses debt financing. Since financial leverage is one of the sources of the unsystematic risk associated with the firm, leverage ratios are obviously important to stockholders. As the firm uses ever-increasing amounts of debt, it become increasingly risky, and stockholders will want to be compensated for bearing that additional risk.

Profitability ratios (e.g., net profit margin, return on assets, or return on equity) measure performance. The ability to generate profitable sales is ultimately the source of the return earned by the firm for its stockholders. The return on assets indicates what the firm has earned on its resources. Since this ratio does not indicate what the firm earned for its stockholders, it is often used in conjunction with the return on equity, which measures what management has earned on the stockholders' investment in the firm.

A high return on equity by itself is not necessarily desirable. If the firm employs a substantial amount of debt financing, this may magnify the return on equity. (Conversely, if the firm were to operate at a loss, the use of debt financing would magnify the loss on the stockholders' equity.) A high return on equity and a high debt ratio may indicate the successful use of financial leverage. If, however, the firm has a high return on equity and a low debt ratio, that indicates the firm has profitable operations and is not using debt financing as a major source of the return to stockholders. This is a less risky situation. Earnings are the result of operating decisions and not financing decisions. Small changes in sales, expenses, or interest rates should not have a large impact on earnings.

The Need for Comparisons: The Problems with Interpretation

Although creditors and stockholders may emphasize different ratios that analyze a firm's financial statements, both should realize that one ratio by itself can be misleading. The usefulness of ratio analysis is the general picture derived from the ratios. Individual ratios may be contradictory, but the total analysis should provide any investor with an indication of the financial position of the firm.

Just as an individual ratio may be meaningless, so may be a set of ratios for a given firm if there is no benchmark with which to compare them. Thus the investor should either (1) compare individual ratios for a firm over a period of time to establish norms for the firm or (2) compare the individual firm's ratios to an industry average. Industry comparisons, however, are not easy to interpret. Many firms have a variety of product lines and may not be readily classified into a particular industry. In addition, industry averages may be dated. Material on industry averages published in the current year must be based on financial statements that are at least one year old. There may be inconsistencies comparing this year's financial statements with previous years' industry averages. Such comparisons will have meaning only if the industry averages are stable over time.

The problem of defining the industry may be illustrated by considering the industry comparisons available through Reuters (http://www.investor.reuters.com), which places Hershey Foods in the food processing industry, which encompasses beverages, crops, fish and livestock, tobacco, and even personal household products. Firms used for the comparison include Heinz, IBP (Iowa Beef), and Kellogg. While Hershey may be classified in the food processing industry, it specializes in candies. Should Hershey be considered comparable to Heinz, IBP, or Kellogg? Are its ratios comparable to industry averages that include firms with perceptibly different products? Whether the answers are yes and Hershey should be compared to industry averages that include firms with different products is left to the analyst or investor using the data.

Problems concerning the use of ratio analysis are not limited to the availability and comparability of industry averages. Differences in accounting practices may also alter a firm's financial statements and thus affect ratio analysis. For example, the choice of leasing instead of buying, larger allowances for doubtful accounts, or the accounting for pension liabilities may have an impact on a firm's financial statements. Although the accounting profession standardizes the construction of financial statements, differences among firms can and do exist, which may raise questions concerning the use of ratio analysis to compare firms.

Even a trend analysis of a firm's financial statements may be suspect. The problems mentioned before also apply to a ratio analysis of one firm over time if it has made accounting changes from one accounting period to the next. Such changes will be noted in the financial statements, but they do raise questions concerning the comparability of ratios computed over a number of years. For example, Hershey Foods sold its pasta operations. Any financial statements that include the pasta operations should be adjusted and the financial ratios recalculated.

Although there can be weaknesses in the use of ratios to analyze a firm's financial statements, the technique is still an excellent starting point to analyze a firm's financial position. The limitations of the data do not necessarily negate the technique. Instead, you need to be aware of the weaknesses so that appropriate adjustments can be made in either the construction of the ratios or the interpretation of the results.

Analysis of Financial Statements, Security Selection, and the Internet

If you do not want to calculate the ratios, you may find many of them at various Internet sites. Most of the basic ratios may be found at no cost. The following table provides selected financial ratios for Hershey Foods that are readily available on the Web.

Ratio	CNBC	MarketWatch	Wall Street City	Yahoo!
Current ratio	2.0	NA	1.99	1.99
Profit margin	11.2%	10.58	NA	11.21
Return on assets	13.0%	15.44	13.56	13.56
Return on equity	35.9%	38.41	37.97	37.97
Debt/Equity	0.74	NA	0.76	NA
Price/Book value	8.8	8.7	8.8	8.82
Price/Earnings	24.8	25.3	24.8	24.87
Price/Sales	2.75	NA	2.7	2.75

The addresses for each site are
CNBC on MSN Money: http://moneycentral.msn.com/investor
CBS MarketWatch: http://www.cbs.marketwatch.com
Wall Street City: http://www.wallstreetcity.com
Yahoo!: http://finance.yahoo.com

It is immediately apparent that not all the ratios are available at each site and that the values can differ. Such differences may be the result of the time periods used, such as the last 12 months, referred to as "trailing twelve months" or TTM, versus the firm's last fiscal year. Different data may be used in the calculation. For example, one source may use earnings without adjusting for extraordinary items while another source may use adjusted earnings. Varying definitions of a particular ratio may also explain differences.

These differences pose a problem if you who want to make comparisons. One obvious solution is for you to compute the ratios, in which case the definitions and time periods can be applied consistently. A more pragmatic solution may be to use one source exclusively. The choice could then depend on which source provides the desired data. For example, one source may provide both the company's ratios and the ratios for the industry.

Once you have determined the appropriate source for the data, ratios can be used to screen companies to isolate firms that meet specific criteria. For example, you can specify a return on equity of at least 20 percent, and a dividend yield of 2.5 percent. The computer then searches the database to identify all firms that meet these specified criteria. If the number is large, the criteria may be made more rigorous or additional criteria may be added to the screening process.

You should realize that a data search does not answer the fundamental question: Is the stock under- or overvalued? (Valuation is considered in the next chapter.) The search only isolates all stocks that meet the specified criteria. If you want to identify all stocks with a dividend yield of 2.5 percent and a return on equity of 20 percent, the resulting list will be based on the current dividend. There is no assurance that the current dividend will be maintained. The return on equity will be based on the firm's income statement and balance sheet, both of which are historical. The next year's earnings could be lower, so the desired return on equity might not be maintained. While screening limits the number of stocks to those that meet the criteria, these filter techniques are at best starting points in the analysis of securities for possible inclusion in a portfolio.

SUMMARY

Fundamental financial analysis selects stocks by identifying the strongest firms within an industry. The analysis starts by considering the direction of the aggregate economy, since security prices respond to economic activity. During periods of prosperity, stock prices tend to rise. Conversely, stock prices will fall when investors anticipate recession and sluggish economic growth.

The aggregate economy is affected by many factors, but the monetary policy of the Federal Reserve and the fiscal policy of the federal government are particularly important. Both the Fed and the federal government pursue the general economic goals of full employment, stable prices, and economic growth. The Federal Reserve affects economic activity through its impact on the supply of money and credit. The federal government affects the economy through taxation and expenditures.

Both monetary and fiscal policy can alter security prices through their impact on interest rates and their impact on firms' earnings (and hence on dividends and growth rates).

Factors that affect an industry also have an impact on the individual firm. Government regulations, labor unions, skilled labor requirements, technological changes, and cyclical demand for an industry's output can and do alter the earnings of a firm. The financial analyst thus considers those characteristics of an industry that play an important role in determining the capacity of the individual firm to succeed and grow within its industry.

The analysis of the individual firm is often built upon an examination of its financial statements using a variety of ratios. While ratios that measure liquidity are primarily of concern to creditors, stockholders are concerned with leverage and profitability. Leverage ratios such as debt to total assets or debt to equity measure the firm's use of debt financing and are indicators of financial risk. Profitability ratios such as the net profit margin or return on equity measure performance. They indicate what management has been able to earn for stockholders.

A firm's ratios may be compared over time (a time-series analysis) or compared with comparable or competitive firms (a cross-sectional analysis). There may be significant problems applying either approach, since a firm is not a static entity but changes over time, and competitors may not be comparable. Few firms have the exact same product lines and often compete with firms in several industries. The Internet may be a ready source of the ratios used to analyze a firm, but various sites may provide different numerical values for the same ratio. You need to use the Internet with caution when obtaining data to analyze and select securities for inclusion in your portfolio.

Learning Objectives

Now that you have completed this chapter, you should be able to:

1. Describe the phases of a business cycle.
2. Define gross domestic product and specify its components.
3. Describe the tools of monetary policy and the mechanics of open market operations.
4. Differentiate the discount rate from the federal funds rate.
5. Explain how monetary and fiscal policy and the federal government's surplus or deficit may affect securities prices.
6. Differentiate cyclical from stable industries and identify factors that may affect the performance of an industry.
7. Apply ratios to analyze the financial statements of a firm.
8. Compare a firm's financial ratios over time and with competing firms.
9. Locate various financial ratios on the Internet.

Internet Application for Chapter 6
The Basics of Fundamental Analysis

To determine if you should purchase any (or all) of the stocks, you need to perform a fundamental analysis and valuation of the firms you are following.

To analyze these firms, obtain the following information:

	BUD	GTRC	HDI	PFE
Price of the stock				
Revenues/sales				
Earnings per share				
Earnings growth rate				
Earnings estimates				
Current annual dividend				
Dividend yield				
Debt ratio				
Return on equity				
Return on assets				

To complete the table, use at least three of the Internet sites provided in Chapter 3. (Do not be surprised if some of the information is not available in a particular site.) After completing the table, answer the following questions.

1. Do the sources provide all the required information, and are the data identical from each source? If not, what might account for the differences?
2. Which firm appears to be growing the fastest?
3. Which firm is the most financially leveraged? Which appears to be the riskiest?
4. Based on profitability, which company appears to be the best performing firm?
5. Is there any reason to prefer one site to another as a source of data?

CHAPTER

7 • • • •

The Valuation and Selection of Common Stock

For many individuals the word *investing* is synonymous with buying and selling common stock. Even if they buy bonds or real estate, *investing* still implies stock. Perhaps one reason for this emphasis is the considerable exposure individuals have to stock. Daily newspapers and the nightly TV news report corporate news, stock transactions, and market averages. Changes in stock market indexes such as the Dow Jones Industrial Average and the S&P 500 stock index are reported throughout the day on various radio channels and cable networks. The same does not apply to the bond markets. Just think about it: how often do you remember the news reporting the Dow Jones bond average?

Suppose you do want to buy a stock and are considering IBM. You need information to facilitate the decision and go to a source such as Yahoo! Finance and type in the IBM ticker symbol. The site provides price quotes and various links such as company profile, analyst ratings, and financials. Financial sounds dull and you already know IBM's profile. You click on analyst ratings and find 20, ranging from "strong buy" to "sell." You also find earnings estimates for the next year, which range from $4.84 to $5.55. You click on an additional link for valuation, which tells you IBM is in a "buy zone" and the buy zone ranges from $66 to $111. If the current price is $104, the stock could decline 40 percent and still be in the buy zone!

You are facing one of the most elusive and perplexing questions facing every investor: what is the stock worth? What is its current value? Without some indication of the current value, the decision to buy will be based on hunches, intuition, or tips. What do you do? A financial psychologist (or cynic) might suggest that you latch onto the specific information that confirms your preconceived desire to buy IBM. But in any event, you must have some notion as to the value of the stock in order to justify the purchase.

In finance the process of valuation is discounting future cash flows. As is illustrated in Chapter 11 on bond valuation, that process is relatively easy for debt instruments because they pay a fixed amount of interest and mature at a specified date. Common stock, however, does not pay a fixed dividend, nor does it mature. These two facts considerably increase the difficulty of (but do not excuse you from) valuing common stock.

This chapter discusses a variety of techniques that range from a dividend-growth model to ratios such as price-to-earnings used to select stocks. Whether any particular method leads to higher investment returns is open to debate. (Remember: the efficient market hypothesis would suggest that few, if any, will lead to superior results.) Even if none of these techniques lead to superior results, your knowing the techniques increases your ability to comprehend a large amount of material available on investing.

INVESTORS' EXPECTED RETURN

Investors purchase stock with the anticipation of a return. As is explained in Chapter 3, that return consists of dividend income and capital gains. That expected return is expressed in the equation reproduced here:

$$E(r) = \frac{E(D)}{P} + E(g)$$

The expected return, $E(r)$, is the sum of the expected dividend yield, $E(D)/P$, and the expected growth rate, $E(g)$. If a stock is selling for $25 and you expect that the firm will pay a $1 dividend and that the stock will grow at 7 percent, your expected return is

$$E(r) = \frac{\$1.00}{\$25} + 0.07 = 11.0\%.$$

This equation points out the importance of the price paid for the stock. Higher prices reduce the dividend yield and reduce the potential capital gain. A broker once recommended a stock to me that was selling for $40. Its price range for the year was $40–$10, so if the current price doubled from $40 to $80, that implies somebody would have experienced an eightfold increase (from $10 to $80) in the value of the stock. Such an increase seemed unlikely to me, so I did not take the recommendation. I thought the stock was overvalued, and the expected return was insufficient to justify buying the stock.

For a stock to be attractive, the expected return must be equal to or greater than the investor's required return. (The required return using the Capital Asset Pricing Model is discussed later in this chapter.) If your required return is 11 percent, an 11 percent expected return meets your required return. You will earn what you want, so the security should be purchased. It is fairly valued. If your expected return were lower, the stock is overvalued and should not be purchased. If the expected return is greater than your required 11 percent, the stock is a steal. (Of course, your expectation may not be fulfilled. Remember, it is expectations that drive us to act, not results.)

In a world of no commission fees and in which the tax on dividends is the same as on capital gains, investors would be indifferent to the source of the return. An investor seeking 11 percent should be willing to accept a dividend yield of zero if the capital gain is 11 percent. Conversely, a capital growth of zero should be acceptable if the dividend yield is 11 percent. And any combination of the two that adds up to 11 percent is also acceptable.

However, because of commissions and taxes, investors are concerned with the source of the return. To realize the capital gain, the investor must sell the shares and pay the commissions, which argues for dividends. In addition, capital gains occur in the future and may be less certain than the flow of dividend income. The uncertainty of future capital gains versus the likelihood of current dividends favors dividends over capital gains.

Prior to the changes in the federal tax laws in 2003, dividends were taxed at a higher rate than long-term capital gains. Currently the highest rate on both is 15 percent. (The rate on short-term capital gains is the individual's marginal tax rate. For many individuals, their tax bracket is higher than the rate on long-term capital gains and dividend income. This difference in the taxation of short-term and long-term capital gains is an obvious incentive to hold the stock for at least a year and a day.) The 15 percent tax rate on dividends and long-term capital gains certainly levels the playing field. Both sources of return are taxed at the same rate; however, there remains a tax argument favoring long-term capital gains. The tax may be deferred until the gains are realized; the tax on dividends cannot be deferred. (It is also naive to expect that the 15 percent rates will remain unchanged indefinitely. You should reconsider the composition of your portfolios as tax laws are changed.)

••VALUATION AS THE PRESENT VALUE OF DIVIDENDS

Value investing focuses on what an asset is worth—its intrinsic value. Emphasis is placed on discounting cash inflows back to the present. For common stock this revolves around discounting future dividends at the appropriate required return. The resulting valuation is then compared with the stock's current price to determine if the stock is under- or overvalued. Thus, valuation compares dollar amounts. That is, the dollar value of the stock is compared with its price. Returns compare percentages. That is, the expected percentage return is compared to the required return. In either case, your decision will be the same. If the valuation exceeds the price, the expected return will exceed the required return.

The process of valuation and security selection is readily illustrated by the simple case in which the stock pays a fixed dividend of $1 that is not expected to change. That is, the anticipated flow of dividend payments is

Year	1	2	3	4	. . .
Dividend	$1	$1	$1	$1	. . .

The current value of this indefinite flow of payments (i.e., the dividend) depends on the discount rate (i.e., the investor's required rate of return). If this rate is 12 percent, the stock's value (V) is

$$V = \frac{\$1}{(1 + 0.12)} + \frac{1}{(1 + 0.12)^2} + \frac{1}{(1 + 0.12)^3} + \frac{1}{(1 + 0.12)^4} + \ldots$$

$$V = \$8.33.$$

This process is expressed in the following equation in which the new variables are the dividend (D) and the required rate of return (k):

(7.1)
$$V = \frac{D}{(1 + k)^1} + \frac{D}{(1 + k)^2} + \ldots + \frac{D}{(1 + k)^\infty}$$

which simplifies to

(7.2)
$$V = \frac{D}{k}.$$

Thus, if a stock pays a dividend of $1 and the investor's required rate of return is 12 percent, then the valuation is

$$\frac{\$1}{0.12} = \$8.33.$$

Any price greater than $8.33 will result in a yield that is less than 12 percent. Therefore, for this investor to achieve the required rate of return of 12 percent, the price of the stock must not exceed $8.33.

There is, however, no reason to anticipate that common stock dividends will be fixed indefinitely into the future. Common stocks offer the potential for growth, both in value and in dividends. For example, if you expect the current $1 dividend to grow annually at 6 percent, the anticipated flow of dividend payments is

Year	1	2	3	. . .
Dividend	$1.06	$1.124	$1.191	. . .

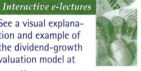
The current value of this indefinite flow of growing payments (i.e., the growing dividend) also depends on the discount rate (i.e., your required rate of return). If this rate is 12 percent, the stock's value is

$$V = \frac{1.06}{(1 + 0.12)^1} + \frac{1.124}{(1 + 0.12)^2} + \frac{1.191}{(1 + 0.12)^3} + \dots$$

$$V = \$17.67.$$

• **dividend–growth valuation model**
A valuation model that deals with dividends and their growth properly discounted back to the present.

Equation 7.1 may be modified for the growth in dividends. This is expressed in Equations 7.3 and 7.4. The only new variable is the rate of growth in the dividend (g), and it is assumed that this growth rate is fixed and will continue indefinitely into the future. Given this assumption, the **dividend-growth valuation model** is

(7.3)
$$V = \frac{D(1 + g)^1}{(1 + k)^1} + \frac{D(1 + g)^2}{(1 + k)^2} + \frac{D(1 + g)^3}{(1 + k)^3} + \dots + \frac{D(1 + g)^\infty}{(1 + k)^\infty}$$

which simplifies to

(7.4)
$$V = \frac{D_0(1 + g)}{k - g}.$$

The stock's intrinsic value is thus related to (1) the current dividend, (2) the growth in earnings and dividends, and (3) the required rate of return. Notice the current dividend is D_0, with the subscript 0 representing the present. The application of this dividend-growth model may be illustrated by a simple example. If your required rate of return is 12 percent and the stock is currently paying a $1 per share dividend growing at 6 percent annually, the stock's value is

$$V = \frac{\$1(1 + 0.06)}{0.12 - 0.06} = \$17.67.$$

Any price greater than $17.67 will result in a total return of less than 12 percent. Conversely, a price of less than $17.67 will produce an expected return in excess of 12 percent. For example, if the price is $20, according to Equation 3.1 the expected return is

$$E(r) = \frac{\$1(1 + 0.06)}{\$20} + 0.06$$

$$= 11.3\%.$$

Because this return is less than the required 12 percent, you would not buy the stock and would sell it if you owned it.

If the price is $15, the expected return is

$$E(r) = \frac{\$1(1 + 0.06)}{\$15} + 0.06$$

$$= 13.1\%.$$

This return is greater than the required 12 percent. The stock offers a superior return and it is undervalued. You would buy the security.

Only at a price of $17.67 does the stock offer a return of 12 percent. At that price it equals the return available on alternative investments of the same risk. The investment will yield 12 percent because the dividend yield during the year is 6 percent and the earnings and dividends are growing annually at the rate of 6 percent. These relationships are illustrated in Figure 7.1, which shows the growth in dividends and prices of the stock that will produce a constant yield of 12 percent. After 12 years, the dividend will have grown to $2.02 and the price of the stock will be $35.55. The total return on this investment remains 12 percent. During that year, the dividend will grow to $2.14, giving a 6 percent dividend yield, and the price will continue to appreciate annually at the 6 percent growth rate in earnings and dividends.

If the growth rate had been different (and the other variables remained constant), the valuation would have differed. The following illustration presents the value of the stock for various growth rates:

Growth Rate	Value of the Stock
0%	$ 8.83
3%	$ 11.78
9%	$ 35.33
11%	$106.00
12%	undefined (denominator = 0)

FIGURE 7.1   Earnings, Dividends, and Price of Stock over Time Yielding 12 Percent Annually

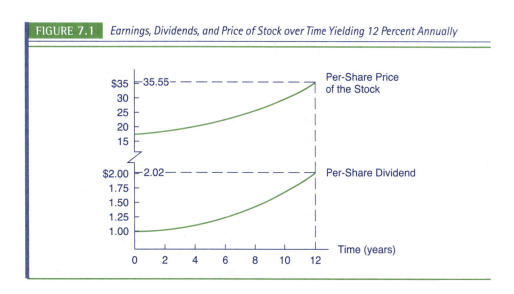

As the growth rate increases, so does the valuation, until the value becomes undefined (an exceedingly large number) when the growth rate equals the required return. This positive relationship indicates that when a stock offers more potential for capital gains, its valuation increases (if the dividend and the required return are *not affected* by the growth).

The dividend-growth valuation model assumes that the required return exceeds the rate of growth (i.e., $k > g$). While this may appear to be a restrictive assumption, it is logical. The purpose of the dividend-growth model is to determine what the stock is worth and then to compare this value to the actual price in order to determine whether the stock should be purchased. If a stock offers 14 percent when you require 12 percent, the valuation is immaterial. It does not matter what the stock costs. Whether the price is $1 or $100,000 is irrelevant because you anticipate earning 14 percent on the amount invested when only 12 percent is required. Valuation can be material only if the growth rate (i.e., the potential capital gain) is less than the required return.

In the preceding illustration, the firm's earnings and dividends grew at a steady 6 percent rate. Figure 7.2 illustrates a case in which the firm's earnings grow annually at an average of 6 percent, but the year-to-year changes stray considerably from 6 percent. These fluctuations are not in themselves necessarily reason for concern. The firm exists within the economic environment, which fluctuates over time. Exogenous factors, such as a strike or an energy curtailment, may also affect earnings during a particular year. If these factors continue to plague the firm, they will obviously play an important role in the valuation of the shares. However, the emphasis in the dividend-growth valuation model is on the flow of dividends and their growth over a period of years. This longer time dimension smoothes out temporary fluctuations in earnings and dividends.

Although the previous model assumes that the firm's earnings will grow indefinitely and that the dividend policy will be maintained, such need not be the case. The dividend-growth model may be modified to encompass a period of increasing or declining growth or one of stable dividends. Many possible variations in growth patterns can be built into the model. Although these variations change the equation and make it appear far more complex, the fundamentals of valuation remain unaltered. Valuation is still the process of discounting future

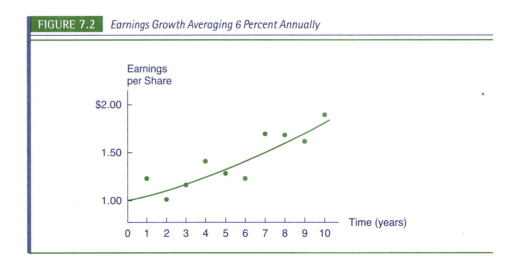

FIGURE 7.2   *Earnings Growth Averaging 6 Percent Annually*

dividends and growth in earnings and dividends back to the present at the appropriate discount rate.

To illustrate such a variation, consider the following pattern of expected earnings and dividends.

Year	Earnings	Yearly Dividends	Percentage Change in Dividends from Previous Year
1	$1.00	$0.40	. . .
2	1.60	0.64	60.0%
3	1.94	0.77	20.3
4	2.20	0.87	13.0
5	2.29	0.905	4.0
6	2.38	0.941	4.0
7	2.48	0.979	4.0

After the initial period of rapid growth, the firm matures and is expected to grow annually at the rate of 4 percent. Each year the firm pays dividends, which contribute to its current value. However, the simple model summarized in Equation 7.4 cannot be used, because the earnings and dividends are not growing at a constant rate. Equation 7.3 can be used, and when these values, along with a required rate of return of 12 percent, are inserted into the equation, the stock's value is

$$V = \frac{\$0.40}{(1 + 0.12)^1} + \frac{\$0.64}{(1 + 0.12)^2} + \frac{\$0.77}{(1 + 0.12)^3} + \frac{\$0.87}{(1 + 0.12)^4}$$

$$+ \frac{\$0.905}{(1 + 0.12)^5} + \frac{\$0.941}{(1 + 0.12)^6} + \frac{\$0.979}{(1 + 0.12)^7} + \dots$$

$$= \$9.16.$$

This answer is derived by dividing the flow of dividends into two periods: a period of super growth (years 1 through 4) and a period of normal growth (from year 5 on). The present value of the dividends in the first four years is

$$V_{1-4} = \frac{\$0.40}{(1 + 0.12)^1} + \frac{\$0.64}{(1 + 0.12)^2} + \frac{\$0.77}{(1 + 0.12)^3} + \frac{\$0.87}{(1 + 0.12)^4}$$

$$= \$0.36 + \$0.51 + \$0.55 + \$0.55.$$

$$= \$1.97.$$

The dividend-growth model is applied to the dividends from year 5 on, so the value of the dividends during normal growth is

$$V_{5-\infty} = \frac{\$0.87(1 + 0.04)}{0.12 - 0.04} = \$11.31.$$

This $11.31 is the value at the end of year 4, so it must be discounted back to the present to determine the current value of this stream of dividend payments. That is,

$$\frac{\$11.31}{(1 + 0.12)^4} = \$11.31(0.636) = \$7.19.$$

The value of the stock, then, is the sum of the two parts.[1]

$$V = V_{1-4} + V_{5-\infty}$$

$$= \$1.97 + 7.19 = \$9.16.$$

As this example illustrates, modifications can be made in this valuation model to account for the different periods of growth and dividends. Adjustments can also be made for differences in risk. You should realize that the model does not by itself adjust for different degrees of risk. If a security analyst applies the model to several firms to determine which stocks are underpriced, there is the implication that investing in all the firms involves equal risk. If the analyst uses the same required rate of return for each firm, then no risk adjustment has been made. The element of risk is assumed to be the same for each company. So how can we adjust the model to account for risk?

THE INVESTOR'S REQUIRED RETURN AND STOCK VALUATION

Interactive e-lectures

See a visual explanation and example of Capital Asset Pricing Model at

http://mayoxtra.swlearning.com

One means to adjust for risk is to incorporate into the valuation model the beta coefficients presented earlier in Chapter 3. In that chapter, beta coefficients, which are an index of the market risk associated with the security, were used as part of the Capital Asset Pricing Model to explain returns. In this context, beta coefficients and the capital asset pricing model are used to specify the risk-adjusted required return on an investment.

The required return has two components: the risk-free rate (r_f) that the investor can earn on a risk-free security such as a U.S. Treasury bill, and a risk premium. The risk premium is also composed of two components: (1) the additional return that investing in securities offers above the risk-free rate, and (2) the volatility of the particular security relative to the market as a whole (i.e., systematic risk as indicated by the beta). The additional return is the extent to which the return on the market (r_m) exceeds the risk-free rate ($r_m - r_f$). Thus, the required return (k) is

$$k = r_f + (r_m - r_f)\beta.$$

Equation 7.5 is the same general equation as the security market line in Chapter 7, which was used to explain a stock's return. In that context, the Capital Asset Pricing Model states that the realized return depends on the risk-free rate, the risk premium associated with investing in stock, and the market risk associated with the particular stock. In this context, the same variables are used to determine the return

---

1. This valuation procedure may be summarized by the following general equation:

$V = V_s + V_n.$

V_s is the present value of the dividends during the period of super growth; that is,

$$V_s = \sum_{t=1}^{n} \frac{D_0(1 + g_s)^t}{(1 + k)^t}$$

V_n is the present value of the dividends during the period of normal growth; that is,

$$V_n = \left[\frac{D_n(1 + g)}{k - g}\right]\left(\frac{1}{(1 + k)^n}\right).$$

The value of the stock is the sum of the individual present values; that is,

$$V_s = \sum_{t=1}^{n} \frac{D_0(1 + g_s)^t}{(1 + k)^t} + \left[\frac{D_n(1 + g)}{k - g}\right]\left(\frac{1}{(1 + k)^n}\right).$$

you require to make the investment. You want a return that covers the expected yield on a risk-free asset, the expected risk premium associated with investing in stock, and the expected market risk associated with the specific stock. The differences between the two uses concerns time and historical versus anticipated values. In one case the expected values are being used to determine if a specific stock should be purchased now. In the other application, historical values are employed to explain the realized return on an investment that was previously made.

The following examples illustrate how you use the equation for the required return. The risk-free rate is 3.5 percent and you expect that the market will rise by 10 percent. (The returns presented in Exhibit 4.2 suggested that over a period of years stocks have yielded a return of 6 to 7 percent in excess of the return on U.S. Treasury bills. Thus, if the bills are currently yielding 3.5 percent, an expected return on the market of 10 percent is reasonable. Treasury bills are covered in more detail in Chapter 10 on government securities.) Stock A is relatively risky and has a beta coefficient of 1.8 while stock B is less volatile and has a beta of 0.8. What return is necessary to justify purchasing either stock? Certainly it would not be correct to require a return of 10 percent for either, since that is the expected return on the market. Since stock A is more volatile than the market, your required return should exceed 10 percent. However, the required return for B should be less than 10 percent; it is less volatile (less risky) than the market as a whole.

Given this information concerning the risk-free rate and the anticipated return on the market, the required returns for stock A and B are

$$k_A = 3.5\% + (10\% - 3.5\%)1.8 = 3.5\% + 11.7\% = 15.2\%$$

and

$$k_B = 3.5\% + (10\% - 3.5\%)0.8 = 3.5\% + 5.2\% = 8.7\%.$$

Thus the required return for stock A and B are 15.2 percent and 8.7 percent, respectively. These required returns are different from each other and from the expected return on the market, because the analysis now explicitly takes into consideration risk (i.e., the volatility of the individual stock relative to the market). Stock A's required rate of return is greater than the expected return on the market (15.2 percent versus 10 percent) because stock A is more volatile than the market. Stock B's required rate of return is less than the return expected for the market (8.7 percent versus 10 percent) because stock B is less volatile than the market as a whole.

The relationship between the required rate of return and risk expressed in Equation 7.5 is illustrated in Figure 7.3 (p. 206). The horizontal axis represents risk as measured by the beta coefficient, and the vertical axis measures the required rate of return. Line *AB* represents the required rates of return associated with each level of risk. Line *AB* uses the information given in the preceding example: The Y-intercept is the risk-free return (3.5 percent), and the slope of the line is the difference between the market return and the risk-free return (10 percent minus 3.5 percent). If the beta coefficient were 1.80, the figure indicates that the required return would be 15.2 percent; if the beta coefficient were 0.8, the required return would be 8.7 percent.

How the risk-adjusted required return may be applied to the valuation of a specific stock using the dividend-growth model is illustrated in the following example. Suppose a firm's current dividend is $2.20, which you expect to grow annually at 5 percent. The risk-free rate is 3.5 percent; you expect the market to rise by 10 percent, and the beta is 0.8 so the required return is 8.7 percent. What is the

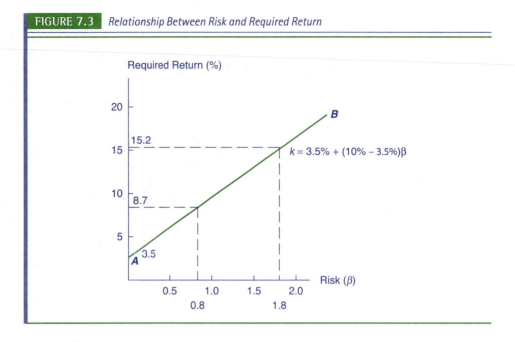

FIGURE 7.3   *Relationship Between Risk and Required Return*

maximum you would be willing to pay for this stock? If you use the dividend-growth model, that price (value) is

$$V = \frac{D_0(1 + g)}{k - g}$$

$$= \frac{\$2.20(1 + 0.05)}{0.087 - 0.035} = \frac{\$2.31}{0.052}$$

$$= \$44.42.$$

At a price of \$44.42 (and only at \$44.42), the expected and required returns are equal. If the market price is below \$44.42, the stock would be considered under-valued and a good purchase. Correspondingly, if the price exceeds \$44.42, the stock is overvalued and should be not purchased. You should sell it short.

●●ALTERNATIVE VALUATION TECHNIQUES

The dividend-growth model is *theoretically* sound: It *discounts future cash flows back to the present at the required return*, and the required return may be adjusted for differences in market risk. While the dividend-growth valuation model permeates textbooks concerning investments, it is rarely used by professional security analysts on pragmatic grounds. Making the model operational is difficult. A problem immediately arises if the stock does not pay a dividend, and many firms do not pay dividends. Without a dividend payment, the numerator is \$0.00, which makes the value equal to \$0.00!

While this problem is obvious, there are additional problems associated with each of the variables in the model. One problem is the choice of the beta coefficient.

As was discussed in Chapter 3, there can be differences in estimated betas for the same stock, which raises a question as to which beta to use. The same question applies to the risk-free rate. Although a short-term rate on federal government securities may be used, investments in stock often have a longer time horizon. The question becomes which to use, a short-term or long-term rate? (A corollary question is this: Is it appropriate to use a short-term rate for valuing a long-term investment?) Even if the analyst does use a short-term rate, there is still the question of which short-term rate: a three-month, a six-month, or any other risk-free short-term rate?

The problems with making the dividend-growth model applicable, however, are not a sufficient basis for discarding it or any other valuation model. Valuation models are built on discounting future cash flows. The analyst is forced to identify real economic forces (e.g., earnings and growth rates) and the returns on alternative investments (e.g., the risk-free rate and the return on the market). Without such analysis, the investor may have to rely on hunches, intuition, and just plain guessing to select assets. Such an approach has no conceptual or theoretical basis.

P/E Ratios

Interactive e-lectures

See a visual explanation and example of price to earnings ratio at

http://mayoxtra.swlearning.com

Value investing is concerned with the components of the dividend-growth model even if the analyst does not apply the actual model. The financial analyst or portfolio manager may employ alternative approaches to identify stocks for possible purchase. One of these approaches is the use of the ratio of the stock's price to earnings per share, or the P/E ratio.

The P/E ratio was introduced in Chapter 1 in the section on the reporting of security transactions by the financial press. Firms in the same industry tend to have similar price/earnings ratios, and a firm's stock tends to trade within a range of price/earnings ratios.

The process by which price/earnings ratios may be used to value a stock is summarized by the following simple equation:

$$P = (m)(EPS),$$

which states that the value of the stock is the product of the earnings per share (*EPS*) and some multiple. This multiple is the appropriate price/earnings ratio. Once the expected earnings and the appropriate multiple are estimated, the intrinsic value of the stock is easily determined. For example, if the financial analyst determines that the appropriate P/E ratio is 10 and the firm will earn $4.50 per share, the value of the stock is

$$(10)(\$4.50) = \$45.$$

The implication is that if the stock is currently selling for $35, it is undervalued and should be purchased. If it is selling for $55, it is overvalued and should be sold.

An alternative method using P/E ratios is to divide the current price by forecasted earnings to express the P/E ratio in terms of future earnings. For example, suppose the price of the stock is $36 when the estimated earnings are $4.50. The P/E using the estimated earnings is $36/$4.50 = 8.0. If the appropriate P/E is 10, a P/E of 8 suggests that the stock is undervalued and that the price of the stock will rise over time as the forecasted earnings are realized. The difference between these two approaches is the starting point. In the first case, the earnings and the appropriate P/E ratio are used to determine a value, which is compared to the current price. In the second case, the current price is divided by the estimated earnings to determine a P/E ratio, which is compared to the appropriate P/E ratio. In either case, the crux of the analysis is (1) the appropriate P/E ratio and (2) earnings.

The use of a P/E approach to valuation and security selection is often found in the financial press (if not the academic press). For example, a financial analyst may recommend purchase of IBM by stating that the "shares trade at 12.7 times our EPS projection of $4.90." A similar statement may be, "The shares appear under-valued at 13 times our earnings estimate of $4.90." Such material is typical of bro-kerage firms' purchase recommendations for common stocks.

The previous discussion considered a unique P/E ratio, but stocks may be treated as if they trade within a range of P/E ratios. Consider the P/E ratios over a ten-year period for Bristol-Myers Squibb in Exhibit 7.1. On the average, the P/E ratio has ranged from a high of 28.2 to a low of 19.1. If the current ratio moves out-side this range, the investor may want to look further at Bristol-Myers Squibb. For example, during 2001, the P/E/ reached 55. During 2002, the range in the P/E ratio was 49–29, so the stock consistently traded above the historic average high P/E. Unless something had changed fundamentally (e.g., the FDA approved a new, major drug), the P/E/ ratio was suggesting that the stock was overvalued. During 2003, the exact opposite occurred when the stock consistently traded for a P/E around 18–16, which would suggest that the stock may have been undervalued.

Weakness in the Use of P/E Ratios

The first major weakness concerning the use of P/E ratios is the appropriate ratio. The preceding illustration employs a P/E ratio of 10, but no explanation is given for why 10 is appropriate. In the Bristol-Myers Squibb illustration, the point is made that the ratio ranged on the average between 28.2 and 19.1 but does not explain why either of these numbers would be the appropriate P/E ratio or why the ratio should stay within the range.

One possible solution is to use the industry average P/E ratio. This is a com-mon solution to the problem of determining an appropriate ratio, but it does implicitly assume that a particular firm is comparable to the firms used to deter-mine the average P/E ratio. Although many firms in an industry are similar, each

EXHIBIT 7.1   Price/Earnings Ratio for Bristol-Myers Squibb

Year	High	Low
2000	36	21
1999	38	28
1998	43	28
1997	30	16
1996	20	14
1995	17	11
1994	21	17
1993	23	18
1992	33	22
1991	21	16
Average	28.2	19.1

is unique in some way. For example, is ConocoPhillips comparable to Exxon-Mobil? Both are large, integrated oil companies, but ConocoPhillips's oil reserves are primarily in Alaska while ExxonMobil's reserves are more diverse. Such differences in resources, markets served, or internal structure do raise the question of comparability. Financial analysts who use industry average P/E ratios may not address this question but view the average P/E ratio as a pragmatic solution to the problem of determining an appropriate P/E ratio for use in security valuation.

The second problem with the use of P/E ratios concerns earnings. There are essentially two problems: (1) the definition of earnings and (2) estimating future earnings. While companies report total and per-share earnings, these "bottom-line" numbers may include extraordinary items that are nonrecurring. Should the earnings be adjusted for these isolated events? For example, Chesapeake Corporation reported EPS of $12.29 in 1991, but these earnings included a $10.03 gain from the sale of its paper and forest products divisions. Without the nonrecurring gain, EPS would have been $2.26. That's a difference of over $10.00 a share!

Obviously, the P/E ratio will be affected by the choice of earnings. Higher earnings will lower the P/E ratio and perhaps suggest that the stock is undervalued, especially if the industry average P/E ratio is higher. If the gain is excluded and EPS are lower, the P/E ratio will be higher. The higher P/E ratio may indicate that the stock is not undervalued. The converse applies to extraordinary charges to income. Chesapeake reported in 2000 a per-share loss of $4.26, which included a charge of $4.87. Without the nonrecurring loss, EPS would have been $0.71. The decline in EPS causes the P/E ratio to be higher (or in this example, undefined), so the stock may appear to be overvalued.

One possible solution is to adjust EPS for extraordinary items and use that figure to calculate the P/E. This is a reasonable approach if the items are unique, non-recurring events. A firm, however, may have extraordinary items on a recurring basis. In one year, bad investments may be written off. In the next year, management may sell a subsidiary for a loss. In the third year, a loss of foreign exchange transactions may decrease earnings. Recurring extraordinary losses may imply poor management, so the use of the actual, *unadjusted* earnings may be appropriate. (One possible means to standardize recurring gains and losses may be to average the earnings over a period of years. Such an approach would acknowledge the extraordinary items but reduce the impact of a large extraordinary gain or loss in a particular year.)

Even if you resolve the problem of defining the appropriate earnings, forecasting future earnings is daunting. By combining an analysis of a firm's financial statement, its position in its industry, and the direction of the economy, a financial analyst may be able to forecast earnings. It is doubtful, however, that you, the individual investor, would have the time or inclination to make such estimates. (Possible methods for estimating the growth in earnings are illustrated later in this chapter.)

Price/Book Ratio

An alternative to P/E ratios for the selection of stocks is the ratio of the price of stock to the per-share book value. (Book value is the sum of stock, additional paid-in capital, and retained earnings on a firm's balance sheet.) Essentially the application is the same as with the P/E ratio. The security analyst compares the price of the stock with its per-share book value. For example, in its Chesapeake 2002 Annual Report, CSK's book value was $37.24. At the end of the year, the price of the stock was $26.48, so the price to book ratio was 0.71 ($26.48/$37.24). A low ratio suggests that the stock is undervalued while a high ratio suggests the opposite. Determining what constitutes a "low" or a "high" ratio is left to the discretion of the analyst. Often, if a stock is selling for less than its book value (i.e., less than 1), it is considered undervalued. However, just because Chesapeake Corporation is selling for less than book value and Coca-Cola with a price/book ratio of 5.85 is selling for more does not necessarily mean that Chesapeake is undervalued while Coke is overvalued.

Price/Sales Ratio

A third valuation ratio is the ratio of the price of the stock to per-share sales (P/S). For example, Chesapeake reported 2002 sales per share of $54.09. Since the year-end price of the stock was $17.85, the price to sales ratio was 0.33 ($17.84/$54.09). (Coca-Cola's per-share sales was $5.61. Since the price of the stock was $43.84, the price-to-sales ratio was $43.84/$5.61 = 7.81.) The price-to-sales ratio offers one particular advantage over the P/E ratio. If a firm has no earnings, the P/E ratio has no meaning, and the ratio breaks down as a tool for valuation and comparisons. The P/S ratio, however, can be computed even if the firm is operating at a loss, thus permitting comparisons of all firms, including those that are not profitable.

Even if the firm has earnings and thus has a positive P/E ratio, the price/sales ratio remains a useful analytical tool. Earnings are ultimately related to sales. A low P/S ratio indicates a low valuation; the stock market is not placing a large value on the firm's sales. Even if the firm is operating at a loss, a low P/S ratio may indicate an undervalued investment. A small increase in profitability may translate these sales into a large increase in the stock's price. When the firm returns to profitability, the market may respond to the earnings, and both the P/E and P/S ratios increase. Thus, a current low price/sales ratio may suggest that there is considerable potential for the stock's price to increase. Such potential would not exist if the stock were selling for a high price/sales ratio.

How the price/sales ratio is used is illustrated in Exhibit 7.2, which gives the price/sales, price/book, and price/earnings ratios for four firms classified in the paper and forest products industry. The exhibit also includes Georgia Pacific, which manufactures paper products and building materials that use timber. (The inclusion of Georgia Pacific illustrates the problem of defining a firm's industry, since virtually all large corporations have operations in several industries.) The ratios are readily available through the Internet. Exhibit 7.2 uses Yahoo!Finance (http://finance.yahoo.com).

As may be seen in the exhibit, Boise Cascade has the lowest P/S and P/B ratios of the paper and forest products firms. These low ratios would suggest that it is the most undervalued of the four paper and forest product firms. Georgia Pacific, however, has the lowest P/E ratio, and its P/S and P/B are only slightly higher than these ratios for Boise Cascade. As is frequently the case, there is no clear reason to prefer Boise Cascade to Georgia Pacific.

While the ratio of price/sales is used as a tool for security selection, the weaknesses that apply to P/E ratios (and to price/book ratios) also apply to price/sales. Essentially, there is no appropriate or correct ratio to use for the valuation of a stock. While some financial analysts believe that a low P/E ratio is indicative of financial weakness, other security analysts draw the opposite conclusion. The same applies to price/sales ratios. Some financial analysts isolate firms with low ratios and then suggest that these firms are undervalued. Other analysts, however, would argue the opposite. Low price/sales ratios are characteristic of firms that

EXHIBIT 7.2	Price/Sales, Price/Book, and Price/Earnings Ratios		

Selected Firms in the Paper and Forest Products Industry			
	Price/Sales	**Price/Book**	**Price/Earnings**
Boise Cascade	0.31	1.39	34.7
Bowater	0.81	1.48	N/E
International Paper	0.79	2.44	60.8
Weyerhaeuser Company	0.70	1.83	29.4
Paper Products and Building Products			
Georgia Pacific	0.43	1.64	21.2

N/E no earnings; firm operated at a loss.

Source: Yahoo!Finance (http://finance.yahoo.com), June 4, 2004.

are performing poorly and not worth a higher price. The low ratio then does not indicate undervaluation but is a mirror of financial weakness.

PEG Ratio

PEG ratio
The price/earnings ratio divided by the growth rate of earnings.

Another alternative valuation technique that came into prominence during the late 1990s is the **PEG ratio**. This ratio is

$$\frac{\text{Price/earnings ratio}}{\text{Earnings growth rate}}.$$

If the stock's P/E ratio is 20 and the per-share earnings growth rate is 10 percent, the value of the ratio is

$$\frac{20}{10} = 2.$$

The PEG ratio standardizes P/E ratios for growth. It gives a relative measure of value and facilitates comparing firms with different growth rates.

If the growth rate exceeds the P/E ratio, the numerical value is less than 1.0 and suggests that the stock is undervalued. If the P/E ratio exceeds the growth rate, the PEG ratio is greater than 1.0. The higher the numerical value, the higher the valuation and the less attractive is the stock. A PEG of 1.0 to 2.0 may suggest the stock is reasonably valued, and a ratio greater than 2.0 may suggest the stock is overvalued. (What numerical value determines under- and overvaluation depends on the financial analyst or investor.)

As with the price/earnings, price/sales, and price/equity ratios, the PEG ratio can have significant problems. Certainly all the questions concerning the use of price/earnings ratios apply to the PEG ratio, since the P/E ratio is the numerator in the PEG ratio. For example, should earnings include nonrecurring items or be adjusted for nonrecurring items? Should the analyst use historical earnings? Should an estimated or expected P/E ratio be used?

Because the PEG ratio standardizes for growth, it offers one major advantage over P/E ratios. The PEG ratio facilitates comparisons of firms in different industries that are experiencing different rates of growth. Rapidly growing companies may now be compared to companies experiencing a lower rate of growth. This comparison is illustrated in Exhibit 7.3, which gives the PEG and P/E ratios for several firms. Several of the firms (e.g., Dominion Resources and EMC) have high P/E ratios and may be considered overvalued based solely on that ratio. However, some firms (e.g., EMC) are expected to grow more rapidly, so when the P/E ratio is standardized for growth, these stocks appear less overvalued. Other firms such as Coca-Cola and Lucent have relatively high PEG and P/E ratios, which would suggest they are overvalued. And at the other extreme, Capital One Financial has a low P/E and a low PEG, which suggests the stock is undervalued. Of course, the investor may want to ask why both ratios are so low for Capital One Financial. The low PEG and the low P/E ratios may be a good starting point but are probably not sufficient to conclude that stock is a good purchase.

You could compute your own PEG ratios, but it is probably more practical to obtain them from an existing source. Possibilities include Yahoo! (**http://finance .yahoo.com**). (See also Exhibit 7.6.) Once again a problem exists concerning which source to use, since PEG ratios from different sources may differ.

In addition, you may have noted an inconsistency in the data in Exhibit 7.3. To compute a P/E ratio, you need earnings. To compute a PEG ratio, you need both a P/E and growth rate. So a question must arise, how can you have a PEG ratio and *not have a P/E ratio*? This is exactly what is reported in Exhibit 7.3 for Tellabs, which has a PEG of 3.7 and no entry for the P/E ratio. The most likely explanation is that the P/E was based on reported earnings. If Tellabs operated at a loss during the previous year, there could be no positive P/E value based on the historical earnings. The PEG ratio, however, may have been based on forecasted earnings, in which case the source could provide a numerical value for the ratio.

EXHIBIT 7.3   Selected PEG Ratios as of May 2004

Firm	PEG Ratio	P/E Ratio
Capital One Financial	0.7	12.0
Coca-Cola	2.4	26.4
ConocoPhillips	1.3	9.9
Dominion Resources	2.4	57.2
EMC	1.6	40.3
ExxonMobil	1.8	14.3
Hershey Foods	2.3	24.5
Honeywell	1.2	47.7
Lucent	3.0	67.4
Tellabs	3.7	N/E

N/E no earnings; firm operated at a loss.

Source: Quicken (http://www.quicken.com), August 10, 2001.

Cash Flow

An alternative to using earnings in security valuation is cash flow and the ability of the firm to generate cash. For young, growing firms, the ability to generate cash may be initially as important as earnings since generating cash implies the firm is able to grow without requiring external financing. After the initial period of operating at a loss but producing positive cash flow, the firm may grow into a prosperous, profitable operation.

The valuation process using cash flow is essentially the same as is used with P/E ratios, except cash flow is substituted for earnings and emphasis is placed on the growth in cash flow rather than the growth of earnings. For example, in its August issue of *Private Client Monthly* a Scott & Stringfellow analyst recommended purchasing XTO Energy stock. Besides the company's successful exploration for and production of natural gas, the analyst pointed out that XTO was trading "below 5 × 2002 discretionary cash flow." In this illustration, 5 times cash flow was being used instead of 5 times earnings to justify purchasing the stock.

The estimation of future cash flow and the determination of the appropriate multiplier are, of course, at the discretion of the investor or analyst. For firms with substantial investments in plant or natural resources, noncash depreciation (and depletion expense) helps recapture the cost of these investments and contribute to the firm's cash flow. The same applies to real estate investments, and funds from operations are often used instead of earnings when valuing properties and real estate investment trusts.

ESTIMATION OF GROWTH RATES

Growth rates have been an integral part of this chapter. Estimated growth in the dividend is an essential part of the dividend-growth model, and a growth rate is necessary to compute the PEG ratio. Unfortunately, calculating a growth rate may be one of the most difficult tasks facing the financial analyst. And this difficulty also applies to you if you want to perform the analysis yourself.

This section covers a variety of methods that may be used to determine growth rates. None of the methods is foolproof, and if you compare your estimates with those found in other sources, they will probably differ. As is so often the case when making investment decisions, you must select among the alternatives. The easiest solution is, of course, to accept the estimates found in other sources and proceed with your analysis. The efficient market hypothesis suggests this may be your best course of action.

Growth as the Product of the Return on Equity and the Retention Ratio

Interactive e-lectures
See a visual explanation and example of growth rate at
http://mayoxtra.swlearning.com

Retained earnings may be used to acquire additional assets. If these assets generate income, they will permit future growth in the firm's cash dividends. Paying cash dividends and internally financing growth are mutually exclusive. If the firm retains earnings, it cannot pay dividends, and if the firm distributes earnings, this source of funds cannot be used to finance expansion of plant and equipment. Of course, the firm could expand by issuing new stock, but then the old stock might be diluted. By not issuing new shares and by retaining earnings, all the potential for growth accrues to the existing stockholders.

The impact of different retention ratios may be seen by considering the following balance sheets.

Assets		Liabilities and Equity	
Assets	$20	Liabilities	$10
		Equity	10
	$20		$20

During the year, the firm earns $2 after deducting all operating and finance expenses. The return on equity, the ratio of earnings divided by equity, is $2/$10 = 20 percent. If the firm retains all its earnings (retention ratio = 1.0 and the payout ratio = 0), the new balance sheet becomes:

Assets		Liabilities and Equity	
Assets	$22	Liabilities	$10
		Equity	12
	$22		$22

Suppose, however, the firm had distributed $0.72 and retained only $1.28 (i.e., the retention ratio is 64 percent and the payout ratio is 36 percent). The new balance sheet becomes:

Assets		Liabilities and Equity	
Assets	$21.28	Liabilities	$10.00
		Equity	11.28
	$21.28		$21.28

The firm's assets and equity have not risen as much because the firm has retained less of its earnings. The future growth in earnings is now less, because management has made a smaller investment in assets.

This relationship between growth (g), the return on equity (ROE), and the retention ratio (RR) is summarized in Equation 7.7:

(7.7)
$$g = \text{ROE} \times \text{RR.}$$

In the first illustration, the growth rate is

$$g = 0.2 \times 1 = 20\%,$$

while in the second illustration, the growth rate is

$$g = 0.2 \times 0.64 = 12.8\%.$$

Unless the return on the equity can be increased, future earnings (and hence future dividends) can only grow at 12.8 percent.

If the firm were able to increase the return on equity, the dividend could be increased without a corresponding decrease in the growth rate. For example, if the return on equity had been 31.25 percent, the firm could distribute 36 percent of its earnings and retain 64 percent and still achieve a 20 percent growth rate (i.e., $0.3125 \times 0.64 = 20\%$). If, however, the return on equity is not increased and management increases the dividend, the higher payment must imply lower retention of earnings. If the firm distributes $1.20, the retention ratio falls to 40 percent, and the rate of growth is reduced to 8 percent ($0.2 \times 0.4 = 8\%$).

What impact will the increased dividend at the expense of growth have on the price of the stock? The answer is indeterminate. Examine the arrows placed in the dividend-growth model:

$$V = \frac{D_0\uparrow(1+g\downarrow)}{k-g\downarrow}.$$

The increase in the dividend (i.e., a higher numerator) argues for a higher stock price, but the lower growth rate, which increases the denominator and decreases the numerator, argues for a lower stock price. The converse also applies. A lower dividend decreases the numerator and suggests a lower price while a higher growth rate means a smaller denominator and an increased numerator, which increases the valuation. Thus, a dividend increment at the expense of the retention of earnings could result in the price of the stock rising or falling.

Alternative Means to Estimate Growth Rates

An alternative means to estimate growth is to analyze past growth and use this information to project future growth. Suppose per-share dividends and their annual percentage change for the firm were as follows:

Year	Dividend	Percentage Change from Previous Year
1994	$0.33	—
1995	0.36	9.1%
1996	0.38	5.6
1997	0.39	2.6
1998	0.42	7.7
1999	0.43	2.4
2000	0.46	7.0
2001	0.52	13.0
2002	0.68	30.8
2003	0.72	5.9
2004	0.72	0.0

The base year is 1994, so the dividend rises from $0.33 to $0.72 over the ten-year period. The annual percentage change, which is given in the third column, varies from year to year. During 2002, the dividend rose over 30 percent, but in the last year the dividend was not increased. The arithmetic average of the ten percentage changes is 8.4 percent.

The arithmetic average of percentage changes can bias the growth rate. (See the discussion of averages in Chapter 4.) If the calculation includes both positive and negative percentage changes, the growth rate is overstated. An alternative method is to compute a geometric average, which avoids the potential bias. If the geometric average of the ten percentage changes is computed, the growth rate is 8.1 percent.

Historical growth rates may also be computed using the future value. The question to be solved is: What is the annual rate of growth if the dividend grew from $0.33 during 1994 to $0.72 during 2004 (i.e., ten completed years)? That is,

$$\$0.33(1+g)^{10} = \$0.72$$
$$(1+g)^{10} = \$0.72/0.33 = 2.182.$$

$$g = \sqrt[10]{2.182} - 1 = 1.081 - 1 = 8.1\%.$$

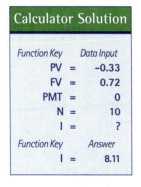

Calculator Solution

Function Key	Data Input
PV =	−0.33
FV =	0.72
PMT =	0
N =	10
I =	?
Function Key	Answer
I =	8.11

The weakness of this approach is that the calculation uses only two observations, the first and last years. An alternate method that uses all of the data estimates an equation that summarizes the observations relating dividends and time. Such an equation yields an estimate of the annual growth rate in the dividend. This technique, least-squares regression analysis, was explained in Chapter 3. How regression may be used to estimate the growth rate is illustrated in the appendix to this chapter. Using this technique yields an annual growth rate of 8.6 percent.

An Application

Which growth rate should you use to value the stock? Currently there are five estimates: 12.8 percent using the return on equity and the retention ratio for the last year, 8.6 percent using regression analysis, 8.4 percent (the arithmetic average percentage change in the dividend), 8.1 percent (the rate using the terminal values of the dividend), and 8.1 percent (the geometric average percentage change). The answer requires judgment because the valuation will differ depending on the choice. Obviously, the lower rate, the more conservative choice, may be appropriate if you anticipate that the pace of economic activity will decline. However, if you believe that the firm's financial condition is improving, the use of a lower growth rate will argue against acquiring the stock.

Since 12.8 and 8.1 are the highest and lowest estimated growth rates, you may decide to drop the two extremes. The remaining estimates are 8.6 and 8.2; however 8.2 is an arithmetic average, so you might prefer 8.1, which is a geometric average and encompasses compounding.

Next you must determine the required return. Earlier in this chapter, the Capital Asset Pricing Model was used to determine the required return. In that model the required return depended on the risk-free rate, the expected return on the market, and the stock's beta. Assume for this discussion that the risk-free rate is 5 percent and that the historical return on the market of 5 to 7 percent above the risk-free rate continues. Under this condition, the expected return on the market is 10 to 12 percent. If the firm's beta is 0.9 and the highest return on the market is used, the required return is

$$k = r_f + (r_m - r_f)\beta$$
$$= 0.05 + (0.12 - 0.05)0.9$$
$$= 11.3\%.$$

Since the required rate of return has been determined and the annual dividend is $0.72, the valuation model may be applied. In this illustration the value of the stock is

$$V = \frac{D_0(1 + g)}{k - g}$$

$$= \frac{\$0.72(1 + 0.081)}{0.113 - 0.081}$$

$$= \$24.32.$$

If the stock is selling for $24, the stock is reasonably priced (i.e., neither undervalued nor overvalued). If the stock is selling for $20, it is undervalued. At $30, it is overvalued.

If the valuation model generates a large divergence between the valuation and the market price (e.g., $40 when the price is $24), you should reconsider the estimates used in the model. A large divergence would indicate that the stock is either well undervalued or overvalued. Such mispricings should be rare because, as discussed in several places in this text, securities markets are competitive and efficient. If a security were undervalued, investors would seek to buy it, which would drive up the price. If a security were overvalued, investors would seek to sell it, which would drive down the price. Thus, if the dividend-growth model indicates a large divergence between the estimated value and the current market price, it would be advisable to determine if the data used in the model are inaccurate.

For example, if you believe that the firm can sustain an 8.6 percent rate of growth, the valuation model yields:

$$V = \frac{\$0.72(1 + 0.086)}{0.113 - 0.086}$$

$$= \$28.96.$$

This valuation indicates that the firm's stock at $24 is undervalued and should be purchased. The question then becomes: Can 8.6 percent be sustained? At 8.1 percent, the valuation is $24.32, which is close to the price of $24. It appears that the market consensus of a sustainable growth rate is around 8.1 percent, for at 8.1 percent the valuation is about $24.

By now it should be obvious that stock valuation is more an art than a science. However, the use of equations such as the dividend-growth model may give valuation an appearance of being more exact than in reality it can be. The model determines a unique value but that number obviously depends on the data used. Instead of determining a unique value, an analyst may employ data derived under varying assumptions and derive a range of values for a given stock. This may lead to investment advice that reads something like "We believe that the stock is fairly priced at $23 to $25 and would buy the stock on any weakness that drives the price below $20." Prices do fluctuate and may briefly create buy or sell opportunities that may offer you an opportunity to open or liquidate positions.

Earnings Estimates, Growth Rates, and the Internet

Suppose you need estimates of future earnings or growth rates as part of a fundamental financial analysis of a stock or to use in a dividend-growth model. Fortunately, several possible complimentary sources of analysts' estimates are available through the Internet. (One means to keep current on available sites is to consult the AAII September/October issue of *Computerized Investing*, which compares comprehensive Web sites. A sampling of Internet sources and the earnings per-share estimates and growth rates for Hershey Foods Company are provided in Exhibit 7.4 (p. 218). You should realize that not all sites give the same information and that the information, which is provided, may vary from the different sources. The data may also be reported in ranges such as the estimated growth of 9.8 to 10.6 percent. This, of course, forces you to choose which data to use in your analysis or revert back to developing your own data. As should be obvious, differences in growth rates will produce different stock values in the dividend-growth model. You need to use some common sense when applying Internet estimates. If the available data suggest that a company's prospects are too good to be true and your

EXHIBIT 7.4	Internet Sources and Analysts' Estimate for Earning per Share for Hershey Foods as of June 2004		

Source	EPS Estimates		Estimated Growth Rates (5 year)
CBS MarketWatch	Current year	$3.97	NA
http://cbs.marketwatch.com	Next year	$4.37	
CNBC/Microsoft	Current year	$3.96	9.9–10.4%
http://moneycentral.msn.com/investor	Next year	$4.36	
Forbes	Current year	$3.96	8.5%
http://www.forbes.com	Next year	NA	
Morningstar	Current year	$3.96	9.8–10.6%
http://www.morningstar.com	Next year	$4.36	
SmartMoney	Current year	NA	9.9%
http://smartmoney.com			
Wall Street City	Current year	$3.96	9.9%
http://wallstreetcity.com	Next year	$4.36	
Yahoo!Finance	Current year	$3.44	10%
http://finance.yahoo.com	Next year	$4.29	

valuations of the stock do not make reasonable sense, do not use the analysis to make investment decisions.

VALUATION, FUNDAMENTAL ANALYSIS, AND EFFICIENT MARKETS

Fundamental analysis is a method for identifying possible securities to include in your portfolio. It facilitates determining if a security should be purchased. That is, the analysis answers the question, is the stock under- or overvalued.

Fundamental analysis and stock valuation are performed in efficient financial markets. Will the analysis result in your earning higher returns? The efficient market hypothesis discussed in Chapter 2 suggests that the answer is No. Remember: fundamental analysis and stock valuation are dependent upon publicly known information concerning the economy, a firm's industry, and its financial condition. According to the efficient market hypothesis, whatever you learn through analyzing existing (public) information has already been factored into a stock's price. Public information, of course, does change, but financial markets are so efficient and securities prices change so rapidly that you will not be able to exploit the new information and earn higher returns.

Are there any exceptions to this general conclusion? The answer to that question is "Possibly Yes." While the majority of evidence supports the efficient market hypothesis, there may be exceptions. These exceptions are frequently referred to as *anomalies*. Two of the most important anomalies are the *P/E effect* and the *small-firm effect*. The *P/E effect* suggests that portfolios consisting of stocks with low price/earnings ratios have a higher average return than portfolios with higher P/E ratios. The *small-firm effect* (or *small cap* for small capitalization) suggests that returns diminish as the size of the firm rises. Size is generally measured by the market value of its stock. If all common stocks on the New York Stock Exchange are divided into five groups, the smallest quintile (the smallest 20 percent of the total firms) has tended to earn a return that exceeds the return on investments in the stocks that compose the largest quintile, even after adjusting for risk.

Subsequent studies have found that the small-firm effect occurs primarily in January, especially the first five trading days. This anomaly is referred to as the *January effect*. However, there is no negative mirror-image December effect (i.e., small stocks do not consistently underperform the market in December) that would be consistent with December selling and January buying. The January effect is often explained by the fact that investors buy stocks in January after selling for tax reasons in December. And there is some evidence that within a size class those stocks whose prices declined the most in the preceding year tend to rebound the most during January.

The *neglected-firm effect* suggests that small firms that are neglected by large financial institutions (e.g., mutual funds, insurance companies, trust departments, and pension plans) tend to generate higher returns than those firms covered by financial institutions. By dividing firms into the categories of highly researched stocks, moderately researched stocks, and neglected stocks (based on the number of institutions holding the stock), researchers have found that the last group outperformed the more well-researched firms. This anomaly is probably another variation of the small-firm effect, and both the neglected-firm effect and the small-firm effect suggest that the market gets less efficient as firms get smaller. Because large financial institutions may exclude these firms from consideration, their lack of participation reduces the market's efficiency.

The *Value Line Investment Survey* weekly ranks all the stocks that it covers into five groups, ranging from those most likely to outperform the market during the next 12 months (stocks ranked "1") to those most likely to underperform the market during the next 12 months (stocks ranked "5"). Several studies have found that using the Value Line ranking system (i.e., selecting stocks ranked "1") generates an excess return, hence the *Value Line effect*. Once again, the smaller firms tended to generate the largest excess return. While the amount of this excess return differed among the various studies, its existence is inconsistent with the efficient market hypothesis. However, it may be exceedingly difficult for the individual investor to take advantage of the anomaly since the Value Line rankings change weekly, which will require substantial transaction costs as the investor frequently adjusts his or her portfolio.

The *overreaction effect* is the tendency of security prices to overreact to new information and is also inconsistent with efficient markets. There are many illustrations in this text of security prices experiencing large changes in response to new information. For example, Guilford Mills announced that it had discovered accounting irregularities that overstated earnings. The stock immediately dropped 18 percent. Is such a decline an overreaction or a correct valuation based on the new information? An overreaction implies the price will correct, and the investor could exploit the overreaction to earn higher returns. Evidence does support this anomaly that the market does overreact, but the overreaction appears to be asymmetric. Investors overreact to bad news but not to good news. This would suggest that Guilford Mill's stock would rebound (at least in the short term). The rebound, however, did not occur and the company eventually declared bankruptcy.

There also appears to be evidence that security prices may drift in a particular direction over a period of time (a *drift* anomaly), especially after a surprise announcement of some magnitude. Bad news is interpreted by the market to be prolonged and stocks continue to decline even if the firm's fundamentals subsequently change. The converse would also be true: The market assumes good news will continue indefinitely. The former situation creates a buying opportunity, while the latter creates a selling opportunity. Presumably, in efficient markets, the change would occur immediately, since the new price embodies the new information. To continue the Guilford Mills example, this inefficiency implies the initial price decline will continue, which suggests that selling the stock short would lead to superior returns. (The overreaction and the drift anomalies appear to be at odds, but that interpretation need not be correct. The subsequent rebound may occur soon following the initial price change after which the price drift resumes.)

book–to–price ratio
The accounting value of a stock dividend by the market price of the stock.

The **book-to-price ratio** considers the ratio of a stock's book value on the firm's balance sheet to the market value of the stock. (This ratio is the reciprocal of the ratio of market value to book value. While both ratios essentially say the same thing from different perspectives, each appears in the financial literature. Price-to-book primarily appears in the professional literature and the popular press. Book-to-price appears in the academic research pertaining to investments.) Stocks with high book-to-market-value ratios are sometimes referred to as *value stocks* to differentiate them from stocks with low ratios of book value to market value, which may be referred to as *growth stocks*. According to this anomaly, the prices of growth stocks are bid up by investors anticipating higher growth in earnings. The higher price reduces the ratio of book value to the stock's market value. As the ratio of book value of equity to market value decreases, the stock becomes more risky because there is increased variability of returns. These riskier stocks should generate higher returns.

In research published in 1992, Fama and French considered the relationship between stock returns and the ratio of book value to the market value for the period 1962–1990.[2] Fama and French's results indicated that firms with low ratios of book value to market value (i.e., the growth stocks) generated lower returns. The immediate implication is that investors who use the ratio of book to market to select securities (i.e., individuals who invest in value stocks) will earn a higher return without bearing additional risk. Such a result is inconsistent with the efficient market hypothesis, which asserts that higher returns are only available if the investor bears more risk.[3]

The Fama and French study is also important for its implications concerning a value strategy versus a growth strategy. The results certainly support a value strategy since they suggest that this approach leads to higher returns. The results also indicate that a growth strategy generates lower returns. Companies classified as growth stocks often have low book-to-price ratios, and these are precisely the stocks that the Fama and French results show produce lower returns and higher risks. The obvious implication is that a growth strategy is inferior. However, research done by Richard Bernstein of Merrill Lynch Capital Markets suggests there may be periods when one strategy generates superior results followed by a period when the opposing strategy produces higher returns.[4]

2. Eugene F. Fama and Kenneth R. French, "The Cross-Section of Expected Returns," *The Journal of Finance* (June 1992): 427–465. The French–Fama study also reported that returns were not related to the beta used in the capital asset pricing model. Low beta stocks generated higher returns, which is inconsistent with the capital asset pricing model.
3. Further support for these results may be found in Josef Lakonishok, "Contrarian Investment, Extrapolation, and Risk," *The Journal of Finance* (December 1994): 1541–1578. This study found that value strategies (investments in firms whose stock price is low relative to earnings and other fundamentals, such as the book value of the equity) did better than growth strategies. For a basic discussion of the value approach, see Robert A. Haugen, *The New Finance: The Case Against Efficient Markets*, 2d ed. (Upper Saddle River, NJ: Prentice Hall, 1999).
4. Richard Bernstein, Style Investing (New York: John Wiley & Sons, 1995); and Richard Bernstein, "Growth & Value," *Merrill Lynch Quantitative Viewpoint* (June 4, 1991).

While evidence does support the efficient market hypothesis, the preceding discussion indicates that there appear to be exceptions. Perhaps the observed exceptions are the result of flaws in the research methodology. Furthermore, any evidence supporting a particular inefficiency cannot be used to support other possible inefficiencies; it applies only to the specific anomaly under study.

Before you rush out to take advantage of these alleged inefficiencies, you should remember several sobering considerations. First, the empirical results are only consistent with inefficiencies; they do not prove their existence. Second, for you to take advantage of the inefficiency, it must be ongoing. Once an inefficiency is discovered and investors seek to take advantage of it, the inefficiency may disappear. Third, transaction costs are important, and you must pay the transaction costs associated with the strategy. If a substantial amount of trading is required, any excess return may be consumed by commissions. Fourth, you still must select individual issues. Even if small firms outperform the market in the first week of January, you cannot purchase all of them. There is no assurance that the selected stocks will be those that outperform the market in that particular year. Fifth, for an anomaly to be useful for an active investment strategy, its signals must be transferable to you. Just because the *Value Line* rankings produce excess returns in an empirical study does not mean that you may be able to receive the information rapidly enough to act on it. The anomaly may exist for those investors with the first access to the information, but not to all investors who receive the recommendations.

SUMMARY

Investors who purchase common stock anticipate a return from dividends and capital appreciation. They will buy a stock if the expected return is equal to or exceeds the required return. Of course, the return investors realize may be less than their expected or required returns. Any realized returns are subject to federal income taxation. Currently the maximum federal tax rate on dividend income and long-term capital gains is 15 percent.

Common stock valuation is based on discounting future cash flows back to the present to determine the current value of the stock. One model, the dividend-growth model, discounts future dividends back to the present at the investor's required return. These dividends depend on the firm's earnings and may grow as the firm prospers. The required return encompasses what the investor may earn on alternative investments and the systematic risk associated with the specific stock.

Alternative approaches to security selection include a variety of ratios such as price to earnings (P/E), price to sales (P/S), price to book value, and P/E to growth (PEG). These ratios are used to compare stocks for possible inclusion in a portfolio. Since growth in earnings and dividends is an integral part of the valuation process, several techniques may be employed to estimate a firm's growth. These include combining the return on equity and the firm's retention ratio, arithmetic and geometric averages, and regression analysis. Since the various methods often produce different estimates of growth, the analyst or individual investor must select the specific estimate to use in the dividend-growth model and the PEG ratio.

Stocks are purchased and sold in competitive financial markets. This competition, the rapid dissemination of information among investors, and rapid changes in stock prices result in efficient stock markets. The efficient market hypothesis suggests that investors cannot expect to outperform the market on a risk-adjusted basis over an extended period of time. Instead, the investor should earn a return that is consistent with the market return and the amount of risk the individual investor bears.

Empirical work tends to support the efficient market hypothesis. These studies provide evidence that investors cannot use public information to earn superior returns. There are, however, several anomalies such as the small firm effect or the use of low P/E ratios that are inconsistent with the efficient market hypothesis. These anomalies suggest that the investor may be able to earn excess returns and that financial markets have pockets of inefficiency.

Learning Objectives

Now that you have completed this chapter, you should be able to:

1. Distinguish between an expected return, required return, and realized return.
2. Calculate a common stock's value using a simple discounted cash flow model.
3. Integrate risk as measured by a stock's beta into the valuation of stock.
4. Explain how to use price to earnings (P/E) ratio, price to sales (P/S ratio), price to book value ratio, and the ratio of P/E to earnings growth (PEG) to select stocks.
5. Calculate earnings and dividend growth rates using several techniques.
6. Identify several possible anomalies to the efficient market hypothesis.

PROBLEMS

1) Given the following data, what should the price of the stock be?

Required return	10%
Present dividend	$1
Growth rate	5%

   a) If the growth rate increases to 6 percent and the dividend remains $1, what should the stock's price be?
   b) If the required return declines to 9 percent and the dividend remains $1, what should the price of the stock be? If the stock is selling for $20, what does that imply?

2) An investor requires a return of 12 percent. A stock sells for $25, it pays a dividend of $1, and the dividends compound annually at 7 percent. Will this investor find the stock attractive? What is the maximum amount that this investor should pay for the stock?

3) A firm's stock earns $2 per share, and the firm distributes 40 percent of its earnings as cash dividends. Its dividends grow annually at 7 percent.
   a) What is the stock's price if the required return is 10 percent?
   b) The firm borrows funds and, as a result, its per-share earnings and dividends increase by 20 percent. What happens to the stock's price if the growth rate and the required return are unaffected? What will the stock's price be if after using financial leverage and increasing the dividend to $1, the required return rises to 12 percent? What may cause this required return to rise?

4) The annual risk-free rate of return is 9 percent and the investor believes that the market will rise annually at 15 percent. If a stock has a beta coefficient of 1.5 and its current dividend is $1, what should be the value of the stock if its earnings and dividends are growing annually at 6 percent?

5) You are considering two stocks. Both pay a dividend of $1, but the beta coefficient of A is 1.5 while the beta coefficient of B is 0.7. Your required return is

$$k = 8\% + (15\% - 8\%)\beta$$

    a) What is the required return for each stock?

    b) If A is selling for $10 a share, is it a good buy if you expect earnings and dividends to grow at 5 percent?

    c) The earnings and dividends of B are expected to grow annually at 10 percent. Would you buy the stock for $30?

    d) If the earnings and dividends of A were expected to grow annually at 10 percent, would it be a good buy at $30?

6) You are offered two stocks. The beta of A is 1.4 while the beta of B is 0.8. The growth rates of earnings and dividends are 10 percent and 5 percent, respectively. The dividend yields are 5 percent and 7 percent, respectively.

    a) Since A offers higher potential growth, should it be purchased?

    b) Since B offers a higher dividend yield, should it be purchased?

    c) If the risk-free rate of return were 7 percent and the return on the market is expected to be 14 percent, which of these stocks should be bought?

7) Your broker suggests that the stock of QED is a good purchase at $25. You do an analysis of the firm, determining that the $1.40 dividend and earnings should continue to grow indefinitely at 8 percent annually. The firm's beta coefficient is 1.34, and the yield on Treasury bills is 7.4 percent. If you expect the market to earn a return of 12 percent, should you follow your broker's suggestion?

8) The required return on an investment is 12 percent. You estimate that firm X's dividends will grow as follows:

Year	Dividend
1	$1.20
2	2.00
3	3.00
4	4.50

For the subsequent years you expect the dividend to grow but at the more modest rate of 7 percent annually. What is the maximum price that you should pay for this stock?

9) Management has recently announced that expected dividends for the next three years will be as follows:

Year	Dividend
1	$2.50
2	3.25
3	4.00

For the subsequent years, management expects the dividend to grow at 5 percent annually. If the risk-free rate is 4.3 percent, the return on the market is 10.3 percent, and the firm's beta is 1.4, what is the maximum price that you should pay for this stock?

10) Management has recently announced that expected dividends for the next three years will be as follows:

Year	Dividend
1	$3.00
2	2.25
3	1.50

The firm's assets will then be liquidated and the proceeds invested in the preferred stock of other firms so that the company will be able to pay an annual dividend of $1.25 indefinitely. If your required return on investments in common stock is 10 percent, what is the maximum you should pay for this stock?

11) H.J. Heinz's annual dividends for 1990–2000 were as follows:

1990	$0.540
1991	0.620
1992	0.700
1993	0.780
1994	0.860
1995	0.940
1996	1.035
1997	1.135
1998	1.235
1999	1.344
2000	1.447

Use these payments to determine the historical growth rate of the dividend. Calculate growth rates based on (1) the average percentage change, (2) beginning and terminal values, and (3) regression analysis. (Regression is illustrated in the appendix to this chapter.) Do the growth rates differ?

Internet Application for Chapter 7
The Valuation and Selection of Common Stock

In the previous chapter you found financial information and ratios concerning the four firms. Locate the following additional information and complete the table.

	BUD	GTRC	HDI	PFE
Price of the stock				
P/E ratio				
P/B ratio				
P/S ratio				
PEG ratio				
Beta				

After completing the table, answer the following questions.

1. Which stock appears to be the least undervalued and the most overvalued according to each valuation ratio?

2. Which stock appears to be the best purchase based on this information?

3. Using the **current** interest rate on the six-month or the one-year Treasury bill and the historic returns on the market provided in Exhibit 4.2, apply the Capital Asset Pricing Model and the dividend-growth model. Develop a range of valuations based on this data. (You need the current risk-free rate because you are making the investment now!)

THOMSON ONE
Business School Edition

Currency with Thomson ONE: Business School Edition

Valuation is a major theme in finance and investments. What an asset (e.g., a stock) is worth permeates investment decisions. This chapter considered several methods to help answer that question and used several ratios to analyze a firm's financial statements. Go to the Thomson ONE: Business School Edition database and compare the following ratios for the pharmaceutical, retail, and telecommunication firms

Return on assets

Return on equity

Debt to total assets

Debt to equity

Price to earnings

Price to book

Estimated growth rate.

(Thomson ONE: Business School Edition provides information from several sources, so you may have to access more than one source to obtain the requested information.) Compare and interpret the data. Based solely on this information, which companies appear to be the best investments?

Appendix 7

Use of Regression Analysis to Estimate Growth Rates

In Chapter 3, regression analysis was used to estimate beta coefficients. In this appendix, it is used to estimate growth rates. The equation to be estimated is

$$D_0(1 + g)^n = D_n.$$

This equation states that the initial dividend (D_0) will grow at some rate (g) for some time period (n) into the future dividend (D_n). This equation may be expressed in the following general form:

$$(a)(b)^x = Y,$$

in which $Y = D_n$, $a = D_0$, $b = (1 + g)$, and $x = n$.

The equation is exponential, which is difficult to estimate, but it may be restated in log-linear form as:

$$\log Y = \log a + (\log b)X.$$

In this form, the least-squares method of regression may be used to estimate a and b. This procedure using dividends (Y) and time (X) is as follows:

Year (X)	Dividend (Y)	Log Y	X^2	X (log Y)
1	0.33	−0.48184	1	−0.48148
2	0.36	−0.44369	4	−0.88739
3	0.38	−0.42021	9	−1.26064
4	0.39	−0.40893	16	−1.63574
5	0.42	−0.37675	25	−1.88375
6	0.43	−0.36653	36	−2.19918
7	0.46	−0.33724	49	−2.36069
8	0.52	−0.28399	64	−2.27197
9	0.68	−0.16749	81	−1.50741
10	0.72	−0.14266	100	−1.42667
11	0.72	−0.14266	121	−1.56934
66	5.41	−3.57168	506	−17.4843

$$\log b = \frac{(n)\Sigma X(\log Y) - (\Sigma \log Y)(\Sigma X)}{(n)\Sigma X^2 - (\Sigma X)^2}$$

$$= \frac{(11)(-17.4843) - (-3.57168)(66)}{(11)(506) - (66)^2}$$

$$= \frac{43.40352}{1210} = 0.035870.$$

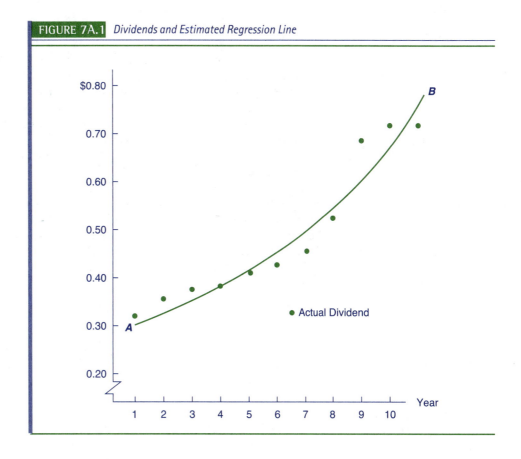

FIGURE 7A.1   *Dividends and Estimated Regression Line*

$$\log a = \frac{\Sigma \log Y}{n} - \frac{(\log b)\Sigma X}{n}$$

$$= \frac{-3.57168}{11} - (0.035870)(66/11)$$

$$= -0.5399.$$

The estimated equation is

$$\log Y = -0.5399 + 0.03587X.$$

The estimated equation is not in the desired form

$$(a)(b)^x = Y$$

to obtain

$$D_0(1 + g)^n = D_n.$$

The estimated equation is in logs and must be converted out of logs.
    Since $10^{-0.5399} = 0.2885$ and $10^{0.03587} = 1.0861$, the equation in the desired form is

$$(0.2885)(1.0861) = D_n.$$

Since $1.0861 = (1 + g)$, g must equal 0.0861 (i.e., $g - 1 = 0.0861$), so the growth rate is 8.61 percent.

Figure 7A.1 plots the dividends over time as well as the estimated equation (line *AB*). Although the observations lie both above and below the estimated line, they tend to follow closely the contour of the line, which suggests that the equation gives a good estimate of the historical rate of growth in the dividend. This conclusion is supported by the coefficient of determination (R_2), which is equal to 0.93—suggesting that 93 percent of the variation in the dividend is explained.

This example illustrates the mechanics of determining the regression equation. The same results may be obtained by using a regression program. Enter the year (1, 2, etc.) as the independent variable and the dividend in *logarithmic form* as the dependent variable. After you obtain the results, convert the equation back to exponential form to determine the rate of growth.

CHAPTER

8 ● ● ●

Technical Analysis

I n Bizet's *Carmen*, three gypsies use cards to foretell their future. One foresees a young lover
who sweeps her off her feet to experience never-ending love. Another foresees a rich, old
gentleman who marries her. She will have diamonds and gold and soon become a widow.
Carmen foresees death.

Wouldn't investing be easier if you could read the cards and foresee the future? Or if you could
find a trading rule that told you when to buy or sell? Then you would not have to perform the analysis described in the previous chapters. The technical approach to security selection purports to do just
that. By analyzing how the market (or a specific stock) has performed in the past, you may forecast
how the market (or a specific stock) will perform in the future. The study of historical data concerning
prices or the volume of transactions is substituted for analysis of financial statements and forecasts of
future dividends and the growth in earnings.

Technical analysis is a very broad topic because there are so many varieties of this type of analysis.
This chapter covers several popular technical approaches to the market and security selection. These
include the Dow Theory, point-and-figure charts, and moving averages. Since these techniques accumulate and summarize data in a variety of charts and graphs, investors who use these techniques are often
referred to as *chartists*.

The discussion in this chapter is primarily descriptive. After presenting several technical approaches,
the chapter considers the empirical studies that seek to verify the techniques. The results of these studies
strongly suggest that *technical analysis does not lead to superior investment results*. However, this lack of empirical support has not stopped the use of technical analysis, and some of its jargon is commonly used by both
professional and lay investors.

THE PURPOSE OF THE TECHNICAL APPROACH

The previous chapters have considered fundamental analysis and methods to value stocks for possible purchase. Such systematic study of the firm's financial condition and potential is the backbone of security analysis and value investing. While these techniques are the fundamental tools of security selection, they tell us little about timing security purchases. If a stock is undervalued, buy it! Timing the purchase is irrelevant.

A different type of analysis uses charts and graphs of price movements, the volume of security transactions, or sales and purchases by selected investors. This approach, especially some of the charts, can appear to be technical, hence the name *technical analysis*. The name does not imply that fundamental analysis is simple. The analysis of financial statements can be complex; however, in the jargon of investments, technical analysis implies a particular approach to security selection that is completely different from the systematic study of a firm's financial statements, its position within its industry, and the aggregate economy. In technical analysis the emphasis is placed on determining when to buy or sell. Such buy or sell signals may be independent of the firm's financial condition. Thus, technical analysis may recommend selling the stock of a financially strong firm if there are indicators that its price will decline.

THE VARIETY OF TECHNICAL ANALYSIS

technical analysis
An analysis of past volume and/or price behavior to identify which assets to purchase or sell and the best time to purchase or sell them.

Technical analysis attempts to predict future stock prices by analyzing past stock prices. In effect, it asserts that tomorrow's stock price is influenced by today's price. That is a very appealing assertion, because it eliminates the need to perform fundamental analysis. No longer do you have to be concerned with ratios, estimating growth, and appropriate discount rates. Instead, you keep a record of specific market factors, such as who is buying and selling the stock, and of specific information on individual stocks, such as the closing price and the volume of transactions. This information is then summarized in a variety of charts and graphs, which in turn tell you when to buy and sell the securities.

There are many different technical approaches to the selection of securities. Only a few will be discussed in this chapter. These are classified into two groups. The first techniques are designed to indicate the general direction of the market. Since security prices move together, the direction of the market is the important, perhaps overriding, factor in the decision to buy and sell securities. This first group of techniques includes the Dow Theory (which is perhaps the oldest of all the technical approaches to the market).

The second group of technical approaches discussed in this chapter is designed not only to discern the direction of the market but also to decide when to buy or sell specific securities. These include point-and-figure charts, bar graphs, and moving averages of stock prices. Before reading further, you should be forewarned that the presentations of the various approaches make their application appear to be easy. In actual practice the buy and sell signal indicated by technical analysis may be less obvious than the illustrations in the text. A technical indicator is constructed with data as they become available. Often, you can look back and see that a pattern has developed (e.g., a sell signal), and if the investor had sold, the correct decision would have been made. Hindsight, however, is 20/20. Seeing the pattern after the fact is not the same as perceiving the pattern as it is unfolding. Of course, you must perceive the indicator as it develops to act on it.

You should also realize that the efficient market hypothesis suggests that using technical analysis will not lead to superior investment results. Most empirical evidence supports this hypothesis. In addition, technical analysis may require frequent trading, which generates commissions and capital gains taxes. The evidence that does support technical analysis suggests that any superior results are small and may not cover the additional commissions and taxes. An obvious implication of these studies is that a strategy of buy and hold produces investment results that are equal to or better than those from trading strategies using technical analysis.

The debate concerning the efficacy of technical analysis will certainly continue, and the Internet increases your access to technical analysis if you make the effort to locate various indicators. The data are readily available; you may track stocks without having to perform any calculations such as a 200-day moving average. The jargon of technical analysis permeates the popular, if not the academic, press on investments. Even if you never use technical analysis as part of your personal investment strategy, you should be aware of this type of analysis and its terminology.

MARKET INDICATORS

The Dow Theory

The Dow Theory is one of the oldest technical methods for analyzing movements in the market. Since the Dow Jones averages are aggregate measures of security prices, the Dow Theory does not predict the direction of change in individual stock prices. What it purports to show is the direction that the market will take. Thus, it is a method that identifies the top of a bull market and the bottom of a bear market.

The Dow Theory developed from the work of Charles Dow, who founded Dow Jones and Company and was the first editor of *The Wall Street Journal.*[1] Dow identified three movements in security prices: primary, secondary, and tertiary. Primary price movements are related to the security's intrinsic value. Such values depend on the earning capacity of the firm and the distribution of dividends. Secondary price movements, or "swings," are governed by current events that temporarily affect value and by the manipulation of stock prices. These price swings may persist for several weeks and even months. Tertiary price movements are daily price fluctuations to which Dow attributed no significance.

Although Charles Dow believed in fundamental analysis, the Dow Theory has evolved into a primarily technical approach to the stock market. It asserts that stock prices demonstrate patterns over four to five years and that these patterns are mirrored by indexes of stock prices. The Dow Theory employs two of the Dow Jones averages, the industrial average and the transportation average. The utility average is generally ignored.

The Dow Theory is built on the assertion that measures of stock prices tend to move together. If the Dow Jones Industrial Average is rising, then the transportation average should also be rising. Such simultaneous price movements suggest a strong bull market. Conversely, a decline in both the industrial and transportation averages

---

1. George W. Bishop, Jr., *Charles H. Dow and the Dow Theory* (New York: Appleton-Century-Crofts, 1960), 225–228.

suggests a strong bear market. However, if the averages are moving in opposite directions, the market is uncertain as to the direction of future stock prices.

If one of the averages starts to decline after a period of rising stock prices, the two are at odds. For example, the industrial average may be rising while the transportation average is falling. This suggests that the industrials may not continue to rise but may soon start to fall. Hence, the smart investor will use this signal to sell securities and convert to cash.

The converse occurs when, after a period of falling security prices, one of the averages starts to rise while the other continues to fall. According to the Dow Theory, this divergence suggests that the bear market is over and that security prices in general will soon start to rise. The investor will then purchase securities in anticipation of the price increase.

There are several problems with this approach. Prior to the creation of the index funds discussed in Chapter 13, you had to select individual securities in anticipation that their prices would follow the market. While in general individual stock prices do follow the market, not all do. (That is the unsystematic risk associated with each stock.) You could be right about the direction of the market and still select the wrong stocks.

This problem no longer exists, since you can take a position on the market as a whole using an index fund. But other problems remain. First, there is the possibility of false (or at least ambiguous) signals. Second, there may be a time lag between an actual turning point and its subsequent confirmation, during which individual stocks and the market may generate substantial price changes.

Barron's Confidence Index

Barron's confidence index

An index designed to identify investors' confidence in the level and direction of security prices.

Barron's confidence index is based on the belief that the differential between the returns on quality bonds and bonds of lesser quality will forecast future price movements. During periods of optimism, investors will be more willing to bear risk and thus will move from investments in higher-quality debt to more speculative but higher-yielding, lower-quality debt. This selling of higher-quality debt will depress its price and raise its yield. Simultaneously, the purchase of poor-quality debt should drive up its price and lower the yield. Thus, the difference between the two yields will diminish.

The opposite occurs when sentiment turns bearish. The investors and especially those who "know" what the market will do in the future will sell poor-quality debt and purchase higher-quality debt. This will have the effect of increasing the spread between the yields, as the price of poor-quality debt falls relative to that of the higher-quality debt.

Barron's confidence index is constructed by using Barron's index of yields on higher- and lower-quality bonds. When the yield differential is small (i.e., when the yields on high-quality debt approach those that can be earned on poor-quality debt), the ratio rises. This is interpreted as showing investor confidence. Such confidence means that security prices will tend to rise. Conversely, when the index declines, that is an indication that security prices will fall.

Like the Dow Theory, Barron's confidence index indicates a tendency; however, it may not give conclusive signals. Since the signals of the Barron's confidence index are often ambiguous or there is a considerable time lag between the signal and the change forecasted, the index can be of only modest use for investors. Like many technical indicators, it may point to the direction that security prices will follow, but it is not a reliable predictor of future stock prices.

Purchase and Sale of Odd Lots

odd-lot theory
A technical approach to the stock market that purports to predict security prices on the basis of odd-lot sales and purchases.

The **odd-lot theory** concerns the purchase and sale of securities by small investors who buy in small quantities (i.e., odd lots, or less than 100 shares). The ratio of odd-lot purchases to odd-lot sales is used as an indicator of the direction of future prices.

The rationale behind the use of the ratio of odd-lot purchases to sales is the assertion that small investors are frequently wrong, especially just before a change in the direction of the market. Such investors will get caught up in the enthusiasm of a bull market and expand their purchases just as the market is reaching the top. The converse occurs at the market bottom. During declining markets, small investors become depressed about the market. After experiencing losses, they sell out as the market reaches its bottom. Such sales are frequently referred to as the passing of securities from "weak" hands to "strong" hands. The weak hands are, of course, the small investors who are misjudging the market, and the strong hands are the large investors who are more informed and capable of making correct investment decisions.

Generally, the ratio of odd-lot purchases to odd-lot sales ranges from 1.4 to 0.6. If the ratio approaches 1.25 to 1.30, that means the small investors are increasing their purchases relative to sales, which is a bearish signal. According to the odd-lot theory, such purchases forecast a decline in stock prices. If the ratio approaches 0.6, odd-lot sales exceed purchases, indicating that the small investor is bearish. Such bearishness on the part of the small investor is then taken as a bullish sign by believers in the odd-lot theory.

Like the Dow Theory and Barron's confidence index, the odd-lot theory illustrates a tendency, but there is also little concrete evidence of its ability to forecast accurately when the market will change. It assumes that purchasers of odd lots make inferior investment decisions, but you should remember that many large investors are also sellers at the market bottom and buyers at the market top. It has even been suggested that the real "odd-lotters" are the institutional investors and that individual investors may profit by doing the opposite of professional money managers.

Investment Advisory Opinions

While the odd-lot theory suggests that the small investor is often wrong, the advisory opinion theory suggests that financial advisors are often wrong. This approach is often referred to as a *contrarian* view, since it takes the opposite side of most financial advisors. The theory suggests that when most financial advisory services become bearish and forecast declining security prices, that is the time to purchase securities. When the majority become bullish and forecast rising security prices, the wise investor liquidates (i.e., sells securities). This technical indicator seems perverse, as it suggests that those most likely to know are unable to forecast the direction of security prices accurately.

Advances/Declines

The advance–decline cumulative series is an indicator based on the cumulative net difference between the number of stocks that rose in price relative to the number that declined. Consider the following summaries of daily trading on the New York Stock Exchange:

	Day	1	2	3	4
Issues advancing		1,200	820	480	210
Issues declining		400	760	950	1,190
Issues unchanged		200	220	370	400
Net advances (declines)		800	60	(470)	(980)
Cumulative net advances (declines)		800	860	390	(590)

During the first day, 800 more stocks rose than declined. While this pattern continued during the second day, the number of stocks rising was less than during the previous day, so the cumulative total registered only a small increment. During the third day, the market weakened, and the prices of more stocks fell than rose. However, the cumulative total remained positive. During the fourth day, the number of stocks that declined rose farther, so that the cumulative total now became negative.

According to technical analysis, the cumulative total of net advances gives an indication of the general direction of the market. If the market is rising, the net cumulative total will be positive and expanding; however, when the market changes direction, the cumulative total will start to diminish and will become negative as prices continue to decline. Of course, the converse applies at market bottoms. When the market declines, the net advances fall (i.e., the negative cumulative total increases). Once the bottom in the market has been reached and security prices start to rise, the number of advances will start to exceed the number of declines, which will cause the net advances to increase. Changes in the direction of advances/declines becomes a barometer of the trend in the market. (This technique is similar to moving averages, which are discussed later in this chapter and which are used to measure both the direction of prices in individual stocks and in the market as a whole.)

SPECIFIC STOCK INDICATORS

The preceding section discussed several technical approaches to the market as a whole. This section considers several techniques which, like the odd-lot theory, may be applied to either the market or individual securities. When applied to the market, their purpose is to identify the general trend. When applied to individual securities, these techniques attempt to time when to buy, when to sell, or when to maintain current positions in a specific security.

Point-and-Figure Charts (X-O Charts)

Most technical analysis has an underlying basis (or perhaps rationalization) in economics. In effect, these analytical techniques seek to measure what can't be measured: changes in supply and demand. Because an increase in demand will lead to higher prices and an increase in supply will lead to lower prices, an analysis that captures shifts in supply and demand will be able to forecast future price movements. **Point-and-figure charts**, also called **X-O charts**, attempt to identify changes in supply and demand by charting changes in security prices.

point-and-figure chart (X-O chart)
A chart composed of Xs and Os that is used in technical analysis to summarize price movements.

If a stock's price rises, that movement is caused by demand exceeding supply. If a stock's price falls, then supply exceeds demand. If a stock's price is stable and trades within a narrow range, the supply of the stock coming onto the market just offsets the current demand. However, when the stock's price breaks this stable pattern of price movements, there has been a fundamental shift in demand and/or supply. Thus, a movement upward suggests a change in demand relative to supply, while a movement downward suggests the opposite.

Point-and-figure charts identify these fundamental changes through the construction of graphs employing Xs and Os. Such an X-O chart is constructed by placing an X on the chart when the price of the stock rises by some amount, such as $1 or $2, and an O on the chart when it declines by that amount. (Some presentations use only Xs.) Such a chart requires tracking the stock on a daily basis, and if the price has changed by the specified amount, an entry is made on the chart.

This procedure is best explained by an illustration. Suppose the price of a stock had the following day-to-day price changes and the investor wanted to construct an X-O chart for price movements of $2. The procedure is illustrated in Figure 8.1.

Daily Closing Prices for January

Date	Prices				
1/1–1/5	$50.13	$51.38	$51.75	$52.50	$54.13
1/8–1/12	53.50	53.13	52.50	51.87	51.13
1/15–1/19	49.50	49.75	47.13	48.75	47.88
1/22–1/26	49.75	46.88	46.12	45.88	44.87

Figure 8.1 is divided into four quadrants, which illustrate the four steps necessary to create the chart.

The first quadrant (A) sets up the axes—time on the horizontal axis and dollars on the vertical axis. *Time is measured in variable units,* since a movement along the X-axis could occur after a week, a month, or a year. The dollar unit depends on the prices of the stock. For lower-priced stocks, the units may be $1, but for higher-priced stocks

FIGURE 8.1 *The Construction of an X-O Chart*

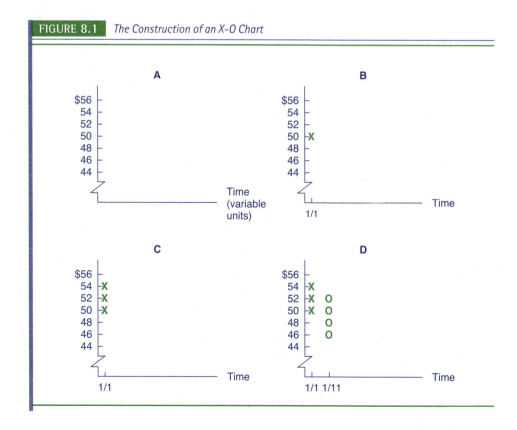

the units may be larger, such as $2 or $3. Since a movement from $40 to $42 is the same percentage increase as a price movement from $20 to $21, the use of the larger increments for higher-priced stocks does not reduce the quality of the X-O chart. In addition, the use of larger units reduces the number of entries necessary to create the chart. In this illustration, a $2 interval is used, so the vertical axis shows the increments in $2 units.

The second quadrant (B) plots the price of the stock on the first day of observation. Since the price of the stock is rising, the chartist enters an X at $50 on the chart. Additional Xs are entered only after the price of the stock rises by $2 (e.g., $50 to $52). All small movements in price both up and down are ignored, and only after the price has risen by $2 is a second X entered on the chart. Thus, although the price of the stock rose during the first three days, no entry is made. The effect of such omissions is both to reduce the work required to construct the chart and to minimize the effect of small daily price fluctuations.

The third quadrant (C) plots the price increases that occurred on days 4 and 5. The price closed above $52 on day 4, so an X is placed on the chart. The same applies to day 5, when the stock closed above $54.

The fourth quadrant (D) illustrates the decline in the stock's price. After reaching a high of $54.50, the price of the stock starts to fall. The chartist now uses only Os instead of Xs to indicate the declining price. Once again, the price must fall by $2 before an entry is made (i.e., the stock must sell for $52 or less, since $54 was the highest X entry). The date on which Os began to be recorded on the chart is noted on the horizontal axis. Once the price reaches $52, an O is placed on the chart. This occurs on January 11. The analyst will continue to place Os on the chart until the present downward trend is reversed and the price of the stock rises by the necessary $2. Then the analyst will start a new column and enter an X to indicate an increase in the stock's price.

In this case, the price of the stock continues to decline. Each time the stock breaks the two-point barrier, another O is placed on the chart. If the price continues to decline, the column will fill up with Os. If the stock's price stabilizes, no entries will be made until a two-point movement occurs.

After a period of stable prices, a deviation signals the direction of future price changes. Such signals are illustrated in Figure 8.2. On the left-hand side (A), after a period of trading between $52 and $58, the price of the stock rises to a new high of $60. This suggests that a new upward price trend is being established, which is a buy signal. On the right-hand side (B), the opposite case is illustrated. The price declines below $52, which suggests that a new downward price trend is being established. If you own the stock, you should sell it.

In both cases illustrated in Figure 8.2, the purchases and sales *appear to be made at the wrong time*. In the case of the purchase, it is made after the stock has already increased in price. Conversely, the sale is made after the stock has declined in price. Thus, purchases are not made at the lows, and sales are not made at the highs. Instead, the purchases appear to be made when the stock is reaching new highs, and the sales are made when the stock is reaching new lows. The rationale for this behavior rests primarily on the belief that the *charts indicate new trends*. Despite the fact that you missed the high prices for the sale and the low prices for the purchase, if the price change that is being forecasted proves accurate, then you will have made the correct investment decision even though the purchases and sales were not made at the exact turning points.

Besides indicating the buy or sell signals when trends are being established, these charts suggest possible trading strategies during the trends, which are also illustrated in Figure 8.2. While the left-hand side shows a price that is obviously ris-

FIGURE 8.2   *Buy and Sell Signals*

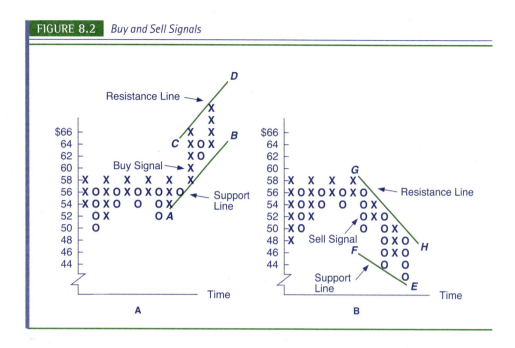

ing, the price is still fluctuating. The right-hand side illustrates a downward trend, but the price is also fluctuating. During the upward trend, each high is higher than the preceding high price, and each low is higher than the preceding low price. Obviously, if you buy this stock and hold it, the return will be positive over this period. However, the return may be increased by judiciously buying at each low, selling at each high, and repeating the process when the cycle within the trend is repeated.

In order to isolate these opportunities, a set of lines has been drawn in Figure 8.2 connecting the high and the low prices that the stock is achieving. These lines are believed to have special significance because they indicate when to make the buy and sell decisions. The bottom lines (*AB* and *EF*), which connect the lowest prices, suggest a price level that generates "support" for the stock. Technical analysis asserts that when the price of the stock approaches a support line, the number of purchases will increase, which will stop further price declines. Hence, the approach of a stock's price toward a support line suggests that a buying opportunity is developing. Should the price reach the line and then start to climb, the investor should buy the stock.

The opposite occurs at the top lines (*CD* and *GH*), which represents "resistance." Since the price of the stock has risen to that level, more investors will want to sell their stock, which will thwart further price advances. Accordingly, you should sell the stock when the price reaches a line of resistance. After the stock has been sold, you then wait for the price to decline to the level of price support (or sell the stock short).

The buy and sell signals indicated by stocks bouncing off of lines *AB* or *EF* and *CD* or *GH* should not be confused with the buy and sell signals that occur when the resistance and support lines are broken. The former is a trading signal; you buy and sell within the trading range. Breaking the resistance or support lines indicates a fundamental shift in supply or demand. Instead of selling the stock when the resistance line is broken, you see the penetration as a strong buy signal. Once the purchases are made, this long position will be maintained until a new price pattern emerges. The opposite occurs when the support line is broken. Any long positions are sold, and you should sell the stock short. (If you are a conservative investor, you may choose not to sell short. Remember, the most you can lose when you buy is the cost of the stock, but the most you could lose if you sell short is, at least theoretically, unlimited.)

Bar Graphs

bar graph
A graph indicating the high, low, and closing prices of a security.

Bar graphs are similar to point-and-figure charts. Like the X-O charts, they require a day-to-day compilation of data and use essentially the same information. Preference for one over the other is a matter of choice.

A bar graph is constructed by using three price observations—the high, the low, and the closing price for the day. If the prices were

Price	Monday	Tuesday	Wednesday	Thursday	Friday
High	$10	$9.50	$9.88	$10.50	$12
Low	9	9	9.25	9.88	10.13
Close	9	9.37	9.87	10	11.50

the bar graphs for each day would be

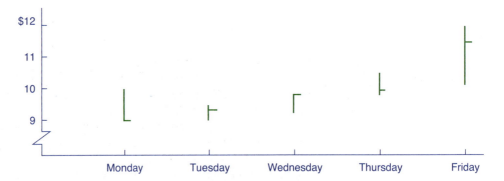

The vertical lines represent the range of the stock's price (i.e., the high and the low prices), and the horizontal lines represent the closing price.

As with the X-O chart, the bar graph is supposed to indicate future price movements in the stock by the pattern that emerges. There are several possible patterns, each with a descriptive name, such as head and shoulder, rounded tops, and descending triangles. Space limits this discussion to only one pattern: the head and shoulder. If you are interested in the variety of patterns, consult a book that explains the different patterns and how they are used to predict future stock prices.[2]

2. Descriptions of various patterns may be found in Clifford Pistolese, *Using Technical Analysis*, rev. ed. (Chicago: Probus, 1994). This paperback includes self-teaching exercises designed to test the reader's ability to spot patterns in stock prices. Other books that explain and illustrate various methods of technical analysis include Steven B. Achelis, *Technical Analysis from A to Z* (Chicago: Probus, 1995); Jake Bernstein, *The Compleat Day Trader: Trading Systems, Strategies, Timing Indicators, and Analytical Methods* (New York: McGraw-Hill Book Company, 1995); Tushar Chande and Stanley Kroll, *The New Technical Trader: Boost Your Profit by Plugging Into the Latest Indicators* (New York: John Wiley & Sons, 1994); Richard Hexton, *Technical Analysis in the Options Market: The Effective Use of Computerized Trading Systems* (New York: John Wiley & Sons, 1995); John J. Murphy, *Technical Analysis of the Financial Markets* (New York: New York Institute of Finance, 1999); Rick Bensignor, ed., *New Thinking in Technical Analysis* (Princeton, NJ; Bloomberg Press, 2000); and Robert D. Edwards and John Magee, *Technical Analysis of Stock Trends*, 8th ed. (Boca Raton, FL: CRC Press, 2001).

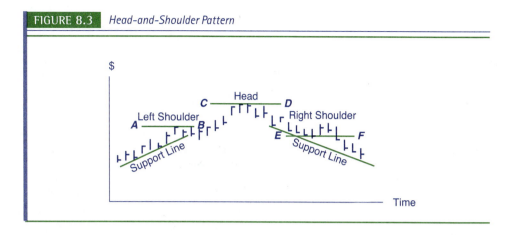

FIGURE 8.3   *Head-and-Shoulder Pattern*

head–and–shoulder pattern
A tool of technical analysis; a pattern of security prices that resembles a head and shoulders.

A **head-and-shoulder pattern** does just what its name implies: The graph forms a pattern that resembles a head and shoulders. Such a pattern is illustrated in Figure 8.3. Initially, the price of the stock rises. Then it levels off before rising to a new high, after which the price declines, levels off, and then starts to fall. To illustrate the head-and-shoulder pattern, several lines have been imposed on the graph. These lines are similar to the lines of resistance and support found on the X-O charts, and X-O charts also develop head-and-shoulder patterns. Line *AB* shows the left shoulder and also represents a line of resistance. However, once it is penetrated, the price of the stock rises to a new high, where it meets new resistance (line *CD*).

When the stock is unable to penetrate this new resistance, the price starts to decline and forms the head. However, after this initial decline in price the stock reaches a new level of support, which forms the right shoulder (line *EF*). When the price falls below line *EF*, the head-and-shoulder pattern is completed. This is interpreted to mean that the stock's price will continue to fall and is taken as bearish sign by followers of this type of analysis.

While the head-and-shoulder pattern in Figure 8.3 indicates that the price of the stock will subsequently fall, the same pattern upside down implies the exact opposite. In this case, penetration of the right shoulder indicates that the price of the stock will rise and is taken as a bullish sign by those who use bar graphs.

Candlesticks

Sometimes the bar graphs are drawn as "candlesticks." Candlestick graphs require four prices: the open, the close, the high, and the low. A thin line (the "shadow") connects the high and low prices. The body of the candlestick connects the opening and closing prices. If the open price exceeds the closing price, indicating that the price fell, the body of the candlestick is filled in (i.e., is black). If the open price is less than the closing price (the price rose), the body is left open (i.e., is white). For example, suppose a stock had the following prices during the week:

	Monday	Tuesday	Wednesday	Thursday	Friday
High	$10.00	$9.50	$10.00	$10.00	$10.00
Open	9.50	9.50	9.50	9.25	9.50
Close	9.25	9.25	9.75	9.50	9.50
Low	9.00	9.00	9.50	9.00	9.00

the candlestick graphs for each day would be

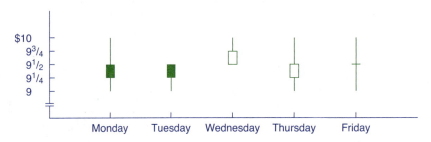

As perhaps would be expected, dark candlesticks (especially long sticks that indicate a large decline from the opening to the closing price) are bearish indicators, while light candlesticks are bullish. Candlesticks may also be used to construct head-and-shoulder patterns and other configurations that technical analysts use to forecast the direction of stock prices.

Moving Averages

moving average
An average in which the most recent observation is added and the most distant observation is deleted before the average is computed.

A **moving average** is an average computed over time. For example, suppose the closing monthly values for the Dow Jones Industrial Average were as follows:

January	9,287	April	9,258	July	9,347	October	9,374
February	9,284	May	9,315	August	9,334	November	9,472
March	9,267	June	9,335	September	9,328	December	9,547

A six-month moving average of the Dow Jones industrials would be computed as follows. The average for the first six months is computed first.

$$\frac{9{,}287 + 9{,}284 + 9{,}267 + 9{,}258 + 9{,}315 + 9{,}335}{6} = \frac{55{,}746}{6} = 9{,}291.$$

Then the average is computed again, but the entry for July (9,347) is added in and the entry for January (9,287) is deleted:

$$\frac{9{,}284 + 9{,}267 + 9{,}258 + 9{,}315 + 9{,}335 + 9{,}347}{6} = \frac{55{,}806}{6} = 9{,}301.$$

The average is now 9,301, which is greater than the average for the preceding six months (9,291).

To obtain the next entry, the average is computed again, with August being added and February being dropped. The average in this case becomes 9,309. By continuing this method of adding the most recent entry and dropping the oldest entry, the averages move through time.

Figure 8.4 presents both the Dow Jones Industrial Average for 1984 through 1994 and the six-month moving average. (The monthly data for continuing the figure are provided in the assignment.) As may be seen from the figure, the moving average follows the Dow Jones industrials. However, when the Dow Jones industrials are declining, the moving average is greater than the industrial average. The converse is true when the Dow Jones Industrial Average is rising: The moving average is less than the industrial average. At several points the two lines cross. For example, the Dow Jones Industrial Average crossed the six-month moving

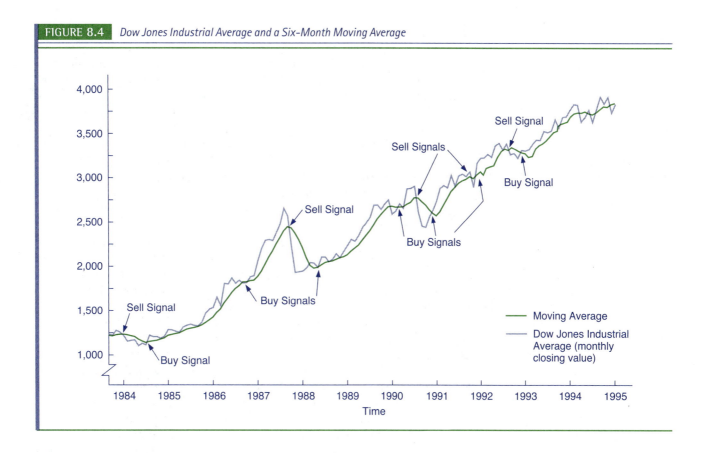

FIGURE 8.4 *Dow Jones Industrial Average and a Six-Month Moving Average*

average in early 1988. Technicians place emphasis on such a crossover, for they believe that it is indicative of a change in the direction of the market. (It may also indicate a change in a specific security's price when the moving average is computed for a particular stock.) In this illustration, there appears to be some validity to the claim of the predictive power of the moving average, as the market rose after the buy signals and fell after the sell signals.

Thanks to the Internet, you do not have to compute moving averages. You can readily find 50-day, 100-day, and 200-day moving averages for time periods such as six months, a year, or five years. Frequently you may customize the data for whatever period you want. There is, however, little evidence that using moving averages of different durations produces inferior or superior results. (If one average were superior, only that average would be computed. The existence of so many moving averages might cause you to ask "Why so many?")[3]

Volume

The preceding techniques emphasized price movements as measured by point-and-figure charts, bar graphs, and moving averages. Technical analysts also place emphasis on the volume of transactions and deviations from the normal volume of

---

3. Moving averages may be combined with other technical indicators. See, for instance, Kenneth Tower, "Applying Moving Averages to Point and Figure Charts," in Rick Bensignor, ed., *New Thinking in Technical Analysis* (Princeton, NJ: Bloomberg Press, 2000).

trading. A large deviation from normal volume is interpreted to mean a change in the demand for or supply of the stock.

Since a price change can occur on small volume or on large volume, the price change itself says nothing concerning the breadth of the change in demand or supply. A price increase on small volume is not as bullish as one accompanied by heavy trading. Conversely, a price decline on small volume is not as bearish as a decline accompanied by a large increase in the number of shares traded. When a price decline occurs on small volume, that indicates that only a modest increase in the supply of the stock was offered for sale relative to the demand. However, if the price decline were to occur on a large increase in volume, that would indicate many investors were seeking to sell the stock, which would be considered bearish.

Short Sales by Specialists

As was explained in Chapter 1, specialists make a market in securities listed on the organized exchanges (i.e., they offer to buy and sell securities for their own accounts). In order to make a market, specialists must be abreast of the events affecting securities. They continually adjust their portfolios in response to the flow of securities to and from the market. It is through this process that they make the market in the individual securities. If they misjudge demand and supply and subsequent price changes, they could suffer large losses.

If specialists believe that the supply of stock will increase and drive down a stock's price, they take short positions in the stock in anticipation of the price decline. Total short sales and specialists' short sales must be reported to the SEC and the NYSE. Generally, about half of all short sales are made by the specialists. If, however, the specialists' proportion of total short sales rises to above 65 percent, technical analysts believe this is a bearish indicator. The high ratio of specialists' short sales indicates that those who may be best able to perceive changes in supply and demand are anticipating price declines. If the ratio of specialists' short sales to total short sales falls to 40 percent, technical analysts interpret that as a bullish sign, indicative of rising future stock prices.

THE VERIFICATION OF TECHNICAL ANALYSIS

At first glance, technical analysis seems so very appealing. All you need is a set of charts and you then follow the signals given by the analysis. Such simple rules for investing literally beg for verification to ascertain if they are, in fact, good predictors.

Several studies have sought to test the validity of technical analysis. The use of computers has eased calculations and made it possible to test several variations of the technical approach. For example, the investigator may have the computer calculate various moving averages (e.g., 200-day, 100-day, or 50-day averages) to determine if one is the best predictor.

The majority of this research has failed to verify the various technical approaches to investing.[4] This conclusion is the basis for the weak form of the

4. For example, see Michael C. Jensen and George A. Bennington, "Random Walks and Technical Theories: Some Additional Evidence," *Journal of Finance* 25 (May 1970): 469–482; Eugene Fama, "The Behavior of Stock Market Prices," *Journal of Business* 37 (January 1965): 34–105; F. E. James, Jr., "Monthly Moving Averages—An Effective Investment Tool?" *Journal of Financial and Quantitative Analysis* (September 1968): 315–326; and J. C. Van Horne and G. G. C. Parker, "The Random Walk Theory: An Empirical Test," *Financial Analysts Journal* (November/December 1967): 87–92. Empirical support for technical analysis may be found in Robert A. Levy, "Random Walks: Reality or Myth," *Financial Analysts Journal* (November/December 1967): 69–77.

efficient market hypothesis discussed in Chapter 2. The large body of empirical evidence has convinced many investors to believe that the technical approach does not lead to superior investment performance and that you would do just as well to buy a randomly selected portfolio and hold it. When commissions are included, the return from following the technical approach may be even less than that earned on a randomly selected portfolio. These conclusions have resulted in a general rejection of technical analysis by many academically trained teachers of finance.

Although technical analysis has found little support in the financial academic community, this may be changing since the publication of studies by respected researchers in investments that supported technical analysis.[5] These studies suggested that a simple set of trading rules using moving averages and support and resistance levels did have forecasting power for changes in the Dow Jones Industrial Average. The results also suggested that traders could improve returns over a buy-and-hold strategy. Unfortunately, the improvement in returns requires frequent trading, which involves transaction costs. Another study found that when transaction costs are factored into the analysis, returns are not improved over buy-and-hold.[6] This result is, of course, consistent with efficient markets. (With the advent of electronic trading and its minimal transaction costs, it may become possible to use trading rules, pay the commissions, and beat a buy-and-hold strategy. Stay tuned.)

One major reason why technical approaches cannot lead to superior investment results is the speed with which security prices change. Information is readily disseminated among the investors, and prices adjust accordingly.[7] Thus, if an investor were to develop an approach that outperformed the market, it would only be a matter of time before the technique would be learned by others. The method would no longer achieve the initial results as additional investors applied it. A system that works (if one can be found) can succeed only if it is not known by many investors, and it is hard to believe that the individual investor will find a technical approach that can beat the market.

Although the technical approach may lack verification, it is still used by some portfolio managers as a supplement to fundamental analysis to help the timing of purchases and sales.[8] One frequently sees advertisements in the financial press or on the Internet for advisory services that employ various technical approaches. Perhaps you should ask why the service is being sold and not being applied exclusively by those who know the "secret." Certainly, if you know how to beat the market, you should be able to earn a substantial return on investments and should not need to sell the secret for monetary gain.

---

5. William Brock, Josef Lakonishok, and Blake LeBaron, "Simple Technical Trading Rules and the Stochastic Properties of Stock Returns," *Journal of Finance* 47 (December 1992): 1731–1764; and Andrew Lo, Harry Mamaysky, and Jiang Wang, "Foundation of Technical Analysis," *Journal of Finance* 55 (August 2000): 1705–1765.
6. Hendrick Bessembinder and Kolok Chan, "Market Efficiency and the Returns to Technical Analysis," *Financial Management* (summer 1998): 5–17.
7. One study found that the technical approach may be a lagging and not a leading indicator of stock prices. In an efficient market, prices may react before the technical indicator gives a signal of the change. Thus, by the time the signal is observed, prices have already responded, and there is no opportunity for the investor to take advantage of the signal. See Ben Branch and Thomas Schneeweis, "Market Movements and Technical Market Indicators," *The Mid-Atlantic Journal of Business* (summer 1986): 31–41.
8. For an integration of fundamental and technical analysis, see Lawrence Stein, *The Fundamental Stock Market Technician* (Chicago: Probus, 1986); and Steven P. Rich and William Reichenstein, "Market Timing for the Individual Investor: Using the Predictability of Long-Horizon Stock Returns to Enhance Portfolio Performance," *Financial Services Review* (1993/1994): 29–43.

THE DOGS OF THE DOW

One investment strategy that recently has come into prominence is the Dogs of the Dow.[9] (Weak stocks or low-priced stocks are sometimes referred to as "dogs.") This simple strategy is neither a technical approach nor a fundamental approach to the selection of securities. Since it requires no analysis of past stock prices, volume of trading, or any other method of technical analysis, it is not readily classifiable as a technical approach. The Dogs of the Dow, however, also avoids the fundamental analysis of financial statements, the valuation of cash flows, and the estimation of future growth rates. Since the Dow dog strategy is mechanical, it is more comparable to technical approaches than to valuation methods for selecting stocks and is included in this chapter.

The Dogs of the Dow strategy requires you to rank all 30 stocks in the Dow Jones Industrial Average from highest to lowest based on their dividend yields (dividend divided by the price of the stock). You then buy an equal dollar amount of the ten stocks with the highest dividend yields. (An alternative strategy is to buy the five lowest-priced "small dogs" of the ten highest-yielding dividend stocks.) After one year, the process is repeated. The Dow stocks are once again ranked, and, if a stock continues to be among the ten highest dividend yields, it is retained. If the stock is no longer among the ten, it is sold and replaced by a new Dow dog that is one of the ten stocks with the highest dividend yields.

This strategy has obvious appeal. First, since it is rebalanced only once a year, commission costs are modest. Second, by waiting one additional day so the portfolio adjustments occur after a year, all capital gains are long-term. Third, by buying the Dow stocks with the highest dividend yields, this yield may offer some downside protection from further price declines. Fourth, buying the Dow dogs is acquiring the stocks in the Dow that are currently out of favor and is consistent with a contrarian strategy.

Does the system work? There is evidence that the Dow dividend strategy produces higher returns than the Dow itself.[10] The evidence, however, also shows that the standard deviations of the returns on the Dow dogs exceeded the standard deviations of the returns on the Dow Jones Industrial Average and the S&P 500 stock index. (A Dow dog portfolio is less diversified, so the expectation would be for greater variability in the returns.) This result is, of course, consistent with efficient markets: More risk-taking generates higher returns. The empirical results also suggest that over long periods, such as a decade, a strategy of buying and holding all the Dow stocks was a better alternative after considering risk, taxes, and transaction costs.

BEHAVIORAL FINANCE

Ken Tower, a technical analyst with CyberTrader and frequent commentator on CNBC and Bloomberg, and I have a running friendly debate concerning the value of technical analysis. He has often visited my classes and illustrated charts and moving averages. He does a better job than I would ever do because he believes

---

9. The Dow dividend strategy was popularized in Michael O'Higgins, *Beating the Dow* (New York: Harper Perennial, 1992). Information concerning the Dow dogs, such as which stocks would currently compose a Dow dog portfolio, may be found at **http://www.dogsofthedow.com**.

10. Evidence that the strategy generates larger returns but the returns are more variable may be found in George Wunder and Herbert Mayo, "Study Supports Efficient Market Hypothesis," *Journal of Financial Planning* (July 1995): 128–135; and Grant McQueen, Kay Shields, and Steven R. Thorley, "Does the Dow-10 Investment Strategy Beat the Dow Statistically and Economically?" *Financial Analysts Journal* (July–August 1997): 66–72.

the analysis does contribute to security selection and portfolio management. As an academic, I have skepticism concerning the efficacy of technical analysis. The evidence for efficient markets is hard to ignore!

However, in a recent class visit, he made one of those telling remarks. Essentially it was that even if the analysis does not necessarily lead to superior results, it would have protected you from the large declines that occurred during 2000-2002. He then showed numerous illustrations in which stocks like Enron, Lucent, and Cisco experienced major declines in price. Ken added that when the prices of these stocks declined, it was natural to think that the declines were buying opportunities ("Everybody loves a sale"), but the charts were not telling you that. Buying these stocks was not a case of "buying on weakness"; instead, the charts were telling you that something fundamental had changed. You might not have known what that change was or why it was occurring, but answering these questions was irrelevant. The charts were telling you to get out.

In one sense, Ken's comments and technical analysis try to help you overcome your personal psychology and how you rationalize investment decisions.[11] Obviously, psychology is important to investing and how you personally make investment decisions. A new discipline, "behavioral finance," has emerged that combines investments and psychology and studies the behavior of individuals as it applies to investment decision making. Behavioral finance stresses that many of us, both individual investors and professional money managers, are subject to bias, incorrect perceptions, and overconfidence. These biases may lead to our over- or underpricing securities. Overconfidence often leads to an inaccurate assessment of risk. If we could only overcome these psychological problems, perhaps we could become better investors.

A large part of behavioral finance is built around investor emotion and how individuals process information. This emotion helps explain why we retain losing positions or select information that confirms our preconceived notions. If you want to buy a penny stock, you can certainly rationalize the purchase. ("It is only $0.24 a share. How much lower can it go?" The answer is obviously $0.00!) The same applies to acquiring land as an investment. ("They aren't making it anymore!") Behavioral finance would suggest that we are not rational and that our irrational behavior leads to inferior investment decisions.[12] My sister could take this irrational behavior to an extreme. She would not sell a stock that had risen. ("I'll have to pay the tax on the gain.") Of course, she would not sell a stock that had declined. ("I paid more; I'd have to take a loss.") By that reasoning, you would never sell anything.

All investors make mistakes. I have never bought a stock because I thought it was going to decline, and I doubt you will ever do so either. But making mistakes is human (no one gets married because they expect to get divorced). Often our decisions are based on expectations that are not fulfilled. As Disraeli expressed it: "What we anticipate seldom occurs; what we least expected generally happens." Technical analysis may help you make better investment decisions by removing the emotion associated with your investment decisions. You follow the system you have selected, and if the charts say *sell*, you sell. Emotion is excluded: *No* attachment to the security, *No* consideration for commissions, and *No* consideration for taxes. You just sell.

---

11. Background material on behavioral finance may be obtained from John R. Nofsinger, *The Psychology of Investing*, 2nd ed. (Upper Saddle River, NJ: Pearson Prentice Hall, 2005) and Hersh Shefrin, *Beyond Greed and Fear* (Oxford University Press, 2002).
12. A portfolio advisor once said to me that during rising markets people "believe in the market. I could make a rabid dog look good and they will 'believe' it is safe."

SUMMARY

Technical analysis seeks to identify superior investments by examining the past behavior of the market and of individual securities. Technical analysts, or "chartists," stress the past as a means to predict the future. This approach is diametrically opposed to the fundamental approach, which stresses future earnings and dividends, (i.e., cash flows) appropriately discounted back to the present.

Several technical approaches (the Dow Theory, Barron's confidence index, and odd-lot purchases versus odd-lot sales) attempt to identify changes in the direction of the market. Because individual security prices move together, the determination of a change in the direction of the market should identify the future movement of individual security prices.

Other technical approaches (X-O charts, bar graphs, and moving averages) may be applied to the market and to individual securities. By constructing various charts and graphs, the technical analyst determines when specific securities should be bought or sold.

A strategy involving the use of Dow Jones Industrial Average stocks selects the ten Dow stocks with the highest yields. These stocks are held for exactly one year, at which time the portfolio is rebalanced to continue holding the Dow stocks with the highest dividend yields.

Whether technical approaches to market timing and security selection lead to superior results (i.e., higher risk-adjusted returns) is an empirical question. With some exceptions, academic research has produced little support for technical analysis. The results of these studies suggest that the investor may achieve similar or superior results by purchasing and holding a well-diversified portfolio of securities.

Learning Objectives

Now that you have completed this chapter, you should be able to:

1. State the purpose of technical analysis.
2. Differentiate among various technical approaches to security selection.
3. Construct X-O charts, bar graphs, and candlesticks.
4. Calculate a moving average.
5. Use technical analysis, especially charts and moving averages, to time the purchase and sale of stock.
6. Construct a portfolio based on the Dogs of the Dow.
7. Discuss technical analysis in an efficient market context.
8. Describe how behavioral finance helps explain why an individual may make poor investment decisions.

ASSIGNMENT

Continue Figure 8.4, using the following data to determine the buy and sell signals. Based on the signals, would you have avoided the market decline experienced during 2000–2002 and caught the market increase during 2003?

Year–month	DJIA	Six-Month Moving Average	Year–month	DJIA	Six-Month Moving Average
94–1	3834	3693	2	8546	7929
2	3832	3723	3	8800	8071
3	3636	3737	4	9063	8341
4	3682	3737	5	8900	8521
5	3758	3749	6	8952	8695
6	3625	3728	7	8883	8857
7	3765	3716	8	7539	8690
8	3918	3731	9	7843	8530
9	3843	3765	10	8592	8452
10	3908	3803	11	9117	8488
11	3739	3800	12	9181	8526
12	3834	3835	99–1	9359	8605
95–1	3843	3848	2	9307	8900
2	4011	3863	3	9786	9224
3	4158	3916	4	10789	9590
4	4329	3986	5	10560	9830
5	4465	4107	6	10971	10129
6	4606	4235	7	10655	10345
7	4727	4383	8	10829	10598
8	4616	4484	9	10337	10690
9	4817	4593	10	10730	10680
10	4801	4672	11	10878	10733
11	5119	4781	12	11497	10821
12	5117	4866	00–1	10941	10869
96–1	5409	4980	2	10128	10752
2	5531	5132	3	10922	10849
3	5645	5270	4	10734	10850
4	5580	5400	5	10522	10791
5	5643	5488	6	10448	10616
6	5655	5577	7	10522	10546
7	5529	5597	8	11215	10727
8	5616	5611	9	10651	10682
9	5882	5651	10	10971	10722
10	6029	5726	11	10414	10704
11	6522	5872	12	10787	10760
12	6448	6004	01–1	10887	10821
97–1	6813	6218	2	10495	10701
2	6878	6429	3	9879	10572
3	6583	6546	4	10735	10533
4	7009	6709	5	10912	10616
5	7330	6844	6	10502	10568
6	7673	7048	7	10523	10508
7	8223	7283	8	9950	10417
8	7622	7407	9	8848	10245
9	7945	7634	10	9075	9968
10	7442	7706	11	9852	9792
11	7823	7788	12	10022	9712
12	7908	7827	02–1	9920	9611
98–1	7907	7775	2	10106	9637

Year–month	DJIA	Six-Month Moving Average	Year–month	DJIA	Six-Month Moving Average
3	10414	9898	2	7891	8195
4	9946	10043	3	7992	8262
5	8925	9889	4	8481	8276
6	9243	9759	5	8851	8268
7	8737	9562	6	8985	8376
8	8664	9322	7	9234	8572
9	7592	8851	8	9416	8827
10	8397	8593	9	9275	9040
11	8896	8588	10	9801	9260
12	8342	8438	11	9782	9416
03–1	8053	8324	12	10454	9660

Source: Yahoo! (http://finance.yahoo.com). For information on the Dow Jones averages and indexes go to http://www.djindexes.com.

Internet Application for Chapter 8 Technical Analysis

Hindsight is 20/20. Technical analysis often appears to be hindsight, that is, the charts appear to have recommended purchases or sales and the signals proved to be correct. However, you make investment decisions in the present and not the past, and the current signals given by the charts may be hard to perceive. Find two technical indicators such as the 200-day moving average and determine if you should be long or short in each of the four stocks.

In addition to the sites that you have previously been using, consider the following specialized sites.

Ask Research   http://www.askresearch.com

Dorsey Wright & Associates   http://www.dorseywright.com

Equity Analytics, Ltd   http://www-analytics.com

Silicon Investor   http://www.siliconinvestor.com.

Currency with Thomson ONE: Business School Edition

This chapter explains several "technical" indicators for selecting stocks such as moving averages. From the Thomson ONE: Business School Edition database, find the 200-day moving average for the fifteen stocks. Based only on this indicator, should you be long or short in each of the stocks? Does the 50-day moving average concur or does that indicator give a contradictory signal?

CHAPTER

9 ● ● ●

The Corporate Bond Market

I In *The Merchant of Venice*, Antonio secured his debt with Shylock with a "pound of flesh." And you thought your credit card interest rate was bad! Perhaps that is why Polonius advised Hamlet "neither a borrower nor a lender be." The terms of a loan can be onerous, but corporations and governments do borrow, often under burdensome terms, to finance investments in plant, equipment, or inventory or for the construction of roads and schools. Internally generated funds are often insufficient to finance such investments on a pay-as-you-go basis. Bonds, which mature at the end of a term longer than one year, permit firms and governments to acquire assets now and pay for them over a period of years. This long-term debt is then retired for corporations by the cash flow that is generated by plant and equipment and for governments by the fees or tax revenues that are collected.

The next three chapters are concerned with bonds and cover (1) the characteristics common to all debt instruments, (2) the risks associated with investing in debt, (3) the mechanics of purchasing bonds, (4) the retirement of debt, and (5) the valuation of bonds. Like stock, bonds may be purchased initially through a private placement or through a public offering. Once the securities are issued, secondary markets develop. While many stocks trade through organized stock markets, the secondary market for bonds is primarily an over-the-counter market. This fact does not limit your ability to invest in bonds. Individuals may readily buy and sell the bonds issued by many corporations and governments just as they may buy and sell shares of stock.

Corporations and governments issue a variety of debt instruments. This chapter is devoted to corporate debt; the subsequent chapter considers bonds issued by the federal, state, and local governments. Corporations issue a wide spectrum of debt instruments. These securities range from secured bonds issued by firms with high credit ratings to bonds with varying features issued by firms with poor credit ratings.

I realize that you might think bonds are not exciting investments or may not be appropriate for you. But I believe you are wrong on both counts. The variety of debt instruments with a wide range of features and the possibility to earn large returns through investing in particular debt instruments suggests these securities can be exciting investments. Bonds can also play an important role in diversifying your portfolio, and in some cases, such as acquiring bonds in a retirement account, they may be more appropriate than acquiring stock.

•••GENERAL FEATURES OF BONDS

Interest and Maturity

All **bonds** (i.e., long-term debt instruments) have similar characteristics. They represent the indebtedness (liability) of their issuers in return for a specified sum, which is called the **principal**. Virtually all debt has a **maturity date**, which is the particular date by which it must be paid off. When debt is issued, the length of time to maturity is set, and it may range from one day to 20 or 30 years or more. (Walt Disney has an outstanding bond that matures in 2093. I doubt we will be around to receive the principal repayment.)

If the maturity date falls within a year of the date of issuance, the debt is referred to as short-term debt. Long-term debt matures more than a year after it has been issued. (Debt that matures in from one to ten years is sometimes referred to as *intermediate debt.*) The owners of debt instruments receive a flow of payments, which is called **interest**, in return for the use of their money. Interest should not be confused with other forms of income, such as the cash dividends that are paid by common and preferred stock. Dividends are distributions from earnings, whereas interest is an expense of borrowing.

When a debt instrument such as a bond is issued, the rate of interest to be paid by the borrower is established. This rate is frequently referred to as the bond's **coupon rate** (e.g., the 7½ percent for the AT&T bond in Exhibit 9.2). The amount of interest is usually fixed over the lifetime of the bond. (There are exceptions; for example, see the section on variable interest rate bonds later in this chapter.) The return earned by the investor, however, need not be equal to the specified rate of interest because bond prices change. They may be purchased at a discount (a price below the face amount or principal) or at a premium (a price above the face amount of the bond). The return actually earned, then, depends on the interest received, the purchase price, and what the investor receives upon selling or redeeming the bond.

The potential return offered by a bond is referred to as the *yield*. Yield is frequently expressed in two ways: the **current yield** and the **yield to maturity**. Current yield refers only to the annual flow of interest or income. The yield to maturity refers to the yield that the investor will earn if the debt instrument is held from the moment of purchase until it is redeemed at par (face value) by the issuer. The difference between the current yield and the yield to maturity is discussed at length in the section on the pricing of bonds in Chapter 11.

There is a relationship between yield and the length of time to maturity for debt instruments of the same level of risk. Generally, the longer the time to maturity, the higher the rate of interest. This relationship is illustrated in Figure 9.1, which plots the yield on various U.S. government securities as of April 2004. This figure, which is frequently referred to as a **yield curve**, shows that the bonds with the longest time to maturity have the highest interest rates. For example, short-term securities (three months to maturity) had yields of 0.92 percent; one-year bonds paid yields of 1.19 percent, and bonds that matured after 20 years paid 4.78 percent.

You expect such a relationship because the longer the time to maturity, the longer you will tie up your funds. To induce you to lend money for lengthier periods, it is usually necessary to pay more interest. Also, there is more risk involved in purchasing a bond with a longer period to maturity, since the future financial condition of the issuer is more difficult to estimate for the longer term. This means that investors will ordinarily require additional compensation to bear the risk associated with long-term debt.

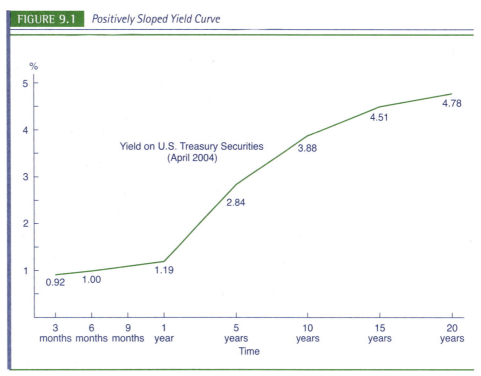

FIGURE 9.1   *Positively Sloped Yield Curve*

Yield on U.S. Treasury Securities (April 2004)

Source: Data derived from *The Wall Street Journal.*

Although such a relationship between time and yield does usually exist, there have been periods when the opposite has occurred (i.e., when short-term interest rates exceeded long-term interest rates). This happened from 1978 to 1979, and again in 1981.

Such a yield curve can be explained by inflation, which exceeded 10 percent in 1981 to 1982. The Board of Governors of the Federal Reserve was pursuing a tight monetary policy in order to fight inflation. It sold short-term government securities (i.e., Treasury bills) in an effort to reduce the capacity of commercial banks to lend. These sales depressed the prices of all fixed-income securities, which resulted in higher yields. The yields on short-term securities rose more than those on long-term securities, and this, coupled with other events in the money and capital markets, resulted in the negative-sloped yield curve. When the rate of inflation abated during the mid-1980s, the yield curve returned to the positive slope that it maintains during most periods.

The Indenture

indenture
The document that specifies the terms of a bond issue.

Each debt agreement has terms that the debtor must meet. These are stated in a legal document called the **indenture**. (For publicly held corporate bond issues, the indenture is filed with the Securities and Exchange Commission.) These terms include the coupon rate, the date of maturity, and any other conditions required of the debtor. One of the more frequent of these requirements is the pledging of collateral, which is property that the borrower must offer to secure the loan. For example, the collateral for a mortgage loan is the building. Any other assets owned by the borrower, such as inventory, may also be pledged to secure a loan. If the borrower defaults on the debt, the creditor may seize the collateral and sell it to recoup the principal. **Default** occurs when the borrower fails to meet not only the payment of interest but *any* of the terms of the indenture. The other conditions of the indenture are just as important as meeting the interest payments on time, and often they may be more difficult for the debtor to satisfy.

Examples of common loan restrictions include (1) limits on paying dividends, (2) limits on issuing additional debt, and (3) restrictions on merging or significantly changing the nature of the business without the prior consent of the creditors. In addition, loan agreements usually specify that if the firm defaults on any other outstanding debt issues, this debt issue is also in default, in which case the creditors may seek immediate repayment. Default on one issue, then, usually puts all outstanding debt in default.

These examples do not exhaust all the possible conditions of a given loan. Since each loan is separately negotiated, there is ample opportunity for differences among loan agreements. During periods of scarce credit, the terms of a loan agreement will be stricter, whereas during periods of lower interest rates and more readily available credit, the restrictions will tend to be more lenient. The important point, however, is that if any part of the loan agreement is violated, the creditor may declare that the debt is in default and may seek a court order to enforce the terms of the indenture.

The Role of the Trustee

Many debt instruments are purchased by investors who may be unaware of the terms of the indenture. Even if individual investors are aware of the terms, they may be too geographically dispersed to take concerted action in case of default. To protect their interests, a **trustee** is appointed for each publicly held bond issue. It is the trustee's job to see that the terms of the indenture are upheld and to take remedial action if the company defaults on the terms of the loan. For performing these services, the trustee receives compensation from the issuer of the debt.

Trustees are usually commercial banks that serve both the debtor and the bondholders. They act as transfer agents for the bonds when ownership is changed through sales in the secondary markets. These banks receive from the debtor the funds to pay the interest, and this money is then distributed to the individual bondholders. It is also the job of the trustee to inform the bondholders if the firm is no longer meeting the terms of the indenture. In case of default, the trustee may take the debtor to court to enforce the terms of the contract. If there is a subsequent reorganization or liquidation of the company, the trustee continues to act on behalf of the individual bondholders to protect their principal.

Forms of Debt

Debt instruments are issued in one of two forms: (1) **registered bonds** or (2) **bearer bonds** to which coupons are attached (therefore, they are also called **coupon bonds**). Registered bonds are similar to stock certificates; the bonds are registered in the owner's name. Delivery of the bonds is made to the registered owner, who also receives the interest payments from the trustee bank. When the bond is sold, it is registered in the name of the new owner by the transfer agent.

While bonds may be registered in the name of the owner, most registered bonds are issued in *book form*. No actual bonds are printed; instead, a computer record of owners is maintained by the issuer or the issuer's agent, such as a bank. If a bond is sold only in book form, the investor cannot take delivery, and the bond must be registered in the street name of the investor's brokerage firm or whoever is holding the bond for the investor. Such a system is obviously more efficient than physically issuing the bond.

Bearer bonds are entirely different. Ownership is evidenced by mere possession of the bond and is transferred simply by passing the debt instrument from the seller to the buyer; no new certificates are issued. Thus, securities in this form are extremely easy to transfer. However, if they are lost, they are like currency. Therefore, the possibility of theft is a concern that requires the owner to be cautious when handling these bonds.

Since the debtor does not know the names of the owners of the bearer securities, coupons for interest payments are attached to the bond. The owner must detach the coupon and send it to the paying agent (the trustee) to collect the interest. In the past, most bonds were of this type. Investors who relied on fixed-interest income for their livelihood were frequently called "coupon clippers," and even today interest payments are referred to as "coupons."

Under current federal law, all newly issued corporate and municipal bonds have to be registered in the name of the owner or whomever holds the bond for the owner (e.g., a brokerage firm). Previously issued bearer bonds with coupons attached still exist; however, the supply is diminishing. It is only a matter of time before all corporate and municipal bonds will be in registered form.

RISK

An important characteristic of all debt is risk: risk that the interest will not be paid (i.e., risk of default); risk that the principal will not be repaid; risk that the price of the debt instrument may decline; risk that inflation will continue, which reduces the purchasing power of the interest payments and of the principal when it is repaid; risk that the bond will be retired (i.e., called) prior to maturity, thereby denying the investor the interest payments for the term of the bond; and risk that interest rates will fall, resulting in lower interest income when the proceeds are reinvested. These risks vary with different types of debt. For example, there is no risk of default on the interest payments and principal repayments of the debt of the federal government. The reason for this absolute safety is that the federal government has the power to tax and to create money. The government can always issue the money that is necessary to pay the interest and repay the principal.[1]

Even though the federal government can refund its debt and hence is free of the risk of default, the prices of the federal government's bonds can and do fluctuate. In addition, the purchasing power of the dollar may decline as a result of inflation, and, therefore, the purchasing power of funds invested in debt also may decline. Thus, investing in federal government securities is not free of risk, since the investor may suffer losses from price fluctuations of the debt or from inflation.

The debt of firms, individuals, and state and local governments involves even greater risk, for all these debtors may default on their obligations. To aid buyers of debt instruments, several companies have developed **credit rating systems**. The most important of these services are Moody, Dun and Bradstreet, and Standard & Poor's. Although these firms do not rate all debt instruments, they do rate the degree of risk of a significant number.

credit rating systems
Classification schemes designed to indicate the risk associated with a particular security.

---

1. The decline in the value of the dollar in foreign countries may reduce the attractiveness of federal obligations. Fluctuations in the value of the dollar, then, do impose risk for foreigners who invest in these securities.

| EXHIBIT 9.1 | Bond Ratings |

Moody's Bond Ratings*

Aaa	Bonds of highest quality	B	Bonds that lack characteristics of a desirable investment
Aa	Bonds of high quality	Caa	Bonds in poor standing that may be defaulted
A	Bonds whose security of principal and interest is considered adequate but may be impaired in the future	Ca	Speculative bonds that are often in default
		C	Bonds with poor prospects of any investment value (lowest rating)
Baa	Bonds of medium grade that are neither highly protected nor poorly secured		
Ba	Bonds of speculative quality whose future cannot be considered well assured		

For ratings Aa through B, 1 indicates the high, 2 indicates the middle, and 3 indicates the low end of the rating class.

Standard & Poor's Bond Ratings[†]

AAA	Bonds of highest quality	BB	Bonds of lower–medium grade with few desirable investment characteristics
AA	High–quality debt obligations		
A	Bonds that have a strong capacity to pay interest and principal but may be susceptible to adverse effects	B	
BBB	Bonds that have an adequate capacity to pay interest and principal but are more vulnerable to adverse economic conditions or changing circumstances	CCC	Primarily speculative bonds with great uncertainties and major risk if exposed to adverse conditions
		C	Income bonds on which no interest is being paid
		D	Bonds in default

Plus (+) and minus (–) are used to show relative strength and weakness within a rating category.

*Source: Adapted from Mergent's *Bond Record*, January 2001.
[†]Source: Adapted from *Standard & Poor's Bond Guide*, January 2001.

Exhibit 9.1 gives the risk classifications presented by Moody and Standard & Poor's. The rating systems are quite similar, for each classification of debt involving little risk (high-quality debt) receives a rating of triple A, while debt involving greater risk (poorer-quality debt) receives progressively lower ratings. Bonds rated triple B or better are considered investment grade, while bonds with lower ratings are often referred to as *junk bonds* or *high-yield securities*. The growth in this poor-quality debt was one of the phenomena within the financial markets during the 1980s. (The variety of features found in junk bonds is covered later in this chapter.)

Even within a given rating, both Moody and Standard & Poor's fine-shade their rankings. Moody adds the numbers 1 through 3 to indicate degrees of quality within a ranking, with 1 representing the highest rank and 3 the lowest. Thus a bond rated A1 has a higher rating than a bond rated A3. Standard & Poor's uses + and – to indicate shades of quality. Thus a bond rated A + has a higher rating than an A bond, which, in turn, has a better rating than an A– bond.

Since the rating services analyze similar data, their ratings of specific debt issues should be reasonably consistent. This consistency is illustrated in Exhibit 9.2, which gives the ratings for several different bond issues. Generally, both Moody and Standard & Poor's assigned comparable ratings, such as the B1 and B+ to the Xerox Credit bond. When the ratings are different, the discrepancies are small. Moody ranked the AT&T bond Baa2, which is lower than the Standard & Poor's BBB+ rating. (BBB would be the comparable rating.)

EXHIBIT 9.2	Ratings for Selected Bonds (as of January 1, 2004)			
Firm	Coupon Rate of Interest	Year of Maturity	Moody's Rating	Standard & Poor's Rating
AT&T	7½%	2006	Baa2	BBB+
Consumers Energy	7⅜	2023	Baa3	BBB−
Dow Chemical	9	2021	A3	A−
Mobil**	8⅝	2021	Aaa	AAA
Viacom	7⅝	2016	A3	A−
Xerox Credit	7.20	2012	B1	B+

*Merged with Exxon to form ExxonMobil.
Source: *Mergent's Bond Record*, January 2004, and *Standard & Poor's Bond Guide*, Year end 2003.

These ratings play an important role in the marketing of debt obligations. Since the possibility of default may be substantial for poor-quality debt, some financial institutions and investors will not purchase debt with a low credit rating. Many financial institutions, especially commercial banks, are prohibited by law from purchasing bonds with a rating below Baa. Thus, if the rating of a bond issued by a firm or a municipality is low or declines from the original rating, the issuer may have difficulty selling its debt. Corporations and municipal governments try to maintain good credit ratings, because high ratings reduce the cost of borrowing and increase the marketability of the debt.

While the majority of corporate and municipal bonds are rated, there are exceptions. If a firm or municipality believes it will be able to market the securities without a rating, it may choose not to incur the costs necessary to have the securities rated. Unrated securities tend to be small issues and, because they lack the approval implied by a rating, probably should be viewed as possessing considerable risk.

Besides the risk of default, creditors are also subject to the risk of price fluctuations. Once debt has been issued, the market price of the debt will rise or fall depending on market conditions. If interest rates rise, the price of existing debt must fall so that its fixed interest payments relative to its price become competitive with the higher rates. In the event that interest rates decline, the opposite is true. The higher fixed-interest payments of the bond make the debt more attractive than comparable newly issued bonds, and buyers will be willing to pay more for the debt issue. Why these fluctuations in the price of debt instruments occur is explained in more detail in Chapter 11, which discusses the valuation of debt instruments.

There is, however, one feature of debt that partially compensates for the risk of price fluctuations. You know that the debt ultimately matures! If the price of the bond decreases and the debt instrument sells for a discount (i.e., less than the face value), the value of the debt must appreciate as it approaches maturity, because on the day of maturity, the full amount of the principal must be repaid.

Since interest rates fluctuate, bondholders may also bear reinvestment rate risk. Of course, this risk does not apply if the investor is spending payments as they are received, but that is often not the case. Instead, the payments are reinvested, and lower interest rates imply you will earn less and accumulate a lower terminal value. The converse would also apply if interest rates were higher. The reinvested payments would earn more and you would accumulate a larger final amount.

Bondholders and creditors also endure the risk associated with inflation, which reduces the purchasing power of money. During periods of inflation the debtor repays the loan in money that purchases less. Creditors must receive a rate of interest that is at least equal to the rate of inflation to maintain their purchasing power. If lenders anticipate inflation, they will demand a higher rate of interest to help protect their purchasing power. For example, if the rate of inflation is 3 percent, the creditors may demand 6 percent. Although inflation still causes the real value of the capital to decline, the higher interest rate partially offsets the effects of inflation.

If creditors do not anticipate inflation, the rate of interest may be insufficient to compensate for the loss in purchasing power. Inflation, then, hurts the creditors and helps the debtors, who are repaying the loans with money that purchases less.

The supposed inability of creditors to anticipate inflation has led to a belief that during inflation it is better to be a debtor. However, creditors invariably make an effort to protect their position by demanding higher interest rates. There is a transfer of purchasing power from creditors to debtors only if the creditors do not fully anticipate the inflation and do not demand sufficiently high interest rates. A transfer of purchasing power *from debtors to creditors* will occur in the opposite situation. If inflation is anticipated but does not occur, many debtors may pay artificially high interest rates, which transfers purchasing power from them to their creditors. Hence, the transfer of purchasing power can go either way if one group inaccurately anticipates the future rate of inflation.

If the investor acquires bonds denominated in a foreign currency, there is the additional risk that the value of the currency will decline relative to the dollar. Payments received in yen, euros, or pounds have to be converted into dollars before they may be spent in the United States, so fluctuations in the value of the currency affect the number of dollars you will receive. Of course, the value of the foreign currency could rise, which means you receive more dollars, but the value could also fall.

All the sources of risk to bondholders (default, fluctuations in bond prices from fluctuations in interest rates, reinvestment rate risk, loss of purchasing power from inflation, and foreign exchange rate risk) are essentially the same as the sources of risk to investors in stock. While a diversified bond portfolio reduces the risk identified with a specific asset (i.e., the risk of default), the risks associated with bond investments in general are not reduced by diversification. Even diversified bond investors must still bear the risks of fluctuations in interest and reinvestment rates, loss of purchasing power from inflation, and declining exchange rates.

THE MECHANICS OF PURCHASING BONDS

Bonds may be purchased in much the same way as stocks. The investor can buy them through a brokerage firm, and some bonds (e.g., federal government securities) can be purchased through commercial banks. The various purchase orders that may be used to buy stock (e.g., the market order or the limit order with a specified price) also apply to the purchase of bonds. Bonds may be bought with cash or through the use of margin.

The bonds of many companies are listed on the New York and American stock exchanges. In addition, there is a large volume of trading in bonds in the over-the-counter markets. Like listed stocks, transactions in bonds are reported by the financial press. The following entry for an AT&T bond is illustrative of the form used to report bond prices:

Bonds	Current Yield	Volume	Close	Net Change
ATT 8.125 22	7.9	20	103	+0.50

The entry is for a $1,000 bond (though bonds generally trade in units greater than $1,000). Bond prices are reported as a percent of face value, so 103 means 103% of $1,000, or $1,030.00. The bond has a coupon rate of 8.125 percent and matures in the year 2022, which is reported as 8.125 22. The current yield is the annual interest payment divided by the price ($81.25 ÷ $1,030.00 = 7.9%). The number of bonds traded was 20, which means that, according to face value, $20,000 worth of these bonds changed ownership.

After the debt has been purchased, the broker sends a **confirmation statement**. Exhibit 9.3 (p. 258) presents simplified confirmation statements for the purchase and subsequent sale of $10,000 in face value worth of Tesoro Petroleum bonds. In addition to a description of the securities, the confirmation statements include the price, the commission, accrued interest, and net amount due.

Bonds earn interest every day, but the firm distributes the interest payments only twice a year. Thus, when a bond is purchased, the buyer owes the previous owner **accrued interest** for the days that the owner held the bond. In the case of the first transaction, the purchase was made after the last interest payment, so the accrued interest amounted to $54.00. This interest is added to the purchase price that the buyer must pay. When the bond is sold, the seller receives the accrued interest. The second transaction occurred soon after the interest payment, and in this case the accrued interest was only $12.00, which was added to the proceeds of the sale.[2]

The profit or loss from the investment cannot be figured as the difference between the proceeds of the sale and the amount that is due after the purchase (i.e., $8,667.00 minus $7,899.00). Instead, an adjustment must be made for the accrued interest. This procedure is illustrated in Exhibit 9.4 (p. 259). First, the accrued interest must be subtracted from the amount due to obtain the cost of the bond. Thus, $7,899.00 minus $54.00 is the cost ($7,845.00) of this purchase. Second, the accrued interest must also be subtracted from the proceeds of the sale. Thus, $8,667.00 minus $12.00 yields the revenues from the sale. To determine the profit or loss, the cost basis is subtracted from the sale value. In this particular instance, that is $8,655.00 (the sale value) minus $7,845.00 (the cost basis), which represents a gain of $810.00.

A few bonds do trade without accrued interest. These bonds are currently in default and are not paying interest. Such bonds are said to trade **flat**, and an F is placed next to them in the transactions reported by the financial press. These bonds are of little interest except to speculators. The risk in buying them is substantial, but some do resume interest payments that can result in substantial returns.

confirmation statement
Statement received from a brokerage firm that specifies a purchase or sale of a security.

accrued interest
Interest that has been earned but not received.

flat
A description of a bond that trades without accrued interest.

•VARIETY OF CORPORATE BONDS

Corporations issue many types of bonds: mortgage bonds, equipment trust certificates, debenture bonds and subordinated debentures, income bonds, convertible bonds, variable interest rate bonds, and zero coupon bonds. These corporate debt

2. Interest on bonds accrues daily. At 5.25 percent, the interest on $10,000 is $525, or approximately $1.44 a day. If the purchase of the bond occurs 37 days after the payment date, the accrued interest owed is $53.28. If the sale occurs 8 days after the interest payment, the accrued interest received is $12.52. Accrued interest amounts in Exhibit 9.3 are rounded to facilitate the calculation of gains (or losses) in Exhibit 9.4.

EXHIBIT 9.3 Simplified Confirmation Statements for the Purchase and Sale of a Bond

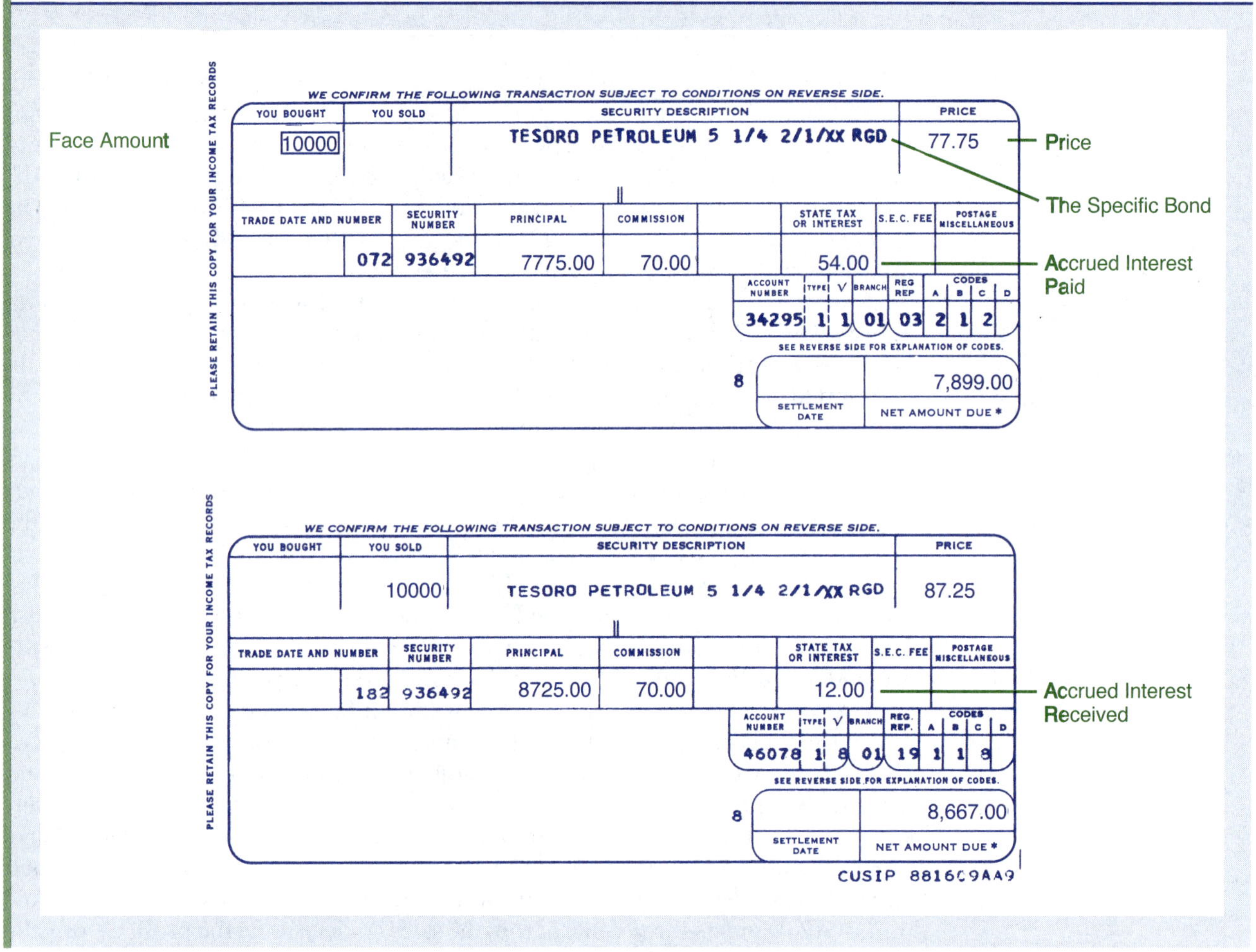
PLEASE RETAIN THIS COPY FOR YOUR INCOME TAX RECORDS

WE CONFIRM THE FOLLOWING TRANSACTION SUBJECT TO CONDITIONS ON REVERSE SIDE.

YOU BOUGHT	YOU SOLD	SECURITY DESCRIPTION	PRICE
10000		TESORO PETROLEUM 5 1/4 2/1/XX RGD	77.75

TRADE DATE AND NUMBER	SECURITY NUMBER	PRINCIPAL	COMMISSION		STATE TAX OR INTEREST	S.E.C. FEE	POSTAGE MISCELLANEOUS
072	936492	7775.00	70.00		54.00		

ACCOUNT NUMBER	TYPE	√	BRANCH	REG REP	CODES A	B	C	D
34295	1	1	01	03	2	1	2	

SEE REVERSE SIDE FOR EXPLANATION OF CODES.

8 SETTLEMENT DATE — NET AMOUNT DUE * 7,899.00

Face Amount — Price — The Specific Bond — Accrued Interest Paid

PLEASE RETAIN THIS COPY FOR YOUR INCOME TAX RECORDS

WE CONFIRM THE FOLLOWING TRANSACTION SUBJECT TO CONDITIONS ON REVERSE SIDE.

YOU BOUGHT	YOU SOLD	SECURITY DESCRIPTION	PRICE
	10000	TESORO PETROLEUM 5 1/4 2/1/XX RGD	87.25

TRADE DATE AND NUMBER	SECURITY NUMBER	PRINCIPAL	COMMISSION		STATE TAX OR INTEREST	S.E.C. FEE	POSTAGE MISCELLANEOUS
182	936492	8725.00	70.00		12.00		

ACCOUNT NUMBER	TYPE	√	BRANCH	REG. REP.	CODES A	B	C	D
46078	1	8	01	19	1	1	8	

SEE REVERSE SIDE FOR EXPLANATION OF CODES.

8 SETTLEMENT DATE — NET AMOUNT DUE * 8,667.00

CUSIP 881609AA9

Accrued Interest Received

Source: Adapted from Scott & Stringfellow, Inc.

instruments are either secured or unsecured. If a debt instrument is secured, the debtor pledges a specific asset as collateral. In case of default, the creditor may seize this collateral (through a court proceeding). Bonds that are not collateralized by specific assets are unsecured. If the debtor were to default, there would be no specific assets the creditors could seize to satisfy their claims on the borrower. Such unsecured debt instruments are supported by the general capacity of the firm to service its debt (i.e., pay the interest and repay the principal). Thus, the capacity of the borrower to generate operating income (i.e., earnings before interest and taxes) is crucial to the safety of unsecured debt obligations.

Mortgage Bonds

mortgage bond
A bond that is secured by property, especially real estate.

Mortgage bonds are issued to purchase specific fixed assets, which are then pledged to secure the debt. This type of bond is frequently issued by utility companies. The proceeds that are raised by selling the debt are used to build power plants, and these plants secure the debt. As the plants generate revenues, the firm

EXHIBIT 9.4	Determination of Profit or Loss on the Sale of a Bond

Cost basis of the bond:	
Amount due	$7,899.00
Less accrued interest	–54.00
	$7,845.00
Revenue from the sale:	
Proceeds of the sale	$8,667.00
Less accrued interest	–12.00
	$8,655.00
Profit (or loss) on the investment:	
Return from the sale of the bond	$8,655.00
Cost basis of the bond	7,845.00
Profit (or loss) on the investment	$810.00

earns the cash flow that is necessary to service (pay interest on) and retire the debt. If the firm defaults on the interest or principal repayment, the creditors may take title to the pledged property. They may then choose to hold the asset and earn income from it (to operate the fixed asset) or to sell it. These options should give you cause for thought: How many creditors could operate a power plant? If the investors choose to sell it, who would buy it?

These two questions illustrate an important point concerning investing in corporate debt. Although property that is pledged to secure the debt may decrease the lender's risk of loss, the creditor is not interested in taking possession of and operating the property. Lenders earn income through interest payments and not through the operation of the fixed assets. Such creditors are rarely qualified to operate the assets should they take possession of them. If they are forced to seize and sell the assets, they may find few buyers and may have to sell at distress prices. Despite the fact that pledging assets to secure debt increases the safety of the principal, the lenders prefer the prompt payment of interest and principal.

Equipment Trust Certificates

equipment trust certificate
A serial bond secured by specific equipment.

Not all collateral has questionable resale potential. Unlike the mortgage bonds that are issued by utility companies, **equipment trust certificates** are secured by assets with substantial resale value. These certificates are issued to finance specific equipment, which is pledged as collateral. Equipment trust certificates are primarily issued by railroads and airlines to finance rolling stock (railroad cars) and airplanes. As the equipment is used to generate cash flow, the certificates are retired. The collateral supporting these certificates is generally considered to be of excellent quality, for, unlike some fixed assets (e.g., the aforementioned utility plants), this equipment may be readily *moved* and sold to other railroads and airlines in the event that the firm defaults on the certificates.

Investors, however, should realize that while equipment may be more readily sold than power plants, these investors could still suffer losses. For example, when Eastern, Pan Am, and several small airlines went bankrupt, they dumped a large number of aircraft on the market, so prices for used aircraft declined. This, of course, meant that even the secured creditors did not receive their principal from the proceeds of the sales of the planes.

Other Asset Backed Securities and Securitization

While equipment trust certificates are secured by equipment such as railroad cars and mortgages are secured by real estate, other assets may also be used as collateral for a debt issue. For example, a firm may issue and sell debt securities backed by its accounts receivable. (The firm may also sell outright the receivables to a financial institution or factor, who, in turn, issues debt instruments secured by the assets.) As the accounts are collected, the funds are used to retire the securities and pay the interest. The advantage to the issuing firm is simple. It obtains the funds immediately and does not have to wait for the collection of the receivables. The advantage to the investors, especially large pension plans, is that they receive an interest-paying security that is relatively safe since it is secured by the underlying assets.

The process of converting illiquid assets such as accounts receivable into liquid assets is called **securitization**. Textron, a manufacturer of Bell helicopters, Cessna aircraft, automotive products, and fastening systems, sells a variety of products, which generates accounts receivable. In its 2003 annual report, Textron reported that it securitized over $765 million in assets. The proceeds of the sales were then used to retire debt previously issued by Textron.

securitization
The process of converting an illiquid asset into a marketable security.

Debentures

Debentures are unsecured promissory notes that are supported by the general creditworthiness of the firm. This type of debt involves more risk than bonds that are supported by collateral. In the case of default or bankruptcy, the unsecured debt is redeemed only after all secured debt has been paid off. Some debentures are subordinated, and these involve even more risk, for they are redeemed after the other general debt of the firm has been redeemed. Even unsecured debt has a superior position to the subordinated debenture. These bonds are among the riskiest debt instruments issued by firms and usually have higher interest rates or other attractive features, such as convertibility into the stock of the company, to compensate the lenders for assuming the increased risk.

debenture
An unsecured bond.

Financial institutions, such as commercial banks or insurance companies, prefer a firm to sell debentures to the general public. Since the debentures are general obligations of the company, they do not tie up its specific assets. Then, if the firm needs additional funds from a commercial bank, it can use specific assets as collateral, in which case the bank will be more willing to lend the funds. If the assets had been previously pledged, the firm would lack this flexibility in financing.

Although the use of debentures may not decrease the ability of the firm to issue additional debt, default on the debentures usually means that all senior debt is in default as well. A common indenture clause states that if any of the firm's debt is in default, all debt issues are also in default, and in this case the creditors may declare that all outstanding debt is due. For this reason, a firm should not overextend itself through excessive amounts of unsecured debt.

Income Bonds

Income bonds are the riskiest bonds issued by corporations. Interest is paid only if the firm earns it. If the company is unable to cover its other expenses, it is not legally obligated to pay the interest on these bonds. Owing to the great risk associated with them, income bonds are rarely issued by corporations. One notable exception is an issue of Disney bonds that could pay as much as 13.5 percent annually if a package

income bond
A bond whose interest is paid only if it is earned by the firm.

of 20 Disney movies grosses over $800 million. If, however, the gross is less, the bonds could yield as little as 3 percent.

Although income bonds are rarely issued by firms, a similar type of security is often issued by state and municipal governments. These are *revenue bonds*, which are discussed later in the next chapter on municipal securities. There is one significant difference between income bonds and revenue bonds. Failure to pay interest does not result in default for an income bond, but it does mean that a revenue bond is in default. Most projects financed by revenue bonds have generated sufficient funds to service the debt, but there have been notable exceptions. Perhaps the most famous default was the multibillion-dollar default by the Washington Public Power Supply System. As of 2004, the defaulted bonds were virtually worthless.

Convertible Bonds

convertible bond
A bond that may be exchanged for (i.e., converted into) common stock.

Convertible bonds are a hybrid-type security. Technically they are debt: The bonds pay interest, which is a fixed obligation of the firm, and have a maturity date. But these bonds have a special feature: The investor has the option to convert the bond into a specified number of shares of common stock. For example, the Nextel Communications 5¼ percent of the year 2010 bond may be converted into 13.44 shares of Nextel common stock. The market price of convertible bonds depends on both the value of the stock and the interest that the bonds pay. If the price of the common stock rises, then the value of the bond must rise. The investor thus has the opportunity for capital gain should the price of the common stock rise. If, however, the price of the common stock does not appreciate, the investor still owns a debt obligation of the company and therefore has the security of an investment in a debt instrument.

Convertible bonds have been popular with some investors, and thus firms have issued these bonds as a means to raise funds. However, convertible bonds are a hybrid security whose value is derived from the stock into which the bond may be converted and its features as a debt instrument. Its value as stock is considered later in this chapter, and its value as a bond is considered in Chapter 11, which covers bond pricing.

Variable Interest Rate Bonds

variable interest rate bond
A long-term bond with a coupon rate that varies with changes in short-term rates.

Generally, the interest that a bond pays is fixed at the date of issuance; however, some corporations issue **variable interest rate bonds**. Citicorp was the first major American firm to offer bonds with variable interest rates to the general public. Two features of the Citicorp bond were unique at the time it was issued: (1) a variable interest rate that was tied to the interest rate on Treasury bills and (2) the right of the holder to redeem the bond at its face value.

The interest rate to be paid by the Citicorp bond was set at 1 percent above the average Treasury bill rate during a specified period. This variability of the interest rate means that if short-term interest rates rise, the interest rate paid by the bond must increase. The bond's owner participates in any increase in short-term interest rates. Of course, if the short-term interest rates decline, the bond earns a lower rate of interest.

The second unique feature of the Citicorp bond was that two years after it was issued, the holder had the option to redeem the bond for its face value or principal. This option recurred every six months. If the owner needed the money more quickly, the bond could have been sold in the secondary market. An important implication of the variable coupon is that the market price of the bond fluctuates less than the price of a fixed coupon bond. As is explained in Chapter 11, the price of a fixed coupon bond fluctuates inversely with interest rates. Such price changes will not occur with a variable rate bond because the interest paid fluctuates with interest rates in general. Hence these bonds avoid one of the major sources of risk associated with investing in bonds: higher interest rates driving down the bond's market value.

Zero Coupon and Discount Bonds

In 1981 a new type of bond was sold to the general public. These bonds pay no interest and are sold at large discounts. The pathbreaking issue was the J.C. Penney **zero coupon bond**. This bond was initially sold for a discount ($330) but paid $1,000 at maturity in 1989. The investor's funds grew from $330 to $1,000 after eight years. The annual rate of growth (i.e., the yield on the bond) was 14.86 percent.[3]

After the initial success of this issue, other firms such as IBM Credit Corporation (the financing arm of IBM) issued similar bonds. In each case the firm pays no periodic interest. The bond sells for discount, and the investor's return accrues from the appreciation of the bond's value as it approaches maturity.

Because the return on an investment in a zero coupon bond depends solely on the accrual of interest and the ability of the firm to retire the debt, the quality of the firm is exceedingly important. Zero coupon bonds issued by firms such as IBM Credit Corporation are of excellent quality and should be retired at maturity. If, however, you purchase zero coupon bonds issued by firms of lesser quality, these bonds may never be redeemed. If the firm were to go bankrupt, you might receive nothing. I purchased a zero coupon Boston Chicken bond for my retirement account. Boston Chicken subsequently went bankrupt, and when the firm was reorganized, the bonds were cancelled. I received not one penny in interest and lost the entire amount invested in the Boston Chicken zero coupon bond.

There is a federal income tax ruling that reduces the attractiveness of zero coupon bonds. The IRS taxes the accrued interest as if it were received. You must pay federal income tax on the accrued interest even though you receive the funds only when the bond matures. Thus zero coupon bonds have little appeal to investors except as part of pension plans. In that case the tax on the accrued interest is deferred until the funds are withdrawn. So the primary reason for acquiring a zero coupon bond is to use it in conjunction with a tax-deferred retirement plan.

Eurobonds

Many U.S. firms also issue bonds in foreign countries to raise funds for foreign investments (e.g., plant and equipment).[4] These bonds fall into two basic types, depending on the currency in which they are denominated. U.S. firms can sell bonds denominated in the local currency (e.g., British pounds or European euros). For example, ExxonMobil reported in its 2002 10-k report that $670 million of its $6.66

---

zero coupon bond
A bond on which interest accrues and is paid at maturity, and is initially sold at a discount.

Calculator Solution

Function Key	Data Input
PV =	−330
N =	8
PMT =	0
FV =	1000
I =	?

Function Key	Answer
I =	14.86

---

3. The yield on a zero coupon is calculated as follows:

$$P_0(1+i)^n = P_n,$$

which is solved for i. In this example,

$$\$330(1+i)^8 = \$1,000$$

$$(1+i)^8 = \$1,000/\$330 = 3.030$$

$$i = \sqrt[8]{3.030} - 1$$

$$i = 0.1486 = 14.86\%.$$

The 14.86 percent may also be derived by using a financial calculator.

4. Bonds are also issued in the United States by foreign firms and these are sometimes referred to as "Yankee" bonds. Other colorful names are also applied to foreign bonds issued in other domestic markets: the "Bulldog" market for foreign bonds issued in the United Kingdom and the "Samurai" market for foreign bonds issued in Japan.

Eurobond
A bond denominated in U.S. dollars but issued abroad.

billion of long-term debt (10.06 percent) was denominated in foreign currencies. The firm can also sell abroad bonds denominated in U.S. dollars called **Eurobonds**. This term applies even though the bonds may be issued in Asia instead of Europe.

When a firm issues a Eurobond, the U.S. firm promises to make payments in dollars. This means that the U.S. investor does not have to convert the payments from the local currency (e.g., British pounds) into dollars. As is explained in Chapter 3, fluctuation in the value of one currency relative to another is a major source of risk that every individual who acquires foreign securities must bear. By acquiring Eurobonds, the U.S. investor avoids this currency risk. However, foreign investors do bear this risk. They have to convert the dollars into their currency, so the yields on Eurobonds tend to be higher than on comparable domestic securities. The higher yield is a major reason why some investors find Eurobonds attractive.

HIGH-YIELD SECURITIES

high-yield securities
Non-investment-grade securities offering a high return.

High-yield securities (sometimes referred to as *junk bonds*) are not a particular type of bond but refer to any debt of low quality (i.e., bonds rated below triple B). These bonds have the same general features associated with investment-grade debt. In addition to the interest payment (the coupon) and the maturity date, junk bonds often have call features and sinking funds. While junk bonds are usually debentures and may be subordinated to the firm's other debt obligations, some do have collateral (i.e., they are mortgage bonds). As is subsequently discussed, some high-yield securities have variations on the basic features associated with all bonds.

High-yield securities may be divided into two classes. First are the bonds that were initially investment grade but whose credit ratings were lowered as the issuing firms developed financial problems. This type of high-yield bond is often referred to as a **fallen angel**. When RJR Nabisco was purchased and taken private, the surviving firm issued substantial new debt that resulted in the downgrading of outstanding RJR Nabisco bonds. The prices of what were previously high-quality debt declined dramatically, and the issues became high-yield securities. Of course, the high yields were to be earned by new buyers and not by the original investors who suffered losses when the prices of the previously issued bonds declined.

fallen angel
Investment-grade security whose quality has deteriorated.

Some fallen angels ultimately go bankrupt. Manville, Public Service of New Hampshire, and Texaco all went bankrupt and defaulted on their debts. However, bonds in default continue to trade, and there is always the possibility that the firm will recover and the price of the bonds will rise. This did occur in the case of Texaco. One of the attractions of the high-yield security market is the possibility that the financial condition of the issuing firm will improve. A higher credit rating should be beneficial to the holders of the firm's debt, because the bonds' prices should increase as the firm's financial condition improves.

The second class of high-yield securities is composed of bonds (and preferred stock) issued by firms with less than investment-grade credit ratings (double B or lower). The maturity dates range from short-term to long-term, and in some cases, the bonds have features that differentiate these securities from the traditional bonds issued by firms with better credit ratings. Four possibilities are the split coupon bond, the reset bond, the increasing rate bond, and the extendible bond.

Split Coupon Bonds

split coupon bond
Bond with a zero or low initial coupon followed by a period with a high coupon.

A **split coupon bond** combines the features of zero coupon and high coupon bonds. During the first three to five years, the bond pays initially no (or a small amount of) interest. The interest accrues like a zero coupon bond. After this initial period, the bond pays a high coupon. For example, Dr Pepper issued a split coupon bond that paid no interest for the first four years and then paid a coupon of 11.5 percent for the next six years, until the bond matured.

These bonds, which are also referred to as *deferred interest bonds*, initially sell at a discounted price that is calculated using the coupon rate in effect when the bond starts to pay cash. For the Dr Pepper bond, the flow of payments per $1,000 bond is

Interest:	
Years 1–4	$0
Years 5–10	$115
Principal repayment at end of year 10:	$1,000

The advantage to the firm issuing split coupon bonds is that debt service is eliminated during the initial period. Split coupon bonds conserve cash, but the accrual of interest is tax deductible to the issuing firm. Split coupon bonds are often issued in leveraged buyouts and other recapitalizations that result in the firm issuing substantial amounts of debt. (The RJR Nabisco buyout resulted in the surviving firm issuing split coupon bonds.)

Split coupon bonds tend to be very costly to the firm issuing them. The high yield to investors means a high cost of funds to the issuers. There is an incentive for the firm to retire the securities as soon as possible. Thus most split coupon bonds have call features that permit the firm to retire the securities before their maturity. For example, Safeway Stores called half of its issue of junior subordinated debentures only 11 months after the bonds were originally issued.

Reset Securities and Increasing Rate Bonds

reset bond
Bond whose coupon is periodically reset.

Although the coupons are fixed when most high-yield securities are issued, there are exceptions. With a **reset bond**, the coupon is adjusted at periodic intervals, such as six months or every year. The coupon is usually tagged to a specified rate, such as the six-month Treasury bill rate plus 5 percent, and there is often a minimum and a maximum coupon. For example, American Shared Hospital Service issued a reset note whose coupon can range from 14 to 16.5 percent.

Since the coupon is permitted to change, price fluctuations associated with changes in interest rates are reduced. The minimum coupon, however, means that if interest rates fall on comparably risky securities, the price of the bond will rise since the coupon becomes fixed at the lower bound. And the same applies when interest rates rise. If the coupon reaches the upper limit, further increases in comparable yields will decrease the bond's price. However, within the specified range the changing coupon should stabilize the price of the bond. Of course, if the firm's financial condition changes, the price of the bond will change independently of changes in interest rates.

increasing rate bond
Bond whose coupon rises over time.

An **increasing rate bond** is a debt security whose coupon increases over time. For example, RJR Holdings issued $5 billion of increasing rate notes. One issue had an initial coupon of 14.5625 percent, but future coupons would be the higher of 13.4375 percent or 4 percent higher than the three-month London Interbank Offer (LIBOR) rate. Subsequent coupons increased by 0.5 percent quarterly for two years and 0.25 percent quarterly for years three and four. Obviously, increasing rate securities are an expensive means for any firm to raise funds, so the investor can anticipate that the issuer will seek to retire the debt as rapidly as possible, which is precisely what occurred as RJR Holdings refinanced after interest rates fell and its financial position improved.

Extendible Securities

extendible security
Bond whose maturity date may be extended into the future.

In the previous discussion, the high-yield securities had differing coupons but fixed maturity dates. Split coupon bonds have periods during which interest accrues but is not paid. Reset and increasing rate notes and bonds have coupons that vary. Each of the types of high-yield securities has a fixed maturity date. However, a firm may issue an **extendible security** in which the term to maturity may be lengthened by the issuer. For example, Mattel issued a bond with an initial maturity date in 1990, but the company could extend the bond for one-, two-, or three-year periods with a final maturity in 1999. Thus the investor who acquired this bond did not know if the bond would be outstanding for one year or six years or longer. Only the final maturity in 1999 was known.

The ability to extend the maturity date is, of course, beneficial to the issuer. If the firm does not have the capacity to retire the debt at the initial maturity date, the date may be extended. This buys time for the firm to find the funds or to refinance the debt. Failure to retire the debt at the final maturity, of course, throws the bond into default.

RETIRING DEBT

Debt issues must ultimately be retired, and this retirement must occur on or before the maturity date of the debt. When the bond is issued, a method for periodic retirement is usually specified, for very few debt issues are retired in one lump payment at the maturity date. Instead, part of the issue is systematically retired each year. This systematic retirement may be achieved by issuing the bond in a series or by having a sinking fund.

Serial Bonds

serial bond
A bond issue in which specified bonds mature each year.

In an issue of **serial bonds**, some bonds mature each year. This type of bond is usually issued by corporations to finance specific equipment, such as railroad cars, which is pledged as collateral. As the equipment depreciates, the cash flow that is generated by profits and depreciation expense is used to retire the bonds in a series as they mature.

The advertisement presented in Exhibit 9.5 (p. 266) for equipment trust certificates issued by Union Pacific Railroad Company is an example of a serial bond. These equipment trust certificates were issued in 1985 and were designed so that one-fifteenth of the bonds matured each year. Thus, the firm retired $2,337,000 of the certificates annually as each series within the issue matured. At the end of 2001, the entire issue of certificates had been retired.

Few corporations, however, issue serial bonds. They are primarily issued by state and local governments to finance capital improvements, such as new school buildings, or by ad hoc government bodies, such as the Port Authority of New York, to finance new facilities or other capital improvements. The bonds are then retired over a period of years by tax receipts or by revenues generated by the investment (e.g., toll roads).

Sinking Funds

sinking fund
A series of periodic payments to retire a bond issue.

Sinking funds are generally employed to ease the retirement of long-term corporate debt. A **sinking fund** is a periodic payment to retire part of the debt issue. One type of sinking fund requires the firm to make payments to a trustee, who

EXHIBIT 9.5   Example of a Serial Bond Issue (Equipment Trust Certificate)

This announcement is under no circumstances to be construed as an offer to sell or as a soliciatation of an offer to buy any of these securities. The offering is made only by the Offering Circular Supplement and the Offering Circular to which it relates.

NEW ISSUE   July 17, 1985

$35,055,000

Union Pacific Railroad Company

Equipment Trust No. 1 of 1985

Serial Equipment Trust Certificates
(Non-callable)

Price 100%

(Plus accrued dividends, if any, from the date of original issuance.)

MATURITIES AND DIVIDEND RATES.

(To mature in 15 equal annual installments
of $2,337,000, commencing July 15, 1987.)

1987	6.500%	1992	7.500%	1997	7.800%
1988	7.000	1993	7.600	1998	7.800
1989	7.125	1994	7.700	1999	7.875
1990	7.300	1995	7.700	2000	7.875
1991	7.375	1996	7.750	2001	7.875

These Certificates are offered subject to prior sale, when, as and if issued and received by us, subject to approval of the Interstate Commerce Commission.

Merrill Lynch Capital Markets

Thomson McKinnon Securities Inc.

Source: Reprinted with permission of the Union Pacific Railroad Company.

invests the money to earn interest. The periodic payments plus the accumulated interest retire the debt when it matures.

Another type of sinking fund requires the firm to set aside a stated sum of money and to randomly select the bonds that are to be retired. The selected bonds are called and redeemed, and the holder surrenders the bond because it ceases to earn interest once it has been called. This type of sinking fund is illustrated in Exhibit 9.6 (p. 268) by an advertisement taken from *The Wall Street Journal*. The specific bonds being retired were selected by a lottery. Once they are chosen, these bonds are called. The owners must surrender the bonds to obtain their principal. If the bonds are not presented for redemption, they are still outstanding and are obligations of the company, but the debtor's obligation is limited to refunding the principal, since interest payments ceased at the call date.

Since each debt issue is different, there can be wide variations in sinking funds. A strong sinking fund retires a substantial proportion of the debt before the date of maturity. For example, if a bond issue is for $10 million and it matures in ten years, a strong sinking fund may require the firm to retire $1 million, or 10 percent, of the issue each year. Thus, at maturity only $1 million is still outstanding. With a weak sinking fund, a substantial proportion of the debt is retired at maturity. For example, a sinking fund for a debt issue of $10 million that matures in ten years may require annual payments of $1 million commencing after five years. In this example, only $5 million is retired before maturity. The debtor must then make a lump sum payment to retire the remaining $5 million. Such a large final payment is called a **balloon payment**.

Repurchasing Debt

If bond prices decline and the debt is selling at a **discount**, the firm may try to retire the debt by purchasing it on the open market. The purchases may be made from time to time, in which case the sellers of the bonds need not know that the company is purchasing and retiring the debt. The company may also offer to purchase a specified amount of the debt at a certain price within a particular period. Bondholders may then tender their bonds at the offer price; however, they are not required to sell their bonds and may continue to hold the debt.[5] The firm must then continue to meet the terms of the debt's indenture.

The advantage of repurchasing debt that is selling at a discount is the savings to the firm. If a firm issued $10 million in face value of debt and the bonds are currently selling for $0.60 on the $1, the firm may reduce its debt by $1,000 with a cash outlay of only $600, resulting in a $400 savings for each $1,000 bond that is purchased. This savings is translated into income, because a reduction in debt at a discount is an extraordinary item that is treated in accounting as income. For example, General Cinema reported a gain of $419.6 million from the purchase of Harcourt Brace Jovanovich's debt at a discount as part of the acquisition of the publisher. The low interest rates of the late 1990s and early 2000s caused bond prices to rise. (See Chapter 11 for the explanation of changes in interest rates and their impact on bond prices.) The increase in bond prices meant the opportunity to repurchase bonds at a discount had disappeared.

On the surface, a firm's retiring debt at a discount may appear desirable. However, using money to repurchase debt is an investment decision, just like buying plant and equipment. If the company repurchases debt, it cannot use the funds for other purposes. Management must decide which is the better use of the money: purchasing other income-earning assets or retiring the debt and saving the interest payments. Unlike a sinking fund requirement (which management must meet), purchasing and retiring debt at a discount is a voluntary act. The lower the price of

balloon payment
The large final payment necessary to retire a debt issue.

discount
The sale of anything below its stated value.

5. If more bonds are tendered than the company offered to buy, the firm prorates the amount of money that it had allocated for the purchase among the number of bonds being offered.

EXHIBIT 9.6   Example of a Sinking Fund Retiring Debt

NOTICE OF REDEMPTION
To the Holders of

New York State Urban Development Corporation

Project Revenue Bonds (Center for Industrial Innovation)

Series 1982 Bonds 11⅛% Due January 1, 2013

(CUSIP NO. 650033BD4)*

Issuing Authority ⟶

Bond Issue ⟶

Coupon ⟶

Maturity Date ⟶

NOTICE IS HEREBY GIVEN THAT, pursuant to the provisions of a resolution adopted by the New York State Urban Development Corporation (the "Corporation"), on November 18, 1982, as amended and restated on December 10, 1982, and entitled "Project Revenue Bond (Center for Industrial Innovation) General Resolution" (the "General Resolution"), as supplemented by a resolution of the Corporation entitled "Series 1982 Project Revenue Bonds (Center for Industrial Innovation) Series Resolution" (the "Series Resolution") authorizing the issuance of the above described Bonds, the Corporation will redeem and the Trustee under the General Resolution has drawn by lot for redemption on January 1, 1993 (the "Sinking Fund Redemption Date"), through the operation of the sinking fund created under the Series Resolution, $465,000 aggregate principal amount of the above described Bonds as set forth below.

Sinking Fund Provision ⟶

Amount to Be Redeemed ⟶

Coupon Bonds called for redemption each bearing the
Prefix A and each in the Denomination of $5,000, are as follows:

386	424	854	3472	3987	4417	5417	5438	5513	6024	6304	6746	6920

Specific Bonds Being Retired ⟶

Registered Bonds called for redemption, in whole or in part, each bearing the
Prefix AR, are as follows:

Bond Number	Denomination	Amount Called	Bond Number	Denomination	Amount Called
26	$ 500,000	$15,000	87	$2,435,000	$30,000
39	50,000	5,000	88	2,460,000	30,000
51	5,000	5,000	89	2,435,000	35,000
81	490,000	10,000	90	2,465,000	20,000
82	95,000	5,000	91	2,405,000	40,000
84	2,430,000	40,000	92	2,450,000	35,000
85	2,420,000	35,000	93	1,945,000	30,000
86	2,480,000	20,000	94	2,415,000	45,000

On the Sinking Fund Redemption Date, there shall become due and payable on each of the above mentioned Bonds to be redeemed, the sinking fund redemption price, namely 100% of the principal amount thereof. Interest accrued on such Bonds to said Sinking Fund Redemption Date will be paid in the usual manner. From and after the Sinking Fund Redemption Date, interest on the Bonds described above shall cease to accrue.

Interest Will Cease to Accrue ⟶

IN ADDITION THE CORPORATION HAS ELECTED TO REDEEM ON JANUARY 1, 1993 (THE "REDEMPTION DATE") ALL REMAINING OUTSTANDING BONDS NOT HERETOFORE CALLED FOR SINKING FUND REDEMPTION AT A REDEMPTION PRICE EQUAL TO 103% OF THE PRINCIPAL AMOUNT THEREOF. INTEREST ACCRUED ON SUCH BONDS TO THE REDEMPTION DATE WILL BE PAID IN THE USUAL MANNER. FROM AND AFTER THE REDEMPTION DATE, INTEREST ON THE BONDS SHALL CEASE TO ACCRUE.

The Bonds specified herein to be redeemed shall be redeemed on or after both the Sinking Fund Redemption Date and the Redemption Date upon presentation and surrender thereof, together, in the case of coupon Bonds, with all appurtenant coupons attached, if any, maturing after January 1, 1993, to Bankers Trust Company, as Trustee and Paying Agent, in person or by registered mail (postage prepaid) at the following addresses:

IN PERSON:

Bankers Trust Company
Corporate Trust and Agency Group
First Floor
123 Washington Street
New York, New York

BY MAIL:

Bankers Trust Company
Corporate Trust and Agency Group
P.O. Box 2579
Church Street Station
New York, NY 10008
Attn: Bond Redemption

If any of the Bonds designated for redemption are in registered form, they should be accompanied by duly executed instruments of assignment in blank if payment is to be made to other than the registered holder thereof.

Coupons maturing January 1, 1993 appertaining to the coupon Bonds designated for redemption should be detached and presented for payment in the usual manner. Interest due January 1, 1993 on registered Bonds designated for redemption will be paid to the registered holders of such registered Bonds in the usual manner.

 NEW YORK STATE URBAN DEVELOPMENT CORPORATION
By: BANKERS TRUST COMPANY, *as Trustee*

the debt, the greater the potential benefit from the purchase, but management must still determine if it is the best use of the firm's scarce resource, cash.

Call Feature

call feature
The right of an issuer to retire a debt issue prior to maturity.

Some bonds may have a **call feature** that allows for redemption prior to maturity. In most cases after the bond has been outstanding for a period of time (e.g., five years), the issuer has the right to call and retire the bond. The bond is called for redemption as of a specific date. After that date, interest ceases to accrue, which forces the creditor to relinquish the debt instrument.

Such premature retiring of debt through a call feature tends to occur after a period of high interest rates. If a bond has been issued during such a period and interest rates subsequently decline, it may be advantageous for the company to issue new bonds at the lower interest rate. The proceeds can then be used to retire the older bonds with the higher coupon rates. Such **refunding** reduces the firm's interest expense.

refunding
The act of issuing new debt and using the proceeds to retire existing debt.

call penalty
A premium paid for exercising a call feature.

Of course, premature retirement of debt hurts the bondholders who lose the higher-yield bonds. To protect these creditors, a call feature usually has a **call penalty**, such as the payment of one year's interest. If the initial issue had a 9 percent interest rate, the company would have to pay $1,090 to retire $1,000 worth of debt. This call penalty usually declines over the lifetime of the debt. Exhibit 9.7 (p. 270) illustrates the call penalty associated with the AT&T 8⅛ of 2020. In 2004 the penalty is $36.40 per $1,000, but it declines to nothing in 2015. Such a call penalty does protect bondholders, and the debtor has the right to call the bond and to refinance debt if interest rates fall sufficiently to justify paying the call penalty.[6]

Several such refinancings occurred during the 1990s when interest rates fell to lows that had not been seen in 20 years. In particular, utility companies that had issued debt when interest rates were higher sold new bonds with lower yields, called the old debt, and paid the call penalty. In 1998, Bell Atlantic retired $125 million of bonds with 7.5 percent coupons. The company paid 101.5 per bond (i.e., $1,015 per $1,000) for a penalty of $15 per bond. Nonutility companies also retired debt whose coupons exceeded the current rate of interest. Texas Instruments retired $200 million of its 12.7 percent bonds. It paid $1,047 to retire $1,000 in face value of debt (i.e., a premium of $47 per bond). These refinancings sufficiently reduced the companies' interest expense to justify paying the call premium.

CONVERTIBLE BONDS

The previous sections discussed a variety of corporate bonds.[7] This section considers bonds with a special feature: You may convert the security into the firm's stock. Generally, convertible securities offer more income than may be earned on the firm's common stock. That is, the interest exceeds the dividend payment. In addition, convertible securities have some potential for capital gains if the price of the underlying stock rises.

---

6. How the call feature may affect the price of a bond is discussed in Chapter 11.
7. Firms may also issue convertible preferred stock, which gives the investor the option to convert the preferred stock into the firm's common stock. Since most of features associated with convertible bonds also apply to convertible preferred stock, the discussion is not repeated. If you learn this material concerning convertible bonds, it is safe to assume that it also applies to convertible preferred stock.

| EXHIBIT 9.7 | Schedule for the Call Penalty of the AT&T 8⅛ Debenture Maturing in 2020 |

Year	Percentage of Face Value	Amount Required to Retire $1,000 of Debt		Amount of Call Penalty
2004	103.640	$1,036.40		$36.40
2005	103.309	$1,033.09		$33.09
2006	102.978	$1,029.78		$29.78
2007	102.647	$1,026.47	_____	$26.47
.	.	.		.
.	.	.		.
.	.	.		.
2010	101.655	$1,016.55		$16.55
.	.	.	_____	.
.	.	.		.
.	.	.		.
2015	100.000	$1,000.00		0.00

Features of Convertible Bonds

Convertible bonds are debentures (i.e., unsecured debt instruments) that may be converted at the holder's option into the stock of the issuing company. Since the firm has granted the holder the right to convert the bonds, these bonds are usually subordinate to the firm's other debt. They also tend to offer a lower interest rate (i.e., coupon rate) than is available on nonconvertible debt. Thus, the conversion feature means that the firm can issue lower-quality debt at a lower interest cost. Investors are willing to accept this reduced quality and interest income because the market value of the bond will appreciate *if the price of the stock rises*. These investors are thus trading quality and interest for possible capital gains.

Since convertible bonds are long-term debt instruments, they have features that are common to all bonds. They are usually issued in $1,000 denominations, pay interest semiannually, and have a fixed maturity date. However, if the bonds are converted into stock, the maturity date is irrelevant because the bonds are retired when they are converted. Convertible bonds frequently have a sinking fund requirement, which, like the maturity date, is meaningless once the bonds are converted.

Convertible bonds are *always callable*. The firm uses the call to force the holders to convert the bonds. Once the bond is called, you must convert, or any appreciation in price that has resulted from an increase in the stock's value will be lost. Such forced conversion is extremely important to the issuing firm, because it no longer has to pay the interest and retire the debt.

Convertible bonds are attractive to some investors because they offer the safety features of debt. The firm must meet the terms of the indenture, and the bonds must be retired if they are not converted. The flow of interest income usually exceeds the dividend yield that may be earned on the firm's stock. In addition, since the bonds may be converted into stock, you will share in the growth of the company. If the price of the stock rises in response to the firm's growth, the value of the convertible bond must also rise. It is this combination of the safety of debt and the potential for capital gain that makes convertible bonds an attractive investment, particularly to investors who desire income and some capital appreciation.

Like all investments, convertible bonds subject the holder to risk. If the company fails, the holder of a bond stands to lose the funds invested in the debt. This is particularly true with regard to convertible bonds, because they are usually subordinate to the firm's other debt. Thus, convertible bonds are riskier than senior debt or debt that is secured by specific collateral. In case of a default or bankruptcy, holders of convertible bonds may at best realize only a fraction of the principal amount invested. However, their position is still superior to that of the stockholders.

Default is not the only potential source of risk to investors. Convertible bonds are actively traded, and their prices can and do fluctuate. As is explained in the next section, their price is partially related to the value of the stock into which they may be converted. Fluctuations in the value of the stock produce fluctuations in the price of the bond. These price changes are *in addition* to price movements caused by variations in interest rates.

The Convertible Bond as Stock—The Conversion Value

conversion value as stock
Value of the bond in terms of the stock into which the bond may be converted.

The value of a convertible bond in terms of the stock, its **conversion value** (C_s), depends on (1) the face value or principal amount of the bond (FV), (2) the conversion (or exercise) price of the bond (P_e), and (3) the market price of the common stock (P_s). The face value divided by the conversion price of the bond gives the number of shares into which the bond may be converted. For example, if a $1,000 bond may be converted at $20 per share, then the bond may be converted into 50 shares ($1,000 ÷ $20). The number of shares times the market price of a share gives the value of the bond in terms of stock. If the bond is convertible into 50 shares and the stock sells for $15 per share, then the bond is worth $750 in terms of stock ($15 × 50).

The conversion value of the bond as stock may be expressed in equation form. The number of shares into which the bond may be converted is called the *conversion ratio*, or

(9.1)
$$\text{Conversion ratio} = \frac{FV}{P_e}.$$

The conversion value of the bond is the product of the conversion ratio and the price of the stock.[8] The conversion value of the bond as stock is expressed in Equation 9.2:

(9.2)
$$C_s = \frac{FV}{P_e} \times P_s$$

The conversion value is illustrated in Exhibit 9.8 (p. 272). In this example a $1,000 bond is convertible into 50 shares (i.e., a conversion price of $20 per share). The first column gives various prices of the stock. The second column presents the number of shares into which the bond is convertible (i.e., 50 shares). The third column gives the value of the bond in terms of stock (i.e., the product of the values in the first two columns). As may be seen in the exhibit, the value of the bond in terms of stock rises as the price of the stock increases.

This relationship between the price of the stock and the conversion value of the bond is illustrated in Figure 9.2 (p. 272). The price of the stock (P_s) is given on the

---

8. The *conversion price* is the face value divided by the number of shares into which the bond may be converted. That is,

$$\text{Conversion price} = \frac{FV}{\text{Conversion ratio}}.$$

If the bond is convertible into 50 shares, the conversion price is

$$\frac{\$1,000}{50} = \$20.$$

| EXHIBIT 9.8 | The Relationship Between the Price of a Stock and the Value of a Convertible Bond as Stock |

Price of the Stock	Shares into Which the Bond is Convertible	Value of the Bond in Terms of Stock
$ 0	50	$ 0
5	50	250
10	50	500
15	50	750
20	50	1,000
25	50	1,250
30	50	1,500

horizontal axis, and the conversion value of the bond (C_s) is shown on the vertical axis. As the price of the stock rises, the conversion value of the bond increases. This is shown in the graph by line C_s, which represents the intrinsic value of the bond in terms of stock. Line C_s is a straight line running through the origin. If the stock has no value, the value of the bond in terms of stock is also worthless. If the exercise price of the bond and the market price of the stock are equal (i.e., $P_s = P_e$, which in this case is $20), the bond's value as stock is equal to the principal amount (i.e., the bond's face value). As the price of the stock rises above the conversion price of the bond, the bond's value in terms of stock increases and *exceeds* the principal amount of the debt.

The market price of a convertible bond cannot be less than the bond's conversion value. If the price of the bond were less than its value as stock, you could sell the stock short, purchase the convertible bond, exercise the conversion feature, and use the shares acquired through the conversion to cover the short sale. You would then make a profit equal to the difference between the price of the convertible bond and the conversion value of the bond. For example, suppose in the preceding example that the bond was selling for $800 when the stock sold for $20. At $20, the bond is worth $1,000 in term of stock ($20 × 50). You would sell 50 shares

| FIGURE 9.2 | The Relationship Between the Price of the Stock and the Conversion Value of the Bond |

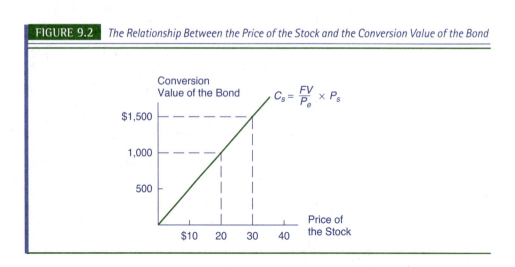

short for $1,000. At the same time you would buy the bond for $800 and immediately convert the bond into 50 shares. After the shares had been received through the conversion of the bond, you would cover the short position and earn $200 (before commissions).

Of course, if you could do that, I could do it. And so could everyone else. As each one of us tried to buy the bonds, their price would increase. The price increase would continue until there was no opportunity for profit. This occurs when the price is equal to or greater than the bond's value as stock. Thus, the conversion value of the bond as stock sets the minimum price of the bond. The market price of a convertible bond will always be at least equal to its conversion value.

However, the market price of the convertible bond is rarely equal to the conversion value of the bond. The bond frequently sells for a premium over its conversion value because the convertible bond may also have value as a debt instrument. As a pure (i.e., nonconvertible) bond, it competes with other nonconvertible debt. Like the conversion feature, this element of debt may affect the bond's price. Its impact is important, for it also has the effect of putting a minimum price on the convertible bond. It is this price floor that gives investors in convertible bonds an element of safety that stock lacks.

THE HISTORY OF SELECTED CONVERTIBLE BONDS

Perhaps the best way to understand investing in convertible bonds is to examine the history of several convertible bonds. The first is a success story, in that the price of the common stock rose and therefore the value of the bond also rose. The second is a not-so-successful story, for the price of the stock declined and so did the value of the bond. However, the story of this bond is not a tragedy, for the bond was still a debt obligation of the company and was retired at maturity even though it was not converted into stock. The third bond illustrates a more typical case in which the bond's price rises but the increase occurs over an extended period of time.

American Quasar was a firm devoted to exploring and drilling for oil and gas. The discovery of oil wells (called *wildcats*) can prove to be highly lucrative; however, the majority of drilling leads only to dry holes (i.e., no oil or natural gas is found). Because of the nature of its operations, American Quasar was a speculative firm at best. Speculative firms, however, need funds to operate, so the firm issued $17,500,000 in face value of convertible bonds. The coupon rate was set at 7¼ percent and the exercise price of the bond was $21 (i.e., it was convertible into 47.6 shares), which was a premium of 17 percent over the approximate price of the stock ($18) at the date of issue.

After the bond was issued, American Quasar's stock did particularly well and the price rose to $32. The value of the convertible bond also increased with the price of the stock. The prices of the bond and the stock moved closely together, and less than two years after being issued the bond was called, which forced conversion of the bond into the stock.

What was the return earned by investors in these securities? Obviously, an investment in either the stock or the bond was quite profitable, since the price of the stock rose so rapidly. The bond's price rose from an initial sale price of $1,000 to approximately $1,500 during the time it was outstanding. The bond paid $72.50 in interest. The holding period return earned over the 15 months on an investment in the bond was

$$\frac{\text{Price appreciation} + \text{Interest earned}}{\text{Cost}} = \frac{\$1,500 - \$1,000 + \$72.50}{\$1,000}$$

$$= \frac{\$572.50}{\$1,000} = 57.25\%.$$

For the stock the holding period return was.

$$\frac{\text{Price appreciation} + \text{Dividends}}{\text{Cost}} = \frac{\$32 - \$18 + \$0}{\$18} = \frac{\$14}{\$18} = 77.7\%.$$

(The bond paid only one year's interest since it was converted prior to the next interest payment, and the stock did not pay any cash dividends while the bond was outstanding.) As may be seen by these calculations, the returns are both positive. The stock did better because the bond was initially sold for a premium over its value as stock. However, an investor who purchased this convertible bond certainly would have little cause for complaint.

While the previous example illustrated how the price of convertible bonds may rise as the price of the stock rises, the Pan American World Airways convertible bonds demonstrate the opposite. The 4½ percent convertible bond was issued when Pan Am was riding the crest of popularity. For investors purchasing either the stock or the bond, Pam Am's popularity vanished, and through years of continued deficits, the price of the stock declined drastically. Both the stock and the bond fell to "bargain basement" prices, as the market expected the firm to default. At that time the bond reached a low of $130 for a $1,000 bond!

Pan Am, however, did not default, and the bond remained an obligation that had to be retired. Thus, when Pan Am did redeem the bond, investors who purchased it initially for $1,000 received their principal. Holders of the Pan Am convertible bonds due in 2010 were not so lucky, because the firm eventually failed and ceased operations in 1991. These bonds thus illustrate that investors who acquire both convertible and nonconvertible bonds of financially weak firms can lose their entire investments if the firm fails.

The American Quasar bond was in existence only briefly because the underlying stock price rose and the bond was converted soon after it was issued. The Pan Am convertible bond lasted the entire term and was retired at par. Between the two extremes is the Seagate Technology convertible bond. Issued in 1993, this 6¾ percent bond continued to trade, with its price moving with the price of the underlying stock. The Seagate convertible illustrates the importance of holding the bond for many years if the bondholder expects to earn a higher return on the bond than on the stock. For example, an investor could have bought the bond in 1993 for $860, while the stock sold for $16. Since the bond was convertible into 23.529 shares, its value as stock was $376 (23.529 × $16). At those prices the bond sold for a premium of $484 ($860 − $376) over the value of the underlying stock. Since the bond paid annual interest of $67.50, it would take over seven years ($484/$67.50) for the interest to offset the premium.

In 1996, the stock had risen to over $60, and Seagate called bonds for $1,013.50 plus accrued interest. At $60, the bonds were worth $1,411.74, so it was obviously advantageous to convert. The call occurred three years after the bonds were issued, so the interest could not cover the premium. The investor who purchased the stock for $16 and sold it for $60 earned an annualized return in excess of 55 percent. The investor who purchased the bond for $860, collected the interest, and sold the bond for $1,412 earned an annualized return of 24.7 percent.

CALLING CONVERTIBLES

Two of the previous illustrations (the American Quasar and Seagate Technology bonds) resulted in the bond's being called. Why do companies call their convertible bonds and when? The answer to the first question is almost self-evident. Calling the bond and forcing it to be converted into stock results in saving the interest payments. Once the bond is converted, interest payments cease. The forced conversion also improves the firm's balance sheet. There is less debt outstanding and additional equity. The debt ratio declines and indicates that the firm is less financially leveraged. This reduction in debt is achieved without a cash outflow to repay the principal.

The mechanics of calling has two considerations. First, the price of the stock must exceed the exercise price of the bond. If the exercise price of a $1,000 convertible bond were $50 and the price of the stock were $40, no one would convert. The bond is convertible into 20 shares ($1,000/$50) and those shares are worth only $800. No investor would convert the bond but instead would accept the call price. If the price of the stock were $80, virtually all investors would convert. The 20 shares are worth $1,600. Few, if any, would accept the call price and not convert the bond.

Once the bond is called, there is the chance that the price of the stock may decline. The call is not instantaneous; it occurs over a period of time such as four weeks. If the price of the above stock were $53, the value of the bond as stock is only $1,060. If the firm called the bond and the price of the stock declined to $49, investors would not convert. This defeats the purpose of the call to force conversion. Management will wait until the price of the stock has risen sufficiently to make it a virtual certainty that the price of the stock will not decline sufficiently that bondholders accept the call price instead of converting.

The second consideration is the actual timing of the call. The call virtually always occurs prior to an interest payment. If the bond pays interest every June 1 and December 1, calling the bond on December 10 occurs after the interest payment is made. It would be better to call the bond prior to December 1. Even calling the bond on November 15 would not avoid the interest payment. The four-week period during which the bondholders may convert would result in their holding the bond until the interest payment is made and then converting the bond. Thus, calls tend to occur more than one month prior to the interest payment (e.g., October 15 in the previous example) but rarely after the interest payment.

Federal Income Taxes and Convertible Bonds

The federal government taxes interest paid by convertible bonds as income, and it taxes any capital gains that occur if the bond is sold for a profit. Does it also levy taxes when the investor converts the bonds into stock? The answer is No. The cost basis of the bond is transferred to the stock.

You buy a convertible bond for $1,000 and it is convertible into 40 shares. The cost basis for the bond is $1,000 and that is used when the bond is sold to determine any capital gains or losses. If you convert the bond, the cost of the 40 shares of stock is also $1,000 ($25 a share). As long as you hold the shares, there has been no taxable transaction. If you sell the 40 shares for $1,600 ($40 a share), your capital gain is $600 ($1,600 – 1,000). If you sell the 40 shares for $10 a share, your capital loss is $600 ($400 – 1,000). Whether these capital gains or losses are short-term or long-term depends on the total time you held the securities. Thus, the determination of long-term or short-term includes both the periods when you held the bond and when you owned the stock.

SUMMARY

This chapter discussed the general features of long-term debt. The terms of a debt issue include the coupon rate of interest and the maturity date. A trustee is appointed for each bond issue to protect the rights of the individual investors. The risks associated with investing in debt are attributable to price fluctuations and inflation as well as to the possibility of default on interest and principal repayment. To help investors, several firms have developed rating services that classify debt issues according to risk.

The mechanics of purchasing debt are very similar to those of buying stocks. However, while stocks are purchased through brokerage firms, some debt instruments (e.g., federal government securities) may be purchased through banks.

Debt may be retired in several ways. Some bonds are issued in a series, with a specified amount of debt maturing each year. Other debt issues have sinking funds that retire part of the bond issue prior to maturity. For some debt issues, the firm has the right to call the bonds prior to maturity. The debtor can also offer to buy the debt back from investors before it matures. Since creditors are as concerned with the return of their principal as they are with the payment of interest, the ability of the firm or government to retire its liabilities is one of the foremost factors in determining the risks associated with investing in debt.

Corporations issue a variety of bonds. Some bonds are supported by collateral (mortgage bonds and equipment trust certificates), but many corporate bonds are not secured (debentures) and are general obligations of the issuer. While the coupon or interest payment is often fixed, there are bonds that pay no interest (zero coupon bonds) and bonds with variable interest payments. High-yield debt instruments, the so-called junk bonds, often have features that differentiate them from the bonds issued by corporations with investment-grade credit ratings.

Convertible bonds are debt instruments with a built-in option. The holder may convert the bond into the firm's stock. While convertible bonds have the essential features of all bonds, their value is also related to the value of the underlying stock. If the price of the stock rises, the value of the convertible bond also appreciates. Convertible bonds thus offer the potential for growth and capital gains that is not possible through an investment in nonconvertible bonds.

Learning Objectives

Now that you have completed this chapter, you should be able to:

1. Describe the features common to all bonds.
2. Explain the purpose of a bond's indenture and the role of its trustee.
3. Identify the sources of risk to the bondholder.
4. Describe the process for buying a bond and the paying or receiving of accrued interest.
5. Differentiate the types of corporate bonds.
6. Contrast features associated with high-yield bonds and features associated with investment-grade bonds.
7. Distinguish among the ways that bonds are retired.
8. Determine a convertible bond's value as stock.
9. Isolate why all convertible bonds have a call feature.

Internet Application for Chapter 9   The Corporate Bond Market

Since bond averages, bond indexes, bond prices, the volume of trading, and other data are not prominently reported in the financial media, you are probably not aware of corporate bonds as a potential investment. Many companies, however, do have bonds outstanding that are traded.

1. Determine if the companies you are following have bonds outstanding. What are the basic features of these bonds (e.g., the coupon, maturity date, or call features)?
2. Are the bonds rated by at least one of the major rating services?
3. If they are rated, rank the bonds based on their ratings and compare the bond ratings and the stocks' beta coefficients. Does there appear to be a relationship between the bond ratings and the stocks' betas?

General information concerning fixed- income securities markets is available from the Bond Market Association: **http://www.bondmarkets.com**. Finding information on specific bonds and their prices is considerably more difficult than obtaining quotes on stocks. If a company has bonds outstanding, they will be enumerated in its annual report. Annual reports may be obtained from the company's Web site or through EDGAR: **http://www.sec.gov**. Mergent Online (**http://mergentonline.com**) also enumerates a company's outstanding bonds. Not all of these bonds, however, may be available for trading. Many issues are privately sold to a financial institution such as a pension plan or insurance company and do not trade in the secondary markets.

THOMSON ONE
Business School Edition

Currency with Thomson ONE: Business School Edition

In Chapter 7, financial ratios are used to analyze a firm's financial condition as a prelude to purchasing the stock. Creditors such as bondholders also use ratio analysis to help determine a firm's capacity to pay interest and retire debt. Go to the Thomson ONE: Business School Edition database and compare the following ratios for each firm:

Current ratio

Quick ratio

Accounts receivable turnover or days sales outstanding

Inventory turnover

Debt to total assets

Debt to equity

Times-interest-earned

(Thomson ONE: Business School Edition provides information from several sources, so you may have to access more than one source to obtain the requested information.) What do these ratios suggest about each firm's use of financial leverage and its capacity to service their debt obligations?

Government Securities

I n the early 2000s, one of the big political issues in Washington was the size of the federal government's deficit. During the later 1990s, the issue was the opposite: what to do with the federal government's surplus. Government deficits occur when disbursements (expenditures) exceed receipts (revenues). Whenever a deficit occurs, someone must finance it. In order to raise funds to cover its deficit, the federal government issues a variety of debt instruments. This variety helps tap different sources of funds that are available in the money and capital markets.

The preceding chapter discussed a variety of corporate debt securities. This chapter extends the discussion to debt securities issued by the federal government, its agencies, and state and municipal governments. Many of the features associated with corporate debt (e.g., interest payments, maturity dates, and call features) apply to government securities. This specific material is not repeated; instead the emphasis is on the features that differentiate government securities from corporate bonds.

The chapter begins with a discussion of the various types of debt securities issued by the federal government. These debt instruments range from EE bonds issued in small denominations to short-term Treasury bills and long-term bonds. The federal government also has created agencies such as the Government National Mortgage Association. These agencies also issue debt securities, whose interest rates generally exceed the rate paid by the bonds of the federal government. The chapter ends with coverage of the debt issued by state and local governments. These bonds, often referred to as "municipal bonds," offer a real alternative to corporation and federal government bonds since they pay interest that is exempt from federal income taxation.

THE VARIETY OF FEDERAL GOVERNMENT DEBT

According to the Economic Report of the President, the federal government made interest payments of $247.7 billion in 2002 on its debt. This sum was substantial and amounted to about 12.3 percent of the total expenditures made by the federal government in that year. The debt was financed by a variety of investors, including individuals, corporations, and financial institutions. To induce this diverse group of investors to purchase its debt, the federal government has issued different types of debt instruments that appeal to the various potential buyers.

For investors, the unique advantage offered by the federal government's debt is its safety. These debt instruments are the safest of all possible investments, for there is no question that the U.S. Treasury is able to pay the interest and repay the principal. The source of this safety is the federal government's constitutional right to tax and to print money. Because there is no specified limitation on the federal government's capacity to create money, only Congress can enact legislation (e.g., the debt ceiling) that restricts the federal government's ability to retire or refinance its debt.

The various types of federal government debt and the amount outstanding of each are illustrated in Exhibit 10.1. As may be seen in the exhibit, there has been an emphasis on the use of short- and intermediate-term (five years or less) financing by the Treasury. This emphasis is partially explained by interest costs. Interest rates on short-term debt are usually lower than those on long-term debt. Hence, the use of short-term financing reduces the Treasury's interest expense. Furthermore, Congress restricts the interest rate that the Treasury may pay on long-term debt, but it does not restrict the interest rate on short-term securities. Thus, during periods of high interest rates, the Treasury may not be permitted to sell long-term securities even if it desires to do so.

NONMARKETABLE FEDERAL GOVERNMENT DEBT

Perhaps the most widely held federal government debt is the series EE bonds. (On November 16, 2001, the Treasury announced that EE bonds sold through financial institutions would be designated as "Patriot Bonds.") Originally Series E bonds were issued in 1941 to help finance World War II. They were sold at a discount in small denominations such as $25, $50, and $100, so virtually every person could save and contribute to the war effort.

EXHIBIT 10.1	The Variety of Federal Government Debt as of		
	Length of Time to Maturity	Value (in Billions of Dollars)	Percentage of Total Debt
Treasury bills	Less than 1 year	$ 927.8	13.9%
Intermediate-term notes	One to 5 years	1,713.7	25.7
Long-term bonds	Over 5 years	582.4	8.7
Savings bonds	Various maturities	155.0	2.4
Other debt*	Various maturities	3,291.2	49.3

*Debt held by U.S. government agencies and trust funds and state and local governments.
Source: *Federal Reserve Bulletin*, November 2003, p. A25.

On January 2, 1980, the Treasury started to issue a new bond, series EE, to replace the series E bonds. Like the E bonds, the new bonds were issued at a discount. The smallest denomination was $50, which cost $25. In November 1982, the Treasury changed the method for computing interest on EE bonds from a fixed rate to a variable rate, which is changed every six months. (You may find the current rate by dialing 1-800-US BONDS. Additional information concerning E and EE bonds may be obtained from savingsbonds.com inc. (**http://www .savingsbonds.com**), which offers a service that provides interest earned, cash-in values, and final maturity dates of all issues of E and EE bonds. The service also tells you which bonds have ceased earning interest.) The variable rate permits the small investor to participate in higher yields when interest rates rise, but the investor will earn less when interest rates fall.

Effective May 1, 1995, the terms of series EE bonds were once again changed, but bonds issued before that date are not affected by the changes. The term of the new EE bonds was set at 17 years. If the bonds are not redeemed at maturity, they will continue to earn interest for an additional 13 years, for a total of 30 years. The interest rate is announced every May 1 and November 1 and applies for the following six months. The new rate is 90 percent of an average of the rate paid by five-year Treasury securities for the preceding three months. Interest is added to the value of the bonds every six months after they are purchased.

An important difference between series EE bonds and other bonds is the lack of a secondary market. If you want immediate cash, the bonds cannot be sold. Instead, you redeem them at a financial institution such as a commercial bank. Nor can the bonds be transferred as a gift, although they can be transferred through an estate. The Treasury also forbids using EE bonds to secure a loan. While corporate bonds may be used as collateral, EE bonds cannot.

In addition to EE bonds, the Treasury issued HH bonds. Unlike EE bonds, which are sold at a discount, HH bonds were sold at par and paid interest twice a year. In 1998, the U.S. Treasury started selling a new security, Series I bonds. Over time the new bonds replaced HH bonds, and the Treasury stopped issuing HH bonds in 2004.

Series I bonds are sold in denominations ranging from $50 to $10,000, and the interest rate is set by the Treasury every May and November for the next six months. The interest payment combines a fixed rate and an additional amount based on the Consumer Price Index. Thus, I bonds offer a guaranteed minimum rate plus an adjustment for inflation. (HH bonds paid a fixed rate with no adjustment for inflation.) The maturity date is 20 years after date of issue but may be extended for an additional 10 years, after which interest payments cease. Interest is exempt from state income taxation and may be excluded from federal income tax if the interest is used to pay qualified higher education expenses.

MARKETABLE SECURITIES

Treasury Bills

Treasury bills
Short-term federal government securities.

Short-term federal government debt is issued in the form of **Treasury bills**. These bills are sold in denominations of $10,000 to $1,000,000 and mature in 3 to 12 months. Like series EE (Patriot) bonds, they are sold at a discount; however, unlike series EE bonds, the discounted price is not set. Instead, the Treasury auctions off the bills, which go to the highest bidders. For example, if an investor bids $9,700 and obtains the bill, he or she will receive $10,000 when the bill matures, which is a yield of 3.1 percent ($300 ÷ $9,700) for the holding period. If the bid price had been higher, the interest cost to the Treasury (and the yield to the buyer) would have been lower.

Once Treasury bills have been auctioned, they may be bought and sold in the secondary market. They are issued in book-entry form and are easily marketed. There is an active secondary market in these bills, and they are quoted daily in the financial press and many city newspapers. For Treasury bills the quotes are given in the following form:

Maturity	Days to Maturity	Bid	Asked	Ask Yield
12/06/05	126	3.49	3.47	3.56

These quotes indicate that for a Treasury bill maturing on December 6, 2005, buyers were willing to bid a discounted price that produced a discount yield of 3.49 percent. Sellers, however, were willing to sell (offer) the bills at a smaller discount (higher price) that returned a discount yield of 3.47 percent. The annualized yield on the bill based on the asked price is 3.56 percent.

The reason for the difference between the discount yield and the annualized yield is that Treasury bills are sold at a discount and are quoted in terms of the "discount yield." The discount yield is not the same as (nor is it comparable to) the annualized yield on the bill or the yield on a bond. The discount yield is calculated on the basis of the face amount of the bill and uses a 360-day year. The simple (noncompound) annualized yield, which is sometimes referred to as the "bond-equivalent yield," depends on the price of the bill and uses a 365-day year.

The difference between the two calculations may be seen in the following example. Suppose a three-month $10,000 Treasury bill sells for $9,800. The discount yield (i_d) is

(10.1)

$$i_d = \frac{\text{Par value} - \text{Price}}{\text{Par value}} \times \frac{360}{\text{Number of days to maturity}}$$

$$\frac{\$10{,}000 - \$9{,}800}{\$10{,}000} \times \frac{360}{90} = 8\%.$$

The annualized yield (i_a) is

(10.2)

$$i_a = \frac{\text{Par value} - \text{Price}}{\text{Price}} \times \frac{365}{\text{Number of days to maturity}}$$

$$\frac{\$10{,}000 - \$9{,}800}{\$9{,}800} \times \frac{365}{90} = 8.277\%.$$

Since the discount yield uses the face amount and a 360-day year, it understates the yield the investor is earning. The discount yield may be converted to the annualized yield by the following equation:

$$i_a = \frac{365 \times i_d}{360 - (i_a \times \text{Days to maturity})}$$

Thus, if the discount rate on a three-month Treasury bill is 8 percent, the annualized yield is

$$i_a = \frac{365 \times 0.08}{360 - (0.08 \times 90)} = 8.277\%,$$

which is the same answer derived using the annual yield equation.[1]

Treasury bills may be purchased through brokerage firms, commercial banks, and any Federal Reserve bank. These purchases may be new issues or bills that are being traded in the secondary market. Bills with one year to maturity are auctioned once a month. Shorter-term bills are auctioned weekly. If the buyer purchases the bills directly through the Federal Reserve bank, there are no commission fees. Brokers and commercial banks do charge commissions, but the fees are modest compared with those charged for other investment transactions, such as the purchase of stock.

Treasury bills are among the best short-term debt instruments available to investors who desire safety and some interest income (i.e., a liquid asset). The bills mature quickly, and there are many issues from which the investor may choose. Thus, the investor may purchase a bill that matures when the principal is needed. For example, an individual who has ready cash today but who must make a payment after three months may purchase a bill that matures at the appropriate time. In doing so, the investor puts the cash to work for three months.

Perhaps the one feature that differentiates Treasury bills from all other investments is risk. These bills are considered the safest of all possible investments, and often referred to as "risk-free" security. There is no question concerning the safety of principal when investors acquire Treasury bills. The federal government always has the capacity to refund or retire Treasury bills because it has the power to tax and the power to create money.

The primary buyers of Treasury bills are corporations with excess short-term cash, commercial banks with unused lending capacity, money market mutual funds, and foreign investors seeking a safe haven for their funds. Individual investors may also purchase them. However, the minimum denomination of $10,000 excludes many savers. Individual investors who desire such safe short-term investments may purchase shares in money market mutual funds that specialize in buying short-term securities, including Treasury bills.

Treasury Notes and Bonds

Intermediate-term federal government debt is in the form of **Treasury notes**. These notes are issued in denominations of $1,000 to more than $100,000 and mature in one to ten years. **Treasury bonds**, the government's debt instrument for long-term debt, are issued in denominations of $1,000 to $1,000,000, and these bonds mature in more than ten years from the date of issue. Notes and bonds are

Calculator Solution

Function Key	Data Input
PV =	-9800
FV =	10000
PMT =	0
N =	.24657
I =	?
Function Key	Answer
I =	8.54

1. The determination of the compound rate (i_c) is

$9,800(1 + i_c)^n = \$10,000,$

in which $n = 90/365$. The solution is

$9,800(1 + i_c)^{90/365} = \$10,000$

$$(1 + i_c)^{0.2466} = \frac{\$10,000}{\$9,800} = 1.0204$$

$$i_c = (1.0204)^{4.0556} - 1 = 0.0854 = 8.54\%.$$

Treasury notes
The intermediate-term debt of the federal government.

Treasury bonds
The long-term debt of the federal government.

issued in book-entry and registered forms. These issues are the safest intermediate- and long-term investments available and are purchased by pension funds, financial institutions, or savers who are primarily concerned with moderate income and safety. Since these debt instruments are so safe, their yields are generally lower than that which may be obtained with high-quality corporate debt. For example, in late 2003, Johnson & Johnson bonds that were rated triple A yielded 5.02 percent, while Treasury bonds with approximately the same time to maturity yielded 4.36 percent.

Like Treasury bills, new issues of Treasury bonds may be purchased through commercial banks and brokerage firms. These firms will charge commissions, but the individual may avoid such fees by purchasing the securities from any of the Federal Reserve banks or their branches. Payment, however, must precede purchase. Unless you submit a competitive bid, the purchase price is the average price charged institutions that buy the bonds through competitive bidding. By accepting this noncompetitive bid, you are ensured of receiving the average yield earned by financial institutions, which try to buy the securities at the lowest price (highest yield) possible.

Once the bonds are purchased, they may be readily resold, as there is an active secondary market in U.S. Treasury bonds. Like corporate stocks and bonds, Treasury bond prices are reported in the financial press, but the reporting is somewhat different. The prices are quoted in 32nds. If a bond were quoted 107:13–107:15 that means the bid price is 107 13/32 and the ask price is 107 15/32. These amounts are $10,740.63 and $10,746.88 per $10,000 face amount of debt.

Treasury bonds are among the safest investments available to investors. As with Treasury bills, there is no question that the federal government can pay the interest and refund its debt, but there are ways in which the holder of Treasury notes and bonds can suffer losses. These debt instruments pay a fixed amount of interest, which is determined when the notes and bonds are issued. The fixed interest means the bonds are subject to interest rate risk. If interest rates subsequently rise, existing issues will not be as attractive, and their market prices will decline. If you must sell the debt instrument before it matures, the price will be lower than the principal amount and you will suffer a capital loss.

You may also lose through investments in Treasury debt when the rate of inflation exceeds the interest rate earned on the bonds. For example, during 1974 the yields on government bonds rose to 7.3 percent, but the rate of inflation for consumer goods exceeded 10 percent. Investors suffered a loss in purchasing power, for interest payments were insufficient to compensate for the inflation.

These two factors, fluctuating interest rates and inflation, illustrate that investing in federal government debt, like all types of investing, subjects the investor to interest rate risk and purchasing power risk. Therefore, although federal government debt is among the safest of all investments with regard to the certainty of payment of interest and principal, some element of risk still exists.

Foreign investors have the additional risk associated with exchange rates when they purchase U.S. federal government securities. If the value of their currency rises relative to the dollar, then the interest and principal repayment is reduced when the dollars are converted into their currency. However, the value of the dollar could rise, in which case the return on the investment is enhanced. During periods of economic uncertainty in other countries, foreign investors will buy dollars both as a safe haven and for the enhanced return that will occur if their currency declines and the value of the dollar rises.

Zero Coupon Treasury Securities

With the advent of Individual Retirement Accounts (IRAs), corporations started issuing zero coupon bonds. Because the Treasury did not issue such bonds at that time, selected brokerage firms created their own zero coupon Treasury securities. For example, Merrill Lynch created the Treasury Investment Growth Receipt (TIGR, generally referred to as *Tigers*). Merrill Lynch bought a block of Treasury bonds, removed all the coupons, and offered investors either the interest to be received in a specific year or the principal at the bonds' maturity. Since payment was limited to the single payment at the specified time in the future, these tigers were sold at a discount. In effect, they were zero coupon bonds backed by Treasury securities originally purchased by Merrill Lynch and held by a trustee.

Other brokerage firms created similar securities by removing coupons from existing Treasury bonds. Some of these zero coupon Treasury securities were given clever acronyms, such as Salomon Brothers' CATS (Certificates of Accrual on Treasury Securities). In other cases they were just called Treasury Receipts (T.R.s). In each case, however, the brokerage firm owns the underlying Treasury securities. The actual security purchased by the investor is an obligation of the brokerage firm and not of the federal government.

Strips

In 1985, the Treasury introduced its own zero coupon bonds, called STRIPS, for Separate Trading of Registered Interest and Principal Securities. Investors who purchase such STRIPS acquire a direct obligation of the federal government. Since these securities are direct obligations, they tend to have slightly lower yields than Tigers, CATS, and the other zero coupon securities created by brokerage firms.

In any case, the primary appeal of these securities is their use in retirement accounts. The interest earned on a zero coupon bond is taxed as it accrues, even though the holder does not receive annual cash interest payments. Thus, there is little reason to acquire these securities in accounts that are not tax sheltered. They are, however, excellent vehicles for retirement accounts, since all the funds (i.e., principal and accrued interest) are paid in one lump sum at maturity. Because any tax on a retirement account is paid when the funds are withdrawn, the tax disadvantage of zero coupon bonds is circumvented. The investor can purchase issues that mature at a desired date to meet retirement needs. For example, a 40-year-old investor could purchase zero coupon government securities that mature when he or she reaches the age of 65, 66, and so on. Such a laddered bond strategy would ensure that the funds were received after retirement, at which time they would replace the individual's earned income that ceases at retirement.

If the investor does acquire zero coupon bonds, that individual should be aware that these securities have the most price volatility of all federal government bonds. As is discussed in Chapter 11, changing interest rates generate fluctuations in bond prices. The longer the term or the smaller the coupon, the greater is the price fluctuation. Zero coupon bonds make no periodic interest payments; thus, for a given term to maturity, their prices are more volatile than coupon bonds with the same maturity.

The reason for a zero coupon bond's increased price volatility in response to changes in interest rates is that the entire return falls on the single payment at maturity. Since the current price of any bond is the present value of the interest and principal payments, the price of a zero coupon bond is solely the result of the present value of the single payment received at maturity. No interest payments will be received during the early years of the bond's life that reduce the responsiveness of the bond's price to changes in interest rates.

Inflation-Indexed Treasury Securities

In addition to traditional marketable debt instruments, the federal government also issues **inflation-indexed securities**, referred to as TIPS (Treasury Inflation-Protection Securities). There are two basic types of marketable federal government inflation-indexed debt. The first is notes, which are issued annually on January 15 and July 15 and mature after ten years. The second is the inflation-indexed bond, which is a 30-year security issued every October 15.

Inflation-indexed notes and bonds pay a modest rate of interest plus make an adjustment for changes in the Consumer Price Index (i.e., the rate of inflation). The interest rate is the "real yield" earned by the investor. The adjustment occurs by altering the amount of principal owed by the federal government; *no* adjustment is made in the semiannual interest *rate*. The amount of the change in the principal depends on the current CPI relative to the CPI when the securities were issued. For example, the ten-year notes issued in January 1999 have a real interest rate of 3⅞ percent. The base CPI to be used for determining subsequent changes in the principal is 164. Two years later, in January 2001, the CPI was 174, and the principal was increased by a factor of 1.06098 (174/164). A $1,000 note was increased to $1,060.98. The investor would then receive interest of $41.075 ($1,060.98 × .03875) instead of the $38.75, which was the amount initially earned when the note was issued.[2] Since the principal and the amount of interest received are increased with the rate of inflation, the investor's purchasing power is maintained.

Inflation-indexed bonds appeal to individuals who are primarily concerned that the rate of inflation will increase so that an investment in a traditional, fixed-rate bond will result in a loss of purchasing power. If, for example, the rate of inflation is 2 percent and an investor purchases a 5 percent, ten-year bond and the rate of inflation rises to 6 percent, the interest is insufficient to cover the higher rate of inflation. The purchasing power of the investor's principal is also eroded. If that investor had acquired an inflation-indexed security, the principal owed and the interest earned would rise sufficiently to cover the increased inflation and provide a modest return.

While federal government inflation-indexed notes and bonds are a means to manage purchasing power risk, there are risks associated with an inflation-indexed bond. The fixed, real rate paid by the bonds is less than the nominal rate that could be earned by an investment in a traditional bond. For example, the rate of interest on a 20-year bond in 2004 was 4.8 percent, which is more than real rate on the inflation-indexed bond. Of course, if the rate of inflation were to increase, the real return on the traditional note would diminish while the inflation-indexed note would continue to earn its 2 percent real rate. If, however, inflation does not increase, the inflation-indexed security produces an inferior return.

Inflation-indexed federal government notes and bonds are, of course, illustrative of an important trade-off investors must accept. To obtain protection and reduce the risk from inflation, you may acquire the indexed bonds. If, however, the rate of inflation does not increase, this strategy earns a lower rate of interest. You could earn a higher rate by not acquiring the indexed bonds, but then you bear the

---

2. This illustration assumes annual interest payments, while the notes (and the bonds) distribute interest semiannually. The index factors for adjusting the principal may be found at **http://www.publicdebt.treas.gov** under the subhead of inflation-indexed notes and bonds.

risk associated with inflation. Although the traditional bond may generate more current interest income, investors who acquire them in preference to the indexed bond bear the risk associated with the loss of purchasing power from inflation.

The possibility also exists that the CPI may decline. If deflation were to occur, the inflation-indexed principal would be *reduced*, which decreases the periodic interest payments. If the inflation-adjusted principal were less than the original par value at maturity of the security, the federal government will repay the initial par value. The buyer is assured of receiving at least the initial amount invested in inflation-indexed securities (when they are issued) if they are held to maturity. Only the periodic interest payments would be reduced.

In addition to these risks, there is a tax disadvantage associated with the federal government's inflation-indexed debt securities. The addition to the principal is considered taxable income even though it is not received until the instrument matures (or is sold). In the preceding example, the principal amount rose from $1,000 to $1,060.89. The $60.89 is taxable income during the two years in which the accretion occurred even though the investor only received interest of 3⅞ percent of the principal value. This tax treatment of the accretion in the principal value may reduce the attractiveness of inflation-indexed notes and bonds except for usage in tax-deferred retirement accounts.

FEDERAL AGENCIES' DEBT

In addition to the debt issued by the federal government, certain agencies of the federal government and federally sponsored corporations issue debt. These debt instruments encompass the entire spectrum of maturities, ranging from short-term securities to long-term bonds. Like many U.S. Treasury debt issues, there is an active secondary market in some of the debt issues of these agencies, and price quotations for many of the bonds are given daily in the financial press.

Several federal agencies have been created to fulfill specific financial needs. For example, the Banks for Cooperatives were organized under the Farm Credit Act. These banks provide farm business services and make loans to farm cooperatives to help purchase supplies. The Federal Home Loan Mortgage Corporation was established to strengthen the secondary market in residential mortgages insured by the Federal Housing Administration. This federal corporation buys and sells home mortgages to give them marketability and thus increase their attractiveness to private investors. The Student Loan Marketing Association was created to provide liquidity to the insured student loans made under the Guaranteed Student Loan Program by commercial banks, savings and loan associations, and schools that participate in the program. This liquidity should expand the funds available to students from private sources.

Federal agency bonds are not issued by the federal government and are *not* the debt of the federal government. Hence, they tend to offer higher yields than those available on U.S. Treasury debt. However, the bonds are extremely safe because they have government backing. In some cases, this is only **moral backing**, which means that in case of default the federal government does *not* have to support the debt (i.e., to pay the interest and meet the terms of the indenture). Some of the debt issues, however, are guaranteed by the U.S. Treasury. Should these issues go into default, the federal government is legally required to assume the obligations of the debt's indenture.

The matter of whether the bonds have the legal or the moral backing of the federal government is probably academic. All these debt issues are excellent credit

federal agency bonds
Debt issued by an agency of the federal government.

moral backing
Nonobligatory support for a debt issue.

risks, because it is doubtful that the federal government would let the debt of one of its agencies go into default. Since these bonds offer slightly higher yields than those available on U.S. Treasury debt, the bonds of federal agencies have become attractive investments for conservative investors seeking higher yields. This applies not only to individual investors who wish to protect their capital but also to financial institutions, such as commercial banks, insurance companies, or credit unions, which must be particularly concerned with the safety of the principal in making investment decisions.

Federal agency debt can be purchased by individuals, but few individual investors do own these bonds, except indirectly through pension plans, mutual funds, and other institutions that own the debt. Many individual investors are probably not even aware of the existence of this debt and the potential advantages it offers. Any investor who wants to construct a portfolio with an emphasis on income and the relative safety of the principal should consider these debt instruments.

Ginnie Mae Securities

Ginnie Mae
Mortgage pass-through bond issued by the Government National Mortgage Association.

One of the most important debt securities issued by a government agency and supported by the federal government is the **Ginnie Mae**, a debt security issued by the Government National Mortgage Association (GNMA or Ginnie Mae), a division of the Department of Housing and Urban Development (HUD). The funds raised through the sale of Ginnie Mae securities are used to acquire a pool of FHA/VA guaranteed mortgages. (FHA and VA are the Federal Housing Administration and Veteran's Administration, respectively.) The mortgages are originated by private lenders, such as savings and loan associations and other savings institutions, and packaged into securities that are sold to the general public and guaranteed by GNMA. The minimum size of each issue is $1 million, and the minimum size of the individual Ginnie Mae securities sold to the public is $25,000.[3]

Ginnie Mae securities serve as a conduit through which interest and principal repayments are made. An investor who buys a Ginnie Mae acquires part of the pool. As interest payments and principal repayments are made to the pool, the funds are channeled to the Ginnie Mae's owners. The investor receives a monthly payment that is his or her share of the principal and interest payment received by the pool. Since such payments may vary from month to month, the amount received by the investor also varies monthly. Thus, the Ginnie Mae is one example of a long-term debt security whose periodic payments are *not fixed*.

Ginnie Mae securities have become particularly popular with individuals financing retirement or accumulating funds in retirement accounts. The reason for their popularity is safety, since the federal government insures the payment of principal and interest. Thus, if a mortgage payer were to default, the federal government would make the required payments. This guarantee virtually assures the timely payment of interest and principal to the holder of the Ginnie Mae.

In addition to safety, Ginnie Maes offer higher yields than federal government securities. Since the yields are ultimately related to the mortgages acquired by

---

3. Individuals with less to invest may acquire shares in a mutual fund that invests in mortgage-backed securities. Since Ginnie Maes convert an illiquid asset (a mortgage loan) into a marketable security, they are an illustration of securitization. Few investors are willing to hold a mortgage, because mortgage notes are difficult to sell. A Ginnie Mae, however, may be readily sold. The effect, then, is to convert an illiquid asset into a marketable asset.

the pool, they depend on mortgage rates rather than on the yields of federal government bills and bonds. This yield differential can be as great as 2 percentage points (sometimes referred to as 200 basis points, with one basis point equaling 0.01 percentage point) over the return offered by long-term federal government bonds.

Ginnie Mae securities are also useful to investors seeking a regular flow of payments, since interest and principal repayments are distributed monthly. The mortgage repayment schedules define the minimum amount of the anticipated payments. However, if the homeowners speed up payments or pay off their loans before the full term of the mortgage, the additional funds are passed on to the holder of the Ginnie Mae securities, which reduces the certainty of the monthly payments. Homeowners can (and do) repay their mortgage loans prematurely. This occurs when individuals move and sell their homes and when interest rates fall. Lower rates encourage homeowners to refinance their mortgages (i.e., obtain new mortgages at the current, lower rate and pay off the old, higher-rate mortgages). Since the old loans are retired, the owners of the Ginnie Mae receive larger principal repayments but can only relend the funds at the current, lower rate of interest. The opposite would occur if interest rates rise. Homeowners will not refinance and prepayments will decline, so the holder of the Ginnie Mae receives lower principal repayments.

Other Mortgage–Backed Securities

While Ginnie Maes were the first mortgage-backed securities, other issues have been created by the Federal Home Loan Mortgage Corporation (FHLMC or *Freddie Mac*), the Federal National Mortgage Association (FNMA, commonly called *Fannie Mae*), and other lending institutions. The FHLMC Participation Certificate (PC) is similar to the Ginnie Mae; they are both conduits through which interest and principal payments pass from the homeowner to the certificate holder. There is, however, one important difference: Freddie Mac PC payments are not guaranteed by the federal government. The absence of this guarantee means that even though the individual mortgages are insured by private mortgage insurance companies, Freddie Mac PCs offer a higher yield than is available through Ginnie Maes.

Mortgage-backed securities are also issued by Fannie Mae. These funds are used to finance mortgages, and like the Freddie Mac Participation Certificate, the bonds are secured by mortgage loans. Since the company is a private corporation (i.e., is not a government agency) whose stock is traded on the NYSE, its debt obligations are not guaranteed by the federal government. Fannie Mae bonds thus offer higher yields than Ginnie Maes. During 1998, FNMA officially changed its name to Fannie Mae. Financial information concerning the company, its securities, and mortgages it issues is available at its Web site: **http://www.fanniemae.com**.

Collateralized Mortgage Obligations (CMOs)

While Ginnie Maes are supported by the federal government so the investor knows that the interest and principal will be paid, the amount of each monthly payment is unknown. Because principal repayments vary as homeowners refinance their homes, the amount of principal repayment received by the investor changes every month. This variation in the monthly cash flow may be a disadvantage to any individual (e.g., a retiree) seeking a reasonably certain flow of monthly cash payments.

A **collateralized mortgage obligation (CMO)** reduces, but does not erase, this uncertainty. Collateralized mortgage obligations are backed by a trust that holds Ginnie Mae and other federal government-supported mortgages. When a CMO is created, it is subdivided into classes (called **tranches**). For example, a $100 million CMO may be divided into four tranches of $25 million each. The principal repayments received by the CMO are initially paid to the first class until that tranche has been entirely retired. Once the first tranche has been paid off, mortgage principal repayments are directed to the holders of the CMOs in the second tranche. This process is repeated until all the tranches have been repaid.

This pattern of payment is illustrated by the following CMO with four tranches. Each tranche consists of a $200,000 loan ($800,000 total outstanding), $100,000 of which is retired each year. Interest is paid annually on the amount of the loan outstanding in each tranche. The rate of interest varies with the expected life of each tranche. The interest rates start at 7 percent for tranche A and rise to 10 percent for tranche D. For accepting later repayment of principal, the investor can expect to earn a higher interest rate. The tranche with the shortest expected life earns the lowest interest rate, while the one with the longest expected life earns the highest rate.

The annual payments to each tranche are as follows if the anticipated payment schedules are made:

Tranche Payment

	A		B		C		D	
Year	Interest	Principal	Interest	Principal	Interest	Principal	Interest	Principal
1	$14,000	$100,000	$16,000	$ 0	$18,000	$ 0	$20,000	$ 0
2	7,000	100,000	16,000	0	18,000	0	20,000	0
3	0	0	16,000	100,000	18,000	0	20,000	0
4	0	0	8,000	100,000	18,000	0	20,000	0
5	0	0	0	0	18,000	100,000	20,000	0
6	0	0	0	0	9,000	100,000	20,000	0
7	0	0	0	0	0	0	20,000	100,000
8	0	0	0	0	0	0	10,000	100,000

This schedule indicates that tranche D is a loan for $200,000 at 10 percent, so the annual interest payment is $20,000 for the first 7 years and $10,000 in year 8. Repayment of principal does not occur until all the preceding tranches are retired. Under the anticipated schedule, the principal repayments of $100,000 occur in years 7 and 8, which is why the interest payment is $10,000 instead of $20,000 in year 8.

Over the eight years, the borrower pays a total of $326,000 in interest for the use of the funds and retires the $800,000 loan. While the owners of the different tranches receive different interest rates, the borrower pays the same rate on the entire loan. The trustee structures the tranches to coincide with the loan payments. In this illustration, the borrower's repayment schedule is as follows:

Year	Principal Owed at the End of the Year	Interest Payment	Principal Repayment
0	$800,000		
1	700,000	$ 72,448	$100,000
2	600,000	63,392	100,000

Year	Principal Owed at the End of the Year	Interest Payment	Principal Repayment
3	500,000	54,336	100,000
4	400,000	45,280	100,000
5	300,000	36,224	100,000
6	200,000	27,168	100,000
7	100,000	18,112	100,000
8	0	9,056	100,000
		$326,016	

The rate of interest on the loan is 9.056 percent on the declining balance. (9.056 percent is a forced number. Generally, the terms of the loan are established and the trustee constructs the tranches to match the borrower's payments. Since the purpose of this example is to illustrate the payments to the tranches, the loan is being forced to approximate the payments to the investors.)

The total interest paid by the borrower is $326,016, and the interest payments approximate those received by the tranches. Notice that the borrower's interest rate of 9.056 percent applies to the entire $800,000 loan, while each tranche receives a different rate of interest. Investors in the early tranches accept a lower rate for a more rapid repayment of principal, while the investors who acquire the longer tranches accept later payments in order to earn a higher rate of interest. The borrower's payments, however, do not make this distinction. The trustee who makes the loan to the borrower establishes the tranches and converts the borrower's debt obligation into a series of securities that different investors with different financial needs find acceptable.

When an investor purchases a CMO, an estimated *principal repayment window* is known. As in the preceding illustration, the schedule gauges when the investor can expect to receive principal repayments and when a particular tranche will be entirely redeemed. As with Ginnie Mae payments, the CMO payment schedule is based on historical repayment data, but the actual timing of the repayments cannot be known with certainty. Lower interest rates will tend to speed up payments as homeowners refinance, while higher interest rates will tend to retard principal repayments.

Since the actual timing of principal repayment is not known, CMOs reduce but do not erase this source of risk. However, less timing risk exists with CMOs than with a Ginnie Mae. When the investor acquires a Ginnie Mae, the repayments are spread over the life of the entire issue. With a CMO, the repayments are spread over each tranche. The investor who acquires a CMO can better match the anticipated need for cash. For example, a 65-year-old retiree may have less immediate need for cash than an 80-year-old. The latter may acquire the first tranche, while the former acquires the third tranche within a CMO. The 65-year-old would receive the current interest component but the principal repayment would be deferred until the first and second tranches were entirely retired.

STATE AND LOCAL GOVERNMENT DEBT

State and local governments also issue debt to finance capital expenditures, such as schools or roads. The government then retires the debt as the facilities are used. The funds used to retire the debt may be raised through taxes (e.g., property taxes) or through revenues generated by the facilities themselves.

Unlike the federal government, state and local governments do not have the power to create money. These governments must raise the funds necessary to pay the interest and retire the debt, but the ability to do so varies with the financial status of each government. Municipalities with wealthy residents or valuable property within their boundaries are able to issue debt more readily and at lower interest rates because the debt is safer. The tax base in these communities is larger and can support the debt.

The Tax Exemption

municipal (tax-exempt) bond
A bond issued by a state or one of its political subdivisions whose interest is not taxed by the federal government.

The primary factor that differentiates state and local government debt from other forms of debt is the tax advantage that it offers to investors. The interest earned on state and municipal government debt is exempt from federal income taxation. Hence, these bonds are frequently referred to as **tax-exempt** or **municipal bonds**. Although state and local governments may tax the interest, the federal government may not. The rationale for this tax exemption is legal and not financial. The Supreme Court ruled that the federal government does not have the power to tax the interest paid by the debt of state and municipal governments. Since the interest paid by all other debt, including corporate bonds, is subject to federal income taxation, this exemption is advantageous to state and local governments, for they are able to issue debt with substantially lower interest rates.

Investors are willing to accept a lower return on state and local government debt because the after-tax return is equivalent to higher yields on corporate debt. For example, if an investor is in the 28 percent federal income tax bracket, the return after taxes is the same for a corporate bond that pays 10 percent as for a state or municipal government bond that pays 7.2 percent: The after-tax return is 7.2 percent in either case.

The willingness of investors to purchase state and local government debt instead of corporate and U.S. Treasury debt is related to their income tax bracket. If an investor's federal income tax rate is 28 percent, a 6.5 percent nontaxable municipal bond gives the investor the same yield after taxes as a 9.03 percent corporate bond, the interest of which is subject to federal income taxation. The individual investor may determine the equivalent yields on tax-exempt bonds and nonexempt bonds by using the following equation:

(10.3)
$$i_c(1 - t) = i_m$$

in which i_c is the interest rate paid on corporate debt, i_m is the interest rate paid on municipal debt, and t is the individual's tax bracket (i.e., the marginal tax rate). This equation is used as follows. If an investor's tax bracket is 28 percent and tax-exempt bonds offer 6.5 percent, then the equivalent corporate yield is

$$i_c(1 - 0.28) = 0.065$$

$$i_c = \frac{0.065}{0.72} = 9.03\%.$$

If the investor lives in a state that taxes income, Equation 10.3 may be modified to include the impact of the local tax. Equation 10.4 includes the impact of the federal income tax rate (t_f) and the state and/or local income tax rate (t_s):

(10.4)
$$i_c(1 - t_f - t_s) = i_m$$

If the investor's federal income tax bracket is 25 percent and the state income tax bracket is 6 percent, then a high-yield, low-quality bond offering 10.0 percent has an inferior after-tax yield to a local municipal bond offering more than 6.9 percent (10.0 percent[1 – 0.25 – 0.06] = 6.9 percent).

Exempting the interest on these bonds from federal income taxation has been criticized because it is an apparent means for the "rich" to avoid federal income taxation. Since the minimum denomination for municipal bonds is $5,000 and dealers may require larger purchases (e.g., $15,000 – $20,000), individuals with modest amounts to invest are excluded from this market except through investing in mutual funds that invest in tax-exempt bonds. The exemption does, however, reduce the interest cost for the state and municipal governments that issue debt, which in effect subsidizes those governments.

Although state and local government debt interest is tax-exempt at the federal level, it may be taxed at the state level. States do exempt the interest paid by their own local governments but tax the interest paid by other states and their local governments. While interest earned on New York City obligations is not taxed in New York, it is taxed in New Jersey. The converse is also true: New Jersey taxes the interest earned on New York City obligations but exempts interest earned on New Jersey municipal bonds.

It should also be noted that state and local governments cannot tax the interest paid by the federal government. While interest earned on series EE bonds and Treasury bills, notes, and bonds is taxed by the federal government, this interest cannot be taxed by state and local governments. In states with modest or no income taxes, this exemption is meaningless. However, in states with high income taxes, such as Massachusetts or New York, this tax exemption may be a major reason for acquiring U.S. Treasury securities. For example, the yield on a Treasury bill on an after-tax basis may exceed the yield on a federally insured certificate of deposit or the yield offered by a money market mutual fund. In such cases, the tax laws will certainly encourage the investor to acquire the federal security, because that investor has both a higher after-tax yield and less risk (i.e., the full faith and credit of the federal government).

Types of Tax–Exempt Securities

State and local governments issue a variety of debt instruments; these can be classified either according to the means by which the security is supported or according to the length of time to maturity (i.e., short- or long-term). State and municipal debt is supported by either the taxing power of the issuing government or the revenues generated by the facilities that are financed by the debt. If the bonds are secured by the taxing power, the debt is a **general obligation** of the government.

A bond supported by the revenue generated by the project being financed with the debt is called a **revenue bond**. Revenue bonds are issued to finance particular capital improvements, such as a toll road that generates its own funds. As these revenues are collected, they are used to pay the interest and retire the principal.

General obligation bonds are commonly thought to be safer than revenue bonds, since the government is required to use its taxing authority to pay the interest and repay the principal. General obligation bonds may have to be approved by popular referendum. Such referendums can be costly, and public approval of the bonds may be difficult to obtain. These characteristics associated with issuing the debt reduce the risk of investing in general obligation bonds. Revenue bonds are supported only by funds generated by the project financed by the sale of the bonds. If the project does not generate sufficient revenues, the interest cannot be paid and the bonds go

general obligation bond
A bond whose interest does not depend on the revenue of a specific project; government bonds supported by the full faith and credit of the issuer (i.e., authority to tax).

revenue bond
A bond whose interest is paid only if the debtor earns sufficient revenue.

into default. For example, the Chesapeake Bay Bridge and Tunnel did not produce sufficient toll revenues, so its publicly held bonds went into default. The default, of course, caused the price of the bonds to fall. Since the bondholders could not foreclose on the bridge, their only course of action was to wait for a resumption of interest payments. After several years elapsed, toll revenues rose sufficiently, such that interest payments to the bondholders were resumed.

Tax-exempt bonds are issued in minimum denominations of $5,000 face value. There is an active secondary market in this debt; however, the bonds are traded only in the over-the-counter market, and only a handful are quoted in the financial press. Small denominations (e.g., $5,000) tend to lack marketability. One municipal bond dealer I know refers to units of $5,000 bonds as roach motels. Once the roach enters the motel, he or she cannot get out. If you buy only a $5,000 face amount, you had better plan to hold the bond to maturity. The secondary market for small units is very thin and there will be a large discount in the bid price if you try to sell the bond.

Although most corporate bonds are issued with a particular term to maturity and a sinking fund requirement, many tax-exempt bonds are issued in a series. With a serial issue, a specific amount of the debt falls due each year. Such an issue is illustrated in Exhibit 10.2, which reproduces an advertisement for bonds sold by the North Carolina Eastern Municipal Power Agency. (These advertisements are placed by the underwriting syndicate to describe a public offering. They are frequently referred to as *tombstones* because of their resemblance to an epitaph on a tombstone.) About half of the $113 million issue is in serial bonds. A portion of the issue matures each year. For example, $2,895,000 worth of the bonds matured on January 1, 2003, and another $5,185,000 matures on January 1, 2013. Serial bonds offer advantages to both the issuer and the buyer. In contrast to corporate debt, in which a random selection of the bonds is retired each year through the sinking fund, the buyer knows when each bond will mature. The investor can then purchase bonds that mature at the desired time, which helps in portfolio planning. Because a portion of the issue is retired periodically with serial bonds, the issuing government does not have to make a large, lump-sum payment. Since these bonds are scheduled to be retired, there is no call penalty. If the government wants to retire additional debt, it can call some of the remaining bonds. For example, if the agency wanted to retire some of these bonds prematurely, it would call the term A bonds that are due in 2021 or the term B bonds due in 2026. (Most issues like the bonds shown in Exhibit 10.2 require that any debt retired before maturity be called in reverse order. Thus, the term bonds with the longest time to maturity are called and redeemed first.)

Although most of the debt sold to the general public by state and local governments is long-term, there are two notable exceptions: tax or revenue anticipation notes. A tax or revenue **anticipation note** is issued by a government anticipating certain receipts in the future—it issues a debt instrument against these receipts. When the taxes or other revenues are received, the notes are retired. The maturity date is set to coincide with the timing of the anticipated receipts so that the notes may be easily retired.

anticipation note
A short-term liability that is to be retired by specific expected revenues (e.g., expected tax receipts).

Tax-Exempt Securities and Risk

While the sources of risk associated with investing in tax-exempt bonds were alluded to in the preceding discussion, it is helpful to summarize them. As is explained in the next chapter, higher interest rates will drive down the prices of existing bonds. This source of risk, of course, applies to all bonds and is not unique to the bonds of state and municipal governments. The investor may reduce this source of risk by purchas-

EXHIBIT 10.2   Tombstone for an Issue of Serial and Term Bonds

Issuing Authority

Tax Exemption

Serial Bonds

Term Bonds

Lead Underwriters

All of these securities have been sold. This announcement appears as a matter of record only.

New Issue

$1,614,620,000

North Carolina Eastern Municipal Power Agency

$113,000,000 Power System Revenue Bonds, Series 1993 A
$1,501,620,000 Power System Revenue Bonds, Refunding Series 1993 B

The Bonds are dated January 1, 1993 for Fixed Rate Bonds and the Date of Delivery for Structured Yield Curve Notes, are due January 1, as shown below and are subject to redemption prior to maturity as described in the Official Statement.

In the opinion of Bond Counsel, under existing statutes and court decisions, interest on the 1993 Bonds is excluded from gross income for federal income tax purposes and is not an item of tax preference for purposes of the federal alternative minimum tax imposed on corporations and taxpayers other than corporations. See "Tax Exemption" in the Official Statement for a description of certain other provisions of law which may affect the federal tax treatment of interest on the 1993 Bonds. In the opinion of Bond Counsel, under existing laws of the State of North Carolina, the 1993 Bonds, their transfer and the income therefrom (including any profit made on the sale thereof) are free from taxation by the State of North Carolina or any political subdivision or any agency of either thereof, excepting inheritance or gift taxes.

$113,000,000 1993 A Bonds

Amount	Due	Interest Rate	Price or Yield	Amount	Due	Interest Rate	Yield or Price	Amount	Due	Interest Rate	Yield
$2,145,000	1997	4.60%	100%	$2,895,000	2003	5⅜%	5.80%	$3,855,000	2008	6⅛%	6.30 %
2,245,000	1998	4.85	100	3,055,000	2004	5¾	5.90	4,090,000	2009	6	6.138†
2,350,000	1999	5.10	100	3,230,000	2005	6	100	4,335,000	2010	6⅛	6.184†
2,470,000	2000	5¼	5.30	3,425,000	2006	6	6.15	4,600,000	2011	6⅛	6.227†
2,600,000	2001	5⅜	5.50	3,630,000	2007	6⅛	6.25	4,880,000	2012	6.20	6.279†
2,740,000	2002	5½	5.65					5,185,000	2013	6.20	6.279†

$55,270,000   6.40% Term Bonds due January 1, 2021 — Yield 6.50%
(Accrued interest to be added)

$1,501,620,000 1993 B Bonds

Amount	Due	Interest Rate	Price	Amount	Due	Interest Rate	Yield	Amount	Due	Interest Rate	Price or Yield
$3,580,000	1995	3.85%	100%	$4,470,000	2000	5¼%	5.30%	$ 39,910,000	2005	6 %	100%
3,715,000	1996	4.35	100	4,705,000	2001	5⅜	5.50	42,600,000	2006	6	6.10
3,880,000	1997	4.60¹	100	4,960,000	2002	5½	5.65	44,760,000	2007	7¼	6.20
4,055,000	1998	4.85	100	5,230,000	2003	5⅜	5.80	123,355,000	2008	7	6.25
4,255,000	1999	5.10	100	5,525,000	2004	5¾	5.90	127,060,000	2009	6⅛	6.30

$248,055,000   6¼% Term Bonds due January 1, 2012 — Yield 6.457%
$ 40,345,000   6 % Term Bonds due January 1, 2013 — Yield 6.437%
$146,625,000   5½% Term Bonds due January 1, 2017 — Yield 6.27 %†
$ 97,790,000   6 % Term Bonds due January 1, 2018 — Yield 6.30 %††
$194,510,000   5½% Term Bonds due January 1, 2021 — Yield 6.45 %
$157,740,000   6 % Term Bonds due January 1, 2022 — Yield 6.41 %
$ 60,180,000   6¼% Term Bonds due January 1, 2023 — Yield 6.33 %†
$ 45,030,000   6¼% Term Bonds due January 1, 2023 — Yield 6.415%
$ 16,875,000   6 % Term Bonds due January 1, 2025 — Yield 6.42 %
$ 16,610,000   6 % Term Bonds due January 1, 2026 — Yield 6.42 %
(Accrued interest to be added)

$55,800,000   6%* ("Bond Rate") Structured Yield Curve Notes due January 1, 2014 — NRO**

†Payment of principal and interest when due will be insured by Financial Guaranty Insurance Company.
††Payment of principal and interest when due will be insured by AMBAC Indemnity Corporation.
*Subject to change as described in the Official Statement.
**Not reoffered.

The 1993 Bonds are offered subject to the approval of legality by Hawkins, Delafield & Wood, New York, New York, Bond Counsel. Certain legal matters in connection with the 1993 Bonds are subject to the approval of Poyner & Spruill, Rocky Mount, North Carolina, North Carolina counsel to Power Agency, and Brown & Wood, New York, New York, counsel to the Underwriters.

Smith Barney, Harris Upham & Co.
Incorporated

Morgan Stanley & Co.
Incorporated

Goldman, Sachs & Co.

J. P. Morgan Securities Inc.

Alex. Brown & Sons
Incorporated

First Charlotte Company
Division of J.C. Bradford & Co.

Interstate/Johnson Lane

J. Lee Peeler & Company, Inc.

Legg Mason Wood Walker
Incorporated

Wheat, First Securities, Inc.

Source: Reprinted with permission of North Carolina Eastern Municipal Power Agency.

ing bonds of shorter maturity, because the prices of bonds with longer terms to maturity fluctuate more. If the investor is concerned with price fluctuations, then shorter-term tax-exempt bonds should be preferred to long-term bonds. The investor, however, should realize that shorter-term bonds generally pay less interest.

The second source of risk is the possibility that the government might default on the interest and principal repayment. Unfortunately, finding information on particular bond issues can be difficult for the individual investor. Municipal bonds are not registered with the Securities and Exchange Commission (SEC) prior to their sale to the general public, and many state and local governments do not publish annual reports and send them to bondholders. Instead, investors may consult the latest issues of Mergent's *Municipal and Government Manual* or *Standard & Poor's Bond Guide*. Fortunately for investors, several firms rate a considerable number of the tax-exempt bonds that are sold to the general public. These ratings are based on a substantial amount of data, for the rating services require the municipal and state governments to provide them with financial and economic information. Since failure of the bond issue to receive a favorable rating will dissuade many potential buyers, the state and local governments supply the rating services with the required information.

The investor can take several steps to reduce the risk associated with default. The first is to purchase a diversified portfolio of tax-exempt bonds, which spreads the risk associated with any particular government. Second, the investor may limit purchases to debt with high credit ratings. If the investor purchases only bonds with AAA or AA credit ratings, there is little risk (perhaps no real risk) of loss from default.

A third means by which the investor may limit the risk of default is to purchase municipal bonds that are insured. Several insurance companies guarantee the payment of interest and principal of the municipal bonds they insure. For example, Monroe Township, New Jersey, bonds are insured by AMBAC and have a AAA rating by Standard & Poor's. AMBAC stands for American Municipal Bond Assurance Corporation, which is part of AMBAC Financial Group, a company traded on the NYSE (ABK). Other municipal bond insurers include MBIA (Municipal Bond Insurance Association), which is also traded on the NYSE (MBI), and FGIC (Financial Guaranty Insurance Co.), which is part of GE Capital.

The investor who acquires insured bonds should realize that lower yields accompany lower risk.[4] As a result of the insurance guarantees, the yield on the bonds will be lower than the yield available on noninsured bonds. The reduction in risk and yields is also affected by the quality of the company offering the insurance. If the insurance company has a lower credit rating than other insurers, the quality of the insurance may be lower, raising the possibility of default by the insurance company should the municipality default.

The existence of these risks does not imply that an investor should avoid tax-exempt bonds.[5] The return offered by these bonds is probably consistent with the amount of risk the investor must bear. If a particular bond were to offer an exceptionally high return, it would be readily purchased and its price driven up so that the return was in line with comparably risky securities. Tax-exempt bonds should be purchased by investors with moderate-to-high incomes who are seeking tax-free income and who do not need liquidity. Like any investment, tax-exempt bonds may fit into an individual investor's portfolio and offer a return (after tax) commensurate with the risk the investor must endure.

4. Insuring municipal bonds decreases the risk to bondholders and reduces required interest payments. However, there may be no net savings to the issuing government if the savings in interest is consumed by the cost of the insurance.
5. The investor also bears the risk associated with inflation and reinvestment rate risk, if the purpose of the bond portfolio is to accumulate funds instead of generating current tax-free income.

SUMMARY

In order to tap funds from many sources, the federal government issues a variety of debt instruments. These range from Series EE and Series I bonds, which are sold in small denominations, to short-term Treasury bills and long-term bonds, which are sold in large denominations. Because there is no possibility of default, federal government debt is the safest of all possible investments. However, you still bear a risk from fluctuations in interest rates and (except for indexed bonds) inflation. If interest rates rise, the prices of marketable federal government bonds will decline. If the rate of inflation exceeds the yield on these securities, investors sustain a loss of purchasing power.

In addition to the debt issued by the federal government, bonds are issued by its agencies. Agency bonds tend to offer slightly higher yields, but they are virtually as safe as the direct debt of the federal government. In some cases, the agency's debt is even secured by the full faith and credit of the U.S. Treasury.

Among the most popular securities issued by a federal government agency are the mortgage pass-through bonds issued by the Government National Mortgage Association, or *Ginnie Mae*. These bonds serve as a conduit through which interest and principal repayments are made from homeowners to the bondholders. Payments are made monthly, so Ginnie Mae bonds are popular with individuals desiring a flow of cash receipts. These bonds expose investors to risk of loss from fluctuating interest rates or from inflation, but the interest payments and principal repayments are guaranteed by an agency of the federal government.

Alternatives to Ginnie Maes are collateralized mortgage obligations (CMOs), which are issued by a trust that holds mortgages guaranteed by the federal government. CMOs are sold in series, or tranches, with the obligations in the shortest tranche being retired before any of the CMOs in the next series are retired.

State and local governments issue long-term debt instruments to finance capital improvements, such as schools and roads. The debt is retired over a period of time by tax receipts or revenues. Some of these bonds are supported by the taxing authority of the issuing government, but many are supported only by the revenues generated by the facilities financed through the bond issues.

State and municipal debt differs from other investments because the interest is exempt from federal income taxation. These bonds pay lower rates of interest than taxable securities (e.g., corporate bonds), but their after-tax yields may be equal to or even greater than the yields on taxable bonds. The nontaxable bonds are particularly attractive to investors in high income tax brackets, because the bonds provide a means to shelter income from taxation.

Learning Objectives

Now that you have completed this chapter, you should be able to:

1. Differentiate the various federal government debt instruments.
2. Calculate the discount yield and the annualized yield on a Treasury bill.
3. Identify the sources of risk to investors who acquire federal government bonds.

4. Identify the source of safety to the investor in federal government debt.

5. Describe the various types of zero coupon bonds involving federal government securities.

6. Isolate the collateral that supports Ginnie Mae bonds and CMO obligations.

7. Distinguish among the debt of the federal government, its authorities, and municipal and state governments.

8. Isolate the primary advantage of stock and local debt and illustrate how to equalize yields on corporate and municipal bonds.

PROBLEMS

1) If a six-month Treasury bill is purchased for $0.9675 on a dollar (i.e., $96,750 for a $100,000 bill), what is the discount yield and the annual rate of interest? What will be these yields if the discount price falls to $0.94 on a dollar (i.e., $94,000 for a $100,000 bill)?

2) An investor is in the 28 percent income tax bracket and can earn 6.3 percent on a nontaxable bond. What is the comparable yield on a taxable bond? If this same investor can earn 8.9 percent on a taxable bond, what must be the yield on a nontaxable bond so that the after-tax yields are equal?

3) An investor in the 35 percent tax bracket may purchase a corporate bond that is rated double A and is traded on the New York Stock Exchange (the bond division). This bond yields 9.0 percent. The investor may also buy a double-A-rated municipal bond with a 5.85 percent yield. Why may the corporate bond be preferred? (Assume that the terms of the bonds are the same.)

4) You are in the 28 percent federal income tax bracket. A corporate bond offers you 6.8 percent while a tax-exempt bond with the same credit rating and term to maturity offers 4.1 percent. On the basis of taxation, which bond should be preferred? Explain.

5) A six-month $10,000 Treasury bill is selling for $9,844. What is the annual yield according to the discount method? Does this yield understate or overstate the true annual yield? Explain.

Internet Applications for Chapter 10   Government Securities

1) Figure 9.1 in the previous chapter illustrates a yield curve. What is the current yield curve based on U.S. Treasury securities? Have yields changed from those used to construct the yield curve in Figure 9.1?

Current yield curves may be constructed from rates found at various sites such as those listed below and the sites given in Chapter 11.

Bureau of the Public Debt   http://www.publicdebt.treas.gov

Federal Reserve   http://www.federalreserve.gov

Federal Reserve Bank of St. Louis   http://www.stls.frb.org/fred

2) You are considering investing in tax-exempt bonds from your state so that you may avoid federal and state income taxes. Locate currently available municipal bonds with approximately 5, 10, and 15 years to maturity. What are their yields? Compare these yields with the yields in question 1.

Possible sites include

FMS Bonds   http://www.fmsbonds.com, which specializes in municipal bonds

BondsOnline   http://www.bonds-online.com

Yahoo!   http://bonds.yahoo.com

CHAPTER

11 • • •

The Valuation of Fixed-Income Securities

I n April 2004, *The Wall Street Journal* reported that a $1,000 federal government bond was selling for $1,287. Another was selling for $1,490! A $1,000 bond issued by General Electric Capital was selling for $1,115. Why would anyone pay these high prices for a $1,000 bond? These investors will receive only $1,000 when the bonds mature. They could have bought a different $1,000 federal government bond for $1,000. And an alternative GE Capital bond was also available, and it cost only $993.

As was learned in previous chapters, a variety of debt instruments are sold to the general public. There exists a very active secondary market for these bonds. Since the bonds trade daily, what establishes their prices? Why do some bonds trade for $1,300 while others trade for much less? Which bonds' prices tend to be more volatile? These are some of the essential questions concerning investing in fixed-income securities, especially bonds.

Although a variety of debt instruments exists, each with its specific name and characteristics, for the purpose of this chapter the term *bond* will be used to represent all types of debt instruments. As will be explained in detail, comparable bonds are priced so their yields are the same. What is important is how much you earn and not how much you pay. The price of any bond (for a given risk class) is primarily related to (1) the interest paid by the bond, (2) the interest rate that investors may earn on comparable, competitive bonds, and (3) the maturity date. Bond pricing is followed by a discussion of the various uses of the word yield, including the current yield, the yield to maturity, and the yield to call.

After the coverage of pricing and yields, the chapter continues with a discussion of yields and risk, duration, and the management of fixed-income portfolios. The chapter ends with the consideration of preferred stock. Since preferred stock pays a fixed dividend, which is analogous to the fixed-interest coupon paid by a bond, the discussion of preferred stock has been deferred until the coverage of bonds and their valuation has been completed. This material includes a brief description of preferred stock and its valuation, the differences between bonds and preferred stock, and an analysis of the ability of the firm to meet preferred stock's fixed dividend payment.

PERPETUAL SECURITIES

Interactive e-lectures

See a visual explanation and example of perpetual security at

http://mayoxtra.swlearning.com

Some securities have an indefinite life. A corporation and its common stock may exist for centuries. Many issues of preferred stock have no maturity dates and are perpetual. There are even a few debt issues that are perpetual. The issuer never has to retire the principal; it only has to meet the interest payment and the other terms of the indenture. The British government issued perpetual bonds called *consols* to refinance (i.e., consolidate) the debt issued to support the Napoleonic Wars. These bonds will never mature, but they do pay interest, and there is an active secondary market in them.

While there are few perpetual bonds, they facilitate illustrating the process of the valuation of debt instruments. Bond valuation is essentially the same as common stock valuation: future cash inflows are discounted back to the present. The discount rate is the return that the investor can earn on comparable securities. (That is, the perpetual interest payments are brought back to the present at the current rate paid by bonds with the same degree of risk.) For example, a perpetual bond pays the following interest payment annually:

Year 1	Year 2	...	Year 20	...	Year 100	...	Year 1000	...
$80	$80		$80		$80		$80	

How much are these interest payments currently worth? To answer the question, the investor must know the rate of interest that may be earned on alternative investments. If the investor can earn 10 percent elsewhere, the present value or price (*P*) is

$$P = \frac{\$80}{(1 + 0.10)^1} + \frac{\$80}{(1 + 0.10)^2} + \ldots + \frac{\$80}{(1 + 0.10)^{20}}$$

$$+ \ldots + \frac{\$80}{(1 + 0.10)^{100}} + \ldots + \frac{\$80}{(1 + 0.10)^{1000}}$$

$$= \$80(0.909) + \$80(0.826) + \ldots + \$80(0.149)$$

$$+ \ldots + \$80(0.000) + \ldots + \$80(0.000)$$

$$= 72.72 + \$66.08 + \ldots + \$11.92 + \ldots + 0$$

$$= \$800.$$

The $80 interest payments received in the near future contribute most to the present value of the bond. Dollars received in the distant future have little value today. The sum of all of these present values is $800, which means that if alternative investments yield 10 percent, an investor would be willing to pay $800 for a promise to receive $80 annually for the indefinite future.

The preceding may be stated in more formal terms. If *PMT* is the annual interest payment and *i* is the rate of return that is being earned on comparable investments, then the present value is

$$P = \frac{PMT}{(1 + i)^1} + \frac{PMT}{(1 + i)^2} + \frac{PMT}{(1 + i)^3} + \ldots.$$

This is a geometric series, and its sum may be expressed as

(11.1)
$$P = \frac{PMT}{i}.$$

Equation 11.1 gives the current value of an infinite stream of equal interest payments. If this equation is applied to the previous example in which the annual interest payment is $80 and alternative investments can earn 10 percent, then the present value of the bond is

$$P = \frac{\$80}{0.10} = \$800.$$

If market interest rates of alternative investments were to increase to 20 percent, the value of this perpetual stream of interest payments would decline; if market interest rates were to fall to 8 percent, the value of the bond would rise. These changes occur because the bond pays a *fixed flow of income*; that is, the dollar amount of interest paid by the bond is constant. Lower interest rates mean that more money is needed to purchase this fixed stream of interest payments, and with higher interest rates, less money is needed to buy this fixed flow of income.

The inverse relationship between interest rates and bond prices is illustrated in Exhibit 11.1, which presents the value of the preceding perpetual bond at different interest rates. As may be seen from the exhibit, as current market interest rates rise, the present value of the bond declines. Thus, if the present value is $1,000 when interest rates are 8 percent, the value of this bond declines to $400 when interest rates rise to 20 percent.

A simple example may show why this *inverse relationship between bond prices and interest rates* exists. Suppose two investors offered to sell two different bond issues. The first is the perpetual bond that pays $100 per year in interest. The second is also a perpetual bond, but it pays $120 per year in interest. If the offer price in each case is $1,000, which bond would you prefer? Obviously, if they are equal in every way except in the amount of interest, you would prefer the second bond that pays $120. What could the seller of the first bond do to make the bond more attractive? The obvious answer is to lower the asking price so that the yield is identical for both bonds. Thus, if the seller were to ask only $833 for the bond that pays

| EXHIBIT 11.1 | Relationship Between Interest Rates and the Price of a Perpetual Bond |

Current Interest Rate (i)	Annual Interest Paid by the Bond (PMT)	Present Price of the Bond $P = \frac{PMT}{i}$
4%	$80	$2,000
6	80	1,333
8	80	1,000
10	80	800
15	80	533
20	80	400

$100 annually, you should be indifferent as to which to purchase. Both bonds would offer a yield of 12 percent (i.e., $100 ÷ $833 for the first bond and $120 ÷ $1,000 for the second bond).

BOND VALUATION

Interactive e-lectures

See a visual explanation and example of bond valuation at

http://mayoxtra.swlearning.com

The vast majority of bonds are not perpetual but have a finite life. They mature, and that repayment of the principal affects their valuation. A bond, then, generates two cash inflows: the interest payments and the principal repayment. The current value or price of a bond is the present value of the interest payments plus the present value of the principal repayment.

This value is expressed algebraically in Equation 11.2. A bond's value is

(11.2)
$$P_B = \frac{PMT}{(1+i)^1} + \frac{PMT}{(1+i)^2} + \ldots + \frac{PMT}{(1+i)^n} + \frac{FV}{(1+i)^n}.$$

in which P_B indicates the current price of the bond; PMT, the interest payment; n, the number of years to maturity; FV, the future value, or the principal repayment; and i, the current interest rate.

The calculation of a bond's price using Equation 11.2 may be illustrated by a simple example. A firm has a $1,000 bond outstanding that matures in three years with a 10 percent coupon rate ($100 annually).[1] All that is needed to determine the price of the bond is the current interest rate, which is the rate being paid by newly issued, competitive bonds with the same length of time to maturity and the same degree of risk. If the competitive bonds yield 10 percent, the price of this bond will be par, or $1,000, for

$$P_B = \frac{\$100}{(1+0.10)^1} + \frac{\$100}{(1+0.10)^2} + \frac{\$100}{(1+0.10)^3} + \frac{\$1,000}{(1+0.10)^3}$$

$$= \$100(0.909) + 100(0.826) + 100(0.751) + 1,000(0.751)$$

$$= \$999.60 \approx \$1,000.$$

If competitive bonds are selling to yield 12 percent, this bond will be unattractive to investors. They will not be willing to pay $1,000 for a bond yielding 10 percent when they could buy competing bonds at the same price that yield 12 percent. For this bond to compete with the others, its price must decline sufficiently to yield 12 percent. In terms of Equation 11.2, the price must be

$$P_B = \frac{\$100}{(1+0.12)^1} + \frac{\$100}{(1+0.12)^2} + \frac{\$100}{(1+0.12)^3} + \frac{\$1,000}{(1+0.12)^3}$$

$$= \$100(0.893) + 100(0.797) + 100(0.712) + 1,000(0.712)$$

$$= \$952.20.$$

Calculator Solution

Function Key	Data Input
PV =	?
FV =	1000
PMT =	100
N =	3
I =	10
Function Key	**Answer**
PV =	−1000

Calculator Solution

Function Key	Data Input
PV =	?
FV =	1000
PMT =	100
N =	3
I =	12
Function Key	**Answer**
PV =	−951.96

---

1. Although most bonds pay interest semianually, this discussion uses annual compounding to facilitate the explanation. Semiannual compounding is illustrated in the next section.

discount (of a bond)
The extent to which a bond's price is less than its face amount, or principal.

Calculator Solution

Function Key	Data Input
PV =	?
FV =	1000
PMT =	100
N =	3
I =	8

Function Key	Answer
PV =	–1051.54

premium (of a bond)
The extent to which a bond's price exceeds the face amount of the debt.

The price of the bond must decline to approximately $952; that is, it must sell for a **discount** (a price less than the stated principal) in order to be competitive with comparable bonds. At that price investors will earn $100 per year in interest and approximately $50 in capital gains over the three years, for a total annual return of 12 percent on their investment. The capital gain occurs because the bond is purchased for $952.20, but when it matures, the holder will receive $1,000.

If comparable debt were to yield 8 percent, the price of the bond in the previous example would have to rise. In this case, the price of the bond would be

$$P_B = \frac{\$100}{(1+0.08)^1} + \frac{\$100}{(1+0.08)^2} + \frac{\$100}{(1+0.08)^3} + \frac{\$1,000}{(1+0.08)^3}$$

$$= \$100(0.926) + 100(0.857) + 100(0.794) + 1,000(0.794)$$

$$= \$1,051.70.$$

The bond, therefore, must sell at a **premium** (a price greater than the stated principal). Although it may seem implausible for the bond to sell at a premium, this must occur if the market interest rate falls below the coupon rate of interest stated on the bond.

You may have noticed that the above answers differ slightly from the answers in the margin that were derived using a financial calculator. The differences are the result of rounding. The numerical values for $1/(1+0.08)^1$ and $1/(1+0.12)^1$ are carried only to three decimals (0.926 and 0.893, respectively), while the financial calculator carries the numbers to more decimals.

These examples illustrate the same general conclusion that was reached earlier concerning bond prices and changes in interest rates. They are inversely related. When the current rate of interest rises, the prices of existing bonds decline. When the market rate of interest fall, bond prices rise. This relationship is illustrated in Exhibit 11.2, which gives the prices of the $1,000 bond at various interest rates. As may be seen in the exhibit, higher interest rates depress the bond's current value. Thus, the bond's price declines from $1,000 to $951.96 when interest rates rise from 10 to 12 percent; the price rises to $1,051.54 when interest rates decline to 8 percent. (Factors that affect the amount of the price change are covered later in this chapter.)

EXHIBIT 11.2   Relationship Between Interest Rates and a $1,000 10 Percent Coupon Bond Maturing after Three Years

Current Interest Rate	Present Price of the Bond
4%	$1,166.51
6	1,106.92
8	1,051.54
10	1,000.00
12	951.96
14	907.13
18	826.06
20	789.35

Source: Prices determined using a financial calculator.

The inverse relationship between the price of a bond and the interest rate suggests a means to make profits in the bond market. All you need to know is the direction of *future* changes in the interest rate. If you anticipate that interest rates will decline, then you are expecting the price of previously issued bonds with a given number of years to maturity and of a certain risk to rise. This price increase must occur in order for previously issued bonds to have the same yield as currently issued bonds. The reverse is also true, for if you anticipate that interest rates will rise, you are also anticipating that the price of currently available bonds will decline. This decline must occur for previously issued bonds to offer the same yield as currently issued bonds. Therefore, if you can anticipate the direction of change in interest rates, you can also anticipate the direction of change in the price of bonds.

You, however, may anticipate incorrectly and thus suffer losses in the bond market. If you buy bonds and interest rates rise, then the market value of your bonds must decline. But you have something in your favor: The bonds must ultimately be retired. Since the principal must be redeemed, an investment error in the bond market may be corrected when the bond's price rises as the bond approaches maturity. The capital losses will eventually be erased. The correction of the error, however, may take years, during which time you have lost the higher yields that were available on bonds issued after the initial investments.

Semiannual Compounding

The valuation of a bond with a finite life presented in Equation 11.2 is a bit misleading, because bonds pay interest twice a year (i.e., semiannually), and the equation assumes that the interest payments are made only annually. However, Equation 11.2 may be readily modified to take into consideration semiannual (or even quarterly or weekly) compounding. This is done by adjusting the amount of each payment and the total number of these payments. To adjust the previous example, each interest payment will be $50 if payments are semiannual, and instead of three annual payments, the bond will make a total of six $50 semi-annual payments. Hence, the flow of payments that will be made by this bond is

Year 1		Year 2		Year 3		
$50	$50	$50	$50	$50	$50	$1,000

This flow of payments would then be discounted back to the present to determine the bond's current value. The question then becomes, what is the appropriate discount factor?

If comparable debt yields 12 percent, the appropriate discount factor is not 12 percent; it is 6 percent. Six percent interest paid twice a year yields 12 percent interest compounded semiannually. Thus, to determine the present value of this bond, the comparable interest rate is divided in half (just as the annual interest payment is divided in half). However, the number of interest payments to which this 6 percent is applied is doubled (just as the number of payments is doubled). Hence, the current value of this bond, which pays interest twice a year (is compounded semiannually), is

$$P_B = \frac{\$50}{(1 + 0.06)^1} + \frac{\$50}{(1 + 0.06)^2} + \frac{\$50}{(1 + 0.06)^3} + \frac{\$50}{(1 + 0.06)^4}$$

$$+ \frac{\$50}{(1 + 0.06)^5} + \frac{\$50}{(1 + 0.06)^6} + \frac{\$1,000}{(1 + 0.06)^6}$$

$$= \$50(0.943) + 50(0.890) + 50(0.840)$$
$$+ 50(0.792) + 50(0.747) + 50(0.705) + 1,000(0.705)$$
$$= \$47.15 + 44.50 + 42.00 + 39.60 + 37.35 + 35.25 + 705$$
$$= \$950.85.$$

With semiannual compounding, the current value of the bond is slightly lower (i.e., \$950.85 versus \$952.20). This is because the bond's price must decline more to compensate for the more frequent compounding. An investor would prefer a bond that pays \$50 twice per year to one that pays \$100 once per year, because the investor would have use of some of the funds more quickly. Thus, if interest rates rise, causing bond prices to fall, the decline will be greater if the interest on bonds is paid semiannually than if it is paid annually.

Equation 11.2 may be altered to include semiannual compounding. This is done in Equation 11.3. Only one new variable, c, is added, which represents the frequency of compounding (i.e., the number of times each year that interest payments are made).

$$(11.3) \qquad P_B = \frac{\frac{PMT}{c}}{\left(1 + \frac{i}{c}\right)^1} + \frac{\frac{PMT}{c}}{\left(1 + \frac{i}{c}\right)^2} + \ldots + \frac{\frac{PMT}{c}}{\left(1 + \frac{i}{c}\right)^{n \times c}} + \frac{FV}{\left(1 + \frac{i}{c}\right)^{n \times c}}$$

When Equation 11.3 is applied to the earlier example, the price of the bond is

$$P_B = \frac{\frac{\$100}{2}}{\left(1 + \frac{0.12}{2}\right)^1} + \frac{\frac{\$100}{2}}{\left(1 + \frac{0.12}{2}\right)^2} + \ldots + \frac{\frac{\$100}{2}}{\left(1 + \frac{0.12}{2}\right)^{3 \times 2}} + \frac{\frac{\$1,000}{2}}{\left(1 + \frac{0.12}{2}\right)^{3 \times 2}}$$

$$= \$50(0.943) + 50(0.890) + \ldots + 50(0.705) + 1,000(0.705)$$
$$= \$950.85,$$

which, of course, is the same answer derived in the immediately preceding example.

FLUCTUATIONS IN BOND PRICES

As the preceding examples illustrate, a bond's price depends on the interest paid, the maturity date of the bond, and the yield currently earned on comparable securities. The illustrations also demonstrated that when interest rates rise, bond prices fall, and when interest rates fall, bond prices rise.

The amount of price fluctuation depends on (1) the amount of interest paid by the bond, (2) the length of time to maturity, and (3) risk. The smaller the amount of interest, the larger the relative price fluctuations will tend to be. The longer the term, or time to maturity, the greater the price fluctuations will be. Riskier bonds may also experience greater fluctuations in price.

This section is concerned with the first two factors that affect price fluctuations, the amount of interest and the term to maturity. The impact of risk is covered in a subsequent section. The effect of the amount of interest and term to maturity may be seen by the following illustrations. In the first case, consider two bonds with equal lives (e.g., ten years to maturity) but unequal coupons. Bond A pays $80 a year (an 8 percent coupon), and bond B pays $140 annually (a 14 percent coupon). Exhibit 11.3 gives the prices of each bond at various rates of interest. For example, if interest rates rise from 10 percent to 14 percent, the price of bond A declines from $877 to $687. Bond B's price falls from $1,246 to $1,000. These are 22 and 20 percent

---

EXHIBIT 11.3   Fluctuations in Bond Prices

Case 1 Differences in Coupons and Equal Maturity Dates

	Prices:	
Current Rate of Interest	Bond A 8 percent coupon 10 years to maturity	Bond B 14 percent coupon 10 years to maturity
4%	$1,324	$1,811
6	1,147	1,589
8	1,000	1,403
10	877	1,246
12	774	1,113
14	687	1,000
16	613	903
18	551	820
20	497	748

Case 2 Differences in Maturity Dates and Equal Coupons

	Prices:	
Current Rate of Interest	Bond A 10 percent coupon 1 year to maturity	Bond B 10 percent coupon 10 years to maturity
4%	$1,058	$1,487
6	1,038	1,294
8	1,018	1,134
10	1,000	1,000
12	982	887
14	965	791
16	948	710
18	932	640
20	917	581

declines, respectively. If interest rates continue to rise, the bonds' prices decline further. At 20 percent, the values of the bonds are $497 and $748. The percent declines in the bond with the lower coupon are greater. (The extreme case would be a zero coupon bond whose price depends solely on the repayment of the principal.)

The length of time to maturity also affects the fluctuation in a bond's price. Consider the two bonds in the second part of Exhibit 11.3. Both bonds pay $100 interest annually (a 10 percent coupon), but bond A matures after one year and bond B matures after ten years. If interest rates are 10 percent, each bond sells for its principal value ($1,000). If interest rates rise to 12 percent, the price of the bonds decline to $982 and $887. The short maturity of bond A, however, cushions the impact of the change in interest rates. At the extreme case of 20 percent, the price of bond A declines only to $917 while the price of bond B declines to $581.

If interest rates fall, the prices of both bonds will rise, but the price of the bond with the longer term will rise more. For this reason, individuals who are speculating on a decline in interest rates will favor bonds with a longer term to maturity, but investors who are concerned with both interest income and safety of principal will prefer short-term debt. These investors are willing to accept less interest income for safety and liquidity. Of course, the extreme form of such investments is the money market mutual fund, which invests solely in short-term investments (e.g., commercial paper and Treasury bills), for such investments offer liquidity that cannot be obtained through investments in longer-term debt.

Bond Valuation Applications to Nontraditional Bonds

In the previous examples of valuation, all the bonds paid interest annually and were retired at maturity. In Chapter 9, bond features were not limited to a fixed payment and maturity date. For example, zero coupon bonds pay no interest, and several high-yield securities (e.g., the split coupon bond, the reset bond, or the extendable bond) have features that differ from the traditional bond.

Although bonds can have these varying features, their valuations remain the same: the present value of future cash flows. For example, what would an investor pay for a $1,000 zero coupon bond that matures after ten years? The answer has to be the present value of the $1,000—that is, the present value of the future cash flow. If the investor requires a return of 7 percent, then the value is

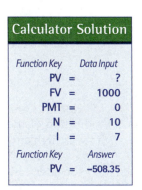

Calculator Solution

Function Key	Data Input
PV =	?
FV =	1000
PMT =	0
N =	10
I =	7
Function Key	Answer
PV =	−508.35

$$P_B = \frac{\$1,000}{(1 + 0.07)^{10}} = \$1,000(0.508) = \$508.$$

If the required return had been 10 percent, the value of the bond would be $1,000(0.386) = $386.

The valuation of split coupon and reset bonds is essentially the same. Consider the Dr Pepper bond in Chapter 9 that illustrated a split coupon bond. That bond paid $0 in interest during the first four years, $115 annually for the next six years, and matured after ten years. How much would an investor pay if the required return were 15 percent? The answer is

$115 × the present value of an annuity for six years at 15 percent

 × the present value of one dollar for four years at 15 percent

 + 1000 × the present value of one dollar at 15 percent for ten years

= **$115(3.785)(0.572) + $1,000(0.247)**

= **$496.**

Calculator Solution

Function Key	Data Input
PV =	?
FV =	1000
PMT_1 =	0
PMT_2 =	0
PMT_3 =	0
PMT_4 =	0
PMT_5 =	115
PMT_6 =	115
PMT_7 =	115
PMT_8 =	115
PMT_9 =	115
PMT_{10} =	115
N =	10
I =	15

Function Key	Answer
PV =	−496

(This solution requires a financial calculator that accepts uneven cash payments.)

If interest rates declined (or the firm's financial condition improved) so the comparable rate is 12 percent, the bond's price would rise to

$$\$115(4.111)(0.636) + \$1,000(0.322) = \$623$$

for a 25.6 percent increase. Of course, the converse is also true; higher yields would cause the price of the split coupon bond to decline.

The valuations of zero coupon and split coupon bonds are essentially no different from the valuation of a regular coupon bond since the payments (their amounts and timing) are known. With a reset bond or an extendable bond, the payments and their timing are not known. The interest payments or the maturity date or both are permitted to vary. While the valuation process remains the present value of future cash inflows, you must make assumptions concerning these inflows. For example, in the case of an extendable bond, you must assume a particular repayment date. If you expect the bond's maturity date to be extended, then the longer term is used to value the bond. Using a shorter term may result in the bond receiving a higher valuation, in which case you would pay too much and realize a smaller return if the maturity is extended.

YIELDS

The word *yield* is frequently used with regard to investing in bonds. There are three important types of yields with which the investor must be familiar: the current yield, the yield to maturity, and the yield to call. This section will differentiate among these three yields.

The Current Yield

The current yield is the percentage that the investor earns annually. It is simply

(11.4)
$$\frac{\textbf{Annual interest payment}}{\textbf{Price of the bond}} \cdot$$

The discounted bond discussed previously has a coupon rate of 10 percent. Thus, when the price of the bond is $952, the current yield is

$$\frac{\$100}{\$952} = 10.5\%.$$

The current yield is important because it gives the investor an indication of the current return that will be earned on the investment. Investors who seek high current income prefer bonds that offer a high current yield.

However, the current yield can be misleading, for it fails to consider any change in the price of the bond that may occur if the bond is held to maturity. Obviously, if a bond is bought at a discount, its value must rise as it approaches maturity. The opposite occurs if the bond is purchased for a premium, because its price will decline as maturity approaches. For this reason it is desirable to know the bond's yield to maturity.

The Yield to Maturity

The yield to maturity considers the current income generated by the bond as well as any change in its value when it is held to maturity. If the bond referred to earlier is purchased for $952 and is held to maturity, after three years the investor will receive a return of 12 percent. This is the yield to maturity, because this return considers not only the current interest return of 10.5 percent but also the price appreciation of the bond from $952 at the time of purchase to $1,000 at maturity. Since the yield to maturity considers both the flow of interest income and the price change, it is a more accurate measure of the return offered to investors by a particular bond issue.

The yield to maturity may be determined by using Equation 11.2.[2] That equation reads

$$P_B = \frac{PMT}{(1+i)^1} + \frac{PMT}{(1+i)^2} + \dots + \frac{PMT}{(1+i)^n} + \frac{FV}{(1+i)^n}.$$

The i is the current rate of interest paid by newly issued bonds with the same term to maturity and the same degree of risk. If the investor buys a bond and holds it to maturity, the yield that is being paid by newly issued bonds (i) will also be the yield to maturity.

Determining the yield to maturity when the coupon rate of interest, the bond's price, and the maturity date are known is not easy, except with the use of a financial calculator. For example, if the bond were selling for $952 and the investor wanted to know the yield to maturity, the calculation would be

$$\$952 = \frac{\$100}{(1+i)^1} + \frac{\$100}{(1+i)^2} + \frac{\$100}{(1+i)^3} + \frac{\$1,000}{(1+i)^3}.$$

Solving this equation can be a formidable task because there is no simple arithmetical computation to determine the value of i. Instead, the investor selects a value for i and plugs it into the equation. If this value equates the left-hand and right-hand sides of the equation, then that value of i is the yield to maturity.

The yield to maturity, however, may be readily computed using a financial calculator. To determine the yield to maturity, enter the amount of each interest payment (PMT = 100), the principal repayment in the future (FV = 1,000), the term to maturity (N = 3), and the current price of the bond (PV = –952), and instruct the calculator to determine the interest (I). (Enter the present value as a negative number, since the calculator is programmed to view the price as a cash outflow and the interest and principal repayment as cash inflows.) When these figures are entered, the calculator determines the interest rate — or the yield to maturity — to be 12.00 percent.[3]

Calculator Solution

Function Key	Data Input
PV =	–952
FV =	1000
PMT =	100
N =	3
I =	?
Function Key	Answer
I =	12.00

2. The yield to maturity is a specific application of the internal rate of return discussed in Chapter 5. Equation 11.2 is simply a restatement of Equation 5.2 for the determination of an investment's internal rate of return.

3. If the bond pays interest semiannually, enter each six-month interest payment (PMT = 50), the principal repayment (FV = 1,000), the term on the bond (N = 6), and the current price of the bond (PV = –952). Instruct the calculator to determine the interest (I). The calculator determines the yield to maturity to be 5.98 percent per period or 11.96 percent compounded semiannually. Notice that the yield to maturity is marginally lower because the timing of the interest payments is slightly faster ($50 after six months followed by the next $50 after twelve months instead of the entire $100 after twelve months.). To equalize the yields, the bond with the semiannual interest payments would sell for a slightly lower price ($951 instead of $952). Since the interest is paid semiannually, you do not have to invest as much to earn a specified return (i.e., 12.00 percent), so the price would be lower. If the prices of the two bonds were the same ($952), you would have overpaid for the bond with the semiannual interest payments and your return would have been lower (11.96 percent versus 12.00 percent).

A Comparison of the Current Yield and the Yield to Maturity

The current yield and the yield to maturity are equal only if the bond sells for its principal amount, or par. If the bond sells at a discount, the yield to maturity exceeds the current yield. This may be illustrated by the bond in the previous example. When it sells at a discount (e.g., $952), the current yield is only 10.5 percent. However, the yield to maturity is 12 percent. Thus, the yield to maturity exceeds the current yield.

If the bond sells at a premium, the current yield exceeds the yield to maturity. For example, if the bond sells for $1,052, the current yield is 9.5 percent ($100 ÷ $1,052) and the yield to maturity is 8 percent. The yield to maturity is less in this case because the loss that the investor must suffer when the price of the bond declines from $1,052 to $1,000 at maturity has been included in the calculation.

Exhibit 11.4 presents the current yield and the yield to maturity at different prices for a bond with an 8 percent annual coupon that matures in ten years. As may be seen in the table, the larger the discount (or the smaller the premium), the greater are both the current yield and the yield to maturity. For example, when the bond sells for $850, the yield to maturity is 10.49 percent, but it rises to 12.52 percent when the price declines to $750.

Discounted bonds offer conservative investors attractive opportunities for financial planning. For example, a person who is currently 60 years old may purchase discounted bonds that mature after ten years to help finance retirement. This investor may purchase several bonds that mature five, six, seven years, and so on, into the future. This portfolio will generate a continuous flow of funds during retirement as the bonds mature.

Discounted bonds generally result from an increase in interest rates. If interest rates fall, bonds would sell for a premium, so the strategy cannot be executed. An alternative but similar strategy uses zero coupon bonds, which always sell for a discount. This strategy is illustrated in Exhibit 11.5, in which the individual needs funds for the years 2010 through 2014 and buys a series of U.S. Treasury zero coupon bonds. For a total outlay of $3,615, the investor will receive $1,000 for each of the five years.

EXHIBIT 11.4   Current Yields and Yields to Maturity for a Ten-Year Bond with an 8-Percent Annual Coupon

Price of Bond	Current Yield	Yield to Maturity
$1,100	7.27%	6.60%
1,050	7.62	7.28
1,000	8.00	8.00
950	8.42	8.77
900	8.89	9.60
850	9.41	10.49
800	10.00	11.46
750	10.67	12.52

EXHIBIT 11.5	Selected U.S. Treasury Zero Coupon Bonds (as of April 1, 2004)		
Coupon Rate	Maturity Year	Price (per $1,000 Face Value)	Yield to Maturity
0%	2010	$806	3.41%
0	2011	764	3.68
0	2012	722	3.94
0	2013	680	4.14
0	2014	643	4.30

Source: *The Wall Street Journal*, April 12, 2004, C8.

The Yield to Call

Some bonds will never reach maturity but are retired before they become due. In some cases the issuer may call the bonds before maturity and redeem them. In other cases, the sinking fund will randomly call selected bonds from the issue and retire them. For these reasons the **yield to call** may be a more accurate estimate of the return actually earned on an investment in a bond.

yield to call
The yield earned on a bond from the time it is acquired until the time it is called and retired by the firm.

The yield to call is calculated in the same way as the yield to maturity except that (1) the expected call date is substituted for the maturity date and (2) the principal plus the call penalty (if any) is substituted for the principal. Note that the anticipated call date is used. Unlike the maturity date, which is known, the date of a call can only be anticipated.

The following example illustrates how the yield to call is calculated. A bond that matures after ten years and pays 8 percent interest annually is currently selling for $935.00. The yield to maturity is 9 percent. However, if the investor believes that the company or government will call the bond after five years and will pay a penalty of $50 per $1,000 bond to retire the debt permanently, the yield to call (i_c) is

$$\$935 = \frac{\$80}{(1 + i_c)^1} + \ldots + \frac{\$80}{(1 + i_c)^5} + \frac{\$1,050}{(1 + i_c)^5}$$

$$i_c = 10.55\%.$$

Calculator Solution

Function Key	Data Input
PV =	−935
FV =	1050
PMT =	80
N =	5
I =	?
Function Key	Answer
I =	10.55

In this example, the yield to call is higher than the yield to maturity because (1) the investor receives the call penalty and (2) the principal is redeemed early and hence the discount is erased sooner. Thus, in the case of a discounted bond, the actual return the investor earns exceeds the yield to maturity if the bond is called and retired before maturity.

However, if this bond were selling for a premium such as $1,147 with a yield to maturity of 6 percent and the firm were to call the bond after five years, the yield to call would become

$$\$1,147 = \frac{\$80}{(1 + i_c)^1} + \ldots + \frac{\$80}{(1 + i_c)^5} + \frac{\$1,050}{(1 + i_c)^5}$$

$$i_c = 5.46\%.$$

Calculator Solution

Function Key	Data Input
PV =	−1147
FV =	1050
PMT =	80
N =	5
I =	?
Function Key	Answer
I =	5.46

This return is less than the anticipated yield to maturity of 6 percent. The early redemption produces a lower return for the investor because the premium is spread out over fewer years, reducing the yield on the investment.[4]

Which case is more likely to occur? If a firm wanted to retire debt that was selling at a discount before maturity, it would probably be to its advantage to purchase the bonds instead of calling them. (See the section on repurchasing debt in the Chapter 9.) By doing so, the firm would avoid the call penalty and might even be able to buy the bonds for less than par. If the firm wanted to retire debt that was selling at a premium, it would probably be advantageous to call the bonds and pay the penalty. If the bonds were selling for more than face value plus the call penalty, this would obviously be the chosen course of action.

You should not expect a firm to call prematurely a bond issue that is selling at a discount. However, if interest rates fall and bond prices rise, the firm may refinance the debt. It will then issue new debt at the lower (current) interest rate and use the proceeds to retire the old and more costly debt. In this case the yield to the anticipated call is probably a better indication of the potential return offered by the bonds than is the yield to maturity.

The preceding example also illustrates the importance of the call penalty. If you bought the bond in anticipation that it would yield 6 percent at maturity (i.e., the investor paid $1,147) and the bond is redeemed after five years for the principal amount ($1,000), the return on the investment is only 4.6 percent. Although the $50 call penalty does not restore the return to 6 percent, the investor does receive a yield of 5.46 percent, which is better than 4.6 percent.

RISK AND FLUCTUATIONS IN YIELDS

Stock investors will bear risk only if they anticipate a sufficient return to compensate for the risk, and a higher anticipated return is necessary to induce them to bear additional risk. This principle also applies to investors who purchase bonds. Bonds involving greater risk must offer higher yields to attract investors. Therefore, the lowest yields are paid by bonds with the highest credit ratings, and low credit ratings are associated with high yields.

This relationship is illustrated by Exhibit 11.6, which presents Standard & Poor's ratings and the anticipated yields to maturity for three bonds that will mature in the year 2013. As may be seen in the exhibit, the bonds with the highest credit ratings have the lowest anticipated yield to maturity. A Wal-Mart bond with a Aa2 rating was selling to yield less than the Baa-rated bond of USX (6.79 percent to 7.57 percent). The difference, or *spread*, in the yields is partially due to the difference in risk between the two bonds. While the Wal-Mart bond is considered to be relatively safe (as judged by its rating), the USX bond is viewed as involving more risk.

Since interest rates change over time, anticipated yields on all bonds vary. However, the yields on bonds involving greater risk tend to fluctuate more. The following table gives the yields on Moody's Aaa-rated and Baa-rated bonds over five-year intervals. (Yields and other information on specific bonds are available in *Mergent's Bond Record*, which is published monthly. Similar information is available in the monthly *Standard & Poor's Bond Guide*.)

Calculator Solution		
Function Key	Data Input	
FV =	1050	
PMT =	80	
N =	5	
I =	6	
PV =	?	
Function Key	Answer	
PV =	−1122	

---

4. If an investor expected the bond to be called for $1,050 after five years and wanted to earn 6 percent, the price would have to be $1,122.

EXHIBIT 11.6	Credit Ratings and Yields to Maturity for Selected Bonds Maturing in the Year 2013

Bond Issue	Standard & Poor's Bond Rating	Yield to Maturity
Wal-Mart 7¼ 13	AA	4.12%
IBM 7½ 13	A+	4.23
USX 9⅛ 13	BBB+	6.20

Source: *Standard & Poor's Bond Guide*, July 2003.

Year	Yield Aaa-rated bonds	Yield Baa-rated bonds	Spread
1982	14.8%	12.9%	1.9%
1987	9.3	10.6	1.3
1992	8.2	9.1	0.9
1997	7.4	8.0	0.6
2002	6.2	7.5	1.3

During the early 1980s, yields rose dramatically and the spread (the difference between the interest rates) rose to 1.9 percent. Yields subsequently fell and the spread declined to less than 1.0 percent. By the early 2000s, interest rates were at historic lows, but the spread between the yields on Aaa-rated and Baa-rated bonds rose to 1.3 percent as investors moved into higher-quality debt and away from poorer-quality investment-grade bonds.

Changes in Risk

Previous sections demonstrated that when interest rates change, bond prices fluctuate in the opposite direction. If interest rates rise after a bond is issued, it will sell for a discount as the price adjusts so that the yield to maturity will be comparable with bonds being currently issued. If interest rates fall after the bond is issued, it will sell for a premium so that once again the yield to maturity is comparable to current interest rates.

The amount of price change depends on the coupon, the term of the bond, and the risk. The smaller the coupon, the greater the price fluctuation for a given maturity and level of risk. The longer the term of the bond, the greater the price fluctuation for a given coupon and level of risk. For given coupons and maturity dates, the prices of riskier bonds tend to fluctuate more.

The coupons and maturity dates of a bond are set when the bond is issued. However, the risk of default on a bond may vary over time as the financial condition of the issuer varies. Firms that were financially sound when their bonds were issued may fall on hard times. Their credit ratings deteriorate. Other firms' financial positions may improve. These changes in risk will, of course, affect the value of outstanding bonds.

That risk and bond rating change is illustrated by Kmart, whose Moody's ratings were as follows

Year	Rating
1993	A3
1994	Baa1
1996	Baa3
2001	Ba2
2002	B2
	Caa1
	Caa3
	Rating withdrawn

During the 1990s the debt of Kmart was considered investment grade, but with the passage of time the rating declined, mirroring the declining financial condition of the firm. During 2001, the rating was reduced to "junk" status and continued to decline until the firm filed for bankruptcy in 2002.

REALIZED RETURNS AND THE REINVESTMENT ASSUMPTION

The yield to maturity makes an important assumption that answers the following questions: What happens to the interest received in year one, year two, and so on (i.e., does the recipient pocket the money or reinvest the funds)? If the funds are reinvested, what rate do they earn? The yield to maturity calculation assumes that *all interest payments are reinvested at the yield to maturity.*[5] This is an exceedingly important assumption because if the payments are not reinvested at that rate, the yield to maturity will not be realized. This also means that when you purchase a bond, the yield to maturity is an expected yield that will not necessarily be the realized yield, even if the bond is held to maturity. The debtor could make all the interest payments and redeem the bond at maturity, but the yield over the lifetime of the bond could be different from the yield to maturity you anticipated when the bond was purchased.

The reinvestment rate assumption is the essential difference between compounding and not compounding. If you buy a $1,000 bond with an 8 percent coupon at par and spend the interest as received, you are earning a simple, non-compounded rate of 8 percent. The yield to maturity, however, assumes that the interest received will be reinvested at 8 percent (i.e., compounded at 8 percent). If the funds are not being reinvested, the compounded yield will be less than the simple 8 percent rate.

The reinvestment rate that you earn could be greater or less than the anticipated yield to maturity. If interest rates rise (and the price of this bond declines), you can reinvest the interest payments at the now higher rate. The yield earned over the lifetime of the bond will exceed the anticipated yield to maturity. If interest rates fall (and the price of this bond rises), you can only reinvest the interest payments at the lower rate. The yield earned over the lifetime of the bond will be less than the anticipated yield to maturity.

Perhaps the best way to see the importance of the reinvestment rate assumption is through several illustrations. In each of the following cases, you purchase

5. The reinvestment assumption also applies to the yield to call, which assumes that cash inflows are reinvested at the yield to call. All time-value calculations assume that inflows are reinvested at the discount rate, or interest rate. If this reinvestment rate is not achieved, then the present value, or future value, or rate of return, or number of years being determined by the calculation to solve a specific problem are inaccurate.

an 8 percent, $1,000 coupon bond that matures after ten years. You want the funds to accumulate and are curious as to how much will be available at the end of the tenth year. Essentially, this question may be restated in the following way: If I invest $80 each year at some rate for ten years and receive $1,000 at the end of the tenth year, how much will I have accumulated? The final amount will depend on the rate earned each year. This is the reinvestment rate.

Case 1: All Interest Payments Are Reinvested at 8 Percent

In this case, the terminal value will be $80 times the interest factor for the future sum of an annuity of $1 at 8 percent for ten years. The future value of this annuity is

$$\$80(14.487) = \$1,158.96.$$

This amount is added to the $1,000 principal received at maturity so you have a total of $2,158.96 at the end of ten years.

What is the return on this investment that initially cost $1,000 and has grown to $2,158.96? As may be seen in the calculator solution, the answer is the anticipated 8 percent.

Case 2: All Interest Payments Are Reinvested at 12 Percent

Suppose immediately after buying the bond, interest rates rise to 12 percent. Of course, the bond would now sell for a discount and you have sustained a loss. But the bond was purchased to receive a flow of interest payments that you intended to reinvest at the current rate. So the loss of value is only a paper loss. The bond is not sold, and the loss is not realized. Instead, the bond is held and the interest payments are now reinvested at the higher rate. What will be the return on this investment? Will this return be equal to the 8 percent yield to maturity that was anticipated when the bond was purchased?

In this case, the terminal value of the interest payments will be $1,403.92. This amount is added to the $1,000 principal received at maturity so you have a total of $2,403.92 at the end of ten years.

What is the return on this investment that initially cost $1,000 and has grown into $2,403.92? The answer is 9.17 percent. The actual yield on this investment over its lifetime (i.e., the realized yield to maturity) exceeds the anticipated 8 percent. Even though interest rates rose, which caused the market value of the bond to fall, the return over the lifetime of the bond exceeds the expected yield to maturity.

Case 3: All Interest Payments Are Reinvested at 5 Percent

In this case, the terminal value of the interest payments will be $1,006.23. The sum of this amount and the $1,000 principal received at maturity is $2,006.23.

What is the return on this investment that initially cost $1,000 and has grown into $2,006.23? The answer is 7.21 percent. Even though interest rates fell and the price of the bond initially rose, the yield on the investment in this bond is only 7.21 percent. The actual return is less than the expected yield to maturity (i.e., the anticipated 8 percent).

These three illustrations are compared in Figure 11.1, which shows the initial $1,000 and the terminal values achieved through the investment of the interest at the different reinvestment rates. Lines *OA*, *OB*, and *OC* represent the growth in each investment at 12 percent, 8 percent, and 5 percent, respectively. The terminal values, $2,403.92, $2,158.92, and $2,006.23, generated through the reinvestment of

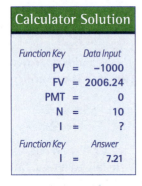

Calculator Solution

Function Key	Data Input
PV =	0
FV =	?
PMT =	80
N =	10
I =	5
Function Key	Answer
FV =	−1006.23

Calculator Solution

Function Key	Data Input
PV =	−1000
FV =	2006.24
PMT =	0
N =	10
I =	?
Function Key	Answer
I =	7.21

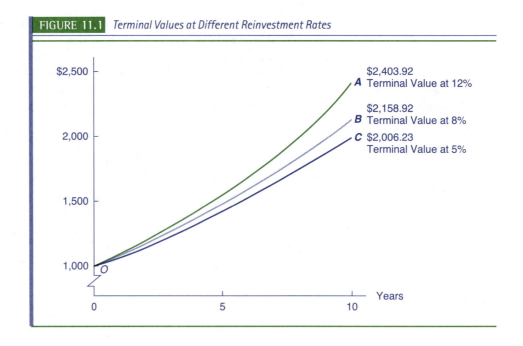

FIGURE 11.1 *Terminal Values at Different Reinvestment Rates*

interest income, are shown on the right-hand side of the figure. Of course, the highest terminal value and consequently the highest realized return occur at the highest reinvestment rate.

Actually, there is little reason to expect you will earn the anticipated yield to maturity. To obtain that yield, interest rates must remain unchanged and the bond must be held to maturity. The probability of these conditions being met is very small. Interest rates change virtually every day, and few bonds remain outstanding to maturity. Most bonds are retired through sinking funds or are called. In either case, only a few bonds of the initial issue may remain outstanding at maturity.

Since many bonds are retired prior to maturity, you may want to purchase only those bonds that are noncallable. Some bonds have this feature written into their indentures. They cannot be retired prior to maturity, in which case there is no uncertainty concerning when these bonds will be redeemed. Since this uncertainty has been erased, such bonds tend to *sell for lower yields*. Thus, you purchase the certainty of when the bond will be retired by forgoing some interest income.

Even if you acquire noncallable bonds, there is still the uncertainty associated with changes in interest rates. Thus, the realized yield over the lifetime of these noncallable bonds may not equal the yield to maturity that was anticipated when the bonds were purchased. A noncallable feature may reduce one source of risk but cannot erase all the possible sources of risk associated with investing in bonds.

There is only one type of bond that erases both the uncertainty of when the bond will be retired and the reinvestment rate. That bond is the noncallable, zero coupon bond. The entire yield occurs at maturity, and the discounted price considers the compounding of the implicit interest. These bonds offer actual yields to maturity that are equal to the expected yields. As long as the issuer does not default (i.e., repays the principal on the maturity date), the yield to maturity will be the realized return.

••DURATION

duration

The average time it takes to collect a bond's interest and principal repayment.

The price volatility of bonds with equal coupons and different terms may be compared on the basis of time. For a given risk class, the price of the bond with the longer term to maturity should be more volatile. Bonds with equal maturities but different coupons may be compared on the basis of the interest payments. For a given risk class, the price of the bond with the smaller coupon will tend to be more volatile. Bonds, however, may have different coupons and different maturity dates. Computing the yield to maturity is one method for comparing bonds. However, the yields to maturity on bonds with different maturities and different coupons may not be comparable, and the yield to maturity does not indicate which bonds' prices tend to be more volatile.

The previous discussion also indicated that the actual return you earn over a bond's lifetime will not equal the yield to maturity if the reinvestment rate differs from the yield to maturity. An alternative calculation that may be used to compare bonds with different coupons and different terms to maturity has been developed. This technique is called the bond's **duration** and it compares bonds with different coupons and different maturity dates by determining each bond's price sensitivity to changes in interest rates.

Duration is defined as the average time it takes the bondholder to receive the interest and the principal. It is a weighted average that encompasses the total amount of the bond's payments and their timing, then standardizes for the bond's price. To illustrate how duration is determined, consider a $1,000 bond with three years to maturity and a 9 percent coupon. The annual payments are as follows:

Year	Payment
1	$ 90
2	90
3	1,090

Currently, the rate of interest on comparable bonds is 12 percent, so this bond's price is $927.95. The bond's duration is the sum of the present value of each payment weighted by the time period in which the payment is received, with the resulting quantity divided by the price of the bond.[6] Thus, for this bond, the duration is determined as follows:

---

6. Duration may be computed when payments are semiannual, in which case the annual payment and interest rate on comparable debt are divided by 2 and the number of payments is multiplied by 2. If this example had used semiannual compounding, the bond's price would be $926.24, and the computation of duration is

Number of Each Payment		Amount of Payment		Present Value Interest Factor at 6 Percent		
1	×	$ 45	×	0.943	=	$ 42.44
2	×	45	×	0.890	=	80.04
3	×	45	×	0.840	=	113.40
4	×	45	×	0.792	=	142.56
5	×	45	×	0.747	=	168.08
6	×	1,045	×	0.705	=	4,420.35
						$4,966.87

$$\text{Duration} = \frac{\$4,966.87/2}{\$926.24} = 5.3624/2 = 2.68 \text{ years.}$$

The duration is marginally smaller because the cash inflows are received slightly faster as the result of semiannual compounding.

Number of Each Payment		Amount of Payment		Present Value Interest Factor at 12 Percent		
1	×	$ 90	×	0.893	=	$ 80.37
2	×	90	×	0.797	=	143.46
3	×	1,090	×	0.712	=	2,328.24
						$2,552.07

$$\text{Duration} = \frac{\$2,552.07}{\$927.95} = 2.75 \text{ years.}$$

A duration of 2.75 years means that the bondholder collects, on the average, all the payments in 2.75 years. Obviously, all the payments are not made exactly at 2.75 years into the future; $90 is received at the end of year one; $90 is received at the end of year two; and $1,090 is received at the end of year three. The weighted average of all these payments is 2.75 years.

The calculation of duration (D) may be formally expressed as:

(11.5)
$$D = \frac{\sum_{t=1}^{m} PVCF_t \times t}{P_B}.$$

The numerator states that the cash flow in each year (CF_t) is stated in present value terms (PV) and weighted by the number of the period (t) in which the payment is received. The individual present values are summed from $t = 1$ to $t = m$ (maturity), and the resulting amount is divided by the current price of the bond (P_B).

Notice that duration is not the sum of the present value of each payment. (That sum is the price of the bond.) Duration takes the present value of each payment and weights it according to when the payment is received. Payments that are to be received farther into the future have more weight in the calculation. If two bonds pay the same coupon but the term of one bond is 10 years while the term of the other is 20 years, the weights given to the payments in years 11 through 20 result in a larger weighted average. The duration, or the weighted average of when all the payments will be received, is longer for the second bond.

The preceding calculation of duration can be tedious. An alternative method simplifies the problem.

(11.6)
$$D = \frac{1+y}{y} - \frac{(1+y) + n(c-y)}{c[(1+y)^n - 1] + y}.$$

Although this equation looks formidable, its application is relatively easy. The variables represent the following:

c = the annual coupon (as a percentage)

n = the number of years to maturity

y = the yield to maturity (reinvestment rate)

Applying the numbers from the preceding illustration yields

$$D = \frac{1 + 0.12}{0.12} - \frac{(1 + 0.12) + 3(0.09 - 0.12)}{0.09[1 + 0.12]^3 - 1] + 0.12}$$

$$= 2.75,$$

which is the same answer (2.75) derived earlier.

By making this calculation for bonds with different coupons and different maturities, the investor standardizes for price fluctuations. Bonds with the same duration will experience similar price fluctuations, while the prices of bonds with a longer duration will fluctuate more. For example, consider the following two bonds. Bond A has a 10 percent coupon, matures in 20 years, and currently sells for $1,000. Bond B has a 7 percent coupon and matures after 10 years with a current price of $815.66.[7] If interest rates rise, the price of both bonds will fall, but which bond's price will fall more? Since the bonds differ with regard to maturity date and coupon, the investor does not know which bond's price will be more volatile.

In general, the longer the term to maturity, the more volatile the bond's price. By that reasoning, bond A will be more volatile. However, lower coupons are also associated with greater price volatility, and by that reasoning bond B's price should be more volatile. Thus, the investor cannot tell on the basis of term and coupon which of these two bonds' prices will be more volatile. However, once their durations have been determined (9.36 and 7.22, respectively), the investor knows that the price of bond A will decline more in response to an increase in interest rates. For example, if interest rates rise to 12 percent, the prices of the two bonds become $850.61 and $717.49, respectively. Bond A's price declined by 15 percent while bond B's price fell by 12 percent, so bond A's price was more volatile.

Since bonds with larger durations are more volatile, you reduce the risk associated with changes in interest rates by acquiring bonds with shorter durations. This, however, is not synonymous with buying bonds with shorter maturities.[8] If two bonds have the same term to maturity, the bond with the smaller coupon will have the longer duration, since a larger proportion of the bond's total payment is repayment of principal. If two bonds have the same coupon, the one with the longer maturity will have the longer duration, as the payments are spread over a longer period of time. However, if one bond has a smaller coupon and a shorter term, its duration could be either greater or smaller than the duration of a bond with a higher coupon and longer term to maturity. Thus, it is possible to buy a bond with a longer term to maturity that has a shorter duration. In such a case, the longer-term bond will experience smaller price fluctuations than the bond with the shorter maturity but longer duration.

Duration and Portfolio Immunization

Pension plan managers or portfolio managers of life insurance companies use duration as a tool of risk management. These professional investors know reasonably well the time and the amount of funds needed for distributions. They then match the duration of their portfolios with the timing of the need for funds. This

---

7. In this illustration it is assumed that the bonds sell for the same yield to maturity. While generally the long-term bond should offer a higher yield, this assumption facilitates comparisons for a given change in interest rates.
8. The only time duration equals the term to maturity occurs when the bond makes no interest payments (i.e., it is a zero coupon bond). All the payments then occur at maturity.

strategy is often referred to as "immunization," because it reduces the risk associated with interest rate fluctuations and the reinvestment of interest payments.

Consider a portfolio manager who needs $2,200 at the end of seven years and purchases at par a high-yield 12 percent coupon bond that matures at the end of seven years. If interest rates remain at 12 percent, the investor will have $2,211 because the coupons are reinvested at 12 percent. The terminal value is

$$\$1,000 + \$120(10.089) = \$2,211.$$

(The $1,000 is the repayment of the principal and the $120[10.089] is the future value of all the interest payments compounded annually at 12 percent.)

If interest rates rise and the portfolio manager reinvests at 14 percent, the terminal value is

$$\$1,000 + \$120(10.730) = \$2,288,$$

and the portfolio manager is even better off. A problem arises when interest rates fall and the coupons are reinvested at a lower rate. For example, if interest rates decline to 8 percent, the terminal value is

$$\$1,000 + \$120(8.923) = \$2,071,$$

and the portfolio manager does not have the required $2,200. The lower reinvestment of the interest payments resulted in an insufficient terminal value.

The portfolio manager could have avoided the shortage by acquiring a bond whose duration (and not its term) is equal to seven years. For example, if the portfolio manager purchases a bond with a 12 percent coupon that matures in 12 instead of 7 years, that bond has a duration of 6.9 years that almost matches when the $2,200 is needed. (The 12 percent 7-year bond has a duration of 5.1 years.) As will be subsequently illustrated, the purchase of the 12-year bond instead of the 7-year bond eliminates the reinvestment risk.

Since the 12-year bond will have to be sold at the end of seven years, the obvious question is: At what price? The price could rise (if interest rates fall) or decline (if interest rates rise). Should the portfolio manager be concerned with interest rate risk (i.e., the fluctuation in the bond's price), which would not apply if the bond matured at the end of seven years? The answer is no. The bond's price of course will change, but the impact of the price fluctuation is offset by the change in the reinvestment of the interest payments. The effect, then, of both reinvestment rate risk and interest rate risk is eliminated.

Suppose interest rates immediately rise to 14 percent after the investor buys the bond. The portfolio manager holds the bond for seven years and reinvests the interest payments at 14 percent. How much will this investor have at the end of seven years? The answer is the sum of the interest payments reinvested at 14 percent for seven years [$120(10.730) = $1,288] plus the sale price of the bond. Since the bond has five years to maturity, its price is

$$\$120(3.433) + \$1,000(0.519) = \$931.$$

Thus, the portfolio manager has $1,288 + $931 = $2,219, which meets the desired amount ($2,200). The loss on the sale of the bond is offset by the increased interest earned when the annual interest payments are reinvested at the higher rate.

Suppose interest rates immediately decline to 8 percent after the bond is purchased. The portfolio manager holds the bond for seven years and reinvests the interest payments at 8 percent. How much will this investor have at the end of seven years? The answer in this case is the sum of the interest payments reinvested at 8 percent for seven years [\$120(8.923) = \$1,071] plus the sale price of the bond. Since the bond has five years to maturity, its price is

$$\$120(3.993) + \$1,000(0.681) = \$1,160.$$

Thus, the portfolio manager has \$1,071 + \$1,160 = \$2,231, which once again meets the desired amount (\$2,200). The gain on the sale of the bond offsets the reduction in interest earned when the interest payments are reinvested at the lower rate.

Notice that in both cases the individual achieves the investment goal of \$2,200 at the end of seven years. Lower reinvestment income from a decline in interest rates is offset by the increase in the price of the bond, while higher reinvestment income from an increase in interest rates is offset by the decline in the price of the bond. Thus, the impact of reinvestment rate risk and interest rate risk is eliminated.

As this discussion indicates, the concept of duration is exceedingly important for any investor who knows when funds will be needed and in what amount. Pension managers know when payments must be made and their amount. Mortality tables help establish the same information for life insurance companies. Portfolio managers immunize their risk exposure and ensure that the desired funds are available when needed. (These portfolio managers, of course, still have the risk of default or incorrect forecasts, such as changes in a mortality table.)

Individual investors will probably find duration less useful. For example, even if parents know when their children will attend college, they do not necessarily know the cost—hence the future value is unknown. In addition, the duration of each bond is not readily available. Thus, individual investors who want to apply this concept will have to perform the calculation themselves and adjust their portfolios as the duration of the bonds in their portfolio fluctuates.

THE VALUATION OF PREFERRED STOCK

As was explained in Chapter 5 on equity, the dividend paid by common stock (if it pays a dividend at all) varies over time and may increase as the firm becomes more profitable and earnings grow. Preferred stock could not be more different. Virtually all preferred stock pays a fixed dividend, which cannot grow, and if the firm does not pay the dividend, it often accumulates. These skipped dividend payments must be made if management ever wants to declare a cash dividend to the common stockholders.

Since preferred stock pays a fixed dividend, it is valued as if it were a debt instrument. The process is the same as is used to value bonds. The future, fixed dividend payments are brought back to the present at the appropriate discount rate. If the preferred stock does not have a required sinking fund or call feature, it may be viewed as a perpetual debt instrument. The fixed dividend (D) will continue indefinitely. These dividends must be discounted by the yield being earned on newly issued preferred stock (k). This process for determining the present value of the preferred stock (P) is:

(11.7)

$$P = \frac{D}{(1 + k)^1} + \frac{D}{(1 + k)^2} + \frac{D}{(1 + k)^3} + \ldots .$$

As in the case of the perpetual bond, this equation is reduced to

$$P = \frac{D}{k}.$$

Thus, if a preferred stock pays an annual dividend of $4 and the appropriate discount rate is 8 percent, the present value of the preferred stock is

$$P = \frac{\$4}{(1 + 0.08)^1} + \frac{\$4}{(1 + 0.08)^2} + \frac{\$4}{(1 + 0.08)^3} + \ldots$$

$$= \frac{\$4}{0.08} = \$50.00.$$

If an investor buys this preferred stock for $50.00, he or she can expect to earn 8 percent ($50.00 × 0.08 = $4) on the investment. Of course, the realized rate of return on the investment will not be known until the investor sells the stock and adjusts this 8 percent return for any capital gain or loss. However, at the current price, the preferred stock is selling for an 8 percent dividend yield.

   If the preferred stock has a finite life, this fact must be considered in determining its value. As with the valuation of long-term debt, the amount that is repaid when the preferred stock is retired must be discounted back to the present value. Thus, when preferred stock has a finite life, the valuation equation becomes

(11.8)
$$P = \frac{D}{(1 + k)^1} + \frac{D}{(1 + k)^2} + \ldots + \frac{D}{(1 + k)^n} + \frac{S}{(1 + k)^n}$$

where S represents the amount that is returned to the stockholder when the preferred stock is retired after n number of years. If the preferred stock in the previous example is retired after 20 years for $100 per share, its current value would be

$$P = \frac{\$4}{(1 + 0.08)^1} + \ldots + \frac{\$4}{(1 + 0.08)^{20}} + \frac{\$100}{(1 + 0.08)^{20}}$$

$$= \$60.73.$$

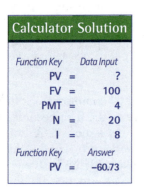

Instead of selling the stock for $50.00, the nonperpetual preferred stock would sell for $60.73. At a price of $60.73, the yield is still 8 percent, but the return in this case consists of a current dividend yield of 6.58 percent ($4 ÷ $60.73) and a capital gain as the price of the stock rises from $60.73 to $100 when it is retired 20 years hence.

Preferred Stock and Bonds Contrasted

Since preferred stock pays a fixed dividend, it is purchased primarily by investors seeking a fixed flow of income, and it is analyzed and valued like any other fixed-income security (i.e., long-term bonds). But preferred stock differs from bonds. Preferred stock is riskier than debt. The terms of a bond are legal obligations of the firm. If the corporation fails to pay the interest or meet any of the terms of the indenture, the bondholders may take the firm to court to force payment of the interest or to seek liquidation of the firm in order to protect their principal.

Preferred stockholders do not have that power, for the firm is not legally obligated to pay the preferred stock dividends. In addition, debt must be retired, while preferred stock may be perpetual. If the security is perpetual, the only means to recoup the amount invested is to sell the preferred stock in the secondary market. The investor cannot expect the firm to redeem the security.

While preferred stock may be perpetual so that the investor cannot expect the firm to retire the stock, it may be callable. This gives the firm the option to retire the preferred stock at its convenience. In a sense this further stacks the deck of cards against the investor. Preferred stock dividends are not assured. If the stock lacks a maturity date, the investor cannot expect the security to be redeemed. And if the preferred stock is callable, the company may redeem the security, but the investor cannot know when such redemption will occur. At least with a bond, the investor has an anticipated interest payment that is a legal obligation and has a known maturity date.

While the above discussion suggests that issuing preferred stock is more advantageous to the firm than issuing debt, there is a major tax consideration that discourages firms from selling preferred stock to raise funds. The interest paid bondholders is a tax-deductible expense, while the dividend on preferred stock is not. Preferred dividends are paid out of earnings. This difference in the tax treatment of interest expense and preferred stock dividends affects the earnings available to the firm's common stockholders. Using debt instead of preferred stock as a source of funds will result in higher earnings per common share.

Consider a firm with operating income (earnings before interest and taxes) of $1,000,000. The firm has 100,000 common shares outstanding and is in the 40 percent corporate income tax bracket. If the firm issues $2,000,000 of debt with a 10 percent rate of interest, its earnings per common share are

Earnings before interest and taxes	$1,000,000
Interest	200,000
Earnings before taxes	800,000
Taxes	320,000
Net income	$480,000
Earnings per common share: $480,000/100,000 =	$4.80

If the firm had issued $2,000,000 in preferred stock that also paid 10 percent, the earnings per common share would be:

Earnings before interest and taxes	$1,000,000
Interest	0
Earnings before taxes	1,000,000
Taxes	400,000
Earnings before preferred stock dividends	600,000
Preferred stock dividends	200,000
Earnings available to common stock	$400,000
Earnings per common share: $400,000/100,000 =	$4.00

The use of preferred stock has resulted in lower earnings per common share. This reduction in earnings is the result of the different tax treatment of interest, which is a tax-deductible expense, and preferred stock dividends, which are not deductible.

SUMMARY

The price of a bond depends on the interest paid, the maturity date, and the return offered by comparable bonds. If interest rates rise, the price of existing bonds falls. The opposite is also true—if interest rates fall, the price of existing bonds rises.

The current yield considers only the flow of interest income relative to the price of the bond. The yield to maturity considers the flow of interest income as well as any price change that may occur if the bond is held to maturity. The yield to call is similar to the yield to maturity, but it substitutes the call date and the call price for the maturity date and the principal.

Discounted bonds may be attractive to investors seeking current income, some capital appreciation, and the return of the principal at a specified date. Since many such bonds are redeemed at maturity, the investor knows when the principal is to be received.

All bond prices fluctuate in response to changes in interest rates and changes in risk, but the prices of bonds with smaller coupons, longer maturities, or poorer credit ratings tend to fluctuate more. These bonds may sell for larger discounts or higher premiums than bonds with shorter maturities or better credit ratings. Such bonds may be attractive investments for individuals who want higher returns and who are willing to bear additional risk.

Investors may determine bonds' duration to ascertain which bonds' prices will fluctuate more. Duration is a weighted average of all of a bond's interest and principal payments standardized by the bond's price. Bonds with smaller durations tend to have smaller price fluctuations in response to changes in interest rates. Duration may also be used to manage reinvestment rate risk by timing a bond's duration with when the funds will be needed.

Preferred stock is legally equity, but because it pays a fixed dividend, it is similar to debt. Preferred stock's value fluctuates with changes in interest rates. When interest rates rise, the price of preferred stock falls; when interest rates decline, the price of preferred stock rises. Because its price behavior is the same as the price behavior of bonds, preferred stock is valued and analyzed as an alternative to long-term debt.

The prime advantage to the firm issuing preferred stock is that it is less risky than debt because preferred stock does not represent an unconditional obligation to pay dividends. The major disadvantage to the issuing firm is that the dividends are not a tax-deductible expense. The primary purpose for purchasing a preferred stock is the flow of dividend income. However, since preferred stock is riskier than debt (from the viewpoint of the individual investor), preferred stock is not a popular investment with individuals.

Learning Objectives

Now that you have completed this chapter, you should be able to:

1. Determine the price of a bond.
2. Isolate the factors that affect a bond's price.

3. Explain the relationship between changes in interest rates and a bond's price.
4. Differentiate among the current yield, yield to maturity, and yield to call.
5. Calculate the current yield, yield to maturity, and yield to call.
6. Explain how the reinvestment of earned interest income affects the investor's realized return.
7. Illustrate the relationship between a bond's duration and its price volatility.
8. Determine the value of a preferred stock.
9. Compare and contrast bonds and preferred stock.

PROBLEMS

1) A $1,000 bond has the following features: a coupon rate of 8 percent, interest that is paid semiannually (i.e., $40 every six months), and a maturity date of ten years.
   a) What is the bond's price if comparable debt yields 8 percent?
   b) What is the bond's price if comparable debt yields 10 percent?
   c) What is the current yield if the bond sells for the prices determined in questions (a) and (b)?
   d) Why are the prices different for questions (a) and (b)?

2) A $1,000 bond has a coupon rate of 10 percent and matures after eight years. Interest rates are currently 7 percent.
   a) What will the price of this bond be if the interest is paid annually?
   b) What will the price be if investors expect that the bond will be called with no call penalty after two years?
   c) What will the price be if investors expect that the bond will be called after two years and there will be a call penalty of one year's interest?
   d) Why are your answers different for questions (a), (b), and (c)?

3) A company has two bonds outstanding. The first matures after five years and has a coupon rate of 8.25 percent. The second matures after ten years and has a coupon rate of 8.25 percent. Interest rates are currently 10 percent. What is the present price of each $1,000 bond? Why are these prices different?

4) If a $1,000 bond with a 9 percent coupon (paid annually) and a maturity date of ten years is selling for $939, what is the current yield and the yield to maturity?

5) A $1,000 zero coupon bond sells for $519 and matures after five years. What is the yield to maturity?

6) Given the following information:

   XY Inc. 5% bond
   AB Inc. 14% bond

   Both bonds are for $1,000, mature in 20 years, and are rated AAA.
   a) What should be the current market price of each bond if the interest rate on triple-A bonds is 10 percent?
   b) Which bond has a current yield that exceeds its yield to maturity?
   c) Which bond would you expect to be called if interest rates are 10 percent?
   d) If CD Inc. had a bond outstanding with a 5 percent coupon and a maturity date of 20 years but it was rated BBB, what would you expect its price to be relative to the XY Inc. bond?

7) a) If a preferred stock pays an annual dividend of $6 and investors can earn 10 percent on alternative and comparable investments, what is the maximum price that should be paid for this stock?

b) If the preferred stock in part (a) had a call feature and investors expected the stock to be called for $100 after ten years, what is the maximum price that investors should pay for the stock?

c) If investors can earn 12 percent on comparable investments, what should be the price of the preferred stock in part (a)? What would be the price if comparable yields are 8 percent? What generalization do these answers imply?

8) Company X has the following bonds outstanding:

Bond A		Bond B	
Coupon	8%	Coupon	Variable—changes annually to be comparable to the current rate
Maturity	10 years	Maturity	10 years

Initially, both bonds sold at $1,000 with yields to maturity of 8 percent.

a) After two years, the interest rate on comparable debt is 10 percent. What should be the price of each bond?

b) After two additional years (i.e., four years after issue date), the interest rate on comparable debt is 7 percent. What should be the price of each bond?

c) What generalization may be drawn from the prices in questions (a) and (b)?

9) A junk bond has the following features:

Principal amount	1,000
Interest rate (the coupon)	9%
Maturity	10 years
Sinking fund	None
Call penalty	One year's interest

a) If comparable yields are 12 percent, what should be the price of this bond?

b) Is there any reason to expect the firm to call the bond if yields are 12 percent?

c) If comparable yields are 7 percent, what should be the price of the bond?

d) Is there any reason to expect the firm to call the bond if yields are 7 percent?

e) If you expected the bond to be called after three years, what is the maximum price you would pay for the bond if the current interest rate is 8 percent?

10) What is the price of the following split coupon bond if comparable yields are 12 percent?

Principal	$1,000
Maturity	12 years
Annual coupon	0% ($0) for years 1–3
	10% ($100) for years 4–12

If comparable yields decline to 10 percent, what is the appreciation in the price of the bond?

11) You purchase a 7 percent $1,000 bond with a term of ten years and reinvest all interest payments. If interest rates rise to 10 percent after you purchase the bond, what is the return on your investment in the bond?

12)   **a)** What is the price of each of the following bonds ($1,000 principal) if the current interest rate is 9 percent?

Firm A	Coupon	6%
	Maturity	5 years
Firm B	Coupon	6%
	Maturity	20 years
Firm C	Coupon	15%
	Maturity	5 years
Firm D	Coupon	15%
	Maturity	20 years
Firm E	Coupon	0% (zero coupon bond)
	Maturity	5 years
Firm F	Coupon	0% (zero coupon bond)
	Maturity	20 years

   b) What is the duration of each bond?
   c) Rank the bonds in terms of price fluctuations with the least volatile bond first and the most volatile bond last as judged by each bond's duration.
   d) Confirm your volatility rankings by determining the percentage change in the price of each bond if interest rates rise to 12 percent.
   e) What generalizations can be made from the above exercise concerning (a) low- versus high-coupon bonds, (b) intermediate- versus long-term bonds, and (c) zero coupon bonds?

The next two problems concern convertible bonds, so if necessary, reread the material in Chapter 9. The problems are straightforward and should increase your understanding of these fascinating securities.

13) A convertible bond has the following features:

Principal	$1,000
Coupon	5%
Maturity date	15 years
Call price	$1,050
Conversion price	$37 (i.e., 27 shares)

Currently the market price of the bond is $1,040, and the market price of the stock is $32.
   a) What is the bond's current yield?
   b) If nonconvertible bonds have a yield to maturity of 7 percent, what would be the current price of this bond if it *lacked the conversion feature*?
   c) What is the value of the bond based on the market price of the stock? (Remember that the bond is convertible into 27 shares.)
   d) Is the bond selling for a price that exceeds its value as debt in (b) and also exceeds its value as stock in (c)?
   e) If the price of the stock rose by 50 percent to $48, what is the minimum increase in the value of the bond?

f) If the price of the stock declined by 50 percent to $16, what is the minimum decrease in the value of the bond if interest rates do not change?

g) Is there any reason to expect the company will call the bond if the price of the stock is $32?

14) A convertible bond has the following features:

Principal	$1,000
Coupon	6%
Maturity date	25 years
Call price	$1,060
Conversion price	$25

Currently the market price of the stock is $30.

a) If the bond lacked the conversion feature, what would be the value of the bond as debt if comparable interest rates were 12 percent?

b) Into how many shares may the bond be converted?

c) What is the value of the bond in terms of the stock?

d) What is the current minimum price that this bond will command if the price of the stock is $30?

e) Is there any reason to anticipate that the issuer will call the bond?

f) If the bond were called, would it be advantageous to convert? What would you receive if you did not convert the bond?

g) If the price of the stock were $10 instead of $30, would you convert the bond if it were called?

h) Given your answer in (g), is there any reason to expect the issuer to call the bond?

Internet Application for Chapter 11   The Valuation of Fixed-Income Securities

You buy bonds through brokerage firms in the same way that you buy stocks. However, bonds are not actively quoted, and many brokerage firms primarily buy and sell bonds from their own inventory. These bonds are usually traded on a net basis, which includes a mark-up or commission. If you buy and sell bonds on a net basis, you do not know the price and the commission, since they are combined. Brokerage firms will locate specific bonds, in which case you pay for the bond plus a commission.

Select a bond to purchase from Chapter 9. Return to the brokerage firms you used in Chapter 1 and determine if you can get a quote for the desired bond. Do not be surprised if you are unable to obtain quotes.

Several possible Internet sources for bond information and prices include:

BondsOnline   **http://www.bonds-online.com**

NASD Bondsinfo   **http://www.nasdbondsinfo.com**

Tradebonds   **http://www.tradebonds.com**

Wall Street Select   **http://bonds.wallstreetselect.com**

Yahoo!   **http://bonds.yahoo.com**

As of August 2004, Yahoo! obtained its bond data from ValuBond. You may go directly to ValuBond at **http://www.valubond.com**. (You may have to register to obtain access to the above sites.)

One final note on investing in specific bonds and obtaining bond quotes: In the late 1980s and early 1990s, I was interested in purchasing high-yield bonds. At that time I had a broker (now deceased) who would obtain price quotes. The quotes often had large spreads (e.g., 60-65) and large minimum purchases (e.g., $50,000). Putting together my high-yield bond portfolio took patience and persistence. Unless you have patience and are able to locate a broker who is willing to obtain quotes for specific bonds, you may prefer to invest in a bond fund. For material on bond funds, see Chapter 12 on investment companies.

12 ● ● ● ●

Investment Companies

I recently had lunch with a friend. Reg is an "Investment Specialist" with an investment company that sells mutual funds. We had the following conversation:

HBM: I don't understand why people pay you to manage their money. They should be able to do that for themselves.

Reg: Do you tune your car?

HBM: No, I take it to the dealer or Dave's if the car is out of warranty.

Reg: I tuned mine once. Ran terrible after that. Cheaper and easier to have someone else do it.

I got the message. Many people just don't have the time to manage their own portfolios; others may believe they don't have the knowledge or they lack the inclination to select individual stocks or bonds. I grew up in an entirely different environment. *All* the members of my family owned individual stocks. If everyone had my family's approach to investing, there would be little need for mutual funds, trust departments, and money management firms that service individual accounts.

Many individuals do not manage their own funds. In some cases they have no choice. My employer withholds funds and contributes to my retirement account, but I must select from the alternatives provided by TIAA-CREF. I cannot select the specific assets for my account. This situation is common. Many employees can invest their 401(k) retirement plans only among the choices provided by their employers. Instead of selecting specific stocks or bonds, these individuals purchase shares in investment companies offered through the retirement plan.

This chapter is an introduction to investment companies. There are two general types of investment companies: closed-end and open-end. The open-end investment company is commonly referred to as a "mutual fund" and is by far the more popular. This chapter covers both types of investment companies, the mechanics of buying and selling their shares, the costs associated with these investments, and the potential sources of return. (The next chapter covers various specialized investment companies such as money market mutual funds or index funds. The large variety of funds offers investors a wide spectrum of alternatives to the purchase of individual stocks and bonds.)

The chapter ends with a brief discussion of liquidating a position in an investment company. While acquiring the shares is obviously important, investments are not an end in themselves. Eventually you will sell or redeem the shares so that the funds may be used to meet your financial objectives.

Before proceeding, I need to make one final comment about Reg and Dave. Dave has skills, experience, and tools; he can tune my car better and more efficiently than I can. That does not mean he is a better mechanic than many of his competitors. I am also certain that Reg has skills, experience, and a wealth of knowledge available to him. Like Dave, he may provide excellent service such as tax and estate planning. This excellent service, however, does not mean that he will consistently make investment decisions that will outperform the market. In reality both Reg and Dave work in competitive markets, and in all probability neither will achieve superior results all the time.

•⦿INVESTMENT COMPANIES: ORIGINS AND TERMINOLOGY

Investment companies are not a recent development but were established in Britain during the 1860s. Initially, these investment companies were referred to as *trusts* because the securities were held in trust for the firm's stockholders. These firms issued a specified number of shares and used the funds that were obtained through the sale of the stock to acquire shares of other firms. Today, the descendants of these companies are referred to as **closed-end investment companies** because the number of shares is fixed (i.e., closed to new investors).

Whereas the first trusts offered a specific number of shares, the most common type of investment company today does not. Instead, the number of shares varies as investors buy more shares from the trust or sell them back to the trust. This **open-end investment company** is commonly called a **mutual fund**. Such funds started in 1924 when Massachusetts Investor Trust offered new shares and redeemed (i.e., bought) existing shares on demand by stockholders.

The rationale for investment companies is simple and appealing. The firms receive the funds from many investors, pool them, and purchase securities. The individual investors receive (1) the advantage of professional management of their money, (2) the benefit of ownership in a diversified portfolio, (3) the potential savings in commissions, as the investment company buys and sells in large blocks, and (4) custodial services (e.g., the collecting and disbursing of funds).

These advantages and services help explain why both the number of mutual funds and the dollar value of their shares have grown dramatically during the last 30 years. According to data available through the Investment Company Institute (**http://www.ici.org**), the total number of funds in 1970 was 361. At the end of 1990, the number had risen to 2,362, and by the beginning of 2003, the number of mutual funds exceeded 8,200. (As of 2003, about 3,000 companies traded on the NYSE. The number of funds more than doubled the number of common stocks traded on the NYSE!) Of the 8,256 funds, 4,756 were equity funds and 2,036 were bond funds. Money market mutual funds accounted for 989, and the balance consisted of hybrid funds whose portfolios encompassed a variety of asset types.

Just as the number of funds has grown, so have their total assets. If the assets of money market mutual funds are excluded, total mutual fund assets grew from $17.9 billion in 1970 to $570.8 billion in 1990. The growth then exploded to $5,233.2 billion in 1999 (a 27.9 percent annual compound rate for 1990–1999). Of course, the bear market of 2000–2002 took its toll on mutual fund assets, which fell to $4,109.6 billion at the end of 2002.

Investment companies receive special tax treatment. Their earnings (i.e., dividend and interest income received) and realized capital gains are exempt from income taxation. Instead, these earnings are taxed through their stockholders' tax returns. Dividends, interest income, and realized capital gains (whether they are distributed or not) of the investment companies must be reported by their shareholders, who pay the appropriate income taxes.

---

closed-end investment company
An investment company with a fixed number of shares that are bought and sold in the secondary securities markets.

open-end investment company
A mutual fund; an investment company from which investors buy shares and to which they resell them.

mutual fund
An open-end investment company.

For this reason, income that is received by investment companies and capital gains that are realized are usually distributed. The companies, however, offer their stockholders the option of having the fund retain and reinvest these distributions. While such reinvestments do not erase the stockholders' tax liabilities, they are an easy, convenient means to accumulate shares. The advantages offered by the dividend reinvestment plans of individual firms, discussed in Chapter 5, also apply to the dividend reinvestment plans offered by investment companies. Certainly the most important of these advantages is the element of *forced savings*. Because you do not receive the money, there is no temptation to spend it. Rather, the funds are immediately channeled back into additional income-earning assets.

One term frequently encountered in a discussion of an investment company is its **net asset value**. The net worth of an investment company is the total value of its stocks, bonds, cash, and other assets minus any liabilities (e.g., accrued fees).[1] The net asset value of any share of stock in the investment company is the net worth of the fund divided by the number of shares outstanding. Thus, net asset value may be obtained as follows:

net asset value
The net worth of a share in an investment company; total assets minus total liabilities divided by the number of shares outstanding.

Value of stock owned	$1,000,000
Value of debt owned	+1,500,000
Value of total assets	$2,500,000
Liabilities	−100,000
Net worth	$2,400,000
Number of shares outstanding	1,000,000
Net asset value per share	$2.40

The net asset value is extremely important for the valuation of an investment company, for it gives the value of the shares should the company be liquidated. Changes in the net asset value, then, alter the value of the investment company's shares. Thus, if the value of the fund's assets appreciates, the net asset value will increase, which may also cause the price of the investment company's stock to increase.

CLOSED-END INVESTMENT COMPANIES

Based on the number of mutual funds and their total assets, open-end investment companies are more important than closed-end investment companies. This discussion, however, begins with closed-end investment companies. These companies developed before mutual funds, and they have characteristics that are similar to the stocks and bonds traded in the securities markets.

As was mentioned in the previous section, a closed-end investment company has a set capital structure that may be composed of all stock or a combination of stock and debt. The number of shares and the dollar amount of debts that the company may issue are specified. In an open-end investment company (i.e., a mutual fund), the number of shares outstanding varies as investors purchase and redeem them. Because the closed-end investment company has a specified number of

---

1. Some investment companies use debt financing to leverage the returns for their stockholders. For example, the High Yield Income Fund (a closed-end investment company) reported in its August 31, 2003, *Annual Report* that the fund has a $24,500,000 loan outstanding. This loan was 29 percent of the fund's total assets. Although the amount that the investment companies may borrow is modest relative to their assets, such use of margin increases the potential return or loss and increases their stockholders' risk exposure.

shares, if you want to invest in a particular company, you must purchase existing shares from current stockholders. Conversely, if you own shares and wish to liquidate the position, you must sell the shares. Thus, the shares in closed-end investment companies are bought and sold, just as the stock of IBM is traded. Shares of these companies are traded on the New York Stock Exchange (e.g., Adams Express) and in the over-the-counter markets (e.g., Z Seven Fund).

Discounts and Premiums

The market price of stock in a closed-end company need not be the net asset value per share; it may be above or below this value. If the market price is below the net asset value of the shares, the shares are selling for a **discount**. If the market price is above the net asset value, the shares are selling for a **premium**.

These differences between the investment company's net asset value per share and the stock price are illustrated in Exhibit 12.1, which gives the price, the net asset value, and the discount or the premium for several closed-end investment companies. Five of the shares sold for a discount (i.e., below their net asset values) and one sold for a premium. The cause of this discount is not really known, but it is believed to be the result of taxation. The potential impact of capital gains taxation on the price of the shares is illustrated in the following example.

A closed-end investment company initially sells stock for $10 per share and uses the proceeds to buy the stock of other companies. If transaction costs are ignored, the net asset value of a share is $10, and the shares may trade in the secondary market for $10. The value of the firm's portfolio subsequently rises to $16 (i.e., the net asset value is $16). The firm has a potential capital gain of $6 per share. If it is realized and these profits are distributed, the net asset value will return to $10 and each stockholder will receive $6 in capital gains, for which he or she will pay the appropriate capital gains tax.

Suppose, however, that the capital gains are not realized (i.e., the net asset value remains at $16). What will the market price of the stock be? This is difficult to determine, but it will probably be below $16. Why? Suppose you bought a share for $16 and the firm then realized and distributed the $6 capital gain. After the distribution of the $6, you would be responsible for any capital gains tax, but the net asset value of the share would decrease to $10.

discount (from net asset value)
The extent to which the price of a closed-end investment company's stock sells below its net asset value.

premium (over net asset value)
The extent to which the price of a closed-end investment company's stock exceeds the share's net asset value.

EXHIBIT 12.1 Net Asset Values and Market Prices of Selected Closed-End Investment Companies as of April 9, 2004

Company	Price	Net Asset Value	(Discount) or Premium as a Percentage of Net Asset Value
Adams Express	$12.80	$14.77	(13.3)%
Gabelli Trust	8.50	8.26	2.9
General American Investors	34.32	34.32	(10.0)
Salomon Brothers Fund	12.23	14.35	(14.3)
Tri-Continental	17.39	20.40	(14.8)
Zweig Total Return	5.21	5.78	(9.9)

Source: *The Wall Street Journal*, April 12, 2004, C8.

Obviously this is not advantageous to the buyer. Individuals may be willing to purchase the shares only at a discount that reduces the potential impact of realized capital gains and the subsequent capital gains taxes. Suppose the share had cost $14 (i.e., it sold for a discount of $2 from the net asset value) and the fund realized and distributed the gain. The buyer who paid $14 now owns a share with a net asset value of $10 and receives a capital gain of $6. Although this investor will have to pay the appropriate capital gains tax, the impact is reduced because the investor paid only $14 to purchase the share whose total value is $16 (the $10 net asset value plus the $6 capital gain).

Although many closed-end investment companies sell for a discount, some do sell for a premium. In Exhibit 12.1, Gabelli Trust sold for $8.50 when its net asset value was $8.26, a premium of 2.9 percent above the net asset value. Often, closed-end investment companies that sell for a premium have a specialized portfolio that appeals to some investors. For example, as of April 2004, the Spain Fund and the Turkish Fund commanded premiums of 11.9 and 17.3 percent, respectively. These funds invest primarily in countries that place restrictions on foreign investments. If you want to acquire shares in firms in these countries (perhaps for potential growth or for diversification purposes), the closed-end investment company is the only viable means to make the investments. The effect may be to bid up the price of the shares so that the closed-end investment company sells for a premium over its net asset value.

Since the shares may sell for a discount or a premium relative to their net asset value, it is possible for the market price of a closed-end investment company to fluctuate more or less than the net asset value. For example, during 2003, the net asset value of Salomon Brothers Fund rose from $10.75 to $14.04 (a 30.6 percent increase), but the stock increased 31.9 percent ($9.12 to $12.03) as the discount fell from 16.2 to 14.3 percent. Since the market price can change relative to the net asset value, an investor is subject to an additional source of risk. The value of the investment may decline not only because the net asset value may decrease but also because the shares may sell for a larger discount from their net asset value.

Some investors view the market price relative to the net asset value as a guide to buying and selling the shares of a closed-end investment company. If the shares are selling for a sufficient discount, they are considered for purchase. If the shares are selling for a small discount or at a premium, they are sold. Of course, determining the premium that will justify the sale or the discount that will justify the purchase is not simple (and may even be arbitrary).

Sources of Returns from Investing in Closed-End Investment Companies

Profits are the difference between costs and revenues. Investing in closed-end investment companies involves several costs. First, since the shares are purchased in the secondary markets, there is the brokerage commission for the purchase and for any subsequent sale. Second, the investment company charges fees to manage the portfolio. These management fees generally range from 0.5 to 2 percent of the net asset value. Third, when the investment company purchases or sells securities, it also has to pay brokerage fees, which are passed on to the investor.

The purchase of shares in closed-end investment companies thus involves three costs that the investor must bear. Some alternative investments, such as savings accounts in commercial banks, do not involve these costs. Although commission fees are incurred when stock is purchased through a broker, the other expenses associated with a closed-end investment company are avoided.

Investors in closed-end investment companies earn returns in a variety of ways. First, if the investment company collects dividends and interest on its portfolio, this income is distributed to the stockholders in the form of dividends. Second, if the value of the firm's assets increases, the company may sell the assets and realize the gains. These profits are then distributed as capital gains to the stockholders. Third, the net asset value of the portfolio may increase, which will cause the market price of the company's stock to rise. In this case, the investor may sell the shares in the secondary market and realize a capital gain. Fourth, the market price of the shares may rise relative to the net asset value (i.e., the premium may increase or the discount may decrease); the investor may then earn a profit through the sale of the shares.

These sources of return are illustrated in Exhibit 12.2, which presents the distributions and price changes over several years for Salomon Brothers Fund from December 31, 1996, through December 31, 2003. As may be seen in the exhibit, the investment company distributed cash dividends of $0.27 and capital gains of $2.63 in 1997. The net asset value rose from $17.26 to $18.51, and the price of the stock likewise rose (from $16 to $17.625). An investor who bought the shares on December 31, 1996, earned a total annual return of 28.3 percent (before commissions) on the investment.[2]

The potential for loss is also illustrated in Exhibit 12.2. If you bought the shares on December 31, 2000, you suffered a loss during 2001. While the fund distributed $0.11 in income and $0.33 in capital gains, the net asset value and the price of the stock declined sufficiently to more than offset the income and capital gains distributions.

MUTUAL FUNDS

Although open-end investment companies (*mutual funds*) are similar to closed-end investment companies, there are important differences. The first concerns their

---

EXHIBIT 12.2   Annual Returns on an Investment in Salomon Brothers Fund, a Closed-End Investment Company

Distributions and Price Changes	2003	2002	2001	2000	1999	1998	1997	1996
Per-share income distributions	$ 0.13	0.11	0.11	0.14	0.18	0.27	$0.27	0.33
Per-share capital gains distributions	–	$ 0.07	0.33	2.41	3.63	3.19	$2.63	2.09
Year-end net asset value	$14.04	10.75	14.07	16.27	19.24	18.76	$18.51	17.26
Year-end market price	$12.03	9.12	12.42	16.25	20.375	18.19	$17.625	16.00
Annual return based on prior year's market price								
a. Dividend yield	1.4%	0.8	0.7	0.7	1.0	1.5	1.7%	2.5
b. Capital gains yield	–	0.5	1.8	11.8	20.2	18.1	16.4%	15.6
c. Change in price	31.9%	–35.2	–13.4	–20.2	12.0	3.2	10.2%	19.6
Total return	33.3%	–33.9	–10.9	– 7.7	33.2	22.8	28.3%	37.7

Source: Salomon Brothers Fund (SBF) annual reports.

---

2. The calculation of the annual return is

$$\frac{\$17.625 + \$0.27 + \$2.63 - \$16}{\$16} = 28.3\%$$

Interactive e-lectures

See a visual explanation and example of mutual funds at

http://mayoxtra.swlearning.com

capital structure. Shares in mutual funds are not traded in the secondary markets. Instead, you purchase shares directly from the fund at the net asset value plus any applicable sales charge. After receiving the money, the mutual fund issues new shares and purchases assets with these newly acquired funds. If you own shares and want to liquidate the position, the shares are sold back to the company at the net asset value minus any applicable sales charge. The shares are redeemed, and the fund pays you from its cash holdings. If the fund lacks sufficient cash, it will sell some of the securities it owns to obtain the money to redeem the shares. The fund cannot suspend this redemption feature except in an emergency, and then it may be done only with the permission of the Securities and Exchange Commission.

The second difference between closed-end and open-end investment companies is the source of the return. As with closed-end investment companies, you may profit from investments in mutual funds from several sources. Any income that is earned from the fund's assets in excess of expenses is distributed as dividends. If the fund's assets appreciate in value and the fund realizes these profits, the gains are distributed as capital gains. If the net asset value of the shares appreciates, you may redeem them at the appreciated price. Thus, in general, the open-end mutual fund offers investors the same means of earning profits as the closed-end investment company does, with one exception. In the case of closed-end investment companies, the price of the stock may rise relative to the net asset value of the shares. The possibility of a decreased discount or an increased premium is a potential source of profit that is available only through closed-end investment companies. It does not exist for mutual funds because their shares never sell at a discount. (They actually sell for a premium if a sales charge is added to the net asset value.) Hence, changes in the discount or premium are a source of profit or loss to investors in closed-end but not in open-end investment companies.

A third important difference between open-end and closed-end investment companies is the cost of investing. Mutual funds continuously offer to sell new shares, and these shares may be sold at their net asset value plus a sales fee, which is commonly called a *loading charge* (also called a *load fee* or simply *load*). This cost and others, such as the 12b-1 fee covered later in this chapter, are disclosed in the fund's prospectus. When you liquidate the position, the shares are redeemed at their net asset value. For most funds no additional fees are charged for the sale.

The loading fee may range from zero for **no-load mutual funds** to between 3 and 6 percent for **load funds**. If the individual makes a substantial investment, the loading fee is usually reduced. For example, the American Balanced Fund (ABALX, or **http://www.americanfunds.com**) offers the following schedule of fees:

no-load mutual fund
A mutual fund that does not charge a commission for buying or selling its shares.

load fund
A mutual fund that charges a commission to purchase or sell its shares.

Investment	Fee
$0–50,000	5.75%
over 50,000	4.5
over 100,000	3.5
over 250,000	2.5

In addition to loading charges, investors in mutual funds have to pay a variety of other expenses. Each mutual fund is required to disclose in its prospectus these various costs, which are generally referred to as "fees and expenses." The costs associated with researching specific assets, brokerage fees charged when the fund buys and sells securities, and compensation to management are all costs that you, the investor, must bear. These expenses are the cost of owning the shares and are in addition to any sales fees (loading charges) you pay when the shares are purchased. The costs are generally expressed as a percentage of the fund's assets. A total expense ratio of 1.6 percent indicates that the fund's expenses are $1.60 for every $100 of assets. It should be obvious that the fund must earn at least $1.60 for each $100 in assets just to cover these costs, so if a fund earns 11.2 percent on its assets, the investor nets 9.6 percent.

The fees and expenses for three no-load mutual funds (Legg Mason High Yield Portfolio, Legg Mason Total Return Trust, and Schwab International Index Fund) are illustrated in Exhibit 12.3. The first three rows list the fees related to purchasing the shares. Because all three funds are no-load funds, there are no sales costs, but the Schwab International Fund does have a fee for early withdrawals. Such exit fees are designed to discourage frequent redemptions by investors seeking short-term gains. If you hold the shares for six months, the charge does not apply.

The management fee compensates the investment advisor for the general management of the fund's affairs. This fee generally runs from 0.5 to 1.0 percent of the fund's assets. Operating expenses cover record keeping, transaction costs, directors' fees, and legal and auditing expenses. The sum of these expenses tends to range from 0.3 to 0.7 percent of the fund's assets; including management and other expenses, the range increases to 0.8 to 1.7 percent of the fund's assets.

While management and other expenses are necessary fees, 12b-1 fees are nonessential costs. As is discussed later in this chapter, these are special charges for marketing and distribution services and may include commissions to brokers who sell the shares. The Schwab fund does not have a 12b-1 fee, but the two Legg Mason funds do. In contrast to the Legg Mason full-service brokerage firm, Schwab's brokers do not work on commission. The 12b-1 fee then compensates the Legg Mason brokers for selling the shares and covers any other expenses associated with advertising and marketing the fund. (The 12b-1 fee is discussed in the section on returns.)

The Portfolios of Mutual Funds

The portfolios of investment companies may be diversified or specialized. Specialized funds such as money market mutual funds or index funds have grown in

EXHIBIT 12.3	Cost Disclosures for Selected No-Load Mutual Funds		
	Legg Mason High Yield Portfolio	**Legg Mason Total Return Trust**	**Schwab International Index Fund**
Sales load	None	None	None
Early withdrawal fees	None	None	0.75%
Exchange fees	None	None	None
Management fees	0.65%	0.75%	0.45
Operating expenses	0.44	0.19	0.50
12b-1 fees	0.50	1.00	None
Total expenses	1.59	1.94	0.95

Source: Each fund's prospectus.

importance and are discussed in the next chapter. The more traditional funds may be classified by investment type or investment *style*. Investment type refers to the class or type of securities the fund acquires, such as income-producing bonds. Investment style refers to the fund's investment philosophy or strategy. Possible styles include the size of the firms acquired by the fund or the approach used to select securities.

Income funds stress assets that generate dividend and/or interest income. As its name implies, the Value Line Income Fund's objective is income. Virtually all of its assets are stocks such as utilities that distribute a large proportion of their earnings and periodically increase the dividend as their earnings grow. Growth funds, however, stress appreciation in the value of the assets, and little emphasis is given to current income. The portfolio of the Value Line Fund consists of common stocks of companies with potential for growth. These growth stocks may include large, well-known companies and smaller companies that may offer superior growth potential.

Even within the class of growth funds, there can be considerable differences. Some funds stress riskier securities in order to achieve faster appreciation and larger returns. For example, Janus Venture seeks capital appreciation by investing in small companies. Other growth funds, however, are more conservative. The Fidelity Fund is a growth fund emphasizing larger companies that are considered to offer capital appreciation but whose earnings are more stable and reliable.

Balanced funds own a mixture of securities that sample the attributes of many types of assets. The Fidelity Balanced Fund owns a variety of stocks, some of which offer potential growth while others are primarily income producers. A balanced fund's portfolio may also include short-term debt securities (e.g., Treasury bills), bonds, and preferred stock. Such a portfolio seeks a balance of income from dividends and interest plus some capital appreciation.

Investment style is built around the size of the firms acquired by the fund or the approach (growth or value) used to select stocks for inclusion in the portfolio. Firm size is referred to as *large cap*, *mid-cap*, or *small cap*. The word "cap" is short for *capitalization*, which refers to the market value of the company. The market value is the number of shares outstanding times the market price. Large cap stocks are the largest companies, with market value exceeding $5 to $10 billion. A small cap stock is a much smaller firm, perhaps with a total value of less than $1 billion. Mid-cap is, of course, between the two extremes. Actually the difference among a small cap, a mid-cap, and a large cap stock is arbitrary. A small cap stock could be less than $1 billion, less than $500 million, or less than $300 million total market value, depending on whose definition is being used. (Some classifications divide stocks into large cap and small cap and exclude mid-cap, and there are classifications that include micro- or mini-cap for even smaller firms.)

Two companies that use paper or produce paper products illustrate this difference in size. Chesapeake Corporation (CSK), a manufacturer of specialty packaging, has 15.2 million shares outstanding; at a price of $23, the total value of the stock is $349.6 million and would be classified as a small cap stock. Georgia Pacific (GP), a manufacturer of disposable paper products and building supplies, has 250.2 million shares outstanding. At a price of $34, the total value is $8.5 billion and would be classified as a large cap stock. It is obvious that CSK is small compared to GP and would not be an acceptable investment for a large cap portfolio even if the portfolio manager believed that the stock was undervalued.

An alternative strategy to capitalization-based investing is *style investing* based on *growth* or *value*. A growth fund portfolio manager identifies firms offering exceptional growth by employing techniques that analyze an industry's growth potential and the firm's position within the industry. A value manager acquires stock that is undervalued. A value approach stresses fundamental analysis and is based on investment tools such as P/E ratios and comparisons of financial statements. (Contrarian investors may be considered value investors since they are identifying strong stocks that are currently out of favor with the investment community.) Many technology stocks illustrate the difference between the growth and value approaches. Amazon.com may appeal to growth portfolio managers because the company was the first to market books via the Internet and has large growth potential. From a value perspective, the firm has no or at best meager earnings and is selling substantially above its value based on its accounting statements. Such a stock would not appeal to value investors.

A fund can have more than one style, such as "small cap–value," which suggests that the portfolio manager acquires shares in small companies that appear to be undervalued. A "small cap–growth" fund would stress small companies offering potential growth but not necessarily operating at a profit.

While various investment styles may seem complementary, a portfolio manager's style can be important, especially when evaluating performance. Presumably, a style portfolio manager offers the investor two things: (1) the style and (2) the investment skill. If a portfolio manager's style stresses small cap growth, that fund's performance should not be compared to the performance of large cap funds. Only through a consistent comparison of funds with similar strategies or styles can the portfolio manager's investment skill be isolated.

THE RETURNS EARNED ON INVESTMENTS IN MUTUAL FUNDS

As was previously explained, investment companies offer several advantages. First, you receive the advantage of a diversified portfolio. Many investors do not have sufficient resources to construct a diversified portfolio, and shares in an investment company permit these investors to own a portion of a diversified portfolio. Second, the portfolio is professionally managed and under continuous supervision. Many investors may not have the time, desire, or expertise to manage their own portfolios, and, except for large portfolios, may lack sufficient assets to obtain individualized professional management. Third, the administrative detail and custodial aspects of the portfolio are performed by the investment company.

However, there are also disadvantages to using investment companies. Their services are not unique but may be obtained elsewhere. For example, the trust department of a commercial bank offers professional management and custodial services. Leaving the securities with the broker and registering them in the broker's name relieves the investor of storing the securities and keeping some of the records. In addition, the investor may acquire a diversified portfolio with only a modest amount of capital. Diversification does not require 100 different stocks. If the investor has $20,000, a reasonably diversified portfolio may be produced by investing in the stock of eight to ten companies in different industries. You do not have to purchase shares in an investment company to obtain the advantage of diversification.

Investment companies do offer the advantage of professional management, but this management cannot guarantee to outperform the market. A particular fund may do well in any given year, but it may do poorly in subsequent years. Several studies have been undertaken to determine if professional management results in superior performance for mutual funds.

The first study, conducted for the SEC, found that the performance of mutual funds was not significantly different from that of an unmanaged portfolio of similar assets.[3] About half the funds outperformed Standard & Poor's indexes, but the other half underperformed these aggregate measures of the market. In addition, there was no evidence of superior performance by a particular fund over a number of years. These initial results were confirmed by later studies.[4] When loading charges are included in the analysis, the return earned by investors tends to be less than that which would be achieved through a random selection of securities.

Exhibit 12.4 provides annualized return and their standard deviations for several classes of funds for two five-year time periods: 1996–2000 and 1998–2002. The impact of the 2000–2002 bear market on fund returns is readily apparent. During both periods, many of the average returns (e.g., large cap and growth) were less than the return on the S&P 500 stock index, and their standard deviations were higher. These data support the general conclusion that in the aggregate, funds do not tend to outperform the market, and this inferior return may be accompanied by increased, not decreased, risk.

These results are easy to misinterpret. They do not imply that the managements of mutual funds are incompetent. The findings give support for the efficient market hypothesis. What these findings imply is that mutual funds and other investment companies may offer investors a means to match the performance of the market and still obtain the advantages of diversification and custodial services. For many individuals, these are sufficient reasons to invest in the shares of investment companies instead of directly in stocks and bonds. These investors do not have to concern themselves with the selection of individual securities.

EXHIBIT 12.4   Returns on Various Types of Low-Load and No-Load Mutual Funds

Fund Classification	Return 1996–2000	Standard Deviation of Return	Return 1998–2002	Standard Deviation of Return
Large cap	17.0%	18.8%	-0.9%	19.1
Small cap	15.1	31.1	1.2	23.8
Growth style	16.1	19.5	-1.5	26.7
Value style	14.4	18.1	2.6	17.4
Balanced	11.8	11.0	2.5	10.9
S&P 500	18.3	17.7	-0.5	18.8

Source: *The Individual Investor's Guide to Low-Load Mutual Funds*, 20th ed. (Chicago: American Association of Individual Investors, 2001), p. 30 and *The Individual Investor's Guide to Top Mutual Funds*, 22nd ed. (Chicago: American Association of Individual Investors, 2003), p. 71.

3. See Irwin Friend et al., *A Study of Mutual Funds* (Washington, DC: U.S. Government Printing Office, 1962).
4. See, for instance, William F. Sharpe, "Mutual Fund Performance," *Journal of Business*, special supplement, 39 (January 1966): 119–138; Michael C. Jensen, "The Performance of Mutual Funds in the Period 1945–64," *Journal of Finance* 23 (May 1968): 389–416; Patricia Dunn and Rolf D. Theisen, "How Consistently Do Active Managers Win?" *Journal of Portfolio Management* 9 (summer 1983): 47–50; and Frank J. Fabozzi, Jack C. Francis, and Cheng F. Lee, "Generalized Functional Form for Mutual Fund Performance," *Journal of Financial and Quantitative Analysis* 15 (December 1980): 1107–1120.

··•SELECTING MUTUAL FUNDS

There are over 8,000 U.S. mutual funds from which to choose. Obviously you cannot buy shares in all of them but must select among the alternatives. While investment companies may relieve you of selecting particular stocks and bonds, they *do not relieve you of having to select among the competing funds*.

Selecting a mutual fund initially requires matching your financial goals and the objectives of the fund. In addition, there are several other factors that can (and should) have an impact on your decision to invest in a particular mutual fund. These include fees and taxation in addition to returns the fund has earned.

Fees and Expenses

If you acquire mutual fund shares, you pay a variety of fees. These may include the loading charge, management fees, 12b-1 fees, and transaction costs incurred by the fund.

Whether the load charge is worth the cost is, of course, open to considerable debate, but there is little evidence that load funds earn a higher return than no-load funds. The load must be justified on the basis of services received. You must find a broker or financial advisor whose advice and help are worth the load fee.

By acquiring no-load funds, the load expense is avoided, but you continue to bear the remaining expenses. Management fees, operating expenses, and transaction costs apply to all funds. While these expenses cannot be avoided, they do differ among the various funds. You should consider these costs, because they obviously decrease returns. Higher-than-average management and operating expenses and frequent portfolio turnover, which generates higher transaction costs, are possible red flags you should take into account when selecting a particular mutual fund for purchase.

You may particularly want to analyze 12b-1 fees, which are marketing expenses and are assessed each year by many no-load funds. Over a period of years, 12b-1 fees can exceed load expenses. Excluding the impact of compounding, a $0.50 annual 12b-1 fee exceeds a $3.00 load fee after six years. If you hold the shares for ten years and pay the 12b-1 fee each year, you would have been better off buying a load fund without the 12b-1 fee. (Unfortunately, some load funds also charge 12b-1 fees.)

Tax Efficiency

Interactive e-lectures

See a visual explanation and example of tax efficiency at

http://mayoxtra.swlearning.com

Mutual fund fees obviously affect an investor's return. Load charges, operating expenses, marketing expenses (12b-1 fees), and commissions paid by the fund reduce the return the investor earns. While funds with lower fees may be preferred, there are reasons why some fees are larger and the increased expense is justified. For example, funds that specialize in foreign investments may have larger expenses because foreign operations cost more and obtaining information on which to base security purchases or sales may be more difficult. Obviously, if you want shares in the foreign fund for some purpose (e.g., diversification), the higher fees may be justified.

While fees affect the fund's return, taxes affect the return the investor retains. Mutual fund returns are before tax, but income and capital gains taxes affect the after-tax return the investor retains. Consider three funds: The net asset value of each is $20 and each earns a return of 10 percent. You buy one share for $20. Fund A consists solely of stocks that are never sold, so at the end of the second year, the fund's net asset value is $22 ($20 × 1.1), and you have stock worth $22.

Fund B collects interest of 10 percent on its investments in bonds. Thus, during the first year, the fund earns $2 and distributes $2. The fund's earnings initially increased its NAV to $22, but after the $2 income distribution, the NAV returns to $20. You reinvest the $2 into 0.1 shares and own 1.1 shares worth $22.

Fund C invests in stock that appreciates 10 percent, then is sold and the gain distributed. The fund's NAV initially increased to $22, but after the $2 capital gain distribution, the NAV returns to $20. You reinvest the $2 into 0.1 shares and have 1.1 shares worth $22.

All three cases end with you owning funds worth $22. However, there is a tax difference. Fund A had no security sales, and you have no tax obligations. Fund B's $2 distribution is subject to income taxes, and Fund C's $2 distribution is subject to capital gains taxation. There is an obvious difference in the investor's tax obligations generated by each fund.

The ability of the fund to generate returns without generating large amounts of tax obligations is the fund's tax efficiency. Obviously, if the fund never realizes any capital gains and does not receive any income, there will be no distributions and you have no tax obligations. This, however, is unlikely. (Even a passively managed index fund may receive dividend income from its portfolio. This income is distributed and the investor becomes liable for taxes on the distribution.) At the other extreme are the funds that frequently turn over their portfolios. Each security sale is a taxable event. *Such frequent turnover implies the fund will not generate long-term capital gains.* The capital gains and the distributions will be short-term and subject to tax at the stockholder's marginal federal income tax rate.

If the fund turns over its portfolio less frequently, the capital gains it realizes and the subsequent distributions may be long-term. Since long-term capital gains are taxed at favorable (lower) rates, the fund's ability to generate long-term instead of short-term capital gains is more favorable from a tax perspective.

"Tax efficiency" is an index that converts mutual fund returns to an after-tax basis by expressing the after-tax return as a percentage of the before-tax return, which permits comparisons based on a fund's ability to reduce stockholder tax obligations. The computation of tax efficiency requires assumptions concerning tax rates. In the following example, an income tax rate is assumed to be 35 percent, and the long-term capital gains tax rate is assumed to be 15 percent. Fund A's return consisted solely of unrealized capital appreciation. Since there is no tax, the after-tax and before-tax returns are equal so the tax efficiency is 100 percent. Fund B's return is entirely subject to income tax of $0.70 (0.35 × $2 = $0.70). While the before-tax return is 10 percent, the after-tax return is 6.5 percent ($1.30/$2). The tax efficiency index is 65 (6.5%/10%). Fund C's return consisted of realized long-term capital gains, which generated $0.30 in taxes (0.15 × $2.00). The after-tax return is 8.5 percent ($1.70/$2), so the tax efficiency index is 85. Since the tax efficiency index for each of the three funds is 100, 65, and 85, on an after-tax basis the performance ranking is A, C, and B.

Under the federal tax law enacted in 2003, if Fund B's income had been dividends on stock investments and not interest on bond investments, the appropriate tax rate would have been 15 percent. In that case the taxes owed would have been $0.30 and the after-tax return would have been 8.5 percent. The tax efficiency index would be 85, the same as the index for Fund C, which had only long-term capital gains. From a tax perspective, the composition of a fund's return is obviously important!

While the tax efficiency index may seem appealing, it has several weaknesses. To construct the tax efficiency index, you need the composition of the returns and the appropriate tax rates in effect when the returns were earned. Tax rates vary with changes in the tax laws, but even without changes in the tax laws, the appropriate income tax rate may differ as you move from one tax bracket to another. The tax efficiency index varies among investors, and published tax efficiency rankings may not be appropriate if your tax bracket differs from those used to construct the index.

A second weakness is that a high tax efficiency index may be achieved when the fund does not realize capital gains. When these gains are realized, the tax efficiency ratio will decline. In terms of the illustration, Fund A's high rating will fall when the gains are realized. Thus, while a high tax efficiency ratio indicates lower taxes in the past, it may also imply higher taxes in the future. For this reason the index needs to be computed over a period of years so that differences in the timing of security sales from one year to the next are eliminated.

A third weakness is that high efficiency may not alter performance rankings. Funds with similar objectives and styles (e.g., long-term growth through investments in large cap stocks) may generate similar tax obligations. Suppose one fund's return is 20 percent while another fund generates 16 percent. All gains are distributed and are long-term. The tax efficiency for both funds is the same, so the relative ranking is unchanged. Unless the second fund can perceptibly save on taxes, its performance will be inferior on both a before- and after-tax basis.

Consistency of Returns

One system for selecting mutual funds may be to purchase shares in a fund that has done well. The premise is that the best-performing funds will continue to do well (i.e., going with the "hot hands"). Certainly the large amount of publicity in the popular financial press given to the funds that do well during a particular time period encourages individuals to invest in those funds. Money does flow into funds that have a superior track record, and, since fees increase as the funds under management grow, it should not be surprising to learn that mutual funds tout any evidence of superior performance.

Consistency of mutual fund performance is intuitively appealing. Such consistency seems to apply to many areas of life. For example, several baseball teams make the playoffs virtually every year. However, the material on efficient markets suggests the opposite may apply to mutual funds. Essentially the question is: If stock market prices have no memory and past stock performance has no predictive power, why should historical mutual fund performance have predictive power? The answer, of course, may be the superior skills of the fund's managers. If fund managers have superior skills, then the portfolios they manage should consistently outperform the portfolios of less-skilled managers.

Studies have been conducted to determine the consistency of fund returns. Nonacademic studies tend to suggest consistency. For example, a study by the Institute for Economic Research indicated that past performance did predict future performance.[5] The results were consistent over different time horizons; for example, 26-week returns forecasted the next 26-week returns and one-year returns predicted the next year returns. Results tended to be best over the longest time horizons. Funds with the highest returns over a period of five years consistently did better during the next two years than the funds with the lowest returns.

---

5. "Mutual Fund Hot Hands: Go with the Winners," Institute for Economic Research (April 1998). Information concerning this study may be obtained from the Institute at 2200 S.W. 10th St., Deerfield Beach, FL 33442.

The results of academic studies, however, are ambiguous. Although some support consistency, others do not.[6] At least one study explained the observed consistency on the basis of the fund's investment objective or style and not on the basis of the portfolio manager's skill.[7] For example, suppose large cap stocks do well while small cap stocks do poorly. Large cap mutual funds should consistently outperform small cap funds. Once the returns are standardized for the investment style, the consistency of the returns disappears. The superior performance of the large cap mutual funds is the result of market movements and not the result of the skill of the portfolio managers. The consistently better-performing large cap stocks give the impression that the large cap mutual funds are the consistently better-performing mutual funds.[8] These findings, of course, support the concept of efficient markets. One set of portfolio managers is not superior to another. Their better performance in one period does not predict superior returns in the next period. Once again, past performance is not indicative of future performance. Past prices have no memory and do not predict future prices.

One major problem facing all studies of the consistency of returns is "survival bias." Suppose an investment management firm has two mutual funds, A and B, which earn 20 and 5 percent, respectively. For some reason (possibly skill, possibly luck) the management of Fund A did perceptibly better than the management of Fund B. Can the investment management firm erase Fund B's performance? The answer is yes! One possibility is to merge Fund B into Fund A. Since Fund A survives, the performance data of B are buried. That is the essence of survival bias—poorly performing funds cease to exist and their performance data disappear.[9]

Does this happen? The answer is unequivocally yes, and there are stunning illustrations. In 1993, the $334 million Putnam Strategic Income Fund was merged into Putnam Equity Income. Prior to the merger, the Putnam Equity Income Fund had only $1 million in assets, so the merger buried the performance of a much larger fund. During the mid-1990s Dreyfus merged or liquidated 14 funds. In late 1998, a plan existed to merge and combine several Steadman funds, which were among the industry's worst-performing funds.[10]

From your perspective, liquidations and mergers are important when interpreting data concerning the consistency of performance. If funds that did poorly

6. A sampling of this research includes: Ronald N. Kahn and Andrew Rudd, "Does Historical Performance Predict Future Performance?" *Financial Analysts Journal* (November–December 1995): 43–51. This study found consistency only in fixed-income funds. William N. Goetzmann and Roger G. Ibbotson, "Do Winners Repeat?" *Journal of Portfolio Management* (winter 1994): 9–18. This study found consistency in both raw returns and after adjusting for risk using the Jensen alpha. W. Scott Bauman and Robert E. Miller, "Can Managed Portfolio Performance Be Predicted?" *Journal of Portfolio Management* (summer 1994): 31–39. This study found consistency over long periods of time (i.e., stock cycles).

7. See, for instance, F. Larry Detzel and Robert A. Weigand, "Explaining Persistence in Mutual Fund Performance," *Financial Services Review* 7, no. 1 (1998): 45–55; and Gary E. Porter and Jack W. Trifts, "Performance of Experienced Mutual Fund Managers," *Financial Services Review* 7, no. 1 (1998): 56–68.

8. An extreme example would be the gold funds. Since the price of gold has stagnated for years, these funds have consistently been among the worst-performing mutual funds. However, if the portfolio manager's job is to operate a gold fund, such consistent inferior performance would be the result of the sector in which the fund invested and not of the portfolio manager's lack of skill. (See the discussion of appropriate benchmarks in the next chapter.)

9. For example, Burton Malkiel has suggested that performance consistency is largely explained by survival bias. His study found that mutual funds tend to underperform the market and that consistency, which may have existed in the 1970's, has subsequently disappeared. See Burton G. Malkiel, "Returns from Investing in Equity Mutual Funds, 1971–1991," *Journal of Finance* (June 1995): 549–572.

10. See "Davis Schedules the Ultimate Fund Killing," *Mutual Funds* (February 1999): 30–32.

cease to exist while funds that do well continue to operate, you may conclude that funds perform better than is the case. Returns from poor funds are ignored. Of course, investors who owned the poorly performing funds will have actual returns that are perceptibly less than the returns reported by the surviving fund.

SELLING/REDEEMING MUTUAL FUND SHARES

You may buy a stock because you think the company is undervalued. If you are right and the price subsequently rises, you could sell the stock and realize the capital gain. You may purchase bonds in anticipation of lower interest rates. You want to lock in the higher yields or speculate that the prices of the bonds will rise as rates decline. You may subsequently sell the bonds in anticipation that interest rates will rise again. Positions in stocks and bonds are sold every trading day. If some investors were not selling, markets would cease to exist—there has to be a seller for every buyer.

Shares in mutual funds may also be liquidated, but since there is no secondary market, the shares are sold back to the fund (i.e., redeemed). Most written material on mutual funds is concerned with acquiring the shares and covers such topics as the features and objectives of various funds, the variety of funds, and the returns they have earned. Not much is written concerning the selling or liquidation of positions in mutual funds. There is, however, no reason to assume that shares once acquired will be held forever; indeed, there are several reasons why you should redeem your shares in mutual funds.

Presumably you acquire the shares to meet financial goals, so the most obvious reason for redeeming the shares is that these goals have been achieved. For example, funds acquired to finance a college education are redeemed to meet that expense. A growth fund acquired while the investor is working may be redeemed when the individual retires and needs a flow of income provided by a bond or balanced fund.

Meeting your financial goal(s) is only one of many reasons for liquidating a position in a mutual fund. For example, investors may acquire a particular mutual fund to meet a specific financial goal, but these objectives are not static. The birth of a child, a death in the family, a change in employment, divorce, or a major illness may alter the investor's financial situation and necessitate a change in the portfolio. A mutual fund that met prior financial objectives may no longer be suitable—in which case, the position is liquidated and the funds invested elsewhere.

Shares may be redeemed for tax purposes. If you have a capital loss from another source, you may liquidate a position in a mutual fund to offset the tax loss. Conversely, if you have a loss in the fund, the shares may be redeemed to offset capital gains from other sources. If there are no offsetting capital gains, the loss may be used to reduce ordinary income (subject to the limitations on capital gain losses offsetting ordinary income as discussed in Chapter 2). The proceeds may be used to invest in an alternative fund with the same or similar goals.

The three previous reasons for liquidating a position (financial goals have been met, financial goals have changed, and tax considerations) apply to the individual investor. There are also reasons for liquidating a position that pertain to the individual fund. A fund's specified objective may change, or the fund's portfolio may not appear to meet its objective. For example, you may question the appropriateness of a growth fund's purchasing shares in a regulated utility. In response, you may redeem the shares to place the proceeds in an alternative fund with a more appropriate portfolio.

The fund may change its investment strategies while maintaining its objective. For example, a growth fund may start using derivative securities in an attempt to increase its return. A large proportion of the fund's portfolio may be invested in foreign securities or in securities of firms in emerging economies. While these strategies may be consistent with the fund's objective, they may be inconsistent with your willingness to bear risk, in which case you may redeem the shares.

A change in the fund's management may also be cause for liquidating a position. While the management of a corporation may be replaced, it may take years for the firm to be transformed—if it is changed at all. For example, it is doubtful that a new management at Hershey's or Heinz will change the basic products sold by these firms. However, a change in a fund's portfolio manager can have an immediate impact, since the portfolio may be easily altered. A fund with a poor performance record may improve while a fund with an excellent record may deteriorate after a change in its principal portfolio manager. For instance, the investor who supports the theory concerning a fund's consistency of performance would consider a change in a fund's portfolio manager to be important and may redeem the shares in response to the change.

Past performance may also induce you to redeem shares. If the fund consistently underperforms its peer group, you may redeem the shares and invest the proceeds elsewhere. The rationale for such a move again supports the consistency argument: Poor-performing funds will continue to underperform. However, you need to define underperformance and its duration. Does underperformance mean 0.5 percent, 2 percent, or a larger percentage? Is consistency two quarters, two years, or longer?

There are still other possible reasons for redeeming shares: (1) the fund's expenses are high relative to the expenses of comparable funds, (2) the fund becomes too large, or (3) the fund merges with or acquires another fund. Once again, you will have to make a judgment as to what constitutes "higher expenses" or "too large" or if the merger is potentially detrimental. If there were obvious answers to these questions, investing would be simple and mechanical. But investing is neither simple nor mechanical, and acquiring shares in mutual funds does not absolve the individual from having to make investment decisions. While you do not determine which specific assets to include in the portfolio, investing in mutual funds requires some active management. A portfolio of mutual funds may require less supervision than a portfolio of individual stocks and bonds, but it should not necessarily be considered a passive investment strategy.

SUMMARY

Instead of directly purchasing securities, you may buy shares in investment companies, which acquire stocks and bonds that meet the fund's (and presumably your) financial objectives. There are two types of investment companies. A closed-end investment company has a specified number of shares that are bought and sold in the same manner as the stock of IBM. An open-end investment company (a mutual fund) has a variable number of shares that are sold to and repurchased (redeemed) from the individual investor.

Investment companies offer several advantages including professional management and diversification. Dividends and interest earned on the fund's assets and realized capital gains are distributed to stockholders, who may have the distributions reinvested in the fund.

Mutual funds may be classified by the types of assets they own, such as bonds, growth stocks, or income stocks. Mutual funds may also be classified according to style, based on the market value (capitalization) of the stocks they acquire. Capitalizations range from large cap to small cap companies. Style investing may also combine growth or value and capitalization, so that some funds are classified as large cap growth funds while others may be small cap value funds.

When you are selecting a mutual fund, you should match the fund's objectives with your financial goals. Other considerations include the fund's expenses and fees, especially 12b-1 fees and loading charges, which reduce your return. You should also consider the fund's tax efficiency, since you pay income and capital gains taxes on the fund's distributions and realized returns. While the fund's objectives, fees, expenses, and the taxation of its distributions may be considerations when selecting a fund, efficient markets suggest that few funds will outperform the market consistently. Historical returns in general support market efficiency as it applies to investments in mutual funds. Although investment companies are professionally managed, historical returns indicate that over a period of years few fund managers consistently outperform the market. And those that do outperform in a particular year rarely repeat those superior results.

Investments should be made to meet specified financial goals. When your financial goals have been met or have changed, positions in specific investment companies may be liquidated. The proceeds may then be invested in different mutual funds that are better designed to meet your new financial goals. Changes in a fund's management, increases in fund expenses, and consistent poor performance are also reasons for liquidating a position in a specific mutual fund and investing the proceeds in an alternative fund.

Learning Objectives

Now that you have completed this chapter, you should be able to:

1. Differentiate between closed-end and open-end investment companies.
2. Identify the sources of return associated with investing in mutual funds and closed-end investment companies.
3. List the advantages offered by investment companies.
4. Explain why a closed-end investment company may sell for a discount but a mutual fund cannot.
5. Distinguish among load fees, 12b-1 fees, and operating expenses.
6. Contrast mutual funds based on investment style.
7. Explain how a fund's tax efficiency may help you select among competing mutual funds.
8. List several factors to consider when selecting a mutual fund for possible investment.
9. List several factors to consider when deciding to redeem shares in a mutual fund.

PROBLEMS

1) What is the net asset value of an investment company with $10,000,000 in assets, $790,000 in current liabilities, and 1,200,000 shares outstanding?

2) If a mutual fund's net asset value is $23.40 and the fund sells its shares for $25, what is the load fee as a percentage of the net asset value (i.e., the amount actually invested in the shares)?

3) If an investor buys shares in a no-load mutual fund for $31.40 and the shares appreciate to $44.60 in a year, what would be the percentage return on the investment? If the fund charges an exit fee of 1 percent, what would be the return on the investment?

4) An investor buys shares in a mutual fund for $20 per share. At the end of the year the fund distributes a dividend of $0.58, and after the distribution the net asset value of a share is $23.41. What would be the investor's percentage return on the investment?

5) Consider the following four investments.

   a) You invest $3,000 annually in a mutual fund that earns 10 percent annually, and you reinvest all distributions. How much will you have in the account at the end of 20 years?

   b) You invest $3,000 annually in a mutual fund with a 5 percent load fee so that only $2,850 is actually invested in the fund. The fund earns 10 percent annually, and you reinvest all distributions. How much will you have in the account at the end of 20 years? (Assume that all distributions are not subject to the load fee.)

   c) You invest $3,000 annually in a no-load mutual fund that charges 12b-1 fees of 1 percent. The fund earns 10 percent annually before fees, and you reinvest all distributions. How much will you have in the account at the end of 20 years?

   d) You invest $3,000 annually in a no-load mutual fund that has a 5 percent exit fee. The fund earns 10 percent annually before fees, and you reinvest all distributions. How much will you have in the account at the end of 20 years?

   In each case you invest the same amount ($3,000) every year; the fund earns the same return each year (10 percent), and you make each investment for the same time period (20 years). At the end of the 20 years, you withdraw the funds. Why is the final amount in each mutual fund different?

Internet Application for Chapter 12   Investment Companies

Families of funds such as Fidelity Investments or Vanguard offer similar products. One advantage associated with investing in the funds of one family is the ease of transferring money from one fund to another. (There is no tax advantage; the sale of one Vanguard fund to move the money into a different Vanguard fund is a taxable transaction unless the investments are in tax-deferred accounts.)

You would like to construct a diversified portfolio of funds that include a growth fund, a bond fund, a value fund, and a specialized health care fund. You are considering several families, including the following:

American Century   http://americancentury.com

Fidelity Investments   http://www.fidelity.com

Janus   http://www.janus.com

T. Rowe Price   http://www.troweprice.com

Schwab   http://www.schwab.com

Strong Funds   http://www.strong-funds.com

The Vanguard Group   http://www.vanguard.com

Answer the following questions for at least three of the families.

1. Do all the families offer the alternatives you want?

2. What was each fund's return for the previous year?

3. Did one family of funds consistently perform better than the other families?

4. Find a measure of risk (e.g., standard deviation of returns or beta co-efficients) and compare the funds' risk-adjusted returns.

Additional information on funds may be found at:

Investment Company Institute   http://www.ici.org

Bloomberg   http://www.bloomberg.com

ICI Mutual Fund Connection   http://www.ici.org

Morningstar   http://www.morningstar.com

Mutual Fund Investor's Center   http://www.mfea.com

Yahoo! Finance   http://finance.yahoo.com

Value Line Investment Research and Asset Management   http://www.valueline.com

CHAPTER

13 • • •

Specialized Investment Companies and Benchmarking Performance

The prior chapter covered the basics concerning investment companies. These mutual funds and closed-end investment companies are an important facet of the financial market. They permit you to have a diversified portfolio without having to select individual stocks and bonds. The industry, however, is not static and has developed a wide range of products designed to entice the funds of investors.

One of the most important developments has been the creation of specialized funds whose purpose is not the construction of a broad-based portfolio. Instead these funds acquire assets other than stocks (money market mutual funds and real estate investment trusts) or own stocks that are limited to a particular segment of the financial markets (mutual funds with foreign investments and socially responsible funds) or stocks based solely on an index of the market (index funds and exchange-traded funds). These funds offer you a real alternative to the traditional investments held by most mutual funds.

This chapter is primarily devoted to these specialized funds. Much of the material in the previous chapter applies to these investment companies. They receive the same favorable tax treatment, have the same types of fees, and are bought and sold in the same manner as equity mutual funds and closed-end investment companies. What differentiates the specialized fund is its purpose and the portfolios it constructs.

The chapter also covers a means to compare investment companies' performance. Although the absolute return is important, the risk assumed to earn that return is also important. The previous chapter suggested that you should not select funds based solely on past performance. This is especially true because past performance may not be indicative of future performance. Instead you should prefer no-load funds with lower fees and higher tax efficiency that meet your financial goals.

Even if you do look at past performance as a guide to selecting funds, a higher return does not necessarily imply superior performance. The return by itself does not take into consideration risk. If a fund's portfolio managers acquire a riskier portfolio, the fund should earn a higher return to compensate you for the additional risk. This chapter ends with a section on three methods for integrating the analysis of the risk associated with a fund's portfolio with the fund's performance. These risk-adjusted measures of performance are important because they facilitate your comparing mutual funds on a risk-adjusted basis.

MONEY MARKET MUTUAL FUNDS AND MONEY MARKET INSTRUMENTS

money market mutual funds
Mutual funds that specialize in short-term securities.

money market instruments
Short-term securities, such as Treasury bills, negotiable certificates of deposit, or commercial paper.

As the name implies, **money market mutual funds** are investment companies that acquire **money market instruments**, which are short-term securities issued by banks, nonbank corporations, and governments. They specialize solely in short-term securities and provide investors with an alternative to savings and time deposits offered by banks. Money market mutual funds thus compete directly with commercial banks and other depository institutions for the deposits of savers, while regular mutual funds offer an alternative means to own stocks and bonds.

Money market funds invest in a variety of short-term securities such as the Treasury bills discussed in Chapter 10. Other short-term securities include the negotiable certificate ("negotiable CDs") issued by commercial banks, commercial paper, repurchase agreements ("repos"), banker's acceptances, and tax anticipation notes.

Commercial paper is an unsecured promissory note issued by a corporation. Since the paper is unsecured, only creditworthy corporations are able to issue commercial paper. Like Treasury bills, commercial paper is initially sold at a discount. With the passage of time, the interest accrues and the discount disappears when the paper is redeemed for its face value. A repo is the sale of a security (such as a Treasury bill) in which the seller agrees to buy back (repurchase) the security at a specific price at a specified future date. The repurchase price is higher than the initial sale price and the difference between the initial sale price and the subsequent repurchase price is the source of the buyer's return.

A banker's acceptance is a short-term promissory note guaranteed by a bank. These acceptances arise through international trade. Suppose a firm ships goods abroad and receives a draft drawn on a specific bank that promises payment after two months. If the firm does not want to wait for payment, it can take the draft to a commercial bank for acceptance. Once the bank accepts the draft (and stamps it "accepted"), the draft may be sold. The buyer purchases the draft for a discount, which becomes the source of the return to the holder. Banker's acceptances are considered to be good short-term investments because they are supported by two parties: the firm on which the draft is drawn and the bank that accepts the draft.

Tax anticipation notes are issued by states or municipalities to finance current operations before tax revenues are received. As the taxes are collected, the proceeds are used to retire the debt. Similar notes are issued in anticipation of revenues from future bond issues and other sources, such as revenue sharing from the federal government. These anticipation notes do not offer the safety of Treasury bills, but the interest is exempt from federal income taxation. Commercial banks and securities dealers maintain secondary markets in them, so the notes may be liquidated should the noteholder need cash.

While money market mutual funds can invest in any of the money market instruments, some do specialize. The Schwab U.S. Treasury Money Fund invests solely in U.S. government securities or securities that are collateralized by obligations of the federal government. Other money market funds invest in a wider spectrum of short-term debt obligations. The Schwab Money Fund usually has few investments in Treasury securities. Instead it purchases negotiable CDs, commercial paper, and repos.

The yields earned on investments in money market funds closely mirror the yields on short-term securities. For example, since the Schwab U.S. Treasury Money Fund invests solely in federal government or federal government-backed securities, its yield mirrors the return on these government securities. This relationship must occur. When the short-term debt matures, the proceeds can only be reinvested at the going rate paid by short-term government securities. Hence changes in short-term interest rates paid by these securities are quickly transferred to the individual money market mutual fund.

Money market fund shares are always priced at $1.00. If, however, the short-term debt instruments held by a money fund were to default, the value of the shares could decline and be worth less than $1.00. In that case investors would sustain a loss. While no one has suffered a loss from purchasing shares in a money market fund, there have been cases in which the sponsor put cash in the fund to cover losses and maintain the $1.00 price. For example, when Mercury Finance Corporation defaulted on its commercial paper, the Strong family of funds covered the losses.

While cash infusions have occurred in the past, you should not conclude that future losses sustained by a money market fund will be covered by the fund's sponsor. However, the regulations under which the funds operate and the commitment of their sponsors certainly suggests that money market funds are among the safest short-term investments available to you to park your cash.

REAL ESTATE INVESTMENT TRUSTS (REITs)

Real estate investment trusts (common called REITs) are closed-end investment companies that specialize in real estate or real estate loans (mortgages). As long as a REIT derives 75 percent of its income from real estate (interest on mortgage loans and rents) and distributes 90 percent of the income as cash dividends, the trust is exempt from federal income tax. Thus, REITs, like mutual funds and other closed-end investment companies, are conduits through which earnings pass to the shareholders.

Shares of REITs are traded on the NYSE or through the Nasdaq stock market. The existence of these markets means that the shares of REITs may be readily bought and sold. This ease of marketability certainly differentiates shares of REITs from other types of real estate investments. While buildings may be bought and sold, there is no ready secondary market for many real estate properties.

Since a REIT distributes virtually all its earned income to maintain its tax status, the result is greater dividend yields than may be available through most stock investments. Selected dividend yields offered by REITs are provided in Exhibit 13.1, and yields in excess of 7 percent are common from investments in REITs.

In addition to higher dividend yields, the tax regulations produce fluctuations in a trust's dividend payments. While other companies tend to maintain stable dividends and increase them only after there has been an increase in earnings that management

EXHIBIT 13.1   Selected REITs and Their Dividend Yields

Firm	Price of Stock as of April 12, 2004	Annual Dividend	Dividend Yield
Commercial Net Lease Realty	$16.87	$1.28	7.0%
First Industrial Realty	34.07	2.74	7.2
HR Properties Trust	9.59	0.80	7.6
United Dominion REIT	15.31	1.17	6.1
Washington REIT	28.31	1.49	5.0

Source: http://www.quicken.com/investments.

anticipates will be maintained, the dividends of REITs will fluctuate with changes in earnings. Higher earnings will lead to higher dividend payments, but lower earnings will decrease dividend payments. While many trusts seek to increase dividend payments periodically, there is the obvious possibility that lower earnings will immediately be translated into lower dividend payments. Shares of REITs, therefore, may not be desirable investments for individuals who need assured and stable sources of dividend income. If, however, you can tolerate fluctuations in your dividend income, you may prefer the shares of REITs since the trusts offer both higher yields and the potential for future dividend growth as rents and property values increase.

Classification of REITs

equity trust
A real estate investment trust that specializes in acquiring real estate for subsequent rental income.

mortgage trust
A real estate investment trust that specializes in loans secured by real estate.

REITs may be grouped according to either the types of assets they acquire or their capital structure. **Equity trusts** own property and rent it to other firms (i.e., they lease their property to others). **Mortgage trusts** make loans to develop property and finance buildings. There is a considerable difference between these two approaches to investing in real estate. Loans to help finance real estate, especially developmental loans, can earn high interest rates, but some of these loans can be very risky. Contractors may be unable to sell or lease the completed buildings, which may consequently cause them to default on their loans. In addition, any inflation in the value of the property cannot be enjoyed by the lender, who owns a fixed obligation.

In an equity trust, the REIT owns the property and rents space. This also is risky because the properties may remain vacant. Unleased property, of course, does not generate revenue, but the trust still has expenses, such as insurance, maintenance, and depreciation. These fixed expenses can generate large fluctuations in earnings of an equity trust. However, should there be an increase in property values, the trust may experience capital appreciation.

The second method for differentiating REITs is according to their capital structures or the extent to which they use debt financing. Some trusts use modest amounts of debt financing, while others use a large amount of leverage. The latter can be very risky investments. If a REIT's loans turn sour and the borrowers default, or if the properties become vacant, the trust may have difficulty meeting its own obligations. Thus, while the use of debt financing magnifies fluctuations in a REIT's cash flow and earnings, low use of financial leverage suggests a REIT is better positioned to survive a period of recession.

These differences among REITs are illustrated in Exhibit 13.2, which presents real estate as a percentage of the trust's assets and its use of debt financing as measured by the debt ratio. The entries are listed in descending order according to their debt ratios. Allied Capital Corporation is a mortgage trust that owns no properties. Its property loans finance commercial real estate, such as offices, retail stores, and hotels. United Dominion REIT is an equity trust (primarily apartments) with over 60 percent of its assets debt financed. Commercial Net Lease Realty is also an equity trust but finances its assets with less debt. While Commercial Net Lease Realty's use of less debt financing suggests that it is less risky than UDR, its commercial properties may be subject to increased vacancy rates. It has more business risk than United Dominion.

INVESTMENT COMPANIES WITH FOREIGN PORTFOLIOS

From a U.S. perspective, there are basically four types of mutual funds with international investments. **Global funds** invest in foreign and U.S. securities. Many

EXHIBIT 13.2	Selected REITs by Type of Assets and Capital Structure	
REIT	Real Estate as a Percentage of Total Assets	Debt Ratio (Debt to Total Assets)
United Dominion REIT	96.6%	67.3%
Washington REIT	93.5	56.6
Commercial Net Lease Realty	85.1	42.5
Allied Capital Corporation	0.0	36.4

Source: 2002 annual reports.

global funds
Mutual funds whose portfolios includedsecurities of firms with international operations that are located throughout the world.

international funds
American mutual funds whose portfolios are limited to non-American firms.

regional funds
Mutual funds that specialize in a particular geographical area.

emerging market fund
Investment company that specializes in securities from less-developed countries.

U.S. mutual funds are global, as they maintain some part of their portfolios in foreign investments. Although these funds do not specialize in foreign securities, they do offer the advantages associated with foreign investments: returns through global economic growth, diversification from assets whose returns are not highly positively correlated with U.S. stocks, and possible excess returns from inefficient foreign financial markets.

In addition to global funds, there are **international funds**, which invest solely in foreign securities and hold no U.S. securities, and **regional funds**, which specialize in a particular geographical area, such as Asia. (There are also mutual funds that specialize in a particular area within the United States, such as the North Star Fund, which invests in firms located in seven upper Midwest states.) The regional funds obviously specialize, and the international funds may also specialize during particular time periods. Thus it is not unusual for an international fund to invest a quarter or more of its assets in the shares of firms in a particular country.

The last type of mutual fund with international investments is the **emerging market fund**, which specializes in securities of firms located in less-developed nations. In many cases, emerging market funds specialize in specific countries, such as the Indonesia Fund or the Turkish Investment Fund. Such funds give you the opportunity to invest in specific markets without specialized knowledge of local firms or laws concerning security transactions in that country. In addition, the governments of some countries with emerging securities markets forbid foreign ownership of securities (perhaps to avoid foreign control or influence). Such governments, however, may grant a specific investment company the right to own securities issued in that country. In such cases, the only means by which the U.S. investor may participate in that specific market is through the ownership of shares in the emerging market fund.

Many of the regional and emerging market funds are closed-end investment companies, whose shares trade on the NYSE. A sampling of such funds is provided in Exhibit 13.3 (p. 356). The exhibit includes funds that specialize in developed economies such as Japan and that specialize in emerging markets such as Malaysia. The price of these shares can be volatile since it depends on both the fund's net asset value and speculative interest in the shares. This speculative interest may cause the shares to sell for a large premium over their net asset value. For example, when the political climate in Germany changed with the fall of the Berlin Wall, the Germany Fund's shares sold for a premium in excess of 80 percent over their net asset value.

Investing in foreign securities offers three possible advantages. The first is the obvious advantage associated with investing in economies and firms experiencing economic growth. The two other advantages, however, may be more important for an individual's portfolio, since economic growth is not unique to foreign firms and foreign economies. (IBM during the 1970s, Limited Brands during the 1980s,

EXHIBIT 13.3   Selected Specialized Country Closed-End Investment Companies Traded on the New York Stock Exchange

Fund	Ticker Symbol
Developed Nations	
Austria Fund	OST
France Growth Fund	FRF
Germany Fund	GER
Italy Fund	ITA
Japan Equity Fund	JEQ
Spain Fund	SNF
Swiss Helvetia Fund	SWZ
United Kingdom Fund	IKM
Emerging Markets	
Brazilian Equity Fund	BZF
Chile Fund	CH
China Fund	CHN
First Philippine Fund	FPF
India Growth Fund	IFN
Indonesia Fund	IF
Jakarta Growth Fund	JGF
Korea Fund	KF
Malaysia Fund	MF
Singapore Fund	SGF
Taiwan Fund	TWn
Thai Fund	TTF
Turkish Investment Fund	TKF

and Microsoft during the 1990s all exhibited superior growth in earnings.) The remaining advantages, then, are (1) excess returns if foreign markets are less efficient than U.S. security markets and (2) reduction in risk through diversification using foreign instead of domestic investments.

Market Efficiency

As explained in Chapter 3, the rapid dissemination of new information and the intense competition among investors produce efficient U.S. financial markets. If new information becomes available that implies a security is undervalued (or overvalued), its price changes rapidly. The opportunity to profit from incorrect valuations disappears before most investors learn the new information. Unless the investor is able to anticipate new information and to adjust his or her position before it becomes generally available, the individual cannot expect to outperform the market consistently. Thus, according to the efficient market hypothesis, higher returns can be achieved only by bearing more risk (i.e., by purchasing assets whose returns tend to be more volatile than the market as a whole).

Foreign markets may not be so efficient. Less analysis may be applied to foreign securities, and the results of the analysis may not be widely disseminated. This suggests that the astute investor may be able to isolate securities that are undervalued or overvalued. If this is true, the opportunity for an excess return would exist. Foreign investments would offer individuals a means to increase returns on their portfolios that is generally not available with domestic investments.

Even if foreign securities markets are not efficient, you may not be able to take advantage of any inefficiencies, especially if you are attempting to identify individual stocks to buy. For this reason you and many other investors may prefer to acquire foreign securities through investment companies. Their management should have better knowledge of a country's companies, their prospects, and financial condition.

Diversification

Even if you cannot take advantage of inefficiencies in foreign markets or if those markets are efficient, there remains a strong argument for including foreign securities in your portfolio: diversification. This advantage depends on the correlation, or more correctly lack of correlation, between American and foreign securities. Consider Figure 13.1, which presents a scatter diagram of returns from the S&P 500 stock index and the EAFE index. EAFE is an acronym for Europe, Australia, and Far East, and the index is composed of stocks from those regions.

FIGURE 13.1 *Scatter Diagram of Annual Returns on the EAFE and S&P 500 Indexes (1978–2000)*

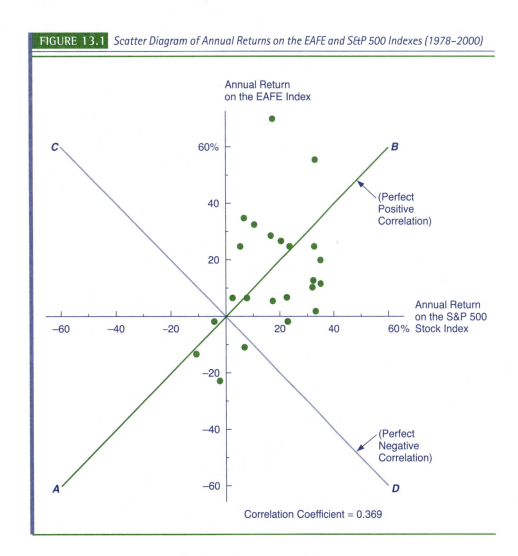

Correlation Coefficient = 0.369

The *X*-axis gives the annual return for the S&P 500 and the *Y*-axis gives the annual return for the EAFE. If the returns on the two indexes were perfectly correlated, all dots would lie on the line *AB*. If the returns were perfectly negatively correlated, all the dots would lie on line *CD*. The dots appear to lie closer to line *AB* than *CD*. The correlation coefficient relating the returns is 0.396, which indicates that there is a positive correlation, but that the correlation is not strong. This lack of strong positive correlation indicates the potential for risk reduction by including foreign stocks in an American equity portfolio and vice versa. Diversification works both ways; including American equities in a Japanese or other foreign stock portfolio also reduces risk.

SOCIALLY RESPONSIBLE FUNDS

Socially responsible investing refers to buying securities in firms that produce socially desirable goods and services or pursue socially desirable policies. Of course, what is considered socially desirable is determined by each individual. For one investor, manufacturers of military and defense products or electric utilities with nuclear facilities may be examples of firms that do not produce socially desirable products. The securities of these firms would be excluded from consideration for possible investments. Another investor, however, may believe that a strong defense is socially responsible or that nuclear power is less polluting than oil and coal-fired generators and would include the securities of defense contractors and nuclear utilities as possible investments.

Socially responsible investing may be applied not only to products but to other facets of business enterprise. Does the firm have a good record for promoting women and minorities? Does the firm perform research on live animals? Does the firm sponsor socially desirable programs, such as research on cancer or AIDS? These are but a few of the possible social considerations individual investors may apply when selecting firms for possible investment.

If socially responsible investing appeals to you, you must determine which firms meet the social goals or criteria you deem important. In one sense, this process is no different from selecting among various stocks and bonds, except social criteria are added to (or substituted for) financial criteria to identify acceptable investments.

If you do not want to select individual socially conscientious firms, a possible alternative is to invest in socially conscientious mutual funds. Of course, you will have to locate a fund with an objective and portfolio that is consistent with your social criteria. A current list of socially responsible funds may be obtained from the Social Investment Forum, a nonprofit organization that promotes the practice of socially responsible investing. The Forum may be reached at its Web site (**http://www.socialinvest.org**).[1]

INDEX AND EXCHANGE-TRADED FUNDS

Few funds outperform the market over an extended period of time, and many do not match the returns earned on comparable benchmarks. These results make

---

1. General information on social investing and social economics may be found through Co-op America (**http://www.coopamerica.org**), the Coalition for Environmentally Responsible Economics (**http://www.ceres.org**), the Investor Responsibility Research Center (**http://www.irrc.org**), and SocialFunds (**http://www.socialfunds.com**).

reasonable sense. In efficient financial markets, few investors, including mutual fund portfolio managers, should consistently outperform the market on a risk-adjusted basis. In addition, as the portfolio manager acquires more securities, the portfolio's composition increasingly mirrors the market as a whole (or the market for the class of securities being acquired).

These results should be not be surprising since, over time, most returns should mirror the market unless the portfolio is riskier that the market. Since investment companies have expenses (e.g., operating expenses and management fees), the return after these costs should be lower than the market return, which is not reduced by any expenses. If you manage your own account and buy and sell stocks through a broker, you also have expenses that reduce your return. You are faced with deciding which strategy, self-management or the delegation of security selection, is more appropriate for you and if the costs are worth the services received.

The inability of many mutual funds to outperform the market or outperform an appropriate benchmark, however, has led to increased interest in index funds, which mirror the market (or a subsection of the market). Their appeal is obvious. It includes (1) portfolio diversification, (2) a passive portfolio whose minimal turnover and minimal supervision result in lower expenses, and (3) lower taxes since the index fund has few realized capital gains.

By 2000, there were about 50 mutual funds that tracked the S&P 500 stock index. Index funds, however, are not limited to funds that mimic the S&P 500. For example, the Dreyfus S&P MidCap Index fund specializes in moderate-sized equities that match the S&P MidCap 400 index. The Vanguard Balanced Index fund mimics a combination of stocks and bonds. The Schwab International Index fund tracks the 350 largest non-U.S. firms.

Since there are so many index funds, the investor may construct a well-diversified portfolio consisting solely of these passive investments. The investor, however, can even move among funds in an effort to market time (e.g., move into stock funds in anticipation of lower inflation and lower interest rates) or to take advantage of anticipated changes in different markets (e.g., sell U.S. index funds and acquire foreign index funds). Thus, the individual can own passive investments but manage them in an active manner. Such a strategy, of course, may seem perverse, but it avoids the expenses associated with the managed funds.

Support for acquiring index funds may be found in both the popular press and professional literature. It is, of course, not surprising to learn that firm believers in efficient markets favor index funds. (See, for instance, Burton Malkiel's *A Random Walk Down Wall Street* [New York: W.W. Norton, 2003]. If you are going to own only one book on investments, this should be it.) John C. Bogle, who was chair and chief executive officer of the Vanguard Group of Investment Companies, also argues persuasively for acquiring index funds.[2] However, his argument may be self-serving, since in 1976, he introduced the first index fund, the Vanguard 500.

Exchange-Traded Funds and Their Portfolios

Financial markets are dynamic. New products are developed, and some catch on while others die. One successful new product has been the exchange-traded fund, which is an outgrowth of the index fund. Index funds permit the individual to take a

---

2. John C. Bogle, "Selecting Equity Mutual Funds," *Journal of Portfolio Management* (winter 1992): 92–100.

position in the market as a whole without selecting individual securities. Purchases or redemptions of an index fund occur only at the end of the day when the fund's net asset value is determined. Standard & Poor's Depository Receipts or SPDRs (commonly pronounced "spiders"), overcame that limitation, since the shares can be bought and sold on an exchange during operating hours. In effect, SPDRs are closed-end index funds that trade like stocks and bonds. That is, they are exchange-traded funds (ETFs).[3]

The first SPDR comprised all the stocks in the S&P 500 stock index. The second SPDR was based on the S&P MidCap stock index and was quickly followed by SPDRs based on subsections of the S&P 500 stock index. The SPDRs covered basic industry, consumer products, cyclical/transportation, energy, financial, industrial, technology, and utility stocks. Because each consists of all the stocks in the S&P 500 stock index that fall into each category, each is a pure play in the particular subsection of the overall index. If you believe that the large energy companies will do well, you do not have to select the specific companies but can buy the energy SPDRs. Since each SPDR is unmanaged, operating expenses should be minimal, and the performance should mirror the return earned on the energy stocks in the S&P 500 stock index.[4]

After the initial success of index funds and SPDRs, the next logical step was to extend the concept to other areas. Today, these is a whole spectrum of exchange-traded funds (also referred to as "exchange-traded portfolios") that track specialized indexes such as the Dow Jones small cap growth fund index or the Wilshire REIT index. Funds even track the *Fortune* 500 and the Merrill Lynch–created HOLDRs (Holding Company Depository Receipts), each of which holds a fixed portfolio of approximately 20 stocks in a sector such as biotech or regional banks. Once the portfolio is acquired, it is maintained indefinitely. There is *no* active management of the portfolio!

Exchange-traded funds have obviously become popular vehicles for investors. Funds based on the Nasdaq 100 (commonly referred to by its symbol QQQ) and the S&P 500 are consistently among the most actively traded securities on the AMEX. However, it cannot be concluded these are riskless investments. From August 2000 to August 2001, the price of the B2B Internet HOLDR declined from a high of $60 to less than $5, a decline in excess of 90 percent!

iShares

After the initial success of index funds and exchange-traded funds, the concept was extended to international investments, as Morgan Stanley developed the iShare (initially called WEBS for World Equity Benchmark Shares). iShares are ETFs that track an index of a country's stock market and may be readily bought and sold on the American Stock Exchange (AMEX). Examples of iShares and their ticker symbols are provided in Exhibit 13.4.

While iShares are index funds, they do not necessarily own every security in a particular index. Instead, the sponsors construct a portfolio that is highly correlated with the index. This strategy reduces commissions and, since the iShares are virtually 100 percent invested, there is minimal turnover, which reduces the cost of managing the fund.

---

3. Information on index funds and exchange-traded funds may be found at IndexFunds, Inc. (http://www.indexfunds.com).
4. SPDRs collect dividends distributed by the stocks they own. These dividends cover the fund's expenses, and any residual is distributed as cash dividends.

EXHIBIT 13.4	Examples of iShares Traded on the AMEX

Australia Index Series	EWA
Austria Index Series	EWO
Belgium Index Series	EWK
Canada Index Series	EWC
France Index Series	EWQ
Germany Index Series	EWG
Hong Kong Index Series	EWH
Italy Index Series	EWI
Japan Index Series	EWJ
Malaysia (Free) Index Series	EWM
Mexico (Free) Index Series	EWW
Netherlands Index Series	EWN
Singapore (Free) Index Series	EWS
Spain Index Series	EWP
Sweden Index Series	EWD
Switzerland Index Series	EWI
U.I. Index Series	EWU

While iShares give you an additional means to invest in foreign markets, they do expose you to risk. The securities in the fund are denominated in the local currency, so your return is affected by change in the value of the index and by any change in the exchange rate. If the value of the dollar were to increase, the dollar value of iShares would decline, because the dollar value of the iShares' portfolio would decline. You could sustain a loss even if the stock market in that particular country were to rise.

(Today iShares are not limited to foreign indexes. You may purchase the shares based on market capitalization, industry sector, or investment style. For example, if you want a position in technology, you may purchase the iShares that track the S&P Global Technology Sector Index. Other iShares split the Russell 3000 index or the S&P 500 index intro growth shares or value shares and track each subgroup. There are even iShares based on interest rates such as 1–3 years Treasury securities, 20+ years Treasury securities, or corporate bonds.)

iShares offer U.S. investors another means to participate in foreign markets. Their prices are expressed in dollars, and that price represents the dollar value of the iShares' portfolio. The securities they own, however, are denominated in the local currency, so an American investor's return is affected by (1) changes in the exchange rate, (2) changes in the value of the index, and (3) any dividends distributed by the stocks in the portfolio. If the value of the dollar were to rise, the value in dollars of an iShares portfolio would decline. Thus, the investor could sustain a loss even though the stock market in that particular country rose.

This exchange rate risk, of course, applies to all foreign investments, but an iShares' management cannot take actions that might offset this risk. Since an iShares portfolio is always fully invested, its management cannot sell the securities and convert to dollars in anticipation that the dollar will rise. The management of a specialized country index fund, however, can liquidate the portfolio and move the funds into dollars to reduce the impact of an increase in the value of the American dollar.

RISK–ADJUSTED PORTFOLIO PERFORMANCE AND THE IMPORTANCE OF BENCHMARKS

The phrases "outperformed the market" or "beat the market" are often used regarding performance. Unfortunately, these phrases imply that the portfolio manager's objective is to earn a return that exceeds the market return. Two important considerations are omitted: (1) what is the appropriate market or benchmark and (2) risk. If the portfolio manager's risk-adjusted return exceeds the appropriate benchmark return, then the fund did outperform (beat) the market.

Three techniques for the measurement of performance that incorporate both risk and return have been developed. These measures, which are often referred to as composite performance measures, are (1) the Jensen index, (2) the Treynor index, and (3) the Sharpe index, each named after the individual who first used the technique to measure performance. All three measures address the questions of the appropriate market index and the measure of risk associated with the portfolio. Thus, all three composite measures provide risk-adjusted measures of performance. They encompass both elements of investment performance: the return and the risk taken to earn that return.

The benchmark frequently used to measure the market is the S&P 500 stock index, since it is a comprehensive, value-weighted index, Because many portfolios are composed of the securities represented in the S&P 500 index, this index is considered to be an appropriate proxy for the market. However, if the portfolios include bonds, real estate, and numerous types of money market securities, the S&P 500 stock index is not the inappropriate benchmark for evaluating portfolio performance.

The differences among the three composite performance measures rest primarily with the adjustment for risk and the construction of the measure of evaluation. The measurement of risk is important because a lower return is not necessarily indicative of inferior performance. Obviously, the return on a money market mutual fund should be less than the return earned by a growth fund during a period of rising security prices. The more relevant question is this: Was the growth fund manager's performance sufficient to justify the additional risk?

All three composite measures are an outgrowth of the Capital Asset Pricing Model (CAPM), presented in Chapter 3. That model specified that the return on an investment (r) depends on (1) the return the individual earns on a risk-free asset, such as a U.S. Treasury bill, and (2) a risk premium. This risk-adjusted return was expressed as

$$r = r_f + (r_m - r_f)\beta$$

in which r_f represents the risk-free rate and r_m is the return on the market. The risk premium depends on the extent to which the market return exceeds the risk-free rate (i.e., $r_m - r_f$) adjusted by the systematic risk associated with the asset (i.e., its beta coefficient). This relationship is shown in Figure 13.2, which replicates Figure 3.19, the security market line. The Y-axis represents the return, and the X-axis represents the risk as measured by beta. Line AB gives all the combinations of return at each level of risk. If the investor bears no risk, the return on the Y-axis represents the risk-free rate, and higher returns are associated with bearing increased risk.

The Jensen Performance Index

Although the CAPM is used to determine the return that is required to make an investment, it may also be used to evaluate realized performance for a

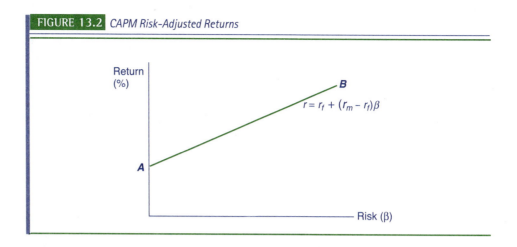

FIGURE 13.2 *CAPM Risk-Adjusted Returns*

well-diversified portfolio: that is, given the realized return and the risk, did the investment earn a sufficient return? The Jensen performance index determines by how much the realized return differs from the return required by the CAPM.[5] The realized return (r_p) on a portfolio (or on a specific investment if applied to the return on an individual asset) is

(13.1)
$$r_p = r_f + (r_m - r_f)\beta + e.$$

Equation 13.1 is basically the same as the CAPM equation except that (1) the *realized* return is substituted for the return and (2) a random error term (e) has been added.[6] In this form, the model is used to evaluate performance and not to determine the required return necessary to make an investment.[7]

If the risk-free return is subtracted from both sides, the equation becomes

(13.2)
$$r_p - r_f = (r_m - r_f)\beta + e.$$

In this form, Equation 13.2 indicates that the actual risk premium earned on the portfolio equals the market risk premium times the beta plus the error term. Since the errors are assumed to be random, the value of e should be zero.

5. Jensen's seminal work on portfolio evaluation may be found in Michael C. Jensen, "The Performance of Mutual Funds in the Period 1945–1964," *Journal of Finance* (May 1968): 389–416.
6. Two methods for computing returns, dollar-weighted and time-weighted rates of return, are discussed in Chapter 4. The dollar-weighted return (the internal rate of return) determines the rate that equates all an investment's cash inflows with its cash outlays. The time-weighted return computes the return for each period and averages these holding period returns. The computation may be an arithmetic or a geometric average, with the latter being preferred because it considers compounding.

   While dollar-weighted or time-weighted rates of return may be used for comparisons, the investor needs to apply the computation consistently. If, for instance, you compute time-weighted rates of return as required by the CFA Institute (formerly the Association for Investment Management and Research), then any comparisons must be made with rates computed using the same method.
7. Application of the Jensen model may require an adjustment in the risk-free rate. Usually, a short-term security, such as a U.S. Treasury bill, is the appropriate proxy for this rate. However, if the time period being covered by the evaluation is greater than a year, it is inappropriate to use a short-term rate, and a different risk-free rate is required for each time interval during the evaluation period. If, for example, the evaluation of the performance of two portfolio managers is being done on an annual basis over five years, a different one-year risk-free rate would have to be used for each of the five years during the evaluation period.

Figure 13.3 reproduces Figure 13.2 and adds line *CD*, which represents Equation 13.1. The two lines, *AB* and *CD*, are parallel, and since the risk-free rate has been subtracted from both sides of Equation 13.1 to derive Equation 13.2, line *CD* has no positive intercept on the *Y*-axis. Equation 13.2 indicates that after subtracting the risk-free rate, higher returns are related solely to the additional risk premium associated with the portfolio. Actual performance, however, may differ from the return implied by Equation 13.2. The possibility that the realized return may differ from the expected return is indicated by

(13.3)
$$r_p - r_f = a + (r_m - r_f)\beta,$$

in which *a* (often referred to as *alpha*) represents the extent to which the realized return differs from the required return or the return that would be anticipated for a given amount of risk.

After algebraic manipulation, Equation 13.3 is often presented in the following form:

(13.4)
$$a = r_p - [r_f + (r_m - r_f)\beta],$$

Jensen performance index
A measure of performance that compares the realized return with the return that should have been earned for the amount of risk borne by the investor.

which is referred to as the **Jensen performance index**. Because alpha is the difference between the realized return and the risk-adjusted return that should have been earned, the numerical value of *a* indicates superior or inferior performance.

If the portfolio manager consistently does better than the capital asset model projects, the *alpha takes on a positive value*. If the performance is consistently inferior, the alpha takes on a negative value. For example, if portfolio manager X achieved a return of 15.0 percent with a beta of 1.1 when the market return was 14.6 percent and the risk-free rate was 7 percent, the alpha is

$$a = 0.15 - [0.07 + (0.146 - 0.07)1.1] = -0.0036,$$

which indicates inferior performance. If portfolio manager Y achieved a 13.5 percent return with a beta of 0.8, the alpha is

$$a = 0.135 - [0.07 + (0.146 - 0.07)0.8] = -0.0042,$$

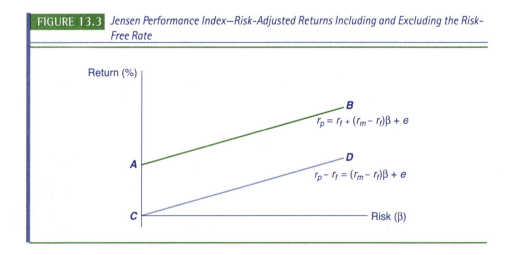

FIGURE 13.3   *Jensen Performance Index—Risk-Adjusted Returns Including and Excluding the Risk-Free Rate*

which indicates superior performance. Even though portfolio manager Y had the lower realized return, the performance is superior on a risk-adjusted basis.

The Jensen performance index permits the comparison of portfolio managers' performance relative to one another or to the market. The numerical values of alpha permit the ranking of performance, with the higher scores indicating the best performance. The sign of the alpha indicates whether the portfolio manager outperformed the market after adjusting for risk. A positive alpha indicates superior performance relative to the market, and a negative alpha indicates inferior performance. Thus, in the previous example, portfolio manager Y's performance was superior not only to portfolio manager X's performance but also to the market. In other words, portfolio manager Y outperformed the market on a risk-adjusted basis.

The Jensen performance index measures risk premiums in terms of beta, so the index assumes that the portfolio is well diversified. Since a well-diversified portfolio's total risk is primarily its systematic risk, beta is the appropriate index of that risk. Thus, the Jensen performance index would be an appropriate measure for large cap growth mutual funds whose portfolios are well diversified. If the portfolio were not sufficiently diversified, portfolio risk would include both unsystematic and systematic risk, and the standard deviation of the portfolio's returns would be a more appropriate measure of risk. Thus, the Jensen performance index is not an appropriate measure of performance for specialized sector funds, such as Fidelity Select Regional Banks, or aggressive small cap growth funds that specialize in a class of stocks, such as Fidelity Emerging Growth.

The Treynor Performance Index

The Treynor and Sharpe indexes are alternative measures of portfolio evaluation. The **Treynor index** (T_i) for a given time period is

(13.5)
$$T_i = \frac{r_p - r_f}{\beta},$$

Treynor index
A risk-adjusted measure of performance that standardizes the return in excess of the risk-free rate by the portfolio's systematic risk.

in which r_p is the realized return on the portfolio and r_f is the risk-free rate.[8] The extent to which the realized return exceeds the risk-free rate (i.e., the risk premium that is realized) is divided by the portfolio beta (i.e., the measure of systematic risk). Thus, if portfolio manager X achieved a return of 15 percent when the risk-free rate was 7 percent and the portfolio's beta was 1.1, the Treynor index is

$$T_x = \frac{0.15 - 0.07}{1.1} = 0.0727.$$

If portfolio manager Y achieved a return of 13.5 percent with a beta of 0.8, the Treynor index is

$$T_Y = \frac{0.135 - 0.07}{0.8} = 0.08125.$$

This indicates that portfolio manager Y outperformed portfolio manager X on a risk-adjusted basis, which is the same conclusion regarding the relative performance of the two portfolio managers derived by the Jensen index of performance. However,

8. Jack L. Treynor, "How to Rate Management Investment Funds," *Harvard Business Review* (January/February 1996): 63–74.

it cannot be concluded from the Treynor index that either portfolio manager out-performed or underperformed the market, because there is no source for comparison. The Treynor performance index must be computed for the market to determine whether the portfolio manager outperformed the market. If, during the time period, the market return was 14.6 percent, then the Treynor index for the market is

$$T_M = \frac{0.146 - 0.07}{1.0} = 0.076.$$

(Notice that the numerical value of the beta for the market is 1.0.) Since the Treynor index for the market is 0.076, portfolio manager X underperformed while portfolio manager Y outperformed the market on a risk-adjusted basis.

The Jensen and Treynor performance measures are very similar. They include the same information: the return on the portfolio, the risk-free and the market returns earned during the time period, and the portfolio's beta. The Treynor measure computes a relative value, the return in excess of the risk-free rate divided by the measure of risk. While the Treynor index may be used to determine whether a portfolio's performance was superior or inferior to the market on a risk-adjusted basis, the numerical value of the index may be difficult to interpret. For example, in the preceding illustration, the Treynor indices for portfolios X and Y were 0.0727 and 0.08125, respectively. When these values were compared to the Treynor index for the market (0.076), the comparisons indicated inferior and superior results, but the results do not indicate by how much each portfolio under- or out-performed the market.

The Jensen measure computes an absolute value, the alpha, which may be easier to interpret and does indicate the degree to which the portfolio over- or under-performed the market. In the example, the alphas of portfolios X and Y were –0.0036 and 0.0042, respectively. Portfolio X performed 0.36 percent less than the market, while portfolio Y performed 0.42 percent better than the market.

The Sharpe Performance Index

The third measure of performance, the **Sharpe performance index** (S_i), is

(13.6)
$$S_i = \frac{r_p - r_f}{\sigma_p},$$

Sharpe performance index
A risk-adjusted measure of performance that standardizes the return in excess of the risk-free rate by the standard deviation of the portfolio's return.

The only new symbol in the index is σ_p which represents the standard deviation of the portfolio.[9] If the previous examples are continued and portfolio manager X's returns had a standard deviation of 30 percent (0.3), while portfolio manager Y's returns had a standard deviation of 25 percent, their respective indices are

$$S_x = \frac{0.15 - 0.07}{0.3} = 0.267$$

and

$$S_Y = \frac{0.135 - 0.07}{0.25} = 0.260.$$

---

9. William F. Sharpe, "Mutual Fund Performance," *Journal of Business* (January 1966): 1119–1138.

Because portfolio manager X has the higher score, the performance is superior to that of portfolio manager Y. The additional return (i.e., 15 versus 13.5) more than compensates for the additional risk (i.e., the higher standard deviation).

The Sharpe ranking of X over Y is opposite to the ranking determined using the Treynor and Jensen indices of performance. In those measurements, portfolio manager Y had the higher score, which indicated better performance. The reason for the difference in the rankings is the measure of risk. The Sharpe performance index uses the standard deviation of the returns as the measure of risk.

Because the measures of risk used in the Sharpe and Treynor indices differ, it is possible for the two indices to rank performance differently. Suppose the average return on a utility fund is 8 percent with a standard deviation of 9 percent. This indicates that during 68 percent of the time, the return ranges from –1 to 17 percent. Returns ranging from –1 to 17 percent may indicate large variability in the return for that type of fund and indicate considerable risk unique to that fund (i.e., a large amount of diversifiable risk). The fund, however, may have a beta of only 0.6, indicating that its returns are less volatile than the market returns. The fund has only a modest amount of nondiversifiable, systematic risk. The large standard deviation may generate an inferior risk-adjusted performance using the Sharpe index because the fund has excessive diversifiable risk. The low beta may generate a superior risk-adjusted return when the Treynor index is used because that index considers only the fund's nondiversifiable risk.

As with the Treynor index, the Sharpe measure of performance does not indicate whether the portfolio manager outperformed the market. No statement can be made concerning performance relative to the market unless the Sharpe performance index also is computed for the market. If the standard deviation of the market return is 20 percent (0.2), the Sharpe index for the market is

$$S_M = \frac{0.146 - 0.07}{0.2} = 0.38.$$

Since this value exceeds the numerical values computed for portfolio managers X and Y (i.e., 0.267 and 0.26), the inference is that both *underperformed* the market on a risk-adjusted basis.

The Benchmark Problem

The Jensen, Treynor, and Sharpe indexes of performance use an index such as the S&P 500 stock index to measure the market. However, this index may not be appropriate. Certainly, a stock index is an inappropriate benchmark for an income fund with a portfolio devoted to bonds. A stock index may even be inappropriate for a portfolio devoted to stock if that portfolio is not similar in composition to the composition of the benchmark (e.g., the specialized funds discussed later in this chapter).

This problem is referred to as the *benchmark problem*, and it permeates all attempts to evaluate portfolio performance. The essence of the problem is that performance of many portfolios should not be compared to a limited aggregate measure of the U.S. stock market. If, for example, a fund invested in European stocks did outperform the S&P 500, it may not have outperformed an aggregate measure of European stocks. The comparison of the fund and the S&P 500 is not meaningful.

These problems may have you wondering: Do I have to compute the performance indices myself? The answer is both Yes and No. It never hurts to do your own analysis. That way you know the data you are using and can at least think about their appropriateness for the comparisons. The *Individual Investor's Guide to the Top Mutual Funds* (published annually by The American Association of Individual Investors, **http://www.aaii.com**) includes (1) a fund's returns for three, five, and ten years, (2) the standard deviation of the returns, (3) the fund's beta. (This handy publication is well worth its modest price. As of 2004, annual membership in the organization costs $50 and includes the *Investor's Guide*.) While these data are not sufficient to compute the three indices, they are a good starting point. Various market returns and risk-free rates are readily available in financial year-end publications. If you do not want to perform the calculations, subscription services from Morningstar (**http://www.morningstar.com**) provide the alphas and the Sharpe index, and they may be sufficient for you to compare funds' performance.

SUMMARY

In the previous chapter, mutual funds may be classified by the types of assets they own, such as bonds or growth stocks, or by their investment style, such as value investing or size of company as indicated by its capitalization. This chapter has a variety of funds with specialized portfolios. These funds stress one facet of the securities markets, such as short-term money market instruments (money market mutual funds), real estate (real estate investment trusts or REITs), socially responsible investments, and foreign securities.

In addition to specialized mutual funds and closed-end investment companies, index funds and exchange-traded funds (ETFs) have evolved. Index funds and ETFs hold portfolios that track an index of the market. While the initial index funds tracked the major measures of the market like the S&P 500, currently index funds track subsets of the market and foreign stock indexes. Index funds and ETFs permit the individual investor to take security positions without having to select individual securities or individual funds. And, unlike mutual funds, the shares of index funds and ETFs are actively traded. You may readily add to your holdings or sell the shares in a specific index fund or ETF.

Although investment companies are professionally managed, the returns they earn over a period of years rarely outperform the market return. While this performance may be judged by comparing absolute returns, this approach omits the impact of risk. Composite measures of performance combine both the return and the risk taken to achieve that return. If the realized return exceeds the risk-adjusted required return, the portfolio manager did outperform the market. Alternative approaches for risk-adjusted portfolio evaluation include standardizing the realized return by a measure of risk such the portfolio's standard deviation (the Sharpe index) or by the portfolio's beta (the Treynor index). The resulting index for each fund may be compared to rank a portfolio manager's performance and determine if he or she outperformed the market on a risk-adjusted basis.

Learning Objectives

Now that you have completed this chapter, you should be able to:

1. List several money market instruments that are acquired by money market mutual funds.
2. Distinguish among the types of real estate investment trusts (REITs) and the advantages they offer investors.
3. Explain how foreign investments may diversify a domestic portfolio.
4. Differentiate between iShares and closed-end country investment funds.
5. Characterize socially responsible investing and how it may be accomplished.
6. Identify the advantages associated with index and exchange-traded funds.
7. Distinguish between an actively managed and a passively managed fund.
8. Compare the performance of funds on the basis of both risk and return.

PROBLEMS

1) You are given the following information concerning several mutual funds:

Fund	Return in Excess of the Treasury Bill Rate	Beta
A	12.4%	1.14
B	13.2	1.22
C	11.4	0.90
D	9.8	0.76
E	12.6	0.95

During the time period the Standard & Poor's stock index exceeded the Treasury bill rate by 10.5 percent (i.e., $r_m - r_f = 10.5\%$).

a) Rank the performance of each fund without adjusting for risk and adjusting for risk using the Treynor index. Which, if any, outperformed the market? (Remember, the beta of the market is 1.0.)

b) The analysis in part (a) assumes each fund is sufficiently diversified so that the appropriate measure of risk is the beta coefficient. Suppose, however, this assumption does not hold and the standard deviation of each fund's return was as follows:

Fund	Standard Deviation of Return
A	0.045 (= 4.5%)
B	0.031
C	0.010
D	0.014
E	0.035

Thus, fund A earned a return of 12.4 percent, but approximately 68 percent of the time this return has ranged from 7.9 percent to 16.9 percent. The standard deviation of the market return is 0.01 (i.e., 1 percent), so 68 percent of the time, the return on the market has ranged from 9.5 to 11.5 percent. Rank the funds using this alternative measure of risk. Which, if any, outperformed the market on a risk-adjusted basis?

Internet Application for Chapter 13   Specialized Investment Companies and Benchmarking Performance

You decide to pursue a passive investment strategy that stresses index funds, but you also want a diversified mix of index funds. Construct a portfolio consisting of an index fund or exchange-traded fund based on (1) European stocks, (2) real estate or real estate investment trusts, (3) Japanese stocks, and (4) emerging markets. Compare the returns on these funds for the past five years with the returns on an index of American stocks.

1. Using the family of funds from the previous chapter, do these investment companies offer specialized funds that meet your needs?

2. In addition to the funds found in question 1, find at least one additional fund or investment company that meets your need.

Possible sources for information on index funds and exchange-traded funds include:

iShares   **http://www.ishares.com**

IndexFunds, Inc.   **http://www.indexfunds.com**

Merrill Lynch's Web site for HOLDRS   **http://www.holdrs.com**

Bank of New York (ADRs)   **http://www.adrbny.com**

Information on real estate funds and real estate investmenttrust funds may be found at the following sites:

National Association of Real Estate Investment Trusts
http://www.nareit.com

REITNet   **http://www.reitnet.com**

ING Clarion (ING Clarion Real Estate Income Fund, symbol: IIA)
http://www.crainvest.com

Scudder RREEF real estate funds I and II (symbols: SRQ and SRO)
http://www.scudder.com.

THOMSON ONE
Business School Edition

Currency with Thomson ONE: Business School Edition

Real estate investment trusts (REITs) are an important means to invest in properties. Using the Thomson ONE: Business School Edition database, compare the following REITs and answer the subsequent questions.

Commercial Net Leases (NNN)

Equity One (EQY)

New Plan Excel (NXL)

United Dominion Resources (UDR)

Washington REIT (WRE)

What were the trust's per-share earnings, per-share funds from operations, and dividends for the last three years? What proportion of each trust's assets is debt financed?

What is the beta coefficient for each trust? Are these beta coefficients consistently greater than 1.0 or less than 1.0 and what does you answer imply?

3 • • •

Derivatives

P art 3 is devoted to derivative securities. As their name implies, derivatives are based on another asset, and a derivative's value is dependent on the value of that underlying asset. Initially, Part 3 is devoted to options. An option is a contract that gives the holder the right to buy or sell a security at a specified price within a specified time period.

Options can be very speculative investments, and only those individuals who are willing and able to bear the risk should consider buying and selling them to take advantage of anticipated price movements. Options, however, may also be used in conjunction with other securities to manage risk. Thus, options are both a means to speculate on price movements in stocks and a means to reduce risk. Chapter 14 covers the basic features and positions using options, the Black-Scholes option valuation model, and a variety of strategies using options. Because options offer the possibility of a large return, those investors who are willing to bear the risk may find this material to be the most fascinating in the text.

Chapter 15 considers an alternative speculative investment: the futures contract. This contract is for the delivery of a commodity, such as wheat, or a financial asset, such as U.S. Treasury bills. Like options, the value of a futures contract is derived from the value of the underlying commodity. Futures contracts can produce large and sudden profits or losses, and they require that the individual actively participate in the day-to-day management of the investments. While futures contracts are considered very speculative, they may be combined with other assets to hedge positions and reduce risk. Thus, futures contracts, like options, may be used as a means to speculate or to manage risk.

CHAPTER

14 •••

An Introduction to Options*

In January 2001, you could have bought an option to buy Cisco Systems stock at $50 for $625. Eight months later, the option was selling for $80 (an 87 percent price decline). In January 2001, you could have bought an option to sell Cisco Systems stock at $50. That option would have cost you $1,638, but in August 2001, that option was worth over $3,400 (a 108 percent price increase). Why did the prices of these options change so dramatically and in opposite directions? This chapter will help you answer that question.

An option is often defined as the right to choose. In the securities markets, an option is the right to buy or sell stock at a specified price within a specified time period. The value of an option is derived from (that is, depends on) the underlying security for which the option is a right to buy or sell. Hence, options are often referred to as *derivative* securities. Options take various forms, including calls, puts, and warrants. Some securities, such as convertible bonds, have options built into them.

Investors in options do not receive the benefits of owning the underlying stock. These investors purchase the option because they expect the price of the option to rise (and fall) more rapidly than the underlying stock. Since options offer this potential leverage, they are also riskier investments; an individual could easily lose the entire amount invested in an option.

This chapter serves as an introduction to options and initially covers the features that are common to put and call options: their intrinsic value, the leverage they offer, and the time premiums they command. The subsequent sections develop this material by (1) discussing the Black-Scholes option valuation model, (2) explaining how stock, bond, and option markets are interrelated so that changes in one are transmitted to the other markets, and (3) illustrating several strategies that employ options.

With the formation of the Chicago Board Options Exchange (CBOE), a secondary market was created for the purchase and sale of call and put options. These options permit you to take long and short positions and to construct positions that reduce risk. The CBOE transformed the securities market, and its initial success led to the trading of options on other exchanges. New types of options were created, such as the stock index option, which is not based on a specific company's stock but on an index of the market as a whole. These index options permit you to take long or short positions on the market as a whole without having to trade individual securities. Index options are also a means to hedge a portfolio to reduce the risk associated with the market.

* This chapter uses material from Herbert B. Mayo, *Using the Leverage in Warrants and Calls to Build a Successful Investment Program* (New Rochelle, NY: Investors Intelligence, 1974). Permission to use this material has been graciously given by the publisher.

The importance of options to investing and risk management cannot be stressed too much. However, you should realize that this chapter is only an introduction to a complex and fascinating topic. Numerous books are devoted to options, and many finance programs have individual courses devoted to options and their use in risk management.

Even this initial introduction produces a long chapter, and reviewers disagreed on the coverage. As the author I am ultimately responsible for the coverage, but I do receive comments and suggestions from a variety of sources. For example, the publisher obtains reviews of the manuscript from instructors at a variety of schools. As you would expect, reviewers often contradict each other because they come from different perspectives. The disagreement concerning the coverage of options was greater than usual. One said, "My goal is to explain how puts and calls work . . . the coverage . . . could be much less detailed." Another suggested that "the coverage of derivatives at the introductory level should be minimal." But a third reviewer commented, "I am not concerned about anything being too long," and one even suggested that I "put in the binomial pricing model." Obviously there was no consensus on the amount of coverage or content.

I opted for length, because it is easier for your instructor (or you) to cut than to add. You should, however, be forewarned that much of the material is difficult, perhaps the most difficult material in the text. But it is exciting and useful material, and as you pursue your career, you will learn that options permeate virtually every facet of finance. You cannot know too much about these derivative securities.

•◦CALL OPTIONS

An **option** is the right to buy or sell stock at a specified **exercise** price (frequently referred to as the *strike* price) within a specified time period. At the end of the time period, the option expires on its **expiration date**. A **call** option is an option to buy a specified number of shares (usually 100) at a specified price within the specified time period. The owner has the right to *call forth* the shares and purchase them. The opposite option, which is called a **put**, grants the right to sell a specified number of shares (usually 100) at a specified price within a specified time period. A put is an option to *place or put* with someone else shares owned by the holder of the option. (Puts are discussed later in this chapter.)

Notice the phrase "within a specified time period" in the preceding definitions. American call and put options may be exercised any time prior to expiration. Comparable European options may be exercised only "at expiration." This difference means an investor could exercise an American call option prior to a dividend payment and receive the dividend. Such is not the case with European call options. Although American options are infrequently exercised prior to expiration, this increased flexibility makes American options more valuable than European options.

The minimum price that an option will command is its **intrinsic value**. This intrinsic value for a call option is the difference between the price of the stock and the call's per-share strike price. If a call is the right to buy stock at $30 and the stock is selling for $40, then the intrinsic value is $10 ($40 – $30). This value is not the same as the call's market price, which is referred to as the **premium**.

If the stock is selling for a price greater than the per-share exercise price, the call has positive intrinsic value. This may be referred to as the option's being *in the money*. If the common stock is selling for a price that equals the strike price, the

---

option
The right to buy or sell something at a specified price within a specified time period.

exercise (strike) price
The price at which the investor may buy or sell stock through an option.

expiration date
The date by which an option must be exercised.

call option
An option sold by an individual that entitles the buyer to purchase stock at a specified price within a specified time period.

put option
An option to sell stock at a specified price within a specified time period.

intrinsic value
What an option is worth as stock.

premium
The market price of an option.

option is *at the money*. And if the price of the stock is less than the strike price, the call has no intrinsic value. The option is *out of the money*. No one would purchase and exercise an option to buy stock when the stock could be purchased for a price that is less than the strike price. However, as is explained subsequently, such options may still trade.

The relationships among the price of a stock, the strike price (i.e., the exercise price of an option), and the option's intrinsic value are illustrated in Exhibit 14.1 and Figure 14.1 (p. 376). (While put and call options generally trade in units of 100 shares, all the text illustrations are on a per-share basis. The reporting of option prices in the financial press is also on a per-share basis.) In this example, the option is the right to buy the stock at $50 per share. The first column of the exhibit (the horizontal axis on the graph) gives various prices of the stock. The second column presents the strike price of the option ($50), and the last column gives the intrinsic value (i.e., the difference between the values in the first and second columns). The values in this third column are illustrated in the figure by line *ABC*, which shows the relationship between the price of the stock and the option's intrinsic value. It is evident from both the exhibit and the figure that as the price of the stock rises, the intrinsic value of the call also rises. However, for all stock prices below $50, the intrinsic value is zero, since security prices are never negative. Only after the stock's price has risen above $50 does the call's intrinsic value become positive.

The market price of a call must approach its intrinsic value as the option approaches its expiration date. On the day that the call is to expire, the market price can be only what the option is worth as stock. It can be worth only the difference between the market price of the stock and the exercise price. This fact means that the investor may use the intrinsic value of a call as an indication of the option's future price, for the investor knows that the market price of the call must approach its intrinsic value as the option approaches expiration.

Because of arbitrage, the intrinsic value sets the minimum price that the security will command. **Arbitrage** is the act of simultaneously buying and selling a commodity or security in two different markets to make a profit from the different prices offered by the markets. In the case of an option, the two markets are the

● **arbitrage**
Simultaneous purchase and sale to take advantage of price differences in different markets.

| EXHIBIT 14.1 | The Price of a Stock and the Intrinsic Value of a Call to Buy the Stock at $50 per Share |

Price of the Stock	minus	Per–Share Strike Price of the Call	equals	Per–Share Intrinsic Value of the Call
$ 0		$50		$ 0
10		50		0
20		50		0
30		50		0
40		50		0
50		50		0
60		50		10
70		50		20
80		50		30
90		50		40

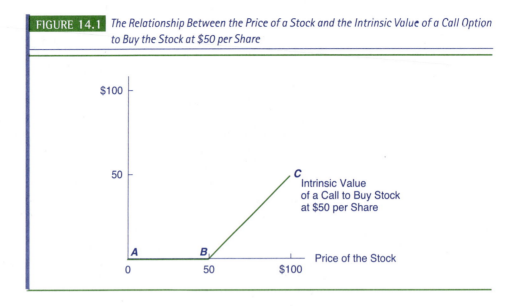

FIGURE 14.1 The Relationship Between the Price of a Stock and the Intrinsic Value of a Call Option to Buy the Stock at $50 per Share

market for the stock and the market for the option. The essence of the arbitrage position is a short sale in the stock and a long position (i.e., a purchase) in the option. After these transactions are effected, the arbitrageur will exercise the call. Then the shares acquired by exercising the option will be used to cover the short position in the stock.

This act of arbitrage may be clarified by using the simple example presented in Exhibit 14.2. If the price of the stock is $60 and the strike price of the call is $50, the intrinsic value is $10. If the current market price of the call is $6, an investor can buy the option and exercise it to acquire the stock. By doing so the investor saves $4, for the total cost of the stock is $56 (i.e., $6 for the call and $50 to exercise the option). The investor then owns stock that has a market value of $60.

If the investor continues to hold the stock, the $4 saving can evaporate if the stock's price falls. However, if the investor simultaneously buys the call and sells the stock short, the $4 profit is guaranteed. In other words, the investor uses arbitrage, the required steps for which are presented in Exhibit 14.2. The investor sells the stock short at $60 and purchases the option for $6 (step 1). The stock is borrowed from the broker and delivered to the buyer. Then the investor exercises the call (step 2) and covers the short position with the stock acquired by exercising the option (step 3). This set of transactions locks in the $4 profit, because the investor sells the stock short at $60 per share and simultaneously purchases and exercises the call for a combined cost of $56 per share. By selling the stock short and purchasing the option at the same time, the investor ensures that he or she will gain the difference between the intrinsic value and its price. Through arbitrage the investor guarantees the profit.

Of course, the act of buying the call and selling the stock short will drive up the call's price and put pressure on the price of the stock to fall. Thus, the opportunity to arbitrage will disappear, because arbitrageurs will bid up the price of the option to at least its intrinsic value. Once the price of the call has risen to its intrinsic value, the opportunity for a profitable arbitrage disappears. However, if the price of the call were to fall again below its intrinsic value, the opportunity for arbitrage would reappear, and the process would be repeated. Thus, the intrinsic value of an

EXHIBIT 14.2	The Steps Required for Arbitrage	
Givens		
Price of the stock		$60
Per-share strike price of the option		50
Price of the option		6
Step 1		
Buy the option for $6		
Sell the stock short for $60		
Step 2		
Exercise the option, thereby acquiring the stock for $50		
Step 3		
After acquiring the stock, cover the short position		
Determination of Profit or Loss		
Proceeds from the sale of the stock		$60
Cost of the stock		
Cost of the option	$6	
Cost to exercise the option	50	
Total cost		56
Net profit		$4

option becomes the minimum price that the option must command, for arbitrageurs will enter the market as soon as the price falls below the intrinsic value.

If the price of the call were to exceed its intrinsic value, arbitrage would offer no profit, nor would an investor exercise the option. If the call to buy the stock in the previous examples were to sell for $5 when the price of the common stock was $50, no one would exercise the call. The cost of the stock acquired by exercising the call would be $55 (i.e., $50 + $5). The investor would be better off buying the stock outright than purchasing the call and exercising it.

Actually, the opportunity for the typical investor to execute a profitable arbitrage is exceedingly rare. Market makers are cognizant of the possible gains from arbitrage and are in the best possible position to take advantage of any profitable opportunities that may emerge. Hence, if the opportunity to purchase the call for a price less than its intrinsic value existed, the purchases would be made by the market makers, and the opportunity to arbitrage would not become available to the general public. For the general investor, the importance of arbitrage is not the opportunity for profit that it offers but the fact that it sets a *floor* on the price of an option, and that floor is the minimum or intrinsic value.[1]

LEVERAGE

leverage
Magnification of the potential return on an investment.

Options offer investors the advantage of **leverage**. The potential return on an investment in a call may exceed the potential return on an investment in the underlying stock. Like the use of margin, this magnification of the potential gain is an example of leverage.

---
1. As is explained later in this chapter on the Black-Scholes option valuation model, prior to the expiration date the minimum price *must exceed* the option's intrinsic value.

Exhibit 14.3, which illustrates the relationship between the price of a stock and a call's intrinsic value, also demonstrates the potential leverage that call options offer. For example, if the price of the stock rose from $60 to $70, the intrinsic value of the option would rise from $10 to $20. The percentage increase in the price of the stock is 16.67 percent ([$70 – $60] ÷ $60), whereas the percentage increase in the intrinsic value is 100 percent ([$20 –$10] ÷ $10). The percentage increase in the intrinsic value of the option exceeds the percentage increase in the price of the stock. If the investor purchased the call for its intrinsic value and the price of the stock then rose, the return on the investment in the option would exceed the return on an investment in the stock.

Leverage, however, works in both directions. Although it may increase the investor's potential return, it may also increase the potential loss if the price of the stock declines. For example, if the price of the stock in Exhibit 14.3 fell from $70 to $60 for a 14.2 percent decline, the intrinsic value of the call would fall from $20 to $10 for a 50 percent decline. As with any investment, the investor must decide if the increase in the potential return offered by leverage is worth the increased risk.

Time Premium Paid for a Call Option

If an option offers a greater potential return than does the stock, investors may prefer to buy the option. In an effort to purchase the option, investors will bid up its price, so the market price will exceed the option's intrinsic value. Since the market price of an option is frequently referred to as the *premium*, the extent to which this price exceeds the option's intrinsic value is referred to as the **time premium** or time value. Investors are willing to pay this time premium for the potential leverage the option offers. This time premium, however, reduces the potential return and increases the potential loss.

The time premium for a call is illustrated in Exhibit 14.3, which adds to Exhibit 14.1 a hypothetical set of prices in column 4. The hypothetical market prices are greater than the intrinsic values of the call because investors have bid up the prices. To purchase the call, an investor must pay the market price and not the

time premium
The amount by which an option's price exceeds the option's intrinsic value.

EXHIBIT 14.3	The Relationship Between the Price of a Stock, the Value of a Call and the Hypothetical Market Price of the Call

		Call	
Price of the Common Stock	Per–Share Strike Price	Intrinsic Value	Hypothetical Market Price
$10	$50	$0	$0
20	50	0	0.02
30	50	0	0.25
40	50	0	1
50	50	0	6
60	50	10	15
70	50	20	23
80	50	30	32
90	50	40	41
100	50	50	50

intrinsic value. Thus, in this example when the market price of the stock is $60 and the intrinsic value of the option is $10, the market price of the call is $15. The investor must pay $15 to purchase the call, which is $5 more than the option's intrinsic value.

The relationships in Exhibit 14.3 between the price of the stock and the call's intrinsic value and hypothetical price are illustrated in Figure 14.2. The time premium is easily seen in the graph, for it is the shaded area indicating the difference between the line representing the market price of the option (line *DE*) and the line representing its intrinsic value (line *ABC*). Thus, when the price of the stock and call are $60 and $15, respectively, the time premium is $5 (the price of the call, $15, minus its intrinsic value, $10).

As may be seen in the figure, the amount of the time value varies at the different price levels of the stock. However, the amount of the time premium declines as the price of the stock rises above the option's strike price. Once the price of the stock has risen considerably, the call may command virtually no time premium over its intrinsic value. At $100 per share, the call is selling at approximately its intrinsic value of $50. The primary reason for this decline in the time premium is that as the price of the stock and the intrinsic value of the option rise, the potential leverage is reduced. In addition, at higher prices the potential price decline in the call is greater if the price of the stock falls. For these reasons investors become less willing to bid up the price of the option as the price of the stock rises, and hence the amount of the time premium diminishes.

The time premium decreases the potential leverage and return from investing in options. If, for example, this stock's price rose from $60 to $70 for a 16.7 percent gain, the call's price would rise from $15 to $23 for a 53.3 percent gain. The percentage increase in the price of the option still exceeds the percentage increase in the price of the stock; however, the difference between the two percentage increases is

FIGURE 14.2 *The Relationships Among the Price of the Stock and the Call's Intrinsic Value and Hypothetical Price*

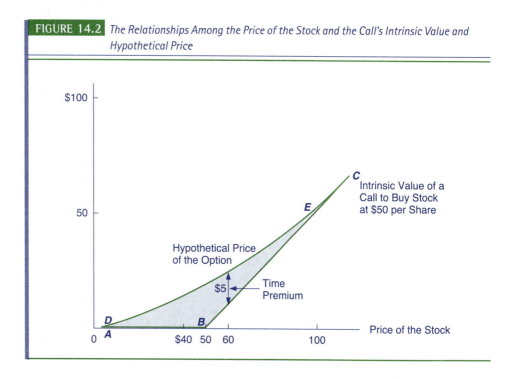

smaller, since the call sells for more than its intrinsic value. The time premium has substantially reduced the potential leverage that the option offers investors.

Investors who are considering purchasing calls should ask themselves what price increase they can expect in the option if the price of the underlying stock should rise. For the option to be attractive, its anticipated percentage increase in price must exceed the anticipated percentage increase in the price of the stock. The call must offer the investor leverage to justify the additional risk. Obviously an investor should not purchase the call if the stock's price is expected to appreciate in value more rapidly than the option's price. The previous example illustrates that the time premium paid for a call may substantially decrease the potential leverage. Thus, recognition of the time premium that an option commands over its intrinsic value is one of the most important considerations in the selection of an option for investment.

Purchasing Calls

Investors who want to leverage their position in a stock purchase calls. If the price of the stock rises, the price of the call will also increase. Since the cost of the call is less than the cost of the stock, the percentage increase in the call may exceed that of the stock, so the investor earns a greater return on the call than on the underlying stock. (This, of course, assumes the price increase in the stock is sufficient to offset the call's time premium.) If the price of the stock declines, the value of the call also declines. However, since the cost of the call is less than the stock, the absolute loss on the investment in the call may be less than the absolute loss on the stock.

To see the potential for profit and loss, consider a call option to buy stock at $50 when the price of the stock is $60 and the call sells for $15. (These numbers were used in Exhibit 14.3 and Figure 14.2 to illustrate the time premium paid for a call.) The investor buys the call (i.e., establishes a long position in the option) to take advantage of the potential leverage. As was previously explained, a price increase in the stock from $60 to $70 causes the price of the call to rise from $15 to $23—respective price increases of 16.7 and 53.5 percent. If the price of the stock were to decline from $60 to $50, the price of the call would decline from $15 to $6—respective price decreases of 20 and 60 percent. Leverage cuts both ways.

The previous example assumes that the price of the stock changed soon after the call was purchased so that the time premium continues to exist. Such will not be the case if these prices of the stock occur at the call's expiration. At expiration, the call will only sell for its intrinsic value. The call will sell for $20 when the stock sells for $70, and for $0 if the stock sells for $50 or less.

The potential profits and losses at expiration on the purchase of the call for $15 when the stock sells for $60 are illustrated in Figure 14.3. As long as the price of the stock is $50 or less, the entire investment in the call ($15) is lost. As the price of the stock rises above $50, the loss is reduced. The investor breaks even at $65, because the intrinsic value of the call is $15—the cost of the option. The investor earns a profit as the price of the stock continues to rise above $65. (Remember that in this illustration the starting price of the stock was $60. The price has to rise only by more than $5 to assure the investor of a profit on the position in the call.)

Figure 14.4 replicates Figure 14.3 and adds the profits and losses from buying the stock at $60. Both involve purchases and therefore are long positions in the securities. If the price of the stock rises above or declines below $60, the investor earns a profit or sustains a loss. The important difference between the lines indicating the profit and losses on the long positions in the two securities is the possible

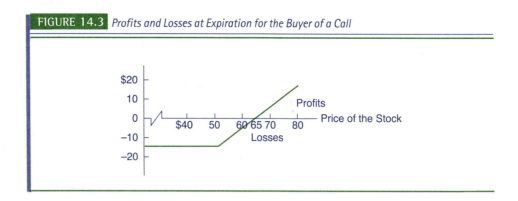

FIGURE 14.3 *Profits and Losses at Expiration for the Buyer of a Call*

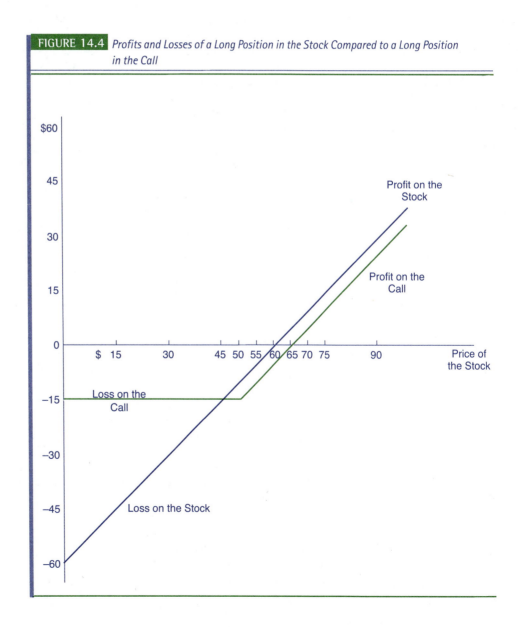

FIGURE 14.4 *Profits and Losses of a Long Position in the Stock Compared to a Long Position in the Call*

large dollar loss from buying the stock compared to the limited dollar loss on the call. In the worst-case scenario, the investor could lose $60 on the stock but only $15 on the call.

Writing Calls

In order for you to buy a call option, there has to be a seller. You buy stock and bonds in secondary markets for these securities. And as is discussed in more detail later in this chapter, there exist secondary markets for put and call options. This section, however, is devoted to the creation of call options. Puts are covered in the next section.

You and I cannot create stocks and bonds. Firms issue them and the securities subsequently trade on organized exchanges in the over-the-counter markets. You and I can create options and sell them. In the jargon of options, the act of issuing and selling a call is referred to as *writing* the option. While a long position in a call (i.e., a purchase) gives the investor an opportunity to profit from the leverage the option offers, the sale of the call (i.e., the short position) produces revenue for the writer.

There are two ways to write options. The first is the less risky strategy, which is called **covered option writing**. The investor buys (or already owns) the underlying stock and then sells the option to buy that stock. If the option is exercised, the investor supplies the stock that was previously purchased (i.e., *covers* the option with the stock). The second method entails selling the call without owning the stock. This is referred to as **naked option writing**, for the investor is exposed to considerable risk. If the price of the stock rises and the call is exercised, the option writer must buy the stock at the higher market price in order to supply it to the buyer. With naked option writing the potential for loss is considerably greater than with covered option writing.

The reason for writing options is the income to be gained from their sale. The potential profit from writing a covered option may be seen in Exhibit 14.4 (p. 383), which continues the illustration used in the discussion of buying a call. In this example the investor purchases the common stock at the current market price of $60 per share and simultaneously sells for $15 a call to buy the shares at the strike price of $50. Possible future prices for the stock at the expiration of the call are given in column 1. Column 2 presents the net profit to the investor from the purchase of the stock. Column 3 gives the value of the call at expiration, and column 4 presents the profit to the investor from the sale of the call. As may be seen in column 4, the sale of the call is profitable to the investor as long as the price of the common stock remains below $65 per share. The last column gives the net profit on the entire position. As long as the price of the common stock stays above $45 per share, the entire position will yield a profit before commission fees. The maximum amount of this profit, however, is limited to $5. Thus, by selling the call the investor forgoes the possibility of large gains. For example, if the price of the stock were to rise to $70 per share, the holder of the call would exercise it and purchase the 100 shares from the seller at $50 per share. The seller would then make only $5 ($50 proceeds when the option is exercised + $15 from the sale of the option – $60 cost of the stock).

If the price of the stock were to fall below $45, the entire position would result in a loss to the seller. For example, if the price of the common stock fell to $40, the investor would lose $20 on the purchase of the stock. However, $15 was received from the sale of the call. Thus, the net loss is only $5. The investor still owns the stock and may now write another call on that stock. As long as the investor owns the stock, the same shares may be used over and over to cover the writing of

covered option writing
Selling an option for which the seller owns the securities.

naked option writing
The selling (i.e., writing) of an option without owning the underlying security.

EXHIBIT 14.4	Profit on a Covered Call (at Expiration) Consisting of the Purchase of Shares of Stock and the Sale of One Call to Buy Shares at $50 a Share

Price of Stock at Expiration of the Call	Net Profit on the Stock	Value of the Call at Expiration	Net Profit on the Sale of the Call	Net Profit on the Position
$35	$-25	$ 0	$15	$-10
40	-20	0	15	-5
45	-15	0	15	0
50	-10	0	15	5
55	-5	5	10	5
60	0	10	5	5
65	5	15	0	5
70	10	20	-5	5

options. Thus, even if the price of the stock does fall, the investor may continue to use it to write more options. The more options that can be written, the more profitable the shares become. For individuals who write covered call options, the best possible situation would be for the stock's price to remain stable. In that case the investors would receive the income from writing the options and never suffer a capital loss from a decline in the price of the stock on which the option is being written.

The relationship between the price of the stock and the profit or loss on writing a covered call is illustrated in Figure 14.5 (p. 384), which plots the first and fifth columns of Exhibit 14.4. As may be seen from the figure, the sale of the covered option produces a profit (before commissions) for all prices of the stock above $45. However, the maximum profit (before commissions) is only $5.

Option writers do not have to own the common stock on which they write calls. Although such naked or uncovered option writing exposes the investor to a large amount of risk, the returns may be considerable. If the writer of the preceding option had not owned the stock and had sold the option for $15, the position would have been profitable as long as the price of the common stock remained below $65 per share at the expiration of the call. The potential loss, however, is theoretically infinite, for the naked option loses $100 for every $1 increase in the price of the stock above the call's exercise price. For example, if the price of the stock were to rise to $90 per share, the call would be worth $4,000 ($40 per share × 100 shares). The owner of the call would exercise it and purchase the 100 shares for $5,000. The writer of the call would then have to purchase the shares on the open market for $9,000. Since the writer received only $1,500 when the call was sold and $5,000 when the call was exercised, the loss would be $2,500. Therefore, uncovered option writing exposes the writer to considerable risk if the price of the stock rises.[2]

The relationship between the price of the stock and the profit or loss on writing a naked call option is illustrated in Figure 14.6 (p. 384). In this case the option

---

2. This risk may be reduced by an order to purchase the stock at $65. If the price of the stock rises, the stop-loss order is executed so that the option writer buys the stock and the position in the call is no longer naked.

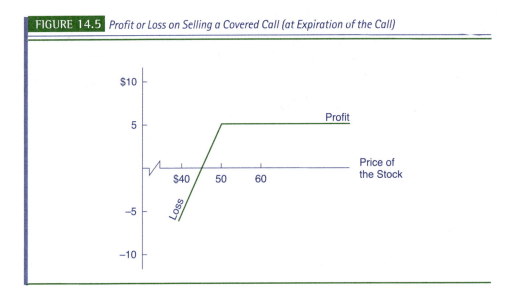

FIGURE 14.5 *Profit or Loss on Selling a Covered Call (at Expiration of the Call)*

writer earns a profit (before commissions) as long as the price of the stock does not exceed $65 at the expiration of the call. Notice that the investor earns the entire $15 if the stock's price falls below $50. However, the potential for loss is considerable if the price of the stock increases.

Investors should write naked call options only if they anticipate a decline (or at least no increase in) the price of the stock. These investors may write covered call options if they believe the price of the stock may rise but are not certain of the price increase. And they may purchase the stock (or the option) and not write calls if they believe there is substantial potential for a price increase.

When Figures 14.3 and 14.6 are combined in Figure 14.7, it becomes apparent that the potential profits and losses from selling a naked call present a mirror image of the losses and profits from purchasing the call. The short position (the sale of the call) exactly mirrors the long position (the purchase). Excluding the impact of

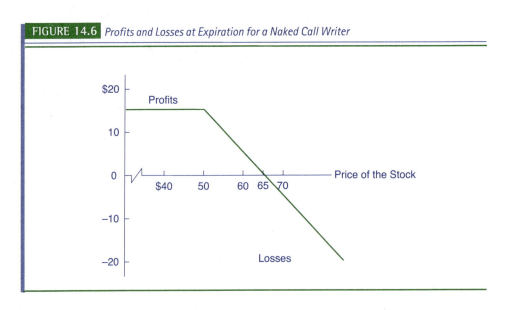

FIGURE 14.6 *Profits and Losses at Expiration for a Naked Call Writer*

FIGURE 14.7 *Profit or Loss on the Purchase of a Call and on the Sale of a Naked Call*

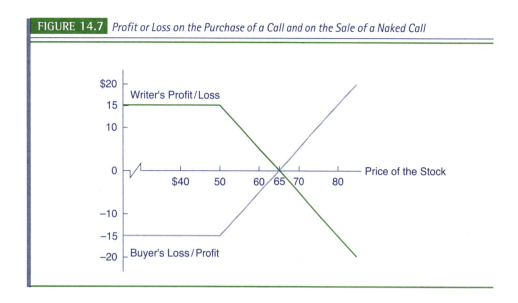

commissions, the profits earned by one participant come at the expense of the investor with the opposite position. The buyer is anticipating that the price of the stock will rise and seeks to take advantage of the call's potential leverage. The writer is anticipating that the price of the stock will not rise. Both cannot be right, so the source of profits to one of the participants has to be the source of the loss to the other.

If, however, the writer had sold the call covered, the profits and losses are not directly opposite. The covered writer has a type of hedged position that reduces the risk associated with fluctuations in the price of the stock. The covered writer seeks to take advantage of the option's time premium and accepts a smaller profit. In the previous illustration, that maximum profit was $5—the option's time premium. The naked writer, however, could earn $15 if the price of the stock declined and would earn the $5 time premium even if the price of the stock did not rise (i.e., remained stable). The potential profits and risks assumed by the naked and covered writers are obviously different. Theoretically, the naked writer has no limit to the possible loss whereas the covered writer's worst-case scenario occurs in the unlikely event that the price of the stock declines to $0.

··•PUTS

A put is an option to *sell* stock (usually 100 shares) at a specified price within a specified time period. As with a call, the time period is short: three, six, or nine months. Like all options, a put has an intrinsic value, which is the difference between the strike price of the put and the price of the stock. Note that the intrinsic value of a put is the reverse of the intrinsic value of an option to buy (e.g., a call). Compare Exhibits 14.1 and 14.5. The relationship between the price of a stock and the intrinsic value of a put is illustrated in Exhibit 14.5 (p. 386). This put is an option to sell 100 shares at $30 per share. The first column gives the strike price of the put, the second column presents the hypothetical prices of the stock, and the third column gives the intrinsic value of the put (i.e., the strike price minus the price of the stock).

If the price of the stock is less than the strike price, the put has a positive intrinsic value and is said to be *in the money*. If the price of the stock is greater than the

EXHIBIT 14.5		The Relationship Between the Price of a Stock and the Intrinsic Value of a Put		
Strike Price	minus	Price of the Stock	equals	Intrinsic Value of the Put
$30		$15		$15
30		20		10
30		25		5
30		30		0
30		35		0
30		40		0

strike price, the put has no intrinsic value and is said to be *out of the money*. If the price of the stock equals the strike price, the put is *at the money*. As with call options, the market price of a put is called *the premium*.

As may be seen in Exhibit 14.5, when the price of the stock declines, the intrinsic value of the put rises. Since the owner of the put may sell the stock at the price specified in the option agreement, the value of the option rises as the price of the stock falls. Thus, if the price of the stock is $15 and the exercise price of the put is $30, the put's intrinsic value as an option must be $1,500 (for 100 shares). The investor can purchase the 100 shares of stock for $1,500 on the stock market and sell them for $3,000 to the person who issued the put. The put, then, must be worth the $1,500 difference between the purchase and sale prices.

Buying Puts

Why should an investor purchase a put? The reason is the same for puts as it is for calls: The put offers potential leverage to the investor. Such leverage may be seen in the example presented in Exhibit 14.5. When the price of the stock declines from $25 to $20 (a 20 percent decrease), the intrinsic value of the put rises from $5 to $10 (a 100 percent increase). In this example a 20 percent decline in the price of the stock produces a larger percentage increase in the intrinsic value of the put. It is this potential leverage that makes put options attractive to investors.

As with calls, investors are willing to pay a price that is greater than the put's intrinsic value: The put commands a time premium above its intrinsic value as an option. As with calls, the amount of this time premium varies and, as is later covered in the section on option valuation, depends on such factors as the volatility of the stock's price, and the time to the expiration of the put.

The relationships among the price of the stock, the strike price of the put, and the hypothetical prices for the put are illustrated in Exhibit 14.6. The first three columns are identical to those in Exhibit 14.5. The first column gives the strike price of the put, the second column gives the price of the stock, and the third column gives the put's intrinsic value as an option. The fourth column presents hypothetical prices for the put. As may be seen in Exhibit 14.6, the hypothetical price of the put exceeds the intrinsic value, for the put commands a time premium over its intrinsic value as an option.

Figure 14.8 illustrates these relationships among the price of the common stock, the intrinsic value of the put, and the hypothetical market value of the put. This figure shows the inverse relationship between the price of the stock and the put's intrinsic value. As the price of the stock declines, the intrinsic value of the

| EXHIBIT 14.6 | Relationship Among the Price of the Stock, the Strike Price of the Put, and the Hypothetical Price of the Put |

Strike Price of the Put	Price of the Stock	Intrinsic Value of the Put	Hypothetical Price of the Put
$30	$15	$15	$15.25
30	20	10	12
30	25	5	8
30	30	0	6
30	35	0	3.50
30	40	0	1
30	50	0	–

put increases (e.g., from $5 to $10 when the stock's price declines from $25 to $20). The figure also readily shows the time premium paid for the option, which is the difference between the price of the put and the option's intrinsic value. If the price of the put is $8 and the intrinsic value is $5, the time premium is $3.

As may be seen in both Exhibit 14.6 and Figure 14.8, the hypothetical market price of the put converges with the put's intrinsic value as the price of the stock declines. If the price of the stock is sufficiently high (e.g., $50 in Exhibit 14.6), the put will not have any market value because the price of the stock must decline substantially for the put to have any intrinsic value. At the other extreme, when the price of the stock is low (e.g., $15), the price of the put is equal to the put's intrinsic value as an option. There are two reasons for this convergence. First, if the price of the stock rises, the investor may lose the funds invested in the put. As the price

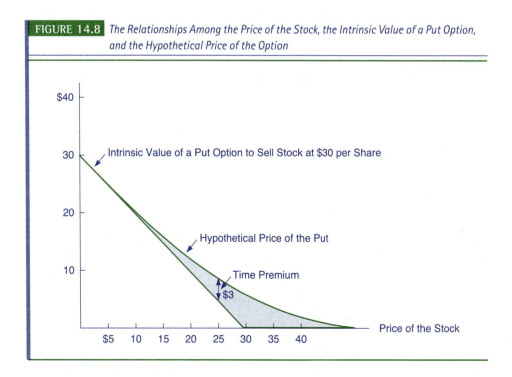

FIGURE 14.8 *The Relationships Among the Price of the Stock, the Intrinsic Value of a Put Option, and the Hypothetical Price of the Option*

EXHIBIT 14.7	Profits and Losses at Expiration from Purchasing a Put	
Price of the Stock	**Intrinsic Value of the Put**	**Net Profit (Loss) on the Purchase**
$15	$15	$7
20	10	2
25	5	-3
30	0	-8
35	0	-8
40	0	-8

of the stock declines below the strike price of the put, the potential risk to the investor if the price of the stock should start to rise becomes greater. Thus, put buyers are less willing to pay a time premium above the put's intrinsic value. Second, as the intrinsic value of a put rises when the price of the stock declines, the investor must spend more to buy the put; therefore, the potential return on the investment is less. As the potential return declines, the willingness to pay a time premium diminishes.

The potential profit and loss from purchasing a put is illustrated in Exhibit 14.7 and Figure 14.9. If the price of the stock is $25 and the strike price of the put is $30, the intrinsic value is $5 (i.e., the put is in the money). Suppose the price of the put is $8, so it commands a time premium of $3. As may be seen in both Exhibit 14.7 and Figure 14.9, the purchase of the put is profitable as long as the price of the stock is less than $22, and the profit rises as the price of the stock declines. In the unlikely case that the price of the stock were to fall to $0, the maximum possible profit is $22 (the strike price minus the cost of the put).

If the price of the stock were to rise, the position sustains a loss. As long as the price of the stock is $30 or greater, the put has no intrinsic value (the put is out of the money). No one would exercise an option to sell at $30 if the stock could be

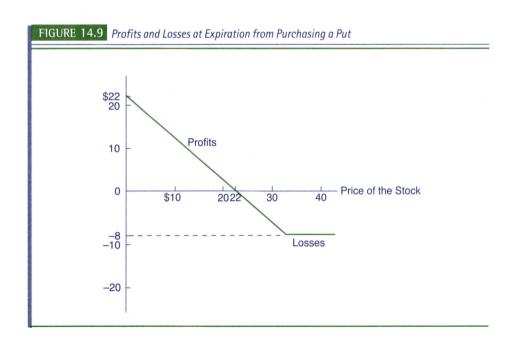

FIGURE 14.9   *Profits and Losses at Expiration from Purchasing a Put*

sold for a higher price elsewhere. The option would have no value and expire. In this case the investor loses the entire cost of the option ($8). This is, of course, the worst-case scenario, but it emphasizes that the most the investor can lose is the cost of the option. As is explained when comparing purchasing a put to selling a stock short, the latter strategy can generate greater losses.

Writing Puts

While the previous section discussed buying a put, this section will consider its opposite—selling a put. As with call options, investors may either buy or sell a put (i.e., they may *write* a put). The investor buys a put in anticipation of a fall in the price of the stock. The investor who writes a put, on the other hand, believes that the price of the stock will *not* fall. The price of the stock could rise, which is certainly acceptable from the writer's perspective, but the emphasis is on the stock's price *not falling*.

The writer may be either naked or covered. If the investor only sells the put, the position is naked. If the writer simultaneously shorts the stock, the writer is covered. If the put were exercised and the writer buys the stock, the writer could then use the stock to cover the short position. However, since covered put writing is rare, the following discussion is limited to naked put writing.

The possible profits and losses from writing a put may be seen by continuing the example in Exhibit 14.7 and Figure 14.9. In that illustration, the investor purchased the put for $8 to sell stock at $30 when the stock was selling for $25. In the opposite case, the investor writes the put to sell the stock at $30, and receives the $8 proceeds. The writer's possible profits and losses are shown in Exhibit 14.8 and Figure 14.10 (p. 390). As long as the price of the stock exceeds $22, the position generates a profit. The profit rises along with the price of the stock and reaches a maximum of $8 when the price of the stock is $30. The position sustains a loss if the price of the stock is less than $22, and the loss increases as the price of the stock declines. The maximum possible loss is $22 if the price of the stock were to fall to $0.

Figure 14.11 (p. 390) combines the two previous graphs to illustrate the profits and losses to both the buyer and the writer of the put. Like the purchase and sale of a call in Figure 14.7, it should be immediately apparent that the writer's profits and losses mirror the buyer's losses and profits. If the stock sells for $22 at the expiration of the put, the option's intrinsic value is $8—which is exactly what the buyer paid and the writer received. Neither buyer nor seller earns a profit or sustains a loss (before commissions on the trades). If the price of the stock is less than $22, the buyer earns a profit at the writer's expense. If the price of the stock exceeds $22, the writer earns a profit at the buyer's expense. If the price of the

EXHIBIT 14.8	Profits and Losses at Expiration from Selling (Writing) a Put

Price of the Stock	Intrinsic Value of the Put	Net Profit (Loss) on the Sale
$15	$15	$–7
20	10	–2
25	5	3
30	0	8
35	0	8
40	0	8

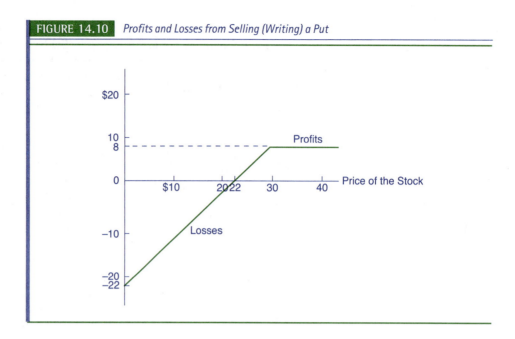

FIGURE 14.10   *Profits and Losses from Selling (Writing) a Put*

stock is $30 or greater, the maximum possible profit to the writer is $8, which is also the buyer's maximum possible loss. If the price of the stock declines to $0, the maximum possible profit to the buyer is $22, which is also the writer's maximum possible loss. Excluding the impact of brokerage commissions on the transactions, the gains and losses offset each other.

Puts Compared with Short Sales

Investors purchase put options when they believe that the price of the stock is going to decline. Purchasing puts, however, is not the only method investors can

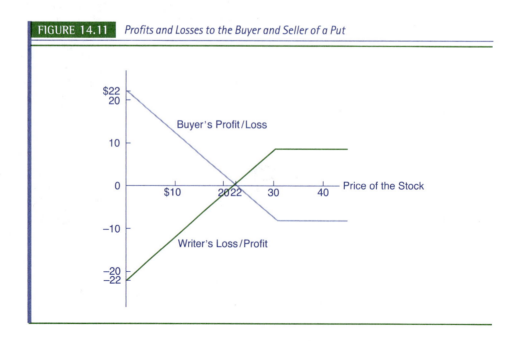

FIGURE 14.11   *Profits and Losses to the Buyer and Seller of a Put*

use to profit from falling security prices. As was explained in Chapter 1, an investor who believes that the price of a stock is going to fall may profit from the decline by selling short. Buying a put is another form of a short position. However, the put option offers the investor two major advantages over selling short. First, the amount of potential loss is less; second, puts may offer a greater return on the investor's capital because of their leverage.

In order to execute a short position, the investor must sell the stock, deliver the borrowed stock, and later purchase the stock to cover the position. The profit or loss is the difference between the price at which the borrowed stock was sold and the price at which the stock is purchased to repay the loan. If the price of the stock declines, the investor reaps a profit, but if the price of the stock rises, the investor suffers a loss. This loss may be substantial if the stock's price rises significantly. For example, if 100 shares are sold short at $30 and later purchased at $50, the investor loses $2,000 plus commissions on the investment. The higher the price of the stock rises, the greater is the loss that the short position inflicts on the investor.[3]

Purchasing a put option does not subject the investor to a large potential capital loss. If the investor purchases for $300 a put that is the option to sell 100 shares at $30, the maximum amount that the investor can lose is $300. If the price of the common stock rises from $30 to $50, the maximum that can be lost with the put is still only $300. However, the loss on the short position is $2,000 when the price of the stock rises from $30 to $50. Puts reduce the absolute amount that the investor may lose.

Besides subjecting the investor to potentially large losses, the short sale ties up a substantial amount of capital. When the investor sells short, the broker will require that he or she put up funds as collateral. The minimum amount that the investor must remit is the margin requirement set by the Federal Reserve, and individual brokers may require that the investor supply more collateral than this minimum. Selling short thus requires the investor to tie up capital, and the larger the amount that the investor must remit, the smaller the potential return on the short position.

Less capital is required to invest in a put. While the amount of margin varies at different time periods, it certainly will not be as low as the price of the put. Thus, purchasing the put instead of establishing the short position ties up a smaller amount of the investor's funds. The potential return is greater if the price of the stock declines sufficiently to cover the cost of the put, because the amount invested is smaller. Puts thus offer the investor more leverage than does the short position.

Short sales, however, offer one important advantage over puts. Puts expire, but a short position can be maintained indefinitely. If an investor anticipates a price decline, it must occur during the put's short life for the investment to be profitable. With a short sale, the investor does not have this time constraint and may maintain the position indefinitely.

THE CHICAGO BOARD OPTIONS EXCHANGE

Prior to the formation of the Chicago Board Options Exchange (CBOE at **http://www.cboe.com**), puts and calls could be purchased only from an options dealer. Each option was different, because the strike price and the expiration date were negotiated with each sale. Once an option was purchased from the dealer, an investor who desired to sell it had difficulty, because there was no secondary market in options.

---

3. Once again the investor may limit this potential loss by establishing an order to purchase the stock should the price rise to some predetermined level.

With the advent of the CBOE, an organized market in put and call options was created. For the first time, investors could buy and sell call and put options through an organized exchange. An investor purchasing a call on the CBOE knew that there would be a secondary market for that option. This ability to sell options that had been previously purchased gave a degree of marketability to options that previously did not exist.

The creation of a secondary market in options led to a large increase in option trading. This initial success of the CBOE exceeded expectations, and soon after its formation, other exchanges started to list options. Currently, put and call options are traded not only on the CBOE but also on other exchanges including the New York, American, Pacific, and Philadelphia stock exchanges.

Today transactions are continuously reported, and investors can easily obtain price quotes for puts and calls. Daily summaries of selected transactions appear in leading newspapers. While the formats differ, Exhibit 14.9 illustrates the type of information that is reported. First there is the company name, which is usually abbreviated: Bk of Am for Bank of America. Below the company name is the closing price of the stock (63). Next come the strike prices and the expiration dates, which are the third Friday in each of the given months (e.g., the options with a strike price of 65 expire on the third Friday in August). The last entries are the volume of trades and the closing prices for the calls and puts. For the August call at 65, 600 calls traded, with the last one selling for 0.60 ($60). For the August put, 350 options traded with the last trade at 2.60 ($260). The number of trades should not be confused with the number of contracts in existence, which is called the **open interest**.

There are no entries for the February puts, which means either there were no trades or the option did not exist. Notice that there is no information for options expiring in October, November, or January and there is no information on options with strike prices other than 60, 65, 70, or 75. This does not imply these options do not exist or that there were no trades. Reported transactions are generally limited by space considerations and may cover only options expiring in the current and following month or six months into the future.

Exhibit 14.9 also shows price relationships between options. For example, if you compare options with the same strike price but different expiration dates, the option with the longer life commands the higher price. Both the September call and the September put with the 60 strike price traded for a higher price than the call and the put with the August expiration date. This is intuitively obvious, since there is more time for the price of the stock to move and cause the value of the option to change. If you compare options with the same expiration date but different strike prices, there is also a relationship between the option prices. For calls,

open interest
Number of contracts with a specified strike price and expiration date on a particular stock.

EXHIBIT 14.9	The Reporting of Option Trading			Call		Put	
Option	Strike	Expiration	Volume	Last	Volume	Last
Bk of Am	60	Aug	1000	3.60	148	0.55
63	60	Sept	500	4.50	20	1.50
63	65	Aug	600	0.60	350	2.60
63	70	Feb	1200	2.90	—	—
63	75	Feb	1400	1.60	—	—

the option with the lower strike price is more valuable (e.g., $3.60 versus $0.60 for the August calls at 60 and 65). For puts, the pricing relationship is the opposite. The August put at 65 sold for $2.60 while the put at 60 sold for $0.55. These relationships hold because as the price of the stock rises, call options with lower strike prices become more valuable but put options with lower strike prices become less valuable. (Option valuation is covered in more detail in the section on the Black-Scholes option valuation model.)

STOCK INDEX OPTIONS

stock index options
Rights to buy and sell based on an aggregate measure of stock prices.

While put and call options were initially created for individual stocks, stock index options have developed. (As is explained in Chapter 15, there are also stock index futures.) These **stock index options** are similar to options based on individual stocks, but the index option is based on an aggregate measure of the market, such as the Standard & Poor's 500 stock index. In addition to puts and calls based on the aggregate market, there are options based on subsets of the market, such as computer technology stocks or pharmaceutical stocks. A listing of selected index options is given in Exhibit 14.10. Stock index options have proved to be particularly popular and account for a substantial proportion of the daily transactions in options.

These options are popular because they permit the investor to take a position in the market or in a group of companies without having to select specific securities. For example, suppose an investor anticipates that the stock market will rise. What does this individual do? He or she cannot buy every stock but must select individual stocks.[4] Remember from the discussion of risk in Chapter 3 that there

EXHIBIT 14.10	Selected Index Options
Traded on the CBOE	
DJ Industrials	
Nasdaq 100	
Russell 2000	
S&P 100 Index	
S&P 500 Index	
Value Line	
Traded on the AMEX	
Internet Index	
Major Market Index	
Japan Index	
MS Technology	
Pharmaceutical Index	
Traded on the Philadelphia Exchange	
Oil Service Index	
Semiconductor Index	
Utility Index	

---

4. The investor could buy an index mutual fund, since such funds construct portfolios that mirror aggregate measures of the stock market.

are two sources of risk associated with the individual stock: nondiversifiable systematic risk and diversifiable unsystematic risk. One source of systematic risk is the tendency of a stock's price to move with the market. Unsystematic risk results from price movements generated by the security that are independent of the market (e.g., a takeover announcement, dividend cut, or large increase in earnings).

If the investor buys a particular stock on the expectation of a rising market, it does not necessarily follow that the individual stock's price will increase when the market rises. Investors construct diversified portfolios to reduce the unsystematic risk associated with the individual asset. As the portfolio becomes more diversified, unsystematic risk is reduced further and the return on the portfolio mirrors the return on the market. (Whether the return on the portfolio exceeds the market depends on the portfolio's beta. If the individual selects stocks with high betas, the diversified portfolio should tend to earn higher returns than the market as a whole in rising markets but sustain larger losses than the market in declining markets.)

Index options offer the investor an alternative to creating diversified portfolios as a means to earn the return associated with movements in the market. For example, if the investor anticipates that the market will rise in the near future, he or she may purchase a call option based on an index of the market as a whole (such as the Standard & Poor's 500 stock index). If the market does rise, the value of the call option also increases. The investor has avoided the unsystematic risk associated with the individual stock. In addition, the investor has avoided the commission costs necessary to construct a diversified portfolio.

If the investor anticipates the market will decline, he or she will purchase a stock index put. If the investor is correct and the market does fall, the value of the stock index put rises. Of course, if the market does not decline but rises instead, the investor loses the amount invested in the put option, but the *maximum that the investor can lose is the cost of the option*. An investor who sells stocks short instead of purchasing stock index put options may be exposed to a large loss if stock prices rise.

Stock index options also give investors a means to manage existing portfolios. This is particularly important for portfolio managers with large holdings or individuals who want to improve the tax management of these holdings. Consider a substantial stock portfolio that has appreciated in value. If the investor anticipates declining stock prices and sells the shares, this is a taxable transaction. Instead of selling the stocks, the investor may sell stock index calls or purchase stock index puts (i.e., construct the protective put strategy discussed later in this chapter). Then if the market declines, profits in these positions will help offset the losses on the individual stocks.

If the investor were to sell stock index call options, the value of these options would decline as the market decreased. The gain on the sale would then offset the loss in individual stocks. If the investor were to purchase stock index put options, the value of the options would increase if the market declined. The loss on the portfolio would be offset by the gain on the put option. (The amount offset would depend on how many put options the investor purchased.) As these two cases illustrate, stock index options offer the investor a means to hedge existing portfolios against a decline in the market without having to liquidate the positions and thus incur the capital gains tax liability. By buying or selling the appropriate stock index option, the investor achieves protection of capital without selling the appreciated securities.

There is one major difference between stock index options and put and call options on specific stocks. With a call option to buy shares of IBM, the owner may exercise the option and buy the stock. With a put option to sell shares of IBM, the owner may exercise the option by delivering shares of IBM stock. Such purchases or deliveries are not possible with a stock index option. The owner of the call cannot exercise it and receive the index. Instead, stock index options are settled in cash. For example, suppose the owner of a call based on the Standard & Poor's 500 index does not sell the option prior to expiration (i.e., does not close the position). At expiration the intrinsic value of the option is determined and that amount is paid by the seller of the option to the owner. Of course, if the option has no intrinsic value at expiration, it is worthless and expires. The seller of the option then has no further obligation to the option's owner. In that case the premium paid for the option (i.e., its price) becomes profit for the seller.

In addition to stock index options, there are options on debt instruments (e.g., Treasury bonds) and foreign currencies. Each of these options permits the investor (1) to take long or short positions on the underlying assets without actually acquiring them or (2) to establish hedge positions that reduce the risk of loss from price fluctuations. For example, if an investor anticipates declining interest rates, he or she will buy a call option to purchase bonds. If interest rates do fall, the value of bonds will rise, increasing the value of the call option. However, if interest rates rise, the investor's maximum possible loss would be limited to the cost of the option.

BLACK–SCHOLES OPTION VALUATION

Interactive e-lectures
See a visual explanation and example of Black-Scholes option valuation at
http://mayoxtra.swlearning.com

Valuation is a major theme in finance and investments. The valuation of bonds, preferred stock, and common stock composes a substantial proportion of the chapters devoted to these securities. The valuation of options is also important but is more difficult than most of the material covered in this text. This section will briefly cover the model initially developed by Fischer Black and Myron Scholes for the valuation of options and subsequently applied to call options.[5] This valuation model, commonly referred to as Black-Scholes, permeates the literature on put and call options. It has also been applied to other areas of finance in which there are options. For example, if a firm has the right to retire a bond issue prior to maturity, the bond has a built-in option. By valuing the option and separating that value from the amount of the debt, the financial analyst determines the cost of the debt.

The following discussion explains and illustrates the Black-Scholes option valuation model. The derivation of the model is not given, so you will have to take the model on faith. You may, of course, pursue its development and subsequent option valuation models in further readings cited in footnote 5.

The question of valuation of an option is illustrated in Figure 14.2 (p. 379). Lines *AB* and *BC* represent the call's intrinsic value, and line *DE* represents the values of the option to buy for the various prices of the stock. The questions are: "Why is line *DE* located where it is? Why isn't line *DE* higher or lower in the

---

5. The initial model was published in Fischer Black and Myron Scholes, "The Pricing of Options and Corporate Liabilities," *Journal of Political Economy* (May/June 1973): 637–654, and is reproduced in Robert W. Kolb, ed., *The Financial Derivatives Reader* (Miami, FL: Kolb, 1992).

More advanced information on option valuation and option strategies may be found in Don M. Chance, *An Introduction to Derivatives and Risk Management*, 5th ed. (Mason, OH: South-Western, 2001), and Robert W. Kolb, *Futures, Options, and Swaps*, 3rd ed. (Malden, MA: Blackwell Publishers, 2000).

Except for price quotations and educational materials, most information on options available through the Internet is by subscription. Sites that may offer some complimentary information include Schaeffer's Investment Research, Inc. (**http://www.schaeffersresearch.com**), McMillan Analysis Corp. (**http://www.optionstrategist.com**), and Option Vue Systems (**http://www.optionvue.com**).

plane? What variables cause the line to shift up or down?" The Black-Scholes model determines the value of the option for each price of the stock and thus locates *DE* in the plane.

In Black-Scholes, the value of a call option (V_o) depends on

P_s, the current price of the stock;

P_e, the option's strike price;

T, the time in years to the option's expiration date (i.e., if expiration is 3 months, $T = 0.25$);

σ, the standard deviation of the stock's annual rate of return; and

r, the annual risk-free rate of interest on an asset (e.g., Treasury bill) with a term equal to the time to the option's expiration.

The relationships between the value of a call (the dependent variable) and each of these independent variables (assuming the remaining variables are held constant) are as follows:

- An increase in the price of the stock (an increase in P_s) increases the value of a call option (V_o). This is true since the intrinsic value of the call rises as the price of the stock rises.

- An increase in the strike price (an increase in P_e) decreases the value of a call option. Higher strike prices reduce the call's intrinsic value for a given price of the stock.

- An increase in the time to expiration (an increase in T) increases the value of a call option. As time diminishes and the call approaches expiration, its value declines.

- An increase in the variability of the stock (an increase in σ) increases the value of a call option. A speculator will find an option on a volatile stock more attractive than an option on a stock whose price tends to be stable. Decreased variability decreases the value of a call.

- An increase in interest rates (an increase in r) increases the value of a call. Higher interest rates are associated with higher call valuations.

Most of the relationships between the independent variables and a call's value seem reasonable with the exception of a change in the interest rate. Throughout this text, an increase in interest rates decreases the value of the asset. Higher interest rates reduce the present value of a bond's interest payments and principal repayment, thus reducing the value of the bond. Higher interest rates increase the required return for a common stock, thus decreasing the valuation of the common stock. This negative relationship between changes in interest rates and a security's value does not hold for call options. Higher interest rates increase the value of an option to buy stock.

The positive relationship between interest rates and the value of a call seems perverse given the previous material in this text, but the relationship makes sense. Remember that the intrinsic value of a call is the difference between the price of the stock and the strike price. The investor, however, does not have to exercise the call immediately but may wait until its expiration. The funds necessary to exercise the call may be invested elsewhere. Higher interest rates mean these funds earn more. You need to invest less at the higher rate to have the funds to exercise the option at expiration. Thus the present value of the strike price (i.e., the funds necessary to exercise the call option) declines as interest rates rise. This reduction in the present value of the strike price increases the value of the call.

It should be noted that dividends are excluded from the Black-Scholes model. In its initial formulation, the valuation model was applied to options on stocks that did not pay a dividend. Hence the dividend played no role in the determination of the option's value. The model has been extended to dividend-paying stocks. Since the extension does not significantly change the basic model, this discussion will be limited to the original presentation.

Black-Scholes puts the variables together in the following equation for the value of a call option (V_o):

(14.1)
$$V_o = P_s \times F(d_1) - \frac{P_e}{e^{rT}} \times F(d_2).$$

The value of a call depends on two pieces: the price of the stock times a function, $F(d_1)$; and the strike price, expressed in present value terms, times a function, $F(d_2)$. While the price of the stock (P_s) presents no problem, the strike price (P_e) expressed as a present value (P_e/e^{rT}) needs explanation. The strike price is divided by the number $e = 2.71828$ raised to rT, the product of the risk-free interest rate and the option's time to expiration. The use of $e = 2.71828$ expresses compounding on a continuous basis instead of discrete (e.g., quarterly or monthly) time periods. The definitions of the functions $F(d_1)$ and $F(d_2)$ are

(14.2)
$$d_1 = \frac{\ln\left(\frac{P_s}{P_e}\right) + \left(r + \frac{\sigma^2}{2}\right)T}{\sigma\sqrt{T}}$$

and

(14.3)
$$d_2 = d_1 - \sigma\sqrt{T}.$$

The ratio of the price of the stock and the strike price (P_s/P_e) is expressed as a natural logarithm (ln). The numerical values of d_1 and d_2 represent the area under the normal probability distribution. Applying Black-Scholes requires a table of the values for the cumulative normal probability distribution. Such a table is readily available in statistics textbooks, and one is provided in Exhibit 14.11 (pps. 398–399) for convenience. Once d_1 and d_2 have been determined and the values from the cumulative probability distribution located, it is these values that are used in the Black-Scholes model [i.e., substituted for $F(d_1)$ and $F(d_2)$ in Equation 14.1].

How the model is applied may be seen by the following example. The values of the variables are

Stock price (P_s)	$52
Strike price (P_e)	$50
Time to expiration (T)	0.25 (three months)
Standard deviation (σ)	0.20
Interest rate (r)	0.10 (10% annually)

EXHIBIT 14.11 Cumulative Normal Distribution

d	F(d)	d	F(d)	d	F(d)	d	F(d)	d	F(d)	d	F(d)	d	F(d)	D	F(d)	d	F(d)	d	F(d)	d	F(d)
-3.09	0.001	-2.51	0.0060	-1.93	0.0268	-1.35	0.0885	-0.77	0.2207	-0.19	0.4247	0.39	0.6517	0.94	0.8264	1.49	0.9319	2.04	0.9793	2.59	0.9952
-3.08	0.001	-2.50	0.0062	-1.92	0.0274	-1.34	0.0901	-0.76	0.2236	-0.18	0.4286	0.40	0.6554	0.95	0.8289	1.5	0.9332	2.05	0.9798	2.6	0.9953
-3.07	0.0011	-2.49	0.0064	-1.91	0.0281	-1.33	0.0918	-0.75	0.2266	-0.17	0.4325	0.41	0.6591	0.96	0.8315	1.51	0.9345	2.06	0.9803	2.61	0.9955
-3.06	0.0011	-2.48	0.0066	-1.90	0.0287	-1.32	0.0934	-0.74	0.2297	-0.16	0.4364	0.42	0.6628	0.97	0.834	1.52	0.9357	2.07	0.9808	2.62	0.9956
-3.05	0.0011	-2.47	0.0068	-1.89	0.0294	-1.31	0.0951	-0.73	0.2327	-0.15	0.4404	0.43	0.6664	0.98	0.8365	1.53	0.937	2.08	0.9812	2.63	0.9957
-3.04	0.0012	-2.46	0.0069	-1.88	0.0301	-1.30	0.0968	-0.72	0.2358	-0.14	0.4443	0.44	0.67	0.99	0.8389	1.54	0.9382	2.09	0.9817	2.64	0.9959
-3.03	0.0012	-2.45	0.0071	-1.87	0.0307	-1.29	0.0985	-0.71	0.2389	-0.13	0.4483	0.45	0.6376	1.00	0.8413	1.55	0.9394	2.1	0.9821	2.65	0.996
-3.02	0.0013	-2.44	0.0073	-1.86	0.0314	-1.28	0.1003	-0.70	0.242	-0.12	0.4522	0.46	0.6772	1.01	0.8438	1.56	0.9406	2.11	0.9826	2.66	0.9961
-3.01	0.0013	-2.43	0.0075	-1.85	0.0322	-1.27	0.102	-0.69	0.2451	-0.11	0.4562	0.47	0.6808	1.02	0.8461	1.57	0.9418	2.12	0.983	2.67	0.9962
-3.00	0.0013	-2.42	0.0078	-1.84	0.0329	-1.26	0.1038	-0.68	0.2483	-0.10	0.4602	0.48	0.6844	1.03	0.8485	1.58	0.9429	2.13	0.9834	2.68	0.9963
-2.99	0.0014	-2.41	0.0080	-1.83	0.0336	-1.25	0.1057	-0.67	0.2514	-0.09	0.4641	0.49	0.6879	1.04	0.8508	1.59	0.9441	2.14	0.9838	2.69	0.9964
-2.98	0.0014	-2.40	0.0082	-1.82	0.0344	-1.24	0.1075	-0.66	0.2546	-0.08	0.4681	0.50	0.6915	1.05	0.8531	1.6	0.9452	2.15	0.9842	2.7	0.9965
-2.97	0.0015	-2.39	0.0084	-1.81	0.0351	-1.23	0.1093	-0.65	0.2578	-0.07	0.4721	0.51	0.695	1.06	0.8554	1.61	0.9463	2.16	0.9846	2.71	0.9966
-2.96	0.0015	-2.38	0.0087	-1.80	0.0359	-1.22	0.1112	-0.64	0.2611	-0.06	0.4761	0.52	0.6985	1.07	0.8577	1.62	0.9474	2.17	0.985	2.72	0.9967
-2.95	0.0016	-2.37	0.0089	-1.79	0.0367	-1.21	0.1131	-0.63	0.2643	-0.05	0.4801	0.53	0.7019	1.08	0.8599	1.63	0.9484	2.18	0.9854	2.73	0.9968
-2.94	0.0016	-2.36	0.0091	-1.78	0.0375	-1.20	0.1151	-0.62	0.2676	-0.04	0.484	0.54	0.7054	1.09	0.8621	1.64	0.9495	2.19	0.9857	2.74	0.9969
-2.93	0.0017	-2.35	0.0094	-1.77	0.0384	-1.19	0.117	-0.61	0.2709	-0.03	0.488	0.55	0.7088	1.10	0.8643	1.65	0.9505	2.2	0.9861	2.75	0.997
-2.92	0.0018	-2.34	0.0096	-1.76	0.0392	-1.18	0.119	-0.60	0.2743	-0.02	0.492	0.56	0.7123	1.11	0.8665	1.66	0.9515	2.21	0.9864	2.76	0.9971
-2.91	0.0018	-2.33	0.0099	-1.75	0.0401	-1.17	0.121	-0.59	0.2776	-0.01	0.496	0.57	0.7157	1.12	0.8686	1.67	0.9525	2.22	0.9868	2.77	0.9972
-22.9	0.0019	-2.32	0.0102	-1.74	0.0409	-1.16	0.123	-0.58	0.281	-0.00	0.5	0.58	0.719	1.13	0.8708	1.68	0.9535	2.23	0.9871	2.78	0.9973
-2.89	0.0019	-2.31	0.0104	-1.73	0.0418	-1.15	0.1251	-0.57	0.2843	0.01	0.504	0.59	0.7224	1.14	0.8729	1.69	0.9545	2.24	0.9875	2.79	0.9974
-2.88	0.002	-2.30	0.0107	-1.72	0.0427	-1.14	0.1271	-0.56	0.2877	0.02	0.508	0.60	0.7257	1.15	0.8749	1.7	0.9554	2.25	0.9878	2.8	0.9974
-2.87	0.0021	-2.29	0.0110	-1.71	0.0436	-1.13	0.1292	-0.55	0.2912	0.03	0.512	0.61	0.7291	1.16	0.877	1.71	0.9564	2.26	0.9881	2.81	0.9975
-2.86	0.0021	-2.28	0.0113	-1.70	0.0446	-1.12	0.1314	-0.54	0.2946	0.04	0.516	0.62	0.7324	1.17	0.879	1.72	0.9573	2.27	0.9884	2.82	0.9976
-2.85	0.0022	-2.27	0.0116	-1.69	0.0455	-1.11	0.1335	-0.53	0.2981	0.05	0.5199	0.63	0.7357	1.18	0.881	1.73	0.9582	2.28	0.9887	2.83	0.9977
-2.84	0.0023	-2.26	0.0119	-1.68	0.0465	-1.10	0.1357	-0.52	0.3015	0.06	0.5239	0.64	0.7389	1.19	0.883	1.74	0.9591	2.29	0.989	2.84	0.9977
-2.83	0.0023	-2.25	0.0122	-1.67	0.0475	-1.09	0.1379	-0.51	0.305	0.07	0.5279	0.65	0.7422	1.20	0.8849	1.75	0.9599	2.3	0.9893	2.85	0.9978
-2.82	0.0024	-2.24	0.0125	-1.66	0.0485	-1.08	0.1401	-0.50	0.3085	0.08	0.5319	0.66	0.7454	1.21	0.8869	1.76	0.9608	2.31	0.9896	2.86	0.9979
-2.81	0.0025	-2.23	0.0129	-1.65	0.0495	-1.07	0.1423	-0.49	0.3121	0.09	0.5359	0.67	0.7486	1.22	0.8888	1.77	0.9616	2.32	0.9898	2.87	0.9979
-2.80	0.0026	-2.22	0.0132	-1.64	0.0505	-1.06	0.1446	-0.48	0.3156	0.1	0.5398	0.68	0.7517	1.23	0.8907	1.78	0.9625	2.33	0.9901	2.88	0.998
-2.79	0.0026	-2.21	0.0136	-1.63	0.0516	-1.05	0.1469	-0.47	0.3192	0.11	0.5438	0.69	0.7549	1.24	0.8925	1.79	0.9633	2.34	0.9904	2.89	.9981
-2.78	0.0027	-2.20	0.0139	-1.62	0.0526	-1.04	0.1492	-0.46	0.3228	0.12	0.5478	0.7	0.758	1.25	0.8943	1.8	0.9641	2.35	0.9906	2.9	.9981
-2.77	0.0028	-2.19	0.0143	-1.61	0.0537	-1.03	0.1515	-0.45	0.3264	0.13	0.5517	0.71	0.7611	1.26	0.8962	1.81	0.9649	2.36	0.9909	2.91	0.9982
-2.76	0.0029	-2.18	0.0146	-1.60	0.0548	-1.02	0.1539	-0.44	0.33	0.14	0.5557	0.72	0.7642	1.27	0.898	1.82	0.9656	2.37	0.9911	2.92	0.9982
-2.75	0.003	-2.17	0.0150	-1.59	0.0559	-1.01	0.1562	-0.43	0.3336	0.15	0.5596	0.73	0.7673	1.28	0.8997	1.83	0.9664	2.38	0.9913	2.93	0.9983
-2.74	0.0031	-2.16	0.0154	-1.58	0.0571	-1.00	0.1587	-0.42	0.3372	0.16	0.5636	0.74	0.7703	1.29	0.9015	1.84	0.9671	2.39	0.9916	2.94	0.9984
-2.73	0.0032	-2.15	0.0158	-1.57	0.0582	-0.99	0.1611	-0.41	0.3409	0.17	0.5675	0.75	0.7734	1.30	0.9032	1.85	0.9678	2.4	0.9918	2.95	0.9984
-2.72	0.0033	-2.14	0.0162	-1.56	0.0594	-0.98	0.1635	-0.40	0.3446	0.18	0.5714	0.76	0.7764	1.31	0.9049	1.86	0.9686	2.41	0.992	2.96	0.9985

$d_2 \rightarrow$ (at 0.59, 0.7224) $d_1 \rightarrow$ (at 0.69, 0.7549)

z	P	z	P	z	P	z	P	z	P	z	P	z	P	z	P	z	P	z	P	z	P
-2.71	0.0034	-2.13	0.0166	-1.55	0.0606	-0.97	0.166	-0.39	0.3483	0.19	0.5753	0.77	0.7793	1.32	0.9066	1.87	0.9693	2.42	0.9922	2.97	0.9985
-2.7	0.0035	-2.12	0.0170	-1.54	0.0618	-0.96	0.1685	-0.38	0.352	0.2	0.5793	0.78	0.7823	1.33	0.9082	1.88	0.9699	2.43	0.9925	2.98	0.9986
-2.69	0.0036	-2.11	0.0174	-1.53	0.063	-0.95	0.1711	-0.37	0.3557	0.21	0.5832	0.79	0.7852	1.34	0.9099	1.89	0.9706	2.44	0.9927	2.99	0.9986
-2.68	0.0037	-2.10	0.0179	-1.52	0.0643	-0.94	0.1736	-0.36	0.3594	0.22	0.5871	0.80	0.7881	1.35	0.9115	1.9	0.9713	2.45	0.9929	3	0.9987
-2.67	0.0038	-2.09	0.0183	-1.51	0.0655	-0.93	0.1762	-0.35	0.3632	0.23	0.591	0.81	0.791	1.36	0.9131	1.91	0.9719	2.46	0.9931	3.01	0.9987
-2.66	0.0039	-2.08	0.0188	-1.50	0.0668	-0.92	0.1788	-0.34	0.3669	0.24.	0.5948	0.82	0.7939	1.37	0.9147	1.92	0.9726	2.47	0.9932	3.02	0.9987
-2.65	0.004	-2.07	0.0192	-1.49	0.0681	-0.91	0.1814	-0.33	0.3707	0.25	0.5987	0.83	0.7967	1.38	0.9162	1.93	0.9732	2.48	0.9934	3.03	0.9988
-2.64	0.0041	-2.06	0.0197	-1.48	0.0694	-0.90	0.1841	-0.32	0.3745	0.26	0.6026	0.84	0.7995	1.39	0.9177	1.94	0.9738	2.49	0.9936	3.04	0.9988
-2.63	0.0043	-2.05	0.0202	-1.47	0.0708	-0.89	0.1867	-0.31	0.3783	0.27	0.6064	0.85	0.8023	1.40	0.9192	1.95	0.9744	2.5	0.9938	3.05	0.9989
-2.62	0.0044	-2.04	0.0207	-1.46	0.0721	-0.88	0.1894	-0.88	0.3821	0.28	0.6103	0.86	0.8051	1.41	0.9207	1.96	0.975	2.51	0.994	3.06	0.9989
-2.61	0.0045	-2.03	0.0212	-1.45	0.0735	-0.87	0.1922	-0.29	0.3859	0.29	0.6141	0.87	0.8078	1.42	0.9222	1.97	0.9756	2.52	0.9941	3.07	0.9989
-2.60	0.0047	-2.02	0.0217	-1.44	0.0749	-0.86	0.1949	-0.28	0.3897	0.3	0.6179	0.88	0.8106	1.43	0.9236	1.98	0.9761	2.53	0.9943	3.08	0.999
-2.59	0.0048	-2.01	0.0222	-1.43	0.0764	-0.85	0.1977	-0.27	0.3936	0.31	0.6217	0.89	0.8133	1.44	0.9251	1.99	0.9767	2.54	0.9945	3.09	0.999
-2.58	0.0049	-2.00	0.0228	-1.42	0.0778	-0.84	0.2005	-0.26	0.3974	0.32	0.6255	0.90	0.8159	1.45	0.9265	2	0.9772	2.55	0.9946		
-2.57	0.0051	-1.99	0.0233	-1.41	0.0793	-0.83	0.2033	-0.25	0.4013	0.33	0.6293	0.91	0.8186	1.46	0.9279	2.01	0.9778	2.56	0.9948		
-2.56	0.0052	-1.98	0.0239	-1.40	0.0808	-0.82	0.2061	-0.24	0.4052	0.34	0.6331	0.92	0.8212	1.47	0.9292	2.02	0.9783	2.57	0.9949		
-2.55	0.0054	-1.97	0.0244	-1.39	0.0823	-0.81	0.209	-0.23	0.409	0.35	0.6368	0.93	0.8238	1.48	0.9306	2.03	0.9788	2.58	0.9951		
-2.54	0.0055	-1.96	0.0250	-1.3	0.0838	-0.80	0.2119	-0.22	0.4129	0.36	0.6406										
-2.53	0.0057	-1.95	0.0256	-1.37	0.0853	-0.79	0.2148	-0.21	0.4168	0.37	0.6443										
-2.52	0.0059	-1.94	0.0262	-1.36	0.0869	-0.78	0.2177	-0.20	0.4207	0.38	0.648										

Critical Values of z for

Significance Level	Two Tails	Lower Tail	Upper Tail
0.10	±1.65	-1.28	+1.28
0.05	±1.96	-1.65	+1.65
0.01	±2.58	-2.33	+2.33

Thus the values of d_1 and d_2 are

$$d_1 = \frac{\ln\left(\frac{52}{50}\right) + \left(0.1 + \frac{0.2^2}{2}\right) \times 0.25}{0.2\sqrt{0.25}}$$

$$= \frac{0.0392 + (0.1 + 0.02)0.25}{0.1} = 0.692$$

and

$$d_2 = 0.692 - 0.2\sqrt{0.25} = 0.692 - 0.1 = 0.592.$$

The values from the normal distribution are[6]

$$F(0.692) \approx 0.755$$

$$F(0.592) \approx 0.722.$$

These values are represented by d_1 and d_2 in Figure 14.12, which shows the areas under the normal probability distribution for both d_1 and d_2. (The total shaded area represents d_1, while the checkerboard area represents d_2.)

The probability distribution seeks to measure the probability of the option being exercised. If there is a large probability that the option will have positive intrinsic value at expiration, the numerical values of $F(d_1)$ and $F(d_2)$ approach 1, and the option's value will approach the price of the stock minus the present value of the strike price:

$$V_o = (P_s)(1) - \frac{(P_e)}{e^{rT}}(1) = (P_s) - \frac{P_e}{e^{rT}}.$$

FIGURE 14.12   *A Normal Curve with the Areas for d_1 and d_2*

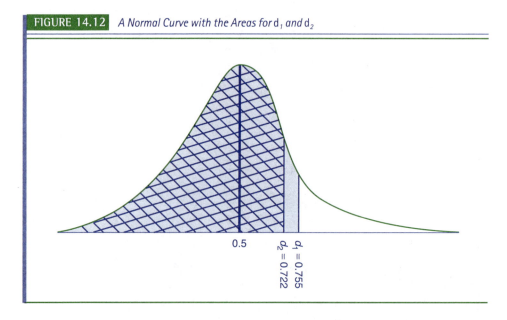

6. $F(0.69) = 0.7549$ and $F(0.59) = 0.7224$, which approximates the values given in the text.

If there is little probability that the option will have positive intrinsic value at expiration, the numerical values of d_1 and d_2 will approach 0, and the option will have little value:

$$V_o = (P_s)(0) - \frac{(P_e)}{e^{rT}}(0) = 0.$$

Given the values for $F(d_1)$ and $F(d_2)$ determined from the normal distribution, the value of the call option is

$$V_o = (\$52)(0.755) - \frac{50}{2.71828^{(0.1)(0.25)}}(0.722) = \$4.00.$$

If the call is selling for more than $4.00, it is overvalued. If it is selling for less, it is undervalued.

If the price of the stock had been $60, the Black-Scholes model determines the value of the option to be $11.25. If the price of the stock were $40, the value of the option is $0.04. By altering the price of the stock, the various values of the option are determined. As shown in Figure 14.13, the different prices of the stock generate the general pattern of option values illustrated by line *DE* in Figure 14.2.

If one of the other variables (i.e., T, σ, P_e, and r) were to change while holding the price of the stock constant, the curve representing the value of the option would shift. If the life of the option had been nine months instead of three months, the curve would shift up. Increased price volatility, a lower strike price, or higher interest rates would also shift the Black-Scholes option valuation curve upwards. A shorter time to expiration, a lower interest rate, a higher strike price, or smaller volatility would shift the curve downward.

These relationships are illustrated in Exhibit 14.12 (p. 402), which shows the impact of each variable on a call's value using Black-Scholes. This illustration uses the previous example and is divided into five cases. In each case one of the variables is changed while all the others are held constant. The value derived in the

FIGURE 14.13 *Black-Scholes Option Values*

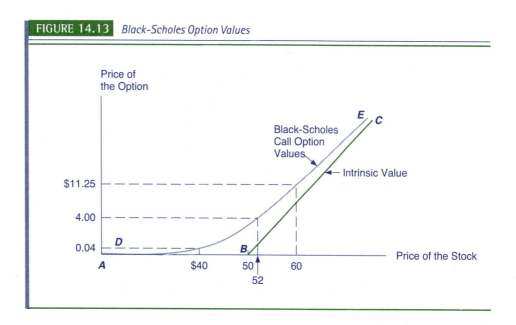

EXHIBIT 14.12   Black-Scholes Option Valuations

Initial values:

Price of the stock	$52.00
Strike price	$50.00
Time to expiration	0.25 (three months, or 90 days)
Standard deviation	0.20
Risk-free interest rate	0.10 (10 percent annually)
Black-Scholes valuation	$4.00

Case 1: Price of the stock is altered

Stock Price	Black–Scholes Option Value
$40	$0.04
45	0.55
50	2.62
52	4.00
55	6.50
60	11.25
65	16.22
70	21.22

Case 2: Strike price is altered

Strike Price	Black–Scholes Option Value
$40	$12.98
45	8.18
50	4.00
55	1.37
60	0.31
65	0.03
70	0.01

Case 3: Time to expiration is altered

Days	Black–Scholes Option Value
360	$8.08
270	6.86
180	5.53
90	4.00
60	3.41
30	2.74
15	2.36
7	2.14
1	2.01

Case 4: Standard deviation is altered

Standard Deviation	Black–Scholes Option Value
1.0	$11.56
0.6	7.71
0.3	4.87
0.2	4.00
0.15	3.62
0.1	3.34
0.05	3.22
0.001	3.21

Case 5: Interest rate is altered

Interest Rate	Black–Scholes Option Value
0.20	$4.91
0.15	4.45
0.12	4.18
0.10	4.00
0.08	3.83
0.06	3.66
0.04	3.50
0.02	3.33
0.001	3.18

initial illustration is underlined in each case. In case 1, the price of the stock varies from $40 to $70, and as the price of the stock rises, so does the valuation of the option. When the option is way out of the money (i.e., when the stock is selling for $40), the valuation is a minimal $0.04. The value rises to $11.25 when the stock sells for $60. At a stock price of $70, the option is way in the money with an intrinsic value of $20, and the Black-Scholes valuation is $21.22.

In case 2, the strike price varies from $40 to $70. As would be expected, the value of the option declines with higher strike prices. While the option is worth $12.98 when the strike price is $40, the option is virtually worthless at a strike price of $70.

Case 3 illustrates the decline in the value of the option as it approaches expiration. A year prior to expiration, the option at $50 is worth $8.08 when the stock sells for $52. This value declines to $4.00 when three months remain. With two weeks to expiration, the option is worth $2.36, and at expiration, the option is only worth its $2.00 intrinsic value.

In case 4, the variability of the underlying stock's return is altered. While greater variability usually decreases the attractiveness of a security, the opposite occurs with call options. Increased variability means there is a greater chance the underlying stock's price will rise and increase the intrinsic value of the option. Thus, increased variability is associated with higher option valuations, and lower variability is associated with lower option valuations. This relationship is seen in case 4. As the standard deviation of the stock's return declines, so does the value of the option.

In the last case, the interest rate is changed. As was explained earlier, a higher interest rate decreases the present value of the strike price and increases the value of the call option. This relationship is seen in case 5. At an annual interest rate of 20 percent, the option is worth $4.91, but this value decreases as the interest rate declines.

While Black-Scholes may appear formidable, it is easily applied because computer programs have been developed to perform the calculations. All the variables but one are readily observable. Unfortunately, the standard deviation of the stock's return is not observable, so you will have to develop a means to obtain that data to apply the model.

One method to overcome that problem is to reverse the equation and solve for the standard deviation. If you know the price of the stock, the strike price, the price of the option, the term of the option, and the interest rate, Black-Scholes may be used to solve for the standard deviation of the returns. Historical data are then used in Black-Scholes to determine the implied historical variability of the underlying stock's returns. If it can be assumed that the variability has not changed, then that value for the standard deviation is assumed to be the correct measure of the stock's current variability and is used to determine the present value of an option.[7]

An Application of Black–Scholes: Expensing Employee Stock Options

Many firms grant stock options to select employees as a type of deferred compensation of "incentive-based compensation." The strike price is set equal to or greater

---

7. For a discussion of the use of implied variability, see Robert W. Kolb, *Futures, Options, and Swaps*, 3rd ed. (Malden, MA: Blackwell Publishers, 2000), 400–402; or William F. Sharpe, Gordon J. Alexander, and Jeffery V. Bailey, *Investments*, 5th ed. (Upper Saddle River, NJ: Prentice Hall, 1999), 627–628.

than the market price of the stock. Since there is no positive intrinsic value, the recipient has no immediate tax obligation. (If the strike price were less than the market price of the stock, the option would have positive intrinsic value, which would be taxable.) If the company does well and the price of its stock rises, the value of these incentive options also increases, and the employee will have been compensated for contributing to the firm's success.

Since many firms grant top management incentive-based stock options, a question arises: Does this practice have a cost to the firm? Are these options expenses? Your initial answer may be No; the option has no intrinsic value and the firm has no cash outflow when the options are issued, so there is no expense.

The answer is not that simple. The Black-Scholes option valuation model indicates that out-of-the-money options do have value. What matters is the difference between the price of the stock and the present value of the strike price. Since incentive options often have five to ten years to expiration, the present value of the strike price is often considerably lower than the current price of the stock. Awarding that value to the employee certainly implies there is a cost to the issuing firm. (Another perspective is to argue that the firm could sell the option and use the proceeds to compensate the employee. The firm now has a cash outflow and an obvious expense.)

Why is it important to conclude that incentive stock options should be expensed? The answer is the potential impact on the issuing firm's earnings. *Expensing the options lowers the firm's reported earnings.* The accounting profession has acknowledged that incentive-based compensation involves a cost. As of June 2004, reporting requirements obligate the issuing firm to estimate the cost of incentive-based compensation. However, the firm has to report the impact on earnings only *in the footnotes* to its financial statements. The firm does not have to report the expense on its income statement, so unless you read the footnotes, the reduction in earnings will go undetected.

While American firms are not required to expense options, you can expect that this requirement will be changed. Starting in 2005, companies using international accounting standards created by the International Accounting Standards Board (IASB) must expense stock options. Although the rule does not apply to American companies, the change will put pressure on the U.S. Financial Accounting Standard Board (FASB) to adopt similar regulations. Stockholders of a few American firms have even voted in favor of expensing options, and some firms (e.g., Coca-Cola) voluntarily expense option. Technology firms, however, strongly oppose expensing, since these companies have used incentive stock options extensively.

The potential impact on earnings is illustrated in the following table, which provides 2003 per-share earnings before and after expensing options for three nontechnology and three technology firms.

	Earnings per share as reported adjusted	Earnings per share for expensing options
ConocoPhillips	$6.96	$6.92
Georgia Pacific	1.01	0.98
Limited Brands	1.38	1.33
LSI Logic	(0.82)	(1.32)
Sun Microsystems	(1.07)	(1.25)
Wind River	(0.31)	(0.63)

The table illustrates that the potential impact on earnings is much larger for the tech firms. ConocoPhillip's per-share earnings are reduced by less than 1 percent, but expensing options more than doubles Wind River's reported loss. Hence it is not surprising that tech firms strongly argue against expensing options.

If options are expensed, the question becomes how to determine their value. Currently Black-Scholes is the model most accepted by U.S. firms for valuing options, but the model does have weaknesses. For example, applying the model requires an assumption concerning the stock's future price volatility. Also, the recipient may exercise an incentive-based option prior to expiration. The Black-Scholes model requires using a specific date. The expiration date is generally used because it is known, but the actual date the employee will exercise the option cannot be known.

••Put–Call Parity

Once the value of a call has been determined, so has the value of a put with the same strike price and term to expiration, because the price of the stock, put, and call are interrelated.[8] A change in the value of one must produce a change in the value of the others. If such a change did not occur, an opportunity for a riskless arbitrage would exist. As investors sought to take advantage of the opportunity, prices would change until the arbitrage opportunity ceased to exist.

The relationship between the prices of a put and a call, the price of the underlying stock, and the option's strike price is referred to as put–call parity. In effect, put–call parity says a pie may be cut into pieces of different sizes, but the total pie cannot be affected. According to put–call parity, the price of a stock is equal to the price of the call plus the present value of the strike price minus the price of the put:

(14.4)
$$P_s = P_c + \frac{P_e}{(1 + i)^n} - P_p.$$

In the previous example, the price of the stock was $52, the strike price of the call was $50, and the value of the call was $4 when the annual rate of interest was 10 percent and the option expired in three months. The values imply that the price of a three-month put to sell the stock at $50 must be

$$\$52 = \$4.00 + \frac{\$50}{(1 + 0.1)^{0.25}} - P_p$$

$$P_p = -\$52 + \$4.00 + \$48.82 = \$0.82.$$

Rearranged, the equation says that the price of the stock plus the price of the put minus the price of the call and the present value of the strike price must equal 0. That is,

$$0 = P_s + P_p - P_c - \frac{P_e}{(1 + i)^n}.$$

---

8. Put–call parity ensures that if the value of a call is determined, the value of the put must also be determined. Since the Black-Scholes model calculates the value of a call, the value of a put with the same strike price and expiration date is also determined. For this reason, software that applies the Black-Scholes model includes the value of a put with the same strike price and expiration date.

If the equation does not hold, an opportunity for arbitrage exists. Consider the following example. A stock sells for $105; the strike price of both the put and call is $100. The price of the put is $5, the price of the call is $20, and both options are for one year. The rate of interest is 11.1 percent (11.1 percent is used because the present value of $100 at 11.1 percent is $100/1.111 = $90, which is easier to work with in this illustration). Given these numbers, the equation holds:

$$0 = \$105 + 5 - 20 - 90.$$

If the call sold for $25, then an opportunity for arbitrage would exist. The investor (or the computer) perceives the disequilibrium and executes the following trades:

1. Buy the stock	Cash outflow	$105
2. Buy the put	Cash outflow	5
3. Sell the call	Cash inflow	25
4. Borrow $90 at 11.1%	Cash inflow	90

(Notice there is an important assumption that the investor can either lend funds and earn 11.1 percent or *borrow* funds at that rate.) There is a net cash inflow of $5 ($25 + 90 − 105 − 5), so the investor has committed no cash and has actually received funds.

What are the potential profits from this position a year from now when the options expire and the investor closes the positions at stock prices of $110, $105, and $90? The question is answered as follows:

Price of the Stock	Profit on the Stock Purchased	Profit on the Call Sold	Profit on the Put Purchased	Interest Paid	Net Profit
$110	$ 5	$15	$−5	$−10	$5
105	0	20	−5	−10	5
90	−15	25	5	−10	5

At the highest price ($110), the investor makes $5 on the stock that was purchased for $105. Since the call's intrinsic value is $10, $15 is made on the sale of the call. Since the put's intrinsic value is $0, $5 is lost on the purchase of the put. Interest paid was $10 ($ 90 × 0.111), so the net profit on all the positions is $5. At the lowest price ($90), the investor loses $15 on the stock. Since the call's intrinsic value is $0, $25 is made on the sale of the call. Since the put's intrinsic value is $10, $5 is made on the put. Ten dollars was paid in interest, so the net profit is $5. By similar reasoning, if the price of the stock remains at $105, the net profit on the position is $5. No matter what happens to the price of the stock, the investor nets $5. There is no cash outlay and no risk; the $5 is assured.

In the previous illustration the call was overpriced, which led to an arbitrage opportunity. Suppose the put were overpriced and sold for $10. Once again an opportunity for arbitrage would exist. The following trades are executed:

1. Sell the stock (short)	Cash inflow	$105
2. Sell the put	Cash inflow	10
3. Buy the call	Cash outflow	20
4. Lend $90 at 11.1%	Cash outflow	90

There is a net cash inflow of $5 ($105 + 10 – 20 – 90), so the investor has once again committed no funds but has actually received cash.

What are the potential profits from this position? The answer may be illustrated as follows:

Price of the Stock	Profit on the Stock (Short)	Profit on the Call Purchased	Profit on the Put Sold	Interest Received	Net Profit
$110	$–5	$–10	$10	$10	$5
105	0	–15	10	10	5
90	15	–20	0	10	5

At the $110 price of the stock, the investor loses $5 on the stock. Since the call's intrinsic value is $10, $10 is lost on the purchase of the call. Since the put's intrinsic value is $0, $10 is made on the sale of the put. Ten dollars was collected in interest, so the net profit is $5. At $90, the investor earns $15 on the stock, but loses $20 on the call. Since the put's intrinsic value is $10, there is no gain or loss on the put, and $10 was collected in interest. Once again the net profit is $5. No matter what happens to the price of the stock, the investor nets an assured $5.

Both examples illustrated an opportunity for a riskless arbitrage. In either case, the act of executing the positions would cause the prices of the securities to change until the opportunity ceased to exist and the condition that

$$0 = P_s + P_p - P_c - \frac{P_e}{(1 + i)^n}.$$

is fulfilled. In the first example, the call was overpriced, and in the second example, the put was overpriced. In actuality, if any of the securities was mispriced, there would be an opportunity for arbitrage.

Put–call parity may also be used to show interrelationships among financial markets and why a change in one must be transferred to another. Suppose the Federal Reserve uses open-market operations to lower interest rates. The Fed buys short-term securities, which drives up their prices and reduces interest rates. This means the equilibrium prices in the preceding example will no longer hold. The lower interest reduces the present value of the strike price. At the existing prices, investors would borrow funds at the new lower rate, buy the stock, sell the call, and buy the put. Executing these transactions generates a net cash inflow and ensures the individual of a profitable riskless arbitrage. Of course, the act of simultaneously trying to buy the stock and the put and to sell the call alters their respective prices until the arbitrage opportunity is negated. The effect of the Federal Reserve's action in one market will then have been transferred to the other financial markets.

•• ADDITIONAL OPTION STRATEGIES

Even if arbitrage drives option markets toward an equilibrium so that the investor cannot take advantage of mispricings, fairly priced options may still be used in a variety of strategies. This section covers several other strategies involving options. These include the *protective put*; the *straddle*, which combines buying (or selling) both a put and a call; and the *collar*, which involves the stock and both a put and a call, is a means to limit the impact of a decline in the price of the stock. Although these additional strategies do not exhaust all the possible strategies using options, they do give an indication of the variety of possible alternatives available that employ puts and calls.

Protective Puts

Purchasing put options may be viewed as a speculative investment strategy. The buyer profits as the value of the underlying stock declines, which causes the value of the put to rise. Since the long-term trend in stock prices is to increase as the economy expands, purchasing a put seems to be betting against the natural trend in a stock's price.

Although purchases of puts by themselves may be speculative, they may, when used in conjunction with the purchase of stock, reduce the individual's risk exposure. Such a strategy—the simultaneous purchase of the stock and a put—is called a *protective put* because it conserves the investor's initial investment while permitting the investor to maintain a long position in a stock so the profit can grow.

Suppose an individual buys a stock for $40 but does not want to bear the risk associated with a decline in the price of the stock. This investor could purchase a put, whose value would rise if the price of the stock were to decline. Suppose there is a six-month put with a strike price of $40 that is currently selling for $2.50.[9] Exhibit 14.13 presents the benefit of buying the put in combination with the stock. The first two columns give the price of the stock and the profit (loss) on the position in the stock. The third and fourth columns give the intrinsic value of the put at its expiration and the profit (loss) on the position in the put. The last column gives the net profit (loss), which is the sum of the profits (losses) on the positions in the stock and the put.

As shown in the last column of the exhibit, the worst-case scenario is a loss of $2.50. No matter how low the price of the stock falls, the maximum loss to the investor is $2.50. If the price of the stock rises, the maximum possible profit is unlimited. The only effect, then, is that the potential profit is reduced by $2.50, the price of the put. (This reduction in potential profit may be seen by comparing

EXHIBIT 14.13	Profit and Loss Resulting from a Protective Put			
Price of the Stock	Profit on the Stock	Intrinsic Value of the Put	Profit on the Put	Total Profit
$20	($20)	$20	$17.50	–$2.50
25	(15)	15	12.50	–2.50
30	(10)	10	7.50	–2.50
35	(5)	5	2.50	–2.50
40	0	0	(2.50)	–2.50
45	5	0	(2.50)	2.50
50	10	0	(2.50)	7.50
55	15	0	(2.50)	12.50
60	20	0	(2.50)	17.50

9. This strategy requires the existence of a put option on the stock. Obviously, it cannot be executed for stocks for which there are no put options.

columns 2 and 5.) What the investor has achieved by purchasing the put in conjunction with the purchase of the stock is the assurance of a maximum loss of $2.50.

This protective put strategy may be viewed as an alternative to placing a stop-loss order to sell the stock at $37.50. The advantage of the protective put is that the investor is protected from the price of the stock falling, the stock being sold, and the price subsequently rising. Day-to-day fluctuations in the price of the stock have no impact on the protective put strategy. The disadvantage is that the put ultimately expires, whereas the limit order may be maintained indefinitely. Once the put expires, the investor no longer has the protection and would once again be at risk from a decline in the price of the stock. To maintain the protection, the investor could buy another put. In the previous example, the cost of the put was $2.50. If the put were in existence for six months, expired, and the investor bought another put for the same price, the annual cost of the protection is $5.[10] The limit order, however, has no costs—although the investor may periodically have to instruct the broker to reinstate the limit order.

There is not a clear answer as to whether the limit order or the protective put is the better strategy. The limit order involves no cost but does subject the investor to being sold out on a dip in the price of the stock. The protective put avoids the risk of being sold out by a temporary price decline but requires the investor to pay the cost of the option, which reduces the potential profit from the position in the stock.

Straddles

A *straddle* consists of a purchase (or sale) of a put and a call with the same exercise price and the same expiration date. If the investor buys both options, it is possible to earn a profit if the price of the stock rises or falls. The price increase may generate a profit on the call, and the price decline may generate a profit on the put.

Investors construct straddles if they expect the stock's price to move but are uncertain as to the direction. Consider a stock that is trading for $50 as the result of takeover rumors. If the takeover does occur, the price of the stock should rise. That argues for a long position in the stock. If the anticipated takeover does not occur and the rumors abate, the price of the stock will probably decline. That argues for a short position.

A long or a short position by itself may inflict losses if the investor selects the wrong position. To avoid this, the investor purchases both a put and a call. A price movement in either direction generates a profit (if the price movement covers the two premiums), and the maximum possible loss is the cost of the two options.

To see these potential profits and losses, consider the following stock and two options to buy and sell the stock:

Price of the stock	$52
Price of a call at $55	$ 1.50
Price of a put at $55	$ 5.50

Instead of purchasing or shorting the stock, the investor buys both options. The possible profits and losses at the expiration of the options for various prices of the stock are as follows:

---

10. The protective put is similar to buying car or home insurance. The individual must renew the policy in order to maintain the coverage. The cost of insuring one's home, however, is perceptibly less (as a percentage of the value of the asset) than the cost of using the protective put to reduce the risk of loss from a decline in security prices.

Price of the Stock	Intrinsic Value of the Call	Profit (Loss) on the Call	Intrinsic Value of the Put	Profit (Loss) on the Put	Net Profit (Loss)
$40	$0	$(1.50)	$15	$9.50	$8
45	0	(1.50)	10	4.50	3
48	0	(1.50)	7	1.50	0
50	0	(1.50)	5	(.50)	(2)
52	0	(1.50)	3	(2.50)	(4)
55	0	(1.50)	0	(5.50)	(7)
60	5	3.50	0	(5.50)	(2)
62	7	5.50	0	(5.50)	0
65	10	8.50	0	(5.50)	3
70	15	13.50	0	(5.50)	8

The position generates a profit as long as the stock price exceeds $62 or is less than $48 (i.e., the range of stock prices that generates a loss is $48 < P_s < $62). If the price of the stock moves either above $62 or below $48, the investor is assured of a profit. The maximum possible loss is $7, which occurs when the price of the stock equals the options' strike price at their expiration. At that price, neither option has any intrinsic value and both expire, so the investor loses the entire amount invested in both options.

The profits and losses from purchasing a straddle are illustrated in Figure 14.14. As may be seen in the figure, the position sustains a loss if the price of the stock is greater than $48 or less than $62, with a maximum possible loss of $7. There is no limit to the potential profit if the price of the stock rises, and the position could generate a profit of $48 in the unlikely case that the price of the stock declines to $0.

FIGURE 14.13 *Profit or Loss from Purchasing a Straddle*

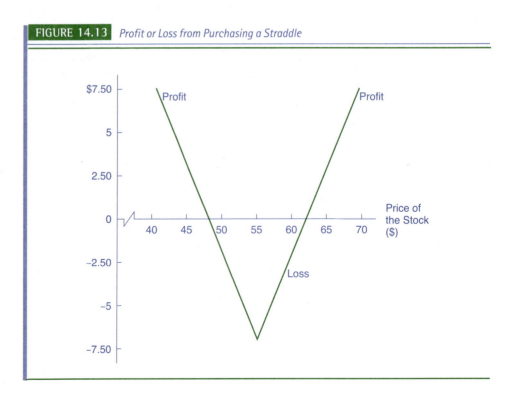

Why would the investor construct a straddle in which it is possible to sustain a loss, even if the price fluctuates but does not fluctuate sufficiently to cover the cost of the two options? The answer is that the investor anticipates a large movement in the price of the stock but is uncertain as to the direction. This position offers potential profit if such a price change occurs and limits the loss if the anticipated change does not materialize.

If the investor expects the price of the stock to be stable, that individual writes a straddle. The investor sells a put and a call. This strategy is, of course, the opposite of buying a straddle and its profit/loss profile is the exact opposite:

Price of the Stock	Intrinsic Value of the Call	Profit (Loss) on the Call	Intrinsic Value of the Put	Profit (Loss) on the Put	Net Profit (Loss)
$40	$0	$ 1.50	$15	$(9.50)	$(8)
45	0	1.50	10	(4.50)	(3)
48	0	1.50	7	(1.50)	0
50	0	1.50	5	.50	2
52	0	1.50	3	2.50	4
55	0	1.50	0	5.50	7
60	5	(3.50)	0	5.50	2
62	7	(5.50)	0	5.50	0
65	10	(8.50)	0	5.50	(3)
70	15	(13.50)	0	5.50	(8)

The writer of the straddle profits as long as the price of the stock exceeds $48 but is less than $62. The maximum possible profit is $7, which occurs when the price of the stock is $55 and both options expire worthless. Of course, the writer could sustain a large loss if the price of the stock makes a large movement in either direction.

Collars

If you look at a shirt, there is an opening for the head and the cloth covers the shoulders. Both shoulders are protected but there is room for the individual's head. A collar in investments is similar. The individual is protected on both sides from price movements.

A collar is constructed when an investor owns a stock and for some reason (possible reasons are considered later) wants to hedge against a movement in the stock's price. The investor constructs a collar by selling a call at one strike price and buying a put at a lower strike price. Since this strategy involves both a purchase and a sale, the cash flows offset each other, resulting in either a small cash inflow or, at worst, a modest cash outflow. Consider the following options and their prices:

Strike Price	Price of a Call	Price of a Put
$45	NA	$2
50	$3	NA

The stock is currently selling for $48, and the investor owns 100 shares. The collar requires the investor to sell the call at $50, a $3 cash inflow, and purchase the put at $45, a $2 cash outflow. The result is a net cash inflow of $1. (This small inflow may cover the commissions, in which case the investor has no net cash outflow.)

The investor now has three positions: (1) a long position in the stock, (2) a short position in the call, and (3) a long position in the put.

The profit/loss profile of these positions at the expiration of the options for various prices of the stock is as follows:

Price of the Stock	Profit on the Stock	Call	Put	Net Profit
$60	$12	($7)	($2)	$3
55	7	(2)	(2)	3
50	2	3	(2)	3
48	0	3	(2)	1
45	(3)	3	(2)	(2)
40	(8)	3	3	(2)
35	(13)	3	8	(2)

In this illustration, if the price of the stock rises, there is a modest gain. If the price of the stock declines, there is a modest loss. The investor's aim to avoid a possible large loss has been achieved.

Why would an investor construct a collar? There are several reasons, which revolve around the timing of sales and limits on the investor's ability to sell. Consider the situation of an investor who bought the preceding stock at $20 and would like to sell at $48. The sale, however, produces a capital gain, which the investor would prefer to defer to the next taxable year. Constructing the collar locks in the price and the profit on the stock because if the price does change, the profits/losses on the various components cancel each other. The original appreciation in the stock from $20 to $48 is retained and the taxes are deferred until the positions are unwound, which could occur in the next taxable year.

Another, and more likely, reason for constructing the collar is to protect a gain when the investor is forbidden to sell the stock. Prior to an initial public offering, a firm may issue employees stock as compensation or grant employees options to buy the stock. For instance, a firm expects to go public and sell stock at $50 and grants current employees shares based on the following formula. Each employee is to receive stock based on 40 percent of that individual's prior year's compensation. That dollar value then will be divided by $50, the initial anticipated price of the IPO, to determine the number of shares that will be granted prior to the initial public offering. If an employee earned $80,000, the number of shares to be received is 640 shares (0.4[$80,000/$50]). The employee, however, cannot immediately sell the shares. Shares are restricted units, one third of which may be sold on the anniversary dates of the initial public offering for the next three years. The employee can only sell 213 shares a year for the next three years.[11]

Suppose six months after the initial public offering the price of the stock is $72. The employee would like to sell and realize the $22 profit, but the stock cannot be sold. Of course, further price increases would be welcome, but a price decline could inflict a loss or at least reduce existing gains. By constructing a collar, these employees are able to freeze the price of the stock until they are able to sell it. While they forgo the possibility of further gains, they lock in existing profits. Since the investment objective is to hedge against a price decline, the collar protects these employees against the possibility of a price decline.

---

11. The purpose of such restrictions is to avoid the dumping of stock right after an initial public offering, especially if the price of the stock rises.

A third reason for constructing a collar is essentially a variation on the previous case. Many top executives receive additional compensation in the form of stock options instead of cash. These stock options are similar to calls and give the executives the right to buy the stock at specified prices for specified time periods. While the calls traded on the CBOE and other exchanges are of relatively short duration, options granted executives often may be exercised after many years.

Once again, the use of collars protects the investors from a price decline. If an executive exercises a profitable stock option, there may be legal or tax reasons why the stock may not be immediately sold. By constructing the collar, the executive freezes the current price of the stock and protects the gain.

Collars are also used in merger agreements to lock in a specified price or range of stock prices. When Georgia Pacific (GP) offered to buy Fort James, the terms established a maximum price of $40. GP offered $29.60 plus 0.2644 shares of Georgia Pacific for every share of Fort James. If GP sold above $40, the number of shares would be decreased. The effect is to set a maximum cost and a minimum cost to Georgia Pacific. If GP sold for more than $40, the reduction in the number of shares limits the upside cost to $40. Thus, if GP were to sell for $50, the stockholders of Fort James would receive $29.60 plus 0.208 shares. The 0.208 shares would be worth $10.40, which plus the $29.60 is a total of $40. At the other extreme, in the unlikely case that the price of Georgia Pacific stock collapsed, the stockholders of Fort James would receive $29.60. The effect is to guarantee Fort James stockholders $29.60 to $40 and to limit the cost to Georgia Pacific of the acquisition from $29.60 to $40. Such merger agreements, which guarantee a minimum but limit the upside price, are common when the acquiring firm offers to swap its stock for the other firm's stock.

Comparing Strategies

Protective puts, straddles, and collars are option strategies that expand the potential uses for puts and calls. If you can work your way through these illustrations, you should be able to compare potential outcomes from any of a variety of strategies using options. For one final test, consider the following four possibilities involving a stock you like and expect to rise in price.

The strategies are (1) buy the stock, (2) buy the stock and sell the call (the covered call), (3) buy the call, or (4) sell the put. Selling the put may seem perverse. You expect the price of the stock to rise, but instead of taking a long position in the stock, you are taking a short position in the put! Does this strategy make sense? Comparing the possible outcomes from each strategy will help answer that question.

The cash outflows from each strategy are as follows:

Buy the stock:	$86
The covered call:	$86 – $10.50 = $75.50
Buy the call:	$10.50
Sell the put:	($8.25)

While the first three strategies result in cash outflows, the sale of the put generates a cash *inflow*.

The possible profits and losses (before commissions) from each strategy are given in the following profit–loss profile:

Price of the Stock	Bought the Stock	Covered Call	Bought the Call	Sold the Put
$110	$24	$9.50	$14.50	$8.25
100	14	9.50	4.50	8.25
95.50	9.50	9.50	.00	8.25
90	4	9.50	(5.50)	8.25
86	0	9.50	(9.50)	8.25
80	(6)	4.50	(10.50)	3.25
76.75	(9.25)	1.25	(10.50)	.00
75.50	(10.50)	.00	(10.50)	(1.25)
70	(16)	(5.50)	(10.50)	(7.75)
60	(26)	(15.50)	(10.50)	(17.75)

Each strategy is profitable if the price of the stock rises. Of course, in absolute dollars, buying the stock produces the largest potential gain (and largest potential loss), but that strategy requires the largest cash outlay.

Analyzing the profit–loss profile indicates that selling the put is a viable alternative strategy for taking a position in a stock you like. Consider the following:

1) Selling the put is similar to the covered call, but selling the put generates a cash inflow of $8.25 while the covered call requires a $75.50 cash outflow. If you earn more than $1.25 on the difference in cash outflows, the sale of the put is the superior strategy.

2) Buying the call produces the lowest possible loss, but the price of the stock must rise to above $95.50 for the strategy to generate a profit. For the sale of the put, the price does not have to rise at all for the strategy to be profitable. Buying the call beats selling the put only if the price of the stock exceeds $103.75.

3) If the price of the stock were to fall, buying the stock or the call produces losses. The covered call and the sale of the put provide some protection from the price decline, but if the price declines below $75.50, all the strategies generate losses.

4) At $75.50 the put may be exercised, forcing you to buy the stock for $85. But your actual cost is $76.75 ($85 – $8.25). For four months you had the use of the $8.25 from the sale of the put and the $86 you would have spent to buy the stock. Instead of buying the stock you liked for $86 (or buying the call for $10.50 and losing the entire amount), you get the stock for a lower price, $76.75.

As this brief discussion indicates, selling a put on a stock you like is a viable strategy. It may seem backwards to sell an option on a stock you expect to go up, but if you are correct, you make money without a cash outflow. If you are wrong, you may end up buying the stock at a lower price. Although it is not quite "Heads I win, tails you lose," it is a reasonable strategy for a stock you believe is undervalued.

SUMMARY

In the securities markets, an option gives the holder the right to buy or sell a stock (or index of stocks) at a specified price within a specified time period. The value of an option depends on the value of the underlying security, so options are often referred to as *derivative* securities. A call is an option written by an individual to buy stock. A put is an option to sell stock. A call writer may either own the underlying stock and write *covered* call options or not own the stock and write *naked* call options. If the call writer does not own the stock, that individual is exposed to a large potential loss should the price of the stock rise dramatically.

Options permit investors to buy and take long positions without acquiring the stock. Options also permit investors to sell and take short positions without selling the stock. Investors purchase options in anticipation of price changes. Options are a means for buyers to leverage the potential profits and limit the potential losses. Writers seek to take advantage of the time premiums that buyers are willing to pay for the options. Options may be used to hedge against a price change. For example, the owner of a stock may acquire a put to protect against a decline in the stock's price.

The intrinsic value of an option to buy is the difference between the price of the stock and the strike (exercise) price of the option. As the price of the stock rises, the value of the call rises. The intrinsic value of a put is the reverse: the difference between the strike price and the price of the stock. As the price of the stock declines, the value of the put rises.

Options tend to sell for more than their intrinsic values — that is, they command a *time premium*. This time premium works against the holder of the option, because it reduces the option's potential leverage. This premium declines with the passage of time, because on the expiration date the option must sell for its intrinsic value. Unless the price of the underlying stock changes sufficiently, the disappearance of the time premium inflicts a loss on the investor who purchased the option.

Since the creation of the Chicago Board Options Exchange (CBOE), put and call options have been traded on organized exchanges. These secondary markets have increased the popularity of options because investors know there are markets in which they may liquidate their positions. The initial success of option trading has led to the creation of varied types of puts and calls, such as stock index options. These index options are puts and calls based on an aggregate measure of the stock market instead of a specific security. Stock index options offer investors a means to manage their exposure to systematic risk by permitting them to take positions in the market as a whole.

The Black-Scholes option valuation model specifies that the value of a call option is positively related to the price and to the volatility of the underlying stock. As the price of the stock rises, the value of the call option rises. The same relationship holds for variability of returns, as options on volatile stocks command higher valuations. Call option values are also positively related to the life of the option.

As the term of the option diminishes and the option approaches expiration, the option's value declines.

While an increase in interest rates generally depresses the value of a financial asset, this negative relationship does not apply to options to buy stock. An increase in interest rates increases the value of the call option, because higher rates reduce the present value of a call's strike price. The lower strike price then increases the value of the option to buy the stock.

Put–call parity explains the interrelationships among financial markets. In equilibrium, the price of the underlying stock, the price of the puts and calls on the stock, and the present value of the strike price (as affected by the rate of interest) must balance or an opportunity for a risk-free arbitrage would exist. As investors seek to execute the arbitrage, the prices of the various securities are affected. An implication of put–call parity is that any change in one of the markets (e.g., an increased demand for stocks) must be transmitted to the other markets.

Strategies using options include writing a covered call and the protective put. Other possible option strategies are straddles and collars. Straddles involve buying or selling a put and a call on the same stock. Collars permit investors who own stock but cannot sell it to lock in the current price. All these strategies using options alter the individual's potential returns and risk exposure from investing in financial assets. Options, thus, are both a means to speculate on anticipated price movements in the underlying stocks and to manage the risk from actual price movements in the underlying stocks.

In addition to being used to value publicly traded calls, the Black-Scholes model may be applied to options issued by firms as part of incentive-based compensation packages. If the firm is successful and the value of its stock rises, the value of the options also increases. Since incentive options are compensation, an accounting question arises: Should the cost of the options be expensed? Expensing requires a valuation, and the Black-Scholes model is often used as a means to value incentive options in order to determine their cost.

Learning Objectives

Now that you have completed this chapter, you should be able to:

1. Define the word *option* as it applies to securities and differentiate among an option's market value, intrinsic value, and time premium.
2. Differentiate the profit and loss profiles from writing a covered call option and a naked call option.
3. Explain the relationship between the price of a stock, a call option, and a put option.
4. Compare buying a put with selling short.
5. Explain the importance of secondary markets to the development of puts and call options.
6. Identify the advantages offered by stock index options.
7. Determine the relationship between the value of an option and the variables specified in the Black-Scholes option valuation model.
8. Calculate the value of a call option using the Black-Scholes option valuation model.
9. Illustrate how arbitrage ensures that the markets for stocks, debt instruments, and options are interlinked.
10. Determine the profits and losses from option strategies such as a protective put, a straddle, and a collar.

PROBLEMS

1) A particular call is the option to buy stock at $25. It expires in six months and currently sells for $4 when the price of the stock is $26.

    a) What is the intrinsic value of the call? What is the time premium paid for the call?

    b) What will the value of this call be after six months if the price of the stock is $20? $25? $30? $40?

    c) If the price of the stock rises to $40 at the expiration date of the call, what is the percentage increase in the value of the call? Does this example illustrate favorable leverage?

    d) If an individual buys the stock and sells this call, what is the cash out-flow (i.e., net cost) and what will the profit on the position be after six months if the price of the stock is $10? $15? $20? $25? $26? $30? $40?

    e) If an individual sells this call naked, what will the profit or loss be on the position after six months if the price of the stock is $20? $26? $40?

2) What are the intrinsic values and time premiums paid for the following options?

Option	Price of the Option	Price of the Stock
Calls: XYZ, Inc., 30	$7.00	$34
XYZ, Inc., 35	2.50	34
Puts: XYZ, Inc., 30	1.25	34
XYZ, Inc., 35	4.25	34

If the stock sells for $31 at the expiration date of the preceding options, what are the profits or losses for the writers and the buyers of these options?

3) The price of a stock is $51. You can buy a six-month call at $50 for $5 or a six-month put at $50 for $2.

    a) What is the intrinsic value of the call?

    b) What is the intrinsic value of the put?

    c) What is the time premium paid for the call?

    d) What is the time premium paid for the put?

    e) If the price of the stock falls, what happens to the value of the put?

    f) What is the maximum you could lose by selling the call covered?

    g) What is the maximum possible profit if you sell the stock short?

    h) After six months, the price of the stock is $58.

    i) What is the value of the call?

    j) What is the profit or loss from buying the put?

    k) If you had sold the stock short six months earlier, what would your profit or loss be?

    l) If you sold the call covered, what would your profit or loss be?

4) A put is the option to sell stock at $40. It expires after three months and currently sells for $2 when the price of the stock is $42.

    a) If an investor buys this put, what will the profit be after three months if the price of the stock is $45? $40? $35?

    b) What will the profit from selling this put be after three months if the price of the stock is $45? $40? $35?

5) A stock that is currently selling for $47 has the following six-month options outstanding:

	Strike Price	Market Price
Call option	$45	$4
Put option	45	2

a) Which option(s) is (are) in the money?
b) What is the time premium paid for each option?
c) What is the profit (loss) at expiration given different prices of the stock—$30, $35, $40, $45, $50, $55, and $60—if the investor buys the call and the put?
d) What is the range of stock prices that will generate a profit if the investor sells the call and the put?
e) What is the range of stock prices that will generate a profit if the investor buys the stock and sells the call?

6) An investor buys a stock for $36. At the same time a six-month put option to sell the stock for $35 is selling for $2.
a) What is the profit or loss from purchasing the stock if the price of the stock is $30, $35, or $40?
b) If the investor also purchases the put (i.e., constructs a protective put), what is the combined cash outflow?
c) If the investor constructs the protective put, what is the profit or loss if the price of the stock is $30, $35, or $40 at the put's expiration? At what price of the stock does the investor break even?
d) What is the maximum potential loss and maximum potential profit from this protective put?
e) If, after six months, the price of the stock is $37, what is the investor's maximum possible loss?

7) A call option is the right to buy stock at $50 a share. Currently the option has six months to expiration, the volatility of the stock (standard deviation) is 0.30, and the rate of interest is 10 percent (0.1 in Exhibit 14.12).
a) What is the value of the option according to the Black-Scholes model if the price of th estock is $45, $50, or $55?
b) What is the value of the option when the price of the stock is $50 and the option expires in six months, three months, or one month?
c) What is the value of the option when the price of the stock is $50 and the interest rate is 5 percent, 10 percent, or 15 percent?
d) What is the value of the option when the price of the stock is $50 and the volatility of the stock is 0.40, 0.30, or 0.10?
e) What generalizations can be derived from the solutions to these problems?

8) In the body of this chapter, disequilibrium of the following equation indicated an opportunity for a riskless arbitrage:

$$0 = P_s + P_p - P_c - \frac{P_e}{(1+i)^n}.$$

The equation was illustrated as follows. A stock sells for $105; the strike price of both the put and call is $100. The price of the put is $5, the price of the call is $20, and both options are for one year. The rate of interest is 11.1 percent, so the present value of the $100 strike price is equal to $90. Given these values, the equation holds:

$$0 = \$105 + 5 - 20 - 90.$$

The opportunity for the riskless arbitrage was then illustrated by two cases, one in which the call was overpriced ($25) and one in which the put was overpriced ($10). For each of the following sets of values, verify that a riskless arbitrage opportunity exists by determining the profit if the price of the stock rises to $110, falls to $90, or remains unchanged at $105.

	Price of the Stock	Price of the Call	Price of the Put	Interest Rate
a.	$105	$10	$5	11.1%
b.	105	20	3	11.1
c.	105	20	5	5.263
d.	105	20	5	19
e.	112	20	5	11.1
f.	101	20	5	11.1

9) A straddle occurs when an investor purchases both a call option and a put option. Such a strategy makes sense when the individual expects a major price movement but is uncertain as to the direction. For example, a firm may be a rumored takeover candidate. If the rumor is wrong, the stock's price could decline and make the put profitable. If the rumor is correct and a takeover bid does occur, the price of the stock may rise and the call become profitable. There is also the possibility (probably small, at best) that the price of the stock could rise and subsequently fall, so the investor earns a profit on both the call and the put. The following problem works through a straddle.
   Given the following:

Price of the stock	$250
Price of a six-month call at $50	5
Price of a six-month call at $50	
3.50	

the individual establishes a straddle (i.e., buys one of each option).
   a) What is the profit (loss) on the position if, at the expiration date of the options, the price of the stock is $60?
   b) What is the profit (loss) on the position if, at the expiration date of the options, the price of the stock is $40?
   c) What is the profit (loss) on the position if, at the expiration date of the options, the price of the stock is $50?

10) As a well-paid executive, you received stock options that you recently exercised. However, you cannot legally sell the stock for the next six months. Currently the stock is selling for $38.25. A call to buy the stock at $40 is selling for $3.38 and a put to sell the stock at $35 is selling for $1.94. How could you use a collar to reduce your risk of loss from a decline in the price of the stock? Verify that the collar does achieve its objective.

Internet Application for Chapter 14   An Introduction to Options
Select one of the securities you have been following that you believe is under-valued (or overvalued) and whose price you expect to rise (or to fall). Instead of buying the stock, consider buying a call option (or a put option).

Using the sources from Chapter 4, locate prices for options that have one month, three months, and six months to expiration. You may also find prices at the Chicago Board Options Exchange Web site (**http://www.cboe.com**). Do not be surprised if one or more of the options do not exist. For strike prices, use three options:

1. an option that is close to the current price of the stock (i.e., an option that is virtually "at" the money or slightly "in" or "out" of the money),
2. an option that is approximately $5 out of the money, and
3. a option that is approximately $5 in the money.

You should have prices for 15 options. Answer the following questions.

1. If the price of the stock rises (falls) by 30 percent *after six months* have passed, what happens to the price of each option?
2. If the price of the stock rises (declines) 10 percent *immediately* after purchasing the option, what happens to the price of each option? Which option(s) would probably have generated the highest percentage loss?
3. If the price of the stock is *unchanged* during the year, how much would you have lost on each option? Why do you know that you would have sustained a loss? What would have been your percentage losses?

Supplemental Internet Application for Chapter 14

This assignment asks you to determine the values of call options on Cisco (CSCO), Coca-Cola (KO), or Microsoft (MSFT) using the Black-Scholes valuation model. That model was explained and illustrated in the body of the chapter. The data necessary to apply the model are (1) the price of the stock, (2) the option's strike price, (3) the term of the option, (4) the risk-free interest rate, and (5) the volatility of the underlying stock. The data are readily observable except the volatility of the underlying stock.

The CBOE publishes estimates of a stock's historical volatility. Go to the Chicago Board Options Exchange Website (**http://www.cboe.com**) and locate each company's historical volatility under "Market Data." This volatility data may be used in Black-Scholes to estimate an option's value (provided that past volatility is an accurate measure of current volatility).

Since the CBOE volatility data are annualized, you should apply them only to an option with a comparable expiration date (i.e., a one-year option). Choose a one-year call (referred to as a Long-term Equity AnticiPation Security or LEAPS) for each stock. Since you now have the strike price, the term (one year), and the volatility, all you need is the price of the stock and the one-year rate on a U.S. Treasury security. Determine the value of each option using Black-Scholes and compare that valuation to the current market price of the option. If they are different, what might that imply about the stock's volatility?

15 • • •

Commodity and Financial Futures

D o you want excitement and rapid action? Would you prefer to speculate in pork bellies (i.e., bacon) instead of investing in the stock of Swift or Armour? Then investing in commodity futures may satisfy this speculative desire. These futures contracts are among the riskiest investments available, as prices can change rapidly and produce sudden losses or profits.

There are two participants in the futures markets: the speculators who establish positions in anticipation of price changes and the hedgers who seek to employ futures contracts to reduce risk. The hedgers are growers, producers, and other users of commodities. They seek to protect themselves from price fluctuations, and by hedging they pass the risk of loss to the speculators. The price of a futures contract ultimately depends on the demand for and supply of these contracts by the hedgers and speculators.

This chapter is an elementary introduction to investing in futures contracts. The chapter describes the mechanics of buying and selling the contracts, the role of margin, the speculators' long and short positions, and how the hedgers use the contracts to reduce risk. Next follows a discussion of financial futures, since commodity contracts are not limited to physical assets. There are also futures contracts for the purchase and sale of financial assets and foreign currencies. There are even futures based on the Standard & Poor's 500 stock index or the New York Stock Exchange Composite Index.

Before reading this chapter, you should realize that futures contracts are not appropriate investments for the vast majority of individual investors. However, you may indirectly participate in these markets. Many corporations use futures contracts to help manage risk from commodity price fluctuations, changes in interest rates, and changes in currency prices. Portfolio managers also use futures contracts to reduce risk from fluctuations in securities prices. This usage is often disclosed in the financial statements you receive from corporations and mutual funds. So, while you may never personally participate in futures markets, you will have a better understanding of financial statements if you have a basic knowledge of these contracts and how they are used for speculation and for hedging.

WHAT IS INVESTING IN COMMODITY FUTURES?

futures contract
An agreement for the future delivery of a commodity at a specified date.

A commodity may be purchased for current delivery or for future delivery. Investing in commodity futures refers to a contract to buy or to sell (deliver) a commodity in the future. For this reason these investments are sometimes referred to as *futures*. A **futures contract** is a formal agreement between a buyer or seller and a commodity exchange. In the case of a purchase contract, the buyer agrees to accept a specific commodity that meets a specified quality in a specified month. In the case of a sale, the seller agrees to deliver the specified commodity during the designated month.

Investing in commodity futures is considered to be very speculative. For that reason investors should participate in this market only after their financial obligations and primary financial goals have been met. There is a large probability that the investor will suffer a loss on any particular purchase or sale of a commodity contract. Individuals who buy and sell commodity contracts without wanting to deal in the actual commodities are generally referred to as *speculators*, which differentiates them from the growers, processors, warehousers, and other dealers who also buy and sell commodity futures but really wish to buy or sell the actual commodity.

The primary appeal of commodity contracts to speculators is the potential for a large return on the investment resulting from the leverage inherent in commodity trading. This leverage exists because (1) a futures contract controls a substantial amount of the commodity and (2) the investor must make only a small payment to buy or sell a contract (i.e., there is a small margin requirement). These two points are discussed in detail later in this chapter.

Interactive e-lectures

See a visual explanation and example of forwards and futures at

http://mayoxtra.swlearning.com

THE MECHANICS OF INVESTING IN COMMODITY FUTURES

Like stocks and bonds, commodity futures may be purchased in several markets. One of the most important is the Chicago Board of Trade (CBT) (**http://www.cbt.com** or **http://www.cbot.com**), which executes contracts in agricultural commodities, such as corn, soybeans, and wheat. Other commodities are traded in various cities throughout the country. Over 50 commodities are traded on ten exchanges in the United States and Canada. As may be expected, the markets for some commodity futures developed close to the area where the commodity is produced. Thus, the markets for wheat are located not only in Chicago but also in Kansas City and Minneapolis. The market for several commodity futures is in New York City, where cocoa, coffee, sugar, potatoes, and orange juice are bought and sold.

Like stocks and bonds, commodity contracts are purchased through brokers. The broker (or a member of a brokerage firm) owns a seat on the commodity exchange. Membership on each exchange is limited, and only members are allowed to buy and sell the commodity contracts. If the investor's broker lacks a seat, then that broker must have a correspondent relationship with another broker who does own a seat.

The broker acts on behalf of the investor by purchasing and selling contracts through the exchange. The investor opens an account by signing an agreement that requires the contracts to be guaranteed. Since trading commodity contracts is considered to be speculative, some brokers will open accounts only after the investor has proved the capacity both to finance the account and to withstand any losses.

Once the account has been opened, the individual may trade commodity contracts. These are bought and sold in much the same way as stocks and bonds; however, the use of the words *buy* and *sell* is misleading. The individual does not buy or sell a contract, but enters a contract to buy or sell. A buy contract specifies that the individual will *accept* delivery and hence "buy" the commodity. A sell contract specifies that the individual will *make* delivery and hence "sell" the commodity.

A commodity order specifies whether the contract is a buy or a sell, the type of commodity and the number of units, and the delivery date (i.e., the month in which the contract is to be executed and the commodity is bought or sold). The investor can request a market order and have the contract executed at the current market price, or he or she may place orders at specified prices. Such orders may be for a day or until the investor cancels them (i.e., the order is good till canceled). Once the order is executed, the broker provides a confirmation statement for the sale or purchase and charges a commission for executing the order. This fee covers both the purchase and the sale of the contract.

Although a futures contract appears to involve a buyer and a seller, the actual contract is made between the individual and the exchange. If an individual buys a contract, the exchange guarantees the delivery (the sale). If an individual sells a contract, the exchange guarantees to take delivery (the purchase). When a contract is created, the exchange simultaneously makes an opposite contract with another investor. While the exchange has offsetting buy and sell contracts, the effect is to guarantee the integrity of the contracts. If one of the parties were to default (for example, the buyer), the seller's contract is upheld by the exchange.

Commodity Positions

The investor may purchase a contract for future delivery. This is the long position, in which the investor will profit if the price of the commodity and hence the value of the contract rises. The investor may also sell a contract for future delivery. This is the short position, in which the seller agrees to make good the contract (i.e., to deliver the goods) sometime in the future. This investor will profit if the price of the commodity and hence the value of the contract decline. These long and short positions are analogous to the long and short positions that the investor takes in the security market. Long positions generate profits when the value of the security rises, whereas short positions result in profits when the value of the security declines.

futures price
The price in a contract for the future delivery of a commodity.

The way in which each position generates a profit can be seen in a simple example. Assume that the **futures price** of wheat is $3.50 per bushel. If a contract is purchased for delivery in six months at $3.50 per bushel, the buyer will profit from this long position if the price of wheat *rises*. If the price increases to $4.00 per bushel, the buyer can exercise the contract by taking delivery and paying $3.50 per bushel. The speculator then sells the wheat for $4 per bushel, which produces a profit of $0.50 per bushel.

The opposite occurs when the price of wheat declines. If the price of wheat falls to $3.00 per bushel, the individual who bought the contract for delivery at $3.50 suffers a loss. But the speculator who sold the contract for the delivery of wheat (i.e., who took the short position) earns a profit from the price decline. The speculator can then buy wheat at the market price (which is referred to as the **spot price**) of $3.00, deliver it for the contract price of $3.50, and earn a $0.50 profit per bushel.

spot price
The current price of a commodity.

If the price rises, the short position will produce a loss. If the price increases from $3.50 to $4.00 per bushel, the speculator who sold a contract for delivery suffers a loss of $0.50 per bushel, because he or she must pay $4.00 to obtain the wheat that will be delivered for $3.50 per bushel.

Actually, the preceding losses and profits are generated without the goods being delivered. Of course, when a speculator buys a contract for future delivery, there is always the possibility that this individual will receive the goods. Conversely, if the speculator sells a contract for future delivery, there is the possibility that the goods will have to be supplied. However, such deliveries occur infrequently, because the speculator can offset the contract before the delivery date. This is achieved by buying back a contract that was previously sold or selling a contract that is owned.

This process of *offsetting existing contracts* is illustrated in the following example. Suppose a speculator has a contract to buy wheat in January. If the individual wants to close the position, he or she can sell a contract for the delivery of wheat in January. The two contracts cancel (i.e., offset) each other, as one is a purchase and the other is a sale. If the speculator actually received the wheat by executing the purchase agreement, he or she could pass on the wheat by executing the sell agreement. However, since the two contracts offset each other, the actual delivery and subsequent sale are not necessary. Instead, the speculator's position in wheat is closed, and the actual physical transfers do not occur. (This process is analogous to the writer of an option buying back the option. In both cases the investor's position is closed.)

Correspondingly, if the speculator has a contract for the sale of wheat in January, it can be canceled by buying a contract for the purchase of wheat in January. If the speculator were called upon to deliver wheat as the result of the contract to sell, the individual would exercise the contract to purchase wheat. The buy and sell contracts would then cancel each other, and no physical transfers of wheat would occur. Once again the speculator has closed the initial position by taking the opposite position (i.e., the sales contract is offset by a purchase contract).

Because these contracts are canceled and actual deliveries do not take place, it should not be assumed that profits or losses do not occur. The two contracts need not be executed at the same price. For example, the speculator may enter a contract for the future purchase of wheat at $3.50 per bushel. Any contract for the future delivery of comparable wheat can cancel the contract for the purchase. But the cost of the wheat for future delivery could be $3.60 or $3.40 (or any conceivable price). If the price of wheat rises (e.g., from $3.50 to $3.60 per bushel), the speculator with a long position earns a profit. However, if the speculator has a short position (i.e., a contract to sell wheat), this individual sustains a loss. If the price declines (e.g., from $3.50 to $3.40 per bushel), the short seller earns a profit, but the long position sustains a loss.

The Units of Commodity Contracts

To facilitate trading, contracts must be uniform. For a particular commodity the contracts must be identical. Besides specifying the delivery month, the contract must specify the grade and type of the commodity (e.g., a particular type of wheat) and the units of the commodity (e.g., 5,000 bushels). Thus, when an individual buys or sells a contract, there can be no doubt as to the nature of the obligation. For example, if the investor buys wheat for January delivery, there can be no confusion with a contract for the purchase of wheat for February delivery. These are two different commodities in the same way that AT&T common stock, AT&T preferred stock, and AT&T bonds are all different securities. Without such standardization of contracts there would be chaos in the commodity (or any) markets.

The units of trading vary with each commodity. For example, if the investor buys a contract for corn, the unit of trading is 5,000 bushels. If the investor buys a contract for lumber, the unit of trading is 110,000 board feet. A list of selected commodities, the markets in which they are traded, and the units of each contract are given in Exhibit 15.1. While the novice investor may not remember the units for a contract, the experienced investor is certainly aware of them. As will be explained later, because of the large units of many commodity contracts, a small change in the price of the commodity produces a considerable change in the value of the contract and in the investor's profits or losses.

Reporting of Futures Trading

Commodity futures prices and contracts are reported in the financial press in the same general form as stock and bond transactions. Typical reporting is as follows:

	Open	High	Low	Settle	Change	LIFETIME High	Low	Open Interest
Corn (CBT) 5,000 bu; cents per bushel								
Jan	233.0	231.5	230.5	230.50	−3.00	243	210.75	36,790
Mar	240.0	241.5	236.5	237.25	. . .	270	205.0	10,900
May	244.5	244.5	241.0	241.75	+0.25	286	221.0	5,444

The reporting is for corn traded on the Chicago Board of Trade (CBT). The unit of trading is 5,000 bushels (bu), and prices are quoted in cents. The opening price for January delivery was 233.5¢ ($2.335) per bushel, while the high, low, and closing (settle) prices were 231.5¢, 230.5¢, and 230.5¢, respectively. This closing price was 3¢ below the closing price on the previous day. The high and low (prior to the reported day of trading) for the lifetime of the contract were 243¢ and 210.75¢, respectively. The **open interest**, which is the number of contracts in existence, was 36,790.

This open interest varies over the life of the contract. Initially, the open interest rises as buyers and sellers establish positions. It then declines as the delivery date approaches and the positions are closed. This changing number of contracts is illustrated in Figure 15.1 (p. 426), which plots the spot and futures prices and the open interest for a September contract to buy Kansas City wheat. When the contracts were initially traded in November, there were only a few contracts in existence. By June the open interest had risen to over 10,000 contracts. Then, as the

open interest
The number of futures contracts in existence for a particular commodity.

EXHIBIT 15.1	Selected Commodities, Their Markets, and Their Units of Trading

Commodity	Market	Unit of One Contract
Corn	Chicago Board of Trade	5,000 bushels
Soybeans	Chicago Board of Trade	5,000 bushels
Cattle	Chicago Mercantile Exchange	40,000 pounds
Coffee	New York Board of Trade	37,500 pounds
Copper	COMEX (Div. of New York Mercantile Exchange)	25,000 pounds
Platinum	New York Mercantile Exchange	50 troy ounces
Silver	COMEX (Div. of New York Mercantile Exchange)	5,000 troy ounces
Lumber	Chicago Mercantile Exchange	110,000 board feet
Cotton	New York Board of Trade	50,000 pounds

remaining life of the contracts declined, the number of contracts fell as the various participants closed their positions. By late September only a few contracts were still outstanding.

As is explained in the section on pricing, futures prices tend to exceed spot prices. If speculators anticipate higher prices, they will buy contracts for future delivery. This anticipation of inflation and the cost of storing commodities usually drives up futures prices relative to the spot price, so the futures price exceeds the current price.

Figure 15.1, however, illustrates that this relationship does not always hold. The figure gives the futures price and the spot price of Kansas City wheat, and, except for a brief period, the spot price exceeds the futures price. This inversion of the relationship occurs if speculators believe the price of the commodity will decline. These speculators sell contracts now to lock in the higher prices so they may buy back the contracts at a lower price. This selling of the futures contracts drives their price down below the spot price.

The futures price must converge with the spot price as the expiration date of the contract approaches. As with options such as puts and calls, the value of the futures

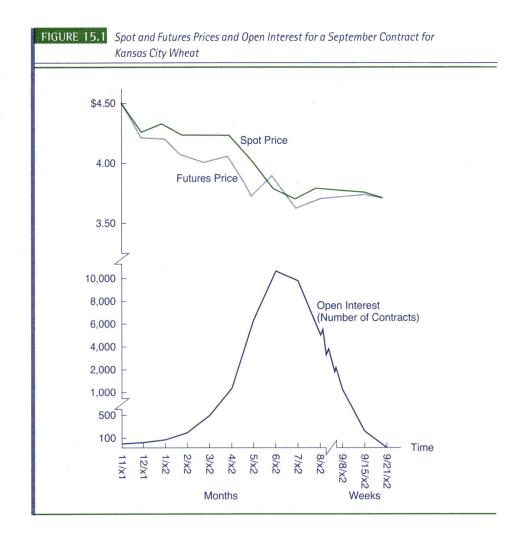

FIGURE 15.1   *Spot and Futures Prices and Open Interest for a September Contract for Kansas City Wheat*

contract can be worth only the value of the underlying commodity at the expiration date. This pattern of price behavior is also illustrated in Figure 15.1. In March, April, and May there was a considerable differential between the two prices. However, in late September the futures and spot prices converged and erased the differential.

The Regulation of Commodity Markets

The commodity exchanges, like stock exchanges, are subject to regulation. Until 1974, federal laws pertaining to commodity exchanges and commodity transaction laws were enforced by the Commodity Exchange Authority, a division of the Department of Agriculture. In 1974, Congress created the Commodity Futures Trading Commission (**http://www.cftc.gov**) to control entry into and operation of the futures markets. As with the regulation of security transactions, the regulations do not protect investors or speculators from their own folly. Instead, the regulations establish uniform standards for each commodity. The regulatory authority also has control over trading procedures, the hours of trading, and the maximum allowable daily price movements.

·•⦿LEVERAGE

margin
Good faith deposit made when purchasing or selling a commodity contract.

Commodities are paid for on delivery. Thus, a contract for future delivery means that the goods do not have to be paid for when the individual enters the contract. Instead, the investor (either a buyer or a seller) provides an amount of money, which is called **margin**, to protect the exchange and the broker and to guarantee the contract. This margin should not be confused with the margin that is used in the purchase of stocks and bonds. In the trading of stocks and bonds, margin represents the investor's equity in the position, whereas margin for a commodity contract is a deposit to show the investor's good faith and to protect the broker against an adverse change in the price of the commodity.

In the stock market, the amount of margin required varies with the price of the security, but in the commodity markets, the amount of margin does not vary with the dollar value of the transaction. Instead, each contract has a fixed minimum margin requirement. These margin requirements in 2004 for selected commodities and financial futures are given in Exhibit 15.2 (p. 428). Thus, an investor who purchases a futures contract for cocoa must put up $1,400. These margin requirements are established by the commodity exchanges but cannot be below the minimums established by the Commodity Futures Trading Commission. Individual brokers may require more, especially for small accounts.

The margin requirements are only a small percentage of the value of the contract. For example, the $1,400 margin requirement for cocoa gives the owner of the contract a claim on 10 metric tons of cocoa. If cocoa is selling for $1,400 a metric ton, the total value of the contract is $14,000. The margin requirement as a percentage of the value of the contract is only 10.0 percent ($1,400/$14,000). This small amount of margin is one reason why a commodity contract offers so much potential leverage.

The potential leverage from speculating in commodity futures may be illustrated in a simple example. Consider a contract to buy wheat at $3.50 per bushel. Such a contract controls 5,000 bushels of wheat worth a total of $17,500 (5,000 × $3.50). If the investor buys this contract and the margin requirement is $1,000, he or she must remit $1,000. An increase of only $0.20 per bushel in the price of the commodity produces an increase of $1,000 in the value of the contract. This $1,000

| EXHIBIT 15.2 | Margin Requirements for Selected Commodity Contracts |

Commodity	Margin Requirement	Financial Futures	Margin Requirement
Cocoa	$1,400	S&P 500	$17,813
Cotton	1,960	Federal funds	540
Hogs	1,080	Treasury bonds	2,565
Lumber	1,125	Municipal bonds	4,000
Silver	1,350	Eurodollar	1,080
Soybeans	743	British pound	1,350
Wheat	979		

is simply the product of the price change ($0.20) and the number of units in the contract (5,000). The profit on the contract if sold is $1,000.

What is the percentage return on the investment? With a margin of $1,000 the return is 100 percent, because the investor put up $1,000 and then earned an additional $1,000. An increase of less than 6 percent in the price of wheat produced a return on the speculator's money of 100 percent. Such a return is the result of leverage that comes from the small margin requirement and the large amount of the commodity controlled by the contract.

Leverage, of course, works both ways. In the previous example, if the price of the wheat declines by $0.10, the contract will be worth $17,000. A decline of only 2.9 percent in the price reduces the investor's margin from $1,000 to $500. To maintain the position, the investor must deposit additional margin with the broker. The request for additional funds is referred to as a **margin call**. Failure to meet the margin call will result in the broker's closing the position. Since the contract is supported only by the initial margin, further price declines will mean that there is less collateral to support the contract. Should the investor (i.e., the buyer or the seller) default on the contract, the exchange becomes responsible for its execution. The margin call thus protects the exchange.

Actually, there are two margin requirements. The first is the minimum initial deposit, and the second is the maintenance margin. The **maintenance margin** specifies when the investor must deposit additional funds with the broker to cover a decline in the value of a commodity contract. For example, the margin requirement for wheat is $1,000 and the maintenance margin is $750. If the investor owns a contract for the purchase of wheat and the value of the contract declines by $250 to the level of the maintenance margin ($750), the broker makes a margin call. This requires the investor to deposit an additional $250 into the account, which restores the initial $1,000 margin.

Maintenance margin applies to both buyers and sellers. If, in the previous example, the price of wheat were to rise by $250, the speculators who had sold short would see their margin decline from the initial deposit of $1,000 to $750. The broker would then make a margin call, which would require the short sellers to restore the $1,000 margin. Once again this protects the exchange, since the value of the contract has risen and the short seller has sustained the loss.

These margin adjustments occur daily. After the market closes, the value of each account is totaled. In the jargon of futures trading, each account is *marked to the market*. If a position has gained in value, funds are transferred into the account. If a position has lost value, funds are transferred out of the account. The effect is to

margin call
A request by a broker for an investor to place additional funds or securities in an account as collateral against borrowed funds or as a good faith deposit.

maintenance margin
The minimum level of funds in a margin account that triggers a margin call.

transfer the funds from the accounts that have sustained losses to those accounts that have experienced gains. If, as a result of the transfer of funds, the account does not meet the maintenance margin requirement, the broker issues a margin call that the individual must meet or the broker will close the position.

The process of marking to the market and daily cash flows may be seen in the following example for a futures contract for 5,000 bushels of a commodity (e.g., wheat or corn). The futures price is $3.00, the margin requirement is $1,500, and the maintenance margin requirement is $800. There are two speculators, one of whom expects the price to rise and buys the contract (i.e., is long) and the other who is short and sells the contract. Both make the initial $1,500 margin payment, so at the end of the first day their respective positions are

Day 1 Futures price: $3.00

Value of the contract:	$15,000
Margin positions:	

Speculator Long	Speculator Short
$1,500	$1,500

During the second day, the futures price rises to $3.05 and the margin accounts are as follows:

Day 2 Futures price: $3.05

Value of the contract:	$15,250
Margin positions:	

	Speculator Long	Speculator Short
Beginning balance	$1,500	$1,500
Change in balance	+250	–250
Required deposits	–	–
Voluntary withdrawals	250	–
Ending balance	$1,500	$1,250

Notice that Speculator Long has gained $250 while Speculator Short has lost $250 and the appropriate adjustments are made at the end of the day as each account is marked to the market. Since both accounts have more than $800, both meet the maintenance margin requirement, so no deposits of additional funds are needed. Speculator Long, however, may remove $250, since the account exceeds the initial margin requirement. These funds may be invested (e.g., in a money market account) to earn interest.

During the third day, the futures price continues to rise to $3.20 a bushel, so the value of the contract is $16,000. The positions for each account are now

Day 3 Futures price: $3.20

Value of the contract:	$16,000
Margin positions:	

	Speculator Long	Speculator Short
Beginning balance	$1,500	$1,250
Change in balance	+750	–750
Ending balance	$2,250	$500

Speculator Long may remove an additional $750 since the account again exceeds the margin requirement. Speculator Short's position is now less than the maintenance margin requirement. He or she will have to restore the account to the initial margin ($1,500), which will require an additional $1,000. After these changes the accounts will be

	Speculator Long	Speculator Short
Beginning balance	$1,500	$1,250
Change in balance	+750	−750
Balance	2,250	500
Required deposits	—	1,000
Voluntary withdrawals	−750	—
Closing balance	$1,500	$1,500

Notice that Speculator Long's $1,000 gain equals Speculator Short's $1,000 loss. If the futures price had declined from $3.00 to $2.80, the cash flows would have been reversed. Speculator Short would have $2,500 in the account and could remove $1,000, while Speculator Long would have only $500. Speculator Long would receive a margin call for $1,000 to restore the account to $1,500.

Whether the speculator chooses to meet the margin call is, of course, that person's decision, but a primary purpose of daily marking all positions to the market is to let the process of transferring funds occur. If a participant fails to meet a margin call, the broker closes the position, so that losses will not continue to increase (and put the brokerage firm at risk). Since speculators are highly aware of their risk exposure and often rapidly close positions, the probability they will receive a margin call is small. Such speculators rapidly close losing positions in order to limit their losses.

daily limit
The maximum daily change permitted in a commodity futures price.

While commodity prices can and do fluctuate, limits are imposed by the markets on the amount of price change permitted each day. The **daily limit** establishes the maximum permissible price increase or decrease from the previous day. The purpose of these limits is to help maintain orderly markets and to reduce the potentially disruptive effects from large daily swings in the price of the futures contract.[1]

Once the price of the futures contract rises by the permissible daily limit, further price increases are not allowed. This does not necessarily mean that trading ceases, because transactions can still occur at the maximum price or below should the price of the commodity weaken. The same applies to declining prices. Once the daily limit has been reached, the price cannot continue to fall, but transactions can still occur at the lowest price or above should the price strengthen. For example, when the 1992 Florida orange crop came in at the higher end of expectations, orange juice futures prices quickly fell. Contracts for January, February, and March delivery declined by the 5¢ daily limit. Although trading could have continued at the lowest price, trading ceased because no one was willing to buy at that level and speculators anticipated further price declines. The same result occurred during the 2003 mad cow disease scare. Even though the Chicago Mercantile Exchange *increased* the daily limit, the futures price of beef declined to the new daily limit and trading ceased. The same principle applies to price increases. In 1995, Hurricane Erin threatened lumber supplies, the price of September lumber rose by the $10 daily limit, and trading ceased.

---

1. The daily limit applies to many futures prices but not all, especially financial futures based on federal government debt and stock index futures.

●●HEDGING

One major reason for the development of commodity futures markets was the desire of producers to reduce the risk of loss through price fluctuations. The procedure for this reduction in risk is called **hedging**, which consists of taking opposite positions at the same time. In effect, a hedger simultaneously takes the long and the short position in a particular commodity.

Hedging is best explained by illustrations. In the first example, a wheat farmer expects to harvest a crop at a specified time. Since the costs of production are determined, the farmer knows the price that is necessary to earn a profit. Although the price that will be paid for wheat at harvest time is unknown, the current price of a contract for the future delivery of wheat is known. The farmer can then sell a contract for future delivery. Such a contract is a hedged position, because the farmer takes a long position (the wheat in the ground) and a short position (the contract for future delivery).

Such a position reduces the farmer's risk of loss from a price decline. Suppose the cost to produce the wheat is $2.50 per bushel and September wheat is selling in June for $2.75. If the farmer *sells* wheat for September delivery, a $0.25 per bushel profit is assured, because the buyer of the contract agrees to pay $2.75 per bushel on delivery in September. If the price of wheat declines to $2.50, the farmer is still assured of $2.75. However, if the price of wheat rises to $3.10 in September, the farmer still gets only $2.75. The additional $0.35 gain goes to the owner of the contract who bought the wheat for $2.75 but can now sell it for $3.10.

Is this transaction unfair? Remember that the farmer wanted protection against a decline in the price of wheat. If the price had declined to $2.40 and the farmer had not hedged, the farmer would have suffered a loss of $0.10 (the $2.40 price minus the $2.50 cost) per bushel. To obtain protection from this risk of loss, the farmer accepted the modest profit of $0.25 per bushel and relinquished the possibility of a larger profit. The speculator who bought the contract bore the risk of loss from a price decline and received the reward from a price increase.

Users of wheat hedge in the opposite direction. A flour producer desires to know the future cost of wheat in order to plan production levels and the prices that will be charged to distributors. However, the spot price of wheat need not hold into the future, so this producer *buys* a contract for future delivery and thereby hedges the position. This is hedging because the producer has a long position (the contract for the future delivery of wheat) and a short position (the future production of flour, which requires the future delivery of wheat).

If the producer buys a contract in June for the delivery of wheat in September at $2.75 per bushel, the future cost of the grain becomes known. The producer cannot be hurt by an increase in the price of wheat from $2.75 to $3.10, because the contract is for delivery at $2.75. However, the producer has forgone the chance of profit from a decline in the price of wheat from $2.75 to $2.40 per bushel.

Instead, the possibility of profit from a decline in the price of wheat rests with the speculator who sold the contract. If the price of wheat were to decline, the speculator could buy the wheat in September at the lower price, deliver it, and collect the $2.75 that is specified in the contract. However, this speculator would suffer a loss if the price of September wheat rose over $2.75. The cost would then exceed the delivery price specified in the contract.

These two examples illustrate why growers and producers hedge. They often take the opposite side of hedge positions. If all growers and producers agree on prices for future delivery, there would be no need for speculators; but this is not the case. Speculators buy or sell contracts when there is an excess or an insufficient supply. If the farmer in the preceding example could not find a producer to buy the contract for the future delivery of wheat, a speculator would buy the contract and accept the risk of a price decline. If the producer could not find a farmer to supply a contract for the future delivery of wheat, the speculator would sell the contract and accept the risk of a price increase.

Of course, farmers, producers, and speculators are simultaneously buying and selling contracts. No one knows who buys and who sells at a specific moment. However, if there is an excess or a shortage of one type of contract, the futures price of the commodity changes, which induces a certain behavior. For example, if September wheat is quoted at $2.75 per bushel, but no one is willing to buy at that price, the price declines. This induces some potential sellers to withdraw from the market and some potential buyers to enter the market. By this process, an imbalance of supply and demand for contracts for a particular delivery date is erased. It is the interaction of the hedgers and the speculators that establishes the price of each contract.

FINANCIAL AND CURRENCY FUTURES

financial futures
Contract for the future delivery of a financial asset.

currency futures
Contract for the future delivery of foreign exchange.

In the previous discussion, commodity contracts meant futures contracts for the delivery of physical goods such as wheat and corn. However, there are also **financial futures**, which are contracts for the future delivery of securities such as Treasury bills, and **currency futures**, which are contracts for the future delivery of currencies (e.g., the British pound or the European euro). Examples of these contracts and where they are traded are provided in Exhibit 15.3.

The market for financial futures, like the market for commodity futures, has two participants: the speculators and the hedgers. It is the interaction of their demand for and supply of these contracts that determines the price of a given futures contract. The speculators are taking positions in anticipation of price changes and the hedgers are taking positions to reduce the impact of price changes. The hedgers in financial futures tend to be large financial institutions and fixed-income portfolio managers. As interest rates and bond prices change, the yields from lending and the cost of borrowing are altered. To reduce the risk of loss from fluctuations in interest rates, borrowers and lenders establish hedge positions in financial futures to lock in a particular interest rate. They reduce the risk associated with changes in interest rates. The hedgers in currency futures are large multinational firms that make and receive payments in foreign currencies. These firms use futures contracts to lock in the price of the currency and thereby avoid the risk associated with fluctuations in exchange rates.

Speculators, of course, are not seeking to reduce risk but reap large returns for taking risks. The speculators are bearing the risk that the hedgers are seeking to avoid. The speculators try to correctly anticipate changes in the value of currencies and the direction of changes in interest rates and to take positions that will yield profits. The return they earn (if successful) is then magnified because of the leverage offered by the small margin requirements necessary to establish the positions.

How financial futures may produce profits for speculators may be illustrated with an example using an interest rate futures contract for the delivery of U.S. Treasury bonds. Suppose a speculator expects interest rates to fall and bond prices to rise. This individual would *buy* a contract for the delivery of Treasury bonds in the future, establishing a *long* position. (Do not confuse yourself; it is easy to get

| EXHIBIT 15.3 | Selected Financial and Currency Futures |

Contract	Market
U.S. Treasury bonds	Chicago Board of Trade
U.S. Treasury notes	Chicago Board of Trade
U.S. Treasury bills	International Monetary Market at the Chicago Mercantile Exchange
Bank CDs	International Monetary Market at the Chicago Mercantile Exchange
Eurodollar	International Monetary Market at the Chicago Mercantile Exchange
British pound	International Monetary Market at the Chicago Mercantile Exchange
Canadian dollar	International Monetary Market at the Chicago Mercantile Exchange
Japanese yen	International Monetary Market at the Chicago Mercantile Exchange
Swiss franc	International Monetary Market at the Chicago Mercantile Exchange

the positions backwards because you anticipate a *decline in interest rates* and the word "decline" implies taking a short position.) If interest rates do fall and bond prices rise, the value of this contract increases because the speculator has the contract for the delivery of bonds at a lower price (i.e., higher yield). If, however, interest rates rise, bond prices fall and the value of this contract declines. The decline in the value of the contract inflicts a loss on the speculator who bought the contract when yields were lower.

If the speculator expects interest rates to rise, that individual *sells* a contract for the future delivery of Treasury bonds (i.e., establishes a *short* position). If interest rates do rise and the value of the bonds declines, the value of this contract must decline, but the speculator earns a profit. This short seller can buy the bonds at a lower price and deliver them at the price specified in the contract. Or the speculator may simply buy a contract at the lower value, thereby closing out the position at a profit. Of course, if this speculator is wrong and interest rates fall, the value of the bonds increases, inflicting a loss on the speculator, who must now pay more to buy the bonds to cover the contract.

The same general principles apply to currency futures. Suppose the price of the British pound is $2. A speculator who anticipates that the price of the pound will rise establishes a long position in the pound. This individual buys a contract for the future delivery of pounds. The futures price may be $2.02 or $1.96. It need not necessarily equal the current, or spot, price. (If many speculators expect the price of the pound to rise, they will bid up the futures price so that it exceeds the current price. If speculators expect the price of the pound to fall, they will then drive down the futures price.) If this speculator buys the futures contract for $2.02 and is correct (i.e., the price of the pound rises), that individual makes a profit. If, for example, the price of the pound were to rise to $2.20, the value of the contract may rise by $0.18 per pound. At expiration the futures and spot prices must be equal. Thus, if the pound is $2.20 on the expiration date, the value of the contract must be $2.20 per pound. Of course, if the speculator is wrong and the price of the pound declines to $1.80, the value of the contract also declines, and the speculator suffers a loss.

If the speculator had anticipated a decline in the value of the pound, that individual would establish a short position and sell contracts for the future delivery of pounds. If the speculator is right and the value of the pound declines, the speculator may close the position for a profit. Since pounds are now worth less, the speculator may buy the cheaper pounds and deliver them at the higher price specified in the contract. If the speculator had been wrong and the price of the pound had risen, that individual would have suffered a loss, as it would have cost more to buy the pounds to make the future delivery required by the contract.

Financial and currency futures, like all futures contracts, offer the speculator an opportunity for profit from a change in prices. Although such securities are not suitable for the portfolios of most individuals, they do offer more sophisticated investors an opportunity for large returns. Whether the returns justify the large risks is, of course, a decision that each individual investor must make.

While most individuals think of futures contracts as a means to speculate on price changes, financial futures may be used to reduce the risk of loss from an increase in interest rates. Consider an investor who desires a flow of income and has constructed a large portfolio of bonds. The portfolio's market value would decline if interest rates rose. To offset the potential loss, the investor could hedge using financial futures. Since the individual has a long position in the bonds, the investor must take a short position in the futures. Therefore, the investor sells contracts for the future delivery of bonds. If interest rates rise (and therefore cause the value of the bonds to fall), the value of the futures contracts also falls. Since the investor has a short position in the contracts, the individual profits from the rising interest rates. The profits on the futures contracts then offset the decline in the value of the bonds.

STOCK MARKET FUTURES

stock index futures
A contract based on an index of security prices

Futures contracts are also based on an index of the stock market (e.g., the Value Line stock index, the Standard & Poor's 500 stock index, or the New York Stock Exchange Composite Index). These **stock index futures** contracts offer speculators and hedgers opportunities for profit or risk reduction that are not possible through the purchase of individual securities. For example, the S&P 500 stock index futures contracts have a value that is 250 times the value of the index. Thus, if the S&P 500 stock index is 1,000, the contract is worth $250,000. By purchasing this contract (i.e., by establishing a long position), the holder profits if the market rises. If the index were to rise to 1,100, the value of the contract would increase to $275,000. The investor would then earn a profit of $25,000. Of course, if the NYSE Index should decline, the buyer would experience a loss.

The sellers of these contracts also participate in the fluctuations of the market. However, their positions are the opposite of the buyers (i.e., they are short). If the value of the S&P 500 stock index were to fall from 1,000 to 900, the value of the contract would decline from $250,000 to $225,000, and the short seller would earn a $25,000 profit. Of course, if the market were to rise, the short seller would suffer a loss. Obviously, if the individual anticipates a rising market, that investor should buy the futures contract. Conversely, if the investor expects the market to fall, that individual should sell the contract.

NYSE Index futures contracts are similar to other futures contracts. The buyers and sellers must make good faith deposits (i.e., margin payments). As with other futures contracts, the amount of this margin ($17,800) is modest relative to the value of the contract. Thus, these contracts offer considerable leverage. If stock prices move against the investor and his or her equity in the position declines, the individual will have to place additional funds in the account to support the contract. Since there is an active market in the contracts, the investor may close a position at any time by taking the opposite position. Thus, if the investor had purchased a contract, that long position would be closed by selling a contract. If the investor had sold a contract, that short position would be closed by buying a futures contract.

There is one important difference between stock market index futures and commodity futures contracts. Settlement at the expiration or maturity of the contract occurs in cash. There is no physical delivery of securities as could occur with a futures contract to buy or sell wheat or corn. Instead, gains and losses are totaled and are added to or subtracted from the participants' accounts. The long and short positions are then closed.

One reason for the development of commodity futures markets was the need by producers and users of commodities to hedge their positions against price fluctuations. Stock index futures (and other financial and currency futures) developed in part for the same reason. Portfolio managers buy and sell stock index futures in order to hedge against adverse price movements. For example, suppose a portfolio manager has a well-diversified portfolio of stocks. If the market rises, the value of this portfolio rises. However, there is risk of loss if the market were to decline. The portfolio manager can reduce the risk of loss by selling an NYSE Composite Index futures contract. If the market declines, the losses experienced by the portfolio will be at least partially offset by the appreciation in the value of the short position in the futures contract.

To execute such a hedge, the portfolio manager uses a futures contract that matches the composition of the portfolio. The NYSE Composite Index contract is suitable for a well-diversified stock portfolio but would not be appropriate for a specialized portfolio. Instead, the portfolio manager, who is responsible for a portfolio of smaller companies, would more likely use futures on the S&P Midcap index, which gives more weight to smaller companies.

To hedge using stock index futures, the portfolio manager divides the value of the portfolio by the value of the contract to determine the number of contracts to sell. For example, if the value of the portfolio is $1,000,000 and the futures contracts are worth $85,000, the individual would sell 11 to 12 contracts ($1,000,000/ $85,000 = 11.76). It may not be possible to exactly hedge the portfolio, since the futures contracts may be unavailable in the desired units. In this example, the portfolio manager would not be able to sell 11.76 futures contracts, but would have to sell either 11 or 12 contracts. This question of units is less of a problem for managers of large portfolios. If the portfolio's value had been $100,000,000, the number of contracts would be 1,176 ($100,000,000/$85,000 = 1,176.47), and the difference between 1,176 and 1,177 is immaterial. The problem facing this portfolio manager will be the market's ability to absorb such a large number of contracts. Is there sufficient demand at current prices to absorb $100,000,000 worth of futures contracts? If the answer is no, then prices will change (which changes the required number of contracts) or the portfolio manager will not be able to hedge completely the long position in the stocks.

In addition to the number of contracts, the portfolio manager must consider the volatility of the portfolio relative to the market. The preceding illustration implicitly assumes that the value of the portfolio exactly follows the index on which the futures contract is based. In effect, the example assumes that the portfolio's beta equals 1.0. If the beta is greater than 1.0, more contracts must be sold to hedge against a price decline, since the value of the contracts sold short will decline less than the value of the portfolio. If the portfolio's beta is less than 1.0, fewer contracts must be sold, since the value of the market will decline more than the value of the portfolio.

The entire process of hedging is illustrated in Exhibit 15.4, in which two portfolio managers want to hedge $2,000,000 portfolios against a price decline. Portfolio A has a beta of 1.25, while portfolio B has a beta of 0.75. Since the portfolio betas differ, portfolio A requires that 9 contracts be sold, while portfolio B requires the selling of only 5. The market subsequently declines by 10 percent from 1,100 to 990. Each portfolio sustains a loss, but the short positions in the futures contracts generate profits that offset the losses. Except for the problem of units, each investor has successfully hedged against the price decline but has also forgone the opportunity for a gain. If the market had risen, the increase in the value of the contracts would offset the gain in the stocks. Hedging with stock index futures works in both directions but is the most appropriate strategy when the portfolio manager expects a price decline and is unwilling to sell the portfolio. For example, the portfolio manager may wish to hedge during a period of greater uncertainty but does not want to sell the securities and generate taxable capital gains.

Besides selling the index futures contract (establishing a short position in futures), the portfolio manager could have hedged by writing an index call option (establishing a covered call position) or by purchasing an index put option (establishing a protective put position). Each of these strategies is designed to protect against a decline in the market as a whole. Each offers potential advantages and has disadvantages, so there is no clear argument to use one exclusively. Selling a futures contract is an easy position to establish and tends to have low transaction costs. If, however, the market were to rise, the loss on the futures contract will offset the gain on the market. Selling the futures eradicates the upside potential.

Selling the call generates income from the sale but the downside protection is limited. If the market were to decline sufficiently to offset the proceeds of the sale of the call, the portfolio will sustain a loss. In addition, if the market rises, the value of the call will increase, which offsets the gain in the portfolio. The protective put does not limit the upside potential. If the market were to rise, the increase in the value of the portfolio is not offset by an equal decrease in the value of the put. But buying the put requires a cash outlay, and the process must be repeated (and cash outlays increased) if the portfolio manager wants to retain the protection from a market decline.

EXHIBIT 15.4   Using Stock Index Futures to Hedge $2,000,000 Portfolios

	Portfolio A	Portfolio B
Value of portfolio:	$2,000,000	$2,000,000
Beta:	1.25	0.75
Value of S&P 500 stock index contract:	$250 × 1,100 = $275,000	$250 × 1,100 = $275,000
Number of contracts necessary to hedge:	($2,000,000/$275,000)(1.25) = 9.09	($2,000,000/$275,000)(0.75) = 5.45
Number of contracts sold:	9	5
Gain on futures contracts sold short after market declines by 10 percent to 900:	$275,000 × 9 − 990($250)9 = $247,500	$275,000 × 5 − 990($250)5 = $137,500
Loss on portfolio:	[$2,000,000(1 − 0.1) − $2,000,000] (1.25) = −$250,000	[$2,000,000(1 − 0.1) − $2,000,000] (0.75) = −$150,000
Net gain (loss)	$247,500 − $250,000 = ($2,500)	$137,500 − ($150,000) = ($12,500)

••THE PRICING OF FUTURES

Several factors may affect a futures contract's price. For example, expectations have been discussed as motivating speculators. The expectation of higher prices leads speculators to take long positions, and the expectation of lower prices results in their establishing short positions. Thus, the futures price mirrors what speculators anticipate prices will be in the future. In addition, the futures price and the spot price are not independent of each other. Such factors as the cost of carrying the commodity link the spot and futures prices. The pricing of futures contracts is an involved topic. The following material covers only the basics so an investor can have an understanding of the pricing of a futures contract. More detailed discussions may be found in texts devoted solely to derivatives.[2]

The following discussion is based on a commodity whose spot price is $100; the futures contract is for delivery after one year. Suppose individuals expect the price of the commodity to be $110 after one year. What should be the current price of a one-year futures contract? The answer is $110. Consider how individuals would react if the price were $108. They would buy the futures contract and, after one year, when the price of the commodity was $110, they would exercise the contract to buy the good for $108 and promptly sell it for $110, making a $2 profit. If the futures price exceeded $110 (e.g., $113), they would reverse the procedure and sell the futures contract. After one year, they would buy the commodity for $110, deliver it for the contract price of $113, and clear $3. For any futures price other than $110, speculators would take positions in the futures contracts. Only if the futures price equals the expected price in the future will the market be in equilibrium and speculators will take no action.

For this reason, futures prices are often considered to be measures of what investors, speculators, and other market participants currently expect the price of the commodity to be in the future. That is, the current futures prices are an indication of what the future holds. The process of using futures prices as a forecasting tool is sometimes referred to as "price disclosure." The current futures price discloses what market participants believe the future price will be.

If expectations concerning future prices were to change, then the futures price must also change. A major failure of the coffee crop would be expected to increase the future price of coffee, so the expectation of high prices would drive up the current futures price. Of course, if the price of coffee did not rise, those speculators who bought in anticipation of the price increase would lose, while those who sold in anticipation that the price increase would not occur would win.

An additional factor that affects futures prices is the cost of carrying the commodity. In the previous examples, the speculator took only one side, that is, he or she bought or sold the futures in anticipation of a price change and the futures price mirrored the speculator's expected price change. Suppose the individual could buy the commodity now for $100 *and* sell the futures contract at $110. If the price rises to $110, the investor wins because the commodity that cost $100 can be delivered for $110. If the price exceeds $110, this individual still gets $110 and earns the $10. If the price is less than $110, the profit remains $10 because the price is set in the contract at $110. What is the catch?

The problem is the cost of carrying the commodity. If the individual buys the commodity for $100, those funds will not be earning interest (if the investor uses his

2. For a more detailed discussion of futures pricing, see Don M. Chance, *An Introduction to Derivatives and Risk Management*, 6th ed. (Mason, OH: South-Western Publishing, 2004); or Robert W. Kolb, *Futures, Options, and Swaps*, 3rd ed. (Malden, MA: Blackwell Publishers, Inc., 2000).

or her own money) or will be requiring interest payments if the funds were borrowed. Suppose the interest rate is 8 percent. Now the individual can borrow $100, buy the commodity for $100, enter into a contract to deliver the commodity after a year for $110, and clear a $2 profit. Thus, if the *futures price exceeds the spot price plus the cost of carry*, then an opportunity for a risk-free arbitrage exists. You will buy the commodity and sell the futures (i.e., long the commodity and short the futures). The act of executing these positions will drive up the spot price of the commodity and drive down the futures price. Speculators who anticipate a price of $110 in the future will gladly buy the futures contract for less than $110, since they anticipate earning the difference between $110 and whatever amount they buy the contract for.

If the interest rate were 12 percent, you would reverse the procedure. You sell the commodity at the current spot price (receiving the $100) and buy a contract for future delivery at $110 (i.e., short the commodity and long the futures). Next invest (lend) the money received from the sale at 12 percent. At the end of the year, you receive the commodity that previously had been sold and make $2 on the transaction. Although the cost of the commodity was $110 and you received only $100 from the sale, you earned $12 on the sale proceeds and netted $2 on the set of transactions.

Once again the act of executing these positions affects the prices of the commodity. Selling the commodity in the spot market will decrease its price, and buying the futures contract will increase its price. As the futures price increases, the speculators, who anticipate the price will be $110, gladly supply (i.e., sell) the contracts as the futures price rises above $110.

In the previous illustration, the cost of carry was limited to the rate of interest. Although that limitation may apply to a financial contract, it does not apply to a contract for a commodity. For commodities, the cost of carry includes interest expense and warehouse expenses, insurance, and shipping.

Consider the preceding case in which the spot price was $100, the futures price was $110, and the interest rate was 8 percent; you bought the commodity with borrowed funds and sold the futures contract. Now, however, add a $9 cost of warehousing and shipping the commodity. These additional expenses alter the potential for an arbitrage profit. The futures price must exceed $117 for you to earn a profit. If you sell the futures contract for $120, you can buy the commodity today for $100 with borrowed funds, pay the $8 interest, cover the $9 in other expenses, and earn a $3 profit without bearing any risk. However, now the futures price must greatly exceed the spot price for the arbitrage opportunity to exist.

SUMMARY

Investing in futures involves entering contracts for future delivery. The speculator may take a long position, which is the purchase of a contract for future delivery, or a short position, which is the sale of a contract for future delivery. The long position generates profits if the price rises, while the short position results in a gain if the price falls.

Commodity and financial futures contracts are purchased through brokers who own seats on commodity exchanges. The contracts are supported by deposits, which are called *margin*, that signify the investor's good faith. The margin requirement is only a small fraction of the value of the contract, and this produces considerable potential for leverage. A small change in the price of the commodity produces a large profit or loss relative to the small amount of margin. For this reason, commodity contracts are considered very speculative.

Hedging plays an important role in commodity futures markets. Growers, miners, and users of commodities often wish to reduce their risk of loss from price fluctuations and thus hedge their positions. Growers sell contracts for future delivery, and users buy contracts for future delivery. Frequently, it is the speculators who are buying and offering the contracts sought by the hedgers. In this way the risks that the hedgers seek to reduce are passed on to the speculators.

Besides commodity futures there are financial futures, currency futures, and stock index futures. Financial futures are contracts for the delivery of financial assets, such as U.S. Treasury bills and bonds. Currency futures are contracts for the future delivery of foreign moneys, such as Japanese yen or British pounds. Stock index futures are based on a broad measure of the market (e.g., the New York Stock Exchange Composite Index). Speculators who anticipate movements in interest rates, foreign currencies, or the stock market can speculate on these anticipated price changes by taking appropriate positions in futures contracts. As with all commodity contracts, the potential return may be quite large, but the risk of loss is also large. Speculating in commodity futures is probably best left to those investors who understand these potential risks and can afford to take them.

Learning Objectives

Now that you have completed this chapter, you should be able to:

1. Define a futures contract.
2. Differentiate between the long and the short positions in a futures contract.
3. Explain the role of margin and the process of having an account "marked to the market."
4. Contrast the role of margin in the stock market and the futures markets.
5. Distinguish spectators from hedgers and describe the role played by each in the futures markets.
6. Identify forces that determine the price of a futures contract.
7. Demonstrate how speculators earn profits or suffer losses in the futures markets.
8. Illustrate how hedgers use futures contracts to reduce the risk of loss from price fluctuations.
9. Explain how you can take a position in the securities markets through using stock index futures.

PROBLEMS

1) You expect the stock market to decline, but instead of selling a stock short, you decide to sell a stock index futures contract based on the New York Stock Exchange Composite Index. The index is currently 6,000, and the contract has a value that is $250 times the amount of the index. The margin requirement is $20,000 and the maintenance margin requirement is $5,000.

   a) When you *sell* the contract, how much must you put up?
   b) What is the value of the contract based on the index?
   c) If after one week of trading the index stands at 6,010, what has happened to your position? How much have you lost or profited?
   d) If the index rose to 6,070, what would you be required to do?
   e) If the index declined to 5,940 (1 percent from the starting value), what is your percentage profit or loss on your position?
   f) If you had purchased the contract instead of selling it, how much would you have invested?
   g) If you had purchased the contract and the index subsequently rose from 6,000 to 6,070, what would be your required investment?
   h) Contrast your answers to parts (d) and (g).

2) This problem illustrates hedging with currency futures. The questions lead you through the process of hedging. While this material was not explicitly covered in the text material, your instructor may use this problem to show how hedging may reduce the risk of loss from fluctuations in the price of a foreign currency. You expect to receive a payment of 1,000,000 British pounds after six months. The pound is currently worth $1.60 (i.e., £1 = $1.60), but the six-month futures price is $1.56 (i.e., £1 = $1.56). You expect the price of the pound to decline (i.e., the value of the dollar to rise). If this expectation is fulfilled, you will suffer a loss when the pounds are converted into dollars when you receive them six months in the future.
   a) Given the current price, what is the expected payment in dollars?
   b) Given the futures price, how much would you receive in dollars?
   c) If, after six months, the pound is worth $1.35, what is your loss from the decline in the value of the pound?
   d) To avoid this potential loss, you decide to hedge and sell a contract for the future delivery of pounds at the going futures price of $1.56. What is the cost to you of this protection from the possible decline in the value of the pound?
   e) If, after hedging, the price of the pound falls to $1.35, what is the maximum amount that you lose? (Why is your answer different from your answer to part (c)?)
   f) If, after hedging, the price of the pound rises to $1.80, how much do you gain from your position?
   g) How would your answer be different to part (f) if you had not hedged and the price of the pound had risen to $1.80?

3) One use for futures markets is "price discovery," that is, the futures price mirrors the current consensus of the future price of the commodity. The current price of gold is $350 but you expect the price to rise to $400. If the futures price were $390, what would you do? If your expectation is fulfilled, what is your profit? If the futures price were $418, what would you do? What futures price will cause you to take no action? Why?

4) The current price of wheat is $3.70 and the expenses for carrying wheat (combined cost of storage, insurance, shipping) are 20 percent of the price. Based on this information, what should be the price of wheat after a year? What would you do if the futures price were $4.55?

Internet Application for Chapter 15   Commodity and Financial Futures

Futures are exceedingly risky investments, especially since the small margin requirements result in the large use of financial leverage. Go to the following exchanges and answer the following questions.

1. Corn and wheat are traded on which exchange(s)? What are the size of each contract and the margin requirement (or "performance bond") for each contract? What is the current or spot price of each commodity and what is the futures price for a contract for delivery approximately three months into the future? What is the value of the contract?

2. Repeat the above questions using stock index futures.

3. After one week has passed, what are the values of the contracts? What are the percentage changes in the futures prices and the percentage returns based on the margin requirements? Which sides, the long or the short, sustained a loss?

Web addresses for the exchanges are

Chicago Board of Trade   **http://www.cbt.com**

Kansas City Board of Trade   **http://www.kcbt.com**

Chicago Mercantile Exchange   **http://www.cme.com**

(You may have to use the site maps to find the requested information or look under entries such as "contract specifications" or "clearing.")

Postscript

H ow would you answer the following questions?

- Your team has just scored a touchdown to close the gap to 14 to 13. There are about 2½ minutes left on the clock. Do you go for a near-certain extra point to tie the game or do you call a less-certain two-point play?
- You have just received $20,000, and a friend suggests that you buy this $2 stock that will double, maybe even triple, within a year. Do you take your friend's advice?

The answer to the first question is not obvious. I would go for the two-point conversion. It's a game and the object is to win. Of course, if my job depended on the outcome, I might go for the tie and take my chances on getting the ball back or wait until overtime. If you have read the material in this text, the answer to the second question is obvious: Don't do it!

Investing is not a game whose objective is to win. While one objective is price appreciation and wealth accumulation, all investments have two components: the return and the risk necessary to earn that return. The management of risk is as important, perhaps even more important, than focusing on winning (i.e., the return). The objective is to construct a well-diversified portfolio that offers a reasonable return over an extended period of time. You can take that $20,000 and construct a diversified portfolio through the acquisition of investment companies such as mutual funds or you can invest $2,000 in ten different common stocks. The probability that these strategies will double or triple your money in a year is virtually nil, but then so is the probability that you will lose the entire amount.

In addition to the trade-off between risk and return, you need to remember that financial markets are very efficient. This is both a blessing and a curse. The blessing is that over time you should earn a return that mirrors the market return plus (or minus) an adjustment for the risk you bear. More aggressive portfolios should produce higher returns, but at a given point in time, that strategy could general greater losses. Since you accumulate assets over a period of time and liquidate those assets over time, you should not always be buying at the highs nor selling at the lows. The impact of the highs and lows should be offset, and the return should compensate you for the risk. It is, of course, your decision as to how much risk you feel comfortable taking, and only you can make that determination.

The curse of efficient markets is that most investment strategies designed to outperform the market don't work. If you strive to develop a skill (e.g., playing the piano or playing tennis) or if you learn more about something (e.g., impressionist painters), you should improve and enjoy the results of your efforts.

Efficient markets, however, suggest this may not be true concerning investments. More knowledge need not lead to superior investment returns, but that knowledge may improve your ability to better manage risk and avoid losses.

Having completed this text, you should know more about investing and the various assets and alternative strategies available to you. It is your obligation to put this knowledge to work. The magic of compounding means that small amounts consistently saved and invested grow into large sums. This process, however, requires self-discipline and patience. If you can avoid the temptation to go for broke, to get caught up in fads, or to chase the latest "new" or "hot" idea, you should do well over time. Ultimately, that is the purpose of learning about investing.

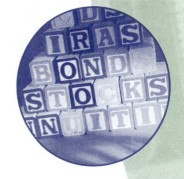

Review: The Time Value of Money

Time plays an important role in finance and investments. For example, investments are made today and returns are earned in the future. The time value of money links the present and the future. It is the mechanism for taking the present into the future and for bringing the future back to the present. Four basic time value cases are explained and illustrated in this review: (1) the future value of $1, (2) the present value of $1, (3) the future sum or value of an annuity, and (4) the present value of an annuity.

Being able to solve time value problems should facilitate your ability to understand investments, develop financial plans, and value securities. To solve the problems, you may use a financial calculator, computer programs such as Excel, or interest tables. In this review, interest tables are used to illustrate the mechanics and financial calculator solutions are provided in the margin.

You should realize that not every problem may readily fit into a preprogrammed calculator. For example, a financial calculator may limit the number of periods in which you have to enter variable cash flows. Interest tables also have weaknesses; the values in the tables are discrete, such as 4 and 5 percent and 9 and 10 years. You cannot use interest rates such as 4.6 percent or periods such as 9 years and 5 months (unless you interpolate).

While financial calculators, computer programs, and interest tables facilitate the calculations, you must set up the problem. Even after correctly setting up the problem and obtaining the answer, you have to interpret the results. For example, if a problem asks you to compare investing $1,000 in an IRA for ten years at 10 percent to investing $1,400 in an IRA for ten years at 8 percent, the final amounts in each account can be determined using financial calculators, computer programs, or interest tables. But you will have to make the comparison and draw any conclusions.

THE FUTURE VALUE OF $1

If $100 is deposited in an account that pays 5 percent annually, how much money will be in the account at the end of the year? The answer is easy to determine: $100 plus $5 interest, for a total of $105. That is,

Initial principal + (Interest rate × Initial principal) = Principal after one year.

compounding
The process by which interest is paid on interest that has been previously earned.

How much will be in the account after two years? This answer is obtained in the same manner by adding the interest earned during the second year to the principal at the beginning of the second year — that is, $105 plus 0.05 times $105 equals $110.25. After two years the initial deposit of $100 will have grown to $110.25; the savings account will have earned $10.25 in interest. This total interest is composed of $10 representing interest on the initial principal and $0.25 representing interest that has accrued during the second year on the $5 in interest earned during the first year. This earning of interest on interest is called **compounding**. Money that is deposited in savings accounts is frequently referred to as being compounded, for interest is earned on both the principal and the previously earned interest.

The words *interest* and *compounded* are frequently used together. For example, banks may advertise that interest is compounded daily for savings accounts, or the cost of a loan may be expressed as 6 percent compounded quarterly. In the previous example, interest was earned only once during the year; thus it is an example of interest that is compounded annually. In many cases, interest is not compounded annually but quarterly, semiannually, or even daily. The more frequently it is compounded (i.e., the more frequently the interest is added to the principal), the more rapidly the interest is put to work to earn even more interest.

How much will be in the account at the end of 25 years? By continuing with this method, it is possible to determine the amount that will be in the account at the end of 25 or more years, but doing so is obviously a lot of work. Fortunately, there are easier ways to ascertain how much will be in the account after any given number of years. The first is to use an interest table called the future value of $1 table.

The first table in Appendix A gives the interest factors for the future value of $1. The interest rates at which $1 is compounded periodically are read horizontally at the top of the table. The number of periods (e.g., years) is read vertically along the left-hand margin. To determine the amount to which $100 will grow in 25 years at 5 percent interest compounded annually, multiply $100 by the interest factor, 3.386, to obtain the answer $338.60. Thus, if $100 were placed in a savings account that paid 5 percent interest annually, there would be $338.60 in the account after 25 years.

Interest tables for the future value of $1 are based on a simple equation. The general formula for finding the amount to which $1 will grow in n number of years, if it is compounded annually, is

(R.1)
$$P_0(1 + i)^n = P_n.$$

Thus, the general formula for finding the future value of $1 for any number of years consists of (1) the initial dollar (P_0), (2) the interest ($1 + i$) and (3) the number of years (n). Taken together, $(1 + i)^n$, the interest rate and time, are referred to as the *interest factor*.

As may be seen in the first table in Appendix A, the value of $1 grows with increases in the length of time and in the rate of interest. These relationships are illustrated in Figure R.1. If $1 is compounded at 5 percent interest (*AB* on the

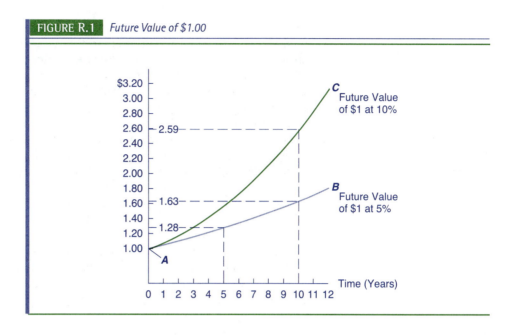

FIGURE R.1   *Future Value of $1.00*

graph), it will grow to $1.28 after five years and to $1.63 after ten years. However, if $1 is compounded at 10 percent interest (*AC* on the graph), it will grow to $2.59 in ten years. These cases illustrate the basic nature of compounding: The longer the funds continue to grow and the higher the interest rate, the higher will be the final (terminal) value.

Doubling the interest rate more than doubles the amount of interest that is earned over a number of years. In the example just given, the interest rate doubled from 5 percent to 10 percent; however, the amount of interest that will have accumulated in ten years rises from $0.63 at 5 percent to $1.59 at 10 percent. This is the result of the fact that compounding involves a geometric progression. The interest $(1 + i)$ has been raised to some power (n).

Future value problems may also be easily solved with the use of a financial calculator designed for business applications. These calculators have been programmed to solve time value problems. (Some financial calculators also have other business applications, such as determining depreciation expense and statistical analysis. Many employers expect new hires to be able to use financial calculators, so an inability to use them may put you at a disadvantage.)

Although there are differences among models, financial calculators generally have five special function keys:

N   I or %   PV   PMT   FV

These keys represent the time period (N), the interest rate (I or %), the amount in the present (PV for *present value*), the periodic payment (PMT for *annuity*, which will be discussed later), and the amount in the future (FV for *future value*).

To illustrate how easy financial calculators are to use, consider the preceding illustration of the future value of $1 in which $100 grew to $338.60 after 25 years when the annual interest rate was 5 percent. Using a financial calculator, enter the present amount (PV = –100), the interest rate (I = 5), and time (N = 25). Since there are no annual payments, be certain that PMT is set equal to zero (PMT = 0). Then instruct the calculator to determine the future value (FV = ?). The calculator should arrive at a future value of $338.64, which is almost the same amount derived using the interest table for the future value of $1. (The difference is the result of the interest tables being rounded to three places.)

You may wonder why the present value was entered as a negative number. Financial calculators consider payments as *either cash inflows or cash outflows*. Cash inflows are entered as positive numbers, and cash outflows are entered as negative numbers. In the example, the initial amount is an outflow because you invest the $100. The resulting future amount is a cash inflow since you receive the terminal amount. That is, you give up the $100 (the outflow) and after 25 years receive the $338.64 (the inflow).

Problems involving time value permeate this text and are illustrated with the use of interest tables and with financial calculators. Illustrations using interest tables clarify the basic concept, while the illustrations that employ the financial calculator indicate how easily the answer may be derived. The financial calculator illustrations use the following general form:

PV = ?
FV = ?
PMT = ?
N = ?
I = ?

followed by the answer. When applied to the preceding illustration, the form is

PV = $–100
FV = ?
PMT = 0
N = 25
I = 5

FV = $338.64

The final answer is separated from the data that is entered, and each example is placed in the margin so that it does not break the flow of the written material.

THE PRESENT VALUE OF $1

In the preceding section, $1 grew, or compounded, over time. This section considers the reverse. How much is $1 that will be received in the future worth today? For example, how much will a $100 payment 5 years hence be worth today if you can earn 10 percent annually? This question incorporates the time value of money, but instead of asking how much $1 will be worth at some future date, it asks how much that future $1 is worth today. This is a question of **present value**. The process by which this question is answered is called **discounting**. Discounting determines the worth of funds that are to be received in the future in terms of their present value.

In the earlier section, the future value of $1 was calculated by Equation R.1:

present value
The current worth of an amount to be received in the future.

discounting
The process of determining present value.

$$P_0(1 + i)^n = P_n.$$

Discounting reverses this equation. The present value (P_0) is determined by dividing the future value (P_n) by the interest factor $(1 + i)^n$. This is expressed in Equation R.2:

(R.2)
$$P_0 = \frac{P_n}{(1 + i)^n}$$

The future is discounted by the appropriate interest factor to determine the present value. If the interest rate is 10 percent, the present value of $100 to be received five years from today is

$$P_0 = \frac{\$100}{(1 + 0.1)^5}$$

$$= \frac{\$100}{1.611}$$

$$= \$62.07.$$

As with the future value of $1, interest tables and financial calculators ease the calculation of present values. The second table in Appendix A gives the interest factors for the present value of $1 for selected interest rates and time periods. The interest rates are read horizontally at the top, and time is read vertically along the left-hand side. To determine the present value of $1 that will be received in five years if the current interest rate is 10 percent, multiply $1 by the interest factor, which is found in the table under the vertical column for 10 percent and in the horizontal column for five years. The present value of $100 is

$$\$100 \times 0.621 = \$62.10.$$

The $100 you will receive after five years is currently worth only $62.10 if the interest rate is 10 percent. This is the same answer that was determined with Equation R.2 (except for rounding).

To solve this problem using a financial calculator, enter the future amount (FV = 100), the interest rate (I = 10), and the number of years (N = 5). Set the payments equal to zero (PMT = 0), and instruct the calculator to compute the present value (PV = ?). The calculator should determine the present value to be –62.09; once again the answer is virtually the same as that derived from the interest tables. Notice that the calculator expresses the present value as a negative number. If you receive a $100 cash inflow after ten years, that will require a current outflow of $62.09 if the rate of interest is 10 percent.

As may be seen in Equation R.2, the present value of $1 depends on (1) the length of time before it will be received and (2) the interest rate. The farther into the future the dollar will be received and the higher the interest rate, the lower the present value of the dollar. This is illustrated by Figure R.2 (p. 450), which gives the relationship between the present value of $1 and the length of time at various interest rates. Lines AB and AC give the present value of $1 at 4 percent and 7 percent, respectively. As may be seen in this graph, $1 to be received after 20 years is worth considerably less than $1 to be received after five years when both are

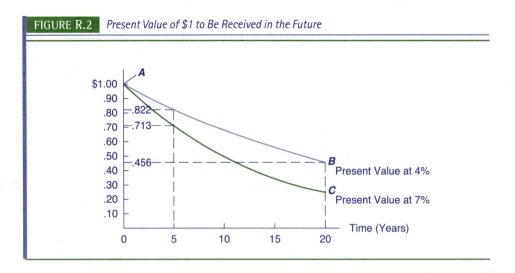

FIGURE R.2   *Present Value of $1 to Be Received in the Future*

discounted at the same percentage rate. At 4 percent (line *AB*) the current value of $1 to be received after 20 years is only $0.456, whereas $1 to be received after five years is worth $0.822. Also, the higher the interest rate (i.e., discount factor), the lower the present value of $1. For example, the present value of $1 to be received after five years is $0.822 at 4 percent, but it is only $0.713 at 7 percent.

THE FUTURE SUM OF AN ANNUITY

annuity
A series of equal annual payments.

future sum of an annuity
Compound value of a series of equal annual payments.

annuity due
A series of equal annual payments with the payments made at the beginning of the year.

ordinary annuity
A series of equal annual payments in which the payments are made at the end of each year.

How much will be in an account after three years if you deposit $100 annually and the account pays 5 percent interest? This is similar to the future value of $1 except that the payment is not one lump sum but a series of payments. If the payments are equal, the series is called an **annuity**. The question is an illustration of the **future sum of an annuity**.

To determine how much will be in the account you must consider not only the interest rate earned but also whether deposits are made at the beginning of the year or the end of the year. If each payment is made at the beginning of the year, the series is called an **annuity due**. If the payments are made at the end of the year, the series is an **ordinary annuity**. What is the future sum of an annuity if $100 is deposited in an account for three years starting right now? What is the future sum of an annuity if $100 is placed in an account for three years starting at the end of the first year? The first question concerns an annuity due, while the second question illustrates an ordinary annuity.

The flow of payments for these two types of annuities is illustrated in Exhibit R.1. In both cases, the $100 is deposited for three years in an account that pays 5 percent interest. The top half of the figure shows the annuity due, while the bottom half illustrates the ordinary annuity. In both cases, three years elapse from the present to when the final amount is determined and three payments are made. The difference in the timing of the payment results in a difference in the interest earned. Because in an annuity due the payments are made at the beginning of each year, the annuity due earns more interest ($31.01 versus $15.25) and thus has the higher terminal value ($331.01 versus $315.25). The greater the interest rate and the longer the time period, the greater will be this difference in terminal values.

| EXHIBIT R.1 | The Flow of Payments for the Future Value of an Annuity Due and an Ordinary Annuity |

	Annuity Due				
	1/1/×0	1/1/×1	1/1/×2	1/1/×3	Sum
	$100.00	5.00	5.25	5.51	$ 115.76
		100.00	5.00	5.25	110.25
			100.00	5.00	105.00
Amount in the account	$100.00	205.00	315.25	331.01	$331.01

	Ordinary Annuity				
	1/1/×0	1/1/×1	1/1/×2	1/1/×3	Sum
	–	$100.00	5.00	5.25	$ 110.25
			100.00	5.00	105.00
				100.00	100.00
Amount in the account	–	$100.00	205.00	315.25	$315.25

The procedures for determining the future sum of an annuity due (FSAD) and the future sum of an ordinary annuity (FSOA) are stated formally in Equations R.3 and R.4, respectively. In each equation, PMT represents the equal, periodic payment, i represents the rate of interest, and n represents the number of years that elapse from the present until the end of the time period. For the annuity due, the equation is

(R.3) $$\text{FSAD} = PMT(1 + i)^1 + PMT(1 + i)^2 + \cdots + PMT(1 + i)^n.$$

When this equation is applied to the previous example in which $i = 0.05$, $n = 3$, and the annual payment $PMT = \$100$, the accumulated sum is

$$\text{FSAD} = \$100(1 + 0.05)^1 + 100(1 + 0.05)^2 + 100(1 + 0.05)^3$$
$$= \$105 + 110.25 + 115.76$$
$$= \$331.01.$$

For the ordinary annuity the equation is

(R.4) $$\text{FSOA} = PMT(1 + i)^0 + PMT(1 + i)^1 + \cdots + PMT(1 + i)^{n-1}.$$

When this equation is applied to the preceding example, the accumulated sum is

$$\text{FSOA} = \$100(1 + 0.05)^0 + 100(1 + 0.05)^1 + 100(1 + 0.05)^{3-1}$$
$$= \$100 + 105 + 110.25$$
$$= \$315.25.$$

Although it is possible to derive the future sum of an annuity in this manner, it is very cumbersome. Fortunately, interest tables and financial calculators facilitate these calculations. In the third table in Appendix A we find the interest factors for the future sum of an ordinary annuity for selected time periods and selected interest rates. (Interest tables are usually presented only for ordinary annuities. How these tables may be used for annuities due is discussed later.) The number of periods is read vertically at the left, and the interest rates are read horizontally at the top. The future value of the ordinary annuity at 5 percent interest for three years (three annual $100 payments with interest being earned for two years) is $100 times the interest factor found in Table 3 of Appendix A for three periods at 5 percent. This interest factor is 3.153; therefore, the future value of this ordinary annuity is $100 times 3.153, which equals $315.30. This is the same answer that was derived by determining the future value of each $100 deposit and totaling them. (The slight difference in the two answers is the result of rounding.)

To use the financial calculator to solve for the ordinary annuity, enter the number of years (N = 3) the rate of interest (I = 5), and the amount of each payment (PMT = –100). Because there is no single initial payment, enter zero for the present value (PV = 0), and instruct the calculator to solve for the future value (FV = ?). When this data is entered, the calculator determines that the future value is $315.25. (The calculator requires you to express the $100 payment as a negative number because it is assuming you are making a cash outflow of $100 each period and receiving a $315.25 cash inflow at the end of the three years.)

The value of an ordinary annuity of $1 compounded annually depends on the number of payments (i.e., the number of periods over which deposits are made) and the interest rate. The longer the time period and the higher the interest rate, the greater will be the sum that will have accumulated in the future. This is illustrated by Figure R.3. Lines AB and AC show the value of the $1 annuity at 4 percent and 8 percent, respectively. After five years the value of the annuity will grow to $5.87 at 8 percent but to only $5.42 at 4 percent. If these annuities are continued for another five years, they will be worth $14.49 and $12.01, respectively. Thus, both the rate at which the annuity compounds and the length of time affect the annuity's value.

FIGURE R.3   *Future Sum of an Ordinary Annuity of $1*

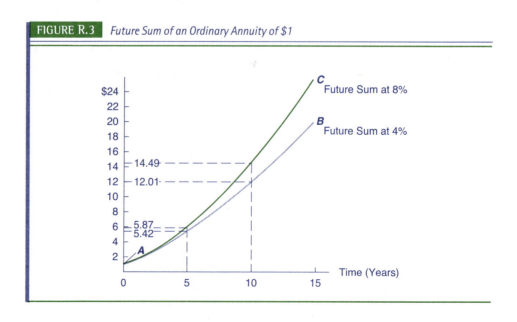

While Table 3 in Appendix A is constructed for an ordinary annuity, it may be converted into a table for an annuity due by multiplying the interest factor given in the table by $(1 + i)$. For example, in the illustration of the $100 deposited annually in the savings account for three years, the interest factor for the ordinary annuity was 3.153. This interest factor may be converted for an annuity due at 5 percent for three years by multiplying 3.153 by $1 + 0.05$. That is,

$$3.153(1 + 0.05) = 3.3107.$$

When this interest factor is applied to the example of $100 deposited in the bank at 5 percent for three years with the deposits starting immediately, the resulting terminal value is

$$\$100(3.3107) = \$331.07.$$

This is the same answer as derived by making each calculation individually and summing them. (Once again the small difference in the two answers is the result of rounding.)

To use a financial calculator to solve for the future value of an annuity due, use the key that informs the calculator that the payments are to be made at the beginning rather than the end of each time period. Enter the amount of the payment (PMT = –100), the rate of interest (I = 5), and the number of years (N = 3). Set the present value equal to zero (PV = 0) and instruct the calculator to solve for the future value.

The difference between the terminal value of the two kinds of annuity payments can be quite substantial as the number of years increases or the interest rate rises. Consider a retirement account in which the saver places $2,000 annually for 20 years. If the deposits are made at the end of the year (an ordinary annuity) and the rate of interest is 7 percent, the terminal amount will be

$$\$2,000(40.995) = \$81,990.$$

However, if the deposits had been made at the beginning of each year (an annuity due), the terminal amount would be

$$\$2,000(40.995)(1 + 0.07) = \$87,729.30.$$

The difference is $5,739.30! Almost $6,000 in additional interest is earned if the deposits are made at the beginning, not at the end, of each year.

The difference between the ordinary annuity and the annuity due becomes even more dramatic if the interest rate rises. Suppose the account offered 12 percent instead of 7 percent. If the deposits are made at the end of each year, the terminal value is

$$\$2,000(72.052) = \$144,104.$$

If the payments are at the beginning of the year, the terminal value will be

$$\$2,000(72.052)(1 + 0.12) = \$161,396.48.$$

The difference is now $17,292.48.

⋅⋅●THE PRESENT VALUE OF AN ANNUITY

In investment analysis, the investor is often not concerned with the future value but with the **present value of an annuity**. The investor who receives periodic payments often wishes to know the current (i.e., present) value. As with the future sum of an annuity, this value depends on whether the payments are made at the beginning of each year (an annuity due) or at the end of each period (an ordinary annuity).

The present value of an annuity is simply the sum of the present value of each individual cash flow. Each cash inflow is discounted back to the present at the appropriate discount factor and the amounts summed. Suppose you expect to receive $100 at the end of each year for three years and want to know how much this series of payments is worth if you can earn 8 percent in an alternative investment. To answer the question, you discount each payment at 8 percent:

Payment	Year	Interest Factor	Present Value
$100	1	0.926	$ 92.60
100	2	0.857	85.70
100	3	0.794	79.40
			$257.70

The process determines the present value to be $257.70. That is, if you invest $257.70 now and earn 8 percent annually, you can withdraw $100 at the end of each year for the next three years.

This process is expressed in more general terms by Equation R.5. The present value (PV) of the annual payments (PMT) is then found by discounting these payments at the appropriate interest rate (i) for n time periods.

(R.5)
$$PV = \frac{PMT}{(1 + i)^1} + \ldots + \frac{PMT}{(1 + i)^n}$$

$$= \sum_{t=1}^{n} \frac{PMT}{(1 + i)^t}$$

When the values from the previous example are inserted into the equation, it reads

$$PV = \frac{\$100}{(1 + 0.08)} + \frac{\$100}{(1 + 0.08)^2} + \frac{\$100}{(1 + 0.08)^3}$$

$$= \frac{\$100}{1.080} + \frac{\$100}{1.166} + \frac{\$100}{1.260}$$

$$= \$257.70$$

Since the payments are equal and made annually, this example is an annuity, and the present value is simply the product of the payment and the interest factor. Interest tables have been developed for the interest factors for the present value of an annuity (see the fourth table in Appendix A). Selected interest rates are read horizontally along the top, and the number of periods is read vertically at the left. To determine the present value of an annuity of $100 that is to be received for three years when interest rates are 8 percent, find the interest factor for three years at 8 percent (2.577) and then multiply $100 by this interest factor. The present value of this annuity is $257.70, which is the same value that was derived by obtaining each of the individual present values and summing them. The price that you would be willing to pay at the present time in exchange for three future annual payments of $100 when the rate of return on alternative investments is 8 percent is $257.70.

To use the financial calculator to solve for the present value of the ordinary annuity, enter the number of years (N = 3), the rate of interest (I = 8), and the amount of each payment (PMT = 100). Since there is no single future payment, enter zero for the future value (FV = 0), and instruct the calculator to solve for the present value (PV = ?). When this data is entered, the calculator determines that the present value is –257.71. (Once again the calculator expresses the $257.71 as a negative number because it is assuming you make an initial cash outflow of $257.71 and receive a $100 cash inflow each period. If you enter the $100 payment as a negative number, the present value will be a positive number. The calculator will then assume you initially received a $257.71 cash inflow through a loan and are making a $100 cash repayment or outflow each period.)

The present value of an annuity is related to the interest rate and the length of time over which the annuity payments are made. The lower the interest rate and the longer the duration of the annuity, the greater the present value of the annuity. Figure R.4 illustrates these relationships. As may be seen by comparing lines *AB* and *AC*, the lower the interest rate, the higher the present dollar value. For example, if payments are to be made over five years, the present value of an annuity of $1 is $4.45 at 4 percent but only $3.99 at 8 percent. The longer the duration of the annuity, the higher the present value; hence, the present value of an annuity of $1 at 4 percent is $4.45 for five years, but it is $8.11 for ten years.

Many payments to be received in investments occur at the end of a time period and not at the beginning and thus illustrate ordinary annuities. For example, the annual interest payment made by a bond occurs after the bond is held for a while,

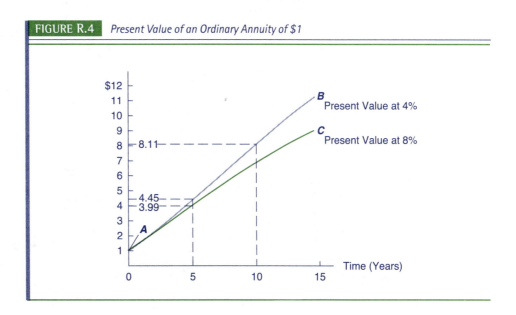

FIGURE R.4   *Present Value of an Ordinary Annuity of $1*

and distributions from earnings (e.g., dividends from stock are made after, not at the beginning of, a period of time). There are, however, payments that may occur at the beginning of the time period, such as the annual distribution from a retirement plan; these would illustrate annuities due.

The difference in the flow of payments and the determination of the present values of an ordinary annuity and an annuity due are illustrated in Exhibit R.2. In each case, the annuity is for $2,000 a year for three years and the interest rate is 10 percent. In the top half of the exhibit, the payments are made at the end of the year (an ordinary annuity), while in the bottom half of the exhibit, the payments are made at the beginning of the year (an annuity due). As may be seen by the totals, the present value of the annuity due is higher ($5,470 versus $4,972). This is because the payments are received sooner and, hence, are more valuable. As may also be seen in the illustration, because the first payment of the annuity due is made immediately, its present value is the actual amount received. Because the first payment of the ordinary annuity is made at the end of the first year, that amount is discounted, and, hence, its present value is less than the actual amount received.

The interest tables for the present value of an annuity presented in this text (and in other finance and investment texts) apply to ordinary annuities. These interest factors may be converted into annuity due factors by multiplying them by $(1 + i)$. Thus the interest factor for the present value of an ordinary annuity for $1 at 10 percent for three years (2.487) may be converted into the interest factor for an annuity due of $1 at 10 percent for three years as follows:

$$2.487(1 + i) = 2.487(1 + 0.1) = 2.736.$$

When this interest factor is used to determine the present value of an annuity due of $2,000 for three years at 10 percent, the present value is

$$\$2,000(2.736) = \$5,472.$$

EXHIBIT R.2 Flow of Payments and Determination of the Present Value of an Ordinary Annuity and an Annuity Due at 10 Percent for Three Years

Ordinary Annuity

1/1/×0	1/1/×1	1/1/×2	1/1/×3
$1,818 ← (0.909) 2,000			
1,652 ←		(0.826) 2,000	
1,505 ←			(0.751) 2,000
$4,972			

Annuity Due

1/1/×0	1/1/×1	1/1/×2	1/1/×3
$2,000			
1,818 ← (0.909) 2,000			
1,652 ←		(0.826) 2,000	
$5,470			

The present value of an ordinary annuity of $2,000 at 10 percent for three years is

$$\$2,000(2.487) = \$4,974.$$

These are essentially the same answers given in Exhibit R.2; the small differences result from rounding.

To use a financial calculator to solve for the present value of the annuity due, use the key that informs the calculator that the payments are to be received at the beginning rather than the end of each time period. Enter the amount of the payment to be received (PMT = 2,000), the rate of interest (I = 10), and the number of years (N = 3). Set the future value equal to 0 (FV = 0), and instruct the calculator to solve for the present value.

••ILLUSTRATIONS OF COMPOUNDING AND DISCOUNTING

The previous sections have explained the various computations involving time value, and this section will illustrate them in a series of problems that you may encounter.

1. You buy a stock for $10 per share and expect the value of the stock to grow annually at 9 percent for ten years, at which time you plan to sell it. What is the anticipated sale price? This is an example of the future value of $1 growing at 9 percent for ten years. The future value is

$$P_n = P_0(1 + i)^n,$$
$$P_{10} = \$10(1 + 0.09)^{10}$$
$$= \$10(2.367) = \$23.67,$$

in which 2.367 is the interest factor for the future sum of $1 at 9 percent for ten years. You anticipate selling the stock for $23.67.

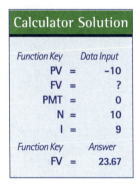

Calculator Solution

Function Key	Data Input
PV =	−10
FV =	?
PMT =	0
N =	10
I =	9
Function Key	Answer
FV =	23.67

2. You sell a stock for $23.67 that was purchased ten years ago. A return of 9 percent was earned. What was the original cost of the investment? This is an example of the present value of $1 discounted back at 9 percent for ten years. The initial value is

$$P_0 = \frac{P_n}{(1 + i)^n}$$

$$= \frac{\$23.67}{(1 + 0.09)^{10}}$$

$$= \$23.67(0.422) = \$9.99 \approx \$10,$$

in which 0.422 is the interest factor for the present value of $1 discounted at 9 percent for ten years. The investment cost $10 when it was purchased ten years ago.

Calculator Solution

Function Key	Data Input
PV =	?
FV =	23.67
PMT =	0
N =	10
I =	9
Function Key	Answer
PV =	−10

You should realize that Questions 1 and 2 are two views of the same investment. In Question 1 the $10 investment grew to $23.67. In Question 2 the value at the time the stock was sold was brought back to the value of the initial investment. Another variation of this question would be as follows. If you bought stock for $10, held it for ten years, and then sold it for $23.67. What was the return on the investment? In this case the values of the stock at the time it was bought and sold are known, but the rate of growth (the rate of return) is unknown. The answer can be found by using *either* the future value of $1 table or the present value of $1 table. (The choice of which table to use is avoided if you use a financial calculator. See the Calculator Solution in the margin.)

If the future value table is used, the question is at what rate (x) will $10 grow in ten years to equal $23.67. The answer is

$$P_0(1 + x)^n = P_n,$$
$$\$10(1 + x)^{10} = \$23.67,$$
$$(1 + x)^{10} = 2.367.$$

The interest factor is 2.367, which, according to the future value of $1 table for ten years, makes the growth rate 9 percent. This interest factor is located under the vertical column for 9 percent and in the horizontal column for ten years.

If the present value table is used, the question asks what discount factor (x) at ten years will bring $23.67 back to $10. The answer is

$$P_0 = \frac{P_n}{(1 + x)^n},$$

$$\$10 = \frac{\$23.67}{(1 + x)^{10}},$$

$$0.422 = \frac{1}{(1 + x)^{10}}.$$

The interest factor is 0.422, which may be found in the present value of $1 table for ten years in the 9 percent column (i.e., the growth rate is 9 percent). Thus, this problem may be solved by the proper application of either the future value or present value tables.

3. An employer starts a pension plan for a 45-year-old employee. The plan requires the employer to invest $1,000 at the end of each year. If that investment earns 8 percent annually, how much will be accumulated by retirement at age 65?

This is an example of the future value of an ordinary annuity. The payment is $1,000 annually and grows at 8 percent for 20 years. The fund will be

$$FV = PMT(1 + i)^0 + \ldots + PMT(1 + i)^{n-1}$$
$$= \$1,000(1 + 0.08)^0 + \ldots + \$1,000(1 + 0.08)^{19}$$
$$= \$1,000(45.762) = \$45,762.$$

(45.762 is the interest factor for the future sum of an ordinary annuity of $1 compounded annually at 8 percent for 20 years.)

4. The same employer places a lump sum in an investment that earns 8 percent and draws on the funds to make the annual payments of $1,000. After 20

Calculator Solution

Function Key	Data Input
PV =	−10
FV =	23.67
PMT =	0
N =	10
I =	?
Function Key	**Answer**
I =	9%

Calculator Solution

Function Key	Data Input
PV =	0
FV =	?
PMT =	−1000
N =	20
I =	8
Function Key	**Answer**
FV =	45,761.96

years all the funds in the account will be depleted. How much must be deposited initially in the account?

This is an example of the present value of an ordinary annuity. The annuity is $1,000 per year at 8 percent for 20 years. Thus, the present value (i.e., the amount of the initial investment) is

$$PV = \sum_{t=1}^{n} \frac{PMT}{(1 + i)} + \ldots + \frac{PMT}{(1 + i)^n}$$

$$= \frac{\$1,000}{1 + 0.08} + \ldots + \frac{\$1,000}{(1 + 0.08)^{20}}$$

$$= \$1,000(9.818) = \$9,818,$$

in which 9.818 is the interest factor for the present value of an ordinary annuity of $1 at 8 percent for 20 years. Thus, the employer need invest only $9,818 in an account now that earns 8 percent to meet the $1,000 annual pension payment for the next 20 years.

Notice the difference between the answers in Examples 3 and 4. In Example 3, a set of payments earns interest, and thus the future value is larger than just the sum of the 20 payments of $1,000. In Example 4, a future set of payments is valued in present terms. Since future payments are worth less today, the current value is less than the sum of the 20 payments of $1,000.

Also notice that if the employer sets aside $9,818 today and earns 8 percent annually for 20 years, the terminal value is $45,761.28, which is essentially the same amount derived in the third illustration. From the employer's viewpoint, the $9,818 may be used to cover a required $1,000 annual payment or used to accumulate a required $45,762 future value. Essentially, either approach achieves the required terminal value.

5. An investment pays $50 per year for ten years, after which $1,000 is returned to the investor. If you can earn 9 percent, how much should this investment cost? This question really contains two questions: What is the present value of an ordinary annuity of $50 at 9 percent for ten years, and what is the present value of $1,000 after ten years at 9 percent? The answer is

$$PV = \sum_{t=1}^{n} \frac{PMT_1}{(1 + i)^1} + \ldots + \frac{PMT_n}{(1 + i)^n} + \frac{FV_n}{(1 + i)^n}$$

$$= \frac{\$50}{(1 + 0.09)} + \ldots + \frac{\$50}{(1 + 0.09)^{10}} + \frac{\$1,000}{(1 + 0.09)^{10}}$$

$$= \$50(6.418) = \$1,000(0.422) = \$742.90.$$

(6.418 and 0.422 are the interest factors for the present value of an ordinary annuity of $1 and the present value of $1, respectively, both at 9 percent for ten years.)

This example illustrates that an investment may involve both a series of payments (an annuity component) and a lump-sum payment. This particular investment is similar to a bond, the valuation of which is discussed in

Calculator Solution

Function Key	Data Input
PV =	?
FV =	0
PMT =	1000
N =	20
I =	8
Function Key	Answer
PV =	-9815.15

Calculator Solution

Function Key	Data Input
PV =	?
FV =	1000
PMT =	50
N =	10
I =	9
Function Key	Answer
PV =	-743.29

Chapter 11. Other examples of valuation and the computation of rates of return are given in Chapter 5, which considers investments in common stock.

6. A corporation's dividend has grown annually at the rate of 5 percent. If this rate is maintained and the current dividend is $5.40, what will the dividend be after ten years? This is a simple future value of $1 problem. The dividend will grow to

$$P_n = P_0(1 + i)^n,$$
$$= \$5.40(1 + 0.05)^{10}$$
$$= \$5.40(1.629) = \$8.80.$$

(1.629 is the interest factor for the future value of $1 at 5 percent for ten years.) Although such a growth rate in future dividends may not be achieved, this problem illustrates how modest annual increments can result in a substantial increase in your dividend income over a number of years. (In the calculator solution, if you enter the 5.40 as a positive number, the answer is a negative 8.80. Either is acceptable as long as you interpret the answer correctly.)

Calculator Solution

Function Key	Data Input
PV =	−5.40
FV =	?
PMT =	0
N =	10
I =	5

Function Key	Answer
FV =	8.80

NONANNUAL COMPOUNDING

You should have noticed that in the previous examples compounding occurred only once a year. Since compounding can and often does occur more frequently — for example, **semiannually**—the equations that were presented earlier must be adjusted. This section extends the discussion of the compound value of $1 to include compounding for time periods other than a year.

Converting annual compounding to other time periods necessitates two adjustments. First, a year is divided into the same number of time periods that the funds are being compounded. For semiannual compounding a year consists of two time periods, whereas for quarterly compounding the year comprises four time periods.

After adjusting for the number of time periods, you adjust the interest rate to find the rate per time period. This is done by dividing the stated interest rate by the number of time periods. If the interest rate is 8 percent compounded semiannually, then 8 percent is divided by 2, giving an interest rate of 4 percent earned in *each* time period. If the annual rate of interest is 8 percent compounded quarterly, the interest rate is 2 percent (8% ÷ 4) in each of the four time periods. These adjustments may be expressed in more formal terms by modifying Equation R.1 as follows:

semiannual compounding
The payment of interest twice a year.

(R.1)
$$P_0\left(1 + \frac{i}{c}\right)^{n \times c} = P_n.$$

The only new symbol is c, which represents the frequency of compounding. The interest rate (i) is divided by the frequency of compounding (c) to determine the interest rate in each period. The number of years (n) is multiplied by the frequency of compounding to determine the number of time periods.

The application of this equation may be illustrated in a simple example. You invest $100 in an asset that pays 8 percent compounded quarterly. What will the future value of this asset be after five years — that is, $100 will grow to what amount after five years if it is compounded quarterly at 8 percent? Algebraically, this is

Calculator Solution

Function Key	Data Input
PV =	−100
FV =	?
PMT =	0
N =	20
I =	2
Function Key	Answer
PV =	148.59

$$P_n = P_0\left(1 + \frac{i}{c}\right)^{n \times c}$$

$$= \$100\left(1 + \frac{0.08}{4}\right)^{5 \times 4}$$

$$= \$100(1 + 0.02)^{20}.$$

In this formulation you are earning 2 percent for 20 time periods. To solve this equation, the interest factor for the future value of $1 at 2 percent for 20 years (1.486) is multiplied by $100. Thus, the future value is

$$P_5 = \$100(1.486) = \$148.60.$$

The difference between compounding annually and compounding more frequently can be seen by comparing this problem with one in which the values are identical except that the interest is compounded annually. The question is, then, to what amount will $100 grow after five years at 8 percent compounded annually? The answer is

Calculator Solution

Function Key	Data Input
PV =	−100
FV =	?
PMT =	0
N =	5
I =	8
Function Key	Answer
PV =	146.93

$$P_5 = \$100(1 + 0.08)^5$$
$$= \$100(1.469)$$
$$= \$146.90.$$

This sum, $146.90, is less than the amount that was earned when the funds were compounded quarterly, which suggests the general conclusion that the more frequently interest is compounded, the greater will be the future amount.

•• TIME VALUE PROBLEMS AND SPREADSHEETS

Time value problems may also be solved using a spreadsheet such as Excel. In Excel, time value problems may be solved by using the *fx* function under *insert*. Go to the "financial" function category and for a particular problem enter the appropriate data. Excel then determines the answer. The format is similar to that employed by a financial calculator. Amounts are entered as cash inflows or outflows, with outflows being negative numbers. The data to be entered are

Rate	Interest per period (%)
Nper	Number of periods
Pmt	Periodic payment
Fv or Pv	Future value or Present value
Type	Ordinary annuity or annuity due

(Set type = 0 for an ordinary annuity and = 1 for an annuity due.)

Excel also solves time value problems in which data and the appropriate instructions are entered into cells in a spreadsheet. The unknown is entered first, followed by Rate, Nper, PMT, PV or FV, and type. For example, to answer the question "$1,000 grows to how much in ten years at 10 percent?" use the following form:

FV(Rate, Nper, PMT, PV, Type). The unknown (FV) is outside the parentheses and the knowns are inside.

The process for solving this problem is illustrated as follows:

Columns	A	B	C	etc
Rows				
1	FV(Rate,Nper,PMT,PV,Type)			
2	% per period	10%		
3	N of periods	10		
4	Payment	0		
5	Present value	1000		
6	Type	0		

To solve the problem, enter the cells or the actual data. That is, type =FV (b2,b3,b4,–b5,b6) or type =FV(10%,10,0,–1000,0) in an open cell such as B7. The present value is a negative number because it is assumed the $1,000 investment is a cash outflow that will grow into the future amount. This future value will then be received (cash inflow) at the end of the ten years. Once the data are entered in cells B2 through B6 and the instruction is placed in cell B7, the answer $2,593.74 is determined.

What follows is a series of examples that illustrate using Excel. In each case, a simple problem is stated first. The Excel format is given, followed by the data in the order in which each number will be entered. The Excel instructions are given using the individual cells and using the numbers, cells B7 and B8, respectively. (It is not necessary to do both.) The final entry is the numerical answer.

This basic format is employed by Excel to solve time value of money problems. Preference for spreadsheets over financial calculators may depend on convenience and potential usage. For example, material in a spreadsheet may be copied to other documents; this is not possible using a financial calculator.

Case 1: Determine FV of $1

($1,000 grows to how much in ten years at 10%?)

FV(Rate, Nper, PMT, PV, Type)	
% per period	10%
N of periods	10
PMT	0
PV	1000
Type	0

Excel instruction:
in cells	=FV(b2,b3,b4,–b5,b6)
or numbers	=FV(10%,10,0,–1000,0)
Answer:	$2,593.74

Case 2: Determine PV of $1

($1,000 received after ten years is worth how much today at 10%?)

PV(Rate, Nper, PMT, FV, Type)	
% per period	10%
N of periods	10
PMT	0
FV	1000
Type	0

Excel instruction:
  in cells   =PV(b2,b3,b4,-b5,b6)
  or numbers   =PV(10%,10,0,-1000,0)
Answer: $385.54

Case 3: Determine FV of an annuity of $1

($2,000 received each year grows to how much in ten years at 10%?)

FV(Rate, Nper, PMT, PV, Type)		FV(Rate, Nper, PMT, PV, Type)	
Ordinary Annuity		Ordinary Due	
% per period	10%	% per period	10%
N of periods	10	N of periods	10
PMT	2000	PMT	2000
PV	0	PV	0
Type	0	Type	1

Excel instruction: Excel instruction:
  in cells   =FV(b2,b3,-b4,b5,b6)   in cells   =FV(b2,b3,-b4,b5,b6)
  or numbers   =FV(10%,10,-2000,0,0)   or numbers   = FV(10%,10,-2000,0,1)
Answer: $31,874.85   Answer: $35,062.33

Case 4: Determine PV of an annuity of $1

($2,000 received each year for ten years is worth how much today at 10%?)

PV(Rate, Nper, PMT, PV, Type)		PV(Rate, Nper, PMT, PV, Type)	
Ordinary Annuity		Annuity Due	
% per period	10%	% per period	10%
N of periods	10	N of periods	10
PMT	2000	PMT	2000
FV	0	FV	0
Type	0	Type	1

Excel instruction: Excel instruction:
  in cells   =PV(b2,b3,-b4,b5,b6)   in cells   =PV(b2,b3,-b4,b5,b6)
  or numbers   =PV(10%,10,-2000,0,0)   or numbers   =PV(10%,10,-2000,0,1)
Answer: $12,289.13   Answer: $13,518.05

Case 5: Determine FV of a single payment and an annuity

($1,000 today plus $2,000 each year grows to how much in ten years at 10%?)

FV(Rate, Nper, PMT, PV, Type)		FV(Rate, Nper, PMT, PV, Type)	
Ordinary Annuity		Annuity Due	
% per period	10%	% per period	10%
N of periods	10	N of periods	10
PMT	2000	PMT	2000
PV	1000	PV	1000
Type	0	Type	1

Excel instruction: Excel instruction:
  in cells   =FV(b2,b3,-b4,-b5,b6)   in cells   =FV(b2,b3,-b4,-b5,b6)
  or numbers =FV(10%,10,-2000,-1000,0)   or numbers =FV(10%,10,-2000,-1000,1)
Answer: $34,468.59   Answer: $37,656.08

Case 6: Determine PV of a single payment and an annuity

($2,000 each year plus $1,000 after ten years is currently worth how much at 10%?)

PV(Rate, Nper, PMT, FV, Type)		PV(Rate, Nper, PMT, FV, Type)	
Ordinary Annuity		Annuity Due	
% per period	10%	% per period	10%
N of periods	10	N of periods	10
PMT	2000	PMT	2000
FV	1000	FV	1000
Type	0	Type	1

Excel instruction:
  in cells   =PV(b2,b3,–b4,–b5,b6)
  or numbers=PV(10%,10,–2000,–1000,0)
  Answer: $12,674.68

Excel instruction:
  in cells   =PV(b2,b3,–b4,–b5,b6)
  or numbers =PV(10%,10,–2000,–1000,1)
  Answer: $13,903.59

Case 7: Determine I given PV, FV, and N

a. Single payment
(What is the rate if you invest $500 and receive $1,000 after ten years?)

b. An Ordinary Annuity
(What is the rate if you invest $10,000 and receive $2,000 a year for ten years?)

Rate (Nper, PMT, PV, FV, Type)		Rate (Nper, PMT, PV, FV, Type)	
		Ordinary Annuity	
N of periods	10	N of periods	10
PMT	0	PMT	2000
PV	500	PV	10000
FV	1000	FV	0
Type	0	Type	0

Excel instruction:
  in cells   =RATE(b2,b3,–b4,b5,b6)
  or numbers=RATE(10,0,–500,1000,0)
  Answer: 7.18%

Excel instruction:
  in cells   =RATE(b2,b3,–b4,b5,b6)
  or numbers =RATE(10,2000,–10000,0,0)
  Answer: 15.10%

c. An Annuity Due
(What is the rate if you invest $10,000 and receive $2,000 at the beginning of each year for ten years?)

Rate (Nper, PMT, PV, FV, Type)	
Annuity Due	
N of periods	10
PMT	2000
PV	10000
FV	0
Type	1

Excel instruction:
  in cells   =RATE(b2,b3,–b4,b5,b6)
  or numbers=RATE(10,2000,–10000,0,1)
  Answer: 20.24%

d. Single payment and Ordinary Annuity
(What is the rate if you invest $10,000 and receive $1,000 after ten years and $2,000 a year for ten years?)

Rate (Nper, PMT, PV, FV, Type)
N of periods   10
PMT   2000
PV   10000
FV   1000
Type   0

Excel instruction:
 in cells   =RATE(b2,b3,–b4,b5,b6)
 or numbers=RATE(10,2000,–10000,1000,0)
Answer: 15.72%

e. Single payment and Annuity due
(What is the rate if you invest $10,000 and receive $1,000 after ten years and $2,000 at the beginning of each year?)

Rate (Nper, PMT, PV, FV, Type)
N of periods   10
PMT   2000
PV   10000
FV   1000
Type   1

Excel instruction:
 in cells   =RATE(b2,b3,–b4,b5,b6)
 or numbers=RATE(10,2000,–10000,0,1)
Answer: 20.84%

Case 8: Determine N given PV, FV, and I

a. Single payment
(How long does it take for $500 to grow to $1,000 at 8 percent?)

NPER(I, PMT, PV, FV, Type)
I   8%
PMT   0
PV   500
FV   1000
Type   0

Excel instruction:
 in cells   =NPER(b2,b3,–b4,b5,b6)
 or numbers =NPER(8%,0,–500,1000,0)
Answer: 9.01

b. An Ordinary Annuity
(How long will $10,000 last if you withdraw $2,000 a year and earn 8 percent?)

NPER(I, PMT, PV, FV, Type)
Ordinary Annuity

I	8%
PMT	2000
PV	10000
FV	0
Type	0

Excel instruction:
  in cells   =NPER(b2,b3,−b4,b5,b6)
  or numbers =NPER(8,2000,−10000,0,0)
Answer: 6.64

c. An Annuity Due
(How long will $10,000 last if you withdraw $2,000 at the beginning of each year and earn 8 percent?)

NPER(I, PMT, PV, FV, Type)
Ordinary Annuity

I	8%
PMT	2000
PV	10000
FV	0
Type	1

Excel instruction:
  in cells   =NPER(b2,b3,−b4,b5,b6
  or numbers =NPER(10,2000,−10000,0,1)
Answer: 6.01

d. Single payment and Ordinary Annuity
(How long will $10,000 last if you withdraw $2,000 a year, $1,000 at the end, and earn 8 percent?)

NPER(I, PMT, PV, FV, Type)
Ordinary Annuity

I	8%
PMT	2000
PV	10000
FV	1000
Type	0

Excel instruction:
  in cells   =NPER(b2,b3,−b4,b5,b6)
  or numbers =NPER(8,2000,−10000,1000,0)
Answer: 6.11

e. Single payment and Annuity Due
(How long will $10,000 last if you withdraw $2,000 at the beginning of each year,
$1,000 at the end and earn 8 percent?)

NPER(I, PMT, PV, FV, Type)
Ordinary Annuity

I	8%
PMT	2000
PV	10000
FV	1000
Type	1

Excel instruction:
  in cells   =NPER(b2,b3,–b4,b5,b6)
  or numbers =NPER(8,2000,–1000,1000,1)
Answer: 5.52

••EQUATIONS FOR THE INTEREST FACTORS

All time value problems consist of a combination of present value, future value, or series of payments plus an interest factor. All interest factors consist of the rate of interest and number of periods. Financial calculators and spreadsheets greatly facilitate solving time value problems. There may be situations, however, in which you need the equation for the interest factor. For example, a scientific calculator is not preprogrammed for interest factors but may be used to derive a desired factor. What follows are the actual equations (R.10 through R.13) and an illustration for each of the interest factors.

The equation for the interest factor for the future value of $1 (FVIF) is

(R.10)
$$FVIF = (1 + i)^n.$$

To find the interest factor for 6 percent for three years [i.e., $(1 + 0.06)^3$], first enter 1 plus the interest rate: 1.06. The display should read 1.06. Next, raise this amount to the third power, which is achieved by striking the y^x key and the number 3. Press "equal," and the display should read 1.191, which is the interest factor that may be found in the first table of Appendix A under the column for 6 percent and three years.

The equation for the interest factor of the present value of $1 (PVIF) is

(R.11)
$$PVIF = \frac{1}{(1 + i)^n}$$

The interest factor for the present value is the reciprocal of the interest factor for the future value of $1. To derive the interest factor for the present value of $1 at 6 percent for three years, do the preceding steps used to determine the future value of $1 and then take the reciprocal. If the calculator has the $1/x$ key, press this key, and the reciprocal is automatically determined. If the calculator lacks this key, the reciprocal is found by dividing 1 by the number just derived. In the illustration, the reciprocal for 1.191 is 0.8396 (1/1.191), which is the interest factor for the present value of $1 at 6 percent for three years. You may verify this number by looking under the column for the present value of $1 at 6 percent for three years in the second table in Appendix A, which gives the interest factor as 0.840. The difference is, of course, the result of rounding.

The equation for the interest factor for the future sum of an annuity (FVAIF) is

(R.12)
$$FVAIF = \frac{(1 + i)^n - 1.}{i}$$

Thus, if the interest rate is 5 percent and the number of years is four, then the interest factor is

$$FVAIF = \frac{(1 + 0.05)^4 - 1}{0.05} = \frac{1.2155 - 1}{0.05} = 4.310,$$

which is the same number found in the table for the future value of an annuity for four years at 5 percent.

The equation for the interest factor for the present value of an annuity (PVAIF) is

(R.13)
$$PVAIF = \frac{1 - \dfrac{1}{(1 + i)^n.}}{i}$$

If the interest rate is 6 percent and the number of years is three, then the interest factor is

$$PVAIF = \frac{1 - \dfrac{1}{(1 + 0.06)^3}}{0.06} = \frac{1 - 0.8396}{0.06} = 2.673,$$

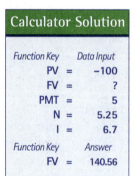

which is the interest factor found in the table for the present value of an annuity at 6 percent for three years.

In addition to facilitating the calculation of interest factors, electronic calculators and spreadsheets also offer a major advantage over the use of interest tables. Interest tables are limited to exact rates (e.g., 5 percent) and whole years (e.g., six years). Unless you interpolate between the given interest factors, the tables cannot provide the interest factor for 6.7 percent for five years and three months. However, this interest factor can be determined by using the electronic calculator or a spreadsheet. The interest factor for the future value of $1 at 6.7 percent for five years and three months may be found as follows:

1. Enter 1.067.
2. Raise 1.067 by 5.25 (i.e., $y^x = 1.067^{5.25}$).
3. Press "equal" to derive the interest factor: 1.4056.

Thus, if $100 is invested at 6.7 percent, compounded annually for five years and three months, the future value is $140.56.

While financial calculators and spreadsheets may ease the burden of the arithmetic, they cannot set up the problems to be solved. You must still determine if the problem concerns future value or present value and whether the problem deals with a lump sum or an annuity. Failure to set up the problem correctly will only lead to incorrect results, so it is imperative that you be able to determine what is being used and which of the various cases applies to the particular problem.

••ADDITIONAL PROBLEMS

Now that we have completed the review, let's do a few additional problems that are similar to the problems in the self-test and similar to problems in the text. After completing the problems, look at the answers to determine if you have grasped how to solve basic time value problems.

Problems

1) If a company paid a dividend of $1 in 2004 and the dividend grows annually by 7 percent, what will be the dividend in 2009?

2) AZ's dividend rose from $1 to $1.61 in five years. What has been the dividend's annual rate of growth?

3) If you want a car costing $15,000, how much must you save annually if your funds earn 5 percent?

4) If you can save $1,500 annually, how much will have been accumulated after four years if the funds earn 7 percent?

5) If the gross private investment in Brazil was $54 billion in 1975 and $136 billion in 1995, what was the annual rate of growth in the nation's investment during the period?

6) A company earned $2.00 per share in 1990 and paid cash dividends of $1.00. In 2000, it earned $5.20 and paid a dividend of $2.16. What is the annual growth rate in earnings and dividends? If the Consumer Price Index was 100 in 1990 and 163 in 2000, has the investor's purchasing power from the dividend payments declined?

7) If an annuity costs $200,000 and yields 7 percent annually for five years, what is the maximum amount you can withdraw each year (assuming the withdrawals are equal)?

8) A firm earns 10 percent annually on its investments. One possible investment offers $50,000 a year for ten years and costs $300,000. Should the firm make this investment?

9) You inherit a trust account that promises to pay $13,000 a year for ten years and then distribute $100,000. If current yields are 10 percent, what is the value of the trust?

10) If a creditor owes $24,000 and annually pays $3,000, how quickly will the loan be retired if the interest rate is 8 percent annually?

11) An annuity offers $1,000 for ten years. If you can earn 12 percent annually on your funds, what is the maximum amount you should pay for this annuity?

12) How much additional interest will you earn on $1,000 at 10 percent for ten years if interest is compounded semiannually instead of annually?

13) If a stadium holds 50,000 and currently 41,000 spectators attend games, how long will it take to fill the stadium if attendance is growing at the rate of 6 percent a year?

14) An employee and employer contribute $3,000 annually for 20 years to a retirement account that earns 9 percent a year. How much will the employee be able to withdraw from the account for 25 years?

Answers to Problems Using Interest Tables and a Financial Calculator

1) This is an example of future value:

   $$\$100(1 + .07)^5 = x$$

   The interest factor for the future value of a dollar at 7 percent for five years is 1.403. Hence

   $$\$100(1.403) = \$1.40$$

   (PV = –100; N = 5; I = 7; PMT = 0; FV = ?; FV = 140.26.)

2) This is an example using future value to solve for the I. Determine the interest factor:

   $$\$100(FVIF) = \$161$$

   The interest factor is $161/$100 = 1.61

   Find 1.61 in the interest table for the future value of a dollar using five years. The growth rate is 10 percent.

   (PV = –100; N = 5; PMT = 0; FV = 161; I = ?; I = 9.99.)

3) This is an example of the future value of an annuity. The question is, what amount (x) times the interest factor for the future sum of an ordinary annuity of $1.00 for four years at 5 percent (interest factor = 4.310) equals $15,000?

   $$x(4.310) = \$15,000$$

   $$x = \$15,000/4.310 = \$3,480$$

   You will have to save $3,480 annually to accumulate the $15,000.

   (PV = 0; N = 4; I = 5; FV = 15000; PMT = ?; PMT = 3480.18.)

4) This problem is also an example of the future value of an annuity:

   $$\$1,500(FVIF\ 7I, 4N) = \$1,500(4.440) = \$6,660$$

   (PV = 0; N = 4; I = 7; PMT = –1500; FV = ?; FV = 6659.91.)

5) This is an example of the future value of $1.

   $$\$54(1 + i)^{20} = \$54(FVIF) = \$136$$

   $$FVIF = \$136/\$54 = 2.52$$

   The growth rate is slightly less than 5 percent annually.

   (PV = –54; N = 20; PMT = 0; FV = 136; I = ?; I = 4.73.)

6) These are all examples of the future value of $1.

   Dividends: $\$1.00(1 + x)^{10} = \$2.16$; FVIF = 2.16

   $$x = 8\%$$

   (PV = –1; N = 10; PMT = 0; FV = 2.16; I = ?; I = 8.01.)

   Earnings: $\$2.00(1 + x)^{10} = \$5.2$; FVIF = 2.60

   $$x = 10\%$$

(PV = –2; N = 10; PMT = 0; FV = 5.2; I = ?; I = 10.03.)

CPI: $100(1 + x)^{10} = 163$; FVIF = 1.63

$x = 5\%$

(PV = –100; N = 10; PMT = 0; FV = 163; I = ?; I = 5.01.)

The dividends and earnings have both grown more rapidly than the Consumer Price Index. The investor's purchasing power has improved (if it is assumed that the value of the stock has not declined to offset the gain in the dividends).

7) This illustrates the present value of an annuity of $1.00. The interest factor at 7 percent for five years is 4.10.

$(FVAIF)(x) = \$200,000$

$4.1x = \$200,000$

$x = \$200,000/4.1 = \$48,780$

You may withdraw $48,778 annually for five years.

(PV = –200000; N = 5; FV = 0; I = 7; PMT = ? PMT = 48778.)

8) This is an example of the present value of an annuity. The interest factor for the present value of the annuity of $1.00 at 10 percent for ten years is 6.145.

$x = \$50,000 \times 6.145$

$x = \$307,250$

The firm should make this investment because the present value of the cash inflow generated by the investment ($307,250) exceeds the cost (cash outflow) of the investment ($300,000).

(PMT = 50000; N = 10; FV = 0; I = 10; PV = ? PV = –307228.)

9) This is another illustration of present value, consisting of an annuity component and a single, lump sum payment.

$\$13,000(6.145) + 100,000(.386) = \$118,485$

The trust is currently worth $118,485.

(PMT = –13000; N = 10; FV = –100000; I = 10; PV = ? PV = 118434.)

10) This is an example of the present value of an annuity in which the number of years is the unknown. Solve for the interest factor:

$\$3,000(PVAIF) = \$24,000$

$PVIF = 24,000/3,000 = 8.$

The number of years to retire the loan is slightly more than 13, using the interest table for the present value of an annuity.

(PMT = –3000; FV = 0; I = 8; PV = 24000; N = ?; N = 13.27.)

11) This problem is similar to #8 but is applied to an investment. The present value of the annuity is

$PVA = \$1,000(5.650) = \$5,650.$

5.650 is the interest factor for the present value of an ordinary annuity at 12 percent for ten years. The investor should pay no more than $5,650 for this investment.

(PMT = 1000; N = 10; FV = 0; I = 12; PV = ? PV = –5650.22.)

12) This problem illustrates the impact of more frequent compounding.

Annual compounding:

$1,000(1 + .1)^{10} = \$1,000(2.594) = \$2,594$

(PV = –1000; N = 10; I = 10; PMT = 0; FV = ?; FV = 2594.)

Semi-annual compounding:

$\$1,000(1 + .1/2)^{10 \times 2} = 1,000(1.05)^{20} =$

$\$1,000(2.653) = \$2,653$

(PV = –1000; N = 20; I = 5; PMT = 0; FV = ?; FV = 2653.)

The difference in interest earned is $59.

13) This an another illustration of using the future value of a dollar to solve for the number of years:

$41,000(1 + .06)^n = 50,000$

FVIF = 50,000/41,000 = 1.220

In less than four years, the stadium will have insufficient seating capacity.

(PV = –41000; I = 6; PMT = 0; FV = 50000; N = ?; N = 3.41.)

14) This problem illustrates the basics of pension plans. The amount accumulated:

$3,000(51.160) = $153,480

PV = 0; I = 9; PMT = -3000; N = 20; FV = ?; FV = 153480.36.)

The annual withdrawals:

$153,480/IFPVA = 153,480/9.823 = $15624.55

Investing only $3,000 a year for 20 years permits you to withdraw over $15,600 a year for 25 years.

(PV = –153480; I = 9; N = 25; FV = 0; PMT = ?; PMT = 15625.22.)

Answers to Additional Problems Using Excel

1	FV(7%,5,0,–100.0)	$140.26
2	RATE(5,0,-100,161,0)	9.99%
3	PMT(5%,4,0,15000,0)	($3,480.18)

(This answer assumes payments are made at the end of each year.)

	PMT(5%,4,0,15000,1)	($3,314.45)

(This answer assumes payments are made at the beginning of each year.)

4	FV(7%,4,–1500,0,0)	$6,659.91

5 RATE(20,0,–54,136,0)   4.73%

6 Earnings per share:
   RATE(10,0,–2,5.20,0)   10.03%

   Dividends:
   RATE(10,0,–1,2.16,0)   8.01%

   CPI:
   RATE(10,0,–100,163,0)   5.01%

7 PMT(7%,5,–200000,0,0) $48,778
   (This answer assumes payments are made at the end of each year.)

   PMT(7%,5,–200000,0,1) $45,587
   (This answer assumes payments are made at the beginning of each year.)

8 PV(10%,10,–50000,0,0) $307,228
   (This answer assumes payments are made at the end of each year.)

   PV(10%,10,–50000,0,1) $337,951
   (This answer assumes payments are made at the beginning of each year.)

9 PV(10%,10,13000,100000,0)   ($118,434)
   (This answer assumes payments are made at the end of each year.)

   PV(10%,10,13000,100000,1)   ($126,422)
   (This answer assumes annuity payments are made at the beginning of
   each year.)

10 NPER(8,24000,–3000,0,0)   13.27
   (This answer assumes payments are made at the end of each year.)

11 PV(12%,10,1000,0,0)   ($5,650.22)
   (This answer assumes payments are made at the beginning of each year.)

   PV(12%,10,1000,0,1)   ($6,328.25)
   (This answer assumes payments are made at the end of each year.)

12 FV(10%,10,0,–1000,0) $2,593.74
   FV(5%,20,0,–1000,0) $2,653.30

13 NPER(6%,0,–41000,50000,0)   3.41

14 FV(9%,20,–3000,0,0) $153,480
   PMT(9%,25,153480,0,0)   ($15,625.22)
   (This answer assumes contributions are made at the end of each year, and
   withdrawals are taken at the end of each year.)

   FV(9%,20,–3000,0,1) $167,294
   PMT (9%,25,167294,0,0)   ($17,031.57)
   (This answer assumes contributions are made at the beginning of each year,
   and withdrawals are taken at the end of each year.)

   FV(9%,20–3000,0,1)   %167,293.59
   PMT(9%,25,167294,0,1)   ($15,625.30)
   (This answer assumes contributions are made at the beginning of each year,
   and withdrawals are taken at the end of each year.)

Appendix A

Mathematical Tables

- THE FUTURE VALUE OF $1

- THE PRESENT VALUE OF $1

- THE FUTURE VALUE OF AN ANNUITY OF $1

- THE PRESENT VALUE OF AN ANNUITY OF $1

The Future Value of $1

Period	1%	2%	3%	4%	5%	6%	7%
1	1.010	1.020	1.030	1.040	1.050	1.060	1.070
2	1.020	1.040	1.061	1.082	1.102	1.124	1.145
3	1.030	1.061	1.093	1.125	1.158	1.191	1.225
4	1.041	1.082	1.126	1.170	1.216	1.262	1.311
5	1.051	1.104	1.159	1.217	1.276	1.338	1.403
6	1.062	1.126	1.194	1.265	1.340	1.419	1.501
7	1.072	1.149	1.230	1.316	1.407	1.504	1.606
8	1.083	1.172	1.267	1.369	1.477	1.594	1.718
9	1.094	1.195	1.305	1.423	1.551	1.689	1.838
10	1.105	1.219	1.344	1.480	1.629	1.791	1.967
11	1.116	1.243	1.384	1.539	1.710	1.898	2.105
12	1.127	1.268	1.426	1.601	1.7496	2.012	2.252
13	1.138	1.294	1.469	1.665	1.886	2.133	2.410
14	1.149	1.319	1.513	1.732	1.980	2.261	2.579
15	1.161	1.346	1.558	1.801	2.079	2.397	2.759
16	1.173	1.373	1.605	1.873	2.183	2.540	2.952
17	1.184	1.400	1.653	1.948	2.292	2.693	3.159
18	1.196	1.428	1.702	2.026	2.407	2.854	3.380
19	1.208	1.457	1.754	2.107	2.527	3.026	3.617
20	1.220	1.486	1.806	2.191	2.653	3.207	3.870
25	1.282	1.641	2.094	2.666	3.386	4.292	5.427
30	1.348	1.811	2.427	3.243	4.322	5.743	7.612

Period	8%	9%	10%	12%	14%	15%	16%
1	1.080	1.090	1.100	1.120	1.140	1.150	1.160
2	1.166	1.188	1.210	1.254	1.300	1.322	1.346
3	1.260	1.295	1.331	1.405	1.482	1.521	1.561
4	1.360	1.412	1.464	1.574	1.689	1.749	1.811
5	1.469	1.539	1.611	1.762	1.925	2.011	2.100
6	1.587	1.677	1.772	1.974	2.195	2.313	2.436
7	1.714	1.828	1.949	2.211	2.502	2.660	2.826
8	1.851	1.993	2.144	2.476	2.853	3.059	3.278
9	1.999	2.172	2.358	2.773	3.252	3.518	3.803
10	2.159	2.367	2.594	3.106	3.707	4.046	4.411
11	2.332	2.580	2.853	3.479	4.226	4.652	5.117
12	2.518	2.813	3.138	3.896	4.818	5.350	5.936
13	2.720	3.066	3.452	4.363	5.492	6.153	6.886
14	2.937	3.342	3.797	4.887	6.261	7.076	7.988
15	3.172	3.642	4.177	5.474	7.138	8.137	9.266
16	3.426	3.970	4.595	6.130	8.137	9.358	10.748
17	3.700	4.328	5.054	6.866	9.276	10.761	12.468
18	3.996	4.717	5.560	7.690	10.575	12.375	14.463
19	4.316	5.142	6.116	8.613	12.056	14.232	16.777
20	4.661	5.604	6.728	9.646	13.743	16.367	19.461
25	6.848	8.623	10.835	17.000	26.462	32.919	40.874
30	10.063	13.268	17.449	29.960	50.950	66.212	85.850

$P_0(1 + i)^n = P_n$ Interest factor $= (1 + i)^n$

The Present Value of $1

Period	1%	2%	3%	4%	5%	6%	7%	8%	9%	10%	12%	14%	15%
1	0.990	0.980	0.971	0.962	0.952	0.943	0.935	0.926	0.917	0.909	0.893	0.877	0.870
2	0.980	0.961	0.943	0.925	0.907	0.890	0.873	0.857	0.842	0.826	0.797	0.769	0.756
3	0.971	0.942	0.915	0.889	0.864	0.840	0.816	0.794	0.772	0.751	0.712	0.675	0.658
4	0.961	0.924	0.889	0.855	0.823	0.792	0.763	0.735	0.708	0.683	0.636	0.592	0.572
5	0.951	0.906	0.863	0.822	0.784	0.747	0.713	0.681	0.650	0.621	0.567	0.519	0.497
6	0.942	0.888	0.838	0.790	0.746	0.705	0.666	0.630	0.596	0.564	0.507	0.456	0.432
7	0.933	0.871	0.813	0.760	0.711	0.665	0.623	0.583	0.547	0.513	0.452	0.400	0.376
8	0.923	0.853	0.789	0.731	0.677	0.627	0.582	0.540	0.502	0.467	0.404	0.351	0.327
9	0.914	0.837	0.766	0.703	0.645	0.592	0.544	0.500	0.460	0.424	0.361	0.308	0.284
10	0.905	0.820	0.744	0.676	0.614	0.558	0.508	0.463	0.422	0.386	0.322	0.270	0.247
11	0.896	0.804	0.722	0.650	0.585	0.527	0.475	0.429	0.388	0.350	0.287	0.237	0.215
12	0.887	0.788	0.701	0.625	0.557	0.497	0.444	0.397	0.356	0.319	0.257	0.208	0.187
13	0.879	0.773	0.681	0.601	0.530	0.469	0.415	0.368	0.326	0.290	0.229	0.182	0.163
14	0.870	0.758	0.661	0.577	0.505	0.442	0.388	0.340	0.299	0.263	0.205	0.160	0.141
15	0.861	0.743	0.642	0.555	0.481	0.417	0.362	0.315	0.275	0.239	0.183	0.140	0.123
16	0.853	0.728	0.623	0.534	0.458	0.394	0.339	0.292	0.252	0.218	0.163	0.123	0.107
17	0.844	0.714	0.605	0.513	0.436	0.371	0.317	0.270	0.231	0.198	0.146	0.108	0.093
18	0.836	0.700	0.587	0.494	0.416	0.350	0.296	0.250	0.212	0.180	0.130	0.095	0.081
19	0.828	0.686	0.570	0.475	0.396	0.331	0.276	0.232	0.194	0.164	0.116	0.083	0.070
20	0.820	0.673	0.554	0.456	0.377	0.312	0.258	0.215	0.178	0.149	0.104	0.073	0.061
25	0.780	0.610	0.478	0.375	0.295	0.233	0.184	0.146	0.116	0.092	0.059	0.038	0.030
30	0.742	0.552	0.412	0.308	0.231	0.174	0.131	0.099	0.075	0.057	0.033	0.020	0.015

Period	16%	18%	20%	24%	28%	32%	36%	40%	50%	60%	70%	80%	90%
1	0.862	0.847	0.833	0.806	0.781	0.758	0.735	0.714	0.667	0.625	0.588	0.556	0.526
2	0.743	0.718	0.694	0.650	0.610	0.574	0.541	0.510	0.444	0.391	0.346	0.309	0.277
3	0.641	0.609	0.579	0.524	0.477	0.435	0.398	0.364	0.296	0.244	0.204	0.171	0.146
4	0.552	0.516	0.482	0.423	0.373	0.329	0.292	0.260	0.198	0.153	0.120	0.095	0.077
5	0.476	0.437	0.402	0.341	0.291	0.250	0.215	0.186	0.132	0.095	0.070	0.053	0.040
6	0.410	0.370	0.335	0.275	0.227	0.189	0.158	0.133	0.088	0.060	0.041	0.029	0.021
7	0.354	0.314	0.279	0.222	0.178	0.143	0.116	0.095	0.059	0.037	0.024	0.016	0.011
8	0.305	0.266	0.233	0.179	0.139	0.108	0.085	0.068	0.039	0.023	0.014	0.009	0.006
9	0.263	0.226	0.194	0.144	0.108	0.082	0.063	0.048	0.026	0.015	0.008	0.005	0.003
10	0.227	0.191	0.162	0.116	0.085	0.062	0.046	0.035	0.017	0.009	0.005	0.003	0.002
11	0.195	0.162	0.135	0.094	0.066	0.047	0.034	0.025	0.012	0.006	0.003	0.002	0.001
12	0.168	0.137	0.112	0.076	0.052	0.036	0.025	0.018	0.008	0.004	0.002	0.001	0.001
13	0.145	0.116	0.093	0.061	0.040	0.027	0.018	0.013	0.005	0.002	0.001	0.001	0.000
14	0.125	0.099	0.078	0.049	0.032	0.021	0.014	0.009	0.003	0.001	0.001	0.000	0.000
15	0.108	0.084	0.065	0.040	0.025	0.016	0.010	0.006	0.002	0.001	0.000	0.000	0.000
16	0.093	0.071	0.054	0.032	0.019	0.012	0.007	0.005	0.002	0.001	0.000	0.000	
17	0.080	0.060	0.045	0.026	0.015	0.009	0.005	0.003	0.001	0.000	0.000		
18	0.069	0.051	0.038	0.021	0.012	0.007	0.004	0.002	0.001	0.000	0.000		
19	0.060	0.043	0.031	0.017	0.009	0.005	0.003	0.002	0.000	0.000			
20	0.051	0.037	0.026	0.014	0.007	0.004	0.002	0.001	0.000	0.000			
25	0.024	0.016	0.010	0.005	0.002	0.001	0.000	0.000					
30	0.012	0.007	0.004	0.002	0.001	0.000	0.000						

$$P_0 = \frac{P_n}{(1+i)^n} \qquad \text{Interest factor} = \frac{1}{(1+i)^n}$$

The Future Value of an Annuity of $1

Period	1%	2%	3%	4%	5%	6%
1	1.000	1.000	1.000	1.000	1.000	1.000
2	2.010	2.020	2.030	2.040	2.050	2.060
3	3.030	3.060	3.091	3.122	3.152	3.184
4	4.060	4.122	4.184	4.246	4.310	4.375
5	5.101	5.204	5.309	5.416	5.526	5.637
6	6.152	6.308	6.468	6.633	6.802	6.975
7	7.214	7.434	7.662	7.898	8.142	8.394
8	8.286	8.583	8.892	9.214	9.549	9.897
9	9.369	9.755	10.159	10.583	11.027	11.491
10	10.462	10.950	11.464	12.006	12.578	13.181
11	11.567	12.169	12.808	13.486	14.207	14.972
12	12.683	13.412	14.192	15.026	15.917	16.870
13	13.809	14.680	15.618	16.627	17.713	18.882
14	14.947	15.974	17.086	18.292	19.599	21.051
15	16.097	17.293	18.599	20.024	21.579	23.276
16	17.258	18.639	20.157	21.825	23.657	25.673
17	18.430	20.012	21.762	23.698	25.840	28.213
18	19.615	21.412	23.414	25.645	28.132	30.906
19	20.811	22.841	25.117	27.671	30.539	33.760
20	22.109	24.297	26.870	29.778	33.066	36.786
25	28.243	32.030	36.459	41.646	47.727	54.865
30	34.785	40.568	47.575	56.085	66.439	79.058

Period	1%	2%	3%	4%	5%	6%
1	1.000	1.000	1.000	1.000	1.000	1.000
2	2.070	2.080	2.090	2.100	2.120	2.140
3	3.215	3.246	3.278	3.310	3.374	3.440
4	4.440	4.508	4.573	4.641	4.770	4.921
5	5.751	5.867	5.985	6.105	6.353	6.610
6	7.153	7.336	7.523	7.716	8.115	8.536
7	8.654	8.923	9.200	9.487	10.089	10.730
8	10.260	10.637	11.028	11.436	12.300	13.233
9	11.978	12.488	13.021	13.579	14.776	16.085
10	13.816	14.487	15.193	15.937	17.549	19.337
11	15.784	16.645	17.560	18.531	20.655	23.044
12	17.888	18.977	20.141	21.384	24.138	27.271
13	20.141	21.495	22.953	24.523	28.029	32.089
14	22.550	24.215	26.019	27.975	32.393	37.581
15	25.129	27.152	29.361	31.772	37.280	43.842
16	27.888	30.324	33.003	35.950	42.753	50.980
17	30.840	33.750	36.974	40.545	48.884	59.118
18	33.999	37.450	41.301	45.599	55.750	68.394
19	37.379	41.446	46.018	51.159	63.440	78.969
20	40.995	45.762	51.160	57.275	72.052	91.025
25	63.249	73.106	84.701	98.347	133.334	181.871
30	94.461	113.283	136.308	164.494	241.333	356.787

$$CS = I(1+i)^0 + I(1+i)^1 + \ldots + I(1+i)^{n-1} \qquad \text{Interest factor} = \frac{(1+i)^n - 1}{i}$$

The Present Value of an Annuity of $1

Period	1%	2%	3%	4%	5%	6%	7%	8%	9%	10%
1	0.990	0.980	0.971	0.962	0.952	0.943	0.935	0.926	0.917	0.909
2	1.970	1.942	1.913	1.886	1.859	1.833	1.808	1.783	1.759	1.736
3	2.941	2.884	2.829	2.775	2.723	2.673	2.624	2.577	2.531	2.487
4	3.902	3.808	3.717	3.630	3.546	3.465	3.387	3.312	3.240	3.170
5	4.853	4.713	4.580	4.452	4.329	4.212	4.100	3.993	3.890	3.791
6	5.795	5.601	5.417	5.242	5.076	4.917	4.766	4.623	4.486	4.355
7	6.728	6.472	6.230	6.002	5.786	5.582	5.389	5.206	5.033	4.868
8	7.652	7.325	7.020	6.733	6.463	6.210	5.971	5.747	5.535	5.335
9	8.566	8.162	7.786	7.435	7.108	6.802	6.515	6.247	5.985	5.759
10	9.471	8.983	8.530	8.111	7.722	7.360	7.024	6.710	6.418	6.145
11	10.368	9.787	9.253	8.760	8.306	7.887	7.499	7.139	6.805	6.495
12	11.255	10.575	9.954	9.385	8.863	8.384	7.943	7.536	7.161	6.814
13	12.134	11.348	10.635	9.986	9.394	8.853	8.358	7.904	7.487	7.103
14	13.004	12.106	11.296	10.563	9.899	9.295	8.745	8.244	7.786	7.367
15	13.865	12.849	11.938	11.118	10.380	9.712	9.108	8.559	8.060	7.606
16	14.718	13.578	12.561	11.652	10.838	10.106	9.447	8.851	8.312	7.824
17	15.562	14.292	13.166	12.166	11.274	10.477	9.763	9.122	8.544	8.022
18	16.398	14.992	13.754	12.659	11.690	10.828	10.059	9.372	8.756	8.201
19	17.226	15.678	14.324	13.134	12.085	11.158	10.336	9.604	8.950	8.365
20	18.046	16.351	14.877	13.590	12.462	11.470	10.594	9.818	9.128	8.514
25	22.023	19.523	17.413	15.622	14.094	12.783	11.654	10.675	9.823	9.077
30	25.808	22.397	19.600	17.292	15.373	13.765	12.409	11.258	10.274	9.427

Period	12%	14%	16%	18%	20%	24%	28%	32%	36%
1	0.893	0.877	0.862	0.847	0.833	0.806	0.781	0.758	0.735
2	1.690	1.647	1.605	1.566	1.528	1.457	1.392	1.332	1.276
3	2.402	2.322	2.246	2.174	2.106	1.981	1.868	1.766	1.674
4	3.037	2.914	2.798	2.690	2.589	2.404	2.241	2.096	1.966
5	3.605	3.433	3.274	3.127	2.991	2.745	2.532	2.345	2.181
6	4.111	3.889	3.685	3.498	3.326	3.020	2.759	2.534	2.339
7	4.564	4.288	4.039	3.812	3.605	3.242	2.937	2.678	2.455
8	4.968	4.639	4.344	4.078	3.837	3.421	3.076	2.786	2.540
9	5.328	4.946	4.607	4.303	4.031	3.566	3.184	2.868	2.603
10	5.650	5.216	4.833	4.494	4.193	3.682	3.269	2.930	2.650
11	5.988	5.453	5.029	4.656	4.327	3.776	3.335	2.978	2.683
12	6.194	5.660	5.197	4.793	4.439	3.851	3.387	3.013	2.708
13	6.424	5.842	5.342	4.910	4.533	3.912	3.427	3.040	2.727
14	6.628	6.002	5.468	5.008	4.611	3.962	3.459	3.061	2.740
15	6.811	6.142	5.575	5.092	4.675	4.001	3.483	3.076	2.750
16	6.974	6.265	5.669	5.162	4.730	4.033	3.503	3.088	2.758
17	7.120	6.373	5.749	5.222	4.775	4.059	3.518	3.097	2.763
18	7.250	6.467	5.818	5.273	4.812	4.080	3.529	3.104	2.767
19	7.366	6.550	5.877	5.316	4.844	4.097	3.539	3.109	2.770
20	7.469	6.623	5.929	5.353	4.870	4.110	3.546	3.113	2.772
25	7.843	6.873	6.097	5.467	4.948	4.147	3.564	3.122	2.776
30	8.055	7.003	6.177	5.517	4.979	4.160	3.569	3.124	2.778

$$PV = \sum_{t-1}^{n} \frac{1}{(1+i)^t} \qquad \text{Interest factor} = \frac{1 - \dfrac{1}{(1+i)^n}}{i}$$

Appendix B

Answers to Selected Problems

Chapter 1

1) **a)** 25% margin: 300%
   c) 75% margin: 100%
2) **b)** 50% margin: –50%
3) At price of stock = $40 and margin requirement of 60%:
   Cash account: –21.2%
   Margin account: –42%
   At price of the stock = $70 and margin requirement of 40%:
   Cash account: 31.2%
   Margin account: 63%
4) At price of the stock = $36: 27.8%

Chapter 2

1) **a)** Capital gains: $4,700
      Tax: $1,316
   b) Tax savings in current year: $1,050
2) **b)** Net long-term loss after net short-term capital gain: $1,000
      Tax savings: $330
   g) Current year tax savings: $990
3) **a)** $280
   d) $560
4) **a)** $500 saved
   b) $0
5) **a)** $10,000 grows to $23,670; the total in all accounts: $172,406 ($172,428 using a financial calculator).
   b) over 25 years (28.3 years)
   c) $19,690
6) Bob: $60,247
   Mary: $77,037
   Difference: $16,790
7) Bob contributes $1,500 for ten years and accumulates $23,906. This amount grows for ten years into $62,012. The final sum is drawn over fifteen years at the rate of $8,153 annually. Mike contributes a larger amount ($2,000) for ten years and accumulates $31,874; however, he must start to withdraw the funds after *five* years, so the final amount grows to $51,349. This final sum is drawn down over twenty years at the rate of $6,031 annually.

Chapter 3

1) 14% in all three cases
2) **a)** 10.3%

3) a) 12.4%
       standard deviation = 3.12
4) a) 50% A/50% B: return = 16%; standard deviation = 3.14
    c) 25% A/75% B: return = 18%; standard deviation = 4.56
6) Return = 12% when beta = 1.5

Chapter 4

1) a) Simple average: $15
        Value-weighted average: $15.60
        Geometric average: $14.50
3) Holding period return: 209%
    Annualized return: 11.96%
4) a) 12% (12.38%)
    c) 9% (8.88%)
5) Dollar-weighted return: 19%
    Time-weighted return: 23.1%
6) Between 9 and 10% (9.4%)
7) b) $85.74
    c) –1.7%
8) Change in price of Stock A: –$50; Stock B: $25
9) Average cost per share: $34.55

Chapter 5

1) a) Cash and retained earnings decline by $1,000,000 to $19,000,000 and
        $97,500,000.
    b) 100,000 shares issued
        Common stock: 1,100,000 shares, $10 par; $11,000,000
        Paid-in capital (new entry): $300,000
        Retained earnings: $97,200,000
2) a) Paid-in capital: $1,800,000
        New price of the stock: $20
    b) Paid-in capital: $2,280,000
        New price of the stock: $54.55
3) 162.9 shares

Chapter 7

1) $21
2) $21.40, which is less than 25. (Don't buy!)
3) a) $28.53
4) Required return: 12%
5) b) Stock A: $7.78
    d) $12.94
7) Required return for B: 12.6%
8) Present value of dividend payments: $7.66
    Value of stock: $68.91
11) Average percentage change: 9.5%
     Beginning and terminal values: 10.4%
     Regression: 10.2%

Chapter 10

1) Discount yield: 6.5%; annualized compound yield: 6.8%
2) Taxable yield: 8.75%
5) 3.12% discount yield
    3.19% annualized yield

Chapter 11

1) **a)** $1,000
    b) $875
    c) Current yield in b.: 9.1%
2) **a)** $1,179 (semiannual compounding: $1,181)
    b) $1,054 (semiannual compounding: $1,055)
    c) $1,142 (semiannual compounding: $1,142)
4) Current yield: 9.6%
5) 14%
    Yield to maturity: 10% (semiannual compounding: 10.04%)
5) 14%
6) **a)** 5% coupon bond: $575 (semiannual compounding: $571)
7) **a)** $60
    b) $75.48
8) **a)** Bond A: $894 (semiannual compounding: $892)
    b) Bond B: $1,000
10) $636
12) **b)** Bond A: 4.4 years
    Bond E: 5.0 years
    c) C, A, E, D, B
13) **a)** 4.8%
    b) $864
    c) $176
    d) $817
    e) $223
    f) At least $1,728
    g) At least $817
    h) Virtually nil

Chapter 12

1) $7.68
2) 6.8%
3) Holding period return: 40.6%

Chapter 13

  a) The risk-adjusted ranking: E, D, C, A, B
  b) The risk-adjusted ranking: C, D, B, E, A

Chapter 14

1) **a)** Intrinsic value: $1; time premium: $3

b)

Price of the stock	Value of the call
$20	$0
30	5
40	15

c) 275%

d) Cash outflow: $22

Price of the stock	Profit
$15	($7)
25	3
26	3
40	3

e) $4, $3, and ($11)

2) XYZ calls: $4 and nil

XYZ puts: nil and $1

If the price of the stock is $31, the losses to the buyers of the calls are ($6) and ($2.50).

If the price of the stock is $31, the profits to the writers of the puts are $1.25 and $0.25.

3) a) $1

b) $0

c) $4

d) $2

e) rises

f) $46

g) $51

h) $8

i) ($2)

j) ($7)

k) $4

4) a) ($2), ($2), and $3

b) $2, $2, and ($3)

6) c) $38

d) ($3)

7) a) If the price of the stock is $50, value of the call: $5.45

b) If the expiration is six months, value of the call: $5.45

c) If the interest rate is 5%, value of the call: $4.82

d) If the standard deviation is 40% (.4), value of the call: $6.79

8) a) Profit if

price of the stock is $110: $10

price of the stock is $105: $10

price of the stock is $90: $10

9) a) $1.50

b) $1.50

c) ($8.50)

10) Maximum loss: $1.81

Chapter 15

1) a) $20,000

b) $1,500,000

          c) Lose $2,500
          e) 67%
          f) $20,000
2) **a)** $1,600,000
     b) $1,560,000
     c) ($250,000)
     d) $40,000
     e) $40,000
     f) $0
     g) $200,000
4) $4.44

Glossary

A

accrued interest: Interest that has been earned but not received.

American Depository Receipts (ADRs): Receipts issued for foreign securities held by a trustee.

annuity: A series of equal annual payments.

annuity due: A series of equal annual payments with the payments made at the beginning of the year.

anticipation note: A short-term liability that is to be retired by specific expected revenues (e.g., expected tax receipts).

arbitrage: Simultaneous purchase and sale to take advantage of price differences in different markets.

arrearage: Cumulative preferred dividends that have not been paid.

B

balloon payment: The large final payment necessary to retire a debt issue.

bar graph: A graph indicating the high, low, and closing prices of a security.

Barron's confidence index: An index designed to identify investors' confidence in the level and direction of security prices.

bearer bond: A bond with coupons attached or a bond whose possession denotes ownership.

bearish: Expecting that prices will decline.

best-effort agreements: Agreement with an investment banker who does not guarantee the sale of a security but who agrees to make the best effort to sell it.

beta coefficient: An index of risk; a measure of the systematic risk associated with a particular stock.

bid and ask: Prices at which a security dealer offers to buy and sell stock.

bond: A long-term liability with a specified amount of interest and specified maturity date.

book-to-price ratio: The accounting value of a stock divided by the market price of the stock.

broker: An agent who handles buy and sell orders for an investor.

bullish: Expecting that prices will rise.

business cycle: An economic pattern of expansion and contraction.

bylaws: A document specifying the relationship between a corporation and its stockholders.

C

call feature: The right of an issuer to retire a debt issue prior to maturity.

call option: An option sold by an individual that entitles the buyer to purchase stock at a specified price within a specified time period.

call penalty: A premium paid for exercising a call feature.

capital gain: The increase in the value of an asset, such as a stock or a bond.

capital loss: A decrease in the value of an asset such as a stock or a bond.

cash budget: A financial statement enumerating cash receipts and cash disbursements.

certificate of incorporation: A document creating a corporation.

charter: A document specifying the relationship between a firm and the state in which it is incorporated.

closed-end investment company: An investment company with a fixed number of shares that are bought and sold in the secondary securities markets.

collateralized mortgage obligation (CMO): Debt obligation supported by mortgages and sold in series.

commissions: Fees charged by brokers for executing orders.

compounding: The process by which interest is paid on interest that has been previously earned.

confirmation statement: A statement received from a brokerage firm detailing the sale or purchase of a security and specifying a settlement date.

contrarians: Investors who go against the consensus concerning investment strategy.

conversion value as stock: Value of the bond in terms of the stock into which the bond may be converted.

convertible bond: A bond that may be exchanged for (i.e., converted into) stock.

coupon bond: A bond with coupons attached that are removed and presented for payment of interest when due.

coupon rate: The specified interest rate or amount of interest paid by a bond

covered option writing: Selling an option for which the seller owns the securities.

credit rating systems: Classification schemes designed to indicate the risk associated with a particular security.

cumulative preferred stock: A preferred stock whose dividends accumulate if they are not paid.

cumulative voting: A voting scheme that encourages minority representation by permitting each stockholder to cast all of his or her votes for one candidate for the firm's board of directors.

current yield: Annual income divided by the current price of the security.

cyclical industry: An industry whose sales and profits are sensitive to changes in the level of economic activity.

D

daily limit: The maximum daily change permitted in a commodity future's price.

date of record: The day on which an investor must own shares in order to receive the dividend payment.

day order: An order placed with a broker that is canceled at the end of the day if it is not executed.

dealers: Market makers who buy and sell securities for their own accounts.

debenture: An unsecured bond.

default: The failure of a debtor to meet any term of a debt's indenture.

deficit spending: Government expenditures exceeding government revenues.

dilution: A reduction in earnings per share due to the issuing of new securities.

director: A person who is elected by stockholders to determine the goals and policies of the firm.

discount: The sale of anything below its stated value.

discount (from net asset value): The extent to which the price of a closed-end investment company's stock sells below its net asset value.

discount (of a bond): The extent to which a bond's price is less than its face amount, or principal.

discount broker: A broker who charges lower commissions on security purchases and sales.

discount rate: The rate of interest that the Federal Reserve charges banks for borrowing reserves.

discounting: The process of determining present value.

distribution date: The date on which a dividend is paid to stockholders.

diversification: The process of accumulating different securities to reduce the risk of loss.

dividend: A payment to stockholders that is usually in cash but may be in stock or property.

dividend-growth valuation model: A valuation model that deals with dividends and their growth properly discounted back to the present.

dividend reinvestment plan (DRIP): A plan that permits stockholders to have cash dividends reinvested in stock instead of received in cash.

dollar cost averaging: The purchase of securities at different intervals to reduce the impact of price fluctuations.

dollar-weighted rate of return: The rate that equates the present value of cash inflows and cash outflows; the internal rate of return.

Dow Jones Industrial Average: An average of the stock prices of 30 large firms.

duration: The average time it takes to collect a bond's interest and principal repayment.

E

efficient market hypothesis (EMH): A theory that security prices correctly measure the firm's future earnings and dividends and that investors should not consistently outperform the market on a risk-adjusted basis.

emerging market fund: Investment company that specializes in securities from less-developed countries.

equilibrium price: A price that equates supply and demand.

equipment trust certificate: A serial bond secured by specific equipment.

equity trust: A real estate investment trust that specializes in acquiring real estate for subsequent rental income.

Eurobond: A bond denominated in U.S. dollars but issued abroad.

ex-dividend: Stock that trades exclusive of any dividend payment.

ex-dividend date: The day on which a stock trades exclusive of any dividends

exercise (strike) price: The price at which the investor may buy or sell stock through an option.

expected return: The sum of the anticipated dividend yield and capital gains.

expiration date: The date by which an option must be exercised.

extendible security: Bond whose maturity date may be extended into the future.

extra dividend: A sum paid in addition to the firm's regular dividend.

F

fallen angel: Investment-grade security whose quality has deteriorated.

federal agency bonds: Debt issued by an agency of the federal government.

federal funds rate: The rate of interest a bank charges another bank for borrowing reserves.

Federal Reserve: The central bank of the United States.

financial life cycle: The stages of life during which individuals accumulate and subsequently use financial assets.

firm commitment: Agreement with an investment banker who guarantees a sale of securities by agreeing to purchase the entire issue at a specified price.

fiscal policy: Taxation, expenditures, and debt management of the federal government.

flat: A description of a bond that trades without accrued interest.

full disclosure laws: The federal and state laws requiring publicly held firms to disclose financial and other information that may affect the value of their securities.

future sum of an annuity: Compound value of a series of equal annual payments.

futures contract: An agreement for the future delivery of a commodity at a specified date.

futures price: The price in a contract for the future delivery of a commodity.

G

general obligation bond: A bond whose interest does not depend on the revenue of a specific project; government bonds supported by the full faith and credit of the issuer (i.e., authority to tax).

Ginnie Mae: Mortgage pass-through bond issued by the Government National Mortgage Association.

global funds: Mutual funds whose portfolios include securities of firms with international operations that are located throughout the world.

good-till-canceled order: An order placed with a broker that remains in effect until it is executed by the broker or canceled by the investor.

gross domestic product (GDP): Total value of all final goods and services newly produced within a country by domestic factors of production.

H

head-and-shoulder pattern: A tool of technical analysis; a pattern of security prices that resembles a head and shoulders.

hedging: Taking opposite positions to reduce risk.

high-yield securities: Non-investment-grade securities offering a high return.

holding period return (HPR): Total return (income plus price appreciation during a specified time period) divided by the cost of the investment.

I

income: The flow of money or its equivalent produced by an asset; dividends and interest.

income bond: A bond whose interest is paid only if it is earned by the firm.

increasing rate bond: Bond whose coupon rises over time.

indenture: The document that specifies the terms of a bond issue.

inflation-indexed securities: Securities whose principal and interest payments are adjusted for changes in the Consumer Price Index.

initial public offering (IPO): The first sale of common stock to the general public.

interest: Payment for the use of money.

internal rate of return: Percentage return that equates the present value of an investment's cash inflows with its cost.

international funds: American mutual funds whose portfolios are limited to non-American firms.

intrinsic value: What an option is worth as stock.

investment banker: An underwriter, a firm that sells new issues of securities to the general public.

IRA: A retirement plan (individual retirement account) that is available to workers.

irregular dividends: Dividend payments that either do not occur in regular intervals or vary in amount.

J

Jensen performance index: A measure of performance that compares the realized return with the return that should have been earned for the amount of risk borne by the investor.

K

Keogh account (HR-10 plan): A retirement plan that is available to self-employed individuals.

L

leverage: Magnification of the potential return on an investment.

limit order: An order placed with a broker to buy or sell at a specified price.

load fund: A mutual fund that charges a commission to purchase or sell its shares

long position: Owning assets for their income and possible price appreciation.

M

maintenance margin: The minimum equity required for a margin position.

margin: The amount that an investor must put down to buy securities on credit.

margin call: A request by a broker for an investor to place additional funds or securities in an account as collateral against borrowed funds or as a good faith deposit.

margin (futures): Good faith deposit made when purchasing or selling a commodity contract.

margin requirement: The minimum percentage, established by the Federal Reserve, that the investor must put up in cash to buy securities.

marginal tax rate: The tax rate paid on an additional last dollar of taxable income; an individual's tax bracket.

market order: An order to buy or sell at the current market price or quote.

maturity date: The time at which a debt issue becomes due and the principal must be repaid.

money market instruments: Short-term securities, such as Treasury bills, negotiable certificates of deposit, or commercial paper.

money market mutual funds: Mutual funds that specialize in short-term securities.

moral backing: Nonobligatory support for a debt issue.

mortgage bond: A bond that is secured by property, especially real estate.

mortgage trust: A real estate investment trust that specializes in loans secured by real estate.

moving average: An average in which the most recent observation is added and the most distant observation is deleted before the average is computed.

municipal (tax-exempt) bond: A bond issued by a state or one of its political subdivisions whose interest is not taxed by the federal government.

mutual fund: An open-end investment company.

N

naked option writing: The selling (i.e., writing) of an option without owning the underlying security.

net asset value: The asset value of a share in an investment company; total assets minus total liabilities divided by the number of shares outstanding.

no-load mutual fund: A mutual fund that does not charge a commission for buying or selling its shares.

noncumulative preferred stock: Preferred stock whose dividends do not accumulate if the firm misses a dividend payment.

NYSE composite index: New York Stock Exchange index; an index of prices of all the stocks listed on the New York Stock Exchange.

O

odd lot: A unit of trading, such as 22 shares, that is smaller than the general unit of sale.

odd-lot theory: A technical approach to the stock market that purports to predict security prices on the basis of odd-lot sales and purchases.

open-end investment company: A mutual fund; an investment company from which investors buy shares and to which they resell them.

open interest: The number of futures contracts in existence for a particular commodity.

open market operations: The buying or selling of Treasury securities by the Federal Reserve.

option: The right to buy or sell something at a specified price within a specified time period.

ordinary annuity: A series of equal annual payments in which the payments are made at the end of each year.

originating house: An investment banker that makes an agreement with a firm to sell a new issue of securities and forms the syndicate to market them.

over-the-counter (OTC) market: The informal secondary market for unlisted securities.

P

paper profits: Price appreciation that has not been realized.

payout ratio: The ratio of dividends to earnings.

PEG ratio: The price/earnings ratio divided by the growth rate of earnings.

point-and-figure chart (X-O chart): A chart composed of Xs and

Os that is used in technical analysis to summarize price movements.

portfolio: An accumulation of assets owned by the investor and designed to transfer purchasing power to the future.

portfolio risk: The total risk associated with owning a portfolio; the sum of systematic and unsystematic risk.

preemptive rights: The right of current stockholders to maintain their proportionate ownership in the firm.

preferred stock: A class of stock (i.e., equity) that has a prior claim to common stock on the firm's earnings and assets in case of liquidation.

preliminary prospectus (red herring): Initial document detailing the financial condition of a firm that must be filed with the SEC to register a new issue of securities.

premium: The market price of an option.

premium (of a bond): The extent to which a bond's price exceeds the face amount of the debt.

premium (over net asset value): The extent to which the price of a closed-end investment company's stock exceeds the share's net asset value.

present value: The current worth of an amount to be received in the future.

present value of an annuity: The present worth of a series of equal payments.

primary market: The initial sale of securities.

principal: The amount owed; the face value of a debt.

private placement: The nonpublic sale of securities.

pro forma financial statement A projected or forecasted financial statement.

progressive tax: A tax whose rate increases as the tax base increases.

proportionate tax: A tax whose rate remains constant as the tax base changes

put option: An option to sell stock at a specified price within a specified time period.

R

rate of return: The annual percentage return realized on an investment.

rate of return (internal rate of return, or IRR): The discount rate that equates the cost of an investment with the cash flows generated by the investment.

realized return: The sum of income and capital gains earned on an investment.

recapitalization: An alteration in a firm's sources of finance, such as the substitution of long-term debt for equity

recession: A period of rising unemployment and declining national output.

refunding: The act of issuing new debt and using the proceeds to retire existing debt.

regional funds: Mutual funds that specialize in a particular geographical area.

registered bond: A bond whose ownership is registered with the commercial bank that distributes interest payments and principal repayments.

registered representative: A person who buys and sells securities for customers; a broker.

registration: Process of filing information with the SEC concerning a proposed sale of securities to the general public.

regressive tax: A tax whose rate declines as the tax base increases.

regular dividends: Steady dividend payments that are distributed at regular intervals.

required return: The return necessary to induce the investor to purchase an asset.

reserve requirement: The percentage of cash that banks must hold against their deposit liabilities.

reset bond: Bond whose coupon is periodically reset.

retention ratio: The ratio of earnings not distributed to earnings.

return: The sum of income plus capital gains earned on an investment in an asset.

revenue bond: A bond whose interest is paid only if the debtor earns sufficient revenue.

rights offering: Sale of new securities to stockholders.

risk: The possibility of loss; the uncertainty of future returns.

round lot: The general unit of trading in a security, such as 100 shares.

S

secondary market: A market for buying and selling previously issued securities.

Securities and Exchange Commission (SEC): Government agency that enforces the federal securities laws.

Securities Investor Protection Corporation (SIPC): The agency that insures investors against failures by brokerage firms.

securitization: The process of converting an illiquid asset into a marketable security.

semiannual compounding: The payment of interest twice a year.

serial bond: A bond issue in which specified bonds mature each year.

share averaging: A system for the accumulation of shares in which the investor periodically buys the same number of shares.

Sharpe performance index: A risk-adjusted measure of performance that standardizes the return in excess of the risk-free rate by the standard deviation of the portfolio's return.

short position: Selling borrowed assets for possible price deterioration; being short in a security or a commodity.

short sale: The sale of borrowed securities in anticipation of a price decline; a contract for future delivery.

sinking fund: A series of periodic payments to retire a bond issue.

specialist: A market maker on the New York Stock Exchange who maintains an orderly market in the security.

speculation: An investment that offers a potentially large return but is also very risky; a reasonable probability that the investment will produce a loss.

split coupon bond: Bond with a zero or low initial coupon followed by a period with a high coupon.

spot price: The current price of a commodity.

spread: The difference between the bid and the ask prices.

Standard & Poor's 500 stock index: A value-weighted index of 500 stocks.

stock: A security representing ownership in a corporation.

stock dividend: A dividend paid in stock.

stock index futures: A contract based on an index of security prices.

stock index options: Rights to buy and sell based on an aggregate measure of stock prices.

stock repurchase: The buying of stock by the issuing corporation.

stock split: Recapitalization that affects the number of shares outstanding, their par value, the earnings per share, and the price of the stock.

stop order: A purchase or sell order designed to limit an investor's loss or to assure a profit on a position in a security.

street name: The registration of securities in a brokerage firm's name instead of in the buyer's name.

surplus: Receipts exceeding disbursements.

syndicate: A selling group assembled to market an issue of securities.

T

tax shelter: An asset or investment that defers, reduces, or avoids taxation.

technical analysis: An analysis of past volume and/or price behavior to identify which assets to purchase or sell and the best time to purchase or sell them.

third market: Over-the-counter market for securities listed on an exchange.

time premium: The amount by which an option's price exceeds the option's intrinsic value.

time-weighted rate of return: Average of individual holding period returns.

tranche: Subdivision of a bond issue.

Treasury bills: Short-term federal government securities.

Treasury bonds: The long-term debt of the federal government.

Treasury notes: The intermediate-term debt of the federal government.

Treynor index: A risk-adjusted measure of performance that standardizes the return in excess of the risk-free rate by the portfolio's systematic risk.

trustee: An appointee, usually a commercial bank, responsible for upholding the terms of a bond's indenture.

U

underwriting: The process by which securities are sold to the general public and in which the investment banker buys the securities from the issuing firm.

V

valuation: The process of determining the current worth of an asset.

value: What something is worth; the present value of future benefits.

variable interest rate bond: A long-term bond with a coupon rate that varies with changes in short-term rates.

venture capitalist: Firm specializing in investing in the securities, especially stock, of small, emerging companies.

voting rights: The rights of stockholders to vote their shares.

Y

yield curve: The relationship between time to maturity

and yields for debt in a given risk class.

yield to call: The yield earned on a bond from the time it is acquired until the time it is called and retired by the firm.

yield to maturity: The yield earned on a bond from the time it is acquired until the maturity date.

Z

zero coupon bond: A bond on which interest accrues and is paid at maturity, and is initially sold at a discount.

Index